MUSCLES IN THE MOVIES

MUSCLES IN THE MOVIES

PERFECTING THE ART OF ILLUSION

JOHN D. FAIR AND DAVID L. CHAPMAN

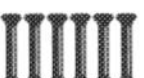

UNIVERSITY OF MISSOURI PRESS

Columbia

Copyright © 2020 by
The Curators of the University of Missouri
University of Missouri Press, Columbia, Missouri 65211
Printed and bound in the United States of America
All rights reserved. First printing, 2020.

Library of Congress Cataloging-in-Publication Data

Names: Fair, John D., author. | Chapman, David L., 1948- author.
Title: Muscles in the movies : perfecting the art of illusion / by John D.
   Fair & David L. Chapman.
Description: Columbia : University of Missouri Press, 2020. | Includes
   bibliographical references and index.
Identifiers: LCCN 2020019216 (print) | LCCN 2020019217 (ebook) | ISBN
   9780826222152 (hardcover) | ISBN 9780826274502 (ebook)
Subjects: LCSH: Human body in motion pictures. | Physical fitness in motion
   pictures. | Motion pictures--History--20th century.
Classification: LCC PN1995.9.B62 F35 2020 (print) | LCC PN1995.9.B62
   (ebook) | DDC 791.43/653--dc23
LC record available at https://lccn.loc.gov/2020019216
LC ebook record available at https://lccn.loc.gov/2020019217

∞™ This paper meets the requirements of the
American National Standard for Permanence of Paper
for Printed Library Materials, Z39.48, 1984.

Typefaces: Minion Pro and Frutiger

To Sarah and Dave

CONTENTS

CONTENTS

ILLUSTRATIONS

PREFACE AND ACKNOWLEDGMENTS

THE APPEARANCE OF muscular and athletic bodies has been an integral part of movie production since the early experiments of Étienne-Jules Marey and Eadweard Muybridge, and Thomas Edison's filming of world-renowned strongman/bodybuilder Eugen Sandow in 1894. Indeed, the motion picture industry had its birth recording the movements of men, women, and animals, and the human physique has continued to fascinate moviegoers to the present day. The developed body has played a pivotal role in many early narrative films. After the turn of the century, Italian filmmakers came to the fore with such action epics as *Cabiria* (1914) and a series of *Maciste* films (1915–28) featuring strongman Bartolomeo Pagano. There were even daring female athletes (like serial queen Pearl White, Australian swimmer Annette Kellerman, and Italian strongwoman Astrea) who occupied the screen in the silent era. By the 1920s Douglas Fairbanks was exerting his muscles with daring on-camera feats, Johnny Weissmuller was winning Olympic gold medals preparing him to be Tarzan, and Tom Tyler won a national weight-lifting championship that would lead to early superhero roles as Captain Marvel and the Phantom. In the 1940s mighty physiques and super strength even found their way into animated cartoons with Mighty Mouse, Popeye, and Superman all using their power and exaggerated heroism to save the day. Ironically, not all cinematic strongmen were heroes, as Anthony Quinn's depiction of a brutish carnival strongman in Federico Fellini's *La strada* (The street, 1954) amply proves.

Arguably the greatest characterization of muscles in the movies, however, was brought to the screen by Mr. America / Mr. Universe Steve Reeves, who as Hercules set the tone for dozens of so-called sword-and-sandal epics, produced mostly in Italy, throughout the 1960s. In the last three decades of the century, Hollywood cashed in on the increased market value of muscles on the screen in a big way with Sylvester Stallone's Rocky (1976–2006) series, Arnold Schwarzenegger's portrayal of *Conan the Barbarian* (1982), Lou Ferrigno's *The Incredible Hulk* (1978–82), and professional wrestler Dwayne "the Rock" Johnson's starring role in dozens of action epics in the early twenty-first century. "In all this, the body was key," reflected Schwarzenegger in 2012. "Looking physically heroic became the aesthetic."[1]

Our approach in this book is twofold, coinciding with the scholarly interests and expertise of the respective authors. As the author of *Sandow the Magnificent: Eugen Sandow and the Beginnings of Bodybuilding*; *American Hunks*; *Venus with Biceps*; and other studies on the display of the built body, David Chapman's major focus has been on the aesthetics and iconography of physical culture.[2] He also brings to bear an extensive knowledge of international bodybuilding and fluency in numerous foreign languages (chiefly, Danish, French, German, and Italian); he has taught history and cinema in public schools in a career spanning four decades. John Fair's scholarship has focused more on America and the functional side of physical culture in such studies as *Muscletown USA: Bob Hoffman and the Manly Culture of York Barbell* and *Mr. America: The Tragic History of a Bodybuilding Icon*.[3] His background includes over five decades as a competitive weightlifter and a teaching career (chiefly in British history) at eight universities. Currently he teaches online physical culture courses at Auburn University and is a resident scholar at the H. J. Lutcher Stark Center for Physical Culture and Sports at the University of Texas at Austin. From differing yet complementary perspectives, the authors share a common goal of revealing the often overlooked prevalence of muscular display and function in film from its inception to the current era.

This enterprise features a division of labor whereby the early chapters on international film in the silent era—including muscular stars, women, and athletes within the burgeoning entertainment genre prior to World War II, as well as the later peplum film phenomenon of the 1960s—are addressed mainly by Chapman. American film in the silent era, portrayals of athletic heroes, superheroes, women in midcentury, and the so-called Schwarzenegger era and beyond are more the province of Fair. In each chapter there will be considerable cross-fertilization of each author's words and ideas with the intent of showing how motion pictures presented, often unwittingly, an idealization of the body, both in appearance and movement. Athletic prowess and a robust physique are universally admired, especially in the United States, and account for much of the box office appeal for action films.

We are not the first to examine the phenomenon of cinematic muscularity, but we have attempted to address the subject with a greater degree of rigor and insight. One of the earlier attempts to look at muscularity in film was a series of ninety-one articles titled "Muscles in the Movies" by artist Charles S. Jenkins Jr. in *Muscular Development* magazine between 1964 and 1972. They consisted of black-and-white portraits and brief biographies showcasing fit-looking men who had appeared in movies or television. In addition to bona fide bodybuilders like Reg Park and Steve Reeves, Jenkins portrayed those with pleasing but unimpressive physiques such as actors Tab Hunter, George Maharis, Sal Mineo and ventriloquist Paul Winchell. Then, in 1975–76, the bodybuilding journalist known as Denie, along with E. P. Bigelow, wrote a series of six articles titled "The History of the Muscle Movies" that appeared in *MuscleMag International.* There have also been studies in French and Italian that covered various elements of the genre, but ours is the first book-length examination in English to look at the phenomenon from an artistic, athletic, and international perspective.

Despite our attempt to be as inclusive as possible, it should be understood at the outset that our coverage is not intended to be comprehensive of all films in which muscles are prominently displayed and used. What follows is just a sampling of actors and motion pictures that are representative of an era or the genre of muscle movies. We also intend to identify some of the major stars whose muscles made a difference in the development of the entertainment industry. Most important, our intent is to show that dazzling performances by perfectly proportioned muscular bodies on the screen better enabled audiences to realize the unreal.

We gratefully acknowledge the following individuals for their insights, inspiration, and assistance in our preparation of this book: Ivo L. Blom, Vrije Universiteit, Amsterdam; Bruce Davis, former executive director of the Academy of Motion Picture Arts and Sciences; Richard Dyer, King's College London; photographer Wayne Gallasch; Bieke Gils, University of South-Eastern Norway; boxing memorabilia collector Bruce Gordon; the late John G. Hagner, Hollywood Stuntmen's Hall of Fame; Christian Hansen, Det Danske Filminstitut; professional wrestler Mark Henry; Ross Higgins, Les Archives Gaies de Québec; Martin Koerber, Die Deutsche Kinemathek, Berlin; John Rodden of Austin, Texas; Anthony Slide of Studio City, California; Jan and Terry Todd and the staff of the H. J. Lutcher Stark Center for Physical Culture and Sports at the University of Texas at Austin; Patricia Vertinsky, University of British Columbia; Thomas Waugh, McGill University; and Tim Wilbur at the website Tim in Vermont. We would also like to thank the Auburn University Library staff; the British Film Institute;

La Cineteca di Bologna; the Harry Ransom Center at the University of Texas at Austin; the Margaret Herrick Library, Beverly Hills, California; Museo Nazionale del Cinema, Turin; and the University of California–Los Angeles Film and Television Archive.

Notes

Unless noted otherwise, all translations are by David L. Chapman.

1. Arnold Schwarzenegger, *Total Recall: My Unbelievably True Life Story*, 337.

2. David L. Chapman, *Sandow the Magnificent: Eugen Sandow and the Beginnings of Bodybuilding* (Urbana: University of Illinois Press, 1994); David L. Chapman, *American Hunks* (Vancouver: Arsenal Pulp Press, 2009); David L. Chapman, *Venus with Biceps* (Vancouver: Arsenal Pulp Press, 2010).

3. John D. Fair, *Muscletown USA: Bob Hoffman and the Manly Culture of York Barbell* (University Park, PA: Penn State University Press, 1999); John D. Fair, *Mr. America: The Tragic History of a Bodybuilding Icon* (Austin: University of Texas Press, 2015).

Style is the form of the ideal, rhythm is its movement

—Victor Hugo *Les Misérables*

MUSCLES IN THE MOVIES

INTRODUCTION

The imitator or maker of the image knows nothing of true existence;
he knows appearances only.

—Plato, *The Republic*

Nobody should come to the movies unless he believes in heroes.

—John Wayne, quoted in Nancy Schoenberger, *Wayne and Ford:
The Films, the Friendship, and the Forging of an American Hero*

FILMMAKERS AND AUDIENCES have long been obsessed with the muscular body. From the first primitive experiments with sequential photography and projected images, it was the developed, athletic body that frequently captivated producers and viewers. Thomas Edison, Étienne-Jules Marey, Georges Méliès, and Eadweard Muybridge all recorded the well-built physique in various forms: wrestlers, boxers, athletes, dancers, runners, and strongmen all appeared in front of the cinematic lens with their muscles in motion. These early films often displayed bodies that were strong, vigorous, aesthetically pleasing, and imbued with magnificent potential. As French film critic Antoine de Baecque has remarked, "Cinema was born muscled, flexing and fully fleshed."[1] Much of this interest was inherited from vaudeville or circus strongmen who performed in theaters and big tops throughout the Western world. At a time when making a living through physical labor was becoming less important, there was a need to reaffirm masculinity on the screen. Although the majority of moviegoers could never attain the spectacular results generated by actors, stuntpeople, or special effects, they could be inspired by representations of extraordinary individuals who possessed great strength, impressive physiques, or superior athleticism. With time, this interest in muscularity has ebbed and flowed, but it remains a constant in art and life. It continues to fascinate movie buffs and to offer insight into how we perceive those who have developed their bodies to such visual potency.

The first real films (as opposed to photographic experiments) were produced almost simultaneously in the mid-1890s by Edison in the United States and Auguste and Louis Lumière in France. It was the American, however, who used entertainers from the vaudeville stage as subjects for his first films. One of the most popular figures from variety theater appeared in early March 1894 at Edison's studio in Orange, New Jersey. The Anglo-German strongman and bodybuilder Eugen Sandow became the first muscular star to be photographed by a motion picture camera. He posed, flexed, twisted his sinewy torso this way and that, and concluded the performance with a back flip. The film was short (thirty-eight seconds), scratchy, and primitive, but it marked the movie industry's initial interest in recording a muscular physique. As it turned out, the filming of Sandow was not an isolated event; cinematic fascination with athletes would extend throughout the medium's history and include some impressive additions.

All art involves illusion and our willingness to surrender to it. Whether we listen to music, observe a ballet, or contemplate a painting, we can submit to an alternate reality despite the awareness of the work's artifice. With films such an illusion is particularly apparent and seductive. If a movie affects us sufficiently, we can be transported to other places, know other people, and submerge ourselves in other dramas. When cinema presents a tale involving outlandishly different individuals, the illusion has the potential to be doubly potent. This book features uniquely strong or muscular individuals who have been fashioned by moviemakers to make us readily accept as plausible their unusual appearances and their unworldly feats.

When observing Gerard Butler's abs in the film *300*, enhanced though they are by computer-generated imagery (CGI), most viewers are prepared to accept the character's strength and beauty with nary a thought of the legerdemain that created them. But even when physiques and cinematic techniques were less developed, the figures on the screen were unlike anything most moviegoers could see in their everyday world. The vast majority of bodies in the films discussed in this book have always been unreal—or at least highly unusual in their appearance or skills. Ordinary, everyday men and women are not the main characters in these dramas. In a sense, they are the bodies of freaks that have been built far beyond the capabilities of others. They are men and women who have spent an inordinate amount of time perfecting their bodies and physical abilities. They are at the peak of their strength and beauty. They are closer to gods than mortals. At least, they are godlike so long as the projector is running and the illusion is artificially maintained. Films of this sort exhibit a romantic view of life—not life as it is, but as it could be. The illusion of reality triumphs over reality itself.

A skilled camera artist can cause an otherwise skeptical viewer to accept that a mighty man can lift a boulder, fight off a swarm of enemies, or survive a withering rain of arrows with little evidence of muscle strain or serious wounds. The feats that cinematic heroes and heroines perform have been carefully manipulated to appear virtually effortless. When Douglas Fairbanks descends to the deck of a pirate ship by ripping through a sail, when Demi Moore transforms herself into a tower of military strength just by doing a few push-ups, or when Steve Reeves pulls down a massive palace using only a couple of chains and his straining muscles, we are being fooled by master actors and filmmakers. Part of the reason for our acquiescence in this ruse is that we love heroes, and want to believe them capable of almost any exploit. With the growth in special effects, the illusions become more sophisticated, but our readiness to believe that what we are seeing is real shows no signs of being suspended. Reality is for the outside world; the cinema is the palace of make-believe.

Men and women who are physically strong, unusually muscular, or highly athletic are central to our interest. This book concentrates on movies in which an actor's muscular body receives conspicuous attention and where a character's physical strength or athleticism is exploited visually. The muscular characters might be primitive ape-men, ancient gladiators, or modern athletes, but virtually all of them display well-developed physiques. This is usually done to impress others (in the film and the audience) and to use their uncommon strength to effect change or destroy adversaries. The bodies of these physical specimens have changed with advancing times, tastes, and techniques for building muscles as well as advancing film techniques such as prosthetic makeup and visual effects. Likewise, physical representations of manliness have changed. Women (and some men) once swooned over actors who seem unsexy to modern eyes. Although it is easy to recognize Rudolph Valentino's dark, dangerous appeal, it is hard to believe that many fans thought Humphrey Bogart or Jimmy Stewart were hot stuff—but they did. When Clark Gable took off his shirt to reveal his remarkably unmuscular chest in *It Happened One Night* (1934), he set a million hearts aflutter. During the Depression and Second World War, male muscularity was less important to moviegoers preoccupied with more immediate concerns over unemployment and national survival. It is easy to see that on rare occasions when the masculine physique was revealed in films, pecs and biceps counted for little; nor did abdominals, especially since most stars hiked up their trousers to navel level (as was the style). Real virility came from action, not appearance. It is sarcastically pitched in a song from the 1948 musical *Kiss Me Kate*: "He may have hair upon his chest, but sister, so has Lassie." These men were selling something other than muscularity; they were exuding manliness as it was perceived at the time and as it pleased audiences. If modern audiences react to vintage sex symbols with a resounding "Meh," then we can only shake our heads and agree with old Tully: "O tempora, o mores."

Interest in purpose-built bodies returned slowly to moviegoers. One of the first clues that fans were paying attention to muscular bodies of their heroes came with the epic portrayals of Kirk Douglas and Burt Lancaster in the 1950s that served as a prelude to the popular sword-and-sandal movies of the 1960s. In these films the heroes were shirtless athletes with rippling sinews usually set in the historical past. It is fitting that the classical era was also the first time in recorded history that anyone attempted to examine the nature of reality and illusion in any profound way. Plato was greatly interested in how we perceive the real world and understand absolute beauty, justice, knowledge, goodness, and truth. He envisioned "two ruling powers" governing man's perception of the world: "one of them is set over the intellectual world, the other over the visible." The latter, he asserted, embodied images consisting of shadows of reality, but the intellect or soul, while aware of visible images, could "behold the things themselves."[2] It should be obvious to even the most guileless of moviegoers that cinematic strongmen and –women are only as substantial as the flickering light in which they consist and as permanent as echoes. Most of them could never exist in the real world—and yet for a while they seem to live and breathe on the screen.

Illusionism is a phenomenon that has sparked much controversy among film theorists.[3] For Australian philosopher Gregory Currie, it hardly exists. What he calls "the myth of illusion" in *Image and Mind* is "the claim that movement in film is an illusion produced by the juxtaposition of static images." He argues that "there is no illusion of movement in cinema; there is real movement, really perceived. Cinematic images are real objects, reidentifiable across time and occupying different positions at different times during the viewing of the shot."[4] Trinity University philosopher Andrew Kania, however, rejects Currie's "assertions that film images simply, literally move"; he instead suggests that "almost no one *really believes* the images are really moving. There is no single reidentifiable image which is moving. And as surely as there is a real world out there, there are illusions." Kania asserts that "we need not, and should not, postulate such strange entities when we can explain the motion of cinematic images in such a simple way: it is an illusion."[5] In *Free Will and Illusion*, Haifa University philosopher Saul Smilansky attributes "enormous importance" to illusion as vital to human function. It "*creates* a mental reality, such as a particular sense of worth and moral depth associated with belief in libertarian free will, which would not exist without it. This in turn translates into people's creation of their social and personal reality" and "our feeling 'at home' in the world, as well as our agency in it, are to a large extent supported and partly even constituted by illusion." Smilansky concludes that libertarian free will depends on the realization of our inability to live without substantial illusion" and acceptance of "the illusoriness of the belief that we can live, in practice, totally without illusion."[6]

Immanuel Kant, Friedrich Nietzsche, Arthur Schopenhauer, and other philosophers have wrestled with the issue of illusion versus reality and of humankind's perennial ability to confuse the two.[7] Of the great thinkers interested in this ancient discourse, Henri Bergson was perhaps most attuned to filmmaking; he conceived a reconstruction of movement by taking a "series of snapshots" and applying "these instantaneous views on the screen, so that they replace each other rapidly." Thus, fixed photographs could be transformed into movement. "Instead of attaching ourselves to the inner becoming of things, we place ourselves outside them in order to recompose their becoming artificially. We take snapshots, as it were, of the passing reality." Bergson argues that the mind is susceptible to a "movie-like" process, and it strives to mimic movements of the real but is always relegated to "the illusion of mobility."[8] Early motion picture developments in France showed Bergson and others how easily reality could be constructed from individual frames projected fast enough to mimic not only motion but life itself. In the final analysis, Kant's thing-in-itself, Schopenhauer's representations of the will—in fact, all attempts to integrate images with reality in art—dissolve into mere illusions. Ultimately, reality is the eternal price that art pays to expression. When Tarzan swings through the tropical forest, he is not really doing so; it is only his projected image that seems to rush through the foliage to save Jane.

Meanwhile, more plebian audiences were being introduced to this new medium through magic lantern shows, which used a series of glass slides and light emanating from oil burner wicks to project movements on a screen. By 1895, estimates the Magic Lantern Society, "there were between 30,000 and 60,000 lantern showmen in the United States, giving between 75,000 and 150,000 performances a year."[9] As photography scholar Frances Terpak observes, the magic lantern "conditioned the modern world to a new kind of visual culture" for "magnificent machines that could cast huge, brightly colored, animated entertainments for hundreds of people."[10] Magic lantern shows, along with theater and vaudeville entertainments, prepared viewers for the kinds of illusions that would appear even more realistic in motion pictures. Soon Sandow and other strongmen and –women would stir the imagination of audiences to a yet undiscovered mimesis of reality that would lift this stratum of humanity out of its dreary routine.

The presence of Herculean forms on the nascent screen owes much to the popularity of the stage, a direct antecedent of film culture where the viewers' need for greater visual realism was becoming more persistent. Audiences were no longer satisfied with sound effects of thunder and lightning and representations of landscapes on set. The demand for realism required "ever more fantastic and spectacular exhibitions," asserts Nicholas Vardac. "The arrival of the motion picture in 1895 was so timely as to appear preordained." Its impact was enhanced by certain producers (like Méliès) who capitalized on this demand by embracing what Vardac calls the "trick film." Time-honored depictions of Superman on the screen take full advantage of such simulacra. By utilizing "fantastical trick elements" a greater sense of realism could be imparted "as if through the eyes of the actor, experiencing the fantasy. In this way, the fantasy became a personal, subjective experience of the audience."[11] Film historian Ben Singer draws on Vardac's ideas to devise his concept of "absorptive realism" as an explanation of how viewers assimilate the lifelike images that compellingly confront them on the screen. Singer contends that when audiences identify most strongly with the films they watch, it produces "illusionism." By this he means that as spectators suspend disbelief when they watch a movie, they become absorbed into its action and realities. In its most extreme form, absorptive realism might cause the viewer to mistake the events on the screen for real life. Thankfully, this rarely happens to those with a normal grasp on reality. But when audiences let themselves go a bit— suspend their disbelief—they can heighten the effects of the movie they are watching by imagining that the action on the screen is (at least while they are watching it) real enough to give them some emotional buy-in. Absorptive realism is therefore the goal of most commercial filmmaking, and owing to their larger-than-life appearance, muscled bodies greatly enhance its impact. Singer's concept also reflects an early observation by journalist Brian Hooker that the moving picture was "primarily a device for visualizing imaginary action as actually taking place."[12] Thus when Pearl White, filmdom's first female action star, writhes in simulated torture, audiences feel sympathy for her despite the fact that we are aware in another part of our brains that we are just watching the play of electrons on a movie screen.

No less in synch with Singer but presenting the obverse side of the same coin is Richard Allen's 1993 essay "Representation, Illusion, and the Cinema." His concept of projected illusion consists of three interlocking modes of virtual experience whereby audiences first take in the dramatic images appearing on screen. This realistic encounter is enhanced by the perception of movement that creates a greater sense of off-screen presence. When a soundtrack is added to these alluring qualities, the scenario is set for an otherworldly cinematic experience. In such a transformed state, "rather than look through the image 'from the outside' at a photographic reproduction of something staged in this world, you perceive the events of the film directly or 'from within.' You perceive a fully realized, though fictional, world that has all the perceptual presentness or immediacy of our own. We call this form of illusion projective illusion." It is a fictional world, Allen contends, where viewers develop an "empathetic identification with one or more characters in the fiction. That is, we actually find ourselves in the mental state of the characters with whom we identify." Whereas action films typically achieve greater viewer interest through violent, suspenseful, or painful scenarios, muscle movies, though often violent, are also able to convey a sense of ecstasy or the sublime by idealizing the human form and its function. Projective illusion is a form of virtual reality where, Allen notes, "our awareness of the photographic basis of the image is overridden by the combination of movement, sound, and projection."[13] While the demeanor and dialogue of eye-catching men and women typically invoke moviegoer fantasies and imaginary scenarios, actors who display and utilize their muscles to enhance viewer involvement further perfect this art of illusion.

While this book's underlying premise is rooted in such concepts as projective illusion and absorptive realism as internalized by audiences, the subject matter embraces the more tangible concept of perceiving the real world. Furthermore, it recognizes that actions appearing to be unattainable by human muscle can be derived through special effects and clever camera artifices, many of which have been around since the beginnings of film. "Moving pictures had barely been invented," notes animator and special effects artist Richard Rickitt, "when enterprising film makers began to experiment with the unique properties of motion picture photography to conjure new and sometimes fantastic images." Likewise, disguises and costuming help to enhance the dark and haunting visage of bodybuilder Dave Prowse as Darth Vader in successive iterations in the *Star Wars* series. This enrichment of reality provided yet another layer of illusion. Throughout the twentieth century, special effects coordinators perfected an endless variety of camera tricks, animatronics, prosthetic makeup, mechanized props, scale models, and pyrotechnics designed to leave audiences in a state of shock and awe and to re-create every semblance of human experience. In the 1950s audiences were even enlisted to produce an illusory impact by watching three-dimensional films with polarized glasses. What producers have not replicated is a believable facsimile of human movement. No mechanical or electronic device can capture the spontaneous action of muscles without destroying the impact of illusion. "Computer-generated humans tend to be used only very briefly, or in long-shot," reckons Rickitt, and thus "detailed scrutiny is impossible."[14]

Technical enhancement is simply the latest of a series of visual representations that can be traced from works of art through photography, the camera obscura, stage productions, and finally to motion pictures where virtually all attempts to convey realism are mediated by illusions. The latest phase of this centuries-long quest for creating visually perfect bodies is closely connected to the way muscles are utilized in movies. Here viewers are often tricked, by stunt people and technical gadgetry, into believing that athletic feats are real and the bodies on display are fit and healthy when they are sometimes the opposite. Although many actors train regularly or at least train for a specific role, stunt doubles are the fittest of the lot. Their lives often depend on it. Yet they create an unreal public image of perfection. Film scholar Ed Sikov recognizes this paradox, that filmmaking is "saddled with the notion that it's purely artificial. The lighting tends to be idealized, the actors' faces are idealized by makeup, the settings are sometimes idealized. Just to describe something as 'a Hollywood vision of life' is to say that it's phony."[15] Yet depictions of muscles in the movies never cease to inspire admiration and imitation. That viewers can indulge in this paradox owes much to absorptive realism, which enables them to enter a fictionalized portrayal of life but also, after being entertained and inspired, to withdraw from it and not lose touch with the real world—much like being awakened from a dream. In the dream world of cinema, viewers strive to believe what they are watching is real; the depiction of real bodies and what muscles can achieve provides one such opportunity. Few moviegoers realized or cared that the legendary Steve Reeves of *Hercules* fame was neither a notable athlete nor much of an actor. The visual impact of his muscles and faux strength was all that mattered. Since Kant and other philosophers identified the distinction between reality and representation, the idealized muscular body depicted in film has provided an endless fascination with the human potential, but it will always remain a distant echo from "the thing-in-itself."

Art and reality have always clashed in the movies. The make-believe world of cinema was a natural battleground, and nowhere was the conflict between illusion and reality more obvious than with photoplay stars. The first cinematic actors were anonymous players who performed in short and primitive films; in time filmgoers wanted to know more about their favorite personalities. Thus the star system was born. As this process settled into Hollywood, and as movies began to be produced abroad in the early twentieth century, studios increased their box office receipts by capitalizing on the visual attraction of their stars' bodies, which were critical to projecting their personalities. Indeed, actor, director, and producer Hobart Bosworth, heralded by pundits as the Dean of Hollywood, stated that "all acting consists in the expression of emotion by means of muscles."[16] For maximum effect, producers injected an abundance of action in silent films where bodily movements, often exaggerated, were a necessary substitute for sound dialogue. By the 1930s action scenes were no less important as a way of creating excitement, often in a dramatic denouement where the hero rescues the girl or foils the villain. Audiences demanded actions that were inspirational and larger than their mundane lives. Why else go to the movies? To ensure profits and vanquish competition, it was necessary to recruit handsome actors with athletic ability and well-endowed bodies. The challenge was to enhance reality, but not all actors—even those truly fit and athletic—could perform the larger-than-life actions required to sustain viewer interest. Furthermore, producers could not risk losing stars or supporting actors to serious injury that would result in costly production overruns. Therefore, it was necessary to create a further cinematic illusion by recruiting stuntmen (and stuntwomen) to double the stars in their most dangerous (and star-enhancing) feats. These professional performers, athletic individuals with finely toned and developed bodies, were the unsung heroes of filmmaking. As producer William Witney observed, "Great athletic ability makes stunt work look so easy that the audience thinks anybody can do it."[17] Stunters, as they came to be called, contributed greatly to making stars. Yet few stars, from Douglas Fairbanks to Arnold Schwarzenegger, would admit they used doubles, as to do so might detract from their heroic status.

Despite waxing and waning interest in men's appearance, certain muscular somatotypes have remained constant throughout motion picture history. The first type is the proletarian body, consisting of a husky physique built by strenuous labor and characterized by thick arms and a barrel chest. Strength, not muscular appearance, is its principal attribute, and the popular Italian character Maciste was an exemplar. This group includes not only the horny-handed sons of labor but those who practiced weightlifting (as opposed to bodybuilding), such as cowboy star Tom Tyler. Joe Bonomo and many other silent strongmen also fit into this category. The second physical paradigm is the athletic body. Possessors of this type are likely to be nimble with mighty forearms and thickly muscled legs produced by years of gymnastic exercise, swimming, football or other athletic activities. These are sport-built bodies, and though pleasantly muscular, they lack a bodybuilder's symmetry or definition. Serial actor Eddie Polo or the strapping Burt Lancaster can be included in this category. The final type, the developed body, includes bodybuilders who have spent years lifting weights and perfecting their physiques into the traditional V-shaped upper body, with broad shoulders, rippling abdominals, thick biceps, and sturdy legs. Steve Reeves and Arnold Schwarzenegger belong in this group. Admittedly, not all action heroes have been buff, but those who display showy muscles and athleticism are more likely to stir the imagination and enhance the potential for viewer absorption. The haptic imagery of muscle films featuring actors with glistening muscles and performing extraordinary feats of strength nearly always provides a more intense and satisfying movie experience.

The films featured in this book have many things in common. One of them is that occasionally the camera pauses (sometimes quickly, sometimes slowly and lovingly) to admire the protagonist's physique. From Sandow's brief performance in Edison's *Black Maria*, the trend extends to scenes like the long, slow, almost erotic pan of Schwarzenegger's recently crucified (and soon to be reanimated) body in *Conan the Barbarian*. From the earliest films to present-day productions, the human body has been a focus of interest and meaning. The actors seem to be screaming, "Look at me! Look what my muscles can do. Look at my body!" Sometimes the actor's body is covered in clothing, but there is always at least one moment when the audience is encouraged to gaze in awe upon the human machine. Here are muscles and athletic abilities that are far beyond the scale of ordinary men and women, and we share in the beauty, sexuality and power of these extraordinarily muscular men and women.

A muscular body might evoke admiration, but muscularly gifted men in films must use their sinews to perform feats relating to the story. Lifting and throwing a boulder or some other heavy object, tossing adversaries around like sticks or effortlessly knocking opponents senseless are actions commonly used to show how cinematic strongmen deal with difficult situations. After all, if a man displays his body for others to enjoy or impress, it is important for him to perform some aggressive or manly deed, lest viewers think the character is just a pretty boy with a gym-perfect body but little ability to use it. The psychosexual anxieties of the audience were often too tender to accept a manly looking hero who could not defend himself or smash things easily. Critics like John Berger and Laura Mulvey have written at length about the "male gaze."[18] "Men *act,* and women *appear*" might be a common way of addressing the issue, but does this apply to many of the muscle epics in this volume in which men appear *as well as* act? A man who partially disrobes risks being seen as "feminine," no matter how many muscles he sports. But if Conan or Rambo smack down deserving villains, smash a few structures, or lay waste to the countryside, they can still prance around with bare pectorals without imperiling their masculinity.[19] What's more, the well-built body strongly reinforces the illusion of seemingly impossible action feats. All this makes audiences feel in sync with the fictional heroes on the screen.

On the other hand, men are not always heroes, women are not always passive objects, and spectators do not always identify with the male. In "Masculinity as Spectacle," Steve Neale warns that identifying with Hollywood's representation of manliness often leaves male viewers feeling inadequate, as the eroticized image of handsome, hirsute masculinity up on the screen is seldom attainable.[20] The same applies to almost any sort of male bonding in movies. When a male character is seen to be very close to a male comrade, the friendship is often terminated by death or disfigurement. Thus, any hint of homoeroticism is avoided as traditional patriarchal order is restored. No matter how masculine the character might appear, there is a fear that the men will start to have affectionate feelings for one another that are not grounded in mere friendship. Powerful male characters can often disrupt more conventional relations between the sexes. In many traditional films the man saves the damsel in distress, and all ends happily in marriage, but the man who refuses to settle down is another common character. In many gladiator or Western movies, mighty and superbly endowed men are often forced (or choose) to move on. As the sun sinks slowly in the west, many athletic heroes trudge off alone or with only a horse or sidekick. The rationale is that they prefer a solitary life and can never be tied down; besides, there are plenty of others who are in desperate need of help. They are blessed with shapely and powerful bodies, but they never feel at home around ordinary mortals. From Maciste and Hercules to Conan and Rambo, the trope of the lonely but hunky hero is played out repeatedly. Just as he rejects an ordinary depiction by his superhuman appearance and abilities, so the hero of muscle movies eschews normal relations. He puts his body on the line in sacrificial duty as a Christlike savior.

But not all bare bodies in a film are there to act solely as saviors; sometimes they are on the screen to titillate us. It would be naive and disingenuous to deny that eroticism is often (perhaps always) present when we view a seminaked human form. It is impossible to know who exactly was watching Bruto Castellani in *Quo vadis* (1913) or Jason Momoa in *Aquaman* (2018); it is likewise impossible to know why. A myriad of motives lead a spectator into the darkened recesses of a cinema theater, but if there is a muscular, seminude actor involved, it is almost certain that scopophilia is involved. This is hardly a new development. As women gained independence and empowerment, one of the ways they expressed liberation was by increasing attendance at the movies. It took little time for producers to note this trend. "In the 1920s," confirms historian Gaylyn Studlar, "the American film industry clearly operated on the assumption that women formed their single most important audience."[21] This trend has continued. A 2018 survey published in the *MPAA Theme Report* revealed that women comprise 51 percent of all moviegoers, so it should be no wonder that shapely men continue to grace the world's screens.[22] Just as men enjoyed watching women in leotards and scantily clad chorus girls on the screen, many women were drawn to Errol Flynn in his Lincoln-green tights and Jean-Claude Van Damme's shirtless, sculpted torso.

Although strength and muscularity are usually the province of men, a surprising number of strongwomen have populated the movies. Only a few years after filming Sandow, Edison studios recorded circus and vaudeville performer Charmion doing a daring striptease in her "Trapeze Disrobing Act." After tossing off several layers of Victorian wardrobe, she revealed herself wearing tights, then posed for the camera in muscular splendor. Charmion was an exception since (unlike men) women normally could not display muscular physiques with equal visibility, but this does not diminish their pioneering roles.[23] Women generally demonstrated strength through athletic or sporting activities, leaving the heavy lifting to their male counterparts. While women could not fit the same somatotype as men (with barrel chests and rippling biceps), they often made up for it in derring-do. The first stars of weekly serial dramas, including Pearl White, Ruth Roland, and Helen Holmes, were often women.[24] Like men, the fate of muscular or sporting women in the movies rose and fell with the times. When women were searching for a persona representing their desire to share power with men, being spunky and in-your-face was fashionable, but when (as in the postwar 1950s) women were expected to retreat behind a man, their ambitions proved illusory, and they turned weak and kittenish.

Another genre that emphasized muscular bodies—this time exclusively male—that emerged in the late 1940s was the gay physique film. Its early purveyors began taking still photographs of seminude men after World War II, but they soon switched to eight- and sixteen-millimeter moving pictures when demand started growing. Physique films emerged from the "posing films" of bodybuilders in contests and studios, but it was soon obvious that gay men were going to be some of the customers. The first physique film that featured an unmistakable gay focus was made in 1949 by Richard Fontaine.[25] Although muscle films marketed to gay men were largely exiled to underground theaters and private showings, it was an audience of inestimable size that craved absorption in a more carnal kind of fantasy.

While muscular men and women have appeared in motion pictures throughout the medium's history, there are three eras when muscularity has been notably popular—the years 1915–25, 1959–65, and after 1977. These surges usually reflected times when masculinity was under attack, at least in moviegoers' minds. The first craze for muscular heroes began in Europe during World War I. Many returning soldiers, maimed in body or spirit, found their jobs were no longer available or taken by women. They sought new paradigms of virility that would reaffirm their ideas of manliness. In Europe and America they found refuge in screen fantasies played out by Bartolomeo Pagano as the mighty Maciste and the athletic escapades of Douglas Fairbanks. Hollywood became a magical kingdom in this era.

Succeeding waves occurred with many new assaults launched against traditional masculinity in the wake of the "greatest generation," which had triumphed over fascism. In *Stiffed: The Betrayal of the American Man*, feminist Susan Faludi argues that since the early 1960s men were losing their dominance in many areas critical for defining masculinity—politics, religion, the military, the community, and the home. To Faludi, the Vietnam War was a "defining event of American masculinity, the bridge that collapsed just as the nation's sons thought they were crossing to manhood."[26] Neither the manly might of Kirk Douglas as Spartacus nor Steve Reeves as Hercules could offer more than fantasy relief. Reeling from Title IX of the Education Amendments of 1972 (which prohibited discrimination based on gender), the passage of *Roe v. Wade* (1973), the Bobby Riggs / Billie Jean King tennis match (1973), and the upsurge of the National Organization for Women, a third wave of macho action films provided hope for sagging male egos. It featured Sylvester Stallone's *Rocky* series (1976–2006), Arnold Schwarzenegger's portrayal of the titular hero in *Conan the Barbarian* (1982), and Dwayne Johnson's starring role in *Hercules* (2014). "Stallone and I were the leading forces in the genre," recalls Schwarzenegger, with many other Hollywood stars muscling up too. "Even guys like Clint Eastwood, who were doing action movies all along, started bulking up and ripping off their shirts and showing off muscles."[27] Their inability to rescue men from the throes of womanhood owes much to the nature of the medium. As Faludi avers, they were caught up in an "ornamental culture" constructed around celebrity and image.[28] The stars of muscle movies are often the silicone implants of cinema—they look good, but they're far from the real thing.

There were other issues raised by the counterculture in the late 1960s that were hardly perceptible in early action films—most notably, race. Although one of the first cinematic strongmen (Maciste) was a white man in black face, muscular heroes in mainstream cinema were almost always white. Admittedly, Paul Robeson, Bruce Lee, and Dwayne Johnson are exceptions. But screen heroes typically represented the triumph of Western white men over "lesser breeds without the law," notes British critic Richard Dyer in discussing early Tarzan films and peplum epics of the 1960s. The villains in many muscular films are often people of color, adhering to the racist stereotypes that portrayed them as foreign, barbaric, and "other." Dyer sees the story of white men surviving in foreign lands as a reflection of imperialism. The physical appearance of actors playing these roles is, he says, indicative of their class since they have leisure time and funds to perfect hypermasculinized bodies.[29] Such media projections perpetuate mythologies of white male supremacy.

Owing to their high action and low introspection, films featuring muscular protagonists are often relegated to the critical dustbin, but these "cheap, trash films" (as one cinema historian dubs them) often reveal as much or more social commentary than so-called art films that enjoy greater prestige among intellectuals.[30] The unsophisticated plots most muscle movies employ reflect values that relegate them to lowbrow status. The target audience for most films featuring strongmen is usually set at the lowest socioeconomic denominator. Men and boys are their principal consumers. Sociologist Herbert Gans describes the normal Hollywood action film as a "hero's fight against crime and related violations of the moral order, or his attempt to save society from a natural disaster, but . . . the issues are always clear." Distinctions between good and evil are sharply delineated, and the protagonist never doubts his rightness or his often violent methods. The hero, sure of his masculinity, is diffident and chivalrous with good girls but sexually aggressive with bad girls. He usually solves problems alone or with a male helper or comic sidekick; distrusts governmental or institutional power and is a law to himself. Although these traits attract largely plebian viewers, there is much of what Gans calls "cultural straddling" since we all indulge in frivolities.[31] It is notably true for "higher" cultures who consume bits of such mindless entertainments as soap operas, football games, or gratuitously violent films. Most muscle movies are merely elaborate professional wrestling matches with handsome, muscular good guys confronting ugly, conniving bad guys who fight it out on the screen. The audience knows who will win, since there are few tragedies featuring muscular heroes. However counterintuitive to reality, the appearance and use of their bodies helps to make this illusion believable.

Many of the cinematic tropes that prominently feature muscles can be traced back to the distant past of Western civilization, to Greek and Roman times, which moviemakers considered heroic. The popularity of these ancient period films continues to thrive, as can be seen in modern films like *Gladiator* (2000) and *300* (2006). A technique relating to both films is the extensive use of CGI. Today's films not only create scenery and sets previously unheard of but can also alter the appearance and exaggerate the movements of actors without tedious workouts to produce such effects. Although the use of special effects to perfect the look and efficacy of male muscles might cause some men to despair of ever matching such a body, movies have always presented a fantasy world that only sometimes resembles the one mortals inhabit. Just as French viewers in 1895 tried to jump out of the way when a locomotive charged directly at them, or the audience screamed and ducked when the revolver was fired at them in *The Great Train Robbery* (1903), it is often difficult to separate art and reality.

The developed body has always represented triumph: the victory of strength over weakness, health over illness, and beauty over ugliness. It also represents the triumph of an individual's willpower over softness, laziness, and complacency. No human is born with a body like those of the stars of muscle films; he or she must build it with determination, persistence, and hard work. Concomitant with a muscular build is the assumption that the person who achieves a body of such beauty, strength, and agility must have the time, training, and nutritional resources to make such physical effort possible. Nevertheless, the illusory effect on viewers is often pervasive and accompanied by a moral. Muscle movie stars are almost always expected to use their physical strength and courage for the betterment of society, and viewers yearn for a Herculean hero who will sweep away the bad and usher in the good. The moral distance from Maciste to Dwayne Johnson is not so very far after all.

Notes

1. Antoine de Baecque, "Projections: La virilité à l'écran," in *Histoire de la virilité*, ed. Alan Corbin, Jean-Jacques Courtine, and Georges Vigarello (Paris: Seuil, 2011), 434.

2. Plato, *The Republic*, 250, 252.

3. For studies that analyze realism in the context of human consciousness, see Kendall L. Walton, "Transparent Pictures: On the Nature of Photographic Realism," *Critical Inquiry* 11, no. 2 (December 1984): 246–77; and Roger Christan Schriner, "Sceptical Alternatives: Strong Illusionism versus Modest Realism," *Journal of Consciousness Studies* 25, nos. 9–10 (2018): 209–27.

4. Gregory Currie, *Image and Mind: Film, Philosophy, and Cognitive Science* (Cambridge: Cambridge University Press, 1995), 34–36, 47.

5. Andrew Kania, "The Illusion of Realism in Film," *British Journal of Aesthetics* 42, no. 3 (July 2002): 246, 254, 256, 258.

6. Saul Smilansky, *Free Will and Illusion* (New York: Oxford University Press, 2000), 292–93, 296. William H. McNeill, late of the University of Chicago, draws a like inference for historians who confront the equally problematic concept of "myth." While conceding that "most historians disdain myths," McNeill asserts that truth actually "resides in myth," that "myths make subsequent experience intelligible" and that "communities live by myths, of necessity." William McNeill, "Make Mine Myth," *New York Times*, December 28, 1981.

7. Immanuel Kant, *Critique of Pure Reason*, trans. Norman Kemp Smith (London: Palgrave Macmillan, 2007), 23, 37, 42, 251; Arthur Schopenhauer, *The World as Will and Representation*, trans. E. F. J. Payne (New York: Dover, 1969), i, 19, 100; Curtis Cate, *Friedrich Nietzsche* (Woodstock, NY: Overlook Press, 2005), 167.

8. Henri Bergson, *Creative Evolution* (New York: H. Holt, 1931), 305–6, 308.

9. Magic Lantern Society, "Before Motion Pictures" (homepage), http://www.magiclanternsociety.org/.

10. Barbara Maria Stafford and Frances Terpak, *Devices of Wonder: From the World in a Box to Images on a Screen* (Los Angeles: Getty Research Institute, 2001), 303. Magic lanterns (or optical lanterns) were also often devised for educational purposes, including lectures on human anatomy, and in smaller versions as a children's toy.

11. A. Nicholas Vardac, *Stage to Screen: Theatrical Method from Garrick to Griffith*, 158, 66, 192.

12. Ben Singer, *Melodrama and Modernity: Early Sensational Cinema and Its Contexts*, 177; Brian Hooker, "Moving-Pictures: A Critical Prophecy," *Century* 93, no. 6 (April 1917): 868.

13. Richard Allen, "Representation, Illusion, and the Cinema," 40–42.

14. Richard Rickitt, *Special Effects: The History and Technique*, 39, 299. It should be noted that the use of CGI has made leaps and bounds since Rickitt's study appeared, to the extent that computer-modeled bodies can now closely mimic recorded human bodies. See Kristen Whissel, *Spectacular Digital Effects: CGI and Contemporary Cinema* (Durham, NC: Duke University Press, 2014).

15. Ed Sikov, *Film Studies: An Introduction* (New York: Columbia University Press, 2010), 4.

16. Hobart Bosworth, "Why Legitimate Actors Fail on the Screen While Many with No Training Succeed," in *The Truth about the Movies by the Stars*, ed. Laurence A. Hughes, 189.

17. William Witney, *In a Door, into a Fight, out a Door, into a Chase: Moviemaking Remembered by the Guy at the Door*, 142. Much of stunting's attraction by the 1960s was pay. Veteran stuntman Gene LeBell, who was making over $200,000 yearly, asks, "Now what the hell did I want to be an actor for? I'm a good stuntman and a lousy actor." Gene LeBell, *The Godfather of Grappling* (Santa Monica, CA: G. LeBell Enterprises, 2004).

18. John Berger, *Ways of Seeing* (New York: Viking, 1973), 45, 47; Laura Mulvey, "Visual Pleasure and Narrative Cinema," 14–30.

19. Several critics have even remarked that if most heterosexual American men are to enjoy watching a handsome, half-naked man on the screen, the character must be punished or undergo some brutal masochistic trial. See, generally, Steven Cohan and Ina Rae Hark, eds., *Screening the Male: Exploring Masculinities in Hollywood Cinema*.

20. Steve Neale, "Masculinity as Spectacle," in Cohan and Hark, eds., *Screening the Male*, 14.

21. Gaylyn Studlar, "The Perils of Pleasure? Fan Magazine Discourse as Women's Commodified Culture in the 1920s," in *Silent Film*, ed. Richard Abel (New Brunswick, NJ: Rutgers University Press, 1996) , 263. Studlar quotes a 1924 *Photoplay* article suggesting that American film audiences comprised 75 percent women. A 1927 article in *Moving Picture World* states that women made up 83 percent of movie audiences.

22. Motion Picture Association of America, "2018 Theme Report: Theatrical Demographic Shares" (PowerPoint presentation), http://www.mpaa.org/wp-content/up loads/2019/03/MPAA-THEME-Report-2018.pdf, 26.

23. Bieke Gils, "Flying, Flirting and Flexing: Charmion's Trapeze Act, Sexuality, and Physical Culture at the Turn of the Twentieth Century," 251–68.

24. Marina Dahlquist, ed., *Exporting Perilous Pauline: Pearl White and the Serial Film Craze*; Jennifer M. Bean, "Technologies of Early Stardom and the Extraordinary Body," 8–57.

25. Harry M. Benshoff and Sean Griffin, *Queer Images: A History of Gay and Lesbian Film in America* (Lanham, MD: Rowman and Littlefield, 2006).

26. Susan Faludi, *Stiffed: The Betrayal of the American Man*, 35, 298.

27. Arnold Schwarzenegger, *Total Recall: My Unbelievably True Life Story*, 337.

28. Faludi, *Stiffed*, 35.

29. See Richard Dyer, *White: Essays on Race and Culture*, and especially the chapter "The White Man's Muscles."

30. Gerald Mast, *A Short History of the Movies*, 364.

31. Herbert J. Gans, *Popular Culture and High Culture: An Analysis and Evaluation of Taste*, rev. and updated ed. (New York: Basic Books, 1999), 116–18.

PART I.

EARLY MOVIE MUSCLES

I. MUSCLES IN MOTION

Movement is life. Moving pictures will satisfy something deep inside all the people in the world. You'll see.

—William Friese-Greene, quoted in Ray Allister,
Friese-Greene: Close-Up of an Inventor

A SIGNIFICANT FEATURE in the development of early film production was the apprehension that much of what we think we observe in human behavior is actually unseen by the eye. Among the first to realize this phenomenon were early filmmakers. Indeed, motion that appeared real as conveyed through the lens of the camera was just an illusion—a persistence of vision that suggested a convergence of time and space. That it was part of the scientific and intellectual revolution that had such a transformative effect on biology (Charles Darwin), physics (Albert Einstein), psychology (Sigmund Freud), and other scientific endeavors of the late nineteenth and early twentieth centuries has never been fully appreciated. Yet the impact of motion pictures on the lives of countless millions of people during the twentieth century and beyond is undeniable.

Moving into Movies

The idea that our eyes can be tricked into seeing motion where none really exists developed slowly and serendipitously. In 1824 British physician Peter Mark Roget determined that the brain retains images for a split second longer than they are cast on the eye. By the outbreak of World War I, gestalt psychologist Max Wertheimer concluded that the eye perceives objects holistically. Thus, the movement of actors that many thousands of moviegoers see on the screen is merely a succession of static images, thereby creating an illusion that the whole has greater salience than the sum of its parts. As film historian David Cook explains, this persistence of vision "prevents us from seeing the dark space between the film frames by causing 'flicker fusion' when the frequency with which the projection light is broken approaches fifty times per second; without this effect, our eyes would perceive the alternation of light and dark on the screen as each projected image succeeded the next," as prevalent in early movies, "known colloquially as 'flickers' or 'flicks.'" This stroboscopic effect, optimally achieved at twelve to twenty-four frames per second, provided the basis for the development of cinematography.[1]

During its century of gestation, the study of muscular motion developed at roughly the same time that physicists were exploring optics, both of which led to unlocking the secrets of cinema. As film scholar Marta Braun points out, these movements were recorded for scientific, not entertainment, purposes and were related to the body's most important muscle, the heart. Impetus was provided by the newly developed science of physiology, an outgrowth of the ancient study of anatomy, which stressed process over stasis and function over form. Early experiments by Jules Janssen and Charles Ozanam in France with wet collodion plate photography led to the 1877 experiments of physiologist Étienne-Jules Marey, whose work with the electrocardiogram enabled him to measure precise movements of the heart muscle. Marey's graphing instruments, notes Braun, "allowed him to monitor movements hidden within the body, and have them trace themselves in a form of writing . . . 'the language of life itself'—which made them intelligible for the first time." Marey, though interested in the external manifestations of these vital functions, was ill prepared by his training as a physician and the nature of his instruments (requiring attachment to the body) to comprehend human and animal locomotion.[2]

Herein lay the significance of his association with Eadweard Muybridge, an English landscape photographer who was recruited in 1878 by former California governor Leland Stanford to solve the perennial question of whether there was any moment at which galloping horses from his racing stable were not touching the ground. By aligning twelve cameras along an outdoor track with shutters activated every twenty-one inches by threads tripped by a moving horse, Muybridge determined moments when the horse's body was suspended in air. After doubling the number of cameras, he serial photographed other animals and gymnasts from the San Francisco Athletic Club. Muybridge then devised a kind of high-speed magic lantern called the zoopraxiscope that rapidly projected images from rotating glass disks to convey the impression of motion. Although the zoopraxiscope was entertaining and presaged the cinema, it lacked (with its multiple cameras) a singular photographic perspective, and irregularities between exposures made the succession of images seem unrealistic. While Muybridge's explanations and representations were not scientific, observes Braun, they were "still the most convincing *illusion* of natural movement that had hitherto been achieved."[3]

Most critically, they served as a template for Marey, who, upon learning of Muybridge's discoveries, shifted his work from chronography to chronophotography. To remedy problems in the zoopraxiscope's design, Marey, by utilizing Janssen's concept of a photographic revolver and a new dry (gelatin bromide) plate, developed his *fusil photographique*, a photographic rifle that took twelve pictures at intervals of 1/720 of a second, enabling him to photograph a bird in free flight. As Braun explains, Marey's camera "made a picture of the changes that occurred in instants of time" by representing "sequential moments in time without the moments in between." Subsequently Marey's experiments extended to humans, utilizing a man dressed in black with joints marked in white in front of a black background to understand the mechanics of walking, running, and jumping. As Richard Dyer notes, "Marey developed film because he wanted to study the body."[4] Whether it was horses, birds, or humans, muscles were at the forefront of early efforts to analyze sequential movement.

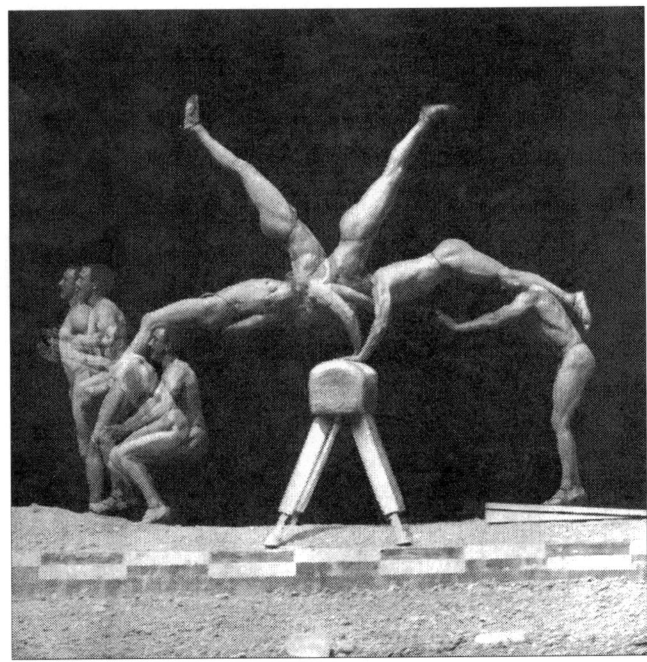

Figure 1.1. Frame from Étienne-Jules Marey's early chronophotographic study of the sequential movements of the human body. Collection of David L. Chapman.

How chronophotography might be applied attracted numerous opinions. Albert Londos and Paul Richer were not so much interested in movement as the human physique. They wanted "to establish a scientific typos of human proportions, at least insofar as the white race is concerned" and to understand, as Braun notes, "the way that light and shadow played over rippling muscles and delineated the expressive images of male force." Georges Demeny, who became Marey's assistant in 1880, believed physiological investigations using chronophotography could promote physical education and stem the degeneration of French citizens and soldiers after the Franco-Prussian War.[5] Demeny's aim, he told Marey, was to "develop the human body harmoniously by movement." To that end, Marey and Demeny employed cadets and officers of the École Joinville-le-Pont, a military academy that trained gymnasts and athletes.[6] This assignment especially interested Demeny, who prepared a manual for military and civic physical education. Although Marey was a pure scientist, he appreciated the practical potential for his investigations and importance of muscular action. As Marey noted, "One must make chronophotographs of the most strong and expert subjects, of gymnastic champions for example. These elite subjects will thus betray the secret of their success, perhaps unconsciously acquired, and which they would doubtless be incapable of defining themselves. The same method could equally well be applied to the teaching of movements necessary for the execution of all manual performances, and in all kinds of sports."[7] By breaking down movements of elite athletes in different sports, Marey and Demeny believed national regeneration would be possible through adoption by those less muscular. Soon their work was replicated in Germany by Ernst Kohlrausch, a gymnastics teacher at the Kaiser Wilhelm Gymnasium in Hanover. Sports, where the body's potential is displayed and often viewed as a military metaphor, seemed to invite chronophotographic application. "Today," Braun observes, "no athlete could do without the assistance of what the camera reveals."[8]

Equipped with a knowledge of chronophotography and suspecting it could do for the eye what his phonograph had done for the ear, Thomas Edison, working through his assistant William K. L. Dickson and utilizing a flexible celluloid film devised by George Eastman, developed a photographic mechanism that illuminated tiny pictures on a revolving drum. Eventually Dickson added perforations to edges of the film, allowing it to feed evenly into a camera. To project these images Dickson and Edison devised a coin-operated device called the kinetoscope, and in France the Lumière brothers, Auguste and Louis, designed a stop-action projector, the cinematograph, that enabled images to be fixed on the viewer's retina momentarily before advancing to the next frame.[9] Dickson and Edison had thus made the transition from science to commercialization, but the kinetoscope had limited use. It was available only in select hotels, department stores, saloons, and amusement arcades, and held only fifty feet of film lasting only forty seconds. It featured everyday life scenes, historical event reenactments, vaudeville routines, and celebrity appearances.[10]

Sandow's Magnificent Muscles

It is significant that the first celebrity to appear in Edison's kinetoscope was the foremost strongman/bodybuilder of the 1890s. Eugen Sandow (Friedrich Wilhelm Müller) was born in Königsberg, East Prussia, in 1867 and traveled throughout Europe in his early years as a circus athlete. He gained fame as a strongman under the tutelage of Professor Attila (Louis Durlacher) by challenging circus performers at English sideshows. From 1889 to 1893 Sandow established his reputation by performing strength feats at music halls and outdoor fairs, but what audiences wanted to see most was the posing routine he added to his act. Upon arriving in the United States under the aegis of showman Florenz Ziegfeld Jr. he performed at the Casino Theatre in New York. The *New York Times* reported that "the curtain went up, revealing the stage steeped in gloom. Then, suddenly, two curtains at the back of the stage were drawn aside, in a blaze of light stood the 'Strong Man,' with his mighty muscles standing out in bold relief in the white glare of an electric light. After performing a number of 'tableaux vivants,' to the accompaniment of slow music and much perspiration, Mr. Sandow left his cabinet, the lights were turned up, and the show began in earnest."[11] No less captivated by the German strongman was the *New York World*, insisting that all previous notions about physical development be abandoned: "Nothing that has ever been seen in New York can be used as a standard of comparison to measure the wonderful young German." But the "proper way" to introduce Sandow was to describe "some of the things which he can do." For example, he had "wrestled with three men at one time, all expert wrestlers, all bigger than he, and has stretched first one and then another flat, using one hand to a man and incidentally preventing the other two from tripping or otherwise throwing him."[12] Such athletic feats along with his magnificent physique soon attracted national attention.

Sandow became a star attraction at Ziegfeld's Trocadero Theater at the 1893 Columbian Exposition in Chicago. It led to a billing at Koster & Bial's, the nation's foremost music hall, and a prolonged tour with a troupe named Sandow's Trocadero Vaudevilles.[13] His strongman stunts and the muscle displays of his nearly naked body were hardly in keeping with Victorian norms of modesty, but they attracted a cross-section of society craving scientific innovation, novel forms of entertainment, and titillation. Sandow recounts that, after each performance, "I gave lectures on anatomy and my system of physical culture in my dressing-room. These lectures were attended by many of the most notable people in America, the crowded audiences including several ladies. I demonstrated how each feat was accomplished, and let the people feel for themselves my muscles, to prove that whilst, when they were relaxed they were as soft as butter, when contracted they were as hard as steel."[14] Sandow's growing fame, not unlike that of Arnold Schwarzenegger seventy years later, stemmed from his physique, but it would not have been possible without a strong athletic background. Both men also shared Germanic cultural roots and were drawn to movies as a means of advancing their careers in America.

For Sandow the opportunity arose on March 6, 1894, at the end of his Koster & Bial's run when he was accompanied by his business manager C. B. Cline, Richard Haines of the North American Phonograph Company, and impresario John Koster to Edison's studio, Black Maria, in West Orange, New Jersey. Here William Dickson shot three films for commercial showings on the kinetoscope and several still photographs.[15] "In point of classical beauty," according to Dickson, "and as a prophetic exposition of what we may expect in the physical regeneration of the race, Eugen Sandow, the modern Hercules, stands foremost. From an anatomical point of view, this great athlete has attained ideal perfection of form, combined with phenomenal strength and grace." Sandow stated that he charged $250 for an exhibition but would "gladly come for nothing for the privilege of shaking the hand of Edison, the greatest man of the age." The strongman then demonstrated that his muscles were not merely for show by playfully picking up Cline and sending him "sailing through the air and out of the door." Upon the film's premier at the kinetoscope parlor on Broadway, the *New York Herald* featured a report titled "The Chance of Sandow's Life" in which it noted that "the strongest man on earth, to quote the play bills, and the greatest inventor of the age met yesterday at Menlo Park, New Jersey. The meeting was an interesting one, and the giant of brain and the giant of muscle found much to admire in each other. Sandow marveled at Edison's inventions, and the Wizard gazed longingly and enviously at the prodigious muscles of the strong man." Dickson's biographer, Paul Spehr, explains that the three filmings of Sandow on March 6 only highlighted "the subtlest part of his act, muscle contractions, chest expansion and posing" and that "the more spectacular components such as lifting large bar-bells, tossing people off stage and balancing horses or grand pianos on his chest, were left for viewing in the theater."[16] Patrons at kineto-scope parlors had to peer through a narrow peephole to see Sandow's weak, flickering image, but the film ran only a few moments, long enough to thrill the patrons. To Spehr and other film historians, it marked "the beginning of commercial motion picture production."[17]

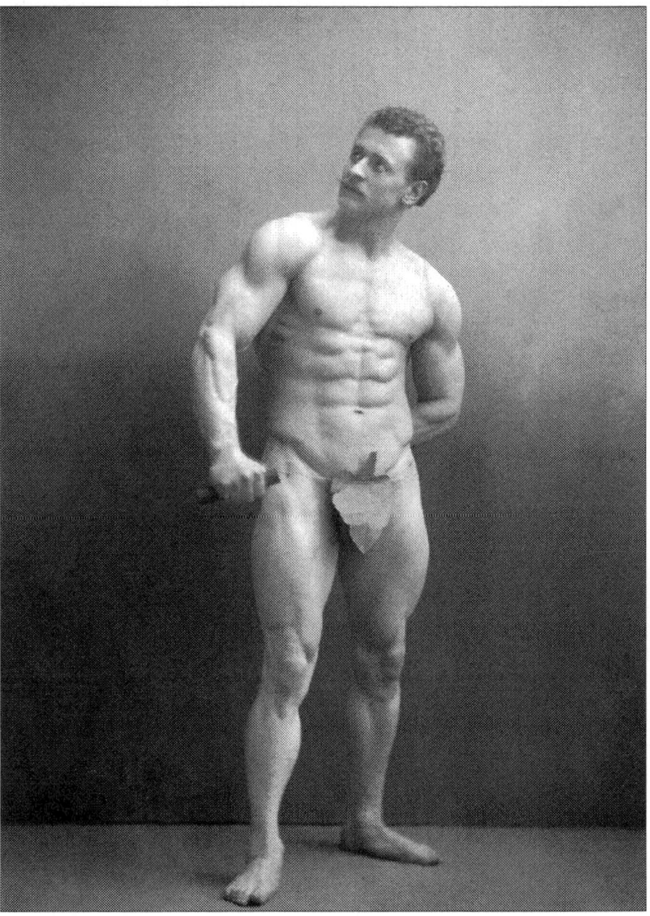

Figure 1.2. Classic photograph of Eugen Sandow at the apex of his fame as a strongman and bodybuilder. Collection of David L. Chapman.

What transpired was not only a display of muscles but a demonstration of what muscles could do. It was consistent with the kinesthetic traditions set by Marey and Muybridge, and Dickson's earlier chronophotographic explorations into the movements of animals, dancers, and humans engaged in daily activities. He had filmed athletes from the Newark Turnverein performing with wands, doing somersaults, using parallel bars, and boxing and followed up his Sandow film with more kinetoscopic productions to attract the paying public: Scottish highland dancing, wrestling, cockfighting, and acrobatic performances, including trapeze acts. That some of Dickson's films, especially ones of Sandow, also had strong homoerotic overtones fueled speculation that he was gay. Spehr, however, argues that "there is no substantiating evidence confirming his sexual orientation." It is less ambiguous that Sandow who, though married, lived for a time in America and Europe with Martinus Sieveking, a Dutch pianist and composer. A revealing portrait in the *New York World* describes them as "bosom friends."[18] Admittedly, emphasis on bodily display and movement was an inherent characteristic of most early films. Given the imperfect quality of images and lack of sound, muscular activity was an effective way to project human expression. "Lacking words," as Charles Musser notes, "actors often resorted to extensive pantomime to convey their thoughts or actions, pushing the use of conventionalized gestures to an extreme."[19]

Several years after their initial encounter, Dickson facilitated a further advance in moving pictures when Sandow's road show encountered an unexpected slump in September 1896 at the Alvin Theater in Pittsburgh. At the insistence of Charles Jefferson, Sandow's manager, Dickson (who had split with Edison and now headed the Biograph Company) made four films of Sandow that were projected on a large screen after his live performance. "Huge, clear, and lifelike" images replaced the "brief, dim peep shows" to which audiences were accustomed on Edison's primitive devices. They were enthralled by this new medium, and "Sandow had stumbled onto an exciting innovation whose time had come."[20] Soon spectators would demand more than just watching movement (even if it involved rippling muscles and acrobatics). It would not be long before story lines would become embodied in the movements of the actors.

While Sandow's strength and physique appear uppermost in retrospect, his lectures and writings indicate that he was trying to convey a profound understanding of physical culture. As an admirer of the Greek ideal of *mens sana in corpore sano* (a sound mind in a sound body), he sought to convince the public that cultivation of the body was inseparable from the mind. The purpose of physical culture, he argued, was to "cultivate the whole of the body so that at last it shall be capable of anything that sound organs and perfectly developed muscles can accomplish." Even strength, that most admirable of physical attributes, must be subjected to willpower. "Muscles are not developed by muscular action alone," he argued. To become strong, a man must learn to "use his mind."[21] For Sandow, there was a higher purpose to this interaction between mind and matter that the medium of motion pictures, which relied on appearances and appealed to curiosity seekers, could hardly convey. He believed that "it is *health* rather than *strength* that is the great requirement of modern men" and the real object of physical culture.[22] However fanciful screen images might be, they could have a powerful and beneficial impact in real life.

Gentleman Jim

With health allegedly his primary concern, and despite his success as a showman, Sandow claimed he never sought fame or pecuniary rewards. Had he merely wanted to make money, he would have become a pugilist, but as he often stated, "No man can be a prizefighter and remain a gentleman."[23] Yet it was boxing, driven by consumer curiosity and, paradoxically, government censorship, that captured the attention of filmmakers at the turn of the century. As boxing historian Dan Streible observes, although spectators seemed more fascinated by "'physical culture' rather than competitive sports," motion pictures "had an affinity for boxing."[24] A possible reason for this attraction was that this medium required no resort to "pantomime" or need to push "conventionalized gestures to an extreme" to satisfy audiences. The actions of boxers were real and by nature exaggerated. That boxers fought with bare knuckles and bare chests only added to their visual impact and appeal, especially considering the modesty that prevailed even in men's swimwear into the 1920s.

By the end of the nineteenth century boxing success increasingly required a strict training regimen and abstemious way of life. Health and fitness were primary concerns, as was the case with Sandow. In *How to Box to Win*, Featherweight Champion Terry McGovern advocated fresh air, pure cold water, and lots of roadwork—twelve miles daily with lips closed and running on the balls of one's feet.[25] David Hutchison's manual, *Boxing*, contradicted the popular notion that "the best equipment for a boxer is ponderous strength, especially of the arms and shoulders." Heavy gymnasium work robbed boxers of suppleness. "Strength is essential, of course, but it is such strength as gives speed and endurance rather than the ability to lift weights or break chains. The best training for the would-be boxer is boxing, plenty of it."[26]

What Hutchison advocated was scientific boxing, introduced by James "Gentleman Jim" Corbett, who shared Sandow's notion of cultivating the mind and body. Corbett argued that boxing "develops every muscle in the human body, it quickens the brain, it sharpens the wits, it imparts force, and above all it teaches self-control." He advised young men to be smart: "Don't try to be a hard hitter before you know what you are going to hit and how you are going to hit." Furthermore, a "good boxer must lead a regular life. . . . Dissipation has ruined more great athletes than all other causes combined." Good boxing started with "good physical health" and "sensible training." Just thirty minutes daily of roadwork or indoor exercise, done "properly and conscientiously," should suffice. Like McGovern, Corbett advised young amateurs to breathe plenty of fresh air, and like Hutchison, not to lift heavy weights. "Dumbbells should not be heavier than two pounds each. Work with something that cultivates speed, and the necessary strength will come with it."[27] Beyond the question of old-time slugging versus the new scientific boxing lay the question of what kind of physique would be most effective in the ring, appealing to fans, and best for a sport that was still illegal in virtually every state.

Whether efficiency would prevail over bigger and stronger muscles would be tested at the much anticipated encounter in New Orleans between Corbett and John L. Sullivan in 1892. At a predeparture exhibition in Brooklyn they flexed their muscles, displaying both power and appearance of power. The *Police Gazette* reported that Sullivan's "back is superbly developed and the great masses of muscle which back his shoulder blades stood out in grandeur. No man of modern times has a finer back." Sullivan predicted he would get to his opponent "good and strong. He can run or do whatever he likes." Corbett, on the other hand, impressed observers by tossing a medicine ball and giving a demonstration of "pushing, hauling and neck-squeezing." He then played handball with John Lawler, the Irish champion, on a temporary court, and "Jim delighted the spectators time and again by his wonderful agility." Al Smith, formerly Sullivan's manager, observed that he had never seen any man "make such a splendid exhibition as Corbett."[28] Later, at Sullivan's sparring match in Madison Square Garden, the *New York Clipper* overheard "murmurs of disappointment." The champion appeared greatly overweight, with folds of fat on the back of his head and his midsection. "His movements seemed slow and listless." Strength seemed to be Sullivan's only advantage. But Corbett had "youth, agility, and endurance." It was apparent that "a perfect man from a physical standpoint was before them."[29] To William Brady, Corbett's manager, he had "the finest physique the Almighty ever put together." Determined to remain at the peak of fitness, Gentleman Jim had a small gymnasium installed in the private railroad car that took him to New Orleans where his defeat of Sullivan marked a triumph of function over form.[30]

It is not surprising that Edison should exploit the newfound heroic status of Corbett's efficient muscles for his fledgling kinetoscope enterprise. Through Brady, Corbett negotiated an agreement offering $5000 to the winner and $250 to the loser in a bout with Peter Courtney, a relatively inexperienced boxer from Trenton, New Jersey. Furthermore, precedent to Babe Ruth's famous called home run in 1932 and the prediction of Muhammad Ali (then Cassius Clay) that he would beat champion Sonny Liston in 1964, it was stipulated that Gentleman Jim would "put the guy out in six rounds" to accommodate kinetoscope's capacity. That is exactly what Corbett did, with under a minute of film remaining.[31] And Edison carefully choreographed the fight to ensure Corbett would be the star, repeatedly shouting the instructions "Hold up that right-hand punch till you get him in the middle of the ring" and "Force him around so that you are facing the camera."[32] While filming Sandow was more an experiment in cinematography, the Corbett-Courtney fight was a commercial venture from which Corbett earned $5000 and over $15,000 in royalties. His biographer pronounced it "the beginning of sports motion pictures."[33]

Meanwhile, as Corbett pursued a stage career as Gentleman Jim, Brady negotiated a bout with challenger Bob Fitzsimmons for March 17, 1897, in Carson City, Nevada. Although Corbett lost in the fourteenth round, it was a technological and financial triumph. Produced by the Veriscope Company, *The Corbett-Fitzsimmons Fight* featured a new widescreen projection and lasted seventy minutes, the longest film shown up to that time. Later versions were cut to twenty minutes to accommodate vaudeville showings. Over the next four years of exposure it earned $750,000, and netted $100,000, a financial bonanza for the Lubin Company, which acquired exclusive rights from promoter Dan Stuart, who lost money on the fight itself. Such was the power of cinema and its projection of moving bodies. Streible called the film a "watershed moment for the fight picture." As Armond Fields notes, *The*

Corbett-Fitzsimmons Fight "was a revelation in movie picture making and its appeal swept the country. Many boxing movies followed, but none caused the same sensation."[34]

No less significant than the newfound profit potential of film was its appeal to an increasingly middle-class clientele, including women, who were often dubbed matinee girls. Boxing was regarded as the most masculine of sporting activities, but Charles Musser argues that *The Corbett-Fitzsimmons Fight* set a precedent for women's spectatorship and entry into the public sphere. They could sample a round or two of filmed bouts shown as matinee features at their neighborhood vaudeville theater. "Suddenly they had access to the forbidden and could peruse the semi-naked, perfectly trained bodies of the male contestants."[35] For them, Corbett's body and persona held a special, perhaps sexual, attraction, argues Streible: "Although journalists never mention the point, nobody seeing either the *Corbett-Fitzsimmons* or *Corbett-Courtney* films could fail to notice the Gentleman's prominently displayed gluteus maximus. The revealing trunks he sports in the filmed bouts were not often worn by other fighters. His daring choice of costume played to his image as a ladies' man."[36] Whether it also appealed to male heterosexual spectators is debatable. Thomas Waugh observes that physique photography, not unlike its cinematic cousin, served as "a lightning rod of (gay) male desire and the eroticized gaze" and represented some of "the first stirrings of the homoerotic construction of the male body."[37] Streible argues that facial disfigurements endured by boxers hardly coincided with most homosexual desires for depictions of male beauty: "The world of boxing was more likely to comport with the traditional patriarchal culture of masculinity than with a gay sub-culture." Even a more sanitized version of Corbett's career portrayed decades later by Errol Flynn in *Gentleman Jim* provides little subtext for homosexual desire.[38]

Charmion

More conducive to conventional male tastes was Edison's three-minute production in 1901 of stage actress Charmion (Laverie Vallee) in *Trapeze Disrobing Act*. Like Sandow and Spanish dancer Carmencita, whom Edison had filmed in 1894, Charmion appeared at Koster & Bial's music hall, near an Edison kinetoscope parlor. This cross-pollination, according to Musser, "introduced a relationship between the world of performance culture and the world of motion pictures."[39] Bieke Gils explains how the new medium also sparked the demise of vaudeville as America's most widespread form of entertainment: "Theatre managers used this new and fascinating technology of film to attract spectators, while continuing to provide staged entertainment. The synergy of vaudeville and cinematography permitted curious audiences to view moving bodies on display."[40] Charmion's performance on a static trapeze consisted of removing several layers of cumbersome turn-of-the-century women's apparel while two male voyeurs enjoyed the striptease from a theater box. When she finally reached the bottom layer of attire, Charmion performed several athletic feats, finishing with outstretched arms.

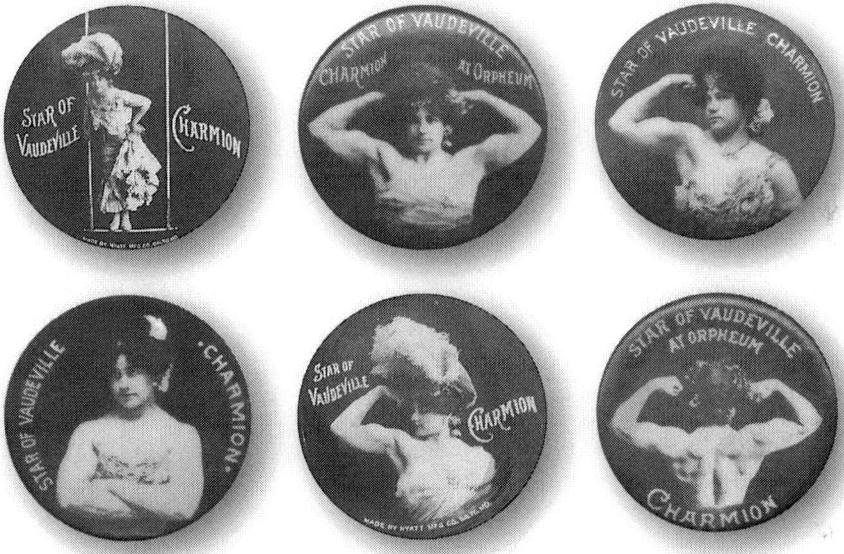

Figure 1.3. Laverie Vallee (better known as Charmion) was filmed in 1901 in her notorious "Trapeze Disrobing Act." She distributed these pinback buttons as publicity for her vaudeville act. Collection of David L. Chapman.

Aside from her pioneering film debut with Edison and her sexually suggestive performance, what made Charmion unique was her athleticism and extraordinary muscular development. "Young women who are ambitious to rival their brothers in muscular development," observed the *New York World*, "would do well to follow the example set by La Petite Charmion" whose "muscles stand out like great knots when she strikes a pugilistic attitude." She had "the muscles of Sandow" with a back and biceps resembling an oak tree and a larger arm than that of Gentleman Jim. Another newspaper report alleged that Charmion had tested her strength against three strongmen, one being Sandow, and she had "nearly half as much leg and back power."[41] Gils notes that "Charmion's most provocative pose was probably the one where she flexed both arms over her shoulders and displayed her naked back, for this suggested that the front of her body was also naked."[42] According to Gils, to offset criticisms of her muscular sexuality and provocative act, Charmion promoted herself as a physical culture advocate and dress reformer, much in the manner of Bernarr Macfadden and George Bernard Shaw. Concurrent with an "increasing fascination with the well-developed muscular body during this era . . . she framed her performances as instructional examples for women who wished to show their strong bodies and learn how to adopt healthy lifestyles." Further to establish credibility, she marketed herself as "the female Sandow." Like that of Sandow, the athletic artistry of Charmion on stage and film, followed by other screen displays of female muscle in 1903 and 1905, boldly challenged Victorian gender norms.[43]

The Inimitable Jack Johnson

A more flagrant challenge to yet another aspect of those norms was the muscular athleticism of legendary black boxer Jack Johnson, both in the ring and in film. Dubbed the Galveston Giant, Johnson had little of the raw aggressive manner of Sullivan or the scientific refinement of Corbett, yet he developed a unique style composed of natural talent, personality, and experience to become the most celebrated and controversial pugilist of his era. Johnson attributed his ability partly to innate strength: "My father was one of the strongest men, physically, I have ever known. He wasn't quite as tall as I am, but he was solidly built and very broad through the shoulders. He carried a barrel of sugar or lard with great ease and could lift a 500-pound bale of cotton with one hand." To illustrate his own strength during a sparring session for his epic fight with Jeff Jeffries, Johnson wedged his right glove between his two-hundred-pound opponent's arm and right side, lifted him, and shook him until Johnson's arm broke free. Though muscular and strong, Johnson did not believe a boxer should develop showy muscles: "A big pile of flesh and muscles, shown off to its best advantage in the footlights, is impressive to an audience, but a connoisseur has no such illusions."[44] He was more concerned with what his muscles could do.

Lacking formal training, Johnson had learned to fight by defending himself on the streets of Galveston, Texas, against bullies. "Fights between kids give them self-confidence and are the first lesson in the struggle for survival," Johnson believed. These encounters, according to Randy Roberts, led to brawls with other black men in alleys and on docks, challenge bouts with circus boxers roaming the country, and sparring matches with better boxers. As Roberts notes, "Though slender, he was well muscled and quick, and he usually won the street fights that came his way."[45] That Johnson became a prizefighter resulted from knowing his boxing ability could afford him to live. While he had virtually no opportunities for formal instruction and gained little knowledge from the black boxers he encountered, he acquired a quick education in pugilism from a white former champion, Joe Choynski, who took on Johnson at the Galveston Athletic Club in 1901. Boxing was illegal in Texas, however, and after Choynski knocked him out in the third round, the police hauled both fighters to jail. "Sheriff Henry Thomas was a delightful man," Johnson recalls. "He gave Joe and me the royal treatment. He allowed the club to send us boxing gloves and every day we would box in the jail yard, surrounded by Police officers and guests. Joe had great affection for me and . . . gave me lessons, showing me the best punches anyone has ever seen in a jail yard." Roberts explains that Johnson's time spent in jail "was like a training camp."[46] Didacticisms imparted by Choynski were critical to Johnson's steady rise to become World Colored Heavyweight Champion in 1903.

There were also cultural factors that affected Johnson's style of fighting. "The ring, like the world," argues Roberts, "was assumed to be the white man's territory, and the black fighter's object was to yield it without suffering physical punishment, allowing his opponent to defeat himself." Through feints and defensive maneuvers, "the black boxer waited for the white fighter to tire before moving on the offensive, but usually he did not turn aggressive even then." Thus Johnson, who never tried for a knockout, "carried opponents in order to deal out more punishment," the object being to hurt rather than end the fight.[47] A desire by black heavyweight champions to avoid crossing the color line and possibly jeopardizing racial stereotypes had relegated Johnson to fighting inferior opponents. Finally, in December 1908, after chasing him around the world, Johnson easily disposed of Canadian Tommy Burns in Sydney, Australia, to become World Heavyweight Champion. "From that moment," notes Gilbert Odd, "he became the most hated man in his own country and there was a world-wide search for a 'white hope' to beat him." By public demand, James Jeffries, a World Heavyweight Champion who had retired undefeated after twenty-two contests, returned to the ring. At 6' 2½" and 220 pounds, Jeffries was regarded as the strongest of the heavyweight champions in build and punching power, but at age thirty-five, and overweight, he was in no condition for a comeback. In Reno, Nevada, on

July 4, 1910, Johnson repeatedly evaded Jeffries's heaviest blows and eventually battered him into submission in round fifteen. "The result," states Odd, "inflamed race riots throughout America and the showing of the film of the fight was prohibited."[48] His victory over "the great white hope," plus his attitude and flamboyant lifestyle, made Johnson an iconoclast.

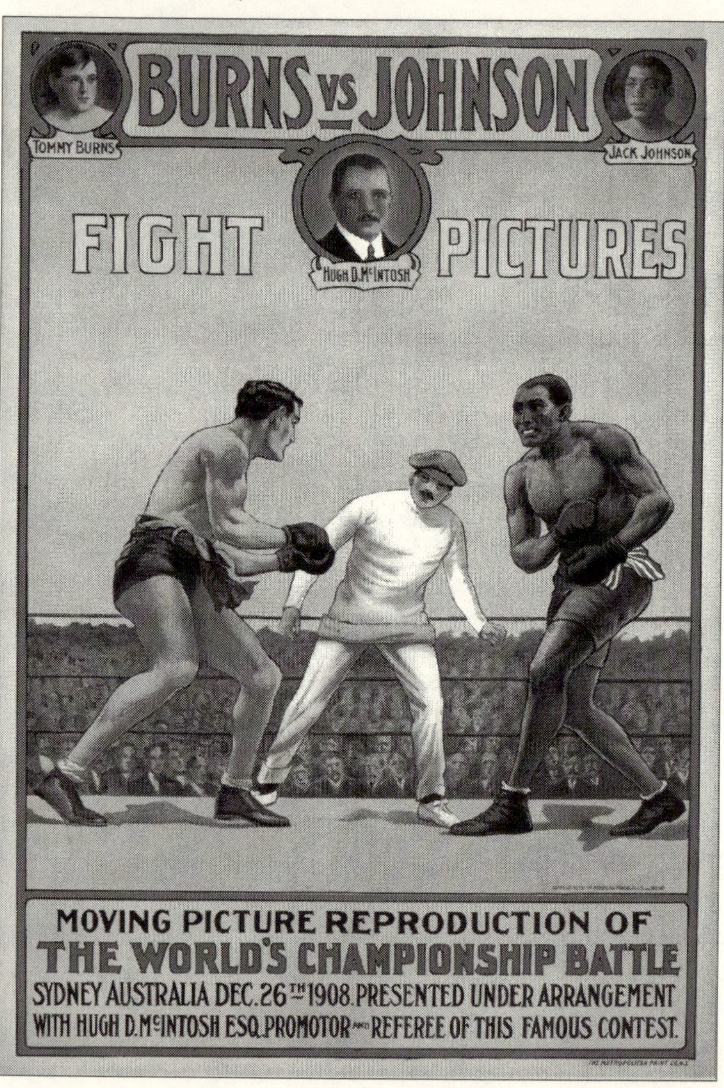

Figure 1.4. Film poster for the 1908 world championship boxing match between Jack Johnson and Tommy Burns. Collection of David L. Chapman.

During the first decade of the twentieth century, as the motion picture industry emerged, boxing films, despite widespread censorship of fights and fight films, proliferated. "The early filmmakers' fascination with capturing the human physique in motion added to the prevalence of boxers in films," notes Streible. "More than one hundred such films were produced by 1907, more than 200 by 1915." Even film reproductions of fights drew heavily; re-creations between 1897 and 1910 "exceeded the number of films shot at ringside."[49] Six films of Johnson's matches were released from his gaining the heavyweight crown to losing it in 1915 to Jess Willard. It is hardly surprising, owing to the social tensions it evoked, that *The Johnson-Jeffries Fight* created a storm of controversy over censorship. But it seems remarkable that it not only jeopardized the sport of boxing but the motion picture industry. "There was never a time," according to *Moving Picture World*, "when the general interests of the moving picture business were more at stake than during the period immediately following the Johnson-Jeffries fight."[50]

What helped keep boxing and motion pictures afloat was the profitability of the medium. For his 1909 bout with Stanley Ketchel, Johnson received a $33,000 purse and $20,000 in proceeds from the film, while he and Jeffries each earned $50,000 in picture profits from their 1910 fight.[51] More important, as Streible notes, "the fight gave professional boxing its greatest exposure" as many white and black curiosity seekers came to see Johnson, who became a larger-than-life-figure and the first black movie star. "At a moment in cinematic history when no images of potent black masculinity had been seen," observes Susan Courtney, "the combination of Johnson's highly cultivated image, his seemingly unconquerable success, and the documentary lure of the fight film footage formed a uniquely powerful image."[52] As former tennis star Arthur Ashe comments in *Hard Road to Glory*, Johnson was "the most significant black athlete in history."[53] Cinematography also granted Johnson a long lease of fame with two Vitagraph comedies—*The Night I Fought Jack Johnson* (1913) and *Some White Hope?* (1915)—that parody the fear white boxers had of him, as well as many fictional renditions and training films. A reminder of Johnson's pride in his strength and physique shows up in the five-minute *Der Meister Boxer der Welt* (The master boxer of the world, 1911), based on his stage show in London.[54] It shows him flexing his biceps and tossing his managers around in comic sequences. Most consequential, however, was the 1970 film *The Great White Hope*, starring Tony Award winners James Earl Jones and Jane Alexander, which provided a lingering aftertaste of how Johnson used his muscularity to instigate a revolution in racial attitudes.[55]

That muscles played a prominent role in the early development of film may be attributed partly to the post–Civil War emergence of competitive athletics and team sports, including boxing, baseball, basketball, and football, and such recreational pursuits as hiking, mountain climbing, and bicycling.[56] Already in motion was a groundswell of interest in filmmaking for scientific, military, and entertainment purposes, leading to what Tom Gunning has termed the "cinema of attractions" that thrived from 1893 to 1908. They featured

> a fascination with visual experiences that seem to fold back on the very pleasure of looking (colors, forms of motions—the very phenomenon of motion itself in cinema's earliest projections); an interest in novelty (ranging from actual current events to physical freaks and oddities); an often sexualized fascination with socially taboo subject matter dealing with the body (female nudity or revealing clothing, decay, and death); a peculiarly modern obsession with violent and aggressive sensations (such as speed or the threat of injury). . . . In effect, attractions have one basic temporality, that of the alternation of present/absence that is embodied in the act of display. In this intense form of present tense, the attraction is displayed with the immediacy of a "Here it is! Look at it."[57]

Such presentations led to simplicity and brevity rather than complexity or extension of action. According to Steven Mintz and Randy Roberts, movies were initially "little more than a novelty, often used as a chaser to signal the end of a show in a vaudeville theater"; they lasted just "seven to ten minutes—too brief to tell anything more than the simplest story."[58] Miriam Hansen concurs that film audiences were "feeding on attractions such as the magical and illusionist power of filmic representation, its kinetic and temporal manipulations" and "the recurring look of actors at the camera." These "'primitive' attractions" were soon displaced by "narrative strategies of viewer absorption and identification."[59] The early Edison productions of Sandow, Corbett, and Charmion, all vaudevillians, easily fit these scholarly profiles. The advent of the nickelodeon, narrative scripts, and the star system, where motion for its own sake (even when it shocked Victorian sexual and racial sensitivities), no longer sufficed to satisfy audience expectations. Viewers wanted to be visually stimulated to think and feel through a carefully woven story. By the time Johnson won his world championship in 1908, the nature of cinema was changing in that muscles might help tell the story, but usually in a more muted fashion.[60]

Notes

1. David A. Cook, *A History of Narrative Film* (New York: W. W. Norton, 1996), 1. For surveys of early cinematic development, see Charles Musser, *The Emergence of Cinema: The American Screen to 1907*, and Charles Musser, *Before the Nickelodeon: Edwin S. Porter and the Edison Manufacturing Company* (Berkeley: University of California Press, 1991).

2. Marta Braun, "The Expanded Present: Photographing Movement," in *Beauty of Another Order: Photography in Science*, ed. Ann Thomas, 153–54.

3. Marta Braun, *Picturing Time: The Work of Etienne-Jules Marey (1830–1904)*, 252. Tom Gunning views Muybridge's achievement as the result of exploring the still medium of photography and its "precarious existence at the intersection of art and science. . . . One might well describe confronting the still image with its extension into an illusion of motion as discovering 'the fundamental conditions and limits of his art.'" Tom Gunning, "Never Seen This Picture Before: Muybridge in Multiplicity," in *Time Stands Still: Muybridge and the Instantaneous Photography Movement*, ed. Phillip Prodger (New York: Oxford University Press. 2003), 267.

4. Braun, *Picturing Time*, 157, 159; Richard Dyer, interview with John D. Fair, London, September 11, 2012.

5. Braun, *Picturing Time*, 167.

6. According to Braun, it was clear to the French War Ministry that Marey's findings "could provide an objective, scientific foundation for the reform of the army. With his cameras and graphing instruments, he had assessed the muscular energy expended in different ways of walking and running and had shown that certain cadences and paces lessened fatigue." Braun, *Picturing Time*, 69, 104.

7. Étienne-Jules Marey, quoted in Braun, "Expanded Present," 167.

8. Braun, "Expanded Present," 170.

9. The cinematograph is usually regarded as an advancement over the kinetoscope as it was both a camera and projector, was portable, and produced a sharper image. Louis Lumière, "The Lumière Cinematograph," in *A Technological History of Motion Pictures and Television*, ed. Raymond Fielding (Berkeley: University of California Press, 1979), 49–51; Jacques Rittaud-Hutinet, ed., *Letters: Auguste and Louis Lumière* (London: Faber and Faber, 1995).

10. Steven Mintz and Randy Roberts, "Introduction: The Social and Cultural History of American Film," in *Hollywood's America: United States History through Its Films*, 3rd ed., ed. Steven Mintz and Randy Roberts, 9.

11. "The Strong Man Appears," *New York Times*, June 12, 1893.

12. *New York World*, June 18, 1893, quoted in Eugen Sandow, *Sandow on Physical Training*, ed. G. Mercer Adam, 107–8.

13. Charles Musser, "'A Personality So Marked': Eugen Sandow and Visual Culture," in *Moving Pictures: American Art and Early Film, 1880–1910*, ed. Nancy Mowll Mathews, 105.

14. Eugen Sandow, *Strength and How to Obtain It*, 125.

15. Paul Spehr speculates that Haines made arrangements to film Sandow at the behest of the Tate/Raff syndicate that was marketing kinetoscopes in New York. Paul C. Spehr, *The Man Who Made Movies: W. K. L. Dickson*, 328.

16. W. K. L. Dickson and Antonia Dickson, *History of the Kinetograph, Kinetoscope and Kinetophonograph* (New York: Crowell, 1895; reprint New York: Museum of Modern Art, 2002), 34; *Orange (NJ) Chronicle*, March 10, 1894, quoted in David L. Chapman, *Sandow the Magnificent: Eugen Sandow and the Beginnings of Bodybuilding*, 76; "The Chance of Sandow's Life," *New York Herald*, April 9, 1894; Spehr, *The Man Who Made Movies*, 337.

17. Chapman, *Sandow the Magnificent*, 77; Spehr, *The Man Who Made Movies*, 325, 327. Marey, who filmed Sandow in 1900, regarded him as "an example of an overdeveloped muscularity that was lacking in well-rounded vigor and overall physiological strength." Étienne-Jules Marey, quoted in Marta Braun, "Chronophotography: Leaving Traces," in Mathews, ed., *Moving Pictures*, 95. Braun adds that in terms of applied scientific knowledge the kinetoscope was "nothing new," but with the financial clout, labor, and space for mass production wielded by Edison, its dissemination and exploitation was "in great part responsible for the enormous progress made in creating a motion picture industry during the following three years." Braun, *Picturing Time*, 191. Likewise, Ray Allister concludes that William Friese-Greene had the inventive genius of Marey and Edison but lacked the financial acumen to market the perforated celluloid film produced from his chronophotographic camera. Ray Allister, *Friese-Greene: Close-Up of an Inventor*, 49. See also Gerald Pratley, "Who Invented the Movies?," *Films in Review* 2, no. 7 (August–September 1951): 13–15; and John Boulting, dir., *The Magic Box* (London: British Lion Film, 1957), starring Robert Donat, with appearances by Peter Ustinov and Laurence Olivier.

18. Spehr, *The Man Who Made Movies*, 53, 325, 330; *New York World*, June 18, 1893, quoted in Sandow, *Sandow on Physical Training*, 110. See also Chapman, *Sandow the Magnificent*, 51–52. Charles Musser makes a stronger, albeit more circumstantial, case for Sandow's homosexuality by linking his behavior to Oscar Wilde's notorious 1895 conviction in England: "Like Wilde, Sandow's homosexual activity had been quite blatant even though it was not quite explicit." Musser, "'A Personality So Marked,'" 109.

19. Musser, *The Emergence of Cinema*, 3.

20. Chapman, *Sandow the Magnificent*, 96–97. In Spehr's view, however, "the reactions were favorable but not overly enthusiastic." Spehr, *The Man Who Made Movies*, 444. Sandow's final filming in 1900 was done by Marey using his *fusil photographique*. Edmond Desbonnet to Gerard Nisivoccia, August 29, 1948, letter in the possession of David L. Chapman.

21. Sandow, *Strength*, 4–5.

22. Sandow, *Sandow on Physical Training*, 5.

23. Sandow, *Sandow on Physical Training*, 18–19.

24. Dan Streible, "On the Canvas: Boxing, Art, and Cinema," in Mathews, ed., *Motion Pictures*, 111–12. The earliest moving representation of boxers appears in Eadweard Muybridge's "Boxing Open Hand (Shoes)" sequence in *Animal Locomotion*.

25. Terry McGovern, *How to Box to Win* (Chicago: Shrewsbury, 1899), 100–101.

26. D. C. Hutchison, *Boxing* (New York: Outing, 1913), 101.

27. James J. Corbett, *Scientific Boxing* (New York: Richard K. Fox, 1912), 11–23. According to physical culturist Thomas Inch, a boxer's regimen consisted of sparring, ball and sack training, shadow boxing, roadwork, medicine ball work, handball, wall machines, and other exercises. Thomas Inch, *Spalding's Book on Boxing and Physical Culture* (Aldershot, UK: Gale and Polden, 1945), 16.

28. Gene Smith and Jayne Barry Smith, eds., *The Police Gazette* (New York: Simon and Schuster, 1972), 157.

29. *New York Clipper*, September 3, 1892, quoted in Armond Fields, *James J. Corbett: A Biography of the Heavyweight Boxing Champion and Popular Theater Headliner*, 56–58.

30. William A. Brady, *Showman: My Life Story*, 79; Patrick Myler, *Gentleman Jim Corbett: The Truth Behind a Boxing Legend*, 51.

31. Fields, *James J. Corbett*, 84–86.

32. Myler, *Gentleman Jim Corbett*, 96.

33. Fields, *James J. Corbett*, 96, 86.

34. Streible, "On the Canvas," 113; Fields, *James J. Corbett*, 107.

35. Musser, *The Emergence of Cinema*, 200. See also Miriam Hansen, "Reinventing the Nickelodeon: Notes on Kluge and Early Cinema," *October* 46 (Autumn 1988): 189.

36. Dan Streible, *Fight Pictures: A History of Boxing and Early Cinema*, 88.

37. Thomas Waugh, "Strength and Stealth: Watching (and Wanting) Turn of the Century Strongmen," *Canadian Journal of Film Studies* 2, no. 1 (1991): 3.

38. Streible, *Fight Pictures*, 94; Raoul Walsh, dir., *Gentleman Jim* (Burbank, CA: Warner Brothers Pictures, 1942). According to Harvey Marc Zucker and Lawrence J. Babich, "If you don't mind Hollywood taking liberties with some facts, *Gentleman Jim* is certainly the most thoroughly enjoyable boxing biography ever put on screen." Harvey Marc Zucker and Lawrence J. Babich, *Sports Films: A Complete Reference*, 1987, quoted in Myler, *Gentleman Jim Corbett*, 211.

39. Charles Musser, "At the Beginning: Motion Picture Production, Representation and Ideology at the Edison and Lumière Companies," in *The Silent Cinema Reader*, ed. Lee Grieveson and Peter Krämer (London: Routledge, 2004), 18. Robert Allen explains that "vaudeville would provide the infant motion picture industry with its most important outlet for exhibition during its first decade." For Edison's *Charmion*, "the burlesque stage provides the rationale for the film's sexual display." Robert C. Allen, *Horrible Prettiness: Burlesque and American Culture* (Chapel Hill: University of North Carolina Press, 1991), 186, 268.

40. Bieke Gils, "Flying, Flirting, and Flexing: Charmion's Trapeze Act, Sexuality and Physical Culture at the Turn of the Twentieth Century," 261.

41. "A Woman in New York with the Muscles of a Sandow," *New York World*, December 19, 1897, quoted in Gils, "Flying, Flirting," 259; *Glens Falls (NY) Morning Star*, May 10, 1898, quoted in Gils, "Flying, Flirting," 259.

42. Gils, "Flying, Flirting," 259; "Strong Women in History: Charmion," *Area Orion* (blog), May 8, 2012, http://areaorion.blogspot.com/2012/05/strong-women-in-history -charmion.html.

43. Gils, "Flying, Flirting," 252–53; *The Physical Culture Girl* (New York: Edison Manufacturing, 1903); *The Athletic Girl and the Burglar, No. 2* (New York: American Mutoscope and Biograph, 1905). In the former, notes Lauren Rabinovitz, the woman "awakens in bed, stretches, rises, hits a punching bag, juggles Indian clubs, and performs calisthenics." In the latter she "works out while a burglar sneaks by her. She sees him, pummels and subdues him with dumbbells, then stands over him raising her arm and dumbbell in a victorious gesture." Lauren Rabinovitz, *For the Love of Pleasure: Women, Movies, and Culture in Turn-of-the-Century Chicago* (New Brunswick, NJ: Rutgers University Press, 1998), 33.

44. Jack Johnson, *My Life and Battles*, trans. and ed. Christopher Rivers (Westport, CT: Praeger, 2007), 2, 98, 104.

45. Randy Roberts, *Papa Jack: Jack Johnson and the Era of White Hopes*, 10.

46. Johnson, *My Life*, 32; Roberts, *Papa Jack*, 15.

47. Roberts, *Papa Jack*, 26, 43.

48. Gilbert Odd, *Boxing: The Great Champions* (London: Hamlyn, 1974), 20, 22.

49. Streible, *Fight Pictures*, 25, 2, 126.

50. "'Man about Town' on the Jeffries-Johnson Fight," *Moving Picture World* 7 (July 23, 1910): 190, quoted in Streible, *Fight Pictures*, 228.

51. Johnson, *My Life*, 87; Streible, *Fight Pictures*, 219; Arthur R. Ashe Jr., *A Hard Road to Glory: A History of the African-American Athlete, 1619–1918*, 38.

52. Streible, *Fight Pictures*, 218, 213, 195; Susan Courtney, *Hollywood Fantasies of Miscegenation: Spectacular Narratives of Gender and Race, 1903–1967* (Princeton, NJ: Princeton University Press, 2005), 54.

53. Ashe, *Hard Road*, 41–42.

54. Thomas R. Cripps, "African Americans on the Silver Screen," in Mintz and Roberts, eds., *Hollywood's America*, ed. 115; Streible, *Fight Pictures*, 240. See also the bibliography of Johnson spin-offs in Streible, *Fight Pictures*, 353n139; and "Lives in Film No. 4: Jack Johnson," *Bioscope*, July 3, 2010, http://www.thebioscope.net/2010/07/03 /lives-in-film-no-4-jack-johnson-2/.

55. Martin Ritt, dir., *The Great White Hope* (Los Angeles: Twentieth Century Fox, 1970); Ken Burns, dir., *Unforgivable Blackness: The Rise and Fall of Jack Johnson* (Arlington, VA: Public Broadcasting System, 2005).

56. Mintz and Roberts, *Hollywood's America*, 3.

57. Tom Gunning, "'Now You See It, Now You Don't': The Temporality of the Cinema of Attractions," in Grieveson and Krämer, eds., *The Silent Cinema Reader*, 44.

58. Mintz and Roberts, *Hollywood's America*, 10.

59. Miriam Hansen, "Benjamin, Cinema and Experience: 'The Blue Flower in the Land of Technology,'" in special issue on Weimar Film Theory, *New German Critique* 40 (Winter 1987): 180.

60. Gunning "'Now You See It,'" 47–49. While Gunning recognizes some elements of narrative implicit during the "cinema of attractions era," Kristin Thompson dates the development of classical narrative from 1909 to 1916. Kristin Thompson, "The Formulation of the Classical Style, 1909–28," in David Bordwell, Janet Staiger, and Kristin Thompson, *The Classical Hollywood Cinema: Film Style and Mode of Production to 1960* (New York: Columbia University Press, 1985), 157, 217.

II. MACISTE AND THE FIRST FORZUTI

As the art of cinematography developed, it became apparent that what appeared on the screen was an illusion within an illusion.

—Kalton C. Lahue, *Bound and Gagged: The Story of the Silent Serials*

CONTRARY TO POPULAR notions, Hollywood has not always been the epicenter of worldwide moviemaking. Simply because America dominated the filmmaking industry in the early to mid-twentieth century, it was not always so. Such illuminating accounts as the documentary series *Cinema Europe: The Other Hollywood* by Kevin Brownlow and David Gill confirm that many of the photographic illusions of human behavior propagated in American cinema originated with European moviemakers who produced the most popular films and stars until World War I.[1] Producers and studios in Britain, Denmark, France, and Germany led the way, but it was Italy, with its strong history of ancient culture, that initially drew attention to the performance of heroic actions by muscular bodies.[2] More than any other figure, this tradition of transforming ancient events to suit the modern tastes was inaugurated in 1914 by the character of Maciste, played by Genoese dockworker Bartolomeo Pagano. But even this mighty character was not the first strongman star in cinematic epics.

Quo vadis

A bull, a girl, and a strongman was the unusual grouping that started the muscle movie craze in 1913. *Quo vadis* was a popular novel that appeared in 1896 and soon afterward became a successful stage play. Seventeen years later the newly organized Cines studio of Turin released its first great movie epic based on the story. It concerns a Roman legionary during Nero's reign who falls in love with a winsome Christian girl. In the end Rome burns and the Christians are thrown to the beasts, but, fortunately, the boy gets the girl. Despite the rather conventional love story, there is an unforgettable scene where the heroine Lygia is condemned to death in the arena by being lashed to the back of a charging bull. She is saved just in time by her faithful servant and fellow Christian, Ursus. Big and strong, he wrestles the bull to the ground, breaking its neck and rescuing his mistress. It was a thrilling episode that made the brawny strongman Bruto Castellani a star. Ursus, as the first benevolent strongman to appear in Italian film, hooked early audiences on historical epics and muscular heroic men.

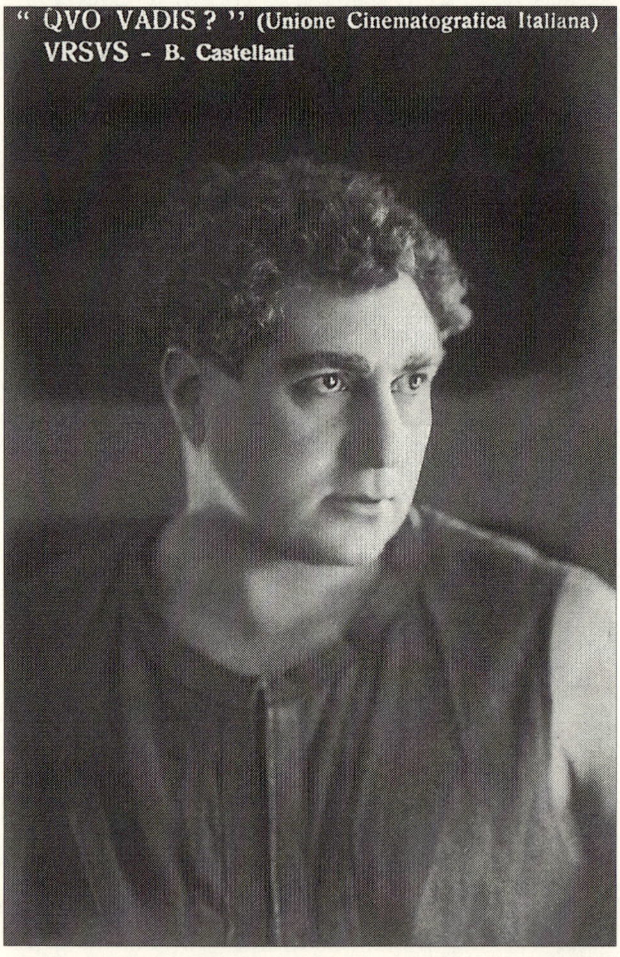

Figure 2.1. Bruto Castellani, the first of the "good giants" in Italian cinema. He played Ursus in the 1913 version of *Quo vadis*. Collection of David L. Chapman.

Quo vadis was among the first of many films set in antiquity. Early French filmmakers also discovered excitement in emperors, gladiators, and classical heroes, but it was the Italians who took the genre to maximum popularity. The *forzuto*, or strongman, became a stock character in many Italian epics, largely because the kindly man of muscle was often the most endearing. It was he who saved the day with his brawn and good-hearted willingness to brave danger for a good cause. In southern Italy these films attracted the poorly educated working classes. They understood physical strength, so seeing a screen character lifting a huge rock and hurling it at villains had meaning. They also yearned for protection from depredations of landlords, tax collectors, and corrupt bureaucrats.[3] There was always plenty of action, but the subtleties of plot were useless on unlettered audiences. Muscles, almost alone, carried the weight of meaning for the epic.

As entertaining as the antics of these *giganti buoni*, or "good giants," were, they would not have attracted much attention if their films had not also appealed to more cultured audiences. Their ancient setting allowed urban middle-class viewers to think they were getting a history lesson along with a cracking good story. Director Enrico Guazzoni was acutely aware of this appeal and determined to give the public an exciting show featuring sex, violence, romance, and adventure—but enough Christian morality to keep censors at bay. It was a formula from which others would later profit. Guazzoni selected the cream of the Cines crop of actors, but his wisest decision was to cast the burly thirtyish Castellani as Ursus.

When the film finally appeared, it created a sensation because of its high-quality, "realistic" acting and two-hour length, far outstripping the normal ten- to thirty-minute one- and three-reelers.[4] The movie was a winning combination of religious themes, decadent orgies, and bloody violence in the Colosseum. A reviewer in the London trade paper *Bioscope* remarked, "No one else knows how to don the tunic like Italian actors!" *Quo vadis* became an instant hit. In London it attracted a huge audience, including King George V and Queen Mary at the Royal Albert Hall. Principal members of the cast were also present, and afterward congratulated by the royal couple. Receiving the most praise was Castellani, whom His Majesty insisted on calling Ursus.[5]

Castellani basically played Ursus for the rest of his career. Sometimes he had a different name, but he was always the same lovable lug. He played Quadrato in *Fabiola* (1918), Cain in *La Sacra Bibbia* (The Holy Bible, 1920), and Tigranes in *Messalina* (1923). Perhaps his best post-Ursus role was in

Il mio antropofago (My cannibal), directed by Giorgio Mannini in 1921. It features a well-known child star named Mimì as the sole survivor of a shipwreck on an island whose only inhabitant is a large and powerful cannibal played by Castellani. Mimi gradually trains her "man Friday" to be a gentleman, and when they are eventually rescued, he can wear evening clothes and act civilized. These successes kept Castellani in the public eye, and when *Quo vadis* was remade in 1924, no one could think of a more appropriate choice for Lygia's rescuer. Unfortunately, time had not been not kind to the once mighty giant. Castellani had gained considerable weight, and in close-ups of his fight with the bull, the strongman is obviously wearing an ill-fitting toupee.[6]

Although he had a successful career as cinema's first benevolent strongman, Castellani was part of a lengthy tradition. Professional strongmen had entertained Italian audiences for centuries, and there had always been an interest in performers who executed seemingly impossible feats of strength on circus and theatrical stages. The crowds at Italian fairs were fond of such groups as the Alcidi, a troupe of strongmen that appeared in Rome in 1792, and Mathevet, a French showman who billed himself in 1827 as L'Ercole degli Ercoli (The Hercules of Herculeses).[7] Often strongmen would reenact scenes from popular novels or plays that required strength and agility. Some used the gimmick of bull wrestling, so when Castellani appeared on film fighting a bull in the arena, audiences recognized this feat because they had seen it elsewhere.[8] In the movie Ursus represents the strength derived from faith in Christ, just as the bull represents rampant pagan sexuality. Ursus not only saves young Lygia from certain death but symbolically preserves her chastity.

Ausonia

In late 1913, another big-budget epic set in ancient Rome was released, *Spartaco, ovvero il gladiatore della Tracia* (Spartacus, or the Thracian gladiator), directed by Giovanni Enrico Vidali. The muscular star of this second *kolossal* (the name the Italians give to a huge film, set in antiquity) was Mario Guaita, who had appeared as costar in two previous films, but it was *Spartaco* that provided a big break. Although the story of a gladiator leading a slave revolt had first been produced in 1909, few expenses were spared for the newer version. The film bears the name of the famous gladiator who led a rebellion in Rome around 70 BCE, but this is where similarities end. In the 1913 version Idamis, the sister of patrician general Crassus, falls in love with

Spartacus, and after he defeats an army sent to crush his rebellion, Spartacus returns to Rome a hero. Shortly afterward he falls afoul of the populace and is nearly thrown to hungry lions in the circus, but he is saved at the last moment by his beloved. All presumably live happily ever after, but the long lines of crucified slaves that figure prominently in the historical account and Stanley Kubrick's 1962 version of *Spartacus* are absent.[9]

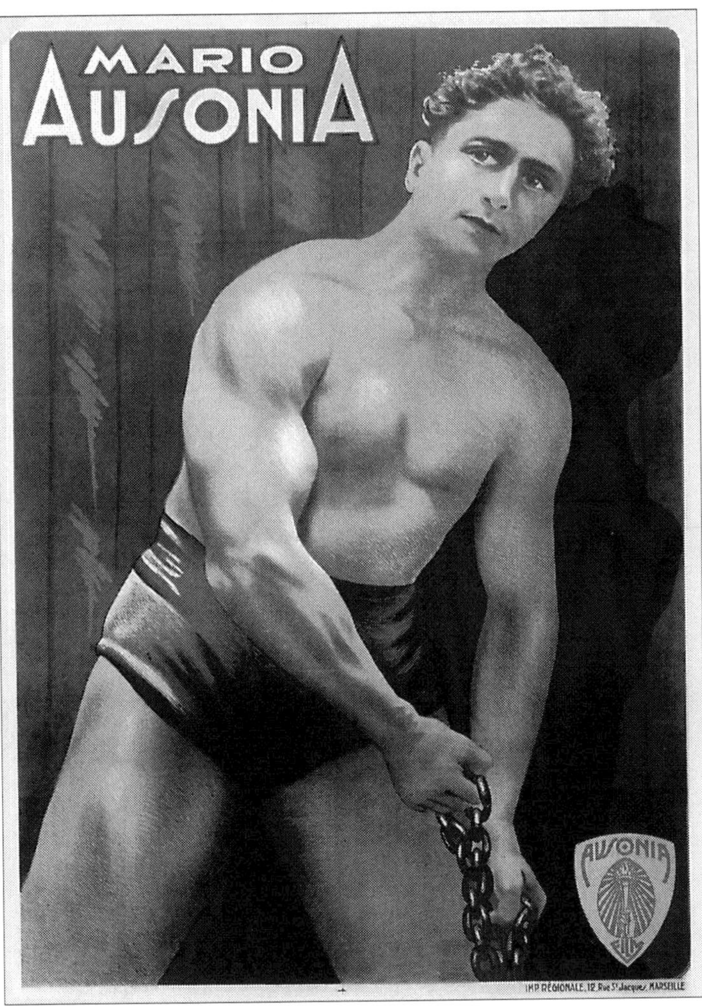

Figure 2.2. Actor and director Mario Guaita Ausonia appeared in many silent adventure films; he was renowned for his shapely physique, as can be seen in this publicity poster from about 1920. Collection of David L. Chapman.

The plot holes in this epic were large enough to accommodate Hannibal's elephants, but the public seemed not to care. The film was greatly successful, thanks largely to the charismatic actor who portrayed the rebel. Guaita was born in Milan in 1881, son of a prominent surgeon and podiatrist. He also began to study medicine around 1900.[10] But Guaita was soon seduced by his love of athletics and the theater. With two other muscular friends he formed the Trio Ausonia around 1905, performing a strength and acrobatics act that created a sensation. In 1908 a French reporter described it as "truly remarkable hand-to-hand balancing work."[11] One of the trio's distinctive features was its use of tableaux vivants, or living pictures. They would often don costumes of Roman gladiators, powder themselves with marble dust and pose motionless as ancient warriors. They were popular with turn-of-the-century audiences because the figures all posed as close to nudity as was legally allowed. Women appeared bare-legged or in tights, and men wore even less. The most muscular and handsome of the trio was Guaita, and when discovered by producer Ernesto Maria Pasquali it was clear that he had star potential.[12] Mario Guaita-Ausonia (as he billed himself) was the first great muscleman of the Italian screen, celebrated as much for his beauty as his acting. Castellani, who had appeared earlier as Ursus, was strong but lacked a beautiful physique. One historian described him as "fat and heavy, practically a giant, a mountain of muscles wrapped in folds of fat."[13] But none of these descriptions could apply to Ausonia. Director Giovanni Vidali often focused the camera on Spartacus's naked muscular arm and chest, enabling viewers to appreciate his powerful physique. In one scene where he uses his strength to bend iron bars, Ausonia gazes briefly at his own massive arm muscle to draw viewers' attention.

The European press soon became aware of Ausonia's appeal. After the film was shown in Budapest in 1914, the *Neues Pester Journal* exclaimed the praises of this paragon of masculinity, declaring that all other male beauties were nothing compared to the young Ausonia: "He is unique in his field, the 'non plus ultra' of handsome men! For physical beauty and for classical features, Mario Ausonia even surpasses the renowned athlete Eugen Sandow."[14] For critics and audiences, this new paradigm of masculine beauty was the film's most striking element, since no actor had ever looked as good. His biceps and well-developed chest were revelations. For modern viewers, the movie displays multiple meanings. Film historian Arthur Pomeroy notes that *Spartaco* serves as the prototype for a long line of "peplum" (sword-and-sandal) films. Like later directors who set their movies in Roman times,

Vidali takes considerable license with historical facts, throws in some genuine details (like classical armor and architecture), and combines an unlikely love story of a slave and a Roman lady. As Pomeroy notes, "It may be argued that there is as much of a tradition for the distortion of history in its literary or dramatic representations as for its respectful recreation." Classicist Maria Wyke sees the film as a political statement since it "valorizes the populist figure of the strongman," placing him at the center of action rather than its periphery. Like Ursus in *Quo vadis*, it glorifies the slave hero. According to Italian critic and historian Gian Piero Brunetta, the most striking thing about the 1913 *Spartaco* is not Ausonia's physical beauty or his "ability to rip out prison bars as if they were bread sticks" but his capacity to communicate his strength to others. In the actor's characterization Spartacus becomes less a rebellious slave and more of a Christ figure who shares his ideal of a perfect society where bondage and injustice are gone. "These are my biceps; these are my triceps—take and eat them," he seems to say. His rebelliousness spreads quickly, and the actor's physical muscularity and charisma "produce a visual hyperbole of extraordinary effectiveness."[15] Brunetta's is an interesting spiritual take on a pre-Christian figure, showing that charisma can inspire followers from all stripes of humanity.

Building on his initial success, Ausonia went on to star in several films that emphasized his athletic abilities and handsome features. The most successful was *L'atleta fantasma* (The phantom athlete), released in 1919. The plot was perfect for displaying his musculature: Jenny, the frivolous daughter of wealthy Lord Ladimoor, is being courted unsuccessfully by timid Harry Audressen (Ausonia). While visiting a museum, Jenny is fascinated by an ancient jewel-encrusted brooch the director wants to sell. Her father buys it for her, but Tesy and Mesy, unscrupulous antique dealers, attempt to steal it. The Phantom Athlete, a masked man with a mighty physique and bare chest, frightens off the robbers. Undeterred, they manage to steal the jeweled ornament, but the athlete recovers the precious object and returns it to Jenny. Still trying to purloin the brooch, the thieves kidnap Jenny and take her to a remote cottage. The Phantom Athlete tries to free her but is taken prisoner. Having been warned in advance, the police capture Tesy and Mesy and Jenny frees the athlete from an underground shaft. Jenny, realizing the valiant hero and Audressen are identical, accepts his declaration of love.[16]

Repeatedly Ausonia sought roles worthy of his muscles, and the reviewers took a great liking to this "cinemathletic oddity."[17] The critic Bertoldo in *La vita cinematografica* explained the almost balletic beauty of Ausonia's movements: "*L'atleta fantasma* entertains and interests one from the first scene to the last. . . . The plot intersects and intertwines without pause; the action is fast and nimble, leading from one surprise to another and maintaining the viewer's rapt attention until the end." Bertoldo concluded, "In addition to being a perfect athlete, Mario Guaita Ausonia proves to be a proper and elegant actor."[18] Ausonia married French screenwriter Renée de Liot and starred in many more films. One of them, *Mes p'tits* (My little ones, 1923), focuses on the sad life of a kindhearted widowed circus strongman (Ausonia) who must raise his two children alone. He suffers many reverses. After losing his job and being falsely accused of murder, his children are taken from him, and after his release from prison, he must search for them. Eventually his innocence is proved, he finds a new love, and he recovers his children. Although many fairground strongmen in books and films were often depicted as stupid, evil brutes who mistreat women and bully almost everyone else, Ausonia's film shines a more benevolent light on the profession.[19] His character uses his strength—both moral and physical—to effect good. Like other good giants, Ausonia thus expands the genre and gives the muscular stage Hercules a sense of pathos that invokes another side to his character—one that most other brawny protagonists chose not to reveal. Ausonia gave the man of muscle a softer, more vulnerable side.

Cabiria

When Ausonia portrayed Spartacus in 1913, the Italian film industry was on an upward trajectory. Production was at full speed, and its standards rivaled the best in the world. Prestigious literary men, playwrights and novelists who previously had turned up their noses at this crass and primitive medium, now were anxious to engage it. Studios throughout Italy were producing hundreds of films yearly, and movie houses were replacing temporary or open-air venues. Simultaneously, cinema's popularity and prestige stimulated bankers, industrialists, and aristocrats to invest in historical epics. "The Roman or Milanese aristocracy," wrote one authority, "who had ambitions of raising Italy to the rank of a great industrial power, was fascinated" by any enterprise that could "make a mark for themselves. Hence, they concentrated on such things as automobiles, aviation and the cinema."[20] What better way of boosting Italy's prestige than images of past grandeur?

A few years earlier, Italy's international stature had been enhanced by an imperial enterprise in Africa. Italians had been involved in colonial adventures for decades, but after a galling defeat in 1896 by native warriors in

Ethiopia, their ardor for conquest cooled. By 1911 Italy was ready to participate again in the scramble for Africa, setting its sights on easier pickings: Cyrenaica and Tripolitana, North African regions controlled by the Ottoman Turks. The Libyan campaign was a short and successful nostrum to restore national vanity. Whether the war was worth the cost in blood and treasure was a question asked by one Italian soldier: "Why should so many people be killed to come and get some sand, four palms and a few lemons?"[21] Despite such sentiments, the Italo-Turkish War had important cultural ramifications since it reminded many Italians of ancient glories. It was, as one scholar noted, a "rhetoric evoking classical fantasies and the Latin world, of suppressing the barbarians and even of the Crusader's cross against the Ottoman crescent."[22] With visions of grandeur reverberating in the Italian psyche, it is little wonder that films about Rome's conquest of Africa would be produced. *Quo vadis* and *Spartaco* became templates for planning an even grander epic to address issues uppermost in many Italian minds: the nation's place in the world and the role of its men.

In 1912, as the war was ratcheting down, Italian director Giovanni Pastrone was mulling over an idea that would eclipse all other films. It would be similar to the huge operatic productions Italy was famous for. Before his involvement in cinema, Pastrone had been a violinist at Turin's Royal Opera House. As historian Maria Prolo notes, Pastrone's "natural disposition for grandiose scenery was perhaps an unconscious recollection of those that were equally imposing which he had seen mounted on the stage of the Teatro Regio." The film Pastrone wanted to produce was *Cabiria*, which proved to be more opulent than the grandest of grand operas. With Libya in mind, the director wanted to showcase Italy's new colonial empire and even went to Paris to see an exhibit of Carthaginian civilization. In June 1913 Pastrone and his backers at Itala Film invited the famous poet Gabriele D'Annunzio to participate in their project with the prospect of "great profit and minimum bother."[23] Although he received fifty thousand gold lire and credit for the screenplay and intertitles, D'Annunzio merely supplied a brief plot summary and named several characters. Among them was a kindhearted giant he called Maciste. This brawny character is a slave of the film's hero, Fulvio Axilla, described by D'Annunzio as his "extremely powerful companion," a dark-skinned freedman of the warlike German tribe the Marsi. Maciste, Prolo notes, "was a pseudonym for the demigod Hercules."[24]

Pastrone had already devised the character and was looking for an actor to play a sympathetic strongman like Ursus in *Quo vadis*. Word went out to talent scouts nationwide to look for a suitable "giant." Finally, a friend encountered Bartolomeo Pagano, a Genoa dockworker. He was a nice young fellow who was exceptionally strong, and his magnificent teeth gave him a "luminous smile." He also possessed an "appalling ignorance" of the world outside the Genoese port district. Pastrone declared him perfect, and sent his protégé a ticket to Turin to prepare for the role of Maciste. A nervous Pagano was introduced to Andrea Cassiano, an acting and gymnastics coach at Itala Film. Seeing his considerable musculature stuffed into a tight-fitting overcoat, Cassiano could not help smiling as the giant stuck out his massive hand while stammering in local dialect, "Vuscià, vuscià" (Respected sir, respected sir). Pagano could neither read nor do simple arithmetic, so every morning from ten to noon he met with a pretty schoolmistress with whom he fell in love. The studios also had their bulky new star take elocution lessons, see a tailor for fitting into elegant suits, and learn how to comport himself in front of a camera and in society.[25]

When filming began in 1913, it was apparent that this preparatory work was justified. The plot is long and complicated. Cabiria, daughter of a wealthy Sicilian land owner, is abducted to Carthage and sold to the high priest of the Temple of Moloch who plans on tossing her into a sacrificial fire. Fortunately, she is rescued by Roman spy Fulvio Axilla and his muscular slave Maciste. Meanwhile, the Romans attack Syracuse and get burned to a crisp by the mirrors of Archimedes. Back in Carthage, beautiful queen Sophonisba provides a refuge for Cabiria, after which Axilla and Cabiria fall in love and sail off toward Rome while a circle of superimposed putti flutter around their boat. Maciste plays his flute, and everyone lives happily ever after.

The Roman hero is valiant, the kidnapped girl is attractive, and the Punic enemies are conniving, ruthless, or just doomed, but the most memorable character is Pagano, who steals every scene throughout the three-hour epic. Film historian Paolo Cherchi Usai minces no words when describing Pagano's contributions: "The success of *Cabiria* was due to the character of the slave Maciste, whose athletic prowess made him a favorite with audiences."[26] Part of the reason for Maciste's popularity was Pagano's enjoyment in portraying him. The actor seemed to be having as much fun as the audience. Furthermore, the muscular star was a force for good. He was a "loyal, morally righteous strong-man with a soft-spot for beauty and a knack for restoring order."[27] An off-putting feature to modern viewers, however, is that Maciste is in blackface, or, more accurately, black-body. To achieve the look of a "Nubian," Pagano rubbed dark makeup over his physique. Thus, his

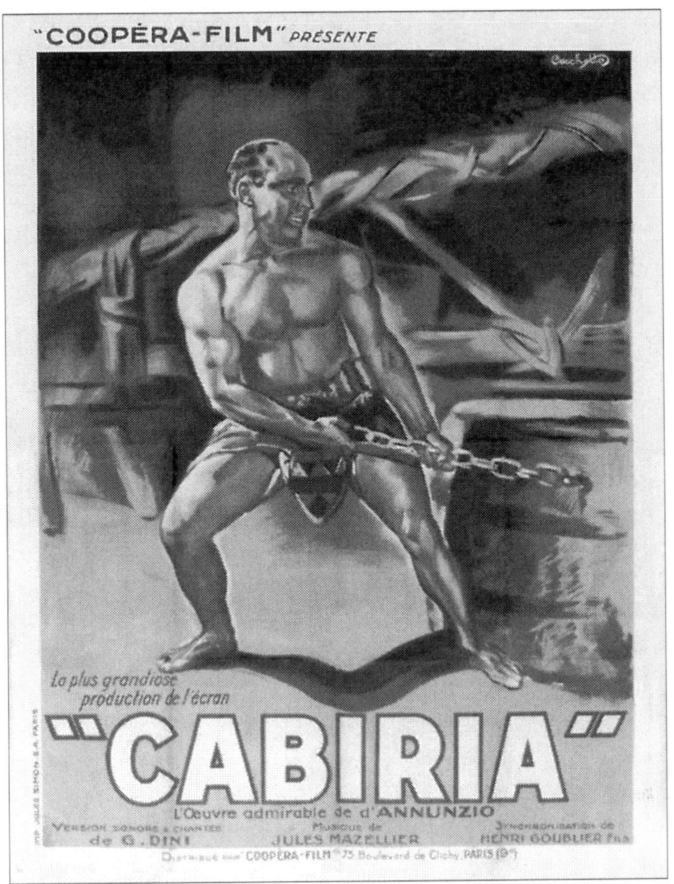

Figure 2.3. Bartolomeo Pagano in his signature role of Maciste, from his first triumph, *Cabiria*. This is a French poster from the 1931 sound reissue of the 1914 epic. Collection of David L. Chapman.

muscles show up better, but race emerges as an issue. To many Americans and Europeans watching *Cabiria* before World War I, it seemed natural that a powerful black man would obediently submit to a white overlord. It was the height of the imperial summer, and it was the way dark-skinned populations were depicted in the Western world. The Americans (in the Philippines), the British (in India), and The Italians (in Libya), expected their subjects to obey and learn from their colonial governors.

Although Maciste is not portrayed as a brute, he follows his master's lead, and even when Fulvio is absent, the black muscleman is obedient. When he is captured helping his master escape and saving Cabiria, Maciste is sentenced to be chained to a Carthaginian gristmill, which he turns for a decade before release. The Numidian slave is so happy to see his master that he exerts his mighty muscles and breaks the bonds that have fettered him to drudgery—and from which, presumably, he might have freed himself long before. Antonia Lant has noted that Maciste's race recalled the body of another famous black man who, like the fictional character, had powerful muscles: "Maciste's nude and powerful physique calls to mind Jack Johnson and American slavery more than that of Rome."[28] Johnson's muscular body would have been familiar to Europeans from early films of his fights. But if Maciste is seen as a visual marker for the American boxer, there are also significant differences. Maciste is portrayed as a fierce fighter but docile, while Johnson was anything but compliant. Whereas Johnson had all the positive and negative attributes of a real person, fictional Maciste is unconstrained by the vagaries of human life. But Maciste is hardly one-dimensional. He is also "a man with a strong personality and a well-developed sense of humor: he makes toys for little Cabiria, jokes with his master, and finds the time to jeer at the priest Karthalo even in the most desperate situations."[29] Owing to his natural acting style, well-constructed character, and jovial charisma, Pagano transcended this film to attain universal popularity. The good giant became one of Italy's most enduring contributions to film. One critic expressed his country's love of Maciste: "When the crisis comes and Italian films remain unremembered and unwanted on the shelves of history, he will be the last to be forgotten."[30]

To promote the film, Pagano as Maciste appeared at cinemas showing *Cabiria*, often in black makeup and a modern suit. By this means the producers attempted to meld the man with the fictional character. The Milanese newspaper *Corriere della sera* noted the natural affection and instant empathy of audiences: "Whether young or old, the audience befriends Maciste; they admire the superb beauty of his Herculean form which makes him a rare champion of our race. . . . They applaud him, feel the agony of his imprisonment, rejoice in his liberation, smile with him, detach his black figure from the screen and turn that into a friendly companion, always accessible in their imagination, in order to tell stories about his deeds and glorify the natural beauty of his actions."[31] Here the journalist differentiates the "Nubian" character of Maciste from the real-life actor. The word *race* (Italian, *razza*) is interesting considering the character's supposed African roots. There seems to be no question about Pagano's Italianness, which adds to the public's affection. He is one of them, a humble dockworker who uses his muscularity to benefit his compatriots—a hero of the working classes.

Maciste Morphs and Matures

Maciste's appeal was palpable as soon as *Cabiria* was released; the only question was how best to exploit the giant's likability. Pastrone and the producers realized they had a star and were determined to keep Pagano and his alter ego in front of the public. Although they understood that Maciste deserved his own film, they had to solve the problem of how to showcase the giant's physicality as well as his warm personality. Because of budget constraints, the next film would be set in contemporary times, and Maciste would remove his dark makeup. Thus, there would be no need for massive sets or elaborate costumes reproducing ancient civilizations. A rationale for abandoning Maciste's African look was that producers were afraid American moviegoers would not like a black hero on their screens. As Lant observes, "In the United States the showing of *Cabiria* with its Numidians and its hero, the slave Maciste, would be strongly influenced by their obsession with skin color." Americans needed to be told that the brawny actor was not really African. In an advertising flier that accompanied a later Maciste movie, they were reassured, "No, he is not a colored giant from Africa—he is a white gentleman."[32] This preoccupation with race would receive even greater notoriety after the 1915 release of D. W. Griffith's *The Birth of a Nation*, in which murderous, miscegenational blacks nearly ruin the postbellum South. No longer is Maciste an African slave who is foreign to European culture; rather, "his racial otherness is rapidly tamed not only ideologically . . . but also physically: his blackness has been utterly erased."[33]

The next problem for producers was how to display Pagano's unique talents. They devised a way for Maciste to travel easily between working-class and middle-class milieus. How could a character's race, era, social class, and appearance be changed without alienating the public? Pastrone's solution was to show Maciste as an actor at Itala Film and allow part of his screen persona to permeate his character. The plot is simple. While working out in the studio gymnasium, Pagano receives a note from a girl who saw his earlier film. She is "a helpless young girl, pursued by powerful malefactors" and hopes Cabiria's savior will also defend her.[34] Like many viewers, she believes the actor's bravery and goodness are not just screen fictions. Help her he does with courageous acts until she is saved from the evildoers.

And if Maciste could assist a single damsel in distress, why not save an entire country? That was the premise of *Maciste alpino* (Alpine Maciste, 1916) starring the amazing forzuto. Maciste and his film crew are shown producing a film in Italy's Dolomite Mountains, near Austria-Hungary, when news arrives that Italy has entered World War I on the Allied side. They inadvertently stray across the border and are captured by enemy troops. Combining patriotism, humor, and pathos, Maciste makes quick work of his captors by thrashing any Austrian within reach. At one point the mighty Italian picks up one of his tormentors by the scruff of the neck and, aided by the special effects of cinematic wizard Segundo de Chomón, boots him out of the room. Maciste then escapes and enlists in the army to fight for his homeland. After a bit of comic business in which all the uniforms that he tries on are too small for his muscular form, he disperses the enemy while rescuing a pretty Italian girl and her patriotic father. Despite its humor and propaganda, the film was brilliantly produced and photographed. Particularly captivating to viewers was a scene where Italian soldiers crossed a mountain gorge while hanging from a rope, advancing hand over hand. Though utterly unrealistic, it made for good watching. No less improvised but effective was the portrayal of Austrian villainy and Italian courage.

In the world of Maciste, war was hardly hell. It was anything but the truth, as bloody debacles at Caporetto and Isonzo soon proved, but no serious viewer could have confused this war with the real one raging on Italy's Alpine frontiers. The film glosses over hideous deadly realities of the conflict and concentrates on heroic, comic, and romantic unrealities. The useless slaughter, inept commanders, and terrible conditions are dispensed with and replaced with easy victory, physical comedy, and absurd bravado. As Gian Piero Brunetta observes, "the problem of the enemy is apparently resolved without the need for hundreds of thousands dead, but simply with two well-aimed fists or a powerful kick up the arse."[35] As one of Italy's first propaganda films, *Maciste alpino* contained enough action and humor to entertain the masses. According to Luca Cottini, it develops a new language for war, as a romp in the mountains against chocolate soldiers straight from a Viennese operetta: "Thanks to Maciste's combination of irony, strength and patriotism," the film provides "not just a model of national identity, but also a symbol of leadership for the Italian nation."[36] Maciste becomes a personification of Italy—young, muscular and fearless. As one of the titles proclaims, "The sons of Italy are all Macistes."

Maciste's appeal was not limited to Italians; it was international from the start. Part of the reason for his worldwide popularity was his depiction of manly virtues. He reveled in unabashed virility, strength, and a willingness to display his bare-chested muscularity on the screen. Thanks to American stars like Douglas Fairbanks, the cinema of athletics had achieved a great popularity at the same time that the Italian star was ascending, and this represented a new force in film in Italy and abroad. Early Italian cinema had been dominated by sultry and tragic divas like Lydia Borelli, Pina Menichelli, and Francesca Bertini who existed in hothouse atmospheres of love, betrayal, and revenge. The second decade of the century saw a rising tide of cinematic masculinity. Fueled in part by the horrors of war and an increasing interest in bodybuilding and physical culture, men were becoming more concerned about their own gender issues.

Maciste therefore represents a public figure who is in the vanguard of this movement and helps lead movies in a more robust direction. His is a cinema of physicality, of action and brute strength. Whereas Fairbanks's usual story arc concerns an immature man-boy who is forced to face his own deficiencies and become a real, two-fisted, hard-as-nails man when the situation deserves it, film historian Jacqueline Reich rightly reckons that Maciste is "100 percent man." There is never much transformation of character in his movies since none is needed. The growth and improvements always occur in those around him—those whom the great giant has rescued either from dastardly villains or themselves.[37]

Maciste and the other good giants have another claim to being champions of masculinity. They all end up displaying their muscles (or physical prowess) in every film. This not only demonstrates their maleness but points out their willingness to be sex objects. The gentle giant is hardly ever put in a situation where he can accept and respond to the love of a woman, but it does not mean he ceases to be a source of erotic excitement—especially among audience members. In his postwar productions Maciste often encounters conniving femmes fatales who attempt to seduce him. Poor Maciste must fight mightily to free himself from the clutches of these malevolent characters. One of the most extraordinary examples is found in *Maciste medium* (Maciste the clairvoyant, 1918) in which he is invited to pose (presumably nude) for a beautiful, sexually voracious artist. "Thank you for coming!" she exclaims in an intertitle. "Would you like to be my guest? For a few days you could pose in my studio with your physique worthy of Michelangelo." He stays and poses, but manages to protect his chastity.[38] Apparently, being asexual and avoiding the occasion of sin is in the job description of a good giant.

Between 1916 and 1921 Pagano starred in ten Maciste films. Most were comedy or adventure movies with little of the farcical or propagandistic content of *Maciste alpino*. Unfortunately, Italy's cinematic preeminence was lost after the Great War. Much of Europe's infrastructure was destroyed, and many of the creative figures—directors, stars, and technicians—moved abroad (many to Hollywood), where they could produce films on a scale previously possible only in the biggest studios at home. Brunetta estimates approximately fifteen hundred Italian films from the 1920s have been preserved, but these "have almost vanished from the historical memory." He blames this slump in popularity on, among other things, rising costs, loss of foreign markets, technical and expressive stagnation, and an inability to adapt to new audiences and lifestyles.[39] But if Italian cinema lost touch with international trends and relied on tired themes and unspectacular techniques, enough remained to sustain the industry. When one film became popular, it was often followed by others called *filone*, or a string of related movies.[40] Producers of Maciste films were hardly alone in employing this device, but when Italian moviemakers struck a vein of gold, they followed it relentlessly. The strongman series starting with *Cabiria* was one of the longest running *filone*, and when the ore ran out in this vein around 1926, it was fated to glisten again in 1958.

Pagano's films were not only popular in Italy; Maciste's bold character was loved in Germany, one of the world's great cinematic centers. Hence a lucrative offer from producers lured Pagano north of the Alps to make four films. But he was never happy in Germany, despising the food, culture, and language. He was also unhappy with the kind of pictures he was making. The Berlin films were the least successful of the series, being slow-paced, poorly photographed, and humorless.[41] Perhaps the best of these productions is *Maciste und die chinesische Truhe* (Maciste and the Chinese trunk), released in 1922. Though hardly a masterpiece, filled as it is with absurd coincidences and mile-wide plot holes, it is noteworthy because it brings Maciste back to being a simple dockworker. Having him masquerade as a workingman while being an aristocrat allows working-class fans to imagine they might bridge the class gap. It is also interesting to see the two Asian characters, portrayed by real Chinese actors. They are not opium fiends or sadistic brutes, just ordinary people.

The connection between reality and the illusory world of film received another impetus when Fascist Party leader Benito Mussolini came to power.

Many writers have noted his uncanny resemblance to Maciste. As film historian Stephen Gundle notes, "If the founder of Fascism seemed like a real-life Maciste, and possibly employed gestures and poses trademarked by Pagano, then the relationship was not only one way."[42] The two men gradually became more alike. Pagano adopted poses staged in Mussolini's bombastic speeches, and the dictator was photographed doing physical stunts. More important, Maciste and Mussolini gloried in their own muscularity, using it to intimidate opponents, preserve order, and help the needy. Psychologist Carl Jung described the Italian dictator as "a man of physical strength" whose "body suggests good muscles. . . . He enjoys a military parade with the zest of a small boy at a circus."[43] Mussolini's strength and muscularity, mixed with a childlike delight in a good show, might also describe his fictional alter ego, Maciste.

In 1922 Mussolini staged his famous March on Rome, after which he seized power and became prime minister. Two years later *Maciste imperatore* (Emperor Maciste) was released. It is a cinematic confection with Maciste posing as king of the mythical country of Sirdagna. The rightful ruler, Otis, living in exile, fears the evil regent Stanos will eliminate him before he can ascend the throne. Since no one has seen the real prince in many years, Otis convinces Maciste to impersonate him. The strongman is between pictures, so he convinces his friend and fellow action star Saetta (Domenico Gambino) to come with him on this adventure. In his new role as monarch, Maciste is so benevolent, fair, and genuinely concerned about his subjects that the people are delighted with him and declare him their emperor. After many adventures featuring the good giant and his sidekick Saetta, Maciste eventually relinquishes the throne to Otis and returns to his movie star life. The timing of the 1924 film demonstrates Maciste's growing identification with the Fascists, since the comparison in the film of a strong, physically intimidating figure seizing control of the government and ruling it as a benevolent dictator is suspiciously coincidental. The popularity of his character was not lost on the real-life Fascists who became increasingly visible in public. Brunetta notes that ordinary citizens in the piazza might catch a glimpse of a group of black-shirted individuals led by a man "dressed up to look like a strongman who from afar might even be Pagano. But the man who spoke from the stage and promised order and forceful action was not Maciste. When the confusion was cleared up, it was too late, and all the cards had been laid out."[44]

The winners of this card game were obvious in 1925 when Mussolini dropped all pretense of ruling democratically and seized power as Il Duce. It also marked his near deification, and the exaltation of his virility, featuring photographs of him running with soldiers, skiing down slopes, swimming at sea, harvesting grapes, and reaping wheat while displaying his naked upper body.[45] But his willingness to strut around bare-chested was not the only similarity between the fictional hero and the dictator. Neither Maciste nor Mussolini had any qualms about using violence to sort out sticky problems. In fact, solving his problems violently was one of Maciste's favorite activities. A friendly rivalry seemed apparent to some citizens. A film company cartoon alluded to this scenario, showing Mussolini perched atop a large barrel marked "castor oil," a concoction often used by black-shirted thugs to torture opponents. Eyeing Maciste dressed in his imperial uniform, Mussolini indicates the barrel and tells his fictional rival, "So you want to be emperor? Well, watch out. There's plenty here for you."[46] The cartoon exploited the thin line that sometimes divides fiction from political reality. Perhaps this brush with Fascist Party threats caused Maciste's makers to be more circumspect; it was an entire year before more films appeared. Energized by new directors and a desire to cash in on their popular star's appeal, 1925–26 proved to be years of great profit and production for Cines, under its new head, Stefano Pittaluga, with four full-length films featuring Maciste. On the surface they were innocuous adventure stories with few overt references to politics or world events, but they took muscle movies in new directions. The involvement of two excellent directors, Guido Brignone and Mario Camerini, guaranteed that creativity and production quality would be high. But Pagano, now nearly fifty years old, was having health problems and starting to have trouble executing the gymnastic and strength feats so prominent in his earlier films.[47]

Maciste's Slow Decline

One of the strongman's later films, *Maciste all'inferno* (Maciste in hell, 1925), is an attempt to recapture the joy of Maciste's earlier works. It became one of Pagano's greatest hits, due largely to a predictable plot, pleasant comedy, and superb camera tricks. *Maciste all'inferno* is a wonderful combination of the grotesque and the sentimental, the comic and the wondrous, and it is closer to the surreal *Diableries* of Georges Méliès than anything else at the time. It was, as one critic declares, "an extremely enjoyable pastiche of expressionism and popular iconography and of Mediterranean sensuality and Gothic Satanism."[48] But its forty-seven-year-old star was tapped out from over ten years of moviemaking. His fatigue stemmed from being one of the few personalities whose presence in a film guaranteed success. Italy's film industry experienced a massive failure in the 1920s as the number of movies produced plummeted. Filmmakers had presented 371 works to the national censorship board in 1920, but by 1930 only eight were reviewed. The reasons for this decline included overtaxation, lack of studio organization, and the wave of American films flooding the Italian market. In 1925 and 1926 Italian output was just thirty-eight and twenty-seven movies, respectively.[49] In this kind of market, producers with a surefire moneymaking formula did not want to stop the series despite the star's many problems. Notwithstanding the cuts and compromises that censors demanded, *Maciste all'inferno* had a great impact. Among its most famous early viewers was the great director Federico Fellini. When asked to name the first film that stuck in his childhood memory, he responded. "I am certain that I remember it exactly because that image has stayed with me etched so deeply that I have tried to reproduce it in all of my films. The film was called *Maciste all'inferno.*"[50]

Pagano's character continued to be popular, and so the actor persevered. Maciste's final films grew increasingly darker and moodier, and *Maciste nella gabbia dei leoni* (Maciste in the lion's cage, 1926) is typical. It is a richly mounted melodrama that mixes adventure, exoticism, ferocious beasts, and pervasive sexuality against a circus backdrop. The circus is a successful venture, and its owner dispatches lion tamer Maciste to Africa to capture new animals for his act. During and after the hunt, we see that both beasts and humans are depicted as willful and cowardly: the animals will turn on their tamers instantly if not overseen by a stern but fair hand. When the firm control of a benevolent leader is removed, chaos results, as when a panicking mob rushes out of the theater after a lion is discovered roaming free. The creature attacks and mauls hapless humans knocked over by the fleeing crowd. Who is more culpable, the beast acting on instinct, or the stupid and craven hordes trying to escape? The message is that it is more dangerous outside the lion's cage than inside. It is only after Maciste uses his strength to capture the lion that order is restored. The implications for Italy are unmistakable: a strong leader is needed to keep passions in check. Italians were perhaps ready for a comfortable cage in which they could be protected from the outside world and from one another. All they had to do was jump through flaming hoops held by their trainer.

It is significant that *Maciste nella gabbia dei leoni* is the first film in which the character is not actually playing the movie star; the character bears no connection to the actor Bartolomeo Pagano. Stella Dagna and Claudia Gianetto note that "Maciste had by this time consolidated his status as a popular character to the point of being able to give up the meta-cinematographic game that saw him as an actor in the diegesis as well as in reality."[51] Another dissimilarity between this movie and its predecessors is the lack of humor. In fact, all later works in the series are darker, crueler, and more pessimistic than the earlier carefree romps, perhaps reflecting the postwar era, but they also show a realization that the good giant cannot solve all the world's problems.

Africa, however, continued as a powerful draw for Italians in the 1920s. In *Maciste contro lo sceicco* (Maciste versus the sheik), also released in 1926, the strongman returns to the Libyan region. Undoubtedly influenced by Rudolph Valentino's *The Sheik* (1921), Douglas Fairbanks's *Thief of Baghdad* (1924), and a general interest in Orientalia (spurred in part by the discovery of King Tut's tomb), Italian screenwriter Mario Camerini crafted a script that placed action in the distant past, where Maciste must save an innocent girl imperiled by oversexed sailors and lustful Arab chieftains. He does everything from bending iron bars and climbing a high wall to fighting a school of sharks. Performing dangerous feats of strength were simply a day's work for Pagano, but there were more serious objectives to the script. As Steven Ricci observes, the powerful protagonist performs deeds that coincide with elements of Fascist physical culture. The action is morally purifying because it responds to corruption. The use of strength is motivated by the need to defend an innocent party. And the action is mostly single-handed, reflecting Italy's desire to solve its own problems.[52] Additionally, the objects of Maciste's rage are mostly foreigners, and this jibes with the Fascist philosophy that Italy was surrounded by adversaries intent on destroying Mussolini's experiment. A dark tone also permeates *Maciste contro lo sceicco*: there is no jolly bonhomie, no ironic humor, and no good-natured self-mockery; it is all deadly serious.[53] Most of the flaws demonstrated by the film's characters are rooted deeply in the human soul, and even a superhuman powerhouse cannot exorcise them all.

By 1926 Pagano was unfit to play the good giant much longer. Despite his diabetes and aging, the public seemed no less eager to see the once barrel-chested but now "barrel-bodied" torso on screen. Thus, he was cast in what became the last film in the Maciste franchise, *Il gigante delle Dolomiti* (The giant of the Dolomites, 1927). With the film industry in a terrible state, producer Stefano Pittaluga bet on a proven winner to give the public what it wanted. The film is a lavish production set in the high reaches of the Dolomites, where for the first time in Maciste filming, the spectacular landscape plays an important role as a rugged backdrop to the action and a reflection of the inhabitants and their conflicts. If the film is visually gorgeous, it cannot boast much by way of a story. As with most of Pagano's films, this one is not plot driven but stunt driven. The stories are mostly variations on the theme of good girl versus bad girl and weak young man needing to be saved from himself (and the bad girl). Maciste uses his strength of character and muscles to save the day and give the villain a drubbing. He also scrambles to the top of a rocky peak, thwarts international criminals, and wrestles a pack of wolves. Unlike his earlier action films, Maciste never appears shirtless in *Il gigante delle Dolomiti*. Directors always liked to show his body to admiring audiences, so he would often remove his shirt or have it torn off in a fight. The great man's body was an emblem of inner beauty and outward strength: his physique was honed by many years of physical labor, a workingman's body not manufactured in a gymnasium. This accounted for much of Maciste's appeal, since it made him instantly recognizable to strong but unsophisticated people worldwide. He might occasionally wear evening dress, appear in society, and participate in social rituals, but he was still seen as a former dockworker and man of the people. Owing to lack of funds and virtually no technology, filmmakers were limited to the raw resource of Maciste's homegrown muscles to provide the major means of conveying cinematic reality.

Reflecting perhaps the declining physical condition of its star, in *Il gigante delle Dolomiti* Maciste is portrayed as a man of sorrow. Death pervades the entire film and provides a beating heart of compassion and forgiveness that is not so obvious in his other movies. Pagano's acting talents have also matured, enabling him to convey suffering concealed under the veneer of courage, strength, and affability. Maciste's body shows the effects of age and injuries endured during his long career. Pagano retired shortly after finishing the film and returned to Genoa to live in comfort at his home, Villa Maciste. He appeared in three more films, but not as Maciste. According to his son Oreste, he "could not work again because of his diabetes, and because he [had] worked without a stunt double, the movies had ruined his strength. Most Genoese called him 'The Giant' more frequently than Maciste."[54] He died at Villa Maciste in 1947.

Maciste's character had made an indelible mark on Italian cinema, and this had been proved beyond all doubt in an earlier lawsuit. In the early 1920s, when Italian filmmaking had dwindled into virtual insignificance, Pagano (and many other actors) had been forced to go to Germany, where the industry was more robust. Itala Film, the company that had made a fortune from the good giant, brought a suit against him, contending that it owned the name and brand of Maciste. In addition to claiming that Pagano no longer looked fit enough to play the character, Itala asserted that "Maciste is always Maciste, and when the contract expires we can always find another one." Eventually an Italian court sided with the star, ruling that Pagano and Maciste were and always would be indistinguishable; Maciste was an individual, not a type, and Pagano was the only actor who could portray him.[55] The judges recognized what the studio executives did not: Maciste was a national treasure and could not be separated from the man who created him.

Despite the court ruling, Pagano's character lived on even after the former dockworker succumbed to illness and passed away. In fact, the fictional being was so popular with audiences worldwide that he spawned imitators who impersonated incarnations of the good giant. Some attempted to hoodwink audiences into thinking they were going to see the original. These reproductions preserved a kind of fiction created by Pagano and his producers that facilitated a transfer between the real actor and his alter ego: artifice yet again trumped reality. Moviegoers could more readily savor these re-creations than another dose of everyday reality. Decades later, when the popularity of gladiator movies reemerged, the name of Maciste was resurrected and the illusion of superhuman strength and physical beauty was perpetuated.

Notes

1. Kevin Brownlow and David Gill, dirs., *Cinema Europe: The Other Hollywood* (London: Photoplay, 1995.

2. Jon Solomon, *The Ancient World in the Cinema* (New Haven, CT: Yale University Press, 2001).

3. Camilla De Rossi, "Quando e Come il Cinema Parla Dialetto," *Italica* 87, no. 1 (Spring 2010): 92–106. Because they were silent epics, there were occasionally problems reading the intertitles. Some rural cinemas hired "translators" to read the standard Italian titles aloud in local dialect.

4. Giovanni Pastrone and Luigi Borgnetto's *La caduta di Troia* (The fall of Troy, 1910) was the first six-hundred-meter film with a running time of about thirty-five minutes. It marked the beginning of full-length films. Roberta E. Pearson, "Historical Films," in *Encyclopedia of Early Cinema*, ed. Richard Abel (London: Routledge, 2005), 299.

5. *Bioscope*, 1913, quoted in Vittorio Martinelli, "Lasciate fare a noi, siamo forti," in *Gli uomini forti*, ed. Alberto Farassino and Tatti Sanguineti, 9.

6. The child star was fourteen-year-old Mimì Pretolani. She reportedly enjoyed working with Castellani, who was "an authentic force of nature," as naive and childlike as his character. Martinelli, "Lasciate fare a noi," 10.

7. Livio Toschi, *La meravigliosa avventura della pesistica italiana* (Rome: Federazione italiana pesistica e cultura fisica, 2007), 19–20.

8. Francisco Ursus and Romulus (Cosimo Molino), whose biographies can be found in Edmond Desbonnet, *Les Rois de la Force* (Paris: Berger-Levrault, 1911), as well as Spanish strongman Andrés Balsa, who styled himself El Moderno Ursus, featured bull wrestling in their acts.

9. The original 1913 film, however, ends tragically with Idamis arriving too late to save her gladiator lover. *Spartacus ou la révolte d'un peuple*, souvenir booklet (Paris: n.p., n.d.), in the collection of David L. Chapman.

10. Ivo Blom, "The Beauty of the Forzuti: Irresistible Male Bodies on and Offscreen," in *Corporeality in Early Cinema: Viscera, Skin, and Physical Form*, ed. Marina Dahlquist, Doron Galili, Jan Olsson, and Valentine Robert, 149.

11. "Notre Galerie Athlétique," *La Culture Physique*, October 1, 1908, 1386. This article attributes the athletes' development to exercises they continued practicing.

12. Giorgio Bertellini, "Pasquali & C. (1908–1921)," in Abel, ed., *Encyclopedia*, 500.

13. Monica Dall'Asta, *Un cinéma musclé: Le surhomme dans le cinéma muet italien (1913–1926)*, 35.

14. Anonymous article, *Neues Pester Journal*, 1914, in Farassino and Sanguineti, eds., *Gli uomini forti*, 111. Ausonia went to Vienna and Budapest for the film's premiere, which received much coverage in the Austro-Hungarian press.

15. Arthur J. Pomeroy, *"Then It Was Destroyed by the Volcano": The Ancient World in Film and on Television* (London: Bloomsbury, 2008), 30–31; Maria Wyke, *Projecting the Past: Ancient Rome, Cinema, and History* (New York: Routledge, 1997), 44–45; Gian Piero Brunetta, *Cent'anni di cinema italiano: Dalle origini alla seconda guerra mondiale*, 116.

16. Predating Superman comics by almost two decades, the Phantom Athlete is arguably the first movie superhero.

17. "Una bizzarria cineatletica" is apparently the film's subtitle, as quoted in the appendix, "Le protagoniste," compiled by Monica Dall'Asta in in *Non solo dive: Pioniere del cinema italiano*, ed. Monica Dall'Asta, 324.

18. Bertoldo, review of *L'atleta fantasma*, *La vita cinematografica*, November 22, 1919, in Farassino and Sanguineti, eds., *Gli uomini forti*, 123.

19. See Blom, "The Beauty of the Forzuti," 152. The most perfectly portrayed brutish strongman is found in Fellini's *La strada* (The street, 1954).

20. Jean Mitry, *Histoire du cinema: Art et industrie* (Paris: Delarge, 1967), 298–99.

21. Christopher Duggan, *The Force of Destiny: A History of Italy since 1796* (London: Allen Lane, 2007), 384.

22. Franco Gaeta, *Il nazionalismo italiano* (Bari, Italy: Laterza, 1981), 39. Gaeta points out that as early as 1847 the Italian national anthem, *Fratelli d'Italia*, contains words reflecting this obsession with Africa and conquest by Roman hero Scipio Africanus during the Punic Wars.

23. Maria Adriana Prolo, "Introduzione," in *Cabiria: Visione storica del III secolo A.C.*, ed. Roberto Radicati and Ruggero Rossi, 6–9. D'Annunzio claimed he only devoted several hours composing "a Greco-Roman drama along the lines of *Quo vadis* for the cinema." Gabriele D'Annunzio, *Scritti giornalistici 1889–1938*, vol. 2 (Milan: Mondadori, 1996), xcviii.

24. Prolo, "Introduzione," 11. In an undated letter to D'Annunzio, Pastrone congratulates the poet's choice of the name Maciste but says, "I had to find another country for him; I made him a mulatto." Paolo Cherchi Usai, *Giovanni Pastrone: Gli anni d'oro del cinema a Torino*, 62.

25. Usai, *Giovanni Pastrone*, 63.

26. Paolo Cherchi Usai, "Italy: Spectacle and melodrama," in *The Oxford History of World Cinema*, ed. Geoffrey Nowell-Smith (New York: Oxford University Press, 1997), 129.

27. Kevin M. Flanagan, "Civilization . . . Ancient and Wicked: Historicizing the Ideological Field of 1980s Sword and Sorcery Films," in *Of Muscles and Men: Essays on the Sword and Sandal Film*, ed. Michael G. Cornelius (Jefferson, NC: McFarland, 2011), 91.

28. Antonia Lant, "Spazio per la razza in Cabiria," in *Cabiria e il suo tempo*, ed. Paolo Bertetto and Gianni Rondolino, 219. Lant cites an early twentieth-century fascination with oriental exoticism as a reason for the film's success.

29. Alberto Barbera and Gian Luca Farinelli, *Maciste: L'uomo forte*, 11.

30. Usai, *Giovanni Pastrone*, 63.

31. "Maciste in persona al Lirico nelle rappresentazioni di 'Cabiria,'" *Corriere della sera*, May 9, 1914, quoted in Cristina Jandelli, *Breve storia del divismo cinematografico* (Venice: Marsilio, 2007), loc. 673, e-book.

32. Lant, "Spazio per la razza in Cabiria," 213; *The Tallygram* (Tally's Broadway Theatre, Los Angeles), October 9, 1916.

33. Giorgio Bertellini, "Colonial Autism: Whitened Heroes, Auditory Rhetoric, and National Identity in Interwar Italian Cinema," in *A Place in the Sun: Africa in Italian Colonial Culture from Post-unification to the Present*, ed. Patrizia Palumbo (Berkeley: University of California Press, 2003), 260.

34. Giovanni Pastrone, dir., *Cabiria* (Turin, Italy: Itala Film, 1914), DVD (Bologna: Museo Nazionale del Cinema / Cineteca Bologna, 2009).

35. Gian Piero Brunetta, quoted in Giovanni Nobili Vitelleschi, "The Representation of the Great War in Italian Cinema," in *The First World War and Popular Cinema: 1914 to the Present*, ed. Michael Paris (New Brunswick, NJ: Rutgers University Press, 2000), 167.

36. Luca Cottini, "La novità di *Maciste alpino*," *Italian Culture* 27, no. 1 (March 2009): 43.

37. Jacqueline Reich, *The Maciste Films of Italian Silent Cinema*, 138–39. As Reich, 169, notes, in the film *Maciste contro la morte* (Maciste versus death, 1920) Maciste portrays a professor of physical culture, with an office including baseball bats, Indian clubs, boxing gloves and weightlifting paraphernalia.

38. Unfortunately, the film has been lost, but a synopsis has been saved. This exchange is quoted in Denis Lotti, *Muscoli e frac: Il divismo maschile nel cinema muto italiano (1910–1929)* (Soveria Mannelli, Italy: Rubbettino, 2016), 122, 144.

39. Gian Piero Brunetta, *The History of Italian Cinema: A Guide to Italian Film from Its Origins to the Twenty-First Century*, trans. Jeremy Parzen (Princeton, NJ: Princeton University Press, 2003), 60–61; Gian Piero Brunetta, *Il cinema muto italiano*, 279.

40. Mikel J. Koven, *La Dolce Morte: Vernacular Cinema and the Italian Giallo Film* (Lanham, MD: Scarecrow, 2006), 5–8.

41. Vittorio Martinelli, "Maciste, le bon géant," Festival International du Film de la Rochelle, http://archives.festival-larochelle.org/festival-1994/maciste.

42. Stephen Gundle, *Mussolini's Dream Factory: Film Stardom in Fascist Italy* (New York: Berghahn, 2013), 44.

43. Carl Jung, quoted in Nicholas Adam Lewin, *Jung on War, Politics and Nazi Germany: Exploring the Theory of Archetypes and the Collective Unconscious* (London: Karnac Books, 2009), 59.

44. Brunetta, *Cent'anni di cinema italiano*, 118.

45. Gigliola Gori, "Model of Masculinity: Mussolini, the 'New Italian' of the Fascist Era," in *Superman Supreme: Fascist Body as Political Icon: Global Fascism*, ed. J. A. Mangan (London: Frank Cass, 2000), 43.

46. Barbera and Farinella, *Maciste: L'uomo forte*, 17.

47. Barbera and Farinella, *Maciste: L'uomo forte*, 16–17.

48. Vittorio Martinelli, "XX Mostra Internazionale del Cinema Libero: Il cinema ritrovato," 1991, Cineteca Bologna, http://www.cinetecadibologna.it/files/festival/Cinema Ritrovato/archivio/fcr1991.pdf.

49. Brunetta, *Cent'anni di cinema italiano*, 132–36.

50. Federico Fellini, *Block-notes di un regista* (Milan: Longanesi, 1988), 56.

51. Stella Dagna and Claudia Gianetto, "Maciste nella gabbia dei leoni," 2009, Cineteca Bologna, http://www.cinetecadibologna.it/vedere/programmazione/app_971/from _2009-07-02/h_0900.

52. Steven Ricci, *Cinema and Fascism: Italian Film and Society, 1922–1943* (Berkeley: University of California Press, 2008), 83.

53. Jean A. Gili, "Les horizons européens de Mario Camerini," in *Mario Camerini*, ed. Alberto Farassino (Crisnée, Belgium: Éditions Yellow Now, 1992), 48.

54. Salvatore Lo Leggio, "Un camallo chiamato Maciste: Bartolomeo Pagano, il re della forza," *Salvatore Lo Leggio* (blog), http://salvatoreloleggio.blogspot.com/2010/03/un-camallo -chiamato-maciste-bartolomeo.html.

55. Reich, *The Maciste Films*, 24.

III. SILENT QUEENS OF SPORT

No athletic type of girl has ever so much as reached first base in motion pictures.

—Lois Shirley, "The Enemy of Beauty—Over-Exercise"

BY THE TIME Hollywood columnist Lois Shirley expressed these sentiments, the Western world was in the throes of the Great Depression, and moviegoers did not want to see athletic women, preferring them in traditional roles. Movie characters might run the gamut from virgin to vamp, but they had to be "womanly." The sporty, boyish flapper was out, and the full-figured "feminine" woman was in. In times of stress and upheaval, no one wanted gender uncertainty. Despite this conservative turn in society and film, strongwomen had already left their mark. Plucky heroines, fearless femme fatales, and women athletes were quite common. In the early twentieth century a few films had dared to recast gender roles and challenge male dominance. These films were tremendously popular, and their stars, the "serial queens," defined a new type of woman. It was no longer based on gentleness or equanimity; as film historian Monica Dall'Asta explains, the role of the serial queen called for "supple muscularity, feline agility and flexible, nimble movements."[1]

Functional Female Muscles

The first athletic woman to use her muscularity to create a cinematic sensation was Charmion, who performed *Trapeze Disrobing Act* for Thomas Edison's cameras in 1901. She was part of a vaudeville craze for strongwomen that flourished around the turn of the century. As the urge to build a stronger and aesthetically pleasing body became popular, filmmakers realized they could combine eroticism and athletics. Among the first to exploit this new interest in physical culture was G. W. "Billy" Bitzer. Although better known as the cameraman for many of D. W. Griffith's famous films, Bitzer was also an accomplished moviemaker. One of his single-reel epics featuring a strong and redoubtable woman is *The Athletic Girl and the Burglar* (1905), in which the actress is larger and more mature than the usual shapely and attractive girls often featured in his films. Although the burglar is trounced by his amazonian "victim," there is a hint of a possible sexual outcome. Another of Bitzer's athletic short subjects is *The Physical Culture Lesson* (1906), in which a man in a dark suit comes to instruct a young lady in calisthenics. Like other early films, it reinforces the erotic possibilities of physical exercise where bodies are offered up in suggestive clothing and risqué poses. Although the images were aimed at male audiences, women were complicit in their creation and consumption. As Sharon Ullman has noted, "Women as well as men were to be in on the joke."[2] In this pre–World War I film, strong, active women could still be used as butts of jokes or in freak shows, but few women were interested in escaping traditional roles. Those who did were often portrayed as dull, overweight, and mannish to emphasize their flaunting of conventionality.

A more outrageous example of female gender transgression from the early days is the mixed-gender boxing film. *The Comedy Set-To* (1898) features a man (Billy Curtis) sparring with a woman (Belle Gordon); they slap one another with open hands until Curtis is felled by an uppercut, and he drops to the mat with an astonished expression. He gets up, shakes hands with Gordon, and they walk off. The "star" of the film was no stranger to the sweet science since Belle Gordon was holder of the *Police Gazette* medal as Champion Lady Bag Puncher of the World. The Edison film catalog markets it as a racy comedy: "Belle is as frisky a little lady as ever donned a boxing outfit, and her abbreviated skirts, short sleeves and low-necked waist make a very jaunty costume."[3]

Edison released another novelty film in 1901, *Gordon Sisters Boxing*, which featured Belle's sisters, Bessie and Minnie, engaging in serious fisticuffs. They appear in short dresses with crinolines and curly hair that belies their aggressive actions as they bob and weave and throw real punches. "The exhibition is very lively from start to finish," the Edison catalog confirms, "the blows fall thick and fast, and some very clever pugilistic generalship is shown." Bessie first gives a punching-bag exhibition, then Minnie and Bessie spar using "scientific" boxing techniques.[4] Despite claims of skill in the fistic arts, these films were designed as comic diversions, not serious boxing displays; Edison also made a series of farcical fight films that pitted multiracial pairs, animals, and even children against each other. No matter how seriously the women in these films took themselves, they were presented as clowns, not athletes. The moviegoing public was not ready for serious fights; it needed some acculturation to understand what occurred in a boxing ring. As Dan Streible explains, "Gags substituted a presumed characteristic of the prize-fighter with its opposite or a variation."[5] The film medium would have to mature before athletic women could be respected.

The New Woman

The idea that a woman could be independent, energetic, and strong stemmed from societal changes that began in the nineteenth century with the "new woman," a precept espoused by rebels who shocked and delighted the public by thumbing their noses at long-held conventions.[6] Fictional versions of these daring women began appearing in the works of Henrik Ibsen, Henry James, George Bernard Shaw, and others, but in films the first manifestations of women beholden to no man first appeared in cinematic serials. Literary works published in weekly or monthly installments had existed since the 1840s, but the first movie serial was *What Happened to Mary?*, which was released in ten episodes in 1912. These "chapter dramas" usually featured exciting episodes that kept viewers on tenterhooks until the next week's installment, at the end of which the story was again left in limbo. The first serials were generally quickly made and low-quality productions. All this changed with the release of *The Perils of Pauline* in 1914, starring Pearl White, a pretty, plucky actress who plays a young woman yearning to be a writer. But when her stepfather mysteriously dies, she avoids first the marriage proposals of his killer and later the murderer's attempts to eliminate her. In each episode the protagonist avoids death in a hairbreadth escape that is always "continued next week." Thanks to their pacing and excitement, Pearl's serials enjoyed worldwide fame, causing a flurry of interest in "chapter films" in which many of the protagonists were women. At the outset of World War I in August 1914, thousands of men marched off to fight for their country, and growing numbers of women took over their jobs. Monica Dall'Asta notes that the "femininization" of European society corresponded to the popularity of Pearl White and other serial queens.[7] For the first time, many women were earning decent wages, and their consequent emancipation made them suddenly visible. By 1916 there were female bank clerks, railroad workers, ticket takers on the metro, tram conductors, and postal workers. Women gloried in their newfound liberation, and many men were noting that women who exerted their muscles and performed nontraditional work could still be beautiful. *Le petit parisien* published racy illustrations of "trouser-wearing women baggage handlers turned into charming, opulent young amazons, who 'call to mind the firm, vigorous flesh of a Rubens.' "[8]

It was into this climate of visible empowerment that Pearl appeared, and it took little time for her to become a new female icon. Strong, dynamic, and brave, she simply wanted some of the freedom men enjoyed. Like many of her female fans, she wanted a life free from the societal and sartorial restrictions that had constrained women for centuries. French critic Marcel Lapierre notes the importance of White's new look: "With her skirt of Scottish wool, her brushed wool blouse and her large velvet beret, she symbolized ideal youthfulness that was ready for adventure. Adolescents (and even grown men) sighed in front of her photograph."[9] Cinematographer Louis Delluc has argued that Pearl was a textbook example of a modern woman: "Her movement, her gestures, her lack of expression . . . and her athletic attributes (boxing, horsemanship, automobile racing, etc.), all made her quite simply perfect for the screen."[10] In many ways, Delluc asserts, White's social impact was more important than her influence on fashion. Images of her vibrant body touched off a wave of imitation. Sport became popular among all segments of society, making athletics an activity in which those of ordinary means might feel a sense of equality. The success of American serials thus coincided with women making social and political headway. The films of Pearl and imitators like Helen Gibson, Juanita Hansen, Ruth Roland, and Marie Walcamp signaled an era of feminine activism while many men were at the front and could not exercise the traditional roles of providers, protectors, and controllers of women. White's athletic films also served as a template for subsequent female stars like Carole Lombard, Mary Pickford, and Ginger Rogers to exhibit similar degrees of dynamism and self-confidence.

The public might have been intrigued with White and her imitators, but modern feminists are often conflicted about them. Ben Singer asserts that the serial queen genre is paradoxical, since "its portrayal of female power is sometimes accompanied by the sadistic spectacle of women's victimization." While the new woman appeared uppity and intimidating to some, she was commanding and confident to others. Stephen Kern has noted that there was a fascination with speed in the early twentieth century, epitomized through increasingly rapid means of transportation like the bicycle, train, automobile, and airplane.[11] These brought both pleasure and danger—much like the new woman. During this era, mobility of space often accompanied social and cultural mobility. Femininity had seldom been linked to action, but the new century and new art form of cinema accomplished this goal. Film historian

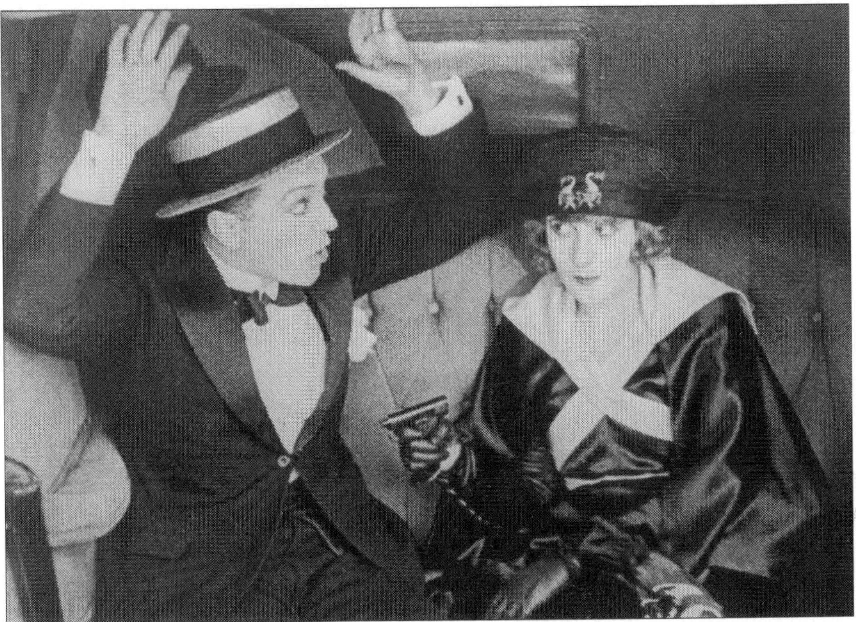

Figure 3.1. Serial queen Pearl White demonstrates her pluck and resourcefulness by pulling a gun on a hapless victim in *The Lightning Raider* (1919). Collection of David L. Chapman.

Vicki Callahan explains that "alterations in space and time represent a kind of ethics, a new morality of pure action that the female body increasingly comes to convey."[12] The new woman integrated form with function.

Musidora

If Pearl White represented female energy and righteousness, other women came from a different direction. These were bad girls who struck terror into the hearts of wealthy matrons, society fat cats, and captains of industry. One of the most extraordinary was Three-Fingered Kate, who starred in several British films between 1908 and 1912. Whereas White and others are victims of male machinations, Kate is "an arch-criminal and mistress of her own destiny."[13] Played by French actress Ivy Martinek, Kate is physically adept (despite missing digits) and intellectually astute, robbing unsuspecting nabobs of ill-gotten gains. She uses her athleticism and undetectable disguises (often donning men's trousers) to outwit hapless male pursuers. Her principal adversary is Sheerluck Finch, an obvious reference to Sherlock Holmes but without the fictional detective's resourcefulness. Elizabeth Miller emphasizes that part of the character's appeal is her "gratuitous and audacious antagonism toward figures of authority."[14] Kate is a dangerous rebel who enjoys tweaking society's nose with what remains of her hand. Her final film shots leave no doubt about her attitude toward forces of order. She faces the camera, holds up her thumb, index finger, and middle finger with palm facing her face and laughs at the audience, flipping off "respectable" society.

Three-Fingered Kate might have been the first cinematic villainess, but there was a French actress who displayed as much cunning and twice the wickedness as Martinek's character. Musidora (Jeanne Roques) was raised in a politically astute family, with parents who encouraged their daughter to express herself artistically. She began her stage career in 1914 but soon switched to film. Eventually Musidora was asked by one of France's best directors of serials to collaborate on the chapter drama *Les vampires* (1915–16). The story tells of a sinister group of bandits who terrorize Paris and a young journalist who tries to thwart them. The greatest sensation of the film is the evil femme fatale Irma Vep (an anagram of the word *vampire*), played with relish by Musidora. Although her stark white face and piercing kohl-marked eyes were remarkable, her skin-tight black silk body stocking caused even more hubbub. The visual impact of Musidora's powerful body was novel and disturbing, a dizzying combination of malevolence and eroticism. This sexy new look was not lost on promoters, who issued a poster that appealed to the public's curiosity. It featured a woman's head encased in a tight-fitting black cowl with an opening for two unearthly eyes. Her neck was encircled by a large red question mark perched above four words: "Qui? Quoi? Quand? Où . . . . ?" (Who? What? When? Where . . . . ?).

In this serial film Paris is crawling with vicious evildoers who operate with impunity and pollute the atmosphere of the city. It was, after all, produced at the height of World War I and reflected the fears many French people had about the pervasiveness of evil and the vipers residing within the bosoms of even happy families. Through the actors' use of masks and disguises, the audience is to intuit that concealment of real identities is everywhere and people are seldom what they seem. In one instance, the vampire gang robs an elegant gathering of socialites by gassing them inside their gilded palace; the bandits wear gas masks, survival tools familiar to citizens of wartime Paris. Like the vampire herself, evil could scale buildings, survive falls from great heights, seep soundlessly into rooms, or perform massive feats of strength. No one was entirely safe from malevolent influences represented by Musidora's terrible alter ego, Irma Vep.

When Musidora appears in her black body stocking, she not only makes an erotic statement but allows herself to move in a free and athletic way. Although she wears the body stocking in only a few scenes in the six-plus-hour series, it is images of the agile Musidora climbing walls, clambering across rooftops, and shinnying down drainpipes that leave the greatest impression. Anne Hollander, in *Seeing through Clothes*, notes that throughout history every reduction in the volume of women's apparel usually corresponded to increasing freedom of motion.[15] Musidora's body stocking represent a near-total liberation of her body, allowing her to move and vault about the screen at will. She has moved far beyond Pearl White's simple narrow skirt, but then Musidora also has the freedom to be as bad as she desires. She is the eternal temptress, the vamp who lures unsuspecting men to moral and physical doom. Musidora is the new woman who has defected to the dark side, the figure many men dread because she is out of control; she is feral, dangerous, and frightening. Whatever cinematic illusion was generated by the real movements of Musidora's body was powerfully reinforced by the existing fears of wartime audiences.

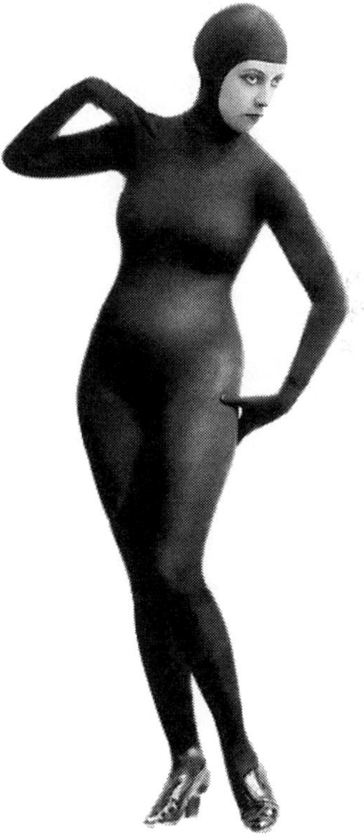

Figure 3.2. Musidora (Jeanne Roques) was most famous for her role as the evil Irma Vep in *Les vampires* (1915), in which she appeared in daring black silk tights. Collection of David L. Chapman.

Protéa

As exciting and erotic as Musidora was, she was not the first movie actress to wear revealing apparel. Josette Andriot in the *Zigomar* series played the title character's evil accomplice wearing her notorious black body stocking.[16] Fetching though she may have been, in that role Andriot was more famous as the star of *Protéa*, a series of spy thriller films released from 1913 to 1919. Victorin-Hippolyte Jasset directed the first of these adventure films and set the tone for later productions. He wisely chose a woman to play the lead. Andriot was a genuine athlete, hired initially for her equestrian skills, but by the time shooting finished, she demonstrated her abilities in acrobatics, cycling, diving, and climbing natural and manmade precipices. She was one of the first female stars renowned for athleticism. Protéa is described in a poem used to advertise the film as having "a nature familiar with every sport, a will that imposes itself on the fiercest of monsters" and being a "Sphinx [who] destroys all things in her path in the name of 'her duty.'" She could "subdue fate as it has subdued both men and beasts."[17] Even allowing for hyperbole, these are unusually vigorous terms to describe a woman in the pre–World War I era.

The most spectacular stunt in this action-packed opus was saved for the series climax. Protéa ends up on a bicycle, pursued by a band of local police detectives who corner her, with the only escape being a wooden bridge extending over a precipice. Her pursuers set fire to the bridge, and the heroine is seemingly trapped. Or is she? With her head lowered to the handlebars, Protéa rides toward the burning bridge, pedaling furiously, intending to leap the gap "in true daredevil style, describing a high arc and landing safely on the other side much to the discomfiture of the waiting sleuths."[18] With such attractions as "infernal" automobiles, mysterious manor houses, chases, explosions, knock-out gas, pursuits on horseback, sword fights, and "stairways that rise up, floors that descend, pillars that spin, and walls that close in," Protéa assumes the aspect of an avenging angel of justice or a dauntless police woman.[19] As one of the first *femmes nouvelles* of French cinema, she was a modern amazon resolved to appropriate all the freedoms of the new century to women. Symbolic of that freedom was the black body stocking worn by Andriot and Musidora. The dark, skintight garment represented a willingness by some women of the early twentieth century to establish an identity that allowed freedom of motion and constituted threat of rebellion to male domination. It also seemed to promise a sexual desirability hitherto hidden. Musidora recognized this erotic potential: "The flimsy silk of my costume must have shaken up the young men of 1916 for a good long while. In that way I created the 'Vamp,' the fickle woman who seduces bad little boys with love."[20]

Queen of the Seas

If Musidora plumbed the depths of human depravity, another cinematic strongwoman explored real depths. Annette Kellerman was born near Melbourne, Australia, in 1886 but came to America as a vaudeville performer in 1906 in a swimming, diving, and dancing act. The following year she achieved notoriety by appearing on a beach near Boston wearing a form-fitting swimsuit revealing her curvaceous body. It was a publicity stunt that got Kellerman arrested, but it gained her fame—and free advertising.[21] The body her swimsuit barely concealed was a paragon of fitness, honed by years of sports participation, and Kellerman took pride in her agile swimmer's physique. In 1908 Harvard professor Dudley Allen Sergeant declared her "the perfect woman," with measurements almost identical to those of the Venus de Milo.[22]

Thanks in part to Kellerman's perfect body and fame garnered in vaudeville, Carl Laemmle at Universal Studios featured her in *Neptune's Daughter* (1914), in which the actress plays a lively water sprite, dancing about while clothed in a few yards of diaphanous fabric. She falls in love with a dry-land king but is thwarted by heartless villains and subjected to mental and physical abuse, after which she emerges triumphant. It was not the plot of this silly film that made Kellerman a sensation and $1 million for the studio but her energetic portrayal of a feisty and fearless naiad who fights for the man she loves. Kellerman's biographer claims she was "Hollywood's first-ever swashbuckling heroine."[23] American audiences had seldom seen a genuinely athletic woman on the screen—one who did her own stunts and ended up saving the protagonist rather than waiting for the man to save her. An even bigger production followed in 1916 with Kellerman starring in *A Daughter of the Gods*, another fairy-tale confection, this time set in a mythical Arabian sheikdom and featuring plenty of action, swimming, and stunts. With a lavish budget of $1 million, it boasted a cast of twenty thousand extras as "gnomes, fairies, battling warriors and beauties" in "entrancing scenes of Oriental splendor."[24] Kellerman's athletic abilities were highlighted as she swam long distances, plummeted over a sixty-foot waterfall, dove from a one-hundred-foot tower, and jumped into a pit of live alligators. Exemplifying the athletic and energetic new woman, Kellerman did stunts with sporting and political implications. The *New York Times* argued that "those who contend that woman is too weak physically to contend with a man at the voting booth and therefore should be denied the franchise should go see Annette Kellerman in *Daughter of the Gods.*"[25]

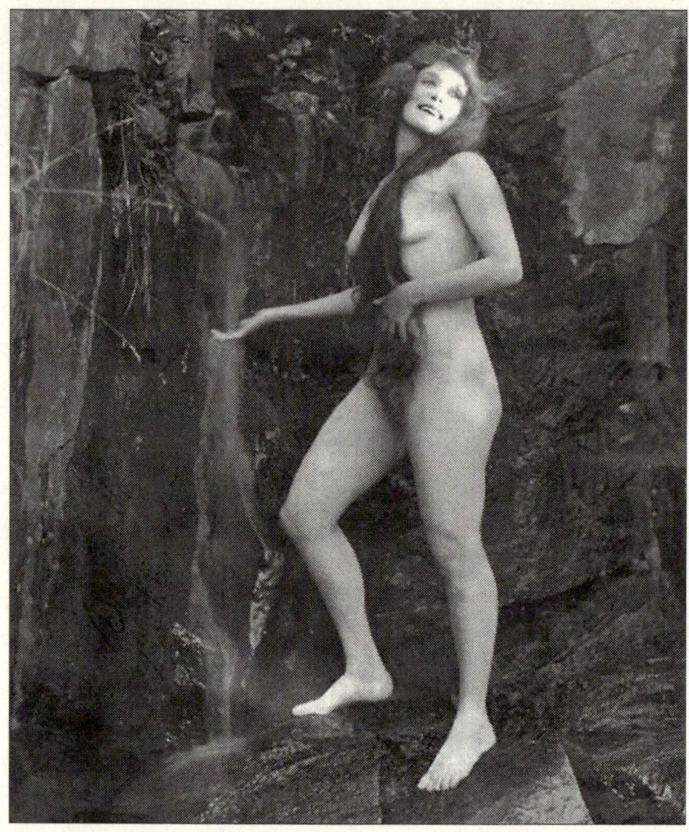

Figure 3.3. Annette Kellerman strikes a nude pose in a photo to promote *A Daughter of the Gods* (1916). Image in the public domain.

All of this added to the film's allure and helped justify its exorbitant budget, but it was the star herself who contributed most to its appeal. One reason for Kellerman's popularity was that she appeared in almost all of them wearing very little. As a result of the use of orthochromatic film, her tights often did not register, and the actress appeared to be naked in some scenes. Kellerman's many "nude" scenes were guaranteed to make the film a succès de scandale. Like American burlesque dancer Sally Rand, who would in the

1930s become famous for her bubble dance, the Australian water nymph was adept at tricking audiences into thinking they were seeing more than they actually were. It never worried Kellerman. In *Neptune's Daughter* she is transformed from a mermaid to a woman with nothing to cover herself other than long tresses of hair. There is also a suggestive disrobing scene which, although shot from a distance, shows her "flitting white and nymph-like through the trees en route to the ocean for a swim."[26] In later films she is clearly nude, despite claims to the contrary. As one reviewer noted, "Clothes may make the man but they don't make a daughter of the gods, at least not the sort Annette depicts." Indeed, the publicity campaign after the film's release made much of her athleticism and "perfect physique." The marketers at the Fox Film studios, eager to engage female patrons, encouraged special publicity ploys. Each movie theater received paper tape measures to distribute to ladies and a life-size cardboard cutout of the star that was to be positioned in the lobby. Women were encouraged to compare their figures to Kellerman's. In many major markets the star lectured on female fitness, thereby increasing her name recognition and film receipts.[27] Kellerman became the epitome of a naturally developed woman despite the artificial glitter and glow of her theatrical setting.

When compared to other blockbusters like *Cabiria* (1914) or *Birth of a Nation* (1915), *Daughter of the Gods* does not hold up well. It was conceived and executed as escapist entertainment featuring a perky female star who performed daring feats of agility and strength on the screen. In 1918 the Australian mermaid tried to spin out another gossamer fantasy set in watery depths. *Queen of the Sea* was greeted with little enthusiasm, especially since audiences could see that it simply rehashed earlier works. The horrors of World War I ended Kellerman's underwater adventures for a time. Audiences could hardly imagine mermaids disporting themselves in the same waves under which U-boats might be lurking. Despite magnificent stunts like a one-hundred-foot dive from a high wire, the movie is considered the actress's first flop.

Kellerman's next film, *What Women Love* (1920), was an attempt to remake her image into "an up-to-date, honest-to-goodness American girl." She plays Annabel Cotton, a tomboy heroine who transforms her milquetoast husband into a he-man. Journalist Janiss Garza divined the film's purpose as "purely an excuse to show off Kellerman's figure in a one-piece bathing suit." The usual stunts, high dives, and underwater struggles to the death rounded out the film, causing Garza to conclude that "the star sounds even more macho than the film's hero!"[28] This film is interesting because gender construction and role reversals are prominent since it is the woman who is active and daring. Seemingly a "real" man is the only one that will satisfy an active woman like Annabel Cotton.

By the time Kellerman made her last movie in 1924, the era of the new woman was over, and she found herself increasingly sidelined by more modern stars. Although no longer heralded as the "perfect woman," she still looked good enough to appear in her revealing bathing costume, but never again nude. *Venus of the South Seas* is an adventure story set on a remote South Pacific island where Shona (Kellerman) is the daughter of a white pearl trader. She meets and falls in love with a rich playboy who visits the island in his yacht. When her father dies, Shona leaves the island to escape the lust-filled clutches of at least two villains. Her rich boyfriend returns in the nick of time, and they defeat the forces of evil. One of the film's most notable segments is a fantasy sequence in which the heroine plays a mermaid, photographed in a large tank to give the star ample opportunity to display her natatory talents. The film's strength, observed *Variety*, "depends entirely upon the aquatic Annette Kellerman and some beautiful water scenes." But it was damned with faint praise as "quite melodramatic" and would "prove of greater interest in the neighborhoods," the latter being a veiled reference to less sophisticated working-class districts.[29] Annette was never a great actress; her appeal came from a mixture of athletics and female vigor. By the time of *Venus of the South Seas*, the mermaid was more of a celebrity than a top-of-the-line movie star, but for many she would remain Australia's most famous citizen.

Ruth Budd

Annette Kellerman was not the only strong female athlete who traded on her good looks and athletic body or made the transition from vaudeville. Ruth Budd began her show business career after 1900 in an acrobatic act with her brother Giles. Unlike other female entertainers, she did not serve as a decorative element for men's work; she was the "understander" (a performer who supports the principal acrobat). Budd represented a new type of gender role, feminine but exhibiting enough physical strength, independence, and assertiveness to confuse or intrigue audiences. In the mid-1910s she launched her solo career as a singing acrobat who always performed her portion of the bill in a revealing union suit and with a cheery demeanor. When she paid a visit to New Zealand in 1917, an anonymous writer called her "the saucy little sponsor of sunshine" who was "radiant, rapturous, refulgent . . . the personification of dainty delightfulness."[30] Sometimes Budd would do a little striptease similar to Charmion's. Female acrobats usually wore tights and revealed more of their bodies than was permitted elsewhere, but Budd knew what limits vaudeville would allow. She would remove her outer garments slowly and salaciously enough to cause a frisson among male customers, but it was usually tame enough for women and children. "Ruth is billed as the girl with the smile," wrote a satisfied critic, adding with a wink, "I didn't notice the smile. Her ankles are lovely." Budd was both naughty and nice. Most patrons accepted her acrobatic costume, but many objected to her disrobing on stage and giving the illusion of impropriety. It was the piquant mixture of boldness and daintiness that made performers like Charmion and Budd unique. Vaudeville historian Alison Kibler confirms that the "combination of masculine action and daring with a feminine manner and appearance made women's acts more shocking to audiences."[31]

Budd's ankles (and the rest of her) were becoming famous, so like many vaudeville artists, she was invited to star in a feature film. *A Scream in the Night* (1919) is a hodgepodge of Darwinian theory and jungle melodrama. Dubbed by *Variety* as "an unusual picture," the bewildering plot features the kidnapping of Senator Newcastle's daughter by mad scientist Professor Silvio, who wants to prove Charles Darwin's theory of natural selection by having the girl mate with an ape. But Budd is the standout in this story. Nearly every reviewer noted her athletic ability, shapely physique, and skimpy attire. "As a forest nymph," wrote one, "Miss Budd is not overburdened with clothing, a leopard skin being her one garment."[32] Although no one seemed clear on how Silvio's experiment could prove Darwinism, natural selection provided women a rationale for strengthening their bodies through exercise. Physical culture would make women better mothers and improve the race.

Budd had appeared in an earlier short feature, *Building Up the Health of a Nation* (1916). With World War I intensifying, many believed America should be prepared for entry into battle. Budd and her brother consequently performed part of their acrobatic routines to inspire such readiness. Her connection to strength, health, and exercise made her a "physical culture girl." She played up her muscularity, and when a reporter asked Budd after the release of her first film what she thought of women's suffrage, the acrobat exhibited her biceps: "Does this arm feel like a clinging vine?" The reporter declared Budd's arms were indeed hard as nails. This connection between a hard body and an independent spirit was exploited by the film's producers, who recommended that promoters emphasize Budd's belief that "women are not the weaker sex." In the film she "accomplishes feats requiring strength and agility that appear to be beyond the girl so winsomely feminine. . . . Certainly no member of her sex and few of the opposite sex can swing through 40 or 50 feet of space."[33] The major theme emerging from *A Scream in the Night* has nothing to do with the Darwinian rigmarole; rather, it concerns the strength of a female body resisting efforts to remake it in order to conform to others' wishes; it is a revolutionary feminist tract molded into an unlikely jungle romance. Budd's character Darwa is an unwitting Pygmalion who refuses to bend to her creator's desires.

Emilie Sannom

During the Great War era, heroines of many adventure films created a new model of femininity. Protagonists were no longer condemned to play purely passive roles; they became agents of action responsible for plot progression. American and European serials featuring determined women who took matters into their own hands proved popular worldwide, and it seemed that nearly every film-producing country featured a copycat Pearl White or Protéa. One of the most successful female daredevils was Emilie Sannom, a Danish actress who achieved international fame as a sturdy athlete, daring acrobat, and fearless aerial stuntwoman. Despite its small size and relatively scarce resources, Denmark was a cinema capital. Film historian Ephraim Katz confirms that "Denmark reigned supreme from 1909 to 1914 as Europe's most prosperous film center. Its films rivaled those of Hollywood, for popularity on the screens of Paris, London, Berlin and New York."[34] At the start of this golden age, Sannom used her daring and dauntless personality to reach stardom. She made about eighty-five films, beginning with primitive farces in 1907 at Nordisk Films Kompagni. In 1911 she played her best role yet as Ophelia in the first cinematic version of *Hamlet*. It was shot at Kronborg Castle, and her part culminated when, in a fit of despair, she threw herself into the castle's muddy moat. This was one of the first feats that would make Sannom "Danmarks Vovehals Nummer Et" (Denmark's number one daredevil). During her career she would scale rooftops and walls, be run over by an express train (lying between the rails), dive into submarine torpedo shafts, and balance on a rope between ship masts, regularly putting herself in danger. As Sannom explained, "I was born with the conviction that whatever happens to me, I'll survive. I'm never going to dissolve in panic, never be disoriented, never become senselessly disturbed."[35] It was all due to unrestrained female muscular willpower.

Indeed, many of Sannom's more dramatic actions proved her steely nerves and fearlessness. In the 1914 film *Pigen fra Hidalgo-Fyret* (The girl from the Hidalgo Lighthouse; English title: *Through Flames to Fame*) she performed one of her most dangerous stunts. Her character is imprisoned in one of the twenty-five-meter-high windmills that dotted the Danish countryside. To escape, she climbs out on one of the mill's sails, then as her weight causes the device to descend, she prepares to jump off as it approaches the ground. But as she gets closer to the end of the blade, it begins to turn dangerously fast, which causes her to be thrown off prematurely. It is easy to see that there were no special effects involved in this maneuver, and Sannom seems genuinely stunned by her fall. Being a trooper and realizing that the camera is still cranking, she picks herself up and staggers off for more breakneck adventures.[36]

In addition to all the action sequences in Sannom's films, they could usually be counted on to include an ample view of her shapely physique, which was often displayed in a one-piece bathing costume. After the war she starred in a series of films as Panopta the lady detective. *Rædselshuset på Søens Bund* (The underwater house of terror), released in 1918, is typical. Despite an unrealistic plot, the film provides several revealing views of Sannom's mastery of movement. She always exhibited a foolhardiness in face of danger that set her apart from other cinematic daredevils. After finishing the *Panopta* series, Sannom went to Rome in 1923 to star in *La fanciulla dell'aria* (Mistress of the air), in which she performed a series of dizzying aerial stunts using airplanes and dirigibles. But it was her gender role reversal that is most intriguing in a 1925 interview for a Danish women's magazine. Unlike other women, Sannom was fearless, plucky and (most fascinating of all) enjoyed wearing "daredevil trousers." When asked what she would do if she were a man, Sannom replied jokingly, "I would be a real, wild cowboy . . . armed to the teeth, hurtling across the prairie after his prey—that would be just right for me. I am at my best either in an airplane, venturing out on one of its wings, on horseback or at sea amid the turbulent waves."[37] Perhaps there was no better place for such a free spirit than the skies. Sannom was a real "amazon of the sky," as she performed daring and terrifying stunts, sometimes suspended in midair, held up only by her arms. She died in a 1931 Danish air show when her parachute failed to open. The epitaph on her headstone hints at her proclivity for death-defying deeds: "Her fear of death was not so great / greater still was her fear of life on Earth."[38]

Italian Strongwomen

As in the other Allied countries, Italy's women felt a "wind of freedom" during and after the Great War, but it was a wind that seemed revolutionary in light of the Mediterranean code of honor, Catholic morality, and the Lombroso school of criminology, which advocated female confinement to prevent prostitution.[39] This female visibility in commerce and industry was reflected in popular culture and especially films. Similar to America and western Europe, a new genre developed featuring strong, dauntless, athletic women. Linda Albertini, a circus acrobat, became the first of this new crop of strong, independent women who used their muscles and ingenuity. In 1917 she teamed up with her real-life partner, former circus acrobat Luciano Albertini, to make *La spirale della morte* (The spiral of death), a patriotic adventure tale in which she plays a circus acrobat who helps a naval lieutenant destroy a fuel depot used by enemy submarines. The film proved a great success, and Luciano achieved fame in numerous films as the athletic character Sansonia. Linda followed him as Sansonette. When Luciano started his own company, she became his leading female star in repetitive scenes that strained credulity with lots of special effects. Nevertheless, Linda threw herself into the work enthusiastically, using her talents on the trapeze. In one aerial performance she flings herself out of a high-flying balloon basket; in another she grabs a rope dangling from a plane overhead as she gallops underneath on horseback and remains suspended for several moments before clambering to safety. By the time of her final Italian film, *Sansonette e i quattro arlecchini* (Sansonette and the four harlequins), she and the public were tiring of outlandish situations and unrealistic adventures. Recognizing Linda's performance as the only redeeming feature of this "twaddle," a reviewer pleaded for her recognition as an artist who should not be buried under a pile of stale plot devices: "If there is something pleasing here, it is thanks to her."[40] Linda eventually followed Luciano to Germany where she appeared in his first four films, but soon afterward her partner replaced her with a more exotic beauty. Still, Linda Albertini's career had lasted longer than those of most other women daredevils. More colorful were the cinematic adventures of Piera Bouvier, described by biographer Tito Alacci as "a fine strapping girl, tall, buxom and with a domineering and fiery temperament."[41] She was discovered on a Genoa street by Ubaldo Maria Del Colle, who was dazzled by her lush, tawny blond hair, her six-foot height, and her haughty gaze, which bespoke an uncompromising and rebellious attitude. After two days she was at work with Alberto Capozzi and shuttling between Genoa, Rome, and Turin, turning out a dozen films as a dancer, noblewoman, revived mummy, princess, and wicked adventuress. A talented sportswoman, Bouvier played opposite Francesco Casaleggio in *L'avventura di Fracassa* (Fracassa's adventure), a pastiche of daredevilry and swashbuckling that demonstrated she was ready for any task, regardless of peril. One reviewer praised the two main actors, but thought the production was cheap and the direction lackluster: "The characters of Fracassa and Farinella are well delineated. . . . It is a pity that the frame that encloses their feats is a bit skimpy and their feats themselves have been underdeveloped."[42] Bouvier received top billing in the 1918 serial film *L'elegante canaglia di Parigi* (The elegant rabble of Paris), in which she looked dazzling in all six episodes wearing black tights. It was directed by Gennaro Righelli, who dragged the story along until he got a better offer in Paris. Fortunately, it was handed over to the more competent Ferdinand Guillaume Polidor for the last two episodes, and he decided to infuse much-needed excitement and reality into the production. No more tricks, no more stand-ins; all scenes were shot with rigorous attention to verisimilitude. Thus, though the film's action was supposedly taking place in Guatemala, Bouvier was forced in midwinter to jump from a bridge outside Rome into the frigid Tiber River. The bridge stood over thirty meters above the freezing water, and "I caught double pneumonia and the mother of my partner Goffredo D'Andrea fainted from fright when she saw what I did," recalled the actress. "But we were incredibly foolish—foolish and happy to have filmed such a memorable scene!" After finishing this film, Bouvier married a wealthy soap manufacturer and retired.[43]

Gisa-Liana Doria was a postwar strongwoman star who flew through the air on a trapeze and piloted airplanes. In her first film, *Il pilota del Caproni n. 5* (The pilot of the Caproni no. 5) she recklessly flew her aircraft against the Red Baron, who pursued her amid a hail of bullets. Doria came from the circus, where she had been part of an acrobatic troupe called the Uccellini; the troupe had appeared in several films that were full of manic, almost frantic, action but short on logic. "The actors seem to be either in the grips of a constant 'delirium tremens' or under the effects of cocaine" noted a critic of the 1921 movie, *A precipizio* (Headlong rush). "But their illogical and violent movements allow us to admire the acrobatic and pugilistic talents of

Gisa Doria and the Uccellini Troupe that one follows with great interest and with much laughter."[44] Adventure films with lots of action, like *La vendetta del massaro* (The tenant farmer's revenge), in which she plays a daring trick rider who gallops at top speed to confront a band of malevolent Mexican bandits, were Doria's forte.

Fede Sedino, another daredevil who began her film career in Turin, first appeared with Mario Guaita-Ausonia, but when he left for Marseilles, Sedino continued on her own with *I milioni della zingara* (The gypsy's millions) and *Il segreto della miniera d'oro* (The gold miner's secret). These quickly made action films were popular in working-class cinemas. Sedino was famous for fast-paced films where she would foil dastardly plots, charge madly on fiery stallions, or leap from cliffs to escape inextricable predicaments. In suburban movie houses Sedino was touted as the Italian Pearl White. Despite restrictions imposed on her because of these "poverty row" productions, she remained an audience favorite. What her films lacked in financial resources they made up in athletic prowess.

Henriette Bonard gave up a modeling career to work in films. Her first roles were in sensational and macabre serials. In 1916 she appeared in *La fidanzata della morte* (Death's betrothed) and *Sua Altezza Reale, il principe Enrico* (His Royal Highness, Prince Henry) which starred the muscular athlete Lionel Buffalo. In 1921 Bonard appeared in two Bartolomeo Pagano films—*Maciste in vacanza* (Maciste on vacation) and *Maciste salvato dalle acque* (Maciste saved from drowning). With regard to athletic energy and versatility, Bonard was unrestrained, offering a vigorous counterpart to male physicality. According to Italian film scholar Stella Dagna, Bonard's beauty and grace threatened to upstage Maciste: "Although the actress specialized in adventure films, her sophisticated ways and her elegant demeanor could not fail to embarrass her partner." Fortunately, director Luigi Romano Borgnetto recognized the tension as Maciste interacted with the beautiful woman. As Dagna notes, "His clumsiness becomes one of the film's comedic resources."[45] Throughout her career Bonard had appeared on screen with many of Italy's greatest strongmen, including Maciste's rival, Luciano Albertini, but she was a strong, athletic woman herself.

Astrea

Female protagonists normally exhibited intelligence, courage, and strength to escape some dreadful trap or certain death. An athletic escapade was almost never done for its own sake—never for the joy of physical exertion.

Although it is true that athleticism and adventurousness were not considered "ladylike" behaviors in the early twentieth century, the women in these films rarely run away from danger, nor do they court it. Shelly Stamp, in analyzing Pearl White and other serial queens, explains that "Pauline's adventures might be said to offer a reflexive treatment of restraint and entrapment."[46] Whether the protagonist is a good girl, like Annette Kellerman, or a villainess like Musidora's Irma Vep, she reacts to troubles and rarely exerts herself physically otherwise. One extraordinary woman, however, broke this pattern. The actress known only as Astrea was a tall, imposing, powerful woman who was neither the beautiful sidekick of a strongman nor a willowy acrobat who used her grace and agility to fight oppression.[47] She resembled an older and more popular character derived from the circus strongwoman and from the nineteenth-century theme of a "superman of the masses" who defends weak and law-abiding citizens. She was one of the world's first female superheroes, a "mastodonic woman" who was in every way except gender another Maciste.[48]

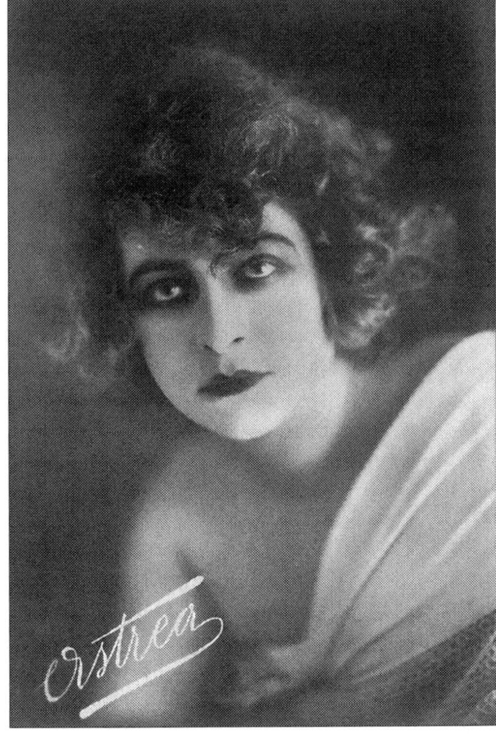

Figure 3.4. Italian actress Astrea (Countess Barbieri). As one of the few female "good giants" in Italian cinema, her screen persona used great strength and stature to fight injustice. Collection of David L. Chapman.

Astrea made four films, beginning with *La riscossa delle maschere* (The revenge of the masks), a reaction to the Italian army's humiliating defeat at Caporetto in 1917. It was intended to revive the nation's depressed morale with a symbolic representation of the Italian masks from the ancient commedia dell'arte. They are miraculously brought to life by Astrea, who portrays the national symbol Italia, complete with castellated crown and a blinding flash of faith and patriotism. Large, formidable, and slightly fearsome, Astrea represents the patriotic women of Italy who lead the revenge of the Italian people, wearing various regional masks. She also demonstrates the female spirit—that same élan that women of all Western countries used to hammer home their rights as citizens deserving participation in the national dialog of voting. "The result is a really vicious little work," remarks critic Vittorio Martinelli, highlighted by "the astonishing muscular demonstrations of its star."[49] In *Justitia* (1919), Astrea's next film, she displays more of her athletic and acting talents. It was celebrated as an excellent comedy, with ample opportunity for adventure and self-deprecating fun. In the plot, Astrea is given the task of protecting a young brother and sister, making sure they receive their sizable inheritance. Attempting to overcome her, a usurper bribes a group of burly circus athletes. But Astrea puts the whole group to flight, thrashing them with her fists without much effort. Her favorite pastimes are pistol shooting and boxing, and woe to anyone who incurs her wrath. During a hunt for the enemy, she must break an enormous chain on a gate, and while she is struggling with it, the camera slowly and lovingly focuses on her muscles, which swell with effort—solid muscles meant to convey strength.[50]

The film was successfully shown throughout Europe. As expressed in the *Bioscope* after its London premiere, "the story is of a sort of female knight who wanders over the world searching for wrongs to right," accompanied by "a clever fool named Birillo." Together this "Donna Quixote" and modern Sancho Panza "trounce a band of arrant knaves using the strength of [Astrea's] muscles and Birillo's cunning." According to Monica Dall'Asta, the most surprising aspect of Astrea was the admiration bestowed on her from male critics. Her muscular power did not obviate her beauty.[51] *Justitia* not only filled the cinemas but inspired thoughtful critics astounded by her strength. Although it was simply another adventure movie, it was different both in its star and its use of humor. The reviewer for *La rivista cinematografica* noted the film was "suffused with a pleasant and genuine comedy. . . . Astrea is Astrea: a strong, nimble, and daring athlete of the first order and at the same time an extremely elegant lady." The *Bioscope* was even more effusive in its praise, noting the "incredible acrobatics by the heroine, a lady Hercules who seems to have mastered the tricks of Houdini; this is the spectacular backdrop for a unique and agreeable adventure film whose thrilling sensations are intelligently interspersed with an irresistible comic vein."[52]

In *L'ultima fiaba* (The last fable, 1920) Astrea is again an athletic and aggressive strongwoman whose outfit consists of jodhpurs, broad-brimmed hat, and khaki shirt, similar to the uniform of the newly formed Boy Scouts, but she also harks back to her real-life heritage as Countess Barbieri by looking comfortable in an elegant evening gown. In the film Astrea attempts to rescue a little girl who is the heir to a very rich man's fortune and who has been kidnapped by a gypsy named Tuffer and his accomplice, an aristocratic lady, in order to get their hands on the child's inheritance. Astrea's combination of farcical situations, role reversals, and slapstick, along with adventure, suspense, and feats of strength, ensured the film's success. Her final film was *I creatori dell'impossible* (The creators of the impossible, 1921) after which she retired, silently abdicating her crown as the queen of muscles.

It seems likely that many films featuring women protagonists who endured discomforts, difficulties, and indignities were playing at least partly for female audiences. The years before World War I were the heyday of the diva in Italy—the beautiful, languid and elegantly dressed woman who suffered and died for love. These films were targeted primarily to women, but those featuring athletic or daredevil women likely had a wider appeal. It is ironic that the greater number of these *forzute*, or strongwomen, films were produced in Italy, which was hardly a bastion of feminism or forward thinking. It was assumed by many Italian men that women were too unintelligent to distinguish between illusions fabricated by filmmakers and everyday reality. Some male writers protested about the racket women and children made when the action of a film was exciting or sentimental. "At a tragic ending, the children and the women present in the theater all combined [to] shed several liters of tears," complained one reviewer in 1925. Another male moviegoer grumbled about the din when heartbreaking events unfolded on the screen, causing women "to howl like a dog whose tail has been stepped on."[53] Elegant women suffering tragic pangs of love or plump mother figures were fine with Italian men, but if the film's protagonist was getting along without a man, that was different. Luciano Doria, columnist for a popular movie magazine, went further than most writers, stating in 1921, "Women (and forgive my brutal honesty) are and will always be inferior beings—like small, charming insects, parasites of that huge and superior animal that is Man."[54] Unfortunately, few Italian women recorded their thoughts on films featuring strongwomen. A hint of their opinions can be found in a 1916 article that speculates on what might be going on in the brains of the female garment workers, stenographers, and bored housewives who saw such films. The female author assumes that as workingwomen watch the heroines on the screen, the single burning question they keep asking themselves is "Why her and not me?"[55] The critic points out that the message of female empowerment was unmistakable and alluring to many women moviegoers. Despite the male dominance and outright misogyny that were common in early twentieth century, at least a few women could find a few models of strength, courage, and independence on-screen in the local cinemas.

Kung Fu Queens

Not all athletic women in silent movies were American or European. Some extraordinary films featuring women with strong character, athletic talent, and muscularity were made in prerevolutionary China. In 1905 a brief scene from a Chinese opera was filmed, but not until after World War I did a fully developed industry evolve in Shanghai. By the mid-1920s Chinese cinema was dominated by martial arts films. The first of them, *Huo shao hong lian si* (The burning of the Red Lotus Temple, 1928) was a curious offshoot of this craze in which women played athletic roles in convoluted adventure stories. One of the most prominent directors was Ren Pengnian, who, with his wife Wu Lizhu, made many films featuring strong, heroic women. Most notable was the thirteen-part serial film *Guangdong daxia* (Northeast hero, 1928–31), which helped make Wu a popular martial arts actress. She personified the modern Chinese sportswoman—fit and able, a role that set her apart from passive heroines of the era. Wu was also renowned for her stunt-work and knowledge of kung fu. She could kick, punch, jab, and jump with ease, and via an elaborate set of piano wires often flew through the air with balletic beauty. These athletic moves earned her the nickname the Oriental Female Fairbanks. Although she never achieved worldwide fame, she was at the forefront of women's empowerment. Lizhu soon had several imitators, as swordswomen and female fighters were the rage in Chinese cinemas.[56]

Nüxia, or female warriors, have an extensive Chinese literary heritage, and gender role reversals have a long Asian tradition. Heroines of Chinese opera were often portrayed by male actors, with gender ambiguity built into many classical roles. Other national interests included physical culture and sports, and eventually Chinese audiences wanted to see their actors perform the same kind of stunts and daredevil feats as Hollywood stars.[57] One means by which female stars performed "manly" stunts was by dressing like men. Wu Suxin successfully used this strategy in the 1929 film *Nüxia bai meigui* (The female knight-errant, White Rose). It opens at Shanghai's Women's Sports Academy, where she is a star athlete, excelling at gymnastics, club swinging, and rifle drill. Wu utilizes her training when she hears that her father's estate is threatened by bandits. She dons a mustache, headscarf, cowboy hat, and trousers, then brandishes a bow and arrows and a broadsword. She then poses in front of her mirror, striking masculine poses and repeatedly "shaping and adjusting her Douglas Fairbanks–type mustache."[58] Wu uses her prowess in martial arts and physical strength to mete out punishment to disrupters of social harmony. The idea that a single person (a lone woman) could fight against wicked landlords and corrupt public officials soon made authorities nervous, and *nüxia* films were quickly quashed by censors. The female knight-errant might have disappeared, but there were other strong role models ready to take their places, and one of these was the athlete.

By the early 1930s Shanghai's golden age of filmmaking had begun, and Western values were making inroads into traditional Chinese culture. Three activities most seductive to urban, newly prosperous Chinese were movies, dancing, and Western-style sports. These recreations are skillfully combined in *Ti yu huang hou* (Queen of sports, 1934), an extraordinary silent film that tells the story of Lin Ying (played by Li Lili), a talented runner and sportswoman from the provinces who enrolls in a Shanghai sports college to pursue her dreams of becoming a champion.[59] She is quickly transformed into a sports celebrity but allows her fame to go to her head. After being seduced by the fast and elegant playboys of upper-class Shanghai, it becomes clear that she has lost her way and forgotten the real meaning of sport. Only after a teammate dies during a competition does Lin Ying rediscover physical culture as vital for reforming the individual and the nation.

Sport can also provide an excuse to celebrate beauty. The camera often pans lovingly across the women's legs as they lie in bed doing air cycling exercises, much like a Rockettes chorus line. Although meant to be sensual, these scenes portray good, healthy exercises in contrast to scenes at posh dance parlors where elegantly dressed crowds smoke, drink, and dance. The film shows that although dancing is a form of physicality, it is a social ill. Film historian Zhang Zhen points out a divide between healthy exercise (competitive sports) and dissolute exercise (ballroom dancing): "While (good) sports were represented as a means to discipline the body and nurture the mind, social dancing stood for excessive pleasure and decadence."[60] *Ti yu huang hou* shows that there was a place for strong, athletic females in sports and politics. Chinese women, like Westerners during and immediately after World War I, kept up their end of the struggle, and the strength they had shown in real life was mirrored by the fictional women they saw in films. It was not really so far from Pearl White to Astrea and Li Lili.

Notes

1. Monica Dall'Asta, "Donne avventurose del cinema torinese," in *Cabiria e il suo tempo*, ed. Paolo Bertetto and Gianni Rondolino, 354.

2. Sharon R. Ullman, *Sex Seen: The Emergence of Modern Sexuality in America* (Berkeley: University of California Press 1997), 27.

3. William Heise, dir., *Comedy Set-To* (New York: Edison Manufacturing, 1898).

4. Thomas A. Edison, dir., *Gordon Sisters Boxing* (New York: Edison Manufacturing 1901), MPEG video available at Library of Congress, "The American Variety Stage: Vaudeville and Popular Entertainment, 1870–1920," http://memory.loc.gov/cgi-bin/query/h?ammem/varstg:@field(NUMBER+@band(varsmp+1628)).

5. Dan Streible, *Fight Pictures: A History of Boxing and Early Cinema*, 98.

6. According to Gail Finney, "The New Woman typically values self-fulfillment and independence rather than the stereotypically feminine ideal of self-sacrifice; believes in legal and sexual equality; often remains single because of the difficulty of combining such equality with marriage; is more open about her sexuality than the 'Old Woman'; is well-educated and reads a great deal; has a job; is athletic or otherwise physically vigorous and, accordingly, prefers comfortable clothes (sometimes male attire) to traditional female garb." Gail Finney, "Ibsen and Feminism," in *The Cambridge Companion to Ibsen*, ed. James McFarlane (Cambridge: Cambridge University Press, 1994), 95–96.

7. Monica Dall'Asta, *Trame spezzate: Archeologia del film seriale*, 143.

8. Margaret H. Darrow, *French Women and the First World War: War Stories of the Home Front* (Oxford: Berg, 2000), 194.

9. Marcel Lapierre, *Les cents visages du cinéma*, 1948, quoted in Dall'Asta, *Trame spezzate*, 145–46.

10. Louis Delluc, "Pearl White," in Écrits cinématographiques II, 1986, quoted in Dall'Asta, *Trame spezzate*, 146.

11. Ben Singer, "Female Power in the Serial-Queen Melodrama: The Etiology of an Anomaly," *Camera Obscura* 8, no. 1 (January 1990): 93; Stephen Kern, *The Culture of Time and Space, 1880–1918* (Cambridge, MA: Harvard University Press, 1983), 111.

12. Vicki Callahan, *Zones of Anxiety: Movement, Musidora, and the Crime Serials of Louis Feuillade* (Detroit: Wayne State University Press, 2005), 101.

13. Alex Marlow-Mann, "Exploits of Three-Fingered Kate, The (1912)," British Film Institute, http://www.screenonline.org.uk/film/id/727128/.

14. Elizabeth C. Miller, *Framed: The New Woman Criminal in British Culture at the Fin de Siècle* (Ann Arbor: University of Michigan Press, 2008), 122.

15. Anne Hollander, *Seeing through Clothes* (New York: Avon, 1980), 154.

16. Georges Sadoul, *Histoire générale du cinéma*, vol. 3, *Le cinéma devient un art*, 342.

17. Jacques Deslandes, "Victorin-Hippolyte Jasset," 1975, quoted in Dall'Asta, *Trame spezzate*, 110.

18. Review of *Protea, Moving Picture World* 18, no. 2 (October 11, 1913): 137. The reviewer adds that after performing this feat, "Mlle. Andriot spent six months in the hospital."

19. Pier Da Castello, "Protéa e l'automobile infernale," *La vita cinematografica*, July 22, 1914, quoted in Dall'Asta, *Trame spezzate*, 110.

20. Musidora, quoted in Sadoul, *Histoire générale du cinéma*, 342.

21. Lisa Bier, *Fighting the Current: The Rise of American Women's Swimming, 1870–1926* (Jefferson, NC: McFarland, 2011), 50.

22. G. P. Walsh, "Kellerman, Annette Marie (1886–1975)," in Australian National-al University, *Australian Dictionary of Biography*, http://adb.anu.edu.au/biography/kellermann-annette-marie-sarah-6911.

23. Emily Gibson, *The Original Million Dollar Mermaid: The Annette Kellerman Story*, 118.

24. Joanna Gilmour, "Naked Ambition," *Portrait* 31 (March–May 2009), http://www.portrait.gov.au/magazines/31/naked-ambition.

25. *New York Times*, quoted in Gibson, *The Original Million Dollar Mermaid*, 149.

26. David S. Shields, "Annette Kellerman," Photography and the American Stage, University of South Carolina, http://broadway.cas.sc.edu/content/annette-kellerman.

27. Gibson, *The Original Million Dollar Mermaid*, 146, 148.

28. Janiss Garza, "What Women Love: Synopsis," http://www.allmovie.com/movie/v116443.

29. *Variety*, June 6, 1924, quoted in "Venus of the South Seas," New Zealand Film Archive, http://web.archive.org/web/20130729091347/http://www.filmarchive.org.nz/feature-project/pages/Venus-SS.php.

30. Anonymous review of Ruth Budd, *Wellington (New Zealand) Evening Post*, November 19, 1917.

31. M. Alison Kibler, *Rank Ladies: Gender and Cultural Hierarchy in American Vaudeville*, 147, 158.

32. Review of *A Scream in the Night, Variety*, October 24, 1919, 190.

33. "She Can Carry Ballot to Box," September 25, 1916, clipping, Ruth Budd Collection, Fort Wayne Historical Society, Fort Wayne, IN, quoted in Kibler, *Rank Ladies*, 143, 164.

34. Ephraim Katz, *The Film Encyclopedia*, 3rd ed. (New York: HarperPerennial, 1998), s.v. "Denmark."

35. Emilie Sannom, quoted in Debora, "Pigen, der ikke kan Gyse," *Tidens Kvinder, n.d.* [1926?], Clippings File, Dansk Filminstitut, Copenhagen, 4.

36. Owen Garth, "Through Flames to Fame," *Picture Stories Magazine*, November 1914, 179–80.

37. "Hvad vilde De gøre, Hvis De var Mand?," *Eva*, October 1925, Clippings File, Dansk Filminstitut, Copenhagen, 14.

38. Inscription by poet Tom Kristensen on Emilie Sannom's headstone, Assistens Cemetery, Copenhagen, quoted in Erik Nørgaard, *Mille, mændenes overmand: Den eventyrlige beretning om skuespillerinden Emilie Sannoms liv* (Copenhagen: Holkenfeldts Forlag, 1992), 114.

39. Françoise Thébaud, "The Great War: Triumph of Sexual Difference," in *History of Women in the West*, vol. 5, 1994, quoted in Monica Dall'Asta, "Donne avventurose del cinema torinese," in Bertetto and Rondolino, eds., *Cabiria e il suo tempo*, 360. Criminologist Cesare Lombroso believed women were less evolved than men and consequently more inclined to vicious habits.

40. Zadig, review of *Sansonette e i Quattro arlecchini*, *La rivista cinematografica*, October 25, 1921, in *Gli uomini forti*, ed. Alberto Farassino and Tatti Sanguineti, 131.

41. Tito Alacci [Alacevich], *Le nostre attrici cinematografiche: Studiate sullo schermo* (Florence: R. Bemporad e Figlio, 1919), 136–37.

42. Il Rondone, review of *L'avventura di Fracassa*, *La vita cinematografica*, January 22, 1920, in Farassino and Sanguineti, eds., *Gli uomini forti*, ed. 123.

43. Piera Bouvier, quoted in Vittorio Martinelli, "Amazzoni dell'aria e danzatrici della prateria," in Farassino and Sanguineti, eds., *Gli uomini forti*, 21.

44. Emilio Pastori, review of *A precipizio*, in Farassino and Sanguineti, eds., *Gli uomini forti*, 133.

45. Stella Dagna, "All'ombra del gigante: Le comprimarie della serie Maciste," in *Non solo dive: Pioniere del cinema italiano*, ed. Monica Dall'Asta, 300.

46. Shelley Stamp, "Serial Heroines, Stars and their Fans," in *The Silent Cinema Reader*, ed. Lee Grieveson and Peter Krämer, 217.

47. Astrea was the stage name of Venetian aristocrat Countess Barbieri. See "In Search of Astrea, Mysterious 'Strongwoman' of the Italian Silent Cinema," June 8, 2016, *Silents, Please!* (blog), http://silentsplease.wordpress.com/2016/06/08/astrea/.

48. Astrea's description as "mastodonic" ("una mastodontica donna") comes from Elena Mosconi, "Dive e antidive: Elettra Raggio e Astrea," in Dall'Asta, ed., *Non solo dive*, 123.

49. Martinelli, "Amazzoni dell'aria," 22.

50. Monica Dall'Asta, *Un cinéma musclé: Le surhomme dans le cinéma muet italien (1913–1926)*, 116.

51. Anonymous review of *Justitia*,*Bioscope*, January 4, 1920, in Farassino and Sanguineti, eds., *Gli uomini forti*, 124; Dall'Asta, "Donne avventurose del cinema torinese," 364.

52. La vedetta, review of *Justitia*,*La rivista cinematografica*, October 25, 1920, in Farassino and Sanguineti, eds., *Gli uomini forti*, 124; Anonymous review of *Justitia*,124.

53. Silvio Aloviso, "La spettatrice muta: Il pubblico cinematografico femminile nell'Italia del primo novecento," in Dall'Asta, ed., *Non solo dive*, 278.

54. Luciano Doria, quoted in Aloviso, "La spettatrice muta," 283.

55. Haydée [Ida Finzi], "La donna e il cinematografo," *Cinemagraf* 1, no. 4 (March 25, 1916): 3, quoted in Aloviso, "La spettatrice muta," 280.

56. Zhang Zhen, *An Amorous History of the Silver Screen: Shanghai Cinema, 1896–1937*, 200–203.

57. Jean Lukitsh, "White Rose Woo, Early Action Star, in 'An Orphan' (1929)," Kung Fu Cinema, http://web.archive.org/web/20150604225224/http://www.kungfucinema.com/electric -shadows/white-rose-woo-early-action-star-in-an-orphan-1929.

58. Weihong Bao, "From Pearl White to White Rose Woo: Tracing the Vernacular Body of Nüxia in Chinese Silent Cinema, 1927–1931," in *Exporting Perilous Pauline: Pearl White and the Serial Film Craze*, ed. Marina Dahlquist, 208–10.

59. The film coincides with the first participation of a Chinese athlete (sprinter Liu Changchun) in the Olympic Games of 1932. Andrew D. Morris, *Marrow of the Nation: A History of Sport and Physical Culture in Republican China* (Berkeley: University of California Press, 2004), 167–84.

60. Zhen, *An Amorous History*, 78.

IV. MUSCLES SPEAK LOUDER THAN WORDS

One of the best things in this little world is enthusiasm. . . . To be
successful you must be happy; to be happy you must be enthusiastic;
to be enthusiastic you must be healthy and to be healthy you must
keep mind and body active.

—Douglas Fairbanks, *Douglas Fairbanks: In His Own Words*

IN THE WAKE of the historic encounter in 1892 between John L. Sullivan, America's first sport superstar, and James J. Corbett, who utilized scientific techniques, boxing became one of the most popular spectator sports. By the outbreak of World War I, largely from attention stirred by Jack Johnson, the fight picture became a desired cinematic subject. Then this form of manly entertainment was dealt a knock-down blow by a federal statute after the controversial match in 1912 between lightweight champion Adolph Wolgast and challenger "Mexican" Joe Rivers in which both boxers knocked each other out simultaneously.[1] Henceforth fight films could only be shown in the state in which they were produced. By 1915, Jimmie Johnson, manager of Madison Square Garden, observed that motion pictures of championship battles, formerly viewed by thousands, virtually ceased to exist and "gone the way of bare-fist fighting" despite technological advances and their popularity. "Who wishes to make an expensive film for one State alone?"[2] Mere reenactments of notable matches failed to capture the suspense and immediacy of a real match. Thus, greater attention shifted to other forms of action on-screen that could both entertain and be controlled.

Francis X. Bushman

The first leading muscle man of the movies, a contemporary and counterpart to the great Bartolomeo Pagano, was Francis X. Bushman, born in Baltimore in 1883. Inspired by Eugen Sandow and Bernarr Macfadden's *Physical Culture* magazine and informed about anatomy from a German weightlifting book, Bushman developed his body in the cellar of his home from an assortment of barbells, dumbbells, and odd pieces of iron and by boxing and wrestling with siblings. "When I lifted weights, I wanted to be a Sandow," he acknowledged. A neighbor recalled seeing him "exercising—using bricks as dumbbells. . . . He picked up two railroad-car wheels with axle between."[3] Bushman explained that he would

> get up at five o'clock in the morning and exercise with barbells and dumbbells for half an hour. Even in the winter with the window half open, I'd work until the sweat ran off my body and down to the floor. Then ice-cold baths. . . . In the evening I'd usually go over to the gym and work out for another three or four hours. And then, before bed, again with the barbells and dumbbells. Sundays I'd run cross-country until I was at the point of collapse. I really did strive for perfection from the time I was conscious of body physical and mind.[4]

In 1903 he won a local strength contest and became a sculptor's model for several years, often posing nude. He also posed nationwide for statues of heroic figures, including those representing Lord Baltimore and Francis Scott Key in his native city.[5] Meanwhile, Bushman was gaining acting experience by playing bit roles in stage productions, and he moved to Union City, New Jersey, near Manhattan. He also earned money as a professional wrestler, and at a local gym he met a young boxer named Doug who was always getting defeated by heavier opponents. Bushman suggested he specialize in tumbling. Later, after seeing Doug perform at the Bijou Theatre on Broadway in *A Gentleman from Mississippi* (1908), he discovered his last name was Fairbanks.[6]

Upon making his own Broadway debut in 1908, Bushman was discovered in Chicago in 1911 by executives of Essanay Film Company who were impressed with his muscular physique. His first film was *His Friend's Wife* (1911). In subsequent appearances in nearly two hundred films (including shorts), Bushman brought a new vitality to photoplay. After signing with Metro Films in 1915 and starring in the $250,000 production of *Romeo and Juliet* (1916), which costarred Beverly Bayne (who would later become his wife), Bushman became a box office idol and was promoted as the Handsomest Man in the World. *Moving Picture World* called it "a great production, one that will rank with the best kinematographic efforts." Above all, Bushman possessed "the physique of a 'well-governed youth'" and "appears to unusual advantage in the scanted garb of the period. . . . 'His leg excels all men's.'"[7] Lon Davis and Debra Davis have dubbed him "an American Greek god," a male counterpart of the Gibson Girl whose visage represented popular perceptions of the ideal female. His "muscular tapered torso, chiseled chin, aquiline profile, hair parted neatly with sideburns and beard cleanly shaven" graced magazine covers and advertisements, and "Bushman personified this image and brought the Gibson Man to the screen." After he was cast as a romantic hero, readers of *Motion Picture Magazine* in 1916 voted Bushman the most popular male film actor, second only to Mary Pickford in overall votes (462,190 to 411,800).[8]

Bushman was not shy about the role physical fitness played in his success. According to *Photoplay*, he was "probably the most perfect physical specimen among the many notable athletes of the studios" in appearance and practice. He was a champion wrestler, distance runner, good shooter, and fine horseback rider. Physical fitness, asserted Bushman, was as important as eating and sleeping. He explained, "In many ways, the ancient Greeks are my ideal of a people. Greek beauty, philosophy, architecture, bodily strength and learning have stood the test of centuries. . . . Their theory can be summed up in an old proverb. . . . 'The body is the urn in which the spirit burns; a spark of divine and eternal fire.' . . . It has brought me results. Keep the body up to standard, and the mind is at its best." Stories of Bushman's magnificent physique and strength abound in family and film lore. His niece, June Bushman Hannan, recalls her Uncle Frank "as always very healthy and body conscious, constantly exercising to stay in shape. He was very strong."[9] An indication of his athleticism occurred while rehearsing a fight scene with former heavyweight champion Jim Jeffries in *Pennington's Choice* (1915). As reported in *Motography*, "Both men were sparring in earnest when Jeffries stepped back a few feet and came forward, his head down, in one of his furious rushes. Bushman squared himself and met the ex-champion with a healthy, full-sized right-hand swing to the jaw, Jeffries straightened up, reeled and pitched forward on the floor." After several minutes and a bucket of water, the ex-champion recovered.[10]

When asked in 1916 how a neophyte could break into the movies, Bushman discussed cultural and personality factors, but he was emphatic that physical attributes were most critical: "A good figure, expressive eyes, preferably regular features, and above all, good habits, are prime requisites." An actor must have "supreme command of his nerves and his muscular system" and a rigorous course of training. "By systematic and even violent exercise, red blood will run through your veins, the nerves will be steeled and the muscles will instantly respond to every command of the mind." The greatest physical challenge on-screen occurred during the filming of *Ben-Hur: A Tale of the Christ* in 1925. Bushman was impressive not only for his athleticism in the climactic chariot race but for his muscularity. The *New York Times* called him "a man of mighty muscle, well-suited to the character of Messala." Other reviews described him as "muscular" and "majestic." He was "really superb" as the villainous Messala and "an actor at all times, but there is something admirable in the way he does it. He has the muscled, theatrical, effects of several years ago, ready to use at a moment's notice."[11] By the time he was blacklisted by Metro-Goldwyn-Mayer (MGM) in 1927 for offending Louis B. Mayer, Bushman was one of the highest-paid stars and lived stylishly on a 260-acre estate with a fleet of lavender limousines. Although his $6 million fortune was eradicated by the Wall Street Crash in 1929, this early man of muscle was widely regarded as the King of the Movies.[12]

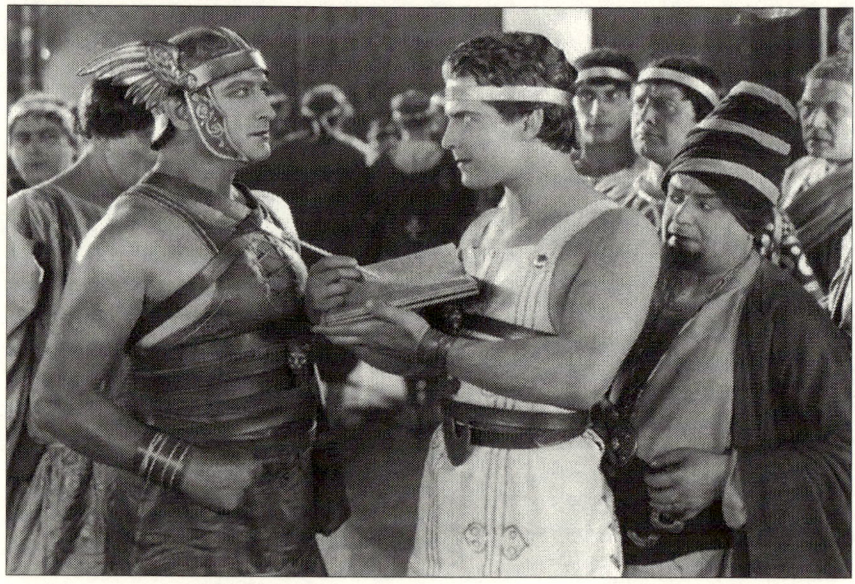

Figure 4.1. Ben-Hur (Ramon Novarro) goads Messala (Francis X. Bushman) into betting his entire fortune on the outcome of a chariot race. Fortunately, Ben-Hur has God on his side; Messala, not so much. Collection of David L. Chapman.

The Club

With the center of the film industry firmly established in Hollywood during World War I, intense action scenes needed to convey the silent narrative to mass audiences who demanded that emerging "stars" be physically fit.[13]

The Los Angeles Athletic Club, affectionately called the Club, was part of a nationwide network of institutions, originating with the New York Athletic Club in 1868, designed to meet the physical and social needs of distinguished male citizens. Located in a twelve-story beaux arts edifice at the corner of Seventh and Olive Streets, the Los Angeles Club, according to *Strength* editor J. C. Egan, was "the most finely equipped in the United States," with five thousand members and "unexcelled" gymnasium facilities. Another account called it the "capitol of the screen rialto . . . where the great and the near-great of filmdom foregather to court physical perfection, enjoy social intercourse," and "exercise their mental attributes," much in the manner of the ancient Greeks. "In the spacious and splendidly equipped gymnasium, the casual visitor is almost certain to bump into some screen notable, 'Hobe' Bosworth may be seen wrestling with Noah Young, the club's champion strongman, or trying to break heavy log chains with his ba-a-are-re han-n-n-d-d-ds. Or he may spy [film star] Bobby Harron keeping down to weight by use of the rowing machine; or Donald Crisp, actor-director, wrestling or doing 'brother' stunts with [actor-director] Elmer Clifton, [D. W.] Griffith juvenile." The club also provided facilities for handball, boxing, swimming, billiards, and weight training. It was a common ground, where members of the film brotherhood could mingle with "business men, authors, newspapermen, mining and oil magnates, doctors, lawyers and the others that make up the backbone of the community."[14]

The physical director at the club was Al Treloar (Albert Toof Jennings), who had won Bernarr Macfadden's 1903 Most Perfectly Developed Man Contest at Madison Square Garden. Earlier he had worked as Sandow's assistant and learned feats of strength and gymnastics. Like Sandow, Treloar's posing routine, imitating Greek statuary and featuring muscle control, was filmed by Thomas Edison's kinetoscope and William K. L. Dickson's American Mutoscope and Biograph Company in 1904 and 1905, respectively.[15] The club was also the site of the first national weightlifting contest conducted by physical culture pioneer David Willoughby. Notable actors who trained at the club included Thomas Meighan, a "Big Irishman" who played opposite Mary Pickford in *M'Liss* (1918); William Russell, an amateur boxing champion and star of *Pride and the Man* (1917); and Al Kaufman, a tall, well-built pugilist who fought Russell in that film.[16] Noah Young, who executed a 294-pound clean and jerk and a 3,200-pound back lift, gained national recognition by winning the heavyweight title at an Amateur Athletic Union contest in San Francisco in 1915. According to Willoughby, the 208-pound strength athlete ran an eight-and-a-half-minute mile at the club while carrying a 150-pound man. From 1918 to 1935 Young appeared, usually as a cop or villain, in 182 Hollywood productions. Finally, club member Tom Tyler, who won the 1928 national heavyweight weightlifting crown and qualified for the 1928 Olympics, appeared usually as a cowboy or superhero in scores of films and television shows from 1924 to 1953.[17] L. E. Eubanks concludes from his survey of the club's muscular habitués that it is not only the actor's personality but his visage that affects his part: "The tools of his trade are the members of his body."[18] Intensive training at the club was deemed vital for stars to create fit bodies for convincing action scenes on-screen. Realism required actors who looked and performed appropriately for the roles they played.

A Health and Fitness Culture

The potential of physically fit movie stars to inspire a healthy lifestyle by actions rather than words was a hallmark of the silent film era. A 1917 *Physical Culture* article by Gordon Reeves calls moving pictures a "wonderful new educative force" to enlighten the public on "the physical aspect of life." Regardless of the narrative, "photoplay, being by its very nature a matter of pictures rather than of words, deals constantly and primarily with the human body in action. The story is told to viewers by the pictured action on the screen," where all aspects and emotions of life "are revealed by the pose and action of the human body." The screen thus becomes "a revelation of the possibilities of the human body." Reeves argues that lack of interest in health and physical culture were "prime causes of the weakness, disease, ugliness and vulgarity of the great physically uncultured majority of mankind." A prime example of the "vital importance of the body" was provided in 1916 by Annette Kellerman in *A Daughter of the Gods*; she becomes a heroine "not because she loves the prince" but "because she can swim. . . . It is a play built on thrills" and "Annette is always the thrill center."[19]

Physical fitness was critical not only for portrayal of action scenes but for enhancement of beauty, especially for women. In 1921 and 1922 *Photoplay* featured a series, "How I Keep in Condition," that featured leading starlets. Corinne Griffith, regarded as one of Hollywood's most beautiful actresses, revealed that she stayed fit by "eating the right kind of food and getting the right kind of exercise"—chiefly, dancing, because it was "the one form of real and beneficial exercise which can be taken with music. . . . I am afraid that raising and lowering dumb-bells would bore me a trifle, and while I like golf and tennis, I take them as odd-time entertainment instead of a regular exercise diet." Dancing also made her happy, and that was "the best sure-fire recipe for beauty." Lila Lee (Augusta Appel), a leading lady who played opposite to such stars as Wallace Reid, Gloria Swanson, and Rudolph Valentino, regarded tennis and horseback riding as ideal forms of exercise. "Fresh air and regular exercise are the most important factors for keeping in condition," she believed, and "these are not so easy for the motion picture player to secure." Days in open-air locations were counterbalanced by weeks in studios on enclosed sets, where conditions were stifling. She tried to keep regular hours, avoid evening parties, and engage in exercises for brain as well as body. Marion Davies (Marion Douras), best known for her relationship with publisher William Randolph Hearst, was a former Ziegfeld girl who had been a successful actress and producer for two decades. "Good health is the bulwark of life," she believed, and regular hours—including seven hours of sleep each night—were essential, as was exercise: "No matter how early I have to be at the studio nor how late I must work, I begin each day either with a ride on horseback or with a walk on the river drive.... I eat only those things that have long since proved beneficial."[20] Bebe Daniels, another starlet and exercise advocate, started her film career at age four and eventually starred opposite Harold Lloyd and Rudolph Valentino. When not working on the set she relied on swimming, fencing, golfing, and riding to stay fit. Fencing, she noted, "causes quickness of action. That quickness develops grace. Rapid movements reduce fat. Riding brings into play practically every muscle in the body." For Nita Naldi, usually cast as a femme fatale, a diet of lamb chops and pineapple kept her slim. Gloria Swanson did not eat much but depended on an active outdoor life to stay slender. "I ride, I swim, I walk, I play tennis," she stated. "I have been in the saddle for six hours, stopping only for luncheon." But she preferred tennis "because of its active nature. It develops a poised mind and a poised body."[21]

"In Hollywood They're So Darned Athletic" is the title of a 1926 *Screenland* article by James Tankersley who toured the studios and witnessed how film stars stayed fit. The Pickford-Fairbanks Studios resembled "a well-equipped public playground," featuring not only horizontal bars and rings but "weights, hammers, punching bags, boxing gloves, foils, racquets of various sizes—everything, including a dog that plays football." Douglas Fairbanks employed a former Olympian as trainer, who accompanied him on trips to the East Coast and Europe. The picture factory of comedian and stuntman Harold Lloyd, according to Tankersley, "really consists of a handball court with a studio annex for Harold who works hours every day on the handball court." After watching Valentino box, he understood "why Jack Dempsey quit fighting and went to acting. He was afraid Valentino would quit acting and go to fighting." Tankersley's tour enabled him to watch Kathryn Perry playing golf; Florence Vidor playing tennis on her home court; Lola Todd, Margaret Quimby, and Marian Nixon skipping rope, running foot races, and turning cartwheels; Olive Borden sprinting; Tom Mix and Hoot Gibson doing some "fancy riding and roping"; and Joan Crawford dancing the Charleston. He also was impressed that Norma Shearer was a swimmer, Jack Holt played polo, Monte Blue boxed, Patsy Ruth Miller was a tennis player, and Buster Keaton played baseball.[22] The variety and extent of their athletic activities helped Tankersley understand how stars managed their beauty and body weight and withstood the rigors of their profession.

Paths to Strength and Beauty

Keeping fit was hardly an obsession that affected only American society. In 1925 an extraordinary documentary was produced in Germany that celebrated physical culture as a metaphor for both personal and national reconstruction. *Wege zu Kraft und Schönheit* (Paths to strength and beauty) was directed by Wilhelm Prager, who divided the film into six parts featuring a comparison of ancient Greece with contemporary Germany, gymnastics for fitness, rhythmic gymnastics, dance, sport, and celebrating life in the open air with health-giving activities. The film posits that ancient societies were ideal places where healthy minds inhabited healthy bodies, and that modern Germany has lost this connection thanks to urbanization and industrialization and thus must recover that once vibrant thread for the country to move on to greater glories. The incipient appeal of National Socialism is never far from the film's thesis.

It begins with a few images of a Greek temple, then quickly turns to a comic scene of a middle-class family on a typically stressful morning. The overweight father struggles with his collar button while his ineffective family frets and offers little except more frustration. Exasperated, he calls his wife a "stupid fool" as the taxi in front honks impatiently.[23] Weak and weedy students go to a crowded school; workers toil in hellish, unhealthy factories; sybaritic wastrels frequent bars, and deformed children suffer in hospitals. This scene of depressing modernity is contrasted with scenes from an ancient gymnasium where muscular and well-formed nude youths exercise in healthy surroundings. The film reinforces the concept that ancient ideals can be reproduced in modern society. To make it more entertaining, there are many sequences featuring topless or nude women who dance, exercise, and generally cavort on the greensward. One of these bare-breasted dancing figures purportedly belonged to Leni Riefenstahl, who would later direct the most famous film featuring the Olympic Games. Although there are male athletes in the footage (including German gymnast Rudolf Kobs), Prager's film is really a celebration of female bodies. Despite its title, it is long on beauty and short on strength. But if there is overobjectification of women, the intertitles come back again and again to the idea that Germans can remake themselves in the image of ancient statues. One contemporary reviewer confirms that the film "shows the place where the building-up of the German people must begin anew."[24]

Germans in the interwar period were greatly influenced by American sport, film, and culture, so it is no surprise that they often looked across the Atlantic for inspiration. Even so, no film as elaborately beautiful and effective on the subject of physical culture had ever been produced. Its unusually long running time of one hundred minutes is a testament to its investment in the subject. If it is a bit too earnest in tone, that is perhaps the way the Germans liked it. If they wanted sheer entertainment, they could have always turned to Hollywood, where the athletic lifestyle was usually portrayed with a bit more fun.

The It Girl and It Guy

Arguably the most famous female film star of the 1920s, the epitome of the free-spirited flapper, was Clara Bow. Idolized as the It Girl, Bow exhibited a naturally fit and youthful image. She grew up a tomboy in the streets of Brooklyn. "When they played baseball in the evening," she recalls, "I was always chosen first and I pitched. I always played with boys. . . . I could lick any boy my size. My right was quite famous." Ironically, her athletic ability and demeanor helped pave her way to show business, enabling her to win a contest where contestants were judged on acting ability, personality, grace, and beauty.[25] Being the It Girl, according to writer Frank Roche, meant "you are well versed in the ways of modern youth," and the public regarded Bow as "the girl signifying the spirit of the age. She is divinely formed; she has pep; in fact, she has everything that the girl of today desires." To retain "that divine form and winsome smile" it was essential that Bow "be more than physically fit at all times." The key to her health and beauty, argued Roche, was the "eighth room" of her rambling Beverly Hills bungalow:

> Clara Bow's gymnasium is one of the most used rooms of her home, as important to her as her hair dresser, her manicurist and her masseuse. . . . In this room devoted to the physical welfare of the screen's "IT" girl are the expected paraphernalia: weights, bars, rings, "horses," mats, Indian clubs, dumb-bells and exercisers. There are also several pairs of boxing gloves. Clara Bow is rather expert in their use. For more than a year, up to a few months ago, she employed a trainer, one Dick Klein, who is in charge of the gymnasium on the Paramount studio lot.

Swimming and diving were Bow's favorite exercises; diving required a combination of grace with muscular and mental coordination: "She would rather win a diving contest from a ten-foot board than to take the finest silver cup that was ever offered in a dance combination." Perhaps the film that most closely identifies Bow with her tomboy roots is the 1927 Paramount Studios production in which she puts on the gloves as *Rough House Rosie*, billed as "the story of a girl who got her men by treating 'em rough!"[26]

Cultural historians, however, are unconvinced that Bow's boxing represented any independence or advancement for women in society. Erik Jensen, in *Body by Weimar*, notes that "a number of female celebrities cultivated their image as pugilists, even if they had little to do with the actual sport."[27] In "Lacing Up the Gloves: Women, Boxing, and Modernity," Irene Gammel points out "the remarkable confidence with which Bow displays her athleticism, kineticism and sexual energy" in a 1927 Malibu Beach photo of her with raised gloves: "Bow's physical pose can thus be read as a prescient self-portrait of a woman whose boldness commanded a price." But Gammel presumes that Bow's boxing films and photographs were designed chiefly for promotional purposes.[28] There were no women's boxing clubs and virtually no women boxers or matches at this time, but Bow's boyish background and representation as a sportswoman provided some plausibility. The appeal of this gender reversal, however, enhanced by her coquettish manner, in striking contrast to the flapper girl look of the 1920s, is undeniable.

Bow's counterpart as male box office idol and unofficial It Guy was Richard Arlen, who starred in *Wings* (1927). He had what sports writer and former Stanford University football player Dick Hyland called "the locker room quality," an acid test by which men judge other men. Within this athletic environment, "either a man has it or he doesn't have it. It can't be put on, and nothing can be substituted for it." After seeing Arlen, at five foot ten and 170 pounds, with "no fat, long muscles, clear eyes, good chest" and "dark

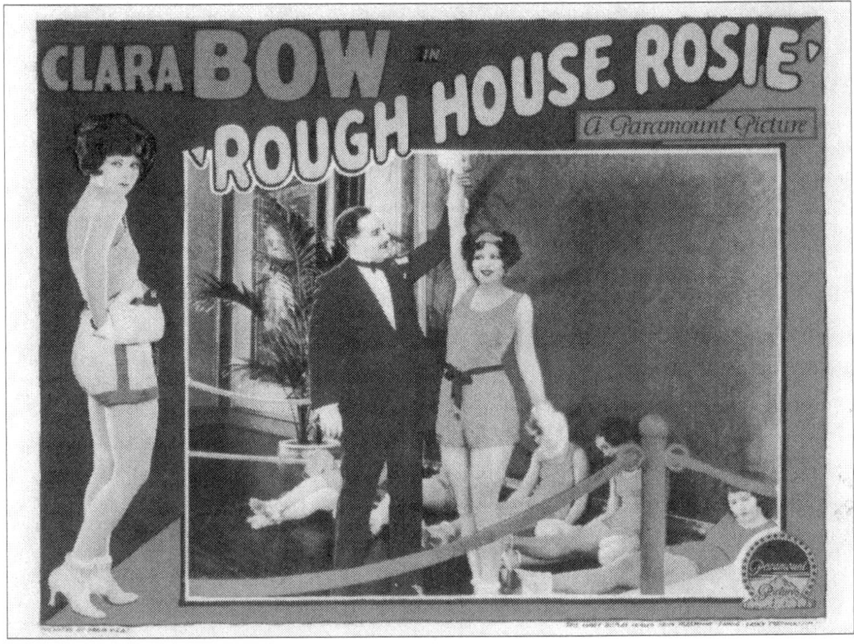

Figure 4.2. Clara Bow demonstrates her pugilistic prowess in this lobby card from the film *Rough House Rosie* (1927). Collection of David L. Chapman.

hair sopping wet" at his golf club, Hyland deemed "he had it, and in this case I don't mean Elinor Glyn's famous definition, but it—the locker room quality."[29] With less emphasis on personality and other intangibles, Ruth Waterbury compares the physical beauty of seventy-two female and sixty-nine male film stars with ancient Greek statues. She concludes that the former's measurements were less than two inches at variance with the Venus di Milo (Aphrodite), and the latter approximated the proportions of the Apollo Belvedere. Waterbury believes that Hollywood was "bringing back the glory that was Greece." For centuries, the human body and the Greek ideal of *mens sana in corpore sano* (a sound mind in a sound body) was scorned, beauty was dethroned, and prudery put in its place, but then

movies came with their demand for beauty, for youth, or health, or artistic productiveness. They happened to settle in a village near the sea. The Greeks had lived near the sea. The cinematropolis rose in a country where the climate made heavy clothing a joke, as it would have been in

Greece. A community grew, made by beauty, urged by beauty, producing beauty. All over the world rose temples of the motion picture where the people went to worship the gods of Hollywood. And the standard rose higher and higher until these modern living gods who reached the heights had to be flawless indeed. To maintain their beauty movie stars had to live sanely, eat wisely, exercise daily, as the Greeks had. In other words, Olympus moved to Hollywood.

Hollywood stars who epitomized this ideal were Joan Crawford, who was within a quarter inch of the Venus ideal, and Arlen, who—with his 38½" chest, 39½" hips, 14" calf, and 8¼" ankle—"outclasses all other male stars, coming within one-half inch of meeting the perfect proportions of the Greek Apollo."[30]

That health and beauty were paramount Hollywood concerns was a continuous theme in *Photoplay* during the 1920s. "No group of people in the world with the exception of the college athletes takes better care of its health than the stars of the motion picture industry" was the view of Dr. Nathan Reynolds, who provided medical care for many stars. "I know many stars who work harder keeping 'in the pink' than do some of our champion fighters," he noted. The key to taking off pounds and youthful appearance was "constant exercise and proper diet." While athletes engaged in rigorous training for limited periods each year, "the screen star's season is twelve months under the searching and relentless eye of the camera." Even ten-year-old Jackie Coogan was featured in an article doing his daily dumbbell drill under his instructor's guidance, striving like his adult counterparts to avoid avoirdupois. As a tribute to the burgeoning body culture of the 1920s, Paramount Pictures produced *The American Venus* (1926), featuring seventy-five "Atlantic City bathing beauties" and Miss America 1925, Fay Lanphier, deemed "the most beautiful girl in the country," in the title role.[31] Lanphier, at least, provided her title, but starring honors went to newcomer Esther Ralston, reported Charley Paddock in 1928. Another unknown, Louise Brooks, " 'took' the picture. Miss Ralston is now a star and Miss Brooks has become one of the most popular leading women in Hollywood." But Lanphier, "better known at that time than a dozen Esthers and Louises, has been forgotten."[32]

How this happened was clear to Paddock, once regarded as the world's fastest human; he had endured rejection as a celebrity in the equally sports-obsessed culture of the 1920s. Although he was a two-time Olympic champion and appeared in five films, none were "big enough to set any part of the world afire," including his hometown of Los Angeles. His "histrionic efforts . . . to cover the ground in fast time as a sprinter did not help me in the least to reach the top in motion pictures." Nor was Gertrude Ederle, the world's greatest swimmer, conqueror of the English Channel, and 1926's most famous woman, more successful. She "had won an undying place in the affections of the American people" and "the world and all that was in it was hers." In her 1927 debut in the romantic comedy *Swim Girl, Swim*, Ederle, like Lanphier, was exploited for name recognition but relegated to a secondary role under star Bebe Daniels. The public was interested in Ederle the swimmer, not Ederle the actress. Likewise, tennis star Bill Tilden, heavyweight boxing champions Jack Dempsey and Benny Leonard, home run king Babe Ruth, and football star Red Grange had only limited success in motion pictures. Even Johnny Weissmuller, who set sixty-nine world records and won five Olympic titles in the 1920s, elicited no interest from movie moguls. Paddock concluded that moviemaking, like any serious undertaking, had to be "studied and mastered. Acting is an art and not a heaven-born gift."[33] Although health, beauty, and athleticism were major assets in pursuing a movie career, being a star athlete did not guarantee success. Few possessed the intangible "it" factor.

The Iodine Squad

An essential ingredient to the acceptance of narrative films in the early decades of the twentieth century was action that often required, in the absence of speech, exaggerated body movements. To enhance audience appeal, filmmakers added elements of risk to action scenes. Doing so meant saving actors with "it" for safe scenes to build the narrative and to employ actors with extraordinary athletic skills to stage daring and exciting climaxes. Thus, a degree of deception, supplementing and fitting the nature of photoplay itself since its origins, seemed imperative. Along with early application of camera tricks and optical artifices, it was stuntmen who perfected the illusions that ensured box office success. Especially in the silent era, stunting was the most physically challenging role in motion pictures, and athletic proficiency was no more necessary than being an actor. "A mistaken idea is that a trained athlete has all the qualifications to make a stunt man," observed stuntman Bob Rose. "Where the athlete practices one thing until he is perfect in it, the stunt man must never fall into the habit of doing things mechanically. Though great muscular development is not important, perfect physical condition is." William Everson regards Richard Talmadge (Sylvester Metzetti), who often doubled for Douglas Fairbanks, as "the greatest athlete of all Hollywood stunt men." He perfected long action sequences involving roof-top chases and fights on moving trains.[34] Though highly skilled, Talmadge never reached stardom. He had, estimates John Baxter, none of Fairbanks's "optimism, good humour and identification with American aspirations."[35]

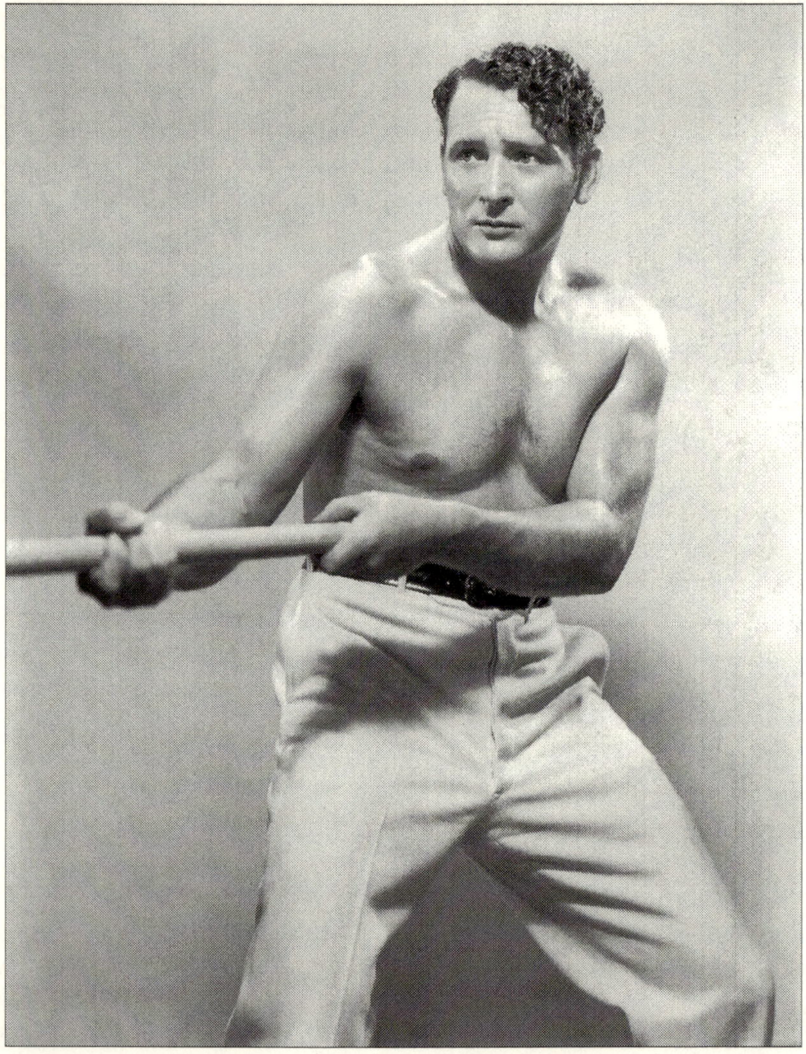

Figure 4.3. Richard Talmadge, dubbed "the greatest athlete of all Hollywood stunt men." Collection of David L. Chapman.

One of the best stuntmen, Richard Grace, emphasized the strict lifestyle required for the role: "The physical condition of the body and the constant attention which must be paid to it to keep it fit is an important factor in our life. The denial which all around stunt men contend with deprives them of many luxuries and oftentimes subjects them to real distress." Intoxicating liquors, tobacco, pie, cake, candy and frozen delicacies headed the list of banned consumables. A foremost trait of stuntmen was their "almost absolute fearlessness." Grace was adept at aerial stunts, such as high dives from over sixty feet and leaping from the wing of one biplane to another. Fellow actor Ray "Red" Thompson, known for stunting in *The General* (1926) with Buster Keaton, handled horses in perilous leaps and once leaped overboard from a speed boat to the back of a whale. With harpoon in hand he "plunged it viciously into the oily flesh just back of the eye. The huge bulk plunged and dove and Thompson, instead of letting go, went down also. When the mammal was next seen above water, 'Red' lunged his weight against the harpoon again, driving it farther into the skull. The battle continued until the whale died." Thompson died, however, while performing a stunt in the Copper River in Alaska in 1927 when his boat was caught in a whirlpool and smashed into rocks and jagged ice. In Grace's estimation, Gene Perkins was the "greatest double in pictures." The secret to Perkins's greatness was his ability to figure out a stunt beforehand, "calculating it perfectly according to time and distance, and in the icy clear-headedness which enabled him to carry it out to the hairline way he had planned it. His nerves—he had none." Yet he died tragically at age twenty-four, trying to mount a Pullman car from a rope ladder dangling from an airplane.[36]

Bob Rose, who performed with Harry Houdini, "the greatest of all stunt men," felt he belonged to a "strange fraternity" of actors. By 1935, after nineteen years of stunting, only six of his original 150 colleagues remained: "I have seen most of the others die, one after another, in performing dangerous feats. Yet . . . I was never seriously injured in doing 560 parachute leaps, eighty plane changes in the air, 150 dives from heights above ninety feet, 180 automobile wrecks, riding horses over cliffs sixty-five times and staging fights atop ninety-foot ship masts and making the proper fall into the water so many times I have lost count." When asked whether there was any standard by which stuntmen were judged by their peers, "Suicide" Buddy Mason replied, "Nope. It's just—well when you get so they call you by your first name when you come into the hospital, then you belong."[37] In defense of using stuntmen for dangerous scenes, Grace argued that it was "absurd to think of most stars doing their own risks." It did not mean they were "physically unfit or unable, but this sort of work is body breaking." There was also the possibility of "tying up production by injuring a player who has an important role." With stars drawing big money and producers spending millions on advertising, the risk was too great. In 1927 Hyland estimated the average stuntman's career lasted less than five years: "He either gets killed or he gets a little sense and quits."[38]

Winna "Winnie" Brown, arguably the greatest stuntwoman, sometimes benefited from an on-site ambulance, notes Adela Rogers St. Johns, but she performed some of the most daring scenes ever recorded: "Perhaps you have sat in your comfortable theater seat and seen the persecuted ingénue jump from the ninth story of a burning building—actually jump right out into space where no net was visible. Winnie Brown!" She was also adept at horse leaps and riding river rapids. As she once explained, lack of recognition for her death-defying artistry never bothered her:

> Most of these here stars don't like for folks to know they use a double. An o' course it ain't their fault most o' the time they do—it's the company makes 'em. If I bust a couple o' ribs or a laig or two, it don't make no difference. I got a swell doctor and he fixes me up cheap. But if one o' them fancy stars gits mashed up or her face scratched, it costs the company a whole wad o' spondolicks. Most o' the girls I've doubled for would have been willin' to tackle it themselves all right, only the company wouldn't hear of it, and besides, those skirts ain't got the trainin'.[39]

Given the scarcity of stuntwomen in the early days, stuntmen frequently substituted for women by wearing a dress or a wig.[40] There were often occasions, however, when female stars performed their own stunts. In 1928 Bebe Daniels, one of the greatest female screen athletes, debated Stanford footballer turned sports writer Dick Hyland on which was more dangerous, motion pictures or football. While Hyland cited one fractured skull and a concussion, five cracked ribs, three displaced vertebrae, a dislocated shoulder, three broken ankles, innumerable sprains, two broken wrists, eight broken fingers, torn muscles galore, a nose broken four times, and a mouthful of teeth weakened by cleated shoes, Daniels probably outscored him with a broken jaw, two concussions, an eyebrow slit by a saber, a severed lip, a dislocated shoulder, torn back muscles, displaced spinal vertebrae, a broken arm, two fingers and a hand broken, pulled leg tendons, a broken leg, four broken toes, and a broken foot. One of her concussions occurred while filming *Miss Brewster's Millions* (1926), when she was riding a bicycle behind the camera truck. "The truck driver had a heavy foot and speeded up," she recalls. "I yelled at him to slow down as I could not pump that fast. He did. With all four brakes. I crashed into the rear of the big thing and everyone had a holiday for a couple of weeks." When asked after filming one of her thrilling scenes whether it was dangerous, Clara Bow exclaimed, "I'll say it was. Why, it was so dangerous that the doubles had doubles."[41] Muscles were important to box office success, but they were often not those of the leading stars.

Joe Bonomo

Coney Island, a southern appendage of Brooklyn and America's playground in the early twentieth century, was the spawning ground for many physical culturists, such as Charles Atlas and Warren Lincoln Travis. Joe Bonomo was born there on Christmas Day 1901 of Turco-Spanish parents who were ice cream and candy makers. Puny and weak as a youth, Bonomo was ridiculed as "toothpicks" and bullied. Inspired by a Polish strongman and a replica of the Apollo Belvedere in the Brooklyn Museum, he built his body through proper eating, exercise, gymnastics, and sports. Also, under Travis's influence, he learned to lift weights and other heavy objects. In high school he lettered in six sports, but he was also absorbed in the antics of carnival and sideshow performers on Coney Island and sought the company of wrestlers and musclemen. At the movies Bonomo's idol was Eddie Polo, the great daredevil for Universal Studios. Bonomo achieved his own breakthrough by winning the Modern Apollo Contest in 1921, sponsored by the *New York Daily News*; the prize included $1,000 and a ten-week screen contract. "I was on my way to fame and fortune in the Land of Make Believe," he recalled. "God was good—the World was good—Life was good!"[42] Bonomo subsequently appeared as a stuntman and extra in thirty-five films, performing fights, escapes from burning buildings, aerial stunts, and the wrestling of wild animals.

As a stand-in for Gene Autry, Lon Chaney, John Wayne, and other stars, Bonomo endured thirty-seven broken bones, including a right arm broken in eleven places, a right leg broken in four, and a broken hip. He also demolished twenty-four cars, eight motorcycles, and three trains, and damaged a hundred automobiles. His contract as a "stock actor" called for him to play any available bit part, including impersonations of "pirates, Gypsies, adagio dancers, doormen, policemen, sailors, cowboys, . . . you name it . . . I played it." He was willing to do "*anything*, and believe me, I did *everything*." The stuntmen he worked with, Bonomo insists,

> were the REAL stars of the Westerns, doubling for the gun toting, spur jangling, swashbuckling Western star whenever a scene was shot where life and limb were at stake . . . and yet their names seldom, if ever, appeared on the screen. Whenever the audience acclaimed their favorite cowboy hero as he thrilled them with death defying stunts, it was really his 'double' they were cheering. . . . We stuntmen were the ones who got the broken bones, who went over the cliffs and rode the rapids. We were the hombres who made those thrilling pictures thrilling.

Probably the most famous of Bonomo's stunt fraternity was Enos Edward "Yakima" Canutt, who won the World's Champion All-Around Cowboy title five times. According to Bonomo, "he could outride, outrope and outshoot any man he ever met. He originated almost all the really spectacular cowboy stunts in film history" and was "largely responsible for the rapid rise of Westerns in popularity." Canutt was never seriously injured, but others were not as lucky. Bert Goodrich, the first Mr. America in 1939 who did stunt work prior to his bodybuilding career, nearly died when his horse slammed into a tree, leaving him with a broken neck and temporary blindness. Still, there was never a shortage of young men willing to take risks or writers "searching the history books for hazardous episodes to put into their scripts," regardless of perils. Many stuntmen sacrificed their lives to create a sense of realism and "provide the thrills that held audiences breathless and brought them clamoring back for more."[43] Such were the vagaries of the film industry, however, that it was the stars, who lived by appearances, and not the stuntmen, who lived by realities, that reaped fame and fortune.

Bonomo performed in hundreds of films and thousands of stunts that required him to be constantly in condition. In the early 1920s he would rise at six o'clock, do some road work and calisthenics, eat breakfast, and be at the studio by eight. He called the picture business a "rugged grind and a demanding taskmaster. But I enjoyed it and never asked more of God or the Industry than that I be kept lucky by the first and busy by the second." He drove a fine car and ate fine food. "For recreation I drove, read, and went dancing or to the movies in the evenings. I went out with girls, but I was always back to my room and asleep by eleven o'clock. The girls shook their heads despairingly but they couldn't shake my resolve." Bonomo styled himself a wrestler, tumbler, acrobat, strongman, boxer, and judo expert, with a special talent for spectacular falls and chair throws. He had the studio build a gymnasium on the lot and recruited a team of acrobats and fighters. He specialized in fight scenes and staged the fight sequences for heavyweight champion Gene Tunney's film serial *The Fighting Marine* (1926). Billed variously as Hercules, the World's Perfect Strongman, or the American Maciste for his circus stunts, Bonomo's strength credentials were redolent of a revered show business tradition: "Before gaping thousands I pulled two ton circus wagons, loaded with kids, through the streets—I broke iron chains with my chest and my 'mighty biceps'—I tore telephone books—I bit the heads off railroad spikes—I pounded nails through thick planks with my bare hands and let men with sledge hammers smash huge rocks into powder, on my bared chest." He also tied iron bars into knots, broke steel chains, and lifted a barbell overhead with a cluster of stagehands hanging on. "For general, all around development and construction of muscles he has found the use of bar bells best," observes William Slater. Bonomo was "a human dynamo. Probably the nearest approach to his physical perfection in filmdom is Douglas Fairbanks who once paid Joe a compliment in remarking, 'I wonder how that fellow keeps going.'"[44]

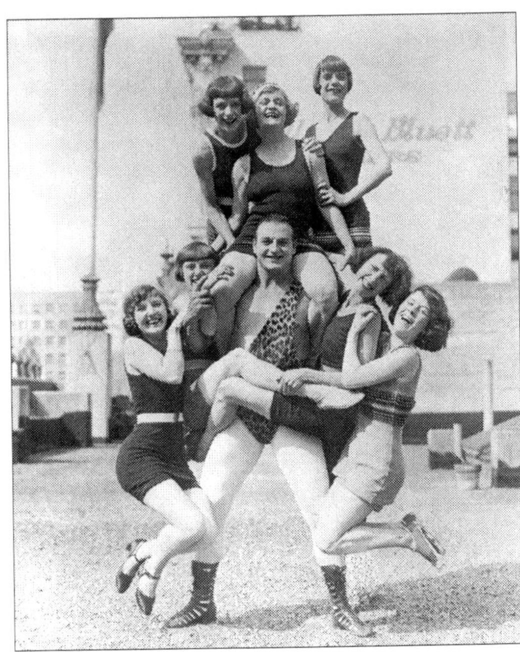

Figure 4.4. Joe Bonomo lifts seven girls on the roof of the Orpheum Theater in Los Angeles in this publicity photo for his 1925 serial *The Great Circus Mystery*. Collection of David L. Chapman.

Although Bonomo's strength and athleticism were real, he was quick to admit that much of what moviegoers see is a version of magic. He contended that "there's no greater magician than the Movie Camera. With its lens a hundred fold quicker than the eye, it tricks you into thinking you are seeing a thousand things that you're really not seeing at all." Behind a "closely guarded Hollywood door" were secrets to "well meant and innocuous frauds" perpetrated on the public for years. Bonomo cited the case of Harold Tumbleweed, a singing cowboy: "He's so nonathletic he's stoop-shouldered from that guitar slung around his neck—and he's been in pictures so many years you wonder if he creaks when he walks. Yet you see this character, who has never jumped onto anything higher than a bar stool, approach his horse from the rear—and a tall horse at that—take a couple of steps, and suddenly, while strumming his theme song, vault through air into his saddle—while the kid in the seat in front of you screeches, 'Look Ma—no hands!'" Likewise, the character playing Super Bird-Man was able to escape his enemies by leaping from a window and soaring over house tops and into the sunset. But Bonomo gave away the magic: "Astounding? Breath taking? It is until, traitor that I am, I give you the three magic words—spring boards, trampolines and piano wires." In fact, Bonomo believed the trampoline was "probably the most extensively used of all stunt apparatus. It covers a multitude of frauds."[45] During a period when muscles meant so much to conveying a movie's narrative, a stuntman's skills had to be supplemented by apparatus to make actions seem even more miraculous.

King of the Cowboys

According to Dick Grace, Tom Mix was "without a doubt the most successful" of all stuntmen.[46] What made Mix unique was not only his countless death-defying feats but an ability to progress from stunting to movie stardom. He was born on January 6, 1880, in Cameron County, Pennsylvania, and elicited an interest in becoming a cowboy when his father became a stable master. After a brief stint in the US Army, he married and moved to Guthrie, Oklahoma, where, according to biographer Robert Birchard, Mix worked as "a wrangler, taught physical culture, and served as Drum Major to the Oklahoma Cavalry Band at the St. Louis Exposition in 1904." He also served briefly as a peace officer and tended bar prior to joining the Miller Brothers 101 Ranch Show, where, as a crack shot and bulldogger, Mix became a "leading performer." In 1910 he joined the Chicago-based Selig Polyscope Company and began making cowboy films.[47] In a review of *The*

"Diamond S" Ranch (1912), James McQuade describes Mix as a "he man of steel muscles and rock-ribbed torso" who performs some "amazing feats of skill, strength, and horsemanship," adding,

> Bulldogging a wild steer is hazardous at all times, but Mr. Mix makes the feat extra hazardous. While his horse is at full gallop, in pursuit of the steer, at the proper moment, Mr. Mix jumps from his mount and lights on the neck of the steer, or on the ground to one side of the animal. In either case he must avoid the long, sharp-pointed horns with his body and be skillful enough to seize them in his hands. Then he twists the animal's neck and forces the creature to the ground. In one instance we see Mr. Mix light on the neck of the steer, causing the animal to turn a complete somersault its full length.[48]

Mix's athleticism is further displayed in the short *Athletic Ambitions*, aka *The Wild Man of the Diamond S Ranch* (1915), where, after practicing physical culture on-screen, he gives "a fine exhibition of his prowess as a sprinter and wins the heart of the girl." From 1910 to 1917 Mix appeared in more than seventy Selig productions, including credits as writer, director, and star. Most of them were short artless affairs shot off-the-cuff in which he performed spectacular stunts but had little time to develop a screen character.[49]

During the next decade, Mix averaged about seven pictures a year with Fox Studios. By this time the popularity of William S. Hart, known for his raw and rugged style as a silent Western star, was waning. Increasingly, audiences preferred the young persona of Mix, "whose films exuded as much pep and energy as Douglas Fairbanks' did," observe George Mitchell and William Everson. "Mix's films for Fox literally *made* that company. . . . They were breezy, cheerful, streamlined affairs, aimed at a wide audience, and were not intended to be re-creations of the real West." Action, excitement, and his "boyish spirit of fun" captivated moviegoers. By 1925 Fox was paying him $25,000 a week. His action scenes and hazardous feats in *The Daredevil* (1920) were "positively amazing," according to a review in *Motion Picture News*, adding, "Riding his horse alongside of a moving freight train he shoots the padlock off the door of a car, rescues the imprisoned girl and places her in the saddle. Then he jumps into the car and eventually captures the highwaymen. The picture is punctuated with thrill after thrill and all of them are executed with the utmost skill and dash."[50] Considerable debate, however, has ensued over whether Mix performed all his own stunts.

According to cowboy actor Ted French, "Tom Mix wouldn't let nobody double him," and many of the stunts were shot at such close range that there was no question of their authenticity. Director George Marshall concurs that "Tom was doing all his own stunts—the horse falls, crashing through glass windows on horseback, and so on. There was no imitation glass during this period either and they didn't dig up the ground to spot a fall. Wherever they were shooting that's where you fell." To Mitchell and Everson, *Sky High* (1922), a breakthrough movie for Mix, lent substance to the claim that he rarely used a double: "Certainly *all* Western stars, at one time or another, have used doubles, but Mix used them much less than most. Mix was quite touchy about this."[51] Special effects designer Roscoe "Rocky" Cline recalls that Mix "most always did the stunts himself," but Cline doubled for Mix in a few underwater scenes. Birchard concludes that "no other Western star ever risked his own life so often in pursuit of a screen thrill."[52]

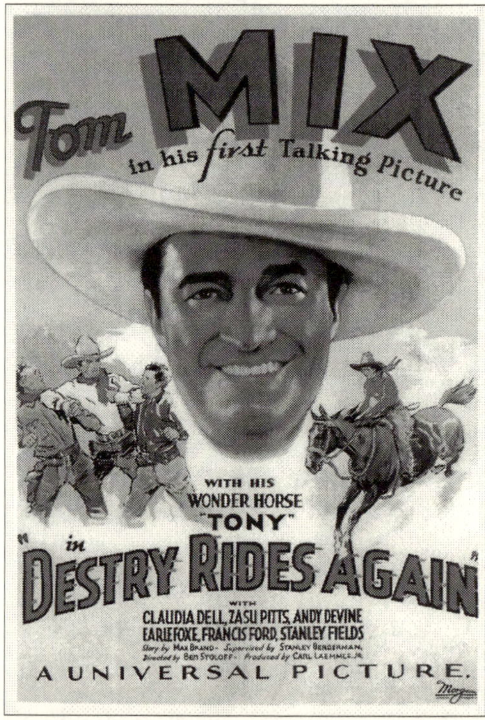

Figure 4.5. King of the Cowboys Tom Mix rides again (presumably with some help from Tony the Wonder Horse) in the 1932 pre-Hays Code Western *Destry Rides Again*. Collection of David L. Chapman.

That Mix was able to avoid being typecast as a stuntman and transition to box office star owes much to his creation of the classic image of the cowboy. He was "a real showman," observes Marshall. Mix was "responsible for the present-day cowboy clothes. I have been in his dressing room when he was working with his tailor designing the tight-fitting pants, the angled pockets, and the shirts with the many buttons—and always very vivid colors." According to Birchard, this classic image was solidified in *Sky High*, in which "Tom took a page from Douglas Fairbanks and *The Mark of Zorro* (1920) and began to blur the line between realism and fantasy."[53] The other image Mix lent to cowboy films was wholesomeness. "From the beginning I decided to make clean pictures," he recalls, adding,

> I decided to give the boys an' grown ups good wholesome entertainment, free from suggestion or anything harmful to a growin' an' fertile minded youth. I tried to convey to the boys an' girls a message of helpfulness. I tried to show them that it was the physically fit man who usually won out. The character I portrayed was always that of a clean minded an' right livin' cow puncher, always tryin' to do the right thing because it was the right thing to do. In no picture have I ever smoked, taken a drink, played cards, or gambled or done anything that I considered unmanly or dishonest or that any boy couldn't copy without harm to himself.[54]

Contrary to the gangster films that flooded the market with tales of sin and depravity before the enactment of the Motion Picture Production Code in 1934, in the early 1930s Mix's moral code set the tone for later cowboy role models such as Gene Autry, Hopalong Cassidy, Roy Rogers, and the Lone Ranger. Critical to Mix's transcending the stunt world was his ability to create his own image and not let Hollywood dictate it. He personified the oxymoron of lighthearted violence in which the good guy wins the gunfight and gets the girl.

King of Hollywood

The actor who most successfully used his muscles to evolve from stunting to film stardom and eventually national icon was Douglas Fairbanks, whose characters complemented those of Mix. According to film theorist Gaylyn Studlar, they "proved their physical and moral mettle as human dynamos employing 'pep,' 'power,' 'punch,' and 'personality' for the forces of good." Even discounting Hollywood's publicity mill, "Fairbanks appeared to be among the most beloved stars of the era, and with few exceptions his films were consistent winners at the box office for almost fifteen years." In 1924, with his close friendship with Charlie Chaplin, the world's funniest man, and his marriage to Mary Pickford, "America's Sweetheart," he was deemed "the most popular man in the world."[55]

Born on May 23, 1883, in Denver, Fairbanks experienced a long apprenticeship on the New York stage from 1900 to 1915, where a golden generation of actors—the likes of Ethel, John, and Lionel Barrymore; Sarah Bernhardt; John Drew Jr.; and Lillian Russell—were starring in theater and vaudeville.[56] Only gradually did his athletic attributes become obvious as an audience attraction. Although there is no evidence that he played organized sports as a youth or broke any high-jumping records, his physical energy was obvious in *A Rose o' Plymouth-Town* (1902), for which leading lady Minnie Dupree referred to his performance as "a bad case of St. Vitus' Dance."[57] In 1906, while performing in *Clothes*, Fairbanks entertained himself during rehearsal breaks by climbing up and down a long flight of stairs on his hands, inducing producer William Brady to offer him a five-year contract. Brady also recalled an instance in *The Cub* (1910) in which Fairbanks had to run upstairs to save a (likely heroine's) life. "Run?" he responded, "what's the matter with jumping?" Brady then "eyed the twelve-foot gap between stage floor and upper floor and expressed some doubts. 'Why, that's simple,' he said, took a little run, caught the edge of the flooring by the stair-opening and pulled up as easy as an alley-cat taking a fence. That made a tremendous hit with the audience." In 1915 Fairbanks's graduation to movies took a physical culture turn when a cameraman filmed him in Central Park leaping over a park bench. A few weeks later Harry Aitken of Triangle Films viewed his athletic dexterity and offered him a contract.[58]

It was a propitious time, with the star system emerging and prior to the advent of the studio contract system in the 1920s. By 1916 Pickford was earning $10,000 a week with Adolph Zukor's Famous Players Film Company and Chaplin was drawing $670,000 a year with the Mutual Film Corporation.[59] Soon Fairbanks was making $15,000 weekly with Triangle through a collaboration with director Allan Dwan, who shared "a similar sense of humor, an athletic nature, and a restless spirit." Dwan recalls he would "move with Doug . . . and surround him with athletes. Stunts *per se* were of no interest to him or to me." What interested them was "a swift, graceful move—the thing a kid visualizes in his hero." Alistair Cooke concurs; congeniality with collaborators was the key, "a willingness to let Fairbanks' own restlessness set the pace of the shooting and his gymnastics be the true improvisations on a simple scenario." From this amiable under-standing "the character of 'Doug' rapidly evolved."[60]

When America entered the war in 1917, Fairbanks wanted to enlist, but President Woodrow Wilson discouraged it, insisting that Fairbanks, along with Canadian-born Pickford and British-born Chaplin, "would be of 'far more service to the nation,'" according to Fairbanks' son, "if they helped with films and propaganda and in cross-country drives, selling Liberty Bonds."[61] Subsequently the trio made short films and conducted bond drives, bringing millions of dollars to government coffers. One of them, held at Fairbanks's Beverly Hills estate in October 1917, was to be a physical culture carnival, featuring Al Treloar, Noah Young, and others of the Los Angeles Athletic Club who were offering fifty- and one-hundred-dollar bonds to anyone who could duplicate their feats. The program also featured daring flyers, bucking bronco riding, boxing and wrestling matches, and "yip-yipping cowboys" to entertain and whip up enthusiasm for the Fourth Liberty Loan.[62] Meanwhile, Fairbanks established his own company to produce films for distribution by Artcraft Pictures, and in 1919 joined with Chaplin, D. W. Griffith, and Pickford to form United Artists Corporation. He could thus sidestep the contract system of major studios that would soon restrict the independence of actors.

Unlike many stage and vaudeville stars, Fairbanks made an effective transition to the silver screen. Over the next two decades he acted in four dozen films and produced, directed, and wrote many others. According to Jeffrey Vance, *His Picture in the Papers* (1916) "solidly established Fairbanks as the American ideal of pep, vim, and vigor," a formula he mastered in numerous blockbusters of the 1920s, including *The Mark of Zorro* (1920), *The Three Musketeers* (1921), *Robin Hood* (1922), *The Thief of Bagdad* (1924), *The Black Pirate* (1926), and *The Gaucho* (1927), all designed to "showcase his energy and athleticism."[63] While his father was filming *The Thief of Bagdad*, Douglas Fairbanks Jr. "loved being asked to join the group that went to his gym." Over the entrance was a sign reading "Basilica Linea Abdominalis" (Temple Dedicated to the Waistline), which led to a facility with rings, bars, and a badminton court. As Fairbanks's son recalls, "The game of DOUG that my father invented was based on badminton but used heavier shuttlecocks and racquets and a larger court." It was briefly popular in the 1920s.[64]

Freedom and imagination to develop his own brand became the hall-mark of Fairbanks's performances. In a 1921 article for *Physical Culture*,

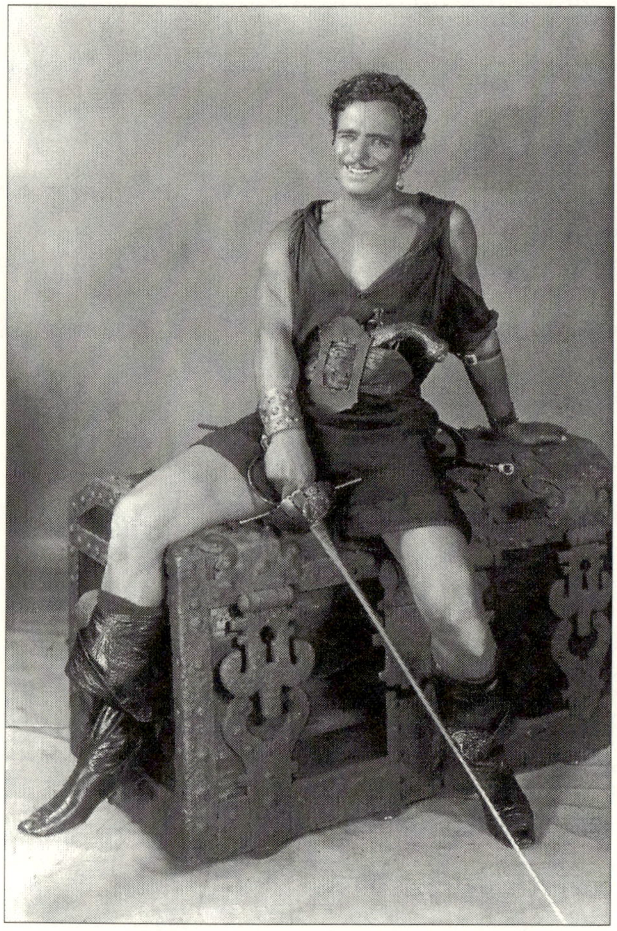

Figure 4.6. This publicity still was made to promote Douglas Fairbanks's stunt-heavy adventure film *The Black Pirate* (1926). Collection of David L. Chapman.

Carl Easton Williams sought to discover how Fairbanks used his amazing physical presence to achieve stardom, noting,

> He is first of all, a personality—one of the two or three most unique personalities on the screen. He is an exponent of whimsical comedy . . . with a dash that represents the spirit of American youth, and then some. . . . The things he does, athletically and acrobatically, are not merely a matter of strength and speed, but of spirit. They are an

expression of a scheme of life, an attitude of mind. . . . The Fairbanks system of keeping fit, then, is a matter of cultivating the Fairbanks spirit. And that spirit is simply the spirit of play.[65]

Mere appearance of muscles was never sufficient to illustrate the Fairbanks spirit. "In exercise, like almost everything else in life," he declared, "it is not the outward form but the spirit behind that counts." Fairbanks once cited a noted physical instructor who wanted to know what exercises would enlarge his arm by an inch. "I was only interested in what I could do with it," Fairbanks responded. "My system of physical culture is play. Do everything you can outdoors in a playful spirit." This playfulness, enhanced by Fairbanks's extraordinary muscular development and spectacular athletic feats, enabled him to promote physical culture in the movies and inspire viewers to adopt a more active lifestyle.[66] For Gaylyn Studlar, Fairbanks's spirit of "perpetual youthfulness and uninhibited, playful physicality" most resembled that of the Boy Scouts and the playful presidency of Theodore Roosevelt: "The 'spirit' that Fairbanks illustrated on film and offscreen was dependent on his ability to convey the attitude that manly physical pursuits were fun. He promoted an optimistic investment in physical culture, not as a grudging fulfillment of the mania for men to be in motion, but as play, which functioned as nothing less, noted one boy reformer, as 'a royal road to health, happiness, and strength of character.' "[67]

Producer Arthur Hornblow Jr. describes Fairbanks as an actor of "a different sort." Reputedly he was "fearfully powerful, exercised in two gymnasiums from morning until night, and went thru life as tho with some extra dynamic force behind him, doing everything so—biff! bang!" One had to know Fairbanks personally, observed Mary Pickford, "to realize the overwhelming dynamism of the man." He was "always climbing, and whoever was with him had to be prepared for some sort of ascent." Fairbanks was a man whose being was defined by "motion."[68]

From a Kantian perspective, however, the nature of this dynamic force remained a mystery. Fairbank's artistry tapped an inner resource or genius of movement that few moviegoers could comprehend. Hornblow believed "the enthusiasm and spirit behind the Fairbanks smile" could not be analyzed. "It's simply the Fairbanks smile—whimsical, mischievous, happy, nonsensical grin that lights up the whole neighborhood whenever it happens. Of course you've seen it on the screen, and you've grinned, too. It's as infectious as German measles!"[69] "Fairbanks' glory," noted Alistair Cooke, "the mystery of his visual fascination, is that he could throw all the text-book tricks on the makeshift apparatus of ordinary life. He appears to the moviegoer to be a sort of Ariel, leaping where he has a mind without any of the natural checks of gravity." He made "virtuoso use of the landscape as a natural gymnasium whose equipment is invisible to the ordinary man," and it was the use of his body as "a crazy but disciplined bow on something that turns into a handy fiddle, that made him an enchanting image." According to Richard Schickel, Fairbanks's athleticism enabled him to create this image, which made him "a truly heroic figure." What impressed Hornblow most was his natural muscularity: "The Fairbanks hobby is the out-of-doors and everything that goes with it. The lithe, brown arm is literally as hard as oak when the rippling muscles are taut, and this bespeaks years of vigorous athletics of all sorts." Fairbanks was adamant that "suspicious mortals" who think every scene in a picture is faked, should know "that it *isn't!*"[70] What he did with his muscles was real.

Another dimension to Fairbanks's makeup and box office appeal, à la Tom Mix, was morality. As Williams explained, "It is noteworthy that the Mary Pickford and Douglas Fairbanks pictures have met with the greatest of success upon a basis of utter wholesomeness. . . . Fairbanks will not tolerate anything that is not utterly clean in any of his productions," an inherent part of the "playful, vigorous line of comedy" he created.[71] Fairbanks believed he had an obligation to serve as a model for American youth, and at the risk of sounding preachy, he repeatedly advised cleanliness "first and most" on the next generation: "The boy who wishes to get to the front in athletics must adopt a program of mental and bodily cleanliness." He believed strong drink was the greatest hindrance to athletic success, and claimed that "personally I have never tasted liquor of any sort." His son confirms that he "never drank" and rarely told a dirty joke. Yet there was a huge exception to his highly disciplined and healthy lifestyle that hastened his affliction with heart disease and death at age fifty-six in December 1939. It was a cruel irony, his son observes, that "few things would be worse for him than his almost constant smoking—from wake up to lights out at night."[72] Yet no such vice, hardly a vice in the 1920s, can gainsay Fairbanks's impact on the display of muscles in the movies and what they could do. According to Studlar, he "not only was emulated by children but by other actors in search of box-office results. To 'out-Fairbanks Fairbanks' became the ultimate commercial compliment and was used to sell as unlikely a Fairbanks rival as Maciste, 'The

Giant Hero of *Cabiria*' in *The Warrior*." As Williams concluded in 1921, "Fairbanks is no longer merely an athletic comedian. He is an American institution."[73]

The Muting of Muscle

Muscular development and athleticism provided a crucial element in the larger-than-life movements that conveyed much of the narrative in silent film. Under this regime there emerged the first motion picture stars and the major studio contract system. With the advent of synchronized dialogue sequence, or talkies, with *The Jazz Singer* (1927), the exaggerated use of muscles in movies was no longer an imperative. As more subtle means of expression emerged, whereby body movement merely complemented speech, numerous stars of yesteryear seemed incapable of adaptation. Francis X. Bushman's physical appeal faded early, especially with female fans, when it was learned that he was married and had five children.[74] It was resurrected briefly in 1925 by his starring role in *Ben-Hur*, but his career suffered following the divorce to his second wife, his MGM blacklisting, and loss of his fortune during the Depression. Although his voice was "full and rich," Bushman, so long identified with the silent screen, was unable to get roles of consequence. That Clara Bow "went down with the Silents" is "an unfounded myth," according to Christina Ball. Though Bow's kinetic acting style was more suited to silent cinema than the more static, dialogue-heavy talkies, she overcame microphone fright and criticism of her untrained voice to make "well-received" movies until 1933. By that time she was battling mental illness and "burnt out by the taxing physical demands" of moviemaking.[75] After surviving many dangerous roles as a stuntman, Joe Bonomo had an opportunity to assume a major role opposite Claudette Colbert in *Cleopatra* (1934). Knowing little about reciting lines, he took acting lessons to develop a more stylized manner and tone down his Brooklyn accent, but to no avail. His retirement followed a broken hip operation and a misfired stunt that almost killed Western star Buck Jones in a fight scene in *The Deadline* (1932). Sound also ended Richard Talmadge's chances of becoming a star actor, and Yakima Canutt was denied the opportunity by an attack of influenza that affected his vocal chords.[76] But his speech impediment had unexpected consequences. It was the coarse masculine voice and tough guy mannerisms of Canutt, who often doubled for John Wayne, that provided much of the screen persona that launched Wayne's career. "I spent weeks studying the way Yakima Canutt walked and talked," Wayne explained in his memoir.

"He was a real cowhand. I noticed that the angrier he got, the lower his voice, the slower his tempo. I try to say my lines low and strong and slow, the way Yak did." Iron Eyes Cody, who played opposite both of them as a Hollywood Indian, confirms that Wayne's "drawling, hesitant speech and that famous hip-rolling walk of his were all pure Yakima Canutt."[77]

Like Bonomo, Bow, and Canutt, Tom Mix did not adapt well to the talkies. The Fox Film Corporation, committed to the new medium and convinced that shooting outdoors would be difficult, did not renew his contract in 1928. For Mix, his thrilling outdoor scenes were his main claim to fame. And, according to Robert Birchard, he was "afraid that his voice would not register well, and concerned that the clicking sound of his dentures would further detract from his appeal as a talkie star." Hence he took his show on the road for three seasons with the Sells-Floto Circus. Mix returned to make more films in the 1930s, but he was "clearly uncomfortable with dialogue" and his voice never fit "the sprightly image he developed on the silent screen."[78] Douglas Fairbanks made the transition to talkies, but he "liked to tell a story visually," according to his son. He saw his films as "essentially pantomime and ballet" and himself "as an athletic dancer leaping with graceful and visually effective movement across the adventures of history." Sound for him was "too literal, too realistic, and too restricting." For Jeffrey Vance, Fairbanks "virtually defined the swashbuckler as a cinematic genre" and would "usher out its initial cycle. Hollywood began to concentrate on talk-laden original scripts, static adaptations of Broadway plays, and musicals" with action films being momentarily cast aside.[79] Amid many other action heroes of the 1920s, it was the panache and skill with which Fairbanks and Mix applied their muscles that created a compelling and believable story for moviegoers. "Douglas Fairbanks and Tom Mix proved that the cowboy and the sword-wielding historical hero were nice, ordinary guys," concludes John Baxter, "and Hollywood lent all its ability to sustaining the illusion of effortless dexterity."[80] It was the muscular dexterity of these stunt stars that most defined the motion pictures and the illusions they created out of life in the silent era. More than any other ingredient, it was the "it" factor, but even Mix and Fairbanks, who had "it" in abundance, barely survived the silent screen era.

Notes

1. "Joe Rivers Dead at 65," *New York Times*, June 26, 1957.
2. Jimmie Johnson, "The Passing of the Fight Picture," *Photoplay*, May 1915, 140–41.

3. Lon Davis and Debra Davis, *King of the Movies: Francis X. Bushman*, 20–21, 25.

4. Francis X. Bushman, quoted in Davis and Davis, *King of the Movies*, 22.

5. Richard J. Maturi and Mary Buckingham Maturi, *Francis X. Bushman: A Biography and Filmography*, 10–19.

6. Davis and Davis, *King of the Movies*, 29.

7. "Francis X. Bushman," *Encyclopaedia Britannica*, http://www.britannica.com/biography/Francis-X-Bushman; George Blaisdell, "Romeo and Juliet," *Moving Picture World* 30, no. 5 (November 4, 1916): 685.

8. Davis and Davis, *King of the Movies*, 41–42; "Popular Player Contest," *Motion Picture Magazine*, February 1917, 126–28.

9. Francis X. Bushman, "How I Keep My Strength," *Photoplay*, June 1915, 59; June Bushman Hannan, quoted in Maturi and Maturi, *Francis X. Bushman*, 10.

10. "Bushman a 'White Hope'?," *Motography* 14, no. 15 (October 9, 1915): 754.

11. Francis X. Bushman, "How to Get IN!," *Motion Picture Magazine*, December 1916, 72; Mordaunt Hall, "The Screen," *New York Times*, December 31, 1925, quoted in Maturi and Maturi, *Francis X. Bushman*, 78. The *Times* reported on November 1, 1925, that MGM employed forty-two cameras, ten thousand extras, and forty-eight horses pulling chariots to acquire fifty-three thousand feet of film for the chariot race. Maturi and Maturi, *Francis X. Bushman*, 74; clippings on *Ben-Hur*, Ms. Collection No. 123, Scrapbook No. 8, Audrey Chamberlin Scrapbooks, Margaret Herrick Library.

12. For details on Bushman's blacklisting and divorce, see Maturi and Maturi, *Francis X. Bushman*, 81–83.

13. In his chapter "Why Hollywood?" Kevin Brownlow mentions "sun, space and somnolence" to describe how the picture industry migrated from New York to the "ideal small-town atmosphere" of Hollywood. Kevin Brownlow, *Hollywood: The Pioneers*, 90.

14. J. C. Egan, "A Coterie of the Strongest Men in the United States: Athletics of the Los Angeles Athletic Club," 18; K. Owen, "The Club, James!" *Photoplay*, February 1917, 67–70.

15. David P. Willoughby, *The Super-Athletes*, 545; "Al Treloar in Muscle Exercises (1905)," Turner Classic Movies, http://www.tcm.com/tcmdb/title/565288/Al-Treloar-in-Muscle-Exercises/.

16. L. E. Eubanks, "Strong Men of the Movies," 28–32.

17. Egan, "A Coterie of the Strongest Men," 19; Willoughby, *The Super-Athletes*, 176; "Noah Young," Internet Movie Database, http://www.imdb.com/name/nm0949927/; "Tom Tyler," Internet Movie Database, http://www.imdb.com/name/nm0878927/. The Los Angeles Athletic Club is also the site where the John R. Wooden Award for outstanding men's and women's college basketball player is bestowed each year.

18. Eubanks, "Strong Men," 28.

19. Gordon Reeves, "The Moving Picture Reveals the Physical Culture Life," *Physical Culture* 37 (February 1917): 39–42. Nearly a century later, Jennifer Barker has underscored Reeves's early observation of how muscles did the talking in silent films: "In order to talk in more specific terms about cinematic and human musculature, we might think

of film's and human's muscularity as they are focused in, and communicated through, gestures. Gestures are a muscular form of speech, for both humans and films. A gesture is an expressive bodily movement that is 'intentional,' in that it is directed toward a world, but not always 'intended,' in the sense of being consciously chosen and performed." Jennifer M. Barker, *The Tactile Eye: Touch and the Cinematic Experience* (Berkeley: University of California Press, 2009), 78.

20. Corinne Griffith, "How I Keep in Condition," *Photoplay*, November 1921, 33; Lila Lee, "How I Keep in Condition," *Photoplay*, December 1921, 102; and Marion Davies, "How I Keep in Condition," *Photoplay*, January 1922, 47.

21. E. W. Bowers, "The Stars Tell How They Keep Those Girlish Lines," *Photoplay*, September 1924, 28–31.

22. James Tankersley, "In Hollywood They're So Darned Athletic," *Screenland*, June 1926, 30–31, 95. In a similar article, Michael O'Shea highlights the athletic credentials of Buck Jones, George O'Brien, George Walsh, and especially Tom Mix. As "one of the greatest exponents of regular exercise outside of the studio and on location," Mix "transported his athletic equipment in specially constructed boxes with Indian clubs, boxing gloves, skipping ropes, handball paraphernalia, a rowing machine, and a punching bag that he used at least an hour a day." Michael O'Shea, "Muscular Movie Marvels: How the Film Stars Keep Physically Fit," *Muscle Builder*, April 1926, 26, 30, 31.

23. Wilhelm Prager, dir., *Wege zu Kraft und Schönheit* (Berlin: Ufa-Kulturfilmabteilung, 1925), YouTube, http://www.youtube.com/watch?v=jaZwJlYMriA.

24. Review of *Wege zu Kraft und Schönheit*, *LichtBild-Bühne*, 1925, quoted in Theodore F. Rippey, "The Body in Time: Wilhelm Prager's *Wege zu Kraft und Schönheit* (1925)," in *The Many Faces of Weimar Cinema: Rediscovering Germany's Filmic Legacy*, ed. Christian Rogowski, 190.

25. Clara Bow, "My Life Story," *Photoplay*, February 1928, 30, 104, and *Photoplay*, March 1928, 116. Described as "the real thing, someone to stir every pulse in the nation" by F. Scott Fitzgerald, Bow became known as the It Girl from her starring role in the 1927 movie *It*. Christina Ball, "The Silencing of Clara Bow," *Gadfly*, March–April 2001, http://www.gadflyonline.com/archive/MarchApril01/archive-clarabow.html.

26. Frank Roche, "How the 'IT GIRL' Keeps Fit," *Strength*, October 1929, 22–23, 79; Frank Strayer, dir., *Rough House Rosie* (Los Angeles: Paramount Studios, 1927), trailer, YouTube, https://www.youtube.com/watch?v=dVCfGZ9l3xI.

27. Erik N. Jensen, *Body by Weimar: Athletes, Gender, and German Modernity*, 95.

28. Irene Gammel, "Lacing Up the Gloves: Women, Boxing, and Modernity," 383–85.

29. Richard [Dick] Hyland, "The Locker Room Quality," *Photoplay*, July 1928, 59, 103. Glyn's classic definition of "it" does not exclude physical attributes, but one need not be "abominably good-looking—it does not depend on intelligence or character or—anything—as you say, it is just 'it.'" Elinor Glyn, *The Man and the Moment* (New York: Macaulay, 1914), 86.

30. Ruth Waterbury, "Olympus Moves to Hollywood," *Photoplay*, April 1928, 34–36, 92.

31. "Health—Hollywood's Greatest Asset," *Photoplay*, November 1926, 32–34; "How Jackie Coogan Keeps Fit," *Photoplay*, October 1924, 70; Frank Tuttle, dir., *The American Venus* (Los Angeles: Paramount Pictures, 1926); "Here Is 'Miss America,'" *Photoplay*, December 1925, 62.

32. Charley Paddock, "Why Athletes Fail in Pictures," 124.

33. Paddock, "Why Athletes Fail," 52–53, 124; Clarence G. Badger, dir., *Swim Girl, Swim* (Los Angeles: Paramount Pictures, 1927).

34. Bob Rose, "Cheating Death for a Living," *Popular Mechanics*, February 1935, 227; William K. Everson, "Stunt Men: They Should Be as Well Known as the Stars for Whom They Often Double," *Films in Review* 6, no. 8 (October 1955): 398.

35. John Baxter, *Stunt: The Story of the Great Movie Stunt Men*, 90. Talmadge made several films capitalizing on his athleticism, but lack of charisma and his German accent kept him from reaching the top.

36. Bob Rose, "Cheating Death for a Living," 227; Dick Hylan, "Risking Life and Limb for $25," Photoplay, November 1927, 31–32. Director Clarence Brown, who worked with Perkins, stated that the greatest danger for the stuntman was "the other fellow. . . . 'I don't worry about myself. It's what the other fellow is going to do that bothers me.'" Clarence Brown, quoted in Hylan, "Risking Life and Limb," 32. Bob Rose concurs that "a stunt man must never rely on someone else." Rose, "Cheating Death," 229.

37. Rose, "Cheating Death," 226; Hylan, "Risking Life and Limb," 30.

38. Grace, "Stunt Men," 130; Hylan, "Risking Life and Limb," 31. As a director of pictures known for "eye-popping action," William Witney concurs that one should "never put an actor at risk if you can use a stuntman." William Witney, *In a Door, into a Fight, out a Door, into a Chase: Moviemaking Remembered by the Guy at the Door*, 2, 27. John Baxter estimates that from 1925 to 1930 there were 10,794 injuries in California film productions, from which fifty-five, mostly stuntmen and -women, died. Baxter, *Stunt*, 16.

39. Winnie Brown, quoted in Adela Rogers St. Johns, "Stunting into Stardom," *Photoplay*, December 1922, 39, 89.

40. Stef Donev, *The Fun of Living Dangerously: The Life of Yakima Canutt*, 4.

41. Dick Hyland, "Pictures or Football?," *Photoplay*, September 1928, 38–40, 109–10; Clara Bow, quoted in Cal York, "Gossip of All the Studios," *Photoplay*, July 1927, 43.

42. Joe Bonomo, *The Strongman: A True Life Pictorial Autobiography of the Hercules of the Screen Joe Bonomo*, 50; Mark H. Berry, "Apollo or Hercules?" *Strength*, July 1929, 29. Although he was a great stuntman, Bonomo was also a great self-promoter; thus his autobiography must be read with skepticism.

43. Bonomo, *The Strongman*, 56–61, 80, 203; Donev, *The Fun of Living Dangerously*, 7. Witney believes that "there will probably never be another stuntman who can compare to Yakima Canutt." Witney, *In a Door*, 63.

44. Bonomo, *The Strongman*, 61, 71, 157, 159–60; William Slater, "Joe Bonomo—Iron Man of the Screen," *Strength*, October 1927, 69–70.

45. Bonomo, *The Strongman*, 82–83, 86–87.

46. Grace, "Stunt Men," 130.

47. Robert S. Birchard, *King Cowboy: Tom Mix and the Movies*, 3–7.

48. James S. McQuade, "A Selig Ranch Picture," *Moving Picture World* 11, no. 6 (February 10, 1912): 471; George Mitchell and William K. Everson, "Tom Mix, of His Many Contributions to the Western, the Greatest Was Showmanship," 388.

49. "Athletic Ambitions," *Moving Picture World* 26, no. 8 (November 13, 1915): 1311; "Movie Stunts," in Selig Polyscope Company advertisement, *Moving Picture World* 33, no. 1 (July 7, 1917): 143.

50. Mitchell and Everson, "Tom Mix," 390–91; *Motion Picture News*, March 20, 1920, cited in Birchard, *King Cowboy*, 155.

51. Birchard, *King Cowboy*, 121; Mitchell and Everson, "Tom Mix," 394. Mix's approach was to "never go back in doing a stunt. I go forward constantly. That is because the human body is so constructed that muscles and bone protect the front of the body. Man was made to advance." Unattributed clipping, British Film Institute Library, quoted in Baxter, *Stunt*, 70.

52. Birchard, *King Cowboy*, 121–22.

53. Birchard, *King Cowboy*, 120–21, 123. According to Baxter, it was the flamboyant outfits worn by stuntman Yakima Canutt that inspired Mix's colorful cowboy wardrobe: "Seeing Yakima Canutt's fancy two-tone shirts when they met in 1923, he promptly had forty made up and started a fashion." Baxter, *Stunt*, 71.

54. Tom Mix, "Making a Million," *Photoplay*, June 1928, 113.

55. Gaylyn Studlar, *This Mad Masquerade: Stardom and Masculinity in the Jazz Age*, 20; Charles K. Taylor, "The Most Popular Man in the World," *Outlook*, December 24, 1924, 683.

56. Jeffrey Vance, *Douglas Fairbanks*, 15–16.

57. Ralph Hancock and Letitia Fairbanks, *Douglas Fairbanks: The Fourth Musketeer* (New York: Holt, 1953), 80. As Fairbanks noted of his student experience, "I was a failure as an athlete." Fairbanks, *Douglas Fairbanks*, 41.

58. William A. Brady, *Showman: My Life Story*, 262–65; Vance, *Douglas Fairbanks*, 22.

59. "Timeline: Mary Pickford," *American Experience*, PBS, July 23, 2004, http://www .pbs.org/wgbh/amex/pickford/timeline/index.html; "C. Chaplin, Millionaire-Elect," *Photoplay*, May 1916, 58.

60. Vance, *Douglas Fairbanks*, 32; Peter Bogdanovich, *Allan Dwan: The Last Pioneer* (New York: Praeger, 1971), 42; Alistair Cooke, *Douglas Fairbanks: The Making of a Screen Character*, 16.

61. Douglas Fairbanks Jr., *The Salad Days*, 48.

62. "Doug's Show Is on Today," clipping, Scrapbook No. 4, Douglas Fairbanks Collection, Margaret Herrick Library.

63. Vance, *Douglas Fairbanks*, 29.

64. Fairbanks also played a daily round of golf or two, often with Fred Astaire or Bing Crosby, his son recalls. He "overexercised . . . to keep his figure like a Greek god's, and early to bed and early to rise was an important part of his daily regimen." Fairbanks, *The Salad Days*, 96, 280.

65. Carl Easton Williams, "Analyzing Douglas Fairbanks," 21–22.

66. Fairbanks, *Douglas Fairbanks*, 161; Douglas Fairbanks, "How I Keep Running on 'High,'" *American Magazine*, August 1922, 38, quoted in Studlar, *This Mad Masquerade*, 41.

67. Studlar, *This Mad Masquerade*, 41

68. Arthur Hornblow Jr., "Douglas Fairbanks, Dramatic Dynamo," 48; Mary Pickford, *Sunshine and Shadow* (New York: Doubleday, 1955), 199, 229, 309.

69. Hornblow, "Douglas Fairbanks," 49.

70. Cooke, *Douglas Fairbanks*, 24–25; Richard Schickel, *His Picture in the Papers*, 54; Hornblow, "Douglas Fairbanks," 50.

71. Williams, "Analyzing Douglas Fairbanks," 84.

72. Douglas Fairbanks, quoted in Schickel, *His Picture in the Papers*, 49; Fairbanks, *The Salad Days*, 96, 347. A 1928 magazine advertisement features Fairbanks saying "'I get more kick from the Lucky Strike flavor than from any other cigarette.' For a slender figure—'Reach for a *Lucky* instead of a sweet.'" Douglas Fairbanks Jr. Collection, Clippings 1917–1990, Douglas Fairbanks Collection, Margaret Herrick Library. Fairbanks allegedly smoked at least three packs a day.

73. Advertisement in the *Exhibitor's Trade Review* 2, no. 17 (September 29, 1917): 1284, quoted in Studlar, *This Mad Masquerade*, 20; Williams, "Analyzing Douglas Fairbanks," 84.

74. Ruth Biery, "What Killed Francis X. Bushman?" *Photoplay*, January 1928, 35, 88.

75. Davis and Davis, *King of the Movies*, 183; Ball, The "Silencing of Clara Bow"; Gammel, "Lacing Up the Gloves," 385.

76. Bonomo, *The Strongman*, 303, 308; Miriam Linna, "Joe Bonomo Is My Hero," 1997, WFMU-FM, https://wfmu.org/LCD/18/bonomo.html; Baxter, *Stunt*, 92–93; Donev, *The Fun of Living Dangerously*, 8.

77. John Wayne, Notes for *My Kingdom*, Folder 2, Maurice Zolotow Papers, University of Texas at Austin, quoted in Garry Wills, *John Wayne: The Politics of Celebrity* (London: Faber and Faber, 1997), 59; Iron Eyes Cody, *Iron Eyes: My Life as a Hollywood Indian* (New York: Everest House, 1982), 91.

78. Birchard, *King Cowboy*, 132, 229, 236. Baxter confirms that "sound finally ended Mix's career" and that his "flat Midwestern voice clashed with the physical image he put forward." Mix's last film was a 1935 serial, *The Miracle Rider*. Baxter, *Stunt*, 72.

79. Douglas Fairbanks Jr., interview with Jeffrey Vance, 1993, in Vance, *Douglas Fairbanks*, 250; see also Vance, *Douglas Fairbanks*, 266.

80. Baxter, *Stunt*, 14.

V. MIGHTY SONS OF MACISTE

It is by imitation far more than by precept, that we learn everything;
and what we learn thus, we acquire not only more effectually, but
more pleasantly.

—Edmund Burke, "On the Sublime and Beautiful"

Luciano Albertini

IN 1918 ITALIAN writer Giovanni Bertinetti made a startling prediction about
how movies could aid physical education: "Every gymnasium will have its
own projection hall where students will learn gymnastic exercises by seeing,
and they can then commit to memory the ones that they will perform." The
cinematograph would be "such an important instrument of social renewal
that those who today consider it to be a mere entertainment or a pernicious
school of youthful corruption will be the first to come under its influence.
The signs are indisputable."[1] Movies did prove to be transformative, however,
and the association of exercise with film that Bertinetti fervently hoped for
became, unexpectedly, a reality. Less than a year later he wrote a screenplay
for a muscular young athlete, Luciano Albertini, that induced more interest
in physical fitness than any possible gymnastic projection room.

Called *Sansone contro i Filistei* (Samson versus the Philistines), it created
a strongman persona for Albertini that would endure throughout his career.
Like many forzuti, he started as a gymnast and acrobat. Albertini was a natural athlete whose father, Nicola, had been a circus strongman who traveled
throughout Europe. Eventually the family settled in Lugo di Romagna, in
Ravenna Province, where Luciano was born (as Francesco Vespignani) in
1882. Albertini often attempted to disguise his circus roots, but his athletic abilities were fostered in a home that encouraged showmanship and
physicality. Young Luciano, as an active sportsman, frequented a gymnastic
club in nearby Forlì and attended classes at the Istituto di Elettrotecnica in
Bologna, enabling him to enlist as an electrician in the Italian Navy. When

his enlistment expired, Albertini enrolled at the École Péchin, a physical culture academy in Lyon, France, where he earned an instructor's diploma. It was here that his body began to be appreciated. "He possessed a harmonious physique," explains one source, "as perfect as a Greek wrestler with solid and weighty muscles, a broad and fit chest, a Herculean build" and "a manly and statuesque beauty" that was sought for modeling at fine arts academies.[2]

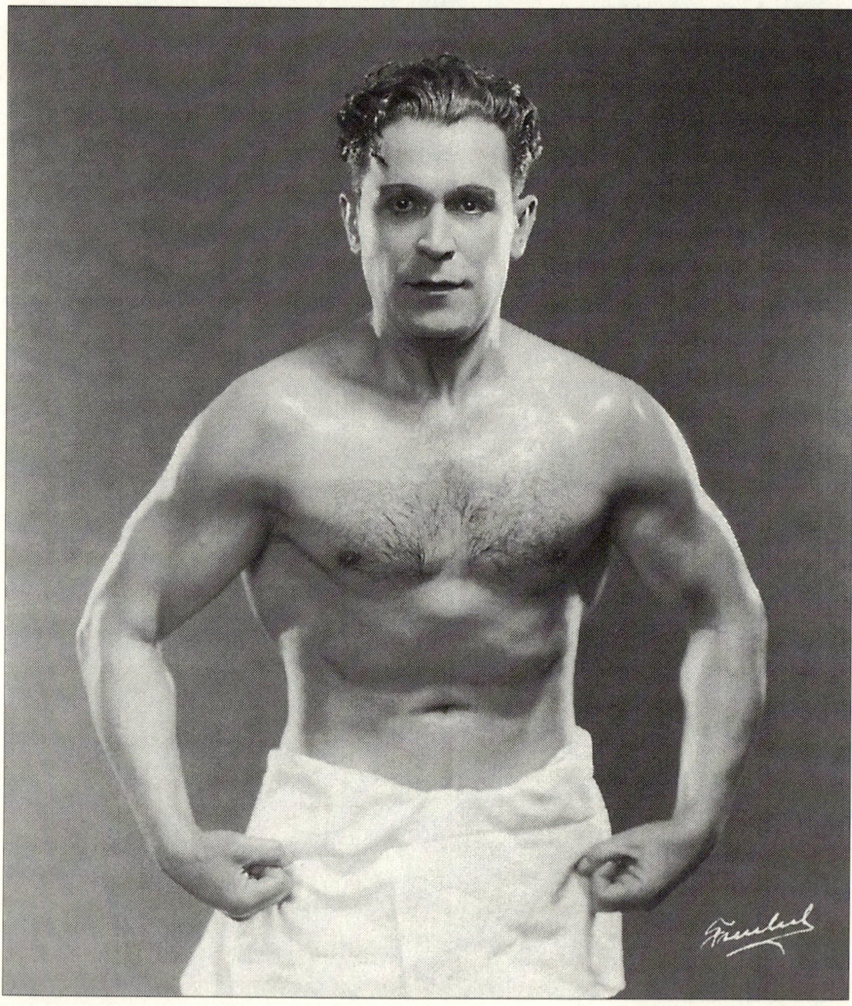

Figure 5.1. Luciano Albertini began his career as a circus acrobat and maintained his superb physique when he transitioned to films. He displays his torso in this publicity still from around 1925. Collection of David L. Chapman.

Around 1905 he began to work for the famous Circus Busch in Berlin, where he formed Les Albertini, an acrobatic troupe on the flying trapeze that traveled throughout Europe for a decade. Albertini's film career began with *La spirale della morte* (The spiral of death) produced in 1917 by Arturo Ambrosio, known for his ancient epics. Unfortunately, the film has been lost, but journalist commentaries indicate it was a pastiche of circus acrobatics and war espionage and a huge success. Called "triumphant" by one critic, "*The spiral of death* is transformed into the *spiral of glory*." The film's star "revealed himself not just as a prodigious gymnast, but as a perfect actor—natural, spontaneous, full of sensitivity and art."[3] By casting Albertini as a muscular athlete working to defeat Italy's enemies by daring actions, he appeared as a rival to Bartolomeo Pagano, aka Maciste, whose war film *Maciste Alpino* (Alpine Maciste) had been released the previous year. As if to underscore that rivalry, Albertini's next film was even more action-packed.

It premiered in early 1918 and introduced Sansone, the role that would make the actor's reputation as a top European athletic star. *Sansone contro i Filistei* (Samson versus the Philistines) proved to be a huge hit, partly because of its modern, working-class situation, but also for its handsome and genial star. Albertini plays a laborer in the fictional Richard's Iron Works. Sansone is stronger and more agile than his fellow workers and "always ready to lend a hand to help a friend or to raise a fist to punish an enemy. And when Sansone raises his fist, it always spells disaster."[4] The story combines modern industrialism with a fairy-tale setting and plot, but Albertini's presence brings a reassuring quality to the end product. By making the main character a working-class man, the producers were attempting to profit from Maciste's popularity as a former dockworker. Albertini wanted to appear in a similar light. An appealing, proletarian hero who was young, handsome, well built, and strong could only add to his public allure. Albertini, however, is not the large, lovable, often blundering hero like his cinematic rival. He introduces acrobatics to the repertoire of the *giganti buoni*, or "good giants"; rather than wrestling a bull by the horns or ripping apart sturdy chains, Albertini was the first of the forzuti to create a persona based on lightness, agility, and celerity. One critic viewed Sansone as "not just a man of unusual strength or of purely material strength, but also an artist of physical strength that he humanizes and embellishes from an interior moral strength."[5] Rather than using strength to solve every problem, Sansone considers all options. While Maciste would apply his muscles to solve problems, Sansone attacks them with subtlety and deliberation. Both of them drew largely on strong inner resources to display and activate their muscles.

Albertini was particularly popular in Great Britain. The star even made a trip to London in December 1918 for the premiere of *Sansonia: The Acrobat of Death* (the British title for *La spirale della morte*). "Italy is famous for her strong men on the films. First Maciste, and now Sansonia," wrote one reviewer. "In both cases a physical drill instructor might envy their chest development and biceps. . . . They are both possessed of prodigious strength and a decided aptitude for screen acting."[6] Albertini's films were sufficiently popular in Italy to allow him to keep churning out a string of modest hits. His next films, *Un drama in wagon lit* (A drama in a railway carriage) and *Il re dell'abisso* (The king of the abyss) were released in 1919. The latter was an old-fashioned adventure film by Giovanni Bertinetti, but the reviewer from Rome's *Apollon* forgave him for churning out such a potboiler, observing that he "had to write a film whose only purpose was to feature Luciano Albertini and to showcase his great acrobatic and wrestling gifts."[7] It appeared that audiences worldwide had an insatiable appetite for movies starring the charismatic acrobat. Bertinetti perceived there were profits to be made, so he formed Albertini-Film, a production company that would make action films based around the talents of Albertini's little "family." One of its first productions in 1919 was *Il protetto della morte* (Protected from death), with a spectacular scene where Luciano Albertini crosses a wire over the sixty-meter Mondrone Gorge in the Piedmontese Alps. To make matters more risky, one end of the wire was attached to a rock and the other to a mule. The plot concerns a man who is impervious to fear and can perform perilous feats to protect the innocent. A *La vita cinematografica* reviewer was impressed with the action sequences: "The thought of imminent death awakens the instincts of preservation and arouses in the human soul a boldness that urges us to confront any danger and encourages us to attempt any daring deed!"[8]

Albertini's next cinematic triumph came late in 1919 with *Sansone e la ladra di atleti* (Sansone and the robber of athletes). Although the film has been lost, it appears to have been about a nefarious villain who attempts to kidnap Italy's leading athletes. Ultimately, Albertini and cyclist Costante Girardengo, known as il Campionissimo (the Greatest Champion) team up to defeat their common enemy. This film is remarkable because it marks the first time in Italian cinema that an adventure film featured a competitive athlete. The appearance of this popular sportsman virtually guaranteed success.

Italians were becoming more interested in sports, making Albertini's film timely. Reviewers were amazed at the innovation of a sporting hero in a fictional film: "Huge numbers of people are rushing to see 'il Campionissimo,' the idol of the masses, Costante Girardengo. Naturally, with him the very clever and daring Luciano Albertini has triumphed." Another critic was delighted to see the workings of a gymnasium where spectators watch "real athletes strengthen their muscles by taking turns on the most modern gymnastic equipment."[9] The principal difference between Pagano and Albertini is that the former represents pure strength, whereas the latter joins stealth, intelligence, and acrobatic flair to the character of the good giant. It was a combination that made the star a darling of the Italian screen.

Albertini's popularity in America was somewhat less assured, and at least one reviewer had trouble determining if the action star's films would catch on across the Atlantic. The critic in *Motion Picture News* commented on a film from 1920, *I figli di Sansonia* (The sons of Sansonia; in America, *The Superman*) and how it would play in Peoria. He declared that the movie was "not to be taken seriously. . . . This plot is so ancient, the action so melodramatic, enacted in a foreign atmosphere and according to foreign technique." But it was "full of thrill stuff of the very kind which has made Doug Fairbanks films so popular." American audiences might ridicule the absurd plot—"the funniest thing in the world is melodrama out of tune, and that's what this one is"—but the star was deemed "a good looking chap" and "certainly some athlete." Although the reviewer never mentioned Albertini's name or those of his fellow cast members, there was "no question but that this is an Italian imitation of Fairbanks pictures," reminding cinema owners of another Italian film that prospered in America. "If you played the 'Maciste' pictures, you will know that they did a whale of a business. We would consider this the same sort of an attraction."[10]

Despite repetitious plots and improbable situations, Albertini-Film still produced several movies a year, but "Albertini's biggest professional frustration was that he was considered just an acrobat (although an exceptional one)," explained one of his costars. He wanted "to act in films that were not just a series of sensational stunts, but which could prove his acting abilities," citing his role as Rolando Candiano in *Il ponte dei sospiri* (The bridge of sighs, 1921).[11] Afterward, Albertini departed for Berlin. Unlike Italy, where moviemaking was slumping, Germany had Europe's most robust film industry. He soon set up Albertini-Film GmbH, which produced popular circus and adventure movies, and then partnered with Anna Gorilowa, a young Hungarian dancer and actress. Their films brought increasing prestige for Albertini. So great was the Italian actor's reputation that talent scouts from America recruited him to star in a prestigious serial called *The Riddle Rider*.[12] "When he considered the American opportunity," recalled Gorilowa, "Albertini thought that he was walking on air. It was to be a Universal production, but with money from [the German production company] Phoebus, and Albertini saw himself at the start of new world recognition and a new career." Unfortunately, upon arrival at Carl Laemmle's studios, he discovered his film would be a lesser serial, *The Iron Man* (1924), and Albertini would not have the principal role. As Mario Quargnolo notes, "The disappointment, the weeping, the stories that poisoned the foreign adventure were countless." Despite the film's silly story line, Universal Studios was determined to make the most of its muscular Italian star, and publicity photos and stories appeared in film magazines.[13] An article in *Picture-Play* introduced Albertini to American filmgoers with three photos—flexing his biceps, in evening dress, and performing a vaudeville stunt. It emphasized the Italian's beauty and grace rather than his muscular power: "Unlike most athletes of such gigantic strength, Albertini is not muscle bound. He moves lightly and swiftly and can vie with fast runners on the track."[14] By marketing him as a muscular male beauty, he was made palatable to female viewers, while his strength and athleticism indicated he was a real man. Albertini was ballyhooed even more in *Universal Weekly*, where readers learned that European adventure films specialized in dangerous leaps and high-altitude feats and Albertini was master of them: "The European idea of thrills is one far different from those of the average American chapterplay."[15]

Physical culture magazines were also interested in this muscular phenomenon. An article titled "Strong Men of the Movies" in *Health and Life* was fulsome in its praise for Albertini. After his acrobatic skills are lauded, readers are told that Italy's other famous strongman, Maciste, is "muscle bound" and incapable of quick or graceful actions. Despite Albertini's "enormous strength, the Italian star is lithe as a panther and every muscle in his body is always usable." This readiness Albertini attributed to his ability to relax and avoid unusable hard knots of muscle.[16] American magazines also attempted to ramp up excitement by portraying Albertini as a real strongman who could perform feats of might and daring without a stuntman. Although many spectacular feats were worked out carefully by the actor with the precision of a circus acrobat, these assertions were largely untrue. Hollywood, after all, was not in the business of truth telling but of convincing people to buy tickets. Gorilowa explains that the American producers assumed Albertini was game for any daredevilry and that after production began he was to jump from the Brooklyn Bridge onto the deck of a passing ship. The serial makers were surprised when Albertini balked. "Perhaps," Gorilowa speculated, "they thought that he did not use a stunt double, while in reality he was not only prudent but also resorted to trickery, and he also used stunt men." The actor's favorite double, Angelo Rossi, arrived at the studios about the same time as his boss, and it was he who performed many of the dangerous feats in Albertini's films. "Rossi," the actor once admitted, "works with his body—I with my face."[17]

Despite exaggerations created by publicity departments, there was little that could save this stinker serial. The only beneficial result of *The Iron Man* was that a husky actor playing the villainous henchman Gaston La Rue (Joe Bonomo) attracted the attention of Universal producers, who decided to feature him as Landow, the Strongman, in the next big serial, *The Great Circus Mystery* (1925). Albertini departed for Germany in 1924, convinced he would find a public more attuned to his brand of athleticism. His first production with Phoebus-Film was *Mister Radio* (1924), an action film that had him bounding over the rocky Dolomite Mountains in northern Italy. As Albertini's work progressed, he showed little interest in varying his successful formula and often recycled stunts. But in *Der Mann auf dem Kometen* (The man from the comet, 1925) Albertini plays a circus acrobat who uses his strength and athleticism to save a helpless infant stolen by an ape and dragged to the top of a tall factory smokestack.[18]

Albertini was especially popular in Germany, where he reportedly lived in a villa on the outskirts of Berlin with "a big courtyard and a gymnasium well stocked with exercise equipment." He enjoyed his star status, but audiences were tiring of his once great persona. Perhaps it is indicative of the passing years and the star's diminishing health that he avoids almost all acrobatic or muscular stunts in *Tempo! Tempo!* (1929), one of his last silent films. Instead of strength, Albertini turns to speed. "The title is apt," writes Georg Herzberg. "This is truly a fast-paced movie." Elegance is also important: "Albertini's ambition is to play the entire movie in silk hat and tails; he avoids all strong-arm tactics, attempting to look particularly elegant at all times."[19]

Around 1930 Albertini's life and career took an unpleasant turn; the sybaritic life he led up to this point was soon a memory. The actor was now fifty years old, and (as Douglas Fairbanks also learned) it was becoming increasingly hard to perform acrobatic stunts. Also, with talkies arriving, Albertini found it difficult to make the transition with his thick Italian accent. Finally, he was showing signs of alcoholism. In 1918 Camillo Bruto Bonzi wrote an article praising Luciano's high ideals at the outset of his career: "His strength is the product of assiduous exercise and great temperance—not counting his natural gifts. A parsimonious eater, he repudiates alcoholic beverages and believes that a man should not consort with women until after he has reached his twenty-fifth year."[20] By the mid-1930s, however, the once temperate star was wandering the streets in a haze of dementia and dipsomania. Renato Lolli, a longtime acquaintance, caught sight of Albertini in a Stuttgart public garden, noting,

> He was wearing a threadbare overcoat; his face was ruddy, perhaps reddened by alcohol. By contrast, his yellow shoes were quite new. He was sitting on a bench alone. It was a very cold day, and it pained me to see such a man engrossed in thought on a freezing morning without adequate clothing. . . . His hands were reddened by fever and they shook with a continuous trembling, especially the left one, which grasped a piece of bread. At his feet a dozen sparrows pecked away peacefully. Every now and then he emitted a little gurgle from his throat due to the jolt from a dry cough."[21]

After Albertini assaulted a doorman, he was institutionalized. By the end of the 1930s he returned to Italy, where he ended his days in a series of hospitals until his death on January 6, 1945. He was buried in a pauper's grave with no one attending the funeral.[22]

At first glance it might seem that Albertini left little by way of legacy. Like other forzuti, he embodied many of the qualities of the ideal modern man: strength, courage, and action. Some critics saw a political element in Albertini's *Sansonia* films because he seemed to represent the Italian Fascist Party's *uomo nuovo* (new man) of the early 1920s. According to Benito Mussolini, the new man was disdainful of death and books and in love with virility, violence, quick thinking, physical resistance, fighting, and war. A statement issued by Albertini's studio tapped into this concept when it described its actor-acrobat as "a remarkable man who lands a fist not just with his muscles, but with his brain. . . . Nature has furnished him with an inventive power and a wonderful imagination." As a new man he was a heroic figure who united "physical strength and intellectual energy." The irony of Albertini's life is that he rose so far but within a generation was forgotten. An athlete, actor, producer and entrepreneur, he was the only Italian strongman who made a Hollywood film. As his biographer laments, Albertini "deserves better than this."[23] In his heyday he was the only credible rival to Maciste.

Carlo Aldini

Carlo Aldini, the third most popular Italian athletic star in the 1920s, used his character's intellect and beautiful muscles to dazzle his enemies. Despite his impressive physique, Aldini usually appeared as a well-dressed aristocrat whose actions reflected constant gallantry. Many of his roles involved saving a helpless woman from marrying an inappropriate and villainous fiancé. Aldini was born on May 6, 1894, in Pieve Fosciana, near Lucca, but the family moved to Bologna, where he attended a technical school and spent much of his free time at the famous gymnastics society Virtus. He was quickly recognized for his athletic skills, especially in track and field, and at the age of fifteen won the regional wrestling and boxing championships. In 1916 he took top Italian honors in the pentathlon. Aldini's sporting prowess, musculature, and grace were exactly what the film industry was looking for in the 1920s with the popularity of forzuti in Italian cinemas and beyond. He first appeared as star in the 1920 "automobile adventure film" *La 63-71-57* (the car's license plate).

It was not until he played the title character in *Ajax* in 1921 that Aldini attracted attention. In this and succeeding films he plays a suave man-about-town who solves mysteries, performs muscular feats, and resolves social conundrums. Like Luciano Albertini and Mario Guaita-Ausonia, Aldini looks as photogenic in a tuxedo as he does when the plot requires him to don tight jerseys or to remove his shirt. It was action that motivated his films, and there was seldom a letup in the stunts, falls, leaps, and lifts performed while saving a damsel in distress or pursuing another benevolent goal. "Innumerable fists, impenetrable mysteries, indescribable daring and incomprehensible plot" is how one reviewer encapsulated Aldini's early film formula.[24] By the mid-1920s, he was compelled to follow Albertini, Pagano, and other compatriots to greener pastures in Germany. But Pagano, although he had appeared in four films, decided to leave the colder climes of Berlin while his next film, *Die närrische Wette der Lord Maciste* (Lord Maciste's foolish wager) was in early production. The newly arrived Aldini stepped into the role, and the movie was renamed *Die närrische Wette der Lord Aldini*.[25]

His next film, directed by Manfred Noa and released in 1924, was destined to become one of the great epics of German silent cinema. *Helena* was a massive undertaking based on Homer's tale of the Trojan War, divided into two parts, *Der Raub der Helena* (The rape of Helen) and *Der Zerstörung Trojas* (The destruction of Troy). Aldini was suited to play the pivotal part of the aloof, heroic Achilles. He appears in a short peplum with his muscular chest and arms in view and performs in a stylized, almost balletic style, using broad gestures and more physicality than other actors. Aldini's character Achilles is distinctive, owing to his seemingly homosexual relationship with his "great friend" Patroclus, with whom he exchanges longing gazes and tender caresses. Despite his muscular physique and obviously masculine demeanor, Aldini's Achilles clearly expresses his manly love for Patroclus, thus presenting one of the few positive roles for a gay man in mainstream cinema of the time. He eschews any of the more common and derisive stereotypes by playing the character in a noble and respectful way. Aldini also displays his fighting and acrobatic skills in a dramatic sequence where he has a one-on-one combat scene with the Trojan champion Hector. Despite its high production values and talented acting, the film found little favor with audiences. The timing of its release could not have been worse, since it coincided with another massive epic, *Die Nibelungen* (The Nibelungs, 1924), directed by Fritz Lang. German nationalism won out over ancient Greek history: Noa's Trojan epic was overshadowed by Lang's paean to Aryan mythology.

From 1924 to 1934 Aldini made thirteen films—almost all in the genre of *Sensationfilme* (adventure films). Quickly made and profitable, they emphasized Aldini's poise, balance, and acrobatic abilities. They also showcased his physique and suavity, and like Albertini, Aldini formed his own production company. Still, he worked in close cooperation with other major Berlin studios, most prominently Phoebus-Film, which also made Albertini's best films. The success of the two Italian athletes in Germany was evident in 1924 when their studio purchased a controlling interest in Berlin's most prestigious cinema, the Marmorhaus (Marble House)—so called because of its splendid stone facade. Although *Filmland* admitted that the new management might leave the provinces in a state of indifference, "for Berliners it means a great deal. Where can we come and see the musclemen Aldini and Albertini from now on? In the Marmorhaus! In recent times, things were really much 'weaker' at this place."[26] Aldini continued to turn out exciting films, one of the best of them being *Die Abenteurer GmbH* (Adventures, Inc.) from 1928, a story based on an Agatha Christie novel, *The Secret Adversary*. Critical reaction was positive. A reviewer from the *Berliner Tageblatt* called it "A crime potboiler with class" with praise for "the gymnast and boxer Carlo Aldini who carries the plot along. He is a colossus—a battleship—who moves with 20,000 horsepower energy." The critic from *Kinematograph* was impressed by Aldini's acrobatic fall via a four-story downspout ending with a plunge into Berlin's freezing River Spree. He imagines the astonishment of passersby on the Weidendamm Bridge if they happened to see a man performing such a spectacular stunt "because the cameras were not apparent, and it was not obvious at first glance that a movie was being shot."[27]

Aldini's first sound film was *Im Kampf mit der Unterwelt* (At war with the underworld), which enjoyed international success. The Italian strongman's last film, a short feature called *Carlos schönstes Abenteuer* (Carlo's most beautiful adventure, 1934), received scant notice, indicating his days as an action star were numbered. It was also evident by the mid-1930s that German audiences were growing weary of *Sensationfilme*, and at age forty, Aldini likely had had enough of the genre. He died of "an irreversible malady" on March 21, 1961. Aldini was the most refined of the Italian musclemen—his closest rival being Ausonia. The true sign of a cinematic strongman comes when he wears very little—as Aldini did in Noa's Trojan epic, displaying his rippling muscles and impressive biceps. As one critic put it, "although he was robust and muscular, he had a graceful physique, a gentleness of behavior and the beauty of a classical sculpture which in *Helena* . . . found its most exact combination."[28]

In interwar Germany filmmaking was flourishing, while the Italian industry was in a near-fatal slump. In the meantime, audiences were clamoring for more adventure films that did not greatly tax the intellect. Actors, technicians, and producers thus converged around Berlin in order to make *Sensationfilme*. After its defeat in World War I, Germany was an economic basket case; no one had much money and hyperinflation rapidly sapped consumers' buying power. This was bad news for some, but good news for the movie industry because it meant that talent, land, and resources were cheap. With the value of currency plummeting disastrously, two realities were apparent: making films in Germany had suddenly become inexpensive, and the public had little material items to spend its money on, so they flocked to the cinemas. Soon there were hundreds of movie studios clustered around Berlin, and during the decade and a half of the Weimar Republic, there were on average 250 films produced every year.[29] Very few of these movies were deathless classics of expressionism, but the demand was there. The principal genres were light comedies, musicals, detective films, and quickly made potboilers. Among these latter were the sorts of movies that Albertini, Aldini, and Maciste made. Movies featuring muscular adventure heroes were very popular, and this was largely for the same reasons that these "good giant" movies were popular in Italy.

Another reason for the success of *Sensationfilme* was that their handsome and often shirtless heroes appealed to the more open and sexually sophisticated audiences of Weimar urban society. This was brought about by a great deal of gender role reassessment at the time. Returning soldiers questioned their personal masculinity, women were forced to work outside the home, and turning to prostitution became the last resort of many starving citizens of both sexes. Berlin was also the home of the world's first gay rights movement; gay people were basking in new but ephemeral freedoms, and film was just one area where these new freedoms were manifested.[30] Many members of German society enjoyed this new emphasis on physicality, sexuality, and liberation. Thus, the growth of the cinema as a means of inexpensive diversion, the free time afforded by unemployment, and the newly awakening sexual freedoms all contributed to the success of German and foreign muscle films. This was a great boon to many of the Italian good giants who had begun their careers south of the Alps but had decided to relocate if in order to make more movies.

Domenico "Saetta" Gambino

If Maciste represented a benevolent strongman and natural Hercules, Domenico Gambino played a smaller, faster, and nimble Mercury—hence the cognomen Saetta (Lightning). Gambino was born in Turin on May 17, 1890, the son of pastry shop proprietors, but when a shabby circus pitched its tents near the family home, Domenico was inspired to enter show business. After playing several roles in a theater company, he encountered a film crew shooting a scene in a Turin park with an actor tumbling awkwardly out of a carriage. Gambino offered to double for the actor and take the fall himself. So pleased was the director that he invited him to do stunts for the entire company. Gambino later pointed out the irony of the situation: "When there was a chance that they might risk their hide, I was put in their place, and of course then they got all the glory. But what a bitter disappointment might the audiences have felt if they had known that lurking behind the noble and statuesque appearance of their bold and beloved star, there was often a gangly young man." Comparing himself to another famous character with a conventionally unattractive appearance, he said, "I was the Cyrano of the Cinema."[31]

In 1910 Gambino was given his own series of comic one-reelers, but he was also turning into a factotum of Italian cinema; if a moviemaker needed an actor, a stuntman, a comedian, or even a talent scout (allegedly, Gambino had a role in discovering Albertini and Pagano), they would often turn to him. This frenetic activity allowed him to form his own production company, Delta Film, in 1918 and accept the stage name of Saetta along with a character based on his own personality. In the end, he would be a people's hero. One critic described Saetta as "good, generous, full of courage who gives everything for others and nothing for himself . . . he happily runs dangers and does not lose his good humor or innate cheerfulness even in the most precarious moments."[32] Saetta's character is much like Maciste's. The diminutive Gambino does not carry the physical weight of the other good giant, but his heart is just as big.

Of all silent era forzuti, Gambino best exemplified the ideals of the futurists, a literary/artistic movement begun in 1909 with Filippo Tommaso Marinetti's "Manifeste de futurisme" (Futurist manifesto) published in Paris. The movement celebrated such modern concepts as speed, technology, strength, and youth. Because of their adherence to some Fascist Party goals, the futurists were accorded more opportunities to exhibit their works. They revered cinema as a means of conveying personal freedom, action, and above all, speed. In *Nuova religione-morale della velocità* (New moral religion of speed, 1916), Marinetti exhorted his compatriots, "Be speedy and you will be strong, optimistic, invincible and immortal." Since the easiest way to achieve high velocity was technology, the futurists were obsessed with trains, airplanes, and especially automobiles. Not surprisingly, artists and poets found Saetta an ideal representative of their philosophy. As Monica Dall'Asta observes, "Saetta runs, runs a long time and at a dizzying rate in astonishing challenges to time. In his irresistible aptitude for running, he is even capable of dominating one of the mechanical engines the most Futurist of all: the automobile."[33] In the film where Gambino's character makes its debut, *Saetta* (1920), he is seen chasing after a car containing the heroine that is careening out of control (the driver being knocked unconscious after an attack). It is zigzagging wildly and threatening to collide with a train, but after a frenzied pursuit, Saetta overtakes the car and brings everything to a safe conclusion. Such high-speed chases became commonplace, and sometimes excessive, in Saetta's films. Noting how one scene resembled slapstick, a critic complained, "We merely note the exaggeration of the chase that is out of all proportion with its goal."[34] If critics were dismayed and confused by Saetta's mixing of genres, audiences could not get enough of it.

Gambino seldom if ever used trick photography; he was an old school athlete who abhorred easy stunts and cinematic jiggery-pokery. He always prepared meticulously before doing a dangerous vault, checking every aspect of the action. Allegedly he made mathematical calculations estimating the necessary speed for a perilous leap or the thickness of the pane of glass he planned on crashing through. The mark of a good stuntman is that he removes as many uncertainties as possible. As one commentator noted, "When things went bad, it was [Gambino] who had to pay personally."[35] In 1924 Gambino joined forces with Pagano to make their only movie together, *Maciste imperatore* (Emperor Maciste). It was a mark of Saetta's popularity that it also had an alternative title, *Maciste imperatore e Saetta suo scudiere* (Emperor Maciste and his sidekick Saetta). Maciste assumes the identity of king of a fictional country in order to reinstate the rightful heir but asks Saetta for help. After many fights, chases, and adventures, they make sure that good triumphs and evil is punished. "Naturally," wrote a reviewer in *La rivista del cinematografo*, "the fists are frequent and very powerful, and Saetta, Maciste's friend, does his part with daring and playful acrobatics."[36]

Gambino was a national hero in Italy that many likened to a more famous foreign film star. "A metropolitan newspaper has compared our Domenico Gambino (Saetta) to Douglas [Fairbanks]!" wrote a journalist after the release of *Saetta impara a vivere* (Saetta learns how to live) in 1924. "To me the difference does not seem to be slight, and certainly not entirely in the American's favor. . . . Gambino has nothing to learn in terms of acrobatics and even less in his acting."[37] Although his films were popular, they were mostly variations on the same theme: Saetta is a poor but honest man who solves injustice by using his wits, strength, and acrobatic skills. Starting in 1920, Gambino began making films at a rapid clip. With the film crisis looming larger in Italy, opportunities were diminishing. The mid-1920s saw the demise of the Italian film industry; additionally, many Italians found themselves surrounded by communists who were trying to shut down the country and its studios. Actor and director Emilio Ghione describes why the movie industry was collapsing: "The Communists were masters of the country and they called strike after strike until the abrupt appearance of the Black Shirts. Meanwhile, all of this gradually brought about the total ruin of Italian cinema."[38] As soon as the Fascist Party was firmly invested, it instituted the Fascio artistico (an organization of proregime artists) with a view to controlling the creative output in all major cities. If an actor wanted to work, he had to make his peace with Mussolini's party, and the higher an actor's profile, the more he was expected to show enthusiasm. Perhaps this is why Gambino donated five hundred lire to the Turin chapter of Fascio artistico.[39]

It appears he never harbored deeply felt sympathies for the Fascists, however. In fact, none of the strongmen or athletic stars of silent Italian cinema ever donned a black shirt. Rather than bow to political pressure to make a film titled *Saetta fascista* (Saetta the Fascist) celebrating the Fascist Party, Gambino slipped out of the country, choosing to follow other actors to Germany when jobs dried up or political crises intervened.[40]

His first production in Germany was an excellent choice: in 1928 Gambino was picked to direct and star in an exciting remake of *Die letzte Galavorstellung des Zirkus Wolfson* (The last gala performance of the Wolfson Circus). Circus films were very popular in the late 1920s, and this one promised an unusual number of thrills. An illustrated Italian newspaper announced in December 1927 during production of his circus film that Saetta suffered a terrible accident when he "had to walk across a wire stretching twenty meters high above the ring. Unexpectedly, the wire snapped, and Saetta fell to the floor, suffering serious injuries." The report was accompanied by a dramatic full-page color illustration of the hapless actor plummeting to the ground as horrified extras witness the calamity.[41] The tightrope fall might have awakened Gambino to the perils of dangerous stunts because they soon largely disappeared from his work. His subsequent movies seemed more appropriate to a man approaching forty, and his next significant film was a 1929 comedy, *Ich hab' mein Herz im Autobus verloren* (I lost my heart in a bus), featuring a pleasant young man who travels at breakneck speed in his race car to make an emergency purchase of some stocks for his rich uncle. By allowing his automobile to do most of the stunts, Gambino could take fewer risks and still maintain the high level of action and suspense his films were famous for. The not-quite-so-smitten reviewer from the *Berliner illustrierte Nachtausgabe* suggested the stunt-driven film might amuse less sophisticated audiences, but certainly not those with much intelligence.[42] Sight gags and thrilling escapades were popular, but talkies were invading the cinema world by 1929, and this was bad news for Saetta, since he did not know German.

Gambino's beloved character Saetta was small, nimble, quick, and nervous—a perfect contrast to muscular heavy strongmen like Maciste. He was also a perfect model for the futurist man as described in 1919 by Mario Carli in "Ardito-futurista": "Fiery eyes, proud and naive, which do not ignore irony; the heart of a dynamo, pneumatic lungs, the liver of a leopard; legs of a squirrel, to climb up all the peaks and climb over all the abysses; somber, virile, sporty elegance, which permits running, freeing oneself from restraints, dancing, haranguing a crowd; loving speed with frenzy."[43] Significantly, this list of futurist qualities appeared the same year that Gambino's character Saetta appeared. It is a situation where art and philosophy borrowed from popular entertainment with mutual enrichment.

Alfredo Boccolini

The field of Italian cinematic strongmen was crowded for a decade and a half, but one of the best was Alfredo Boccolini. Born near the Italian naval base in La Spezia on December 29, 1885, he became an apprentice mechanic aboard a man-o'-war at age sixteen. Owing to his athletic build and size (over six feet tall, and 240 pounds), he was invited to join a German circus where he performed various functions from trapeze artist to lion tamer. When Italy entered World War I, Boccolini rejoined the Italian Navy and was discovered in 1917 by director Augusto Genina who was shooting ship exteriors for his upcoming film, *Il siluramento dell'Oceania* (The sinking of the Oceania). Boccolini's small part impressed both Genina and audiences and led to a role in Albertini's *La spirale della morte*.

In 1918 Boccolini starred in his first film that attracted serious attention as a big, buff lovable hero named Galaor. The muscular and athletic protagonist impressed contemporary critics; as one noted, "The herculean Boccolini is without doubt a handsome man when compared to the strongmen of the screen up until now, taking into account the statuesque perfection of his physique added to his regular and nicely expressive facial features."[44] Of all the good giants of Italian cinema, Galaor was closest in character to Maciste: large, muscular, and kindly, with a penchant for protecting widows and orphans. Boccolini's next film, *Lagrime di popolo* (The people's tears, 1918), revealed to many, including a critic for *La vita cinematografica*, the actor's strong resemblance to Pagano: "There are too many situations in this film in which Galaor is reminiscent of Maciste, and Boccolini's personality ultimately loses itself in imitation."[45]

It hardly mattered to Italian (and international) audiences whether Galaor was a shameless Maciste knockoff; they could not get enough of these lovable titans. If Boccolini had played no other character than Galaor he would have become a mere interesting footnote to the story of cinematic strongmen. Fortunately, he stepped out of his role enough to display some real acting talent between 1921 and 1922. The first was a cast-of-thousands epic called *La nave* (The ship) based on the founding of Venice after Rome's fall. It was a change of pace for Boccolini, who was used to rock 'em and sock 'em action pictures where plots catapulted quickly to an inevitable happy ending. In *La nave* the actor was stuck in a slow-moving historical drama with little opportunity to display his actions. Owing to this role, however, Boccolini was offered a part in *Samson und Delila* (1922), produced and directed by Hungarian Alexander Korda. Like other popular films, it featured a biblical story interspersed with a similar modern setting. But the contemporary story is so flimsy that it pales in comparison with the more interesting tale of Samson and the woman who ruins him.

Boccolini returned to Italy in 1924 to make his final silent film, *Galaor contro Galaor*, in which he plays a double role as good Galaor and his evil lookalike. The plot features a dangerous bandit who assumes Galaor's appearance and commits all sorts of nefarious deeds. After a series of chases and dangerous stunts, the real Galaor captures his demonic doppelgänger. In a film chock-full of action, Boccolini performs a series of astounding vaults, flights, sprints, and dives; races around in automobiles and motorcycles; clambers up a tall smokestack at the Fiat Works in Turin; and even jumps from a great height using a parachute. Perhaps his most impressive stunt, filmed at the Genoa docks of Sestri Ponente, involved swinging between two massive loading cranes. "Galaor is locked in combat with himself," one critic breathlessly announced, "which is another way of saying against everything and everyone. . . . It is a film that one can call without any fear of exaggeration the exploit of a great acrobatic artist."[46] Boccolini literally struggles with his evil twin, a sinister alter ego who embodies his own inner demons. In a genre based on muscularity and physicality, this is a good way of making those bodies represent more than just heroism. This film shows for the first time a benevolent strongman who does not fight monsters, gangsters, villains, or usurpers; instead he fights the evil within. Of course, those who choose not to dig that deeply can still enjoy the film on a superficial level, but it demonstrates that not every strongman film was a simplistic action picture.[47]

After these early triumphs, Boccolini's personal and professional lives unraveled quickly. His first wife and two children died of the Spanish flu. With his second wife, Emma Savani, he was reduced to traveling around to second-string cinemas lecturing on his career and performing strongman tricks such as thrusting his hand in a lighted brazier without harm and bending iron rods. For increasingly apathetic audiences, he was also playing an accordion and singing a few songs, then performing in public squares and carnivals. He made a few feeble attempts at sound films, but his fortunes kept plummeting in a true "spiral of death." He died in poverty in 1956.[48]

Aurèle Sydney

In Italy he was known as the English Maciste, but he made adventure films in England, France, Italy, and Spain, and he was not English. Aurèle Sydney was a man of the world, born on April 17, 1888, in Newcastle, New South Wales. The future cinema star was the child of an Australian woman and her French immigrant husband and named Aurèle William Edmund Labat de Lambert. He allegedly completed his studies at the University of Sydney, then traveled for a year around the "savage isles of the Pacific." In New Caledonia he entered a piano competition and was the unexpected victor. When he returned to Australia he joined a band of Shakespearean actors who took the Bard all over the outback. By 1906 he was in England, where he was described as "a young man with an athletic build. . . . who engages in every manifestation of sport." The young Australian had a sturdy physique, the daring that comes with exuberance, and a slightly exotic appeal. To make ends meet, he accepted the offer of film director Albert Capellani to appear in a slapstick comedy starring André Deed. Sydney played the antagonist to Deed's character Cretinetti in a half dozen films shot in Italy between 1907 and 1909. Like many early actors, he alternated between studio and stage. In 1910 he tried the Paris stage and took the surname Sydney, supposedly suggested by the great actress Sarah Bernhardt: "Cela sonne bien!" (That sounds good!) she explained.[49] In 1915 he was offered a part in a film under the director Abel Gance, *L'énigme de dix heures* (The ten o'clock riddle). Its success helped Sydney secure an even more important role.

In *Ultus, The Man from the Dead* (1915) Morris Morgan is left for dead without food or water in the Australian outback by his deceitful prospecting partner Gilbert Townsend, who returns wealthy to England. After finding him years later, Morris seeks justice and revenge. With the help of an odd gang of criminals, Ultus (as Morris calls himself) goes about the systematic ruination of the man who abandoned him in the desert. Ultus is pursued by the redoubtable private detective Conway Bass, but neither Townsend nor Bass is a match for the daring hero obsessed with vengeance. It was a thrilling story and enjoyed huge success worldwide. It also brought fame to Aurèle Sydney, the tall Australian who played Ultus. Despite his broad acting style and melodramatic emotions, Sydney had a strong screen presence that made him irresistible. He was so successful that six more Ultus installments were released between 1916 and 1917, all of which explored the elaborate revenge that falls upon the dastardly ex-partner Townsend.[50] Director George Pearson was so delighted with *Ultus* that he purchased another studio with better equipment and sturdier scenery. According to studio publicity, new sets were needed because Sydney was "such a he-man that when he came through a door and closed it, either the handle or the door tended to come away in his hand." Sydney briefly became the highest paid actor in British cinema, and his screen appearance was magnetizing. He had the physique of Hercules with a generous head of hair, an aquiline nose, and a bold persona that confronted every danger with strength, agility, and self-confidence.[51] Sydney's character in *Ultus* represented a slight variation on the good giant persona since he was seeking retribution not for downtrodden peasants, widows, or orphans but for personal reasons. There was never any question that his actions were just, but there was a slightly dangerous and hostile edge to his character that set him apart from other muscular do-gooders. The all-too-human desire for just punishment for those who had wronged him made Sydney's character more unusual, believable, and endearing.

There was no one quite like him (except Maciste) on the world stage. Thus, when Cines studio of Rome nabbed him after his British triumphs, it was a coup for Italian cinema. "The English Maciste" made a series of *racconti straordinari* (extraordinary tales), most notably *L'incubo, il drama di una stirpe* (The nightmare, a drama of race), and *Il gioiello di Khama* (The jewel of Khama). Sydney ended his career in Madrid making warmed-over versions of previous movies. While planning several more projects, he died on May 22, 1920. So convincing were Sydney's portrayals of reality that he became one of the most popular athletic stars of the early twentieth century.

Giovanni Raicevich

It is hard to imagine a less likely figure to emerge as a paragon of physical beauty and manly strength, but Giovanni Raicevich was one such star. He was one of the first professional athletes tapped by Italian producers to become the next Maciste. Unfortunately, by the time he appeared in movies, he was too overweight and elderly to be a matinée idol, but he had instant name recognition and was undeniably strong. Like most strongman stars of the 1920s, Raicevich grew up in a working-class home. He was born on June 10, 1881, in the Austro-Hungarian port of Trieste. Raicevich was a mixture of cultures: his father was a seaman from the Croatian island of Lastovo, and his mother was Italian, from the Veneto region. Giovanni developed a love of sport growing up while swimming with friends in the Adriatic Sea. As one biographer notes, "The first contests in the water developed in him the passion for competition—a passion that was encouraged by the fact that he was almost always victorious over the others."[52] He and his elder brothers Emilio and Massimo also became interested in muscle building and wrestling, so they joined the prestigious Società Ginnastica Triestina, where they learned the basics of physical culture. By age seventeen Giovanni's wrestling talents led him to Vienna, where he became the Austrian amateur wrestling champion. When the Milanese professional wrestler Alfredo Palazzoli boastfully challenged Raicevich to a wrestling match, he was almost instantly pinned which convinced the young powerhouse Raicevich that his talents in the arena might be a good way to make a living.[53] At his first match in 1900 in Hamburg, he cut a handsome figure, slim and muscular with a pleasing face and full Hapsburgian lips. His beauty did not go unnoticed by women who saw him perform. In 1901 at the Folies Bergères in Paris he defeated a huge Turkish wrestler. While the crowd applauded wildly, a beautiful woman entered the stage, threw her arms around the startled Raicevich's neck, and began kissing him on both cheeks. This was the famous *grande horizontale* La Belle Otéro, who was fond of muscular young men.[54]

Other victories followed as Raicevich wrestled in various venues of prewar Europe and the Americas. In 1909 he became a major sports figure by winning the world championship in Milan, then wrestling before thousands of spectators at New York's Madison Square Garden. In 1912 Raicevich even fought an inconclusive match with renowned American grappler Frank Gotch.[55] His service in the Italian Army in World War I and affliction with the Spanish flu in its aftermath ended his international competitions and caused him to realize that strength was a temporary gift. He needed to find another means of livelihood.

In 1911 Raicevich demonstrated some of his movements and holds in a short feature, *La lotta e i lottatori* (Wrestling and wrestlers) from Ambrosio Film in Turin.[56] It was not an ambitious project, but it introduced him to the moviegoing public. His next film, *Il leone mansueto* (The timid lion, 1919), was part of the good giant series popularized by Maciste. The story line relates how perpetrators of injustice discover that "once provoked, the strong and courageous 'timid lion' responds with a blow from his terrible paw."[57] Public familiarity with the star's athletic career guaranteed the film's success. Publicity posters presented Raicevich's name in huge red letters as "The World Champion of Greco-Roman Wrestling." The film also showed producers that Maciste had no monopoly on good giant roles. One canny movie man, Gustavo Lombardo, lured Raicevich to his studios in Naples to make films full of ingenious gags, amusing intertitles, and special effects. He also contrasted the characters played by Raicevich with villains played by stars who were recognized as romantic or elegant leads. The surprise of seeing normally sophisticated lovers playing against character added to his films' appeal.[58]

Lombardo's ideas made Raicevich a star, and they went on to produce six films together. In the first, *Il re della forza* (The king of strength, 1920) he struggles to defeat Turkus, the African giant. After a series of adventures, the hero saves the life of Prince Alessio and rescues his mother from kidnappers. The film was full of action and stunts displaying the athlete's muscularity and strength. He variously escapes being crushed by boulders, avoids strangulation by a noose thrown over his head, and rights a cart filled with sacks of flour. The great man's three-word motto—strength, chivalry, and generosity—is ever present.[59] The film also displayed Raicevich as a man of the people, suggesting that some of his actions might alienate bourgeois sensibilities. But peasant and working-class audiences would enjoy seeing Raicevich going to extremes in appearance and behavior. There was no attempt to disguise his obesity, which became a mark of honor. His eating habits were even a source of mirth, as Raicevich became a prodigy of oversized appetites. Maciste had occasionally been filmed consuming huge quantities of food, but, as one reviewer noted, it was nothing compared to the Triestino's gustatory feats: "We are shown Raicevich digging into a mountain of spaghetti; here we have him picking clean an entire goat carcass with his teeth. We cannot envision any of these [cinematic] giants as anything other than gluttons."[60] Intertitles ironically describe "A little plate of beans" and "A bit of meat" while intercutting shots of a huge meal.

Despite the distaste expressed by highbrow critics, audiences enjoyed seeing their hero indulging in Pantagruelian feats. It exemplified his superhuman quality, but it was also part of Raicevich's often self-deprecatory sense of humor. In *Il re della forza* he boasts that he can stop a tram with a single hand. When observers register incredulity, the strongman demonstrates his power by raising his hand and hailing the next tram to a stop. Humor, adventure, and justice are combined in the final scene where Raicevich is locked in a ship's hold by villains who set the vessel afire. When the malefactors organize a magnificent banquet to celebrate their victory, they are surprised by the sudden entrance of the supposedly entrapped hero. He confronts the evildoers, knocks them out, and tosses them out the window, where police collect them in a large life net. The final scene shows the chastened malefactors staring at the audience behind bars; society has been saved by physical violence administered by the good giant.

Raicevich's most famous film, *L'uomo della foresta* (The man of the forest, 1922), was inspired by Edgar Rice Burrough's great adventure story *Tarzan of the Apes*, and his costume was based on the one Elmo Lincoln made famous in the American version. Raicevich appears in a wig and headband along with a capacious leopard skin covering his midsection but exposing one of his pendulous pectorals. The plot features Princess Issiè, whose rightful place has been stolen by an evil minister named Ike. After a series of adventures, she meets Buono, the gentle jungle giant. In the film's most famous scene he is tortured in the arena by having his arms and legs tied to two vicious bulls who charge in opposite directions. Buono unleashes his tremendous power to resist their pull.

Despite its clunky plot and improbable hero, *L'uomo della foresta* was a huge success. Accounts in *La rivista cinematografica* reported that even in relatively large cities like Florence and Bari, the Carabinieri had to be summoned to preserve order as massive waves of spectators attempted to enter the cinemas. Audiences of both genders could not get enough of the kindly but corpulent strongman. The triumph of *L'uomo della foresta* was followed by two moderate successes with the star making forty-five thousand lire a month—at a time when one thousand lire was considered a good monthly salary.[61] When his contract expired in 1922, Raicevich and his brothers established their own studio in Rome. Little is known about its first production, *Il trionfo di Ercole* (The triumph of Hercules, 1922), since the film has been lost, but a surviving photo shows Raicevich posing as the Farnese Hercules, though wearing a fig leaf. Unfortunately, the forty-one-year-old actor did not fit the role since his unsculpted body and general flabbiness made him more a figure of ridicule than respect or beauty. That it was a flop, along with his next two independent productions, must have been a shock.[62] By 1923 the once golden strongman's film career, artistic reputation, and fortune were in shreds. His cinematic adventure had lasted just four years, and he was forced to return to wrestling to recoup money lost in movie production. At least his sporting reputation was intact. Raicevich retired from the arena in 1930 and, owing to ties with Fascist Party officials, he became president of the Federazione di atletica pesante (weightlifting federation), which oversaw the sports of wrestling, weightlifting, and judo. He had survived the war and Spanish flu, but in 1957 he succumbed to an Asiatic form of the disease.

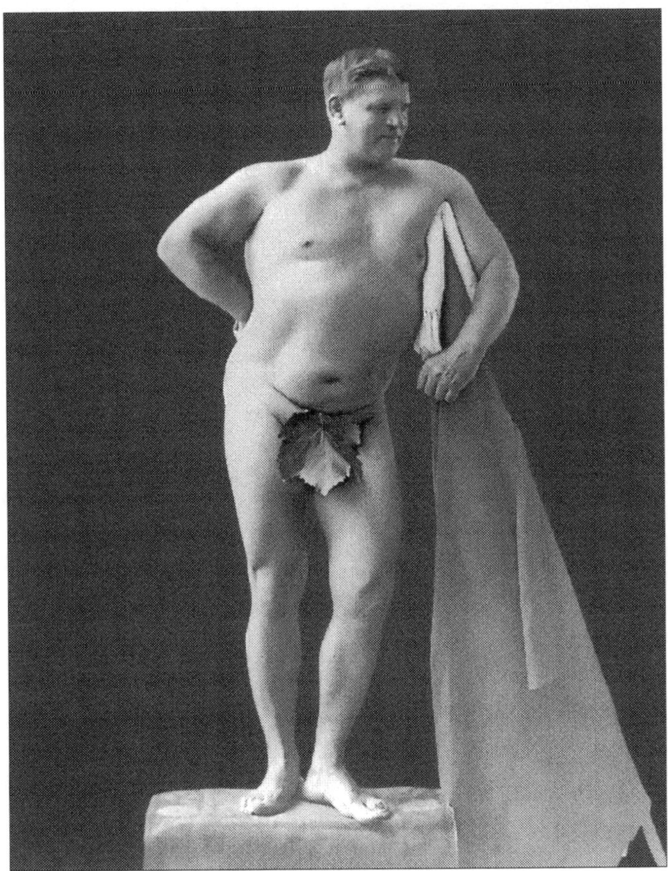

Figure 5.2. Italian wrestler Giovanni Raicevich made this production still for his 1922 film *Il trionfo di Ercole*. Clearly the star was not a slave to conventional canons of male beauty. Collection of David L. Chapman.

By the end of the silent era, the good giants were declining in popularity. Many films featuring *forzuti* between 1914 and 1929 were forgotten in succeeding decades. It was a series that started in Italy but continued with varied success in many countries. Not everyone was as happy with them as the audiences. When Raicevich's *Il leone mansueto* appeared in 1919, critics viewed it with distaste. G. C. Albonetti blamed it on Maciste. "Yes, let us admit it frankly," he complained, "Itala Film delivered a fatal blow to commercial cinema the day they had the deplorable idea to show Maciste's fulsome physique on the silver screen. Because from that day onward there began a real mad rush to look for other men of Herculean stature." It meant that stars like Albertini, Aldini, Raicevich, and Saetta all received exposure in the "limelight of fame." Albonetti could not understand the tastelessness and repetitive plots of their films and was convinced that Raicevich was no better than others. He lamented that *Il leone mansueto* followed the usual derivative formula: "It is an entire film based on chases, abductions and assaults with fists and boots; to our eyes it is just the same old meal that has been heated and reheated too often. We are sick and tired of it!"[63] Albonetti had not learned the golden rule of popular entertainment: if something is successful, repeat it until audiences tire of it, then move on to the next big production. He was unaware that the fad for strong, athletic heroes was fated to continue for another decade before the genre exhausted itself in a welter of unrealistic situations, ridiculous characters, and repetitive plots.

Notes

1. *La vita cinematografica*, December 1918, quoted in Claudio Bertieri, "Dal mito degli Alcidi al cinema verità," in *Coroginnica: Saggi sulla ginnastica, lo sport e la cultura del corpo 1861–1991*, ed. Adolfo Noto and Lauro Rossi (Rome: La Meridiana, 1992), 261.

2. Camillo Bruto Bonzi, "Luciano Albertini (Sansonia)," *La vita cinematografica*, December 1918, in *Gli uomini forti*, ed. Alberto Farassino and Tatti Sanguineti, 166.

3. Bonzi, "Luciano Albertini (Sansonia)," in Farassino and Sanguineti, eds., *Gli uomini forti*, 168. Several sources list the great early drama *Assunta Spina* (1915) as Luciano's first film, but that is inaccurate; it was Alberto Albertini who appeared in that film.

4. *Sansone contro i Filistei, Dramma di strepitose avventure moderne*, advertising pamphlet, Fondazione Maria Adriana Prolo, Museo Nazionale del Cinema, Turin, Italy.

5. Bertoldo, review of *Sansone contro i Filistei, La vita cinematografica*, December 15, 1918, in Farassino and Sanguineti, eds., *Gli uomini forti*, 121.

6. "Strong Man Film Actor," *Fielding (New Zealand) Star*, December 11, 1918.

7. Giuseppe Lega, review of *Il re dell'abisso, Apollon*, June 20, 1919, in Farassino and Sanguineti, eds., *Gli uomini forti*, 125.

8. Farfarello, review of *Il protetto della morte, La vita cinematografica*, March 22, 1920, in Farassino and Sanguineti, eds., *Gli uomini forti*, 125. For the Gorge of Mondrone account, see Mario Quargnolo, *Luciano Albertini: Un divo degli anni "venti,"* 9.

9. Mak, review of *Sansone e la ladra d'atleti, La rivista cinematografica*, August 10, 1921, in Farassino and Sanguineti, eds., *Gli uomini forti*, 125–26; anonymous review of *Sansone e la ladra d'atleti, La vita cinematografica*, September 22, 1919, in Farassino and Sanguineti, eds., *Gli uomini forti*, 126.

10. "Sansonia in 'The Superman,'" *Motion Picture News*, November 15, 1919, 3607–8.

11. Anna Gorilowa, quoted in Quargnolo, *Luciano Albertini*, 10.

12. "Coast Brevities," *Film Daily*, December 2, 1923, 12.

13. Quargnolo, *Luciano Albertini*, 24–25; "Universal 'Baby Star' on Screen a Short Time," *Universal Weekly*, January 5, 1924, 23.

14. "Strong-Man Stuff," *Picture-Play*, March 1924, 100.

15. "Latin Star's Serial Stunts in a Class by Themselves," *Universal Weekly*, January 19, 1924, 16.

16. "Strong Men of the Movies," *Health and Life*, March 1924, 92–93.

17. Gorilowa, quoted in Quargnolo, *Luciano Albertini*, 25; Luciano Albertini, quoted in Quargnolo, *Luciano Albertini*, 12. Albertini regularly used two doubles; both were former acrobatic colleagues from his circus days.

18. Quargnolo, *Luciano Albertini*, 25. This unlikely sequence had been lifted from a 1916 Italian film directed by Alfred Lind, *Il circo della morte, ovvero l'ultima rappresentazione di gala del circo Wolfson* (The circus of death, or the last gala performance of the Wolfson Circus). In the earlier film the child is rescued by an acrobatic actress known as Miss Evelyn.

19. Vittorio Martinelli and Mario Quargnolo, *Maciste & Co.: I giganti buoni del muto italiano*, 14; Georg Herzberg, review of *Tempo! Tempo!*, *Film-Kurier*, 1929, in *Der Film der Weimarer Republik 1929: Ein Handbuch der zeitgenössischen Kritik*, ed. Gerhard Schoenberner, 663–64.

20. Bonzi, "Luciano Albertini (Sansonia)," 166.

21. Renato Lolli, quoted in Quargnolo, *Luciano Albertini*, 14.

22. Michele Giordano, *Giganti buoni: Da Ercole a Piedone (e oltre,) il mito dell'uomo forte nel cinema italiano*, 15.

23. Quargnolo, *Luciano Albertini*, 14.

24. Anonymous review of *Tetuan, il galeotto detective*, *La rivista di letture*, June 1925, in Farassino and Sanguineti, eds., *Gli uomini forti*, 137.

25. Vittorio Martinelli, "Maciste, le bon géant," Festival International du Film de la Rochelle, http://archives.festival-larochelle.org/festival-1994/maciste.

26. "Das endlose Celluloidband, von Cinemax," *Filmland Monatsschrift* 2 (December 1924): 86.

27. Hanns Horkheimer, review of *Abenteurer GmbH*, *Berliner Tageblatt*, 1929, in Schoenberner, ed., *Der Film der Weimarer Republik 1929*, 3; anonymous review of *Abenteurer GmbH*, *Kinematograph*, 1929, in Schoenberner, ed., *Der Film der Weimarer Republik 1929*, 4.

28. Martinelli and Quargnolo, *Maciste & Co.*, 18–19.

29. Corey Ross, "Cinema, Radio and 'Mass Culture' in the Weimar Republic: Between Shared Experience and Social Division," in *Weimar Culture Revisited*, ed. John Alexander Williams, 28–30; Christian Rogowski, *The Many Faces of Weimar Cinema: Rediscovering Germany's Filmic Legacy*, 3–4.

30. Anjeana K. Hans, *Gender and the Uncanny in the Films of the Weimar Republic* (Detroit: Wayne State University Press, 2014), 19–26; Robert Beachy, *Gay Berlin: Birthplace of a Modern Identity* (New York: Vintage, 2014), 167.

31. Camillo Bruto Bonzi, "Conversando con Domenico Gambino," *La vita cinematografica*, January 1921, in Farassino and Sanguineti, eds., *Gli uomini forti*, 173. Because of his short size and slight build, Gambino sometimes doubled for female cast members.

32. Bonzi, "Conversando con Domenico Gambino," 173.

33. Monica Dall'Asta, *Un cinéma musclé: Le surhomme dans le cinéma muet italien (1913–1926)*, 108.

34. Farfarello, unidentified review, *La vita cinematografica*, February 15, 1920, quoted in Dall'Asta, *Un cinéma musclé*, 108.

35. Martinelli and Quargnolo, *Maciste & Co.*, 33. Many daredevils swore they never used trickery or doubles (as did Albertini), but these protestations were rarely true.

36. Anonymous review of *Maciste imperatore*, *La rivista del cinematografo*, March 1929, in Farassino and Sanguineti, eds., *Gli uomini forti*, 143.

37. P. G. Merciai, review of *Maciste imperatore*, *La rivista cinematografica*, June 25, 1924, in Farassino and Sanguineti, eds., *Gli uomini forti*, 143.

38. Emilio Ghione, "Il fascio artistico torinese," *La conquista cinematografica*, October–November 1921, quoted in Gian Piero Brunetta, *Il cinema muto italiano*, 302.

39. Brunetta, *Il cinema muto italiano*, 302–3.

40. Gian Piero Brunetta, *Cent'anni di cinema italiano: Dalle origini alla seconda guerra mondiale*, 152.

41. *Illustrazione del popolo*, supplement to the *Gazzetta del popolo*, December 25, 1927.

42. Anonymous review of *Ich hab' mein Herz im Autobus verloren*, *Berliner illustrierte Nachtausgtabe*, 1929, in Schoenberner, ed., *Der Film der Weimarer Republik 1929*, 303.

43. Sergio Giuntini and Angela Teja, "Boccioni's Coin," in *Sport, Militarism and the Great War: Martial Manliness and Armageddon*, ed. Thierry Terret and J. A. Mangan (London: Routledge, 2012), 85.

44. V., review of *Galaor*, *La vita cinematografica*, July 7, 1918, in Farassino and Sanguineti, eds., *Gli uomini forti*, 120.

45. Bertoldo, review of *Lagrime di popolo*, *La vita cinematografica*, December 22, 1918, in Farassino and Sanguineti, eds., *Gli uomini forti*, 120.

46. *Films Pittaluga*, August 15, 1924, quoted in Chiara Giorgetti, "Galaor contro Galaor," *Enciclopedia del cinema in Piemonte*, http://www.torinocittadelcinema.it/sched afilm.php?film_id=1233&stile=small.

47. "Alfredo Boccolini," in Enrico Lancia, ed., *Dizionario del cinema italiano: Gli attori dal 1930 ai giorni nostri*, vol. 1 (Rome: Gremese, 2003), 78.

48. Martinelli and Quargnolo, *Maciste & Co.*, 24.

49. Blios, "Aurelio Sydney" *Film: Corriere dei cinematografi* 4, no. 36 (November 30, 1917): 8.

50. The episodes are *The Townsend Mystery* (1916), *The Ambassador's Diamond* (1916), *The Grey Lady* (1916), *The Traitor's Fate* (1916), *The Secret of the Night* (1917), and *The Three Button Mystery* (1917). Ken Wlaschin, *Silent Mystery and Detective Movies: A Comprehensive Filmography* (Jefferson, NC: McFarland, 2009), 229.

51. Andrew Marr, *The Making of Modern Britain: From Queen Victoria to VE Day* (London: Macmillan, 2009), 242; Martinelli and Quargnolo, *Maciste & Co.*, 47.

52. "La storia di Giovanni Raicevich," PiacenzAntica, http://www.piacenzantica.it/page.php?233.

53. Livio Toschi, "Giovanni Raicevich 'Il re della forza' nella vita e sui tappeti di lotta si batté per Trieste italiana," *Rassegna storica del risorgimento* 90, no. 1 (2003): 87–96.

54. "Giovanni in lotta con gli uomini e in pace con le donne," *Lo sport fascista*, February 2, 1937, cited in Toschi, "Giovanni Raicevich," 88. Otéro also once tried to arrange a tryst with Eugen Sandow; see David Chapman, *Sandow the Magnificent: Eugen Sandow and the Beginnings of Bodybuilding*, 51–53.

55. Dino Cafagna, *L'uomo più forte del mondo: La leggenda di Giovanni Raicevich da Trieste*, 71.

56. Carlo Gaberschek, "Il Friuli è un set antico," *Messaggero Veneto*, May 1, 2003, http://ricerca.gelocal.it/messaggeroveneto/archivio/messaggeroveneto/2003/05/01/NZ_11_SPEA2.html.

57. Cafagna, *L'uomo più forte del mondo*, 109.

58. Martinelli and Quargnolo, *Maciste & Co.*, 44.

59. Cafagna, *L'uomo più forte del mondo*, 113.

60. Diòniso, review of *Il re della forza*, *La vita cinematografica*, January 22, 1921, in Farassino and Sanguineti, eds., *Gli uomini forti*, 130. Maciste is shown eating enormous meals in many films, the most famous being *Maciste Alpino* (Alpine Maciste, 1916) where he eats the Austrian officer's dinner.

61. Martinelli and Quargnolo, *Maciste & Co.*, 45; Cafagna, *L'uomo più forte del mondo*, 120.

62. It is unclear why the film failed. Perhaps the production values were not high enough or the plot too uninteresting for their target audience. Unfortunately, the company's next production, *Un viaggio nell'impossible* (A trip to the impossible, 1923), also failed. The company folded while its third film, *Ercole al bivio* (Hercules at the crossroads) was in preproduction. Whatever the Raicevich brothers were selling, the public was not buying it. Cafagna, *L'uomo più forte del mondo*, 120–23.

63. G. C. Albonetti, review of *Il leone mansueto*, *La cine-fono*, February 26, 1920, in Farassino and Sanguineti, eds., *Gli uomini forti*, 124.

VI. DAREDEVILS, ACROBATS, AND ATHLETES

Show business is a world of make-believe whose very soul is publicity.

—Hedda Hopper, quoted in George Eells, *Hedda and Louella*

Harry Piel

DURING THE SILENT film era, Germany was the only country that seriously rivaled the American film industry. The quality and quantity of movies produced in Berlin was staggering. They included all genres, from musicals and light comedy to serious art, but some of the most popular films featured stunts, speed, and sportsmen. These *Sensationfilme* were churned out quickly because demand for them seemed endless. Actors like Luciano Albertini, Carlo Aldini, and Bartolomeo Pagano came north to cash in on this phenomenon, but the greatest star of this genre was German-born Harry Piel. Although he lacked acrobatic training, muscularity, and good looks, Piel had energy, charisma, and talent, all of which he employed to create a longer career and more acclaim than almost any other action film star. In the 1920s and 1930s he wrote, directed, and/or starred in over a hundred movies. Children sang about him in nursery rhymes, and he was a protagonist in pulp novels. His films played to huge audiences throughout Europe and even the Soviet Union where a 1920s survey found Piel was extremely popular with children. To the question "What has cinema taught you?" an alarming number of girls responded, "I would like to marry Harry Piel," and many boys said they wanted to *be* Harry Piel. "Harry Pielitis" was an imaginary ailment invented by a *Pravda* journalist who warned of the pernicious effects of fantasy and foreign films on the psyches of good little Bolsheviks.[1] Piel became known as the German Fairbanks.

Born in Düsseldorf on July 12, 1892, Piel was fascinated with acrobatics, lion taming, and performing, and at the age of sixteen ran off with a traveling circus. But his father, who was determined that he should become a middle-class burgher, brought Harry home for punishment. "I was a far too restless character to be able to be a businessman," Piel confirmed. "I remember precisely how upset my father got when he found out that I had just climbed down a downspout to the fourth floor of a house" because of a wager. "My father could not understand me. 'I am ashamed of you!' he said," then confined Harry to his room for eight weeks.[2] This punishment had little effect. After finishing school, Piel enrolled as a cadet in the German Navy, then left for Paris, hoping to learn acrobatics. Instead he met actor-director Léonce Perret, who introduced him to Gaumont and other film studios, where he learned how to write cinema scenarios. Convinced the new medium offered freedom, Piel decided on a movie career. On returning to Germany in 1912 he founded his own production company, Kunst Film Verlags Gesellschaft, and made *Schwarzes Blut* (Black blood). Although this venture failed, Piel became known as a filmmaker who worked efficiently.

Despite Germany's entry into World War I, Piel created numerous movies for foreign producers. His films were full of action, adventure, and danger, and were thus perfect vehicles to divert audiences from the real-life disasters confronting them. When the excitement level in his pictures flagged, Piel would usually blow something up. He soon acquired the reputation of "dynamite director." With the end of the war, Piel decided to star in one of his own potboilers, *Die grosse Unbekannte* (The great unknown, 1919). If moviegoers needed escapist entertainment before the war, they needed it even more after 1918. His movies featured simple, straightforward plots with easily identifiable heroes and villains as well as good girls and heartless vamps. Piel supplied excitement by using his athletic skills to beat the foe, deliver justice, or free helpless damsels. "For him no wall was too high, no river too deep, no airplane too rickety," writes one journalist. "He climbed, chased, ran, flew, and swam after his enemies and thrashed them thoroughly until in the end the last opponent was given a knockout blow and lay on the ground."[3] But there was more to his appeal than action; Piel captured the feelings of many postwar Germans who longed for a hero who would use strength, cunning, and courage to set things right. Soon they would discover what happens when countries allowed strongmen claiming to have all the answers to come to power.

Piel was not glamorous, but he seemed equally at home in jodhpurs and pith helmet as in elegant evening clothes with top hat and cape. Perhaps ordinariness was at the root of his appeal. He was a Middle-European everyman, but one who would fight gangsters and tame tigers, hang between the wheels of a speeding locomotive, and fight in the rigging of a swooping biplane. To make his appeal more universal, parents were assured that Piel would provide good, wholesome family entertainment.[4] Unfortunately, he was not the only star of the adventure films that were so popular worldwide. Americans had a firm hold on the largest action movie markets, with such superstars as Douglas Fairbanks and Tom Mix, and Europeans frequently sought others who could match the German actor feat-for-feat. Two of Piel's strongest rivals were Italians Luciano Albertini and Carlo Aldini. It is little wonder that studio publicity departments whipped up a great deal of ballyhoo. In 1921 Albertini's camp questioned Piel's sporting and athletic credentials. Piel reacted with disdainful coolness, emphasizing his artistry over brute strength:

It is currently customary, both in Germany and abroad, for film actors and directors to hire managers who were managers of professional wrestlers or prizefighters; even worse, it is common that film actors and directors maintain their reputations by challenging others to prove their superiority with cash prizes.

As far as I am concerned, audiences should appreciate my work as artistry, and thanks to the nature of my scripts, sensational actions should not be seen as purely artistic achievements, but they are specifically attuned to using my natural talents and abilities for the practice of sports of every kind.[5]

Shortly afterward Albertini went off to Hollywood to appear in his film serial *The Iron Man* (1924), and the field was open for Piel to continue working with one less challenger.

Unlike the Italian stars of *Sensationfilme*, Piel had no real athletic training, having not come up through the circus or music hall. Although he was fit and active, his gifts were natural, not cultivated. In an interview for *Mon ciné* Piel listed all the sports he played to attain mastery of his body: "I box, I swim, I do rowing, I practice horseback riding, I drive an automobile, ride motorcycles, and do tumbling, skiing and I don't know what else." He also enjoyed the excitement and challenge of being an actor, athlete, director, and producer. He asked only that "I can continue to do all this for as long as my physical strength allows me to."[6] Meanwhile, he was churning out one or two films yearly.

One of his best films at the Phoebus-Film studios was *Achtung Harry! Augen Auf!* (Watch out, Harry! Keep your eyes open!, 1926), in which Piel plays a reporter who infiltrates a gang of ruffians to expose their nefarious deeds. In the film's most exciting segment, Piel is tossed into a rat-infested sewer flowing into the harbor and has to escape and rescue the damsel from the villain's clutches before rising tidal waters drown him. Like most of Piel's early films, the main character is almost constantly in motion—jumping, running, fighting, or swimming. Piel's costume consists of a dark shirt that exposes much of his chest and a scarf tied closely around his muscular neck. His jaunty appearance matches his heroic character, and his costume allows him freedom to perform the many stunts that make this film enjoyable. Piel's next film had as much energy and movement as *Achtung Harry!* but it was done at Nero-Film, where he would have greater artistic freedom with his own production unit and a budget of 200,000 marks. Listed by his own name as the star, his first film, *Was ist los im Zirkus Beely?* (What's happening at the Beely Circus?, 1927) had lots of action, suspense, and intrigue. Among the numerous chases, dangers, and hairbreadth escapes is a scene where Piel flees from a tiger only to find himself in a room where the walls are closing in. One perilous escape follows another in quick succession until, by the end of the film, the audience is nearly as exhausted as the main character. The film received generally favorable reviews, with the critic from *Kinematograph* noting that he always found Piel's films "clever, daring and full of freshness."[7]

Piel continued churning out several films yearly. Audiences seemingly could not get enough of his action movies, and Piel made the transition to talkies with little difficulty. His first sound film *Er oder Ich* (Him or me, 1930) was a brilliant success. Piel, playing a double role as prince and petty criminal, seemed a natural for sound. His films continuously attracted moviegoers, without a single dud. In 1933 Piel joined the Nazi Party and became a patron member of the Schutzstaffel, or SS, meaning he remitted a monthly fee.[8] Piel would later pay dearly for his connections to National Socialism. Even before World War II ended, he experienced difficulties. In 1940 his film *Panik* was shut down by German censors. The movie tells the story of a trapper who captures animals for his country's zoos. In its final sequence, an air raid frees the animals. They run around terrifying the citizenry until Piel recaptures them and forces them back into confinement. Nazi film reviewers were horrified that German citizens might believe the fatherland could ever be bombed. By the end of the war, Piel was ruined morally and financially. When Berlin was about to be taken by the Red Army, Piel headed to Hamburg. In November 1945, however, he was arrested by British authorities for his Nazi affiliation. He was sentenced to six months in prison and

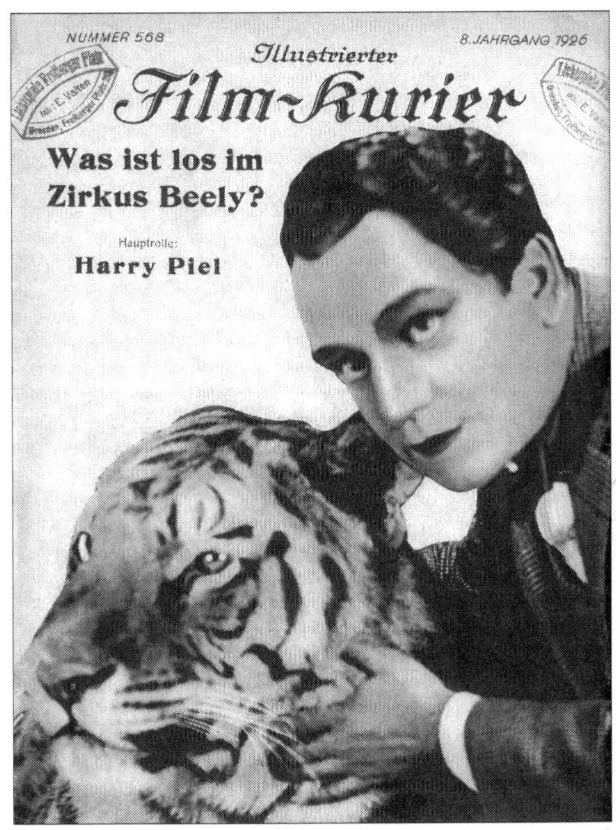

Figure 6.1. German star of action films Harry Piel was perhaps the most popular German star of the 1920s and 1930s. Here he poses with one of his costars in the 1926 hit *Was ist los im Zirkus Beely?* Collection of David L. Chapman.

banned from moviemaking for five years.[9] Although Piel continued making films through a company he founded in the 1950s, the public was no longer enamored of his *Sensationfilme*. Old, tired, and disillusioned, he was unable to navigate a new world of ambiguous heroes, more sophisticated plots, and earthier love stories. A broken man, the once wealthy and famous actor died virtually forgotten and penniless in Munich on March 27, 1963.

Harry Piel was heralded in newspapers as the German Fairbanks or the Rhineland Tarzan, but it hardly accounts for his popularity and longevity. He was neither an acrobat, a stuntman, nor a classically trained actor, but he knew how to tap the hopes and fears of largely working-class audiences. Unlike other athletic stars like Douglas Fairbanks or Rudolph Valentino, Piel did not have a sculpted physique, yet he made his mark as a great athlete of German cinema.[10] He was able to bound around the screen in a graceful series of leaps, vaults, and tumbles and could display a fearless attitude toward wild beasts. His movements on the screen are closer to those of Buster Keaton or Harold Lloyd, but both of those American stars had built personas that avoided conventional heroism. Piel, on the other hand, thrived on rescues, confrontations, and battles that showed his bravery and sense of justice. In this regard he was a more "European" star, resembling Albertini, Aldini, and Pagano's Maciste than any American rival. Piel was an ordinary man who used his gifts of strength and courage to reward virtue and punish vice. He was the strongman who sees injustice, uses his power and audacity to right perceived wrongs against Aryan society—a perfect National Socialist hero. His great energy was also evident in his desire to retain control over his persona and filmmaking. He was often the producer, director, writer, and principal actor. Piel made about 110 films over forty years—showing that he had his fingers firmly on the pulse of his audience.

German Boxers

While the films of Jim Corbett and Jack Johnson had thrilled and entertained American audiences, many Germans had also fallen in love with boxing pictures, and quite a few of them were made between the wars. Unlike earlier filmed matches, these were narrative movies; thus, the stories could be fictional, but the boxers were real. This fascination with pugilism stemmed from a renewed interest in physical culture, a desire to reclaim a toughness and manhood supposedly lost in the Great War, a wish to show German nationalism, and a new openness about appreciation of the male body. As one historian explains this obsession with boxing, "Sports stood at the intersection of nationalism, popular culture, and self-development, functioning as a discursive metaphor on many levels."[11] The Nazis certainly recognized boxing as a virile and aggressive activity; one party member questioned the masculinity of those who did not approve of the sweet science, calling them "Sofaliebhaber und Blümchenflücker" (sofa lovers and flower pickers).[12]

Prizefighter Hans Breitensträter could never be accused of flower picking, and in 1921 he was one of the first German boxers to be featured in the movies. He is one of the main characters in the film *Der Held des Tages* (The hero of the day), in which he engages in a series of brutal slugfests. Like many other German boxers, Breitensträter became popular with the public, especially with those who appreciated his fair-haired good looks and tight, muscular physique. As he must have discovered, the attributes of many fighters could be displayed to great effect in movies, and few pugilists were shy about displaying them. Many in Weimar Germany were obsessed with fitness, health, muscularity, and nudism, and a few athletes figured out that they could increase their reputations and gather huge armies of fans by showing a bit of skin. As historian Erik Jensen has noted, "Boxers were positively entrepreneurial in the commodification of their own well-trained bodies."[13] Breitensträter had the benefit of being a perfect example of an Aryan superman; in addition to being muscular, he was an aggressive fighter and was much admired for his lovely golden locks (Der Blonde Hans being one of his nicknames).

By far the most famous boxer to star in German films was the champion heavyweight Max Schmeling. Much has been written about this powerful fighter, who became world champion in 1930–32 and in 1936 defeated the Brown Bomber, Joe Louis in a legendary bout, only to be defeated by Louis two years later. In 1930 Schmeling starred in *Liebe im Ring* (Love in the ring), in which he plays the son of a fruit seller who also happens to be a talented boxer. He and his girlfriend, a fishmonger's daughter, visit a variety show, where he wins an amateur boxing match; afterward he turns professional. As he rises in the sport, he is tempted to jettison his former sweetheart and live the high life with a beautiful lady of easy virtue. In the end he sees the falsehood of the glamorous life and returns to his humble girlfriend's arms. The story is about boxing, but the real match is between the two women—one a superficial and destructive vixen and the other an honest and loving working-class girl. Boxing thus becomes a metaphor for German urban life in the early 1930s. The film was sufficiently successful and Schmeling was such a popular figure that he made another film in 1934, *Knock-Out: Ein junges Mädchen, ein junger Mann* (Knock out: A young girl, a young man). This time Schmeling is a stagehand at a theater, and when one of the girls (played by his real-life wife, Anny Ondra) is attacked by a masher, Schmeling thrashes him. In doing so he impresses a boxing impresario who immediately agrees to send him to a boxing school to learn the sport's finer points. After many misadventures and mistaken assumptions, Schmeling's character becomes a great star, and the lovers end up together.

Thanks to his successful career in the ring and his popular portrayals in movies, Schmeling became something of a superstar. He and his beautiful actress-wife, Anny Ondra, became one of the most famous power couples of the time, and the two were often welcome in the most sophisticated salons of 1930s Berlin. Boxing films were popular in interwar Germany for numerous reasons. The sport not only celebrated toughness, aggression, and strength but it also came at a time of greater body consciousness.[14] German magazines seemed to fall all over themselves to present nude or seminude photos of popular fighters; this eroticization of the male body came at a time when the country needed to reconstruct the psyches of men who were affected by their defeat in the recent war. Men wanted to be like these tough pugs, and women wanted to possess them. One article described the reactions of women who attended boxing matches in sensual and erotic terms: "excited to the tips of their fingers, lustful, inflamed for the slender one or the blond or the strong one. They are entirely absorbed and never take an eye off the fighters."[15] A similar level of attention must have been present when they saw their favorites in the cinema. During both the silent and the talkie periods, there were "countless pulp stories and films" that featured boxing as a major plot element. Boxing films were suddenly everywhere; among them were Buster Keaton's comedy *Battling Butler* in 1926 and handsome French boxer Georges Carpentier's Warner Brothers musical *Hold Everything* (1930). Even Alfred Hitchcock featured a boxer, Carl Brisson, who had fought earlier in Germany, in his 1927 film *The Ring*. It could not have hurt movie attendance when bare-chested boxers bobbed and weaved on the screens of German cinemas when we consider that Berlin was also the center of a vibrant gay subculture.[16] It is no small wonder that muscular physiques came into their own (at least in movies). Not all male sex idols were former pugilists, however; some were drawn from the world of the circus.

Eddie Polo

By all accounts Eddie Polo was a difficult man—stubborn, opinionated, uncooperative, and confrontational. During his heyday he was also one of Universal Studios' most popular stars. His appeal was international, with fans during the late 1910s and 1920s eagerly awaiting each film and serial. "Eddie Polo is a name to conjure with in Madras," wrote an Indian film critic. "One has only to mention his name to his devotees to hear him acclaimed as their idol."[17] This passion for a stocky former circus acrobat turned actor was echoed all over the world—at least for a time.

Some sources say that Polo was born in Vienna; others say Los Angeles. But according to his own (admittedly unreliable) account, he was born in "the desert in the northern part of California" on February 1, 1875.[18] Not even his name is certain. He was born Edward Wyman or Weimer, but all that this conflicting information shows is that none of it is entirely reliable. Polo was one of six children of a circus family that frequently toured Europe and North America. Although he played fast and loose with facts in his autobiography, one thing seems clear: Polo's early years were difficult. If we are to believe his account, around 1880 the future actor and his four sisters, brother, mother, and father all traveled back to Europe where Polo & Family performed as acrobats and tumblers. After Polo's father was injured in a fall, he "distributed his family among a number of other shows," and at age six he was apprenticed to Henry Wolf, the owner of a small circus, from whom he learned acrobatic and gymnastic skills. After five years with Wolf, Polo ran away, eventually ending up back in America. In New York he performed with various circuses, later joining the Ringling Brothers Circus for seventeen years. Along with his brother Sam, he devised a well-received trapeze act called the Flying Cordovas. Due to his familiarity with the big top, Polo's films repeatedly adopted circus themes. Along with his acrobatic skill, he exhibited a fine physique while performing athletic stunts. He was five foot nine and weighed 175 pounds of mostly solid muscle.[19] With well-developed shoulders and the bulging biceps of a gymnast, it was Polo's eye-catching body that set him apart from other knockabout action stars. He looked the part of a circus acrobat or a hardworking cowboy. He enjoyed displaying his muscular body; his shirt was torn off frequently, and his circus tights left little to the imagination.

After tiring of an acrobat and vaudeville performer's life, Polo, with a wife and child, needed a steadier and less demanding means of making a living. In 1913, at age thirty-eight, he approached Chicago-based Essanay Studios about movie work. He began with bit parts and then turned to stunts to augment his meager salary, mostly in the *Slippery Slim* series of comedies. The next year he switched to Universal Studios, where he did stunt work until he was discovered by the team of actor-director Francis Ford and leading lady Grace Cunard, who were considered masters of early serial films.[20] Polo's big break came when Ford and Cunard witnessed his acrobatic expertise. They soon arranged for a part to be written into their upcoming film serial *The Broken Coin* (1915). As soon as the first episodes appeared and fans saw Polo, they responded by writing letters praising him. The resulting boost to his ego caused the first of many confrontations with Ford and Cunard.[21] As with his other productions, Polo made for a photogenic presence, often revealing his superb musculature. His raw physicality and graceful movements endeared him to fans more than his acting. Much to the surprise and displeasure of company members, Polo acquired a fan base that made him too popular to ignore.

Bowing to public demand, Universal offered him some starring roles. In 1918 Polo appeared in *Bull's Eye*, an eighteen-episode oater that perfectly suited his athleticism. The advertising copy went into overdrive, and he acquired the sobriquet Hercules of the Films, thus placing even more emphasis on his strength and muscular physique. Audiences were promised "sensational stunts that have never yet been shown on any screen" and "unbelievable thrills that defy all precepts of human nerve and daring!"[22] It was a typical Polo story: long on action but meager on plot. But his viewers were rarely put off by flimsy story lines; they were there to see amazing stunts and were seldom disappointed. In the days before sophisticated special effects or rear projection, actors performed stunts the old-fashioned way—simply doing them while the camera cranked away. Polo claims he did not use stuntmen, and most authorities believe him. A *Motography* reporter was impressed by the actor's acrobatics in *Bull's Eye*: "With one end of a lariat looped around the top of a tall tree and the other grasped firmly in his hands, Eddie Polo made a running jump from the top of an eight-foot cliff, circled at nearly horizontal angle through the air and came to earth in a clump of underbrush. Hemmed in at the brink of a cliff by a band of outlaws who were determined to capture him, 'Reckless' Polo took this novel way of escaping from them."[23] Audiences kept coming back to see more daring feats and the actor's physique.

Universal Studios realized it had a tiger by the tail with Polo's egotistical personality and impression on female audiences. As early as November 1917 the public was clamoring for his photos, but the rising star had none "glamorous" enough for fan magazines.[24] In February 1918 the first major article devoted to Polo appeared in *Motion Picture* magazine. It underscores his suavity, strength, courage, and manly beauty. Clearly the publicity department was trying to turn him into a sort of Latin lover, but one who was hearty and brave—100 percent man, with the physique to match. In the article Polo reviewed his career as a circus acrobat, gymnastics instructor, and boxing coach and recounted the time he circled the Eiffel Tower in an airplane and then parachuted a thousand feet. Seemingly the main point was to showcase his magnificent physique. Indeed, the largest illustration was a photo montage of Polo's costar in *The Gray Ghost* (1917), Priscilla Dean, smiling lasciviously at an artfully arranged vignette photo of Polo's bare upper body.[25] The Hercules of the Films was flying high and fast.

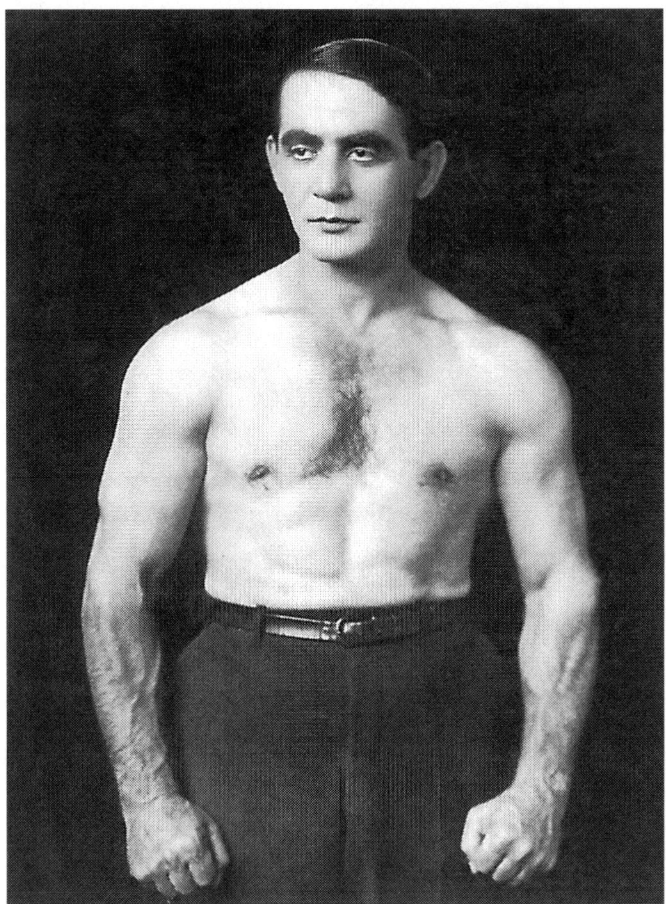

Figure 6.2. Eddie Polo's star burned brightly for a while in the 1920s but rapidly fizzled later in life. He is pictured here around 1920, at the height of his strength, prowess, and fame. Collection of David L. Chapman.

Lure of the Circus (1918) promised to be the actor's greatest work to date. Like other serial films, it is a web of action, mystery, and violence draped over a confusing plot. It combines skullduggery at the circus as well as violence on newly discovered oil fields in Southern California. The film, purporting to display Polo at his heroic and acrobatic best, shows why he was beloved by female and youthful male fans.[26] There is much violence but little logic, and thanks to the many scrapes into which the star throws himself, his shirt is continually being ripped off his muscular deltoids. In 1919 Polo convinced producer Carl Laemmle that he would be a perfect star in more prestigious feature films rather than an endless run of serials. The resulting productions showcased Polo as cowboy Cyclone Smith, but the plots consisted of the same sort of escapes, rescues, and heroism that characterized his serials. Nevertheless, these action-packed horse operas were extremely successful: between 1919 and 1921 Polo made four Cyclone Smith films.[27] After the cowboy films, Polo took advantage of the armistice and sailed to newly pacified Europe, where he was always popular, to do publicity appearances and make *The Vanishing Dagger* (1920). He also appeared in *King of the Circus* (1920), another vehicle in which Polo displayed his acrobatic skills and shapely physique in trapeze artist tights. But Polo was rubbing his employer and fellow players the wrong way. As cinema historian Anthony Slide explains, "as Polo became more popular with filmgoers, he became less popular with the people he was working with; he became conceited and pompous."[28]

The year 1922 marked a dramatic change in Polo's career. Universal's new studio manager, Julius Stern, did not appreciate Polo's demands and overinflated ego and, as one historian verifies, the feeling was mutual: "Eddie just had no use for him."[29] Polo quit abruptly and, with the profits he had earned over five years, started his own company with plans to produce a lavish serial based on the pirate Captain Kidd. The company traveled to Florida and Cuba to film on location, and Polo poured massive amounts of money into the project, but *Captain Kidd* (1922) was a box office flop. After this debacle, Polo's once-brilliant Hollywood career was effectively over.[30] In Europe, where his popularity was still intact, Polo found work and appreciation. Between 1922 and 1932 the onetime serial protagonist appeared in nearly twenty films, sometimes as star. Most of them were quickly made, ephemeral B movies, but they kept Polo (now in his fifties) visible to the public and made enough money to sustain him and his producers.

Perhaps for this reason Polo's old boss at Universal, Carl Laemmle, gave him another chance in 1929. Laemmle drafted a young journalist, Billy Wilder, to write a film starring Polo that his nephew, Ernst Laemmle, would direct. *Der Teufelsreporter: Im Nebel der Grossstadt* (*A hell of a reporter*, or *The daredevil reporter: In the fog of the big city*) resulted in Wilder's first screen credit. It is an amusing story filled with stunts designed for Polo. But Wilder, destined for cinematic immortality as a director, hated the film. "Oh, it was bullshit, absolute bullshit," he insisted. He added with sarcastic exaggeration, "The leading man was an old Hungarian-American cowboy actor by the name of Eddie Polo, and he was already by that time, seventy-five."[31]

When biographer Charlotte Chandler asked him about *Der Teufelsreporter*, Wilder became furious: "You people don't do us any favors by finding this crap. You should bury it!"[32] Most modern sources accept Wilder's judgment that the film was a disaster, but to those who saw it (in 1929 and the years following), it was not nearly as bad; some even perceived sparks of genius. It contains some remarkable acrobatics, amusing gags, and real excitement. According to Kevin Brownlow, the film has "the most amazing stunt I've ever seen in films." With a group of thirteen girls in his charge, Polo gets to the top of a tall building in Berlin. The girls stand on each other's shoulders until they are as high as the building, then Polo uses them as a ladder to climb up and gain access.[33]

Contemporary German critics were more impressed with Polo's physical abilities than his acting, but they were generally pleased with the movie. "Eddie Polo brings physical dexterity to the role by performing some good stunts, but his acting is not all that it should be," wrote a *Berliner Morgenpost* reviewer. In the *Frankfurter Zeitung* Siegfried Kracauer admits that "the fable is somewhat simplistic, but what it lacks in complexity is more than offset by its pace. Eddie rushes about, jumps, drives, climbs and telephones," revealing "a marvelous physical dexterity." Polo's athleticism as well as his "boyish amiability" reminded Kracauer of Harry Piel.[34] Clearly it was not the disaster Wilder complained about, nor was Polo the broken-down has-been who ruined the film. It's possible that Wilder's opinion was tainted by some personal animus between him and Polo. According to historian Gene Phillips, Wilder nursed a grudge against the action star because he had seduced Wilder's girlfriend, so he wanted to expunge both Polo and the picture from memory.[35] Despite the behind-the-scenes drama, many viewers appreciated the film. If nothing else, it shows that even at the end of his career, Polo could display flashes of the skill, strength, and charisma that made him an audience favorite.

Polo remained in Europe until about 1933, by which time the vogue for *Sensationfilme* had passed. When he returned to Hollywood, he only received bit roles and uncredited walk-on parts from the 1940s to the 1950s. Unable to reclaim his former glory, Polo now embodied the washed-up movie star: "Disgusted, disgruntled and mumbling about a conspiracy, he let it be known that he was dropping out of the motion picture business for good."[36] In an odd twist of fate, Polo's name got into the newspapers, but not in a flattering way. An acrobat and trapeze artist adopted the name Eddie Polo and went around the Midwest and South in the late 1940s staging "thrill shows." The impostor performed a truly dramatic stunt: he had himself hoisted up the side of a building, hanging by his hair, and did a "slide for life" down a cable until reaching the ground, attached only by his ample tresses. Fox Movietone News and *Life* magazine even photographed him performing this dangerous feat. Unfortunately, the stunt eventually went wrong, and he fell to his death. Afterward many newspaper obituaries appeared until the real Eddie Polo stepped forward to prove he was still alive. He would meet his real death twenty years later from a heart attack in Hollywood on June 14, 1961.[37]

Everything Is at Stake

In 1932 Luciano Albertini, the great star of Italian adventure films and darling of German fans of *Sensationfilme*, appeared in his final movie, *Es geht um alles* (Everything is at stake), an appropriate title for a work drawing the era of the athletic/acrobatic stars to a close. The genre had begun two decades earlier in Italy, but it continued to thrill and entertain audiences, particularly in central Europe. At first these films usually involved frantic chases, with a clear villain and even clearer hero who would right wrongs and mete out justice with fists and fury. The protagonists were mostly fine physical specimens with broad shoulders, muscular arms, narrow waists, and amazing athletic skills. By the 1930s the genre had run its course; only Harry Piel managed to keep it fresh enough to attract audiences. Another problem was that many *Sensationfilme* stars were foreigners whose mastery of German was often lacking. The arrival of talkies in the late 1920s spelled the end of many careers. The political situation was also heating up in Germany. With the rise to power of the Nazis, many foreign artists felt uncomfortable staying in the fatherland. In 1932 Albertini turned fifty years old—a bit long in the tooth for performing daredevil stunts, so he must have known he either had to retire or move in another artistic direction. In that year he made *Es geht um alles*; it was Albertini's first talkie, but it would be his last work in front of the camera.

Albertini plays the vaudeville magician Handy Bandy, who appears nightly at the prestigious Wintergarten theater in Berlin. He cuts a ridiculous appearance as a tired-looking middle-aged man in pseudo-Egyptian garb, assisted by two equally silly partners, Frank and Eddy (played by Domenico Saetta Gambino and Eddie Polo). The constant chases, reversals, and hairbreadth escapes place this production in the genre of *Sensationfilme*, but the comedy (perhaps inadvertent self-parody) puts it into another category. It is a swan song for the first golden age of the athletic and acrobatic film. The foolish old men represent the previous age, and their ineffective dithering underscores the fate of the genre itself. It ends in defeat for the old-timers, but they get to show off stunts they can still do and demonstrate their comedic gifts. The message is clear: the old ways are over, and a new world filled with disappointments, opportunities, and fresh horrors is on the horizon. Perhaps few realized it in 1932, but everything *really was* at stake.

Notes

1. Denise J. Youngblood, *Movies for the Masses: Popular Cinema and Soviet Society in the 1920s* (Cambridge: Cambridge University Press, 1992), 53–54.

2. Heinz Siegeris, "Harry Piel: Millionen haben ihn geliebt—Millionen haben ihn vergessen," *Heim und Welt*, June 24, 1962, quoted in Matias Bleckman, *Harry Piel: Ein Kino-Mythos und seine Zeit*, 17.

3. Matias Bleckman, "Harry Piel, Der Mann ohne Nerven, in der Reihe 'Deutsche Erfolgsfilme,'" *Berliner Zeitung*, September 29, 2015.

4. "Harry Piel: 12.VII.1892–27.III.1963" (obituary), *Der Spiegel*, April 3, 1963, http://www.spiegel.de/spiegel/print/d-45142987.html.

5. Harry Piel, "Der Film," *LichtBild-Bühne* 11 (March 12, 1921), quoted in Bleckman, *Harry Piel*, 116.

6. Jean Frick, "Harry Piel," *Mon ciné*, November 13, 1924, 10–11.

7. Anonymous review of *Was ist los im Zirkus Beely?*, *Kinematograph*, 1927, quoted at "Une redécouverte: *Que se passe-t-il au cirque Beely?* 1926," Goethe Institute, April 26, 2004, www.goethe.de/.../broschuerentexte_fr, accessed July 25, 2015. The Goethe Institute has since removed the webpage, which was in commemoration of a showing of the newly restored film in 2004. The page was apparently an online version of a printed brochure (hence, "broschuerentexte").

8. See John M. Steiner, *Power Politics and Social Change in National Socialist Germany: A Process of Escalation into Mass Destruction* (The Hague: Mouton, 1975),230n29.

9. Bleckman, *Harry Piel*, 318–25, 335–44.

10. Aside from having his shirt torn open occasionally, the only film where Piel's physique is displayed extensively is the boxing film *Bobby geht los / Skandal in der Arena* (Bobby gets going / Scandal in the arena, 1931), and the results were not aesthetically pleasing.

11. Anton Kaes, Martin Jay, and Edward Dimendberg, "The Cult of the Body: *Lebensreform*, Sports, and Dance" (section introduction), in Anton Kaes, Martin Jay, and Edward Dimendberg, eds., *The Weimar Republic Sourcebook*, 674.

12. Hans Leip, *Max und Anny: Romantischer Bericht vom Aufsteig zweier Sterne* (Hamburg: Broschek, 1935), 16.

13. Erik Jensen, "Sweat Equity," in John Alexander Williams, ed., *Weimar Culture Revisited*, 190.

14. Kaes, Jay, and Dimendberg, "The Cult of the Body," 674.

15. "Impressionen im Ring," *Sport im Bild* 28, no. 11 (March 17, 1922), quoted in Erik N. Jensen, *Body by Weimar: Athletes, Gender, and German Modernity*, 85.

16. Jensen, *Body by Weimar*, 89.

17. Stephen Putnam Hughes, "Silent Film Genre, Exhibition and Audiences in South India," in *Explorations in New Cinema History: Approaches and Case Studies*, ed. Richard Maltby, Daniel Biltereyst, and Philippe Meers (Chichester, UK: Wiley-Blackwell, 2011), 299.

18. Eddie Polo, "The Story of My Life," *Moving Picture Weekly*, July 31, 1920, 26. There are few deserts in northern California, so—assuming this is not mere fiction—it is unclear where his supposed birthplace is.

19. Guillermo J. Reilly, "Serrin y celuloide: Historia de la vida de Eddy Polo," *Cine-Mundial*, May 1922, 271; Kalton C. Lahue, *Bound and Gagged: The Story of the Silent Serials*, 240–41; Gene Scott Freese, *Hollywood Stunt Performers: A Dictionary and Filmography of Over 600 Men and Women, 1922–1996* (Jefferson, NC: McFarland, 1998), 1976.

20. Anthony Slide, *Early American Cinema*, 168. Francis Ford (1882–1953) was the elder brother of director John Ford (1895–1973). Grace Cunard (1894–1967) and the elder Ford were married when she was Universal's most prominent serial queen. Between 1916 and 1918 they wielded great influence at the studio and were sometimes called the Masters of Mystery.

21. Lahue, *Bound and Gagged*, 242.

22. Advertising spread for *The Bull's Eye*, *Motion Picture News*, January 12, 1918, 280–81.

23. "Newslets for Use in Your Program," *Motography* 19, no. 2 (January 12, 1918): 92.

24. "The Answer Man," *Motion Picture*, November 1917, 153.

25. Lillian Conlon, "The Prowess of Polo," *Motion Picture*, February 1918, 47–49.

26. The French press book for the film provides a hint of Polo's proposed audience in 1922: "He will attract the children. He will keep the adults and interest them." *L'idole du cirque*, French press book for the film *Lure of the Circus*, 1922, collection of David L. Chapman.

27. Larry Langman, *A Guide to Silent Westerns* (New York: Greenwood, 1992), 101. Langman lists four films, but they were later recut to make serials.

28. Slide, *Early American Cinema*, 168.

29. Lahue, *Bound and Gagged*, 244.

30. John J. McGowan, *J. P. McGowan: Biography of a Hollywood Pioneer* (Jefferson, NC: McFarland, 2005), 93.

31. Billy Wilder, quoted in Robert Horton, ed., *Billy Wilder: Interviews* (Jackson: University Press of Mississippi, 2001), 145. Polo was actually fifty-four years old.

32. Charlotte Chandler, *Nobody's Perfect: Billy Wilder, a Personal Biography*, 46.

33. Kevin Brownlow, quoted in Chandler, *Nobody's Perfect*, 46.

34. [Gertrud Haupt?], review of *Der Teufelsreporter*, *Berliner Morgenpost*, 1929, quoted in *Der Film der Weimarer Republik 1929: Ein Handbuch der zeitgenössischen Kritik*, ed. Gero Gandert (Berlin: Walter de Gruyter, 1997), 191; anonymous review of *Der*

Teufelsreporter, Frankfurter Zeitung, 1929, in Gandert, ed., *Der Film der Weimarer Republik 1929,* 191.

35. Gene D. Phillips, *Some Like It Wilder: The Life and Controversial Films of Billy Wilder* (Lexington: University Press of Kentucky, 2010), 6.

36. Lahue, *Bound and Gagged,* 247.

37. "Polo Promotional Debut in Memphis Comes Out Winner," *Billboard,* April 17, 1948, 46; Lahue, *Bound and Gagged,* 248; "Hair Raising Act," *Life,* April 12, 1948, 142. See also "Polo Dies from Fall at Peak of Wire Act," *Billboard,* July 16, 1949, 52; Daniel Blum, *Screen World* (Cheshire, CT: Crown, 1962), 225.

PART II.

MUSCLES OF ACTION AND ALLURE

VII. THE ATHLETIC BODY

Bodies are created beautiful, and if we will exercise as much care in preserving bodies as we do in beautifying our faces and hands and other commonly exposed parts of our bodies, we may retain physical beauty.

—Jean Harlow, quoted in James M. Fidler,
"Will Hollywood Accept Nudism?"

AS HOLLYWOOD EMERGED from the silent pictures into the talkie-enriched narratives of the 1930s, it was less essential to express movement vividly and more necessary to build drama and tension through speech and accompanying gestures. Greater emphasis could now be devoted to using the body to reinforce voices and advance the dramatic narrative. Portrayals of the body increasingly expressed the beauty of form as well as function. While the athleticism, personality, and grin of Douglas Fairbanks proved a winning combination in the 1920s, it no longer satisfied audiences who wanted to understand what these athletic characters were feeling beneath their muscles. "It was radio that did it," insists Kevin Brownlow. "Radio that attuned the public to the sound of canned dialogue and made them miss it at the movies."[1] Paradoxically, musclemen—though perfectly capable of expressing themselves in speech—often did little talking. While action scenes enabled them to exhibit their skills, greater attention was focused on integrating their athletic bodies into the context of romance, glamour, and heroic outcomes.

The Latin Lover

In the early 1920s few film actors exploited their bodies and emotive abilities better than Rudolph Valentino. "I am a motion picture star today only because of thorough physical training which I received in my boyhood," he claimed in 1924. Descended from sturdy ancestors who trained for Italian military service, Valentino's first instructor was his father, a wrestler endowed with superior "bulk and strength" who selected foods that would build and

185

strengthen his muscles. Rudolph became "a strapping husky boy, full of life and animal spirits, able to go through prolonged periods of exercising." He became proficient in aquatic sports, running, and bicycle and horseback riding, but he was most fond of Greco-Roman wrestling and Italian football. On arriving in America in 1913, Valentino utilized his athleticism as a dancer and dance teacher in Los Angeles and in various screen roles. That he could rise above "doing bits or working in mob scenes" he attributed to "my physique, which I have brought to its present condition by following the laws of nature and common sense." Valentino believed his all-round physical training was most useful in *The Four Horsemen of the Apocalypse* (1921), *The Sheik* (1921), and *Blood and Sand* (1922), which made him a major star. His portrayal of a toreador in the latter required "a strong, agile and vigorous body." As Valentino recalled,

> The mental and physical tension I was under in "The Sheik" was tremendous, for I spent hours daily on the desert sands of California under a blistering sun, almost always on the move and frequently indulging in violent exercises. And those who saw my first big picture, "The Four Horsemen of the Apocalypse," will, I think, admit I had some scenes which put me to the supreme physical test.
>
> And in those pictures, I went through every scene assigned to me without a double, for no double could have possessed a better body to meet the exacting physical requirements than I had.

Exemplary of his athletic versatility was the role Valentino played in *The Young Rajah* (1922), in which he was able "to take my seat as one of the sturdy crew from the University of California, which took part in the picture's spectacular race. In other pictures I utilized my ability to swim, ride and fence." Despite his romantic Hollywood image, he followed a "rigid training plan" that incorporated wrestling, fencing, horseback riding, and a strict diet.[2]

The portrait drawn by Howard Kelly in Bernarr Macfadden's *Physical Culture* magazine, replete with physique photos, places greater emphasis on Valentino's "young body of rippling muscles and steely sinews" and how he developed it from specific exercises. Kelly assures readers that the actor's muscular thighs and calves "are not effects contrived by trick photography" and "not illusions cast by light and shadow." After he and Macfadden tested the firmness of Valentino's muscles with "our own hands," Kelly concluded that Valentino's leg development resulted from "his bicycle riding, swimming, running and soccer foot-ball." Swimming also produced "the husky pads of muscle that protect his shoulder bones." At an early age Valentino began doing the Australian crawl, "a swift overhand stroke of the arms, bringing the shoulder muscles into violent action." Likewise, rowing not only expanded the chest, Kelly argued, but broadened the shoulders. And "wrestling played a role in developing his back shoulder muscles." Swimming and wrestling "gave Valentino's body its beautiful symmetry, and kept certain muscles from bulging out of proportion." What impressed Kelly most, however, was his back development. Beneath his shoulder blades Valentino had a "strong pair of muscles," which the actor attributed to weightlifting, along with his muscular biceps and forearms. Although often enduring harsh living and working conditions as an actor, Valentino believed "health is a security against all adversity. . . . I have not allowed anything to interfere with my 'keep fit' policy." Kelly rated him "one of the most athletic figures of the screen."[3]

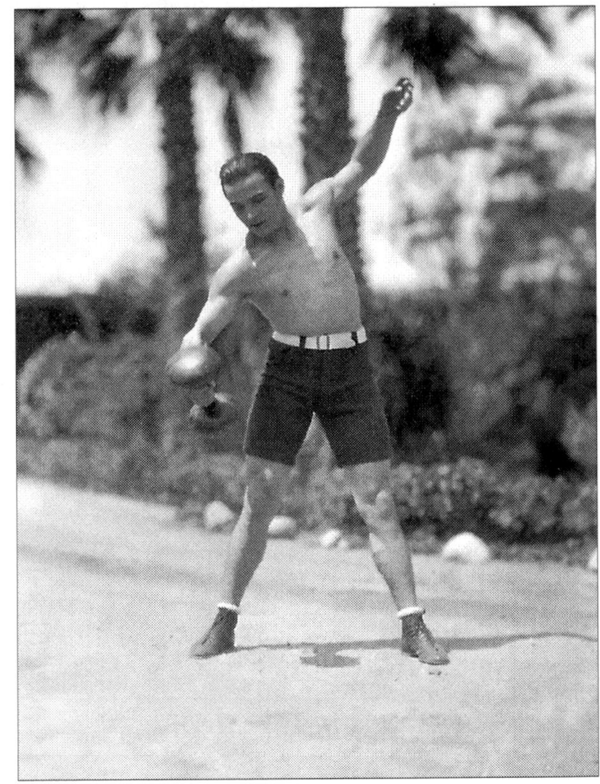

Figure 7.1. For Rudolph Valentino, physical perfection equaled movie stardom and success. He consequently worked at keeping his body in top form. Here he exercises with a dumbbell, around 1923. Collection of David L. Chapman.

Valentino is, however, best known not for his physical culture pursuits but as the first of filmland's great foreign lotharios. His body, in addition to his on-screen presence, was different for American audiences. He was different from good old boy Tom Mix and the dashing Fairbanks. His foreignness made him exciting and dangerous. Although there were "plenty of elegant and polished actors in Hollywood," notes Brownlow, "what aroused so much fascination was his effect on women in the audience. No other star in film history had such a shattering impact." Yet Valentino led a tortuous existence offscreen. Both of his marriages ended in divorce, and while women universally loved him, some men derided his fame. Nor would posterity be kind to his ability as an actor, characterizing him as overwrought with passion and his pictures as "romantic *kitsch*."[4] While it seems doubtful that Valentino's struggles with the studios over control of his career was a contributory factor in his death, it seemed ironic, given his healthy lifestyle, that he fell to peritonitis at age thirty-one in 1926. "Never before was the discourse on fan behavior so strongly marked by the terms of sexual difference," asserts film scholar Miriam Hansen, "and never again was spectatorship so explicitly linked to the discourse on female desire."[5] The viewing of his body at Campbell's funeral parlor in Manhattan turned into pandemonium. "It was a crowd so filled with emotion, that you weren't at all sure what they might do," observed Adela Rogers St. Johns. "Hysterical crowds behave badly at funerals."[6]

George O'Brien

Another muscular figure who emerged from the silent screen was George O'Brien. Born in San Francisco in 1899, his father was a policeman, six feet tall and weighing 220 pounds, and once an amateur boxer. He encouraged young George's interest in athletics and took him to movies, where he read him the intertitles. "My father taught us what he knew about boxing," O'Brien later recalled, "including how to use the left hand. One person I knew in those days was Jim Corbett. I learned a lot from him." Corbett encouraged O'Brien to join the Columbia Park Boys Club, where he learned calistenics, wrestling, tumbling, and other skills that prepared him for his movie career. At age twelve O'Brien became interested in weight training, again with his father's support. "It gives the young man a chance to test his strength and build up a powerful body in a short time," George believed, enabling him to "lay the foundation for a healthy, husky, physical being which will pay dividends in later life." In high school he lettered in four sports and learned cowboy skills—horseback riding, roping, and bulldogging—on a ranch near

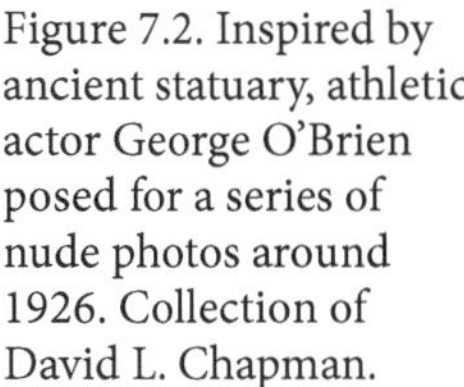

Figure 7.2. Inspired by ancient statuary, athletic actor George O'Brien posed for a series of nude photos around 1926. Collection of David L. Chapman.

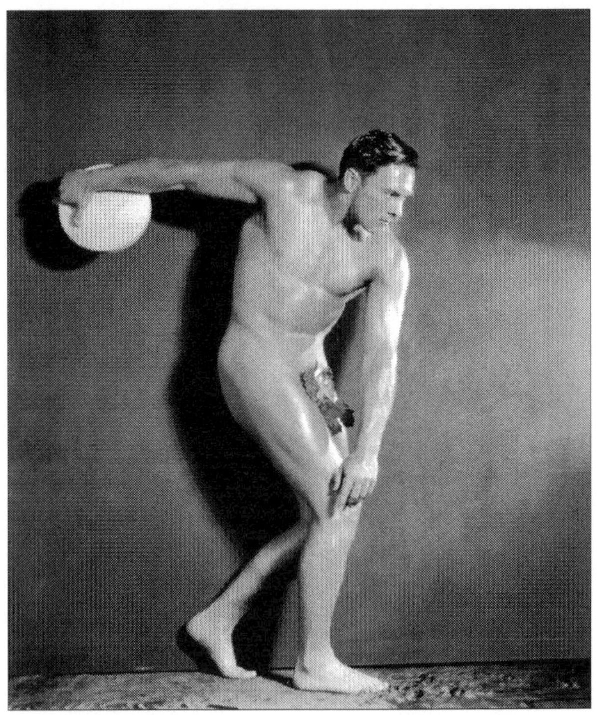

his home in Los Gatos.[7] During World War I, O'Brien parleyed his athletic talents in the US Navy, playing basketball and winning the light heavyweight boxing championship of the Pacific Fleet.

After his time in the navy he entered motion pictures as a cameraman for cowboy stars Buck Jones and Tom Mix and eventually starred in *The Iron Horse* in 1924, a popular Western under top director John Ford. He starred in four more Fox Film Corporation productions that year, and in 1925 starred in *The Fighting Heart* as a romantic ring hero.[8] After another boxing movie, *Is Zat So?* (1927), Alma Talley in *Picture Play* deemed George "A Physically Perfect Young Man," an Apollo who "doesn't go around being physically perfect any more than he goes about being the erstwhile heavyweight champion of the Pacific fleet." A charming and modest young man, "the strong-man roles he is always called upon to play rather amuse him. Usually, of course, he plays a prize fighter, appropriately enough; other strong-man stunts are constantly being written into his scenarios."[9] In both Western and boxing films, O'Brien liked to perform his own stunts, and in *The Roughneck* (1924), a South Seas adventure film, he executed his most daring feat by leaping sixty feet from a ship deck. It was "a boy's idea of adventure," noted the *New York Times*. "After observing all that Mr. O'Brien experiences as Jerry Delaney, one concludes that he needs his deep chest and brawny arms." To friends and colleagues, he was known as the Chest.[10]

Screenland writer Delight Evans even attributes O'Brien's motion picture breakthrough to his physique; to Ford he "looked like just about the strongest set of muscles in Hollywood." Most of O'Brien's evenings were spent at Tom Mix's gymnasium "instead of at parties," and he was "a handball fiend and basketball star. Apparently the only sport in which he does not indulge is flying."[11] After O'Brien's appearance in *The Painted Lady* (1924), a melodrama with Dorothy Mackaill, his "popularity increased rapidly," according to his biographer: "The studio tended to capitalize whenever possible on his athletic prowess, and his physique was often displayed for no other reason than to show off his body. He was flooded with fan mail, especially from youngsters who wanted to know how they could build a physique like his. . . . George had the physical build of a Greek Hercules, the lithe grace of a dancing master, and the hitting power of a Missouri mule. He was one of the few motion picture actors holding a membership card in the American Athletic Union [*sic*]." The 1925 Fox production of *The Dancers*, a story based on the postwar jazz age and dance craze of the younger generation, had "box office punch," observed *Variety*, and "George O'Brien stands out like a house afire as the hero."[12] His popularity also increased among potential bodybuilders and gay men by his willingness to pose for classic nude portraits for postcards and magazines. The display of O'Brien's manly biceps and chest and other portions of his well-developed body, though shocking for the times, helped to glamorize the male physique and inspire young men to start training. O'Brien's stature and good looks helped him acquire the male lead in F. W. Murnau's 1927 masterpiece *Sunrise*.[13] O'Brien later told Lew Pike, in a *Strength and Health* article, that he had so many fans requesting advice that he created a form letter advising zealots to "visit a gym and seek a competent instructor."[14]

By the end of the 1920s O'Brien's muscular presence was filling a void in masculinity created by the unexpected death of Rudolph Valentino in 1926 and the retirement of Tom Mix in 1929. Unlike many silent stars, he successfully transitioned to the talkies. In 1928 he costarred in *Noah's Ark* with Dolores Costello, and starred in his first talkie, *Salute*, a football film directed by Ford that included newcomers Ward Bond and John Wayne. With his suitable voice, outstanding physique, and athletic skills, O'Brien became a desirable choice for outdoor scripts, and most notably those based on Zane

Grey novels, including *The Lone Star Ranger* (1930), one of the most success-ful Westerns ever produced. "His he-man proclivities," reckoned Hamilton Dana in 1928, "have established him as the most popular of actors so far as the youth of America is concerned." O'Brien went on to star in twenty-two sound films.[15] By 1938, as David Menefee notes, he was making $25,000 per picture, and for sixteen films (1936–39) he earned "nearly a million dollars, a time when the average American wage-earner made $3,000–$5,000 annual-ly." Despite popularity and financial success, "George never strayed from his core values. One of his hobbies had long been weight lifting, and he had built himself into a 240-pound giant." Not unlike Fairbanks and Mix, O'Brien never let scandal intrude on his personal life. He was always conscious of his responsibility to youth and sought to be "the kind of man he wanted their parents to encourage them to emulate."[16] He neither drank nor smoked.

Even after a five-year stint in the navy during World War II, and well into his forties, O'Brien's "husky physique has not lost any of its muscular propor-tions," noted Pike, nor had his commitment to fitness. "O'Brien is still quite a handball player and he indulges in the fast moving game thrice a week at the club after he has completed his wall-pulley exercises, gone through a boxing routine, performed 25 or more pushups and exercised with weights." To George Lowther, in a 1947 *Your Physique* article, O'Brien "did not look a day over thirty" and possessed "a physique that would delight anyone half his age" with 16¾-inch biceps, a forty-six-inch chest, and a 34½-inch waist.[17] His postwar acting career persisted until 1964, highlighted by his appearance in *My Wild Irish Rose* (1947), pronounced by *Variety* as the sort of film that "pleases right off the reel . . . George O'Brien makes a rugged strong man."[18] In 1981 he suffered a stroke and died four years later at age eighty-six in Broken Arrow, Oklahoma. Not unlike Valentino's, O'Brien's beefcake image had a strong appeal to women and gay viewers, but he-men who wanted their bodies to resemble his were no less appreciative.

The Tarzan Tradition

While O'Brien enjoyed a screen life of forty years, perhaps the most collective representation of muscular manhood was the iconic figure of Tarzan. From the release of *Tarzan of the Apes* in 1918 by the National Film Corporation, and through to 1960, there were twenty-eight feature films, four serials, and three feature serials with twelve Tarzans and thirteen Janes. Producer Sy Weintraub observed in 1959 that "Tarzan's history reads like a cross-section of Hollywood," having grossed more than $500 million and viewed by two billion people. "I believe Tarzan is the most durable and commercial of all movie personalities."[19]

The jungle hero sprang from the prolific pen of Edgar Rice Burroughs, a Chicago native who gained recognition as an adventure and science fiction novelist. His portrayal of a manly figure stemmed not from any physical culture background but from his familiarity with ancient Greek epics.[20] Tarzan, argues classicist Erling Holtsmark, was cast "much in the mold of the mythological heroes of antiquity" who have "one foot in the divine world and one in the human world." Burroughs casts his hero with one foot "in the world of animals" and displays an interest in similarities between the language of the apes and classical Greek and Latin. While Tarzan's intellect surpasses that of beasts, his "animal aspect gives him superhuman sensitivities of smell, hearing, and sight, as well as physical strength beyond the imagination of any mere man."[21] His physical attributes are described in *Tarzan of the Apes* (1912), the first of twenty-six books in the series: "His straight and perfect figure, muscled as the best of the ancient Roman gladiators must have been muscled, and yet with the soft and sinuous curves of a Greek god, told at a glance the wondrous combination of enormous strength with suppleness and speed." These kinds of representations suggest that modern casting of a real-life Tarzan in the movies would reveal lots of skin, muscle, and heroic deeds.[22]

Despite sales of three million copies, it was not until 1918 that the National Film Corporation realized the box office potential of *Tarzan of the Apes*. Elmo Lincoln, an Indiana native, became the first screen Tarzan. A protégé of D. W. Griffith, he played the blacksmith in *Birth of a Nation* (1915) and other manly roles displaying his massive chest. "That's quite a chest you have there" was Griffith's initial reaction to seeing him shirtless. Lincoln got the part of Tarzan over thirty-five other actors, chiefly "because of his barrel chest and terrific torso." From the outset, as Walt Morton observes, "the physicality of the actor chosen to portray Tarzan was the central issue in casting for the role."[23] Filming took place near Morgan City, Louisiana, where husky young men from the New Orleans Athletic Club, in lieu of real apes, were hired to don ape skins and swing through trees. Although Lincoln was somewhat awkward in romantic scenes and his wig kept shifting, he displayed strength and agility in fight sequences and reportedly stabbed a lunging lion to death.[24] *Tarzan of the Apes* was one of the first films to gross over $1 million. Lincoln then made two sequels, *The Romance of Tarzan* (1918) and *The Adventures of Tarzan* (1920). But Burroughs was dismissive of Lincoln. He was "far from my conception of the character. Tarzan was not beefy but was light and graceful and well muscled" and "the epitome of grace." Burroughs conceived him as "a man a little over six feet tall and built more like a panther than an elephant." To *Photoplay*, however, Lincoln was "the American Maciste, if any American screen player has the right to be called a rival to the famous Italian strong man of 'Cabiria' fame."[25]

Figure 7.3. Chesty Elmo Lincoln, featured in an ad for *Tarzan of the Apes* (1918), his first Tarzan film. Collection of David L. Chapman.

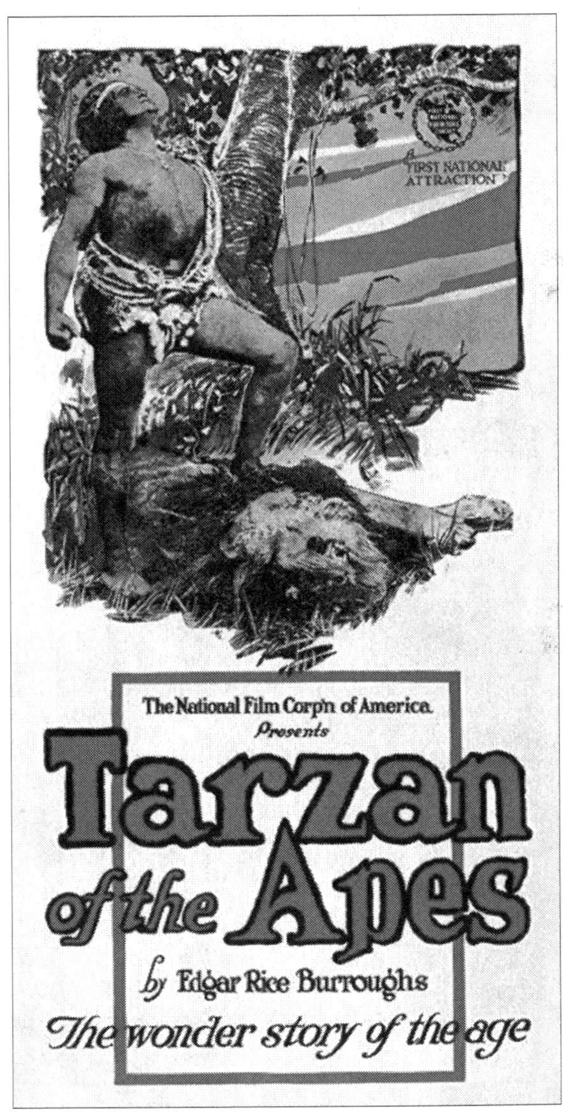

Regardless of Burroughs's views, Lincoln's portrayal served as the catalyst for a slew of Tarzan epics. Soon Goldwyn Pictures released *Revenge of Tarzan* (1920) starring New York City fireman Gene Pollar who was 6' 2½" and weighed 215 pounds, with a thirty-eight-inch waist. Mike Chapman rated him "one of the worst built of all movie Tarzans." Selected mainly for his size, Pollar was the first Tarzan to wear a leopard-skin breechclout, but he was no actor, and *Films in Review* labeled the script "inept and contrived." Burroughs called the picture "a stinker," and Pollar resumed his job as a fireman.[26] In *The Son of Tarzan* (1920) the plot centers on the adventures of Tarzan's son, played successively by youth actors Gordon Griffith and Kamuela Searle, a former stuntman. Playing a secondary role as Tarzan in this fifteen-part serial was Dempsey Tabler, a forty-one-year-old Tennessee athlete who had spent four seasons in light opera. Like previous Tarzans, Tabler performed his own action sequences, and in one fight scene he broke several ribs. An *ERBzine* review calls Tabler "a surprising choice . . . whose feeble physique and poorly designed toupee failed to convince anyone that he was the Lord of the Jungle." According to Chapman, he had "no arm or chest development and a sagging midsection." A tragic incident occurred during the filming when a frightened elephant slammed Searle to the ground, forcing his replacement by a double. Although *Son of Tarzan* was a box office success and Burroughs was pleased, he believed there were "too many Tarzan pictures on the market."[27]

At six foot four and 225 pounds, James Pierce was an All-American basketball center at Indiana University who later, as a coach at Glendale High School, nurtured such future stars as Robert Livingston, Bob Steele, and John Wayne. He also studied acting and was discovered at a party at Burroughs's Tarzana, California, ranch when the host yelled "There's Tarzan!" Burroughs "proceeded to talk me into playing the Apeman," according to Pierce. "He said I looked just like what he had always had in mind."[28] Tapped for the starring role in *Tarzan and the Golden Lion* (1927), Pierce exhibited what Burroughs described as physical perfection. Not unlike ancient Greek heroes, Tarzan possessed "gracefully contoured muscles" suitably situated on a "godlike frame. Not as the muscles of the blacksmith or the professional strong man were the muscles of Tarzan of the Apes," wrote Burroughs, "but rather as those of Mercury or Apollo, so symmetrically balanced were their proportions, suggesting only the great strength that lay in them." So great an advantage was Tarzan's "great height and strength" that in a subsequent battle he vanquished opposing warriors before swinging in circles by his ankles a priest who barred his way.[29] In the movie version, however, Pierce is far from a muscular marvel, and his physical prowess is limited to minor scuffles in contrived battle scenes. Though it was popular with the public, critics lambasted the film. "This wins the hand-embroidered toothpick as being the worst picture of the month" was the view of *Photoplay*. "It is an insult to the human intelligence to expect anyone to sit through this." Burroughs, however, was "convinced that it is going to be the greatest Tarzan picture ever made. We have found a man who really is Tarzan, and whom I believe will be raised to the heights of stardom." Although Pierce never reached stardom, his Tarzan connection was made manifest by his marriage to Burroughs's daughter Joan, with whom he performed 364 fifteen-minute ape-man radio episodes in the 1930s.[30]

Last of the early Tarzans was Frank Merrill, who, at six feet and 185 pounds, had been a national gymnastic champion on the rings, high bar, and rope climbing. With a forty-four-inch chest and 16¼-inch biceps, he was adjudged "the world's most perfect man" at a physical culture contest and deemed "physically perfect" by the president of the Los Angeles Medical Association. He broke into motion pictures in 1920 as a double for Elmo Lincoln in *The Adventures of Tarzan*. Then starring in a fifteen-part serial, *Tarzan the Mighty* (1928), he applied his athleticism to perfecting Tarzan's vine-swinging techniques, thereby enhancing the ape-man's image. According to physical culturist Bob Jones, Merrill "must constantly guard against putting out anything like his full strength in fighting human beings, lest he do them serious damage. He prefers to stack up against wild beasts." Another innovation by Merrill was the Tarzan yell in *Tarzan the Tiger* (1930), produced by the Metro-Goldwyn-Mayer (MGM) sound department for a sound version that included a crude musical score, sound effects, and a few lip-synched lines of recorded dialogue. "Merrill's superb physique," Gabe Essoe believes, was "an important factor" in the "fantastic reception" of *Tarzan the Mighty*."[31] Merrill displayed his strength in nationwide stage demonstrations where he lifted ponderous weights, including straight-arm supine laterals with dumbbells weighing seventy to one hundred pounds. *ERBzine* calls Merrill "one of the greatest all-round athletes in the world" whose "striking appearance and prodigious strength" was no less important to his success in pictures. He was an early "Hercules of the Screen."[32]

Johnny Weissmuller and Buster Crabbe

With the advent of talking pictures came the most widely acclaimed Tarzan. Motivated by success with the jungle epic *Trader Horn* (1931) and capitalizing on excess wild animal footage, MGM intended to provide another sequel of Burroughs's first novel. For Tarzan, ace director William Van Dyke sought "a man who is young, strong, well-built, reasonably attractive, but not necessarily handsome, and a competent actor. The most important thing is that he have a good physique." After testing hundreds of actors and athletes, he chose Peter Johnny Weissmuller, a six-foot-three, 190-pound athlete who had taken up swimming as a scrawny youth on his doctor's advice. He went on to win five gold medals in the 1924 and 1928 Olympics, along with sixty-seven world and fifty-two national titles, and to break individual swimming records in virtually every category he entered. Although he had little acting experience, Weissmuller appeared to have stage (or jungle) presence and was reputedly "the only man who's natural in the flesh and can act without clothes."[33] To film historian Rudy Behlmer, Weissmuller was first rate: "As opposed to other screen Tarzans, he did not appear muscle-bound, and was able to move about in a loose, cat-like manner. There were other subtle touches of an animal nature—the wariness, the quick turning of the head, and the catching of a scent." While a specially built jungle on MGM's back lot and a nearby lake was equipped with swinging rope vines and trapezes, most aerial acrobatics were performed by Alfredo Cardona, who doubled for Weissmuller.[34]

Much of Weissmuller's popularity as Tarzan may be attributed to the co-incidental release of *Tarzan the Ape Man* with the 1932 Olympics in Los Angeles. "Did Johnny Weissmuller make the Olympics popular or did the Olympics make a hero out of Johnny?" asks Gail Hall Wright in a *Screenland* article titled "Hollywood Goes Olympic!" She observed that "stars with Olympic records are top-hole-ace-high-one hundred percent out here now." Production schedules were even arranged for stars to attend the games, and "worship of bodily perfection prevails in California today no less than it did years ago when the Olympic heroes became national idols and the games were regarded as sacred."[35] Another aspect of the new Tarzan's popularity was his appeal to women, often in their teens, who regarded him as "a perfect work of God." According to Ida Zeitlin he was "a man with a flawless body, six feet three inches of brawn and muscle moving with ease and power and grace before their delighted eyes, broad-shouldered, slender-hipped, an ideal of masculine strength and beauty—a new hero, literally fallen from the skies, with 'Gawd, whadda physique!' "[36] These sentiments resonated also with Katherine Albert in *Photoplay*: "Me and eighty million other girls have gone Weissmuller." As a glamorous male figure, his impact was similar to Valentino's. When Weissmuller entered the *Photoplay* offices "work absolutely stopped and three girls fainted." Albert seemed bemused. "Hollywood is a funny town—it's got to have its sex appeal marked in big letters."[37]

There was nothing about the display of Weissmuller's near-naked body that violated the Hays Code,[38] but the underwater swimming sequences in *Tarzan and His Mate* (1934), featuring Maureen O'Sullivan's (and her double's) abbreviated costume in their depiction of Jane, caused the Hays censorship office to reject the picture. MGM appealed, but a jury sustained the rejection. Decades later O'Sullivan "felt it was suitable for the Jungle, although criticism caused them to modify it." In retrospect, she viewed her six-time role as Jane as "mostly very favorable. They were fairy tales. Almost Disney-like."[39]

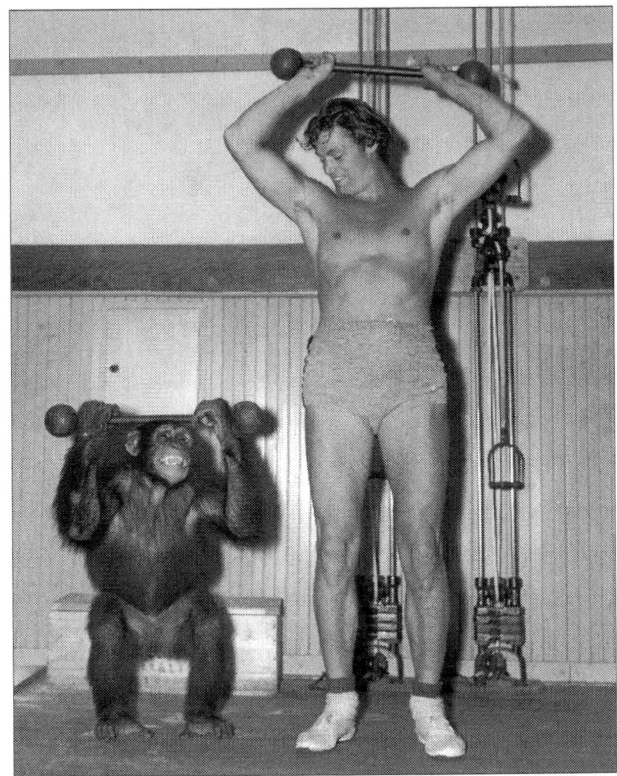

Figure 7.4. Johnny Weissmuller and Cheetah pump iron together in 1938. Collection of David L. Chapman.

Over the next several decades Weissmuller made eleven more Tarzan films, then sixteen Jungle Jim films and a television series. The ape-man was such a popular subject that other studios sought to cash in on the bonanza. In 1933 Paramount Pictures produced a Tarzan-like tale called *King of the Jungle* starring Clarence Linden "Buster" Crabbe, whose swimming skills rivaled Weissmuller's. Raised in Honolulu, Crabbe thrived on the beach life of Waikiki, where, as a lifeguard, he made twenty-two rescues. He went on to swim on the US Olympic team in Amsterdam in 1928 and won a gold medal in the four-hundred-meter freestyle at the 1932 Olympics. While enrolled as a University of California prelaw student, he worked as a stunt double and bit player. His movie break, according to Ben Maddox, occurred "when Paramount was hunting for a competitor to Weissmuller and noticed Buster in the '32 Olympics." Crabbe's success in *King of the Jungle* led to his first serial in *Tarzan the Fearless* (1933). It was an "unthrilling jungle adventure," notes Alan Barbour, where Crabbe had no dialogue aside from meaningless grunts. "The role virtually destroyed Crabbe's possibilities for major stardom since producers pictured him as strictly a physical specimen for audiences to gawk at."[40]

Shortly after Crabbe hung up his leopard skin, audiences had even more to gawk at in *Search for Beauty* (1934), in which he appeared in mainstream cinema's first nude shower scene.[41] This pre–Hays Code sex comedy ostensibly celebrated the human physique, but it also took aim at many other targets. It was apparently spawned by Paramount marketers who thought it would be a great stunt to hold a contest for the best male and female physiques in the "civilized" world (which was coded language for "nonwhites need not apply"). What resulted was a story displaying both beefcake and cheesecake: the men show off their musculature in tiny bathing trunks and the women jiggle away merrily in braless splendor. Crabbe is joined by Ida Lupino, who plays a British diver. A couple of hucksters dupe the two protagonists into collaborating on a health and exercise magazine (modeled on Bernarr Macfadden's *Physical Culture*, with a dash of *True Confessions*) that will be an excuse to sell nudie images and sexy stories.

The film's final scene features beautiful physiques culled from the far corners of the Anglo-Saxon world. The scantily clad beauties of both sexes perform in a floor show that is part Busby Berkeley routine and part Nuremberg Rally: as rows of grimly smiling Aryan athletes march past and perform their choreographed movements, we are meant to admire the fitness and precision of these paragons of white superiority. The film's

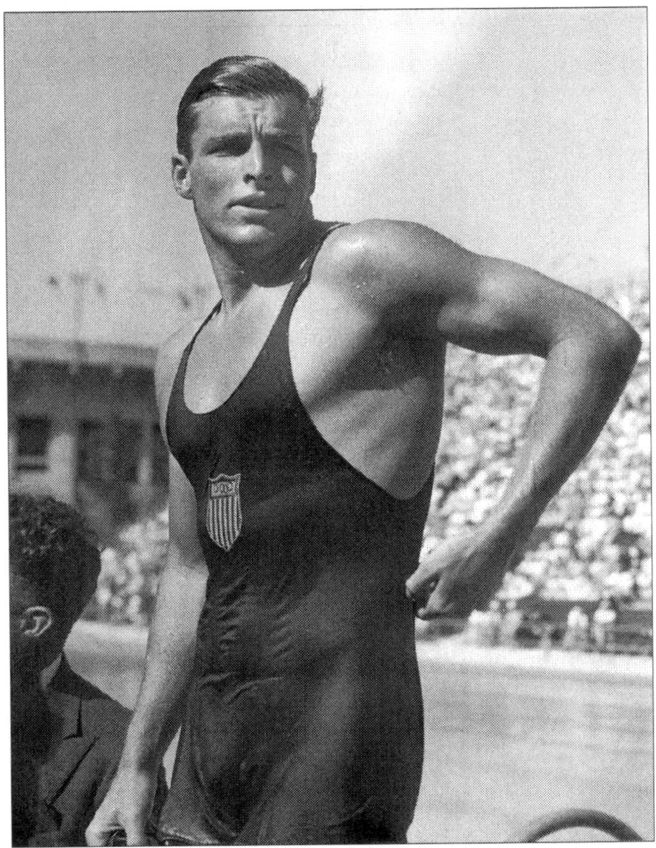

Figure 7.5. Olympian Buster Crabbe began as a swimmer, but later starred in many movies, including Zane Grey Westerns and the serials *Tarzan the Fearless* (1933), *Flash Gordon* (1936–40), *Red Barry* (1938), and *Buck Rogers* (1939). Collection of David L. Chapman.

central conflict pits the celebration of healthy physiques against the objectification of the body for erotic effect. The forces of sweetness, health, and purity prevail over the venal and pornographic urges of the human psyche. The film seems to say you can't have it both ways—either it's sport or it's smut.

Fortunately, unlike Weissmuller, whose Tarzan fame led to frustration with being forever typecast in that role, "what-a-physique" Crabbe used his handsome face and athletic body to star in a variety of action-packed serials—first in a series of Zane Grey Westerns and then a succession of heroic roles in the serials *Flash Gordon* (1936–40), *Red Barry* (1938), and *Buck Rogers* (1939), playing the top three pop fiction heroes of the 1930s. Barbour labels him "The King of the Serials."[42]

Athletic Muscles

Muscles remained evident in Tarzan depictions for the rest of the decade, but they prevailed chiefly with amateur athletes. As Denie Walter, a writer on bodybuilding, notes, "Weissmuller and Crabbe had aesthetic looking proportionate rib cages that added to their powerful look and were supported by adequate legs." But Tarzan actors never had the legs of "an advanced bodybuilder in line and shape."[43] Modern bodybuilding muscles appeared in the 1930s with the inimitable physique of John Grimek, who was little known to those outside the weightlifting subculture and/or to readers of muscle magazines. Readers of movie magazines, however, were soon exposed to the more mainstream likeness of Herman Brix, a football and track and field star at the University of Washington who won a silver medal in the shot put at the 1928 Olympics. Originally cast as Tarzan for the 1932 version, Brix broke his shoulder while filming *Touchdown* (1931), and the part went to Weissmuller. But when Burroughs set up his own company, Burroughs-Tarzan Enterprises, he picked Brix to star in *The New Adventures of Tarzan* (1935) and *Tarzan and the Green Goddess* (1938). Unlike most adaptations, these films closely coincided with their literary origins.[44] Brix also played a Tarzan-like role in the Republic Pictures serial *Hawk of the Wilderness* (1938). Although he later became a versatile film and television actor, his fine physique is most obvious in his early roles. Denie Walter describes it as "a thoroughly magnificently etched piece of nature. It combined deep abdominals with flared pectorals, wide shoulders and, although not massive, good legs. His was easily the most shapely leg development on any actor in this part. Brix's calves were large and symmetrically 'diamonded' in their caste."[45] Glenn Morris, the last of the prewar Tarzans, was the 1936 Olympic decathlon champion and winner of the Sullivan Award as the top amateur athlete in the United States. Hoping to supersede Weissmuller's box office appeal, producer Sol Lesser selected Morris for the leading role in *Tarzan's Revenge* (1938) over baseball great Lou Gehrig, who lacked muscular legs. For the leading lady Lesser complemented Morris's athleticism with Eleanor Holm (Jarrett), winner of the one-hundred-meter backstroke at the 1932 Olympics. Morris "had a very athletic physique," observes Chapman, "with fine symmetry and his build was similar to that of Brix but he was not defined." A review in *Variety* also found favor with Morris, whose "feats on ropes, between trees and elsewhere, including the water, make him a highly acceptable Tarzan. His physique is what the fiction hero calls for, and the females are not unlikely to thrill over the loin-clothed strong man of the jungle." Lesser admitted, however, that Morris was "no actor," and *Liberty* magazine labeled Holm "one of the year's worst actresses." Nor did *Tarzan's Revenge* fare well in later years. Edward Connor declared it "dreadful," with "not one redeeming feature." It was "the worst of the Tarzan series, and could justly be included in a list of the ten worst films of all time."[46]

Fortunately, acting was less important in Tarzan films of the 1920s and 1930s than quality of movement. The films were full of action scenes that required athleticism and display of muscles. As Ron Ely, who later portrayed the ape-man, observed, "athletes rather than actors were cast as Tarzan," especially in the early films. Curiously, the Burroughs novel displaying the most muscles and action was never filmed; in *Tarzan and the City of Gold* (1933) Tarzan is depicted as "tall, magnificently proportioned, muscled more like Apollo than like Hercules . . . he presented a splendid figure of primitive manhood that suggested more, perhaps, the demigod of the forest than it did man."[47] By the late 1930s the athletic physiques of successive Tarzans were inspiring young bodybuilders to display their physiques in regular contests, including Mr. America, which began in 1939. Denie Walter calls Tarzan "the first real quality strength-hero of budding youth in search of identity. Inevitably this leads to a barbell bug bite swelling into the complex physical culture syndrome." That Tarzan's image permeated popular culture is evident in the remark of future bodybuilding mogul Joe Weider after he started weight training in the mid-1930s: "Because of my new muscles, other kids started calling me Tarzan."[48]

The Glamour Girls

As Hollywood entered the 1930s many starlets and leading men still utilized a regimen of regular exercise and proper diet to maintain screen appeal. In a 1932 *Screenland* article titled "The Body Beautiful," Margery Wilson advises female readers that "if you want to keep or recapture youth—exercise! Youth demands movement, lots of it! . . . Youth leaves us in exact ratio to our lack of movement." These sentiments parallel those in an article titled "Keeping Fit in Movie Land" by James MacFarland in *Strength*, a physical culture magazine. McFarland attributes the beauty of modern screen stars to such vigorous activities as swimming, tennis, canoeing, hiking, and playing basketball. What Wilson had in mind, however, was a different kind of movement called "anatomical architecture" involving bending and stretching. "The perfect exercise" she describes, "using every muscle in the body," involves a series of cross-body toe touches that seem unlikely to induce many beneficial results. Light exercise, mainly stretching, is also the theme in "Keeping Fit Beautifully" by Anne Van Alstyne, who claims, "Stretching brings you alive." Early morning and late at night she recommends as the best times for these exercises, and, "Between each stretch, relax completely for a moment to allow the blood to race through the worked muscles." Only by such means, Van Alstyne argues, can the body become "beautifully fit" and can one attain good looks, popularity, and charm.[49]

"Charm? No! No! You Must Have Glamour," insists Katherine Albert in *Photoplay*. "If you want to be popular—be glamorous." Admittedly Hollywood fads changed frequently—from "sweet girls" in the 1920s to "vamps, sweet girls again and now glamour" in the 1930s. Epitomizing this style were the likes of Tallulah Bankhead, Marlene Dietrich, Greta Garbo, and especially Norma Shearer, whose personal and pubic life was imbued "with an aura of glamour." According to Albert, "Her clothes (that loose evening gown she wore in 'A Free Soul'), her spritely, gay manner, her rippling laugh—which, if you ask me, ripples over our screen a little too fluently—her madcap method of living—all these things have surrounded her upon the screen. Shearer, with that sixth sense that has made her what she now is, realized long before the rest of us that this was the new mood." The efficacy of glamour is most evident, Albert concludes, in fan response: "Money, box-office money, speaks." But nowhere does she indicate that Shearer's appeal might reside as much in her physical attributes as in her personality.[50] Sue Wilson, however, in a 1929 *Strength* article, attributes Shearer's screen persona to "physical exuberance," a result of her "indulgence in sporting games and exercise." Outdoor activities—swimming, tennis, golf, and polo—were her favorite pastimes. Unlike other stars who might hop into sports gear for publicity photos, Shearer was a real player. As Wilson notes, "Beauty is skin deep they say, but Miss Shearer will tell you that there is more than that to it. She believes that beauty will fade quickly if a girl does not take the proper amount of exercise."[51] Virtually all Hollywood insiders agreed that beauty was essential to glamour, but the role of exercise in achieving it was a matter of conjecture.

The tendency of most stars was to achieve the greatest amount of health and fitness with the least effort. A consensus emerged that too much vigorous exercise might ruin one's appearance. "Sports of any kind," asserted Anne Van Alstyne, "are all conducive to building strength, beauty of line and elasticity." But one should "be careful about over-doing, since to exercise to the point of exhaustion is to defeat one's purpose." Even Universal star Kathryn Crawford, known for her pep and vigor, cautioned against overtraining. "I am a firm believer in steady exercise," she claimed, "but also believe that the exercise should not be too strenuous. There is just as much danger in over-doing as in not doing enough." Fitness and figure guru Jim Davies concurred. "Remember to try not to overdo exercise," he advised. "The moment you overdo, you will find yourself sore and out of sorts." Relaxation through stretching and deep breathing were essential to Davies's fitness regimen: "I have more calls to soothe screaming nerves than I have to reduce or build up bodies." For the overwrought actor, Davies would put him in a steam cabinet to relax. For readers wishing to emulate his treatments, he recommended a form of antiexercise: "Take a luke-warm shower, put on a light, loose robe, and lie down on your back in bed without a pillow. Adopt the 'spread-eagle' position, with eyes closed and head tipped back, and count up to 500 very slowly, without moving a muscle or a nerve." For a special treatment, Davies met screen star Miriam Hopkins in her dressing room "for a relaxing massage" daily at noon. "Miriam keeps in excellent condition by this means," he explained. "She is naturally slim, so she doesn't go in for exercise." Davies also listed Mary Boland, Claudette Colbert, Gary Cooper, Ida Lupino, and Mae West among his clients. One of his exercises for "keeping generally fit" was the "land crawl," a version of toe touching from a prone position. Comparing his clients with the Venus de Milo, still the universal standard of beauty, Davies deemed Marlene Dietrich, with the measurements 38–30–41, to have the ideal Hollywood figure.[52]

Sylvia of Hollywood

Further criticism of intense physical exertion appears in a 1931 *Photoplay* article titled "The Enemy of Beauty—Over-Exercise," in which Lois Shirley counsels against women's exercise. Champion athletes such as Gertrude Ederle (swimming), Helen Hicks (golf), and Helen Wills (tennis) were allegedly deformed and could not attain Hollywood standards of beauty. A leading proponent of antiathleticism was Sylvia Ulback (Symnove Johanne Waaler), a sort of female equivalent of Jim Davies known alternatively as Sylvia, Sylvia of Hollywood, and even Madame Sylvia. "If you want to be beautiful," she wrote, "don't over-exercise. No woman athlete is beautiful! Swimming, riding, golf and tennis are fine, but shouldn't be overdone. Muscles are horrid things that must be pounded off." Sylvia allowed none of her stars to engage in "violent" exercise. She was adamant that clients do no more than ten minutes of prescribed exercise daily and never "step inside a gymnasium." Rather, she administers "stretching and relaxing exercises." While sports might promote health, Sylvia argued, "they are the deadly foe of beauty."[53]

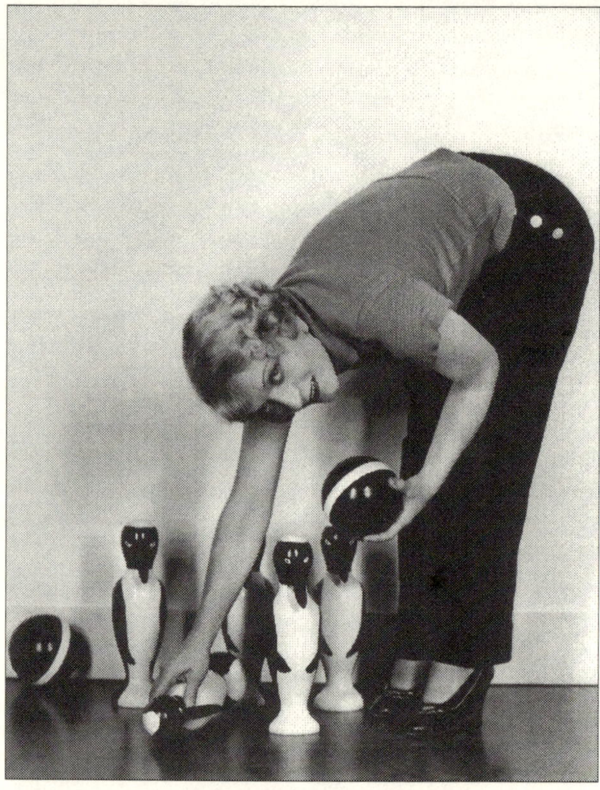

Figure 7.6. Sylvia Ullback, aka Madam Sylvia of Hollywood, posing with duckpins shaped like penguins. Photo by Ray Lee Jackson. Collection of David L. Chapman.

The modus operandi of Hollywood's most notable flesh sculptor is described by her secretary in *Hollywood Undressed* (1931). Sylvia showed up in Hollywood, a diminutive four foot eight and without "much meat on her—but what there is, it's all power." She made her breakthrough in 1925 by pounding and kneading the flesh of Marie Dressler, who was consuming fourteen quarts of "near beer" a day and suffering from gastritis. "You could wring her out like a wash cloth," Sylvia said. Soon she attracted other celebrities seeking beauty and glamour, including Douglas Fairbanks Jr., Hedda

Hopper, Ramon Novarro, Zasu Pitts, Gloria Swanson, and Norma Talmadge. Ina Claire (Fagan) was a special case: having lived a life of "luxurious ease," she needed to shed ten pounds in three days. As Sylvia explained, "The idea seemed to be to spare Miss Claire the exertion of lifting an arm. What Claire wanted . . . was for Sylvia to go to work, not too painfully, mind! And give her a ten-minute absolution for all past sins of overeating and insufficient exercise." It was not so much health that Sylvia's clients wanted; "what they wanted was beauty—melting, luscious beauty." Sylvia administered her vigorous massage in a stucco shack on the Pathé studio lot that became known as the Torture Chamber. As Sylvia posited, "The real reason for the phenomenal success of massage in the film colony is that it's a short-cut to physical conditioning, without which beauty turns into so much lard, and it's a method where the responsibility is shifted to other shoulders. The victims on Sylvia's slab in the back room of the Pathé bungalow took punishment—plenty! But not without howls and shrieks of agony. . . . On a hot, quiet day the outcries from the bungalow would reach the street outside the lot." However much faith Sylvia and her clients had in her methods, massage alone could not induce body shape changes: "The pounding can, and does, effect a speedy correction of overweight, underweight and some of the other deviations from the beautiful normal," but "a waistline bought on the massaging slab won't last from now until next Sunday unless the buyer cooperates in the upkeep." With every treatment Sylvia provided a lecture on diet—what to eat, what not to eat, and how it should be prepared. Notably understated is any coverage on exercise, the rationale being that "exercises and calisthenics are so deadly dull to the majority of individuals that the program of self-improvement is seldom carried out."[54] The assumption was that glamour could be achieved by massage, diet, and stretching.

The Prizefighter and the Lady

Athletic performance, however, remained important for male actors, and muscles in the ring made a comeback in the 1930s with the athlete-cum-star-studded cast of *The Prizefighter and the Lady* (1933). Based on a story by Frances Marion, author of the Academy Award–winning *The Champ* (1931), it's a rags-to-riches tale of a brash and brawny young boxer named Steve Morgan (Max Baer) who wants to reach the top. But his ambitions become entangled in a romantic involvement with Belle Mercer (Myrna Loy), the moll of a powerful local gangster. Morgan wins the heart of the lady, and with her help and that of his fight manager, the Professor (Walter

Huston), fights his way to a bout with reigning heavyweight champion Primo Carnera. His defeat seems assured, however, when he betrays them both through his wayward training practices and philandering. After taking a merciless beating for nine rounds, Morgan is rescued by the professor and the lady, who provide the moral support to match his opponent and salvage a draw and happy outcome. *The Prizefighter and the Lady* is a powerful action film featuring an impressive display of muscles and what they can do, with cameo appearances by former world champions Jack Dempsey, Jim Jeffries, Strangler Lewis, and Jess Willard. Perhaps the most interesting trait of the two male leads, Baer and Carnera, is that neither had acting experience. Furthermore, they were competitors for boxing's greatest prize in real life. Carnera, who was the World Heavyweight Champion (1933–34), was later defeated by Baer (1934–35), lending the film a touch of authenticity.[55]

Reviewers seemed stunned but appreciative of Baer's audacity and the film's producers, much in the manner of *Rocky* four decades later. *Variety* welcomed Baer as "a new he-man lover type. . . . What Baer has is the physique of an Apollo, a very likeable personality and an obvious ability to take direction on a picture stage. The chance to be an actor didn't send him off his nut, or if it did he wasn't permitted to show it. In Myrna Loy and Walter Huston he's surrounded with two of the screen's most proficient troopers, either of whom would ordinarily make the average tyro look like so much spinach. But he stands up with both Huston and Miss Loy and finishes without breathing hard." The complementary roles of Carnera and Dempsey benefited from "never asked to be anything but their own selves."[56] The *New York Times* was unrestrained in praising the film and its foremost practitioner of the manly art:

> Max Baer may have astonished many pugilistic enthusiasts by his defeat of Max Schmeling last June, but the chances are that many more persons will be surprised by his extraordinarily capable portrayal in the picture. . . . This California giant has such an ingratiating personality and an easy way of talking that one forgets signs of fistic encounters on his physiognomy. Mr. Baer is easily the outstanding thespianic graduate of the squared ring. . . . His voice is clear and pleasing and it causes one to wonder whether his success as a player will not interfere with his fighting. Moreover, Mr. Baer is a versatile individual, for when the occasion demands he sings and dances a good deal better than some of those who consider themselves experts.[57]

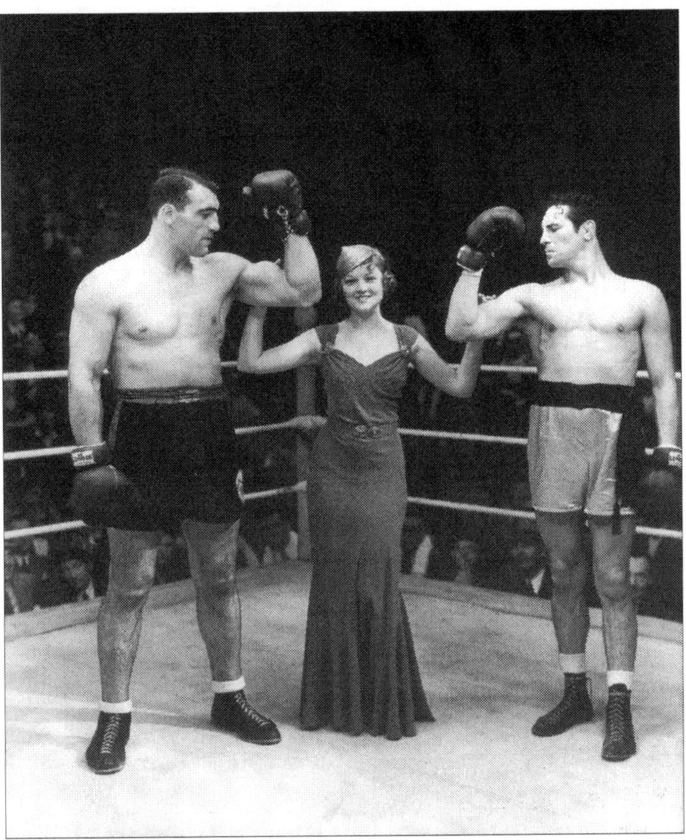

Figure 7.7. Primo Carnera, Myrna Loy, and Max Baer pose for *The Prizefighter and The Lady* (1933). Collection of David L. Chapman.

In the wake of his splendid premier, speculation mounted on whether Baer would abandon boxing for the movies. He responded by becoming World Heavyweight Champion.

Clearly the man of muscle in the film is Max Baer, not Carnera. At "over six feet tall and weighing 195 pounds," notes *Ring* magazine editor Nat Fleischer, he "had the finest physical equipment a ringman could want. Baer had massive shoulders, long and supple muscular arms, slim waist, strong legs, and a deadly right hand."[58] An unexpected bonus provided by *Prizefighter and the Lady* is the lengthy song-and-dance number, in which Baer leads a troupe of chorus girls through a routine with talent rivaling that of Fred Astaire or Gene Kelly. Baer's ability to adapt athletic skills to screen artistry, however, seemed rare in Hollywood. Allison Quirk, echoing earlier sentiments by Charlie Paddock, discusses the problems inherent in this transition in a *Photoplay* article titled "Muscling In," noting that "very few famous specialized athletes have ever gotten to first base in motion pictures." Disregarding such exceptions as former football star Johnny Mack Brown and Johnny Weissmuller, "one reason why many noted athletes have failed to ring the gong in pictures is that the public is not interested in them as actors but only as record-breakers." Unlike Baer, few natural-born athletes are natural-born actors. "Most of them are as self-conscious before the 'mike' as an 1860 bride," quips Quirk. "They spend years of training to build a perfect physical machine for one sport or another—swimming, football, track—and usually at the neglect of other faculties. . . . You can only cash in on a body machine when it's brand new."[59]

But there was more muscular action in *The Prizefighter and the Lady* than meets the casual viewer's eye. Silent film star Victor Varconi contends that mastering movements of the body is essential but insufficient to project the more subtle quality of personality into acting: "I believe so thoroughly in the eyes as the medium of getting over personality that I have shorn from my technique every physical motion that is not absolutely necessary. You can do more with the little muscles around the eyes, the corners of the mouth and the shoulders than with all the rest of the body put together."[60] While the muscularity of Baer and Carnera dominates the consciousness of most viewers, it is the studied eye movements of Otto Kruger and Myrna Loy that provide unconscious links to the film's personality dynamics. Even more subtle is Jack Dempsey's wink to the fighters just before their climactic bout—that upon a knockdown the other boxer must retreat to the opposite corner—reminding fans of the famous "long count" that enabled underdog Gene Tunney to claim the title from Dempsey in 1924.

Tom Tyler, Western Hero

In a Hollywood career spanning four decades, Tom Tyler appeared in over a hundred films, often as the lead. Yet unlike other he-men of his ilk— Buster Crabbe, Buck Jones, Hoot Gibson, Tom Mix, or George O'Brien— he never became a major star. The extent to which his physical culture persona had an impact on his screen life remains uncertain. Tyler was born Vincent Markowski in 1903 to parents of Lithuanian extraction in Port Henry, New York, the location of Arctic City Studios, where the serial *Perils of Pauline* (1914) was filmed, possibly his first awareness of the acting profession.[61] His exposure to physical culture came after his family moved in 1918 to Hamtramck, Michigan, where Tyler won a weightlifting contest. "There was a talent scout sitting in the audience," according to family friend Tom Kozyra. "He came up to Tom afterwards and told him he should go try Hollywood, and that he would give him some names of people to see."[62] With a loan from his sister, Tyler ventured to Los Angeles, where he worked in sundry jobs, from laborer to artist's model, and continued weight training. His first film breaks came as an extra in *Three Weeks* (1924), an Indian in *Leatherstocking* (1924), and a cowboy in *Wild Horse Mesa* (1925), which led to his first starring role in *Let's Go, Gallagher* (1925) with FBO Pictures. A 1925 New York newspaper review called Tyler the new "surprise star" who "strongly resembles George O'Brien, built on a larger and more powerful scale."[63] By this time he was being typecast as a cowboy hero and adopting Tom Tyler as a screen name, possibly inspired by a likeness to Tom Mix, whose stylish cowboy attire, replete with ten-gallon Stetson, he adopted.

Tyler was fated to fall into the lower-tier star system the studios were developing in the early 1920s. They designed it to take advantage of the many talented and attractive wannabes flocking to Hollywood, utilize the nearby desert landscape, and avoid paying the high salaries demanded by major stars. This strategy resulted in the B Western genre. As Western film expert Bobby Copeland notes, "Studio heads decided to raise their own stars in the Mix mold, tying them to contracts and paying them like slaves." Film critic David Robinson concurs, writing, "The B western was a child of poverty—a perfect vehicle for the producer working on a shoestring budget who could not afford a sound stage or construct lavish sets. To make a B western, all he had to do was hire a few actors, rent a half dozen horses and travel a few miles outside Los Angeles, where nature provided the kind of spectacular scenery that could give an extra boost to even the most shaky productions."[64] Tyler's initiation to B Westerns came when FBO was looking for a handsome cowboy hero to complement its leading star, Fred Thomson. As Tyler biographer Mario DeMarco explains, "The brass was certainly impressed by his good looks and physical stature—and asked him one question that set him back a few paces, 'Can you ride a horse?'" Without hesitation, he replied "with a firm, 'Yes,' and was signed by the studio." Tyler had never ridden a horse and had no idea how to mount one.[65] After a few quick lessons at a nearby ranch, however, he was ready to ride in *Galloping Gallagher* (1924). Perhaps more than any Hollywood actor, Tyler epitomized the B Western. For the remainder of the silent era, he starred in three dozen low-budget quickies.

What made Tyler distinctive, however, was his weightlifting exploits. David Willoughby describes him as "about as strong to start with as I was after having trained with weights for eight years." With Willoughby's coaching, Tyler "rapidly improved in strength and lifting power. He had tremendous natural energy, but lacked in skill and balance." He could have become a great lifter, but his film work limited his training to "fits and starts." In his first competition, in May 1925, Tyler did a 199¾-pound right-hand clean and jerk, a 189¼-pound snatch, an eighty-five-pound right-hand press, and a 469½-pound dead lift. For the next three years he remained Amateur Athletic Union heavyweight champion for Southern California and eventually clean-and-jerked 340 pounds. The climax of his lifting career occurred when he won the national title at the 1926 Sesquicentennial Championships in Philadelphia with a three lift (press, snatch, clean and jerk) total of 693½ pounds.[66] Although Tyler qualified for the 1928 Olympics in Amsterdam, the United States sent no weightlifting team.

Nevertheless, he became known as a man of muscle in Hollywood. Tyler's "sensational physique," observes Mike Chapman, was "as good as any male actor who had ever made his way to Tinseltown." Along with "a genetic disposition toward muscularity," the results of his training were "obvious for all

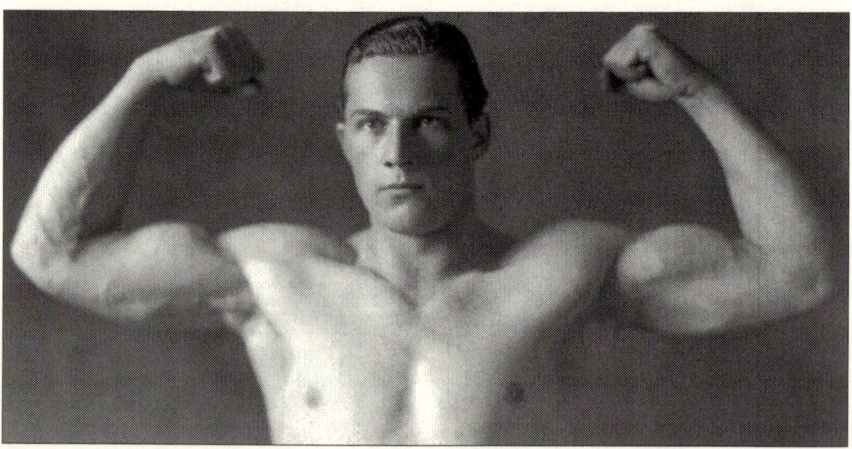

Figure 7.8. Tom Tyler, 1926 National Heavyweight Weightlifting Champion, who played in numerous roles as a cowboy hero, Captain Marvel, and the Phantom. Collection of David L. Chapman.

to see." Unlike other muscle men, notes DeMarco, Tyler never revealed exaggerated muscular proportions on the screen: "He possessed the physique of a fine athlete rather than an 'oversized muscleman.'" Likewise, athlete and Tarzan actor Herman Brix had a high regard for Tyler's muscularity: "Tom had a tremendous physique. He was very powerful, probably the most powerful man in Hollywood at the time. In my opinion, he would have made an ideal Tarzan."[67] Ironically, it was three medalists at the 1928 Olympics, Brix, Crabbe, and Weissmuller, who won starring roles as Tarzan in the 1930s.

Muscles alone, however, were never enough to ensure enduring fame in the rough-and-tumble film industry. "Despite his production," notes journalist Richard Bak, "Tyler is easily overlooked today as just one more obscure laborer in the dream factory of American cinema." The reasons for his relative obscurity are manifold. Weightlifting was his first love, an enjoyable pastime that enabled him to mold an impressive physique, become a sports champion, and gain a modicum of fame.[68] But his relegation to an endless series of B Westerns led him to accept movie roles as a matter of course and financial necessity. Chapman notes that "he wasn't focused on becoming a major star as much as he was on earning a solid living. He was in Hollywood to work, on a regular basis, not to be a prima donna waiting only for the most appealing roles." Bruce Hickey observes that Tyler was "stuck with bottom-dollar productions in his solo starring westerns, and never had a standout series." Additionally, Tyler did not make the transition to talkies smoothly. Ray Slepski, his nephew, points out that "one of the things that hurt him a lot was his voice. It was kind of gravelly." He also seemed to overpronounce his lines.[69] To Beth Marion, Tyler's costar in *Rip Roarin' Buckaroo* (1936), his voice seemed somewhat high and squeaky, but she "always thought, more than over-pronouncing his words, he maybe had a little accent and was trying to overcome that." Similarly, film director Oliver Drake recalls that Tyler "had a slight Lithuanian accent and it seemed no one wanted him for a talkie." Although Tyler sought help from a diction coach, it did not lead to more opportunities. He eventually had to sell his car and give up his Beverly Hills home.[70]

A no less serious shortcoming was Tyler's awkward physical presence on screen. Bobby Copeland points out that Tyler "wasn't cut out for major studio work. He had a monotone voice . . . and he was pretty wooden in love scenes. Actually, despite his impressive physique, he really wasn't that good of a physical actor. He could look awkward in fight scenes. He didn't have major movie-star potential, however that's defined. You know it when you see it. Tom Tyler didn't have it—but his star still shone pretty brightly for a while." Chuck Anderson adds that Tyler "never developed into a proficient screen brawler (like Bob Steele and Tex Ritter), and often appeared to swing and churn rather than pummel his antagonist into submission."[71] What could have been an immense asset for Tyler, as it was for Fairbanks and Mix, was the wholesome image he projected. "I think the real appeal was that the hero always had good, strong values," notes Copeland. "He didn't drink, swear, or carouse. If he hit a guy, he'd pick him up afterwards. Instead of killing the villain, he'd shoot the hat off his head. For kids who didn't really have a role model . . . these figures were like your father, preacher, and Sunday-school teacher, all rolled into one. You'd come out of the theater feeling like your soul had just been cleansed."[72] It was an image that even Tyler's brief "torrid love affair" with femme fatale Marlene Dietrich could not dispel. According to Marion Shilling, his costar in *Rio Rattler* (1935), he was "a handsome, big mass of muscle" but never out of character. He was "always prompt and knew his lines but [was] very quiet." That he never gravitated toward the exuberant and dissolute lifestyle of many stars likely worked to his disadvantage and prevented him from rubbing shoulders with Hollywood kingmakers. While Tyler was cranking out B Westerns in the late 1930s, the star was rising for John Wayne, who, according to Chapman, was "making friends with some powerful people in the business, including John Ford." Wayne was "often invited to spend weekends with the powerful director and his pals on Ford's yacht, drinking, fishing and playing cards." Wayne's breakthrough came when Ford chose him as lead actor in the classic Western *Stagecoach* (1939), with Tyler relegated to a lesser role. Not unlike his earlier casting experience with Tarzan, it was a lost opportunity. Film historians Don Miller and Leonard Maltin regret that Tyler "could have been transformed into a screen image approaching the highest plateaus. That it didn't happen is too bad."[73]

For other athletic actors with intangibles in the interwar period it did happen. Pat O'Brien, sometimes called Hollywood's Irishman in Residence, is not typically regarded as an athletic actor, but football movies became popular in the 1930s and 1940s, and O'Brien starred in the greatest, *Knute Rockne, All American*. Upon its release in 1940 O'Brien gave a pep talk to Notre Dame students—not about football, but about physical culture. After naval service during World War I, he played sub-quarterback for Marquette University against Notre Dame University. As O'Brien explained at the time,

The fact that I played football in my twenties has saved me lots of embarrassment now that I'm forty. In this picture I have to get out there and throw passes, kick, run, even score a touchdown against Army. I have to play with kids in their twenties, too. And had I not, twenty years previous, got in this condition and kept in it I would have looked an awful bum out there, at forty. It would have been pretty embarrassing for me, too, if I'd had to have a double do my playing for me. I *didn't* have to.[74]

This film also fostered one of the most memorable lines in the history of sport—"win just one for the Gipper"—uttered by a young actor who started his career in B Westerns and, by dint of personality, ambition, and political savvy, would later catapult from Hollywood to the White House.

Notes

1. Kevin Brownlow, *Hollywood: The Pioneers*, 264. Brownlow also quotes film critic Cedric Belfrage who, after seeing *The Jazz Singer*, lamented that "the international language was over. This was really a thing which nobody seemed to notice very much, but after all, the human species had lived on the face of the globe for thousands of years and there had never before been a language in which they could all speak to each other" (266).

2. Rudolph Valentino, "Muscles in the Movies: How Physical Culture Made Me a Screen Star," *Muscle Builder*, August 1924, 28, 30, 32.

3. T. Howard Kelly, "Red Blood and Plenty of Sand," *Physical Culture* 49 (February 1923): 27–29, 138. Valentino also authored an exercise book in which he attested that "my athletic experience and all round physical strength have been absolutely indispensable in my work"; Rudolph Valentino, *How You Can Keep Fit* (New York: Macfadden, 1923), 5.

4. Brownlow, *Hollywood*, 184–85.

5. Hansen adds that "Valentino's appeal depends, to a large degree, on the manner in which he combines masculine control of the look with the feminine quality of 'to-be-looked-at-ness.'" Little mention is made of Valentino's body. Miriam Hansen, "Pleasure, Ambivalence, Identification: Valentino and Female Spectatorship," *Cinema Journal* 25, no. 4 (Summer 1986): 1, 12. Likewise, the emphasis of Thomas Slater's study of Valentino's script writer is on redefining masculinity in the wake of the Great War rather than focusing on bodily motion—despite the absence of sound. Thomas J. Slater, "June Mathis's Valentino Scripts: Images of Male 'Becoming' after the Great War," *Cinema Journal* 50, no. 1 (Fall 2010): 99–120.

6. Adela Rogers St. Johns, interview, in David Gill and Kevin Brownlow, dirs., "Episode 6: Swanson and Valentino," in *Hollywood Series: A Celebration of American Silent Film* (London Thames Television / Photoplay Productions, 1979), YouTube, http://www.youtube.com/watch?v=fVqgx20CPVs. See also the chapter "Ballyhoo" in Allan R.

Ellenberger, *The Valentino Mystique: The Death and Afterlife of the Silent Film Idol* (Jefferson, NC: McFarland, 2005), 61–77. City officials estimated roughly 100,000 people eventually viewed Valentino's body.

7. David W. Menefee, *George O'Brien: A Man's Man in Hollywood*, 28–31.

8. Mario DeMarco, *Tom Tyler and George O'Brien: "The Herculeses of the Cinema Range,"* 56–58, 62.

9. Alma Talley, "A Physically Perfect Young Man," *Picture Play*, October 1927, 74.

10. Delight Evans, "Sock-Wham-Bam-Biff-Zumm!" *Screenland*, January 1928, 102; Mordaunt Hall, "The Screen: Strained Adventures," *New York Times*, December 3, 1924; DeMarco, *Tom Tyler and George O'Brien*, 56.

11. Evans, "Sock-Wham-Bam-Biff-Zumm!," 102.

12. Menefee, *George O'Brien*, 70–72; "The Dancers," *Variety*, January 7, 1925, 38.

13. Menefee, *George O'Brien*, 72–73; *Sunrise* was the most prestigious film in which O'Brien starred, and Murnau, a gay man, saw beauty in O'Brien's soul as well as well as his physical features.

14. Lew Pike, "George O'Brien, Movie Muscle Man!" *Strength and Health*, March 1948, 30.

15. Hamilton Dana, "George O'Brien—Athletic Movie Star," *Strength*, December 1928, 23; DeMarco, *Tom Tyler and George O'Brien*, 62.

16. Menefee, *George O'Brien*, 141, 83–84.

17. Pike, "George O'Brien," 18, 29; George Lowther, "How George O'Brien of the Movies Keeps Fit," *Your Physique*, October 1947, 8–9.

18. "Film Reviews, *My Wild Irish Rose*," *Variety*, December 10, 1947, 12.

19. Edward Connor, "The Twelve Tarzans," 463; Sy Weintraub to Marty Weiser, "Tarzan's Greatest Adventure," Miscellaneous (circa 1958), Paramount 1959, Rudy Behlmer Papers, Margaret Herrick Library, f. 195.

20. As John Kasson observes, Burroughs was "always acutely conscious of the gulf between his life as an author and the adventures of his alter ego, Tarzan." John F. Kasson, *Houdini, Tarzan, and the Perfect Man: The White Male Body and the Challenge of Modernity in America*, 160.

21. Erling B. Holtsmark, *Edgar Rice Burroughs* (Boston: Twayne, 1986), 53–54, 57; Erling B. Holtsmark, *Tarzan and Tradition: Classical Myth in Popular Literature* (Westport, CT: Greenwood, 1981), 35, 92–93. In 1937 Burroughs confirmed to Rudolph Altrochi, a University of California professor, that his concept of Tarzan was also influenced by Rudyard Kipling's *The Jungle Book* (1894) and a book about "a sailor who was shipwrecked on the coast of Africa and who was adopted and consorted with great apes." Edgar Rice Burroughs to Rudolph Altrochi, March 29, 1937, quoted in Scott Tracy Griffin, *Tarzan: The Centennial Celebration*, 26.

22. Edgar Rice Burroughs, *Tarzan of the Apes* (New York: Random House, 2003), 104; Kasson characterizes Burroughs's Tarzan as "the ultimate self-taught, self-made man" whose duty is to rescue the others from "one near disaster after another. Their assignment, in turn, is to admire his beautiful and powerful body while he does so." Kasson, *Houdini*, 207.

23. Gabe Essoe, *Tarzan of the Movies: A Pictorial History of More Than Fifty Years of Edgar Rice Burroughs' Legendary Hero*, 14; "Meet Tarzan—All Eleven of 'Em," *Tarzan's Greatest*, No. 533, Paramount 1959, Margaret Herrick Library; Connor, "The Twelve Tarzans," 453; Walt Morton, "Tracking for the Sign of Tarzan: Trans-Media Representation of a Popular Culture Icon," in *You Tarzan: Masculinity, Movies and Men*, ed. Pat Kirkham and Janet Thumim (New York: St. Martin's, 1993), 114.

24. Essoe, *Tarzan*, 14–15.

25. Irwin Porges, *Edgar Rice Burroughs: The Man Who Created Tarzan* (Provo, UT: Brigham Young University Press, 1975), 315f; "A Yankee Maciste," *Photoplay*, July 1919, 91.

26. Mike Chapman, "Gallery of Tarzans," 40; Essoe, *Tarzan*, 23–27; Connor, "Twelve Tarzans," 454.

27. Essoe, *Tarzan*, 30; Bill Hillman, "The Son of Tarzan," *ERBzine* 0589, http://www.erbzine.com/mag5/0589.html; Chapman, "Gallery," 40.

28. Essoe, *Tarzan*, 49.

29. Edgar Rice Burroughs, *Tarzan and the Golden Lion* (New York: Grosset and Dunlap, 1923), 65, 250.

30. "The Shadow Stage," *Photoplay*, May 1927, 135; Bill Hillman, "Tarzan and the Golden Lion," *ERBzine* 0591, http://www.erbzine.com/mag5/0591.html; Essoe, *Tarzan*, 56.

31. Bob Jones, "Frank Merrill—Tarzan of the Apes," *Strength*, February 1930, 33, 70–71; Essoe, *Tarzan*, 59–61.

32. Denie Walter, "The Tarzan Blueprints," 42; Bill Hillman, "Frank Merrill: 'The Hercules of the Screen,'" *ERBzine* 2870, http://www.erbzine.com/mag28/2870.html.

33. Essoe, *Tarzan*, 70.

34. Rudy Behlmer, "The MGM Tarzans," f. 192, Rudy Behlmer Papers, Margaret Herrick Library.

35. Gail Hall Wright, "Hollywood Goes Olympic!," *Screenland*, September 1932, 16–17. See also "What! More Olympic Swimmers?" *Photoplay*, July 1932, 68–69.

36. Ida Zeitlin, "The Newest Hollywood Thrill!" *Screenland*, August 1932, 51. Weissmuller created a similar thrill when he appeared virtually nude in *Glorifying the American Girl* in 1929.

37. Katherine Albert, "Hey! Hey! Here Comes Johnny!" *Photoplay*, June 1932, 29, 118.

38. The Motion Picture Production Code, more commonly known as the Hays Code (after Will H. Hays, the president of the Motion Picture Producers and Distributors of America), was a set of moral guidelines adopted in 1930 but not rigidly enforced until mid-1934.

39. Rudy Behlmer to Henry Hart, April 16, 1965; Joseph I. Breen to Gen. Will H. Hays, April 10, 1934; and Rudy Behlmer to Maureen O'Sullivan, March 14, 1966, Rudy Behlmer Papers, Margaret Herrick Library.

40. Ben Maddox, "Has Hollywood Tamed Its Tarzans?," *Screenland*, June 1934, 92; Alan G. Barbour, *Cliffhanger: A Pictorial History of the Motion Picture Serial*, 1.

41. *Variety* took note of Crabbe's bare behind, reporting that the former Olympian treated viewers to "a few flashes of the lily white in a bathing suit and later under a shower in the locker room." *Variety*, 1934, quoted in Jerry Vermilye, *Buster Crabbe: A Biofilmography* (Jefferson, NC: McFarland, 2008), 65.

42. Barbour, *Cliffhanger*, 1; Evelyn Ballarine, "Going Native," *Screenland*, June 1933, 53. Crabbe later published a book featuring "twenty basic exercises that firm your body and sharpen your mind." Buster Crabbe, *Energistics: The Simple Shape-Up Exercise Plan* (Chicago: Playboy, 1976).

43. Walter, "The Tarzan Blueprints," 43.

44. As Mike Chapman observes, "Brix's portrayal probably comes closest to capturing ERB's image of the adult Tarzan—a wise and cultured man who can revert, on a moment's notice, to the savagery of primitive man." Chapman, "Gallery," 41.

45. Walter, "The Tarzan Blueprints," 43.

46. Bill Hillman, "Tarzan's Revenge," *ERBzine* 0619, http://www.erbzine.com /mag6/0619.html; Chapman, "Gallery," 41; "Tarzan's Revenge," *Variety*, January 12, 1938, 14; Essoe, *Tarzan*, 100, 104; Connor, "Twelve Tarzans," 460.

47. Ron Ely, "Foreword," in Griffin, *Tarzan: The Centennial Celebration*, 6; Edgar Rice Burroughs, *Tarzan and the City of Gold* (New York: Ballantine Books, 1964), 10.

48. Walter, "The Tarzan Blueprints," 41; Joe Weider and Ben Weider, *Brothers of Iron* (Champaign, IL: Sports Publishing, 2006), 24.

49. Margery Wilson, "The Body Beautiful," *Screenland*, March 1932, 66–67; James H. MacFarland, "Keeping Fit in Movie Land," *Strength*, November 1930, 19; Anne Van Alstyne, "Keeping Fit Beautifully," *Screenland*, May 1930, 106.

50. Katherine Albert, "Charm? No! No! You Must Have Glamour," *Photoplay*, September 1931, 38–39, 100.

51. Sue Wilson, "Recreation and Sport—the Keynote of Health Agrees Norma Shearer," *Strength*, December 1929, 22–23.

52. Anne Van Alstyne, "Building for Beauty," *Screenland*, August 1930, 91; Sue Wilson, "Try Kathryn Crawford's Plan," *Correct Eating and Strength*, June 1930, 73; Jim Davies, "Want to Have a Hollywood Figure?," *Screenland*, June 1934, 73–74; Jim Davies, "How to Have That Hollywood Figure!," *Screenland*, August 1934, 27.

53. Lois Shirley, "The Enemy of Beauty—Over-Exercise," 30–31, 112.

54. Sylvia [Ulback], *Hollywood Undressed: Observations of Sylvia as Noted by Her Secretary* (New York: Brentano's, 1931), 10, 90, 124, 128–29, 174–75, 219.

55. See also Carlo Gaberscek, "Carnera e il cinema," in *La leggenda di Primo Carnera*, ed. Roberto Festi (Civezzano, Italy: EsaExpo, 2006).

56. "Talking Shorts, Prizefighter and the Lady," *Variety*, November 14, 1933, 17.

57. Mordaunt Hall, "Max Baer, Myrna Loy and Walter Huston in 'The Prizefighter and the Lady,'" *New York Times*, November 11, 1933. Carnera was no slouch in either his physique or as an actor. The Italian champion appeared in twenty films.

58. Nat Fleischer, Sam E. Andre, and Nat Loubet, *A Pictorial History of Boxing* (New York: Bonanza, 1981), 123.

59. Allison Quirk, "Muscling In," *Photoplay*, January 1933, 102–3.

60. Victor Varconi, "Personality and Talent in Photoplay," in *The Truth about the Movies by the Stars*, ed. Laurence A. Hughes, 127.

61. "Moriah Historical Society," Historic Port Henry–Moriah, http://www.porthenry moriah.com/living-here/about/moriah-historical-society.

62. Tom Kozra, interview, August 14, 2004, in Mike Chapman, *The Tom Tyler Story: From Cowboy Star to Super Hero*, 11.

63. Unidentified New York newspaper review, July 31, 1925, quoted in Chapman, *The Tom Tyler Story*, 19.

64. Bobby J. Copeland, *Trail Talk*, 18; David Robinson, *Hollywood, 1920–1970*, 1997, quoted in Chapman, *The Tom Tyler Story*, 18–19.

65. Mario DeMarco, *Tom Tyler and George O'Brien*, 17.

66. John Bradford, "American Continental Weight Lifters Association Notes," *Strength*, November 1926, 52.

67. Chapman, *The Tom Tyler Story*, 19; DeMarco, *Tom Tyler and George O'Brien*, 15; Herman Brix, quoted in Chapman, *The Tom Tyler* Story, 38.

68. Richard Bak, "A Hero from Hamtramck," *Hour Detroit Magazine*, August 10, 2010, http://www.hourdetroit.com/community/a-hero-from-hamtramck/. A two-page 1927 advertisement by the Milo Barbell Company shows that the commercial possibilities of Tyler's fame was not overlooked: "His physique and unusual physical ability and versatility, which he attributes to Milo bells and methods, have won him recognition among the motion picture companies of the West, which resulted in an actor's contract." Milo Barbell Company, advertisement, *Strength*, January 1927, 78–79.

69. Chapman, *The Tom Tyler Story*, 56; Bruce Hickey, *Wrangler's Roost*, no. 118, quoted in Chapman, *The Tom Tyler Story*, 49; Ray Slepski, quoted in Bak, "A Hero from Hamtramck."

70. Boyd Magers and Michael G. Fitzgerald, *Westerns Women: Interviews with 50 Leading Ladies of Movie and Television Westerns from the 1930s to the 1960s*, 156; Oliver Drake, *Written, Produced and Directed by Oliver Drake* (Baldwyn, MS: Outlaw, 1990), 21.

71. Copeland, *Trail Talk*, 52; Chuck Anderson, "Tom Tyler," The Old Corral, http://www.b-westerns.com/tyler7.htm.

72. Copeland, *Trail Talk* 52.

73. Magers and Fitzgerald, *Westerns Women*, 197; Chapman, *The Tom Tyler Story*, 54; Don Miller, *Hollywood Corral*, 51.

74. Pat O'Brien, quoted in Gladys Hall, "Pat O'Brien's Message," *Screenland*, October 1940, 92.

VIII. THE SUPERHEROES

I'm Popeye the Sailor Man,
I'm Popeye the Sailor Man.
I'm strong to the finich
Cause I eats me spinach.
I'm Popeye the Sailor Man.

—Samuel Lerner, "I'm Popeye the Sailor Man"

CARTOONS—OR FUNNY PAPERS, as we know them—were a product of hard times, emerging after World War I and sustaining society through the worst depression of modern times. Their adaptation to film ensued with the emergence of Mickey Mouse in Walt Disney's classic *Steamboat Willie* (1928). The anxieties of the 1920s and 1930s created a need for entertainment to keep America laughing, and publishers and moviemakers quickly seized on profits that could be made by creating fantasies. Action movies with athletic stars like Douglas Fairbanks were already in place. The transition from these men of muscle (albeit with stunt doubles in tow) to animated and superheroic stars was a natural outgrowth of the Jazz Age, which provided a much-needed escape from reality. Fantasy figures promulgated by Hollywood helped fill an existential void in Western civilization in the aftermath of the worst war in human history. Heroes were in vogue. The new mood of rejuvenation reflected many aspects of the futurism movement of Filippo Tommaso Marinetti and its postwar associations with Italian Fascism. "Speed and power furnished the dominant *motif* of the new age," observes historian Eugen Weber, "and its proponents set out to translate them into prose, verse, and the plastic arts." The "Manifeste de futurisme" (Futurist manifesto, 1909) declared that "we want to exalt the aggressive gesture, the feverish insomnia, the athletic step, the perilous leap, the box on the ear, and the fisticuff. We declare that the world's wonder has been enriched by a fresh beauty: the beauty of speed."[1] Speed was personified in America by Barney Oldfield, whose sixty-mile-per-hour record in 1903 helped popularize race car driving in film, and Sir Malcolm Campbell, whose Bluebird automobile broke the three-hundred-mile-per-hour barrier in 1935, inspired many more speed records by World War II.[2]

Popeye the Sailor Man

The most notable postwar superhero in print was Popeye the Sailor Man, who first appeared as a secondary character on January 17, 1929, in *Thimble Theatre*, a comic strip created by Elzie Crisler Segar for King Features Syndicate and published in William Randolph Hearst's *Evening Journal*. The original stars were Olive Oyl, her brother Castor Oyl, and erstwhile boyfriend Harold Hamgravy, but it was Popeye who quickly gained popularity and led to the cartoon's retitling.[3] Named for his protruding eye, Popeye's signature story line centered on feats of strength he used to assist and rescue others from danger. He was inspired by a familiar character named Frank Fiegel in Segar's hometown of Chester, Illinois. According to Fiegel's 1947 obituary, "he performed amazing feats of strength" in his youth. "Because of his hardened physique he was affectionately known as 'Rocky.' His angular jaw and familiar corn-cob pipe apparently impressed the young Segar." Film commentator Glenn Mitchell adds that like Popeye, Fiegel "mangled the English language and always sought to do the right thing." Once, when some local hoodlums attempted to rob him, he not only escaped unscathed but seriously injured them. Thus, "Rocky became Popeye."[4] Although spinach was recognized as the source of Popeye's strength, it was not initially featured in the plot. Curiously, his physique shows abnormal and unheroic development, with gigantic muscles misplaced in the forearms rather than the biceps typically coveted by strongmen. With these bodily endowments, Popeye would subdue many monstrous and seemingly superior adversaries, including the Sea Hag (a vicious pirate), Alice the Goon (a hairy Amazon), Toar (a massive brute), and his nemesis Bluto, who would become a fixture in all of Popeye's subsequent adventures.

Such was the popularity of Popeye comics by the 1930s that film adaptations seemed inevitable, especially after Disney's introduction of Mickey Mouse. No less innovative were the Fleischer brothers, Max and Dave, who produced the animated antics of Ko-Ko the Clown (1924), Bimbo (1930), and Betty Boop (1930) with Paramount. Popeye's first appearance in a Betty Boop cartoon was titled *Popeye the Sailor* (1933). His arrival is heralded in a newspaper headline, "Popeye a Movie Star, The Sailor with the 'Sock' Accepts Movie Contract." The newspaper photo of Popeye then comes to life as he strolls on board a ship, singing his signature song ("I'm Popeye the Sailor Man," composed by Sammy Lerner) while casually displaying his strength—smashing an anchor into thousands of fish hooks, crushing a nautical clock into tiny alarm clocks, splintering a flagpole into clothespins, and punching a huge fish mounted on a plank into a cascade of sardine cans. What Director Dave Fleischer desired was to "just show his strength," which became the formula for the *Popeye* series.[5] The action centers on the rivalry between Popeye and Bluto for Olive Oyl's affections, first in a brief dockside encounter, then at a carnival where the two suitors compete in games of skill. Later, as Fred Grandinetti recounts, "Popeye joins hula dancer Betty Boop on stage until he sees Bluto running off with Olive. Bluto ties Olive to the railroad tracks and begins pounding on Popeye. As the train fast approaches Olive, Bluto stomps on the sailor, who then casually opens a can of spinach and eats it. With two swings of his fists, he knocks Bluto into a tree (which conveniently becomes a coffin). With another smashing punch, he turns the oncoming train into scrap, then sings, 'I'm Popeye the Sailor Man (*toot, toot*).'"[6] This kind of dramatic ending, with good triumphing over evil, was standard fare for most action films of the era. The *Popeye* series is unique in that it was always done heroically, with muscles alone.

The first official Popeye film, *I Yam What I Yam* (1933), features more display of muscular brawn as the sailor man saves Olive Oyl from a band of Indians, first with his fearsome twister punch, warding off hundreds of arrows, socking some of the tribe into Indian head nickels, and finally, after consuming a can of spinach, smacking down a club-wielding chief who is transformed into the pacifist Mahatma Gandhi. Olive proclaims Popeye her "hero," and he is crowned with a headdress labeled "Big Cheese." What enabled the Fleischers to extricate Popeye from the clutches of *Thimble Theatre* and Betty Boop was not only his immense popularity but the demotion of Betty from sex kitten to ingénue in light of the recently adopted Motion Picture Production Code. "Like Jane in the live-action Tarzan films, her body was immediately covered up; gone was the garter, the short skirt, the décolletage," notes Leonard Maltin. "Her character was transformed into a Goody Two-Shoes."[7] The Popeye flicks should have aroused the ire of censors by its violence, especially as kids' fare, but there was never bloodshed, and no one was ever killed. The villains returned intact for another episode. Cartoon historian Jerry Beck dubs Popeye "the anti-hero. He was a gruff old man. He smoked. . . . He didn't speak normal English. He spoke in Popeyese." According to animation director Eric Goldberg, the sailor was "one of the great moral characters in animation. . . . He always wants to do what's right. Sometimes he has to use violence in order to achieve it." Popeye projected an upbeat image, and his adventures, much like those of B Westerns, depicted him as a lovable, all-American everyman. His success was so immediate and overwhelming that it stunned Walt Disney. Popeye was a bigger draw than Mickey Mouse.[8]

Much of what facilitated the *zoom, pow,* and *boom* so characteristic of Popeye cartoons was the immense strength linked to his consumption of spinach; both were viewed as valuable components of healthy growing bodies. Diet and exercise were a natural complement to Popeye's moral didacticisms. The message was so strong that in 1934 spinach consumption increased by 33 percent in the United States, and Segar started receiving complimentary crates of spinach at his home, notes cartoonist Frank Caruso. After downing a can of spinach in one episode, Popeye even acquired a suit with a cape and a shield emblazoned with a giant *S* on his enlarged chest, a conscious cartoonist confusion of Superman and Spinach. So important was the vegetable to every Popeye plot that it became the equivalent of a supporting character. Occasionally it even assumed a life of its own, explains Grandinetti. In *I Wanna Be a Lifeguard* (1936) "a battered Popeye whistles for his can of spinach, which is in his locker room. Upon hearing the whistle, the can quivers, drops to the ground and rolls toward Popeye." In *Friend or Phony* (1952) "Bluto tricks Popeye into throwing away his can of spinach. The can lands on the back of a moving truck and yells, 'You'll be sorry!' As Bluto uses construction equipment to pound Popeye into the ground, the sailor sends out an SOS via the smoke in his pipe. The spinach can sniffs the smoke, jumps off the back of the truck, hops toward Popeye, pops itself open and pours the spinach inside Popeye's mouth."[9] From 1933 to 1957 Fleischer and Famous Studios produced 234 Popeye films, followed by 412 cartoons after 1960 from television studios. Finally, the first human adaptation occurred when Paramount Pictures produced *Popeye* (1980), a musical comedy starring Robin Williams as the sailor. Constant exposure spawned hundreds of items bearing the likeness of the one-eyed sailor and his crew, including toys, picture books, video games, paint kits, statues, bobblehead dolls, mugs, cookie jars, and Christmas ornaments. Virtually all subsequent superheroes inspired this kind of exploitation directed at the children's market.[10]

The precise impact of Popeye's many manifestations on American youth cannot be determined, but the unmistakable message in virtually all episodes is that strength is desirable and muscles are meant to be used. No less obvious to *Mad* magazine art director Sam Viviano is Popeye's place in the heroic tradition: "He was really the first superhero—super strong and super fast. He beat superman to the punch by nine years." Comic book historian Michael Uslan concurs: "Popeye is our modern day Hercules. If you assume that Hercules and mythological gods like Hercules from the Greeks, the Romans, the Norse, the Egyptians were our first superheroes, then Popeye was truly the first one in the modern era."[11] For American movie audiences, it was their first exposure to animated muscle and might. The widespread popularity of Popeye showed that contrived representations of human behavior were no less capable of absorption by the viewing public than real actors displaying might and muscle.

The Man of Steel

Unlike Popeye, derived from a single hometown strongman, Superman was drawn from a myriad of sources, including Popeye, by a pair of Cleveland schoolboys, Joe Shuster and Jerry Siegel. Their biographer, Brad Ricca, identifies two items in a Sunday edition of the Cleveland *Plain Dealer*, from June 18, 1933, as a source of inspiration. The first was a front-page report that local high school student Jesse Owens, having set a record of 9.4 seconds in the hundred-yard dash, was the world's fastest human. The second item appeared on the comics page, where spinach-eating Popeye outlifted the gigantic Bullo Oxheart, alleged to be the world's strongest man. Historian Larry Tye identifies three fictional influences, including Edgar Rice Burroughs, who created not only Tarzan but also John Carter of Mars, who "traveled in space and was invulnerable. His strength on Mars came from the planet's having less gravity than Earth, the flip side of what would happen to Superman when he reached Earth from Krypton." Burroughs became Siegel's favorite writer and inspired him to create a heavily muscled parody of Tarzan called Goober the Mighty. Author Dennis Dooley concludes that Siegel was "more preoccupied with heroes of gigantic strength and powerful physiques than the average boy his age."[12] Another derivation came from the book *Gladiator* (1930), by Philip Wylie, in which the hero, Hugo Danner, had "the strength of Samson, the speed of Hermes, and skin, like Caeneus's, that was impervious to injury." Eight years later Wylie's "superhuman" became Siegel's "superman." Finally, there was Doc Savage, the Man of Bronze, a creation of Street and Smith Publications in 1933. Savage not only possessed brute strength but "the deductive skills of Sherlock Holmes, the tree-swinging grace of Tarzan, the scientific-sleuthing acumen of Dick Tracy, and the morals of Abraham Lincoln." On the eve of Superman's birth, Tye observes, the world was "awash with heroes."[13]

The schoolboys' favorite actor was the swashbuckling Douglas Fairbanks. "He did *The Mark of Zorro* and *Robin Hood* and had a marvelous one called *The Black Pirate*," Shuster recalled. "He had a stance which I often used in drawing Superman. You'll see in many of his roles—including Robin Hood—that he always stood with his hands on his hips and his feet spread apart, laughing—taking nothing seriously."[14] The figure that Siegel imagined and Shuster drew, according to Les Daniels, was

> the ultimate acrobat and strongman. He was in the tradition of the mighty heroes who are legendary in every culture, from Samson and Hercules to Beowulf, and he fought against crime and tyranny and social injustice. An immigrant of sorts, he became the champion of the American way. "Let's put him in this kind of costume," Shuster remembered suggesting, "and let's give him a big *S* on his chest, and a cape, make him as colorful as we can and as distinctive as we can."[15]

What made Shuster and Siegel's creation so appealing was a surfeit of superlative powers enabling him to supersede rival heroes. "So keen was the ferment and the determination to be noticed," Tye observes, "that the word the Greeks had given us [hero] no longer was enough."[16]

Superman's creators shared a common background and outlook that led to successful collaboration. In addition to similar physical characteristics, both were sons of Jewish tailors who were poor refugees. Tye observes that "both wore glasses, were petrified of girls, and preferred to stay indoors reading when everyone else their age was in the park playing ball, which made them two-for-one targets of schoolyard toughs." Superman compensated for their daily deprivations. Gina Misiroglu notes that Clark Kent, Superman's alter ego, "was the downtrodden 'everyman,' while Superman personified physical power. Superman was an unabashed intimidator you could cheer for, a figure of hope when many Americans felt hopeless."[17] The first breakthrough for the creative duo occurred with the appearance of the first issue of *Action Comics* in June 1938, with a manly looking Superman on the cover wearing a blue body suit and yellow chest plate, with red cape, briefs, and boots. Issue number 7, "Superman Joins the Circus," featured Superman's sense of humor along with his strength as he lifted a set of barbells in one hand and a terrified circus strongman in the other, asking, "Which is the greatest dumbbell?" By 1939 Superman's powers coalesced into "leaping over skyscrapers, running faster than an express train, springing great distances and heights, lifting and smashing tremendous weights, possessing an impenetrable skin," which enabled him to rescue the "helpless and oppressed" and battle "forces of evil and injustice." Superman personified the physical attributes that Siegel lacked. At five foot two and 112 pounds, he started lifting weights to ensure, as Tye notes, "that the body that stared back at him in the mirror really was a model for Superman." Along with copious quantities of milk and steak, he eventually reached 128 pounds. Shuster's deteriorating eyesight hardly deterred his depictions of the man with X-ray vision. Happily, reader response was robust. Within two years Superman was outselling other comics by five times, including those of Dick Tracy, Little Orphan Annie, and Popeye.[18]

Such was the popularity of the Man of Steel that he appeared on radio, portrayed by Clayton "Bud" Collyer, and daily in nationally syndicated newspaper strips that ran until 1966. Meanwhile, Shuster and Siegel relinquished the character's ownership to National Comics Publications in 1947 for merely $130.[19] The first Superman motion picture was launched in 1941 as an animated short by the Fleischer brothers for Paramount. They produced "an exciting, dramatic adventure with plenty of action and special effects," according to Leonard Maltin. "These films are among the best fantasy cartoons ever produced and feature a gallery of spectacular and memorable high-lights. . . . SUPERMAN stands as one of the Fleischer studio's finest achievements."[20] It included such catchphrases as "faster than a speeding bullet" and "more powerful than a locomotive" and introduced a telephone booth as Clark Kent's changing room. Although *Superman* cost an unprecedented $100,000 per ten-minute episode, it inspired a "Supermania" for twenty million fans, observed *Time* in 1942. Their devotion seemed unswerving to "this irrepressible Citizen Fixit, who smacks death rays back into the cannon, restores toppling skyscrapers to their foundations, knits broken bridges together with his bare hands, and who has brought a new cry into the world: 'It's a bird! It's a plane! It's— SUPERMAN!" While plots remained unchanged with Superman always winning, "his idolators (of all ages) seem satisfied to see him flex his muscles" until the series ended in 1943.[21]

Further flexing, in a more realistic medium, emerged in 1948 when Columbia Pictures launched a fifteen-chapter serial of mini-movies. The actor chosen to play Superman was Kirk Alyn, a song-and-dance entertainer who had studied ballet, performed in vaudeville and Broadway, appeared in chorus lines and blackface, and even modeled for muscle magazines.[22] In Hollywood, Alyn had done six pictures for producer Sam Katzman who, along with two National Comics executives, auditioned him. Alyn later recalled that when he got to the studio,

> they stared at me and said, "Yeah, he looks like Clark Kent, but let's see what he looks like with his shirt off." Fortunately, I was in good shape at the time. "Kirk," the guy said, "take your pants off." "I was shocked. "Now, wait a minute . . ." I began. "Look, Kirk," he said, "you're gonna have to wear tights in the movie. I have to see what your legs look like." . . . I found out later that I got the part because I looked the most like Clark Kent. That must have helped a great deal. That and the fact that a lot of the guys they interviewed could barely speak English; a lot of Greek wrestlers, fighters and big muscle men.[23]

On the set Alyn had to perform his own stunts. "I was working with barbells, so I was in good physical shape," he recalled. "And the strong dancer's legs helped me a great deal. I didn't need a trampoline to help me get off the ground. And I did it gracefully! Being Superman, I had to do everything gracefully, because everything was supposed to be easy for him." At times Alyn thought he was Superman. He would "pick people up, leap off cliffs, break things with my hands. And you don't do those things in just one take. You rehearse them four or five times" then "shoot the scene two or three more times until you get it right. Well, it takes an awful lot of strength to do those things in a manner that's really convincing. My ballet training came in handy." He also barely escaped a speeding train and endured agony hanging from wires attached to a breastplate during flying sequences. "Boy, was that murder! It was the hardest thing I ever had to do in show business," he recalled. "You don't know what it's like trying to hold your legs up in the air for nearly eight hours. My neck hurt, my back hurt, my stomach hurt, everything hurt." Although physical hardships did not deter Alyn from making another serial, *Atom Man vs. Superman* (1950), he felt stereotyped and that his career had dead-ended. But his success on the big screen as a live-action hero paved the way for the most popular rendition of the Man of Steel.[24]

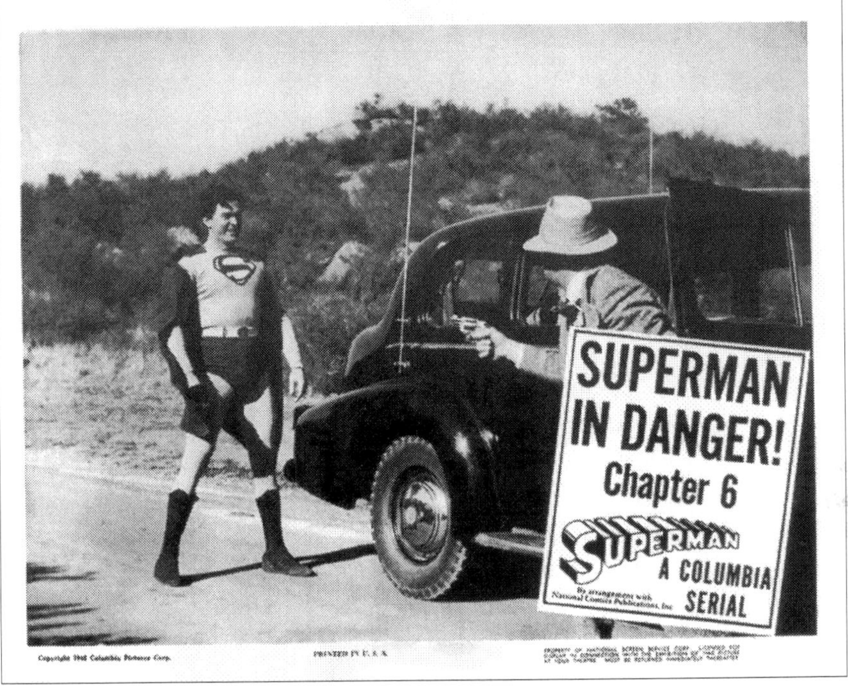

Figure 8.1. Kirk Alyn on a lobby card for the first film adaptation of Columbia Pictures' *Superman* for the series from 1948. Collection of David L. Chapman.

George Reeves

When George Reeves appeared in the first full-length Superman movie, it coincided with a slump in comic book sales and movie attendance. Born in 1914 as George Keefer Brewer in Woolstock, Iowa, his acting career began in high school and at Pasadena Junior College after his divorced mother moved to California. A strapping youth at six foot two, and 195 pounds, he also took up Golden Gloves boxing and wrestling and became a local light-heavyweight champion. But his mother persuaded him to leave the ring after he had continuously broken his nose. George then turned to acting at the prestigious Pasadena Playhouse, where he was recruited to play one of the Tarleton twins and a suitor of Scarlett O'Hara in *Gone with the Wind* (1939). Over the next decade, after a name change to Reeves, he served in World War II and acted in minor movie, radio, and television roles, including Johnny Weissmuller's *Jungle Jim* (1948). His break came in 1951 when filmmakers Robert Maxwell and Tommy Carr chose him to play Superman.

According to producer and journalist Gary Grossman, most of the two hundred applicants were

> professional actors rather than mere musclemen. Just to be sure, however, the two surveyed the studs at the 1951 Mr. America contest in Los Angeles. "But most of them," says Tommy Carr, "appeared to have a serious deficiency in their chromosome count." In any event, the search ended when George Reeves dropped in one day with his agent. . . . From that moment on he was my first choice. He looked like Superman with that jaw of his.[25]

Designed to serve as a pilot for a television series, *Superman and the Mole Men* (1951) was a fifty-eight-minute low budget production in black and white that set the mold for Reeves's most memorable role.

Broadcast on ABC at 8:30 PM, *The Adventures of Superman* was not initially a kids' show, but it quickly caught on not only with the comic book audience but also with adults. Les Daniels calls it "Superman's entry into the modern world." From 1951 to 1958, and through decades of reruns, *Adventures* became a television classic.[26] To cut costs, the producers borrowed costumes from old episodes of *Flash Gordon*, *Captain Marvel*, and *Captain America*, and Reeves wore Kirk Alyn's boots. Much attention was paid to matching Superman's appearance with his miraculous physical powers. Clark Kent's manly demeanor was bolstered by his gray double-breasted suit with padded shoulders, but getting into the Superman costume was an ordeal. Beneath the suit, Reeves wore twenty pounds of rubber latex padding to bolster the look of his arms, shoulders, and chest. The materials gave him a rash, and he sweltered under the hot studio lights, often shedding several pounds of water weight during each filming session.[27] As Grossman points out, "it wasn't easy for a grown man to run around all day in false muscles and a cape. 'George wore stuffing to cover for his sloped shoulders,' muses Whitney Ellsworth. 'He was a great athlete and did all his own jumps—and he did them well. But in uniform he needed the extra help at the shoulders to look like Superman.'" Despite Reeves's athleticism and desire to do his own feats, special effects supervisor Thol Simonson notes that most scenes required stuntmen. Grossman explains that producer Ellsworth tried to reason with Reeves: "'It doesn't make sense, George. Why take a chance to prove you're a he-man?' There'd always be an argument and Ellsworth would lose a pound of sweat in pure worry. 'There was a manhood thing involved

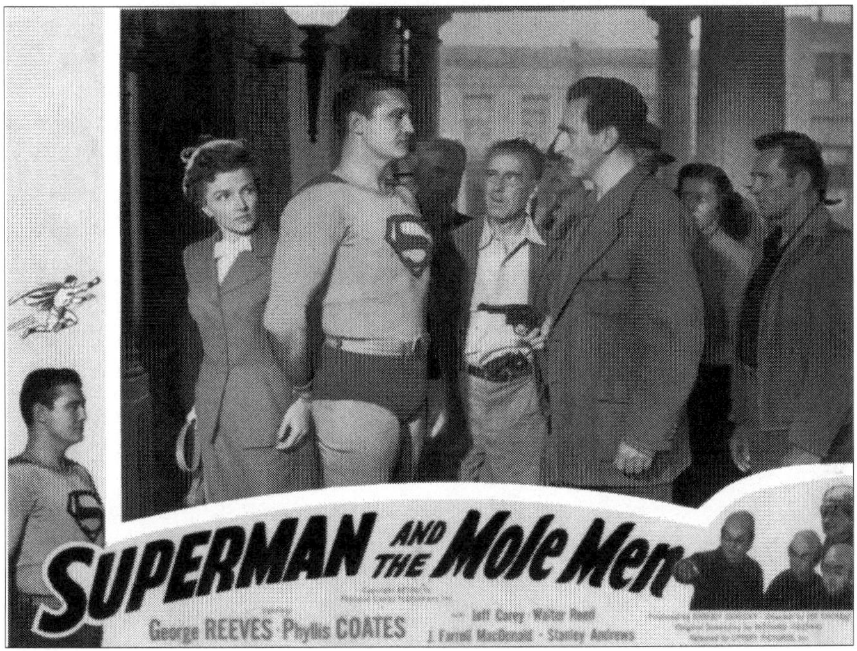

Figure 8.2. Lobby card for *Superman and the Mole Men* (1951), featuring George Reeves and Phyllis Coates. Image in the public domain.

with George,' says Whitney Ellsworth. 'He didn't want a man to double for him in one stinking little scene, but I'd always come back with, 'That isn't it, George, you can twist your ankle and be out for three days leaving us sitting around doing nothing.' "[28] Even so, conditions were probably less demanding than those Alyn endured. Film historian John Field explains that the aerial apparatus was simplified for Reeves to fit into a body mold attached to an invisible steel pole that could twist in flight without using wires. For color filming after 1956, Superman wore bright red boots with heels raised three inches to project a more imposing look, and his new red and blue suit was 100 percent wool. According to Jim Hambrick, curator of the Superman Museum in Metropolis, Illinois, "it took three to five guys after George put his muscles on to get him into that costume." It was so hot on set that he had to sit in front of dry ice and a wind machine between takes to avoid dehydration.[29]

Off the set Reeves was known for his lively social life, but he worked out regularly with trainer Gene LeBell and always exhibited an athletic demeanor in portraying Superman. On the patio of his home in Benedict Canyon, George could be seen in white bathing trunks lifting weights and practicing judo moves while soaking up the California sun. Nor was Reeves shy about displaying his buff body. He showed some interest in the nudist movement in the 1950s and often walked around his house and did yardwork unclothed. As the final season of his contract expired, and anticipating the renewal of another season in 1959, for which he would be directing, Reeves, at age forty-five, was planning a series of publicity matches with Light-Heavyweight Champion Archie Moore and even contemplating a return to wrestling. Hence he increased the intensity of his patio workouts and started roadwork in the canyon.[30] Superman, after all, had to look super, on the screen and in the ring. But all came to naught when Reeves was caught in a love triangle with Toni Mannix, wife of Metro-Goldwyn-Mayer executive Eddie Mannix, and society playgirl Lenore Lemmon, to whom he was engaged. On June 16, 1959, he was found dead in his home from a gunshot wound. Endless controversy swirled over the untimely death of Superman. Official reports deemed it suicide, but much evidence suggested foul play and involvement of organized crime through one of his lovers. Superman did not die with Reeves, however. "The 1950s TV show," observes Tye, "even more than his radio and film work, had taken Superman beyond the rarefied world of comic books and made him a centerpiece of popular culture. Television was now the medium that mattered in America." Sam Kashner and Nancy Schoenberger concur; Reeves had achieved "a kind of immortality. *The Adventures of Superman* would never be off the air, its episodes repeated endlessly in syndicated markets all over the world."[31] And with countless reincarnations of Superman in multiple mediums, artists enhanced his muscularity far beyond anything Shuster and Siegel could have imagined.

"Here I Come to Save the Day"

Among the many derivations of the Man of Steel, Mighty Mouse, a conflation of Superman and Mickey Mouse, was the most popular. Unlike Superman, however, no human could be enlisted to play a mouse; an off-screen narrator was the only voice associated with the superhero's personality. He was the brainchild of Isadore "Izzy" Klein, who had done animation work for Disney and would later produce ten televised episodes of *Popeye*. After joining the story department of Terrytoons in 1940, Klein proposed a spoof of Superman using a fly, which studio owner Paul Terry then transformed into Super Mouse.[32] But Standard Publishing had already appropriated that name for its *Coo Coo Comics* series in 1942. As Popeye and Superman derived their superpowers from spinach and outer space, respectively, Super Mouse—replete with red tights, cape, blue body shirt, white gloves, and a yellow *S* on his chest—became "the Mouse of Steel" by consuming cheese. Jeff Rovin describes this transformation: "When he takes a bite of super cheese, which he carries in his back pocket, the plucky mouse becomes superpowerful: able to fly, deflect bullets with his body, lift prodigious weights (such as pulling a train up a steep hill), see through solid objects, project his voice great distances, tune in to distant sounds with super hearing, and live indefinitely underwater. The hero's 'worst enemy' is the sinister cat Terrible Tom." Terrytoons' version of Super Mouse, released in 1942 as *The Mouse of Tomorrow*, features a similar costume but with Oil Can Harry replacing Terrible Tom as archvillain. As Rovin notes, "A quiet community of mice is being terrorized by cats, and genocide is becoming more and more inevitable. However, when one mouse manages to hide in a supermarket he finds the shelves loaded with super goods. Eating super celery and super soup, and washing with super soap, he tops off his stay with a portion of super cheese. The combination turns him into Supermouse, a spindly runt who nonetheless possesses super strength and ability to fly. After stranding the cats on the moon, he returns to protect the lives and liberty of his fellow mice." By 1944, to preempt legal action from the Superman producers, Super Mouse became Mighty Mouse, dressed in a yellow bodysuit, red trunks, cape, and white gloves, situated on the world's tallest skyscraper and guarding Terrytown, a village inhabited solely by mice.[33]

Mighty Mouse soon emerged as the most popular animal superhero. From 1942 to 1961 he starred in eighty theatrical shorts that became a Saturday morning staple on CBS television from 1955 to 1967. Part of the cartoon's appeal was repetition and the certainty that the superhero would appear on the scene at the decisive moment, just before all hope was lost. Thus he held the distinction of spending less time on screen than other stars—the building of the plot being no less important than his timely appearance to save the day. Paul Terry explained that continued success of this theme was rooted in religious lore: "If you go back through history, when a person is down and there's no more hope, you say, 'It's in God's hands now.' . . . So, taking that as a basis, I'd only have to get the mice in a tough spot and they say, 'Isn't there someone who can help?' 'Yes, there is someone; it's Mighty Mouse!' So down from the heavens he'd come . . . and lick the evil spirit, or whatever it was, and everything would be serene again."[34] Probably the most memorable and powerful lore surrounding Mighty Mouse is the refrain,

> Mister Trouble never hangs around,
> when he hears this Mighty sound,
> Here I come to save the day!
> That means that Mighty Mouse is on the way!
> Yes sir, when there is a wrong to right,
> Mighty Mouse will join the fight!
> On the sea or on the land,
> He's got the situation well in hand!

It resulted from the collaboration of lyricist Marshall Barer and composer Philip Scheib in the late 1940s and became standard fare by the time the series was adapted to television. Barer, noted for the lyrics in *Once upon a Mattress* (1959) and other major productions, regretted that his best-known song was the Mighty Mouse theme, "Here I Come to Save the Day." "Some claim to fame, huh?" Barer once stated. "I'm actually not all that proud of it. I wrote it in the back of a taxicab."[35] The implication seems clear: never underestimate the power of muscles in the movies, especially in an imaginary world for children.

The Dark Knight

Unlike Popeye, Superman, Mighty Mouse, or most other superheroes, Batman displayed no superstrength, superspeed, or ability to fly, yet he possessed "superpowers." "Batman is, after all, a mortal man," concludes physicist James Kakalios. "His complete lack of superpowers accounts in part for his appeal." Neuroscientist E. Paul Zehr concurs: "Certainly, Batman is an athletic figure, but he doesn't necessarily need huge muscles and a six-pack to fight crime."[36] While Zehr analyzes whether a human could ever attain the physical condition and skills of the legendary Dark Knight, it is obvious that the ingenious use of technology facilitated his crime-fighting. An inventory compiled by Rovin includes not only the multifaceted batmobile but the "batplane, batcopter, batboat, batcycle, batrocket, whirly-bat (autogyro), jetpack and wings for powered flight, and a hang-glider; Batman's cape can be used to glide short distances. His utility belt contains a wide array of weapons including suction-cup tips which attach to fingers for climbing, tear gas pellets, smoke grenades, a laser torch, a camera, an infrared flashlight, a two-way radio, a gas mask, a bat-a-rang, and batrope." Additional paraphernalia are provided in a four-story batcave below the Bruce Wayne mansion, which features a crime lab. According to Kakalios, "the use of superpowers themselves involves direct violations of the known laws of physics, requiring a deliberate and willful suspension of disbelief." Comics, however, "needed only a single 'miracle exception'—one thing you have to buy into to make the superhero plausible."[37] Batman's arsenal of superhuman accessories has enabled a suspension of reality in comics and on-screen into the twenty-first century.

The original depictions of the Dark Knight, however, displayed little technological wizardry. Like Shuster and Siegel, Bill Finger and Bob Kane (Kahn), the cocreators of Batman, had similar backgrounds. Both shared a Jewish heritage, graduated from DeWitt Clinton High School in the Bronx, and sought careers in writing and art, respectively. Kane worked briefly for Max Fleischer before designing strips for Detective Comics, Inc., and Finger joined him in 1938 as a ghostwriter. Seeking to build on its successful Superman character in *Action Comics*, editor Vin Sullivan asked Kane to create a similar superhero for the Detective Comics brand. Their first sketches resembled Superman until Kane recalled reading about Leonardo da Vinci's ornithopter, a glider-like flying device with bat-like wings, and remembered one of his favorite films, *The Bat Whispers* (1930), an adaptation of a Mary Roberts Rinehart novel. Another inspiration, observes Les Daniels, was *The Mark of Zorro* (1920): "This film featured an athletic, flamboyant performance by Douglas Fairbanks, which turned him into the biggest action star of the silent screen; the story, about a wealthy fop who transformed himself at night into a masked crusader for justice in Old California, stuck with young Kane. Even such details as the hero entering his hideout through an old grandfather clock were carried over from the film. 'It left a lasting impression on me. Later, when I created the Batman, it gave me the dual identity,' said Kane."[38] Finger recalls that his partner "had an idea for a character called 'Batman,' and he'd like me to see the drawings. I went over to Kane's, and he had drawn a character who looked very much like Superman with kind of . . . reddish tights, I believe, with boots . . . no gloves, no gauntlets . . . with a small domino mask, swinging on a rope. He had two stiff wings that were sticking out, looking like bat wings. And under it was a big sign . . . BATMAN." Influenced by Lee Falk and Ray Moore's popular *Phantom* newspaper strip (1936), Finger persuaded Kane to replace the domino mask with a cowl, employ a cape instead of wings, add gloves, and adopt the name Bruce Wayne, a combination of Scottish patriot Robert the Bruce and Revolutionary War general Anthony Wayne. Under Finger's influence, Batman became a blend of Douglas Fairbanks and Sherlock Holmes. He would have a "Watson" named Robin—mimicking Robin Hood, another Fairbanks character. Along with National Comics writer Gardner Fox, Finger created the batmobile, the batcave, Cat Woman, the Joker, and Gotham City.[39]

The first film adaptation of Batman occurred when Columbia Pictures launched a fifteen-part serial in 1943 starring Lewis Wilson. It featured Batman seeking to foil a plot by a Japanese spy (played by J. Carrol Naish) and a group of traitors to place America under enemy control using a radium-powered death ray, thereby turning Gotham City scientists into zombies. While a 1939 Cadillac is employed by Wayne as his batmobile and production quality is poor, the climbing and jumping sequences seem impressive and believable. They were facilitated by a team of stuntmen. But contrary to the image of a muscular and well-defined physique projected in early comic book characterizations of Batman, the 1943 serial has him wearing a baggy and boring outfit that conveys neither action nor strength. In a 1949 Columbia reboot, *Batman and Robin*, the batmobile is updated to a 1949 Mercury, and the Dark Knight is challenged by a villain called the Wizard who uses a remote-control device to take over planes, trains, and automobiles. Gina Misiroglu calls it "a lackluster production in almost every sense. The cliff-hangers are poorly written, the acting is mediocre, the costumes are bad, the music is weak, and even the director seems to have lost interest." As a consolation, its star, Robert Lowery, regarded by Les Daniels as "a sturdier batman," was a versatile athlete who was stronger and better built than Wilson and once played baseball for the Kansas City Blues.[40]

No obvious athletic or physique attributes were evident, however, when Batman and Robin came to ABC television and Twentieth Century Fox movie screens in 1966. Although the career of Adam West, who starred in both versions, was defined by his characterization, in much the same way as George Reeves became the image of Superman, he displayed no more physical prowess than either of his predecessors. What is distinctive about the West-era Batman is the technology, including a full-fledged batmobile (replacing a family sedan), a batcopter, a batboat, and other innovations made possible by an expanded budget. Machines, not muscles, would henceforth characterize human depictions of the Dark Knight. Both qualities, however, were evident in the animated versions that appeared in the CBS *Batman-Superman Hour* in 1968 and in various iterations for the next decade. Here

Batman is depicted with superhuman athletic abilities and muscles drawn to heroic proportions and complemented by an arsenal of gadgets that would generate a comic book–style popularity for a new generation of kids. Film historian Mark Reinhart rates these cartoons as of "decidedly poor quality— their animation was very cheaply produced, and their scripts were unbearably silly"; even so, "the character's light-hearted 1960s screen works kept right on winning new fans."[41]

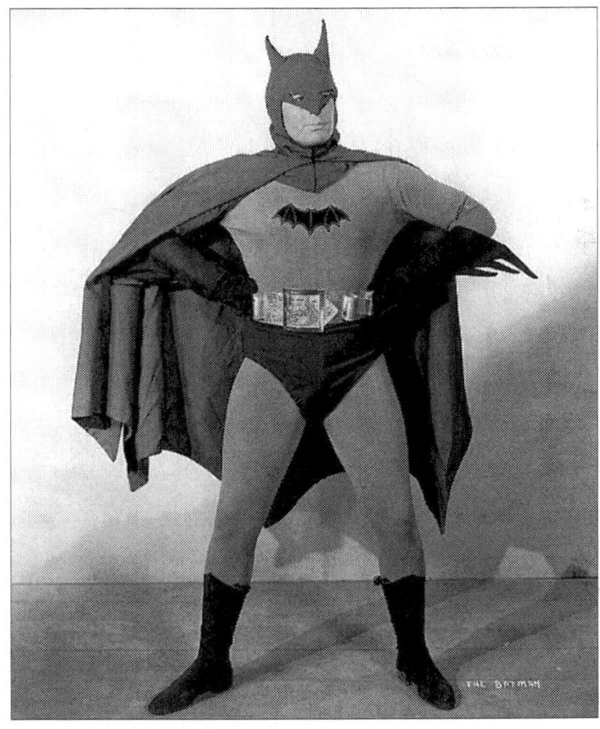

Figure 8.3. Lewis Wilson was the first live-action movie Batman. He starred in a 1943 serial version of the Dark Knight. Collection of David L. Chapman.

No powerful athletic or physique portrayal was possible in subsequent adult-oriented films where human agency was minimized and technology reigned supreme. *Batman*, released in 1989, starred Michael Keaton and featured Kim Basinger and Jack Nicholson. "Perhaps the most unexpected aspect of the film was the casting of Michael Keaton as Batman," observes Daniels. "Conventional wisdom might have demanded a muscle-bound hero rather than a quick-witted leading man who had most often been seen in comedies."[42] But Keaton, the movie, and its 1992 sequel, *Batman Returns*, proved immensely popular, and no one seemed to miss the kind of muscularity exhibited in the countless doodads being marketed to kids and adults. To a Chicago reviewer, oblivious to stuntmen and technology, the 1989 version illustrated how Batman was the best of all comic book heroes: "You see Spider-man can fly with webs. Super Man [*sic*] has super strength and can fly, but Batman just needs himself. He kicks butt by himself."[43] How any human could attain the physical attributes of Batman was analyzed hypothetically by E. Paul Zehr, who concludes that engagement in his activities "on a regular and possibly daily or nightly basis . . . would create such a large physiological stress and entail so many injuries that the possibility of remaining on top for a lifetime or even a very short career as a costumed crimefighter lacking in superpowers is very low."[44] What Zehr overlooks is that superheroes, even those relying on technology, are imaginary figures loosely linked to reality and, like ancient Greek gods, are meant for emulation, not duplication. By no means the least important aspect of introducing so many superheroic fabrications is that they usher in a reliance by moviemakers on special effects to enhance the human body's potential to create illusions.

Wonder Woman

As a complement to Superman, Wonder Woman shares a provenance with other comic book superheroes preceding World War II. Contrived by eccentric professor William Moulton Marston, who also invented the polygraph, she was an Amazon who landed in America in 1941 in her invisible robot plane from an imaginary Paradise Island of women to "fight for peace, justice, and women's rights." What's more, she came equipped with lots of gadgets and trickery. In addition to a plane that allowed her to soar undetected, she had bracelets made of Feminium (found only on Paradise Island) that could stop bullets, a tiara that could serve as a projectile, and a golden lasso that forced truth from anyone it snared. Like Superman and Batman, Wonder Woman had an alter ego, "a secretary named Diana Prince; she worked for U.S. military intelligence. Her gods were female, and so were her curses. 'Great Hera!' she cried. 'Suffering Sappho!' she swore. She was meant to be the strongest, smartest, bravest woman the world had ever seen. She looked like a pin-up girl. In 1942, she was recruited to the Justice Society of America, joining Superman, Batman, the Flash, and Green Lantern; she was the only woman. "She wore a golden tiara, a red bustier, blue underpants, and knee-high, red leather boots. She was a little slinky; she was very kinky."[45] Wonder Woman, derived from Artemis in ancient Greek lore, had the beauty of Aphrodite (who created her), the wisdom of Athena, the strength of Hercules, and the fleetness of Mercury. At age three she could uproot trees, at five she could outrun a deer, and at fifteen she acquired her Feminium bracelets. What motivated Marston was the archetypal depiction of women in comics as lacking force, strength, and power. He sought to "create a feminine character with all the strength of Superman plus all the allure of a good and beautiful woman." Marston hoped to establish a "strong, free, courageous womanhood; and to combat the idea that women are inferior to men, and to inspire girls to self-confidence and achievement in athletics, occupations and professions monopolized by men." An early feminist, Marston meant Wonder Woman to be "psychological propaganda for the new type of woman who should . . . rule the world."[46]

Making her debut in issue 8 of *All-Star Comics* in 1941, Wonder Woman soon became a lead story and became the first female superhero to have her own comic book. That it took so long to establish a corresponding screen presence owes much to women's repressed status in American society over the next several decades. It was not until 1966 that William Dozier, the producer of ABC's *Batman* series, commissioned a script titled "Who's Afraid of Diana Prince?" But the resulting five-minute pilot, intended for television, remained stillborn. Finally Wonder Woman appeared in animation, first through her daughter Wonder Girl in a series of *Teen Titans* segments that aired on CBS in 1967–68, and then as herself in Filmation Associates' *The Brady Kids* series on ABC in 1972–73.[47] In the thirteenth episode, "It's All Greek to Me," Wonder Woman, after rescuing a distressed ship with her golden lasso, accompanies the Bradys in a time travel adventure to ancient Greece to teach them that physical conditioning was as important as mental discipline. After testing their prowess in Olympic events, they learn that a "healthy body plus healthy mind equals success."[48] Wonder Woman then became a constant from 1973 to 1986 in the Hanna-Barbera *Super Friends* series on ABC, along with Aquaman, Batman, and Superman, who fought aliens, androids, and supervillains.

Owing largely to media support, Wonder Woman's profile grew steadily during the 1970s. With the inaugural issue of *Ms.* magazine in July 1972, which featured Wonder Woman on the cover, the superhero reached a new development phase through alliance with the burgeoning women's movement. The first effort to create a live-action television series took the form of a 1974 ABC pilot starring Cathy Lee Crosby, but it was ill-conceived. "Virtually no stunts or special effects were used," notes Misiroglu, "and the low budget was painfully obvious." Although ABC squashed the pilot, it preserved the concept in 1975 by utilizing a meticulous script by veteran writer Stanley Ralph Ross, noted for creating Batman television episodes in the 1960s. *The New Original Wonder Woman* was a spectacular success, owing largely to the performance of newcomer Lynda Carter. As Misiroglu explains, "The nearly six-foot tall brunette seemed born for the role. Carter was tall, shapely, beautiful, and looked right in the star-spangled costume, which designer Donfeld [Donald Lee Feld] had taken almost directly from the comics, with the exception of a red-white-and-blue cape Carter wore for special occasions. Carter had been a singer, dancer, variety show performer, and former Miss World USA before landing the role. Although her acting wasn't rock-solid . . . she made the viewer believe she was Wonder Woman."[49]

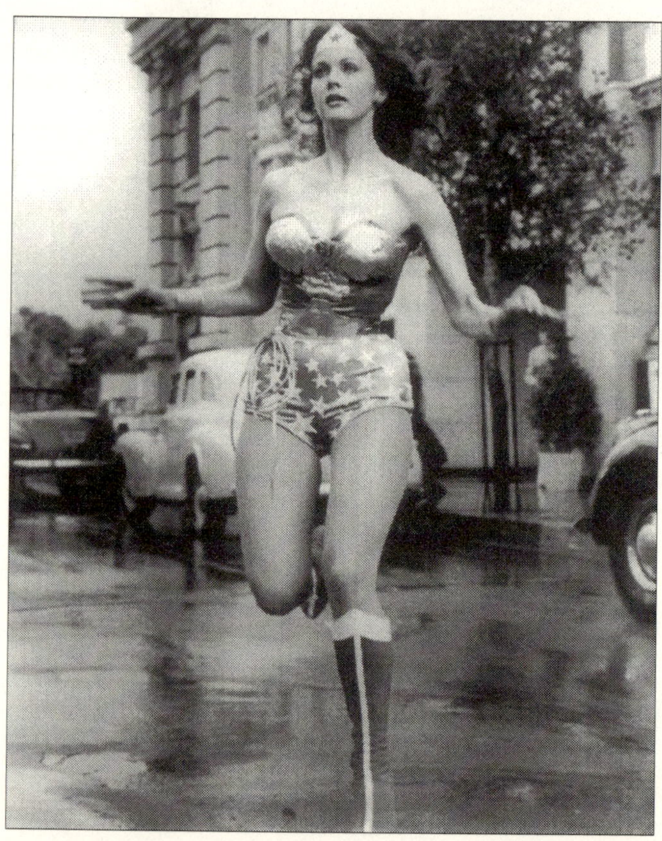

Figure 8.4. Lynda Carter fights evildoers in the 1970 TV series, *Wonder Woman*. Collection of David L. Chapman.

What helped make the superhero believable was the realism infused in stunts where Wonder Woman deflected bullets with her bracelets, hurled her tiara like a boomerang, and roped in villains with her magic lasso. The most spectacular feats, observes Misiroglu, were performed by stuntwoman Jeannie Epper, who "jumped over tanks, buildings, and other assorted obstacles with the greatest of ease." To Epper, however, it was Carter's performance that was amazing: "I think what made her such a hit was she was so beautiful and feminine." Furthermore, she was "very gutsy and very athletic, and a lot of her fight work she did herself," for which "we'd go in and block the fight out . . . and she would just come in and amaze everybody." Epper believed Carter "was the only really live person that could have ever portrayed 'Wonder Woman' and pulled it off."[50] It was with the Carter/Epper duo that Wonder Woman reached the apogee of its physical potential and joined the pantheon of erstwhile male superheroes.

The Big Red Cheese and the Ghost That Walks

Like most comic book superheroes born in the 1930s, Captain Marvel (nicknamed the Big Red Cheese) was derived from the ancient Greeks. The hero begins his journey as ordinary boy Billy Batson until he is transformed by a magic lightning bolt from the wizard Shazam and bestowed with superhuman powers. Merely by uttering the word *SHAZAM* the boy acquired the wisdom of Solomon, the strength of Hercules, the stamina of Atlas, the power of Zeus, the courage of Achilles, and the speed of Mercury. Captain Marvel was a blatant attempt by Fawcett Publications to capture some of the lucrative market created by Detective Comics' Superman. It enlisted artist C. C. Beck and writer Bill Parker to create a superhero modeled after actor Fred MacMurray. Although the first issue in February 1940 had a low print run under Fawcett's new *Whiz Comics* brand, Captain Marvel was an instant success, and the second issue registered sales of over 500,000 copies. Each episode featured the same boy-to-miracle man transformation and triumph over forces of evil. Within two years Captain Marvel was outselling Superman, reaching an amazing 1.3 million copies per issue, twice a month.[51]

Not surprisingly, the Superman powers that be at National Comics, realizing the Big Red Cheese was a serious rival, sued Fawcett for copyright infringement. "From 1941 to 1953," as Misiroglu explains, "Fawcett and DC [i.e., National] battled it out in court, earning their lawyers a small fortune in fees before Fawcett threw in the towel, agreeing to cease publishing the character."[52] Meanwhile, Republic Pictures, after failing to secure the rights to Superman from National Comics, sought to produce a twelve-part serial, *The Adventures of Captain Marvel*, as William Witney explains, by shifting from one superhero to another:

> After all the hassle with Superman being canceled, I couldn't believe the front office buying one that I thought was an infringement on the Superman title. It was called *Captain Marvel*. I hoped the Superman people would hold off a lawsuit long enough for us to make the serial. A lawsuit did come along. . . . My theory was that both Superman and Captain Marvel infringed on the creator of *Popeye the Sailor Man*. Clark Kent went in a phone booth, changed his clothes and became Superman. Billy Batson said "Shazam" and became Captain Marvel. Popeye came years before them to set the precedent. He ate a can of spinach and his muscles bulged and he became Superman and Captain Marvel rolled into one.

For the starring role of Superman, Witney had already interviewed Tom Tyler "and liked him. Tom was clean cut, six-foot-four, and had a beautiful muscular body."[53] To another observer, casting Tyler "as the mighty muscleman was sheer genius." He was so visually suitable and revered by fans that "it is difficult to imagine any other actor in his place." "Tom Tyler fit the part to a 'T,'" Witney later remarked. "If I had to cast the part again, I'd look for his clone."[54]

No less striking was the physical presence of Davy Sharpe, who doubled for Tyler's most risky stunts. "Even at an early age," recalls veteran stuntman John G. Hagner, Sharpe was "well-coordinated, strong and athletically developed. . . . During his mid-teens, he devoted considerable time to his physical training" and during the 1920s won the Amateur Athletic Union tumbling championships. Stunt historian John Baxter concurs that Sharpe was "an all-round stunt man, but he ha[d] a specialty; the acrobatic—leaps, falls from horses, high dives, unrestrained fisticuffs." In *The Perils of Nyoka* (1942), one of the most frenzied serials ever made, Sharpe doubled for literally everyone in the cast—the heroine included.[55] Former child star Frankie Coghlan Jr., who played Billy Batson as Captain Marvel's alter ego, remembered Sharpe as

> an absolutely fearless man who made even the most difficult stunt look easy. He was such a meticulous performer that he was rarely injured. I attribute this to his careful planning and his excellent timing and judgment of distance. My favorite caper that Dave did in Captain Marvel

was in the first chapter when he did a back flip, catching two of the native tribesmen under the chins with well-placed kicks.

And I'll never forget the day he made a headlong dive off the side of a cliff, dressed in the Marvel costume, into a small fireman's net far below, just to get the right camera angle impression of flying.[56]

Sharpe "had the same perfectly proportioned body as Tom," according to Witney. He was only five foot ten, but as long as Sharpe kept moving, no one could detect the size differential. Hagner observes that his stunts were so realistic and reliable that it became a Hollywood cliché: "If you want action-plus guaranteed, get Dave Sharpe."[57] Although he was critical to making Tyler's action scenes convincing, Sharpe insisted that "the one who should really be praised is Tom Tyler. He spent hours strung up in that harness and rigging while being photographed in front of a process screen, and the pain must have been almost unbearable. Yet, he never let out a peep. What a pro!"[58] Owing to the dynamic duo of Tyler and Sharpe, the Big Red Cheese became not only a rival but a fitting complement to the Man of Steel.

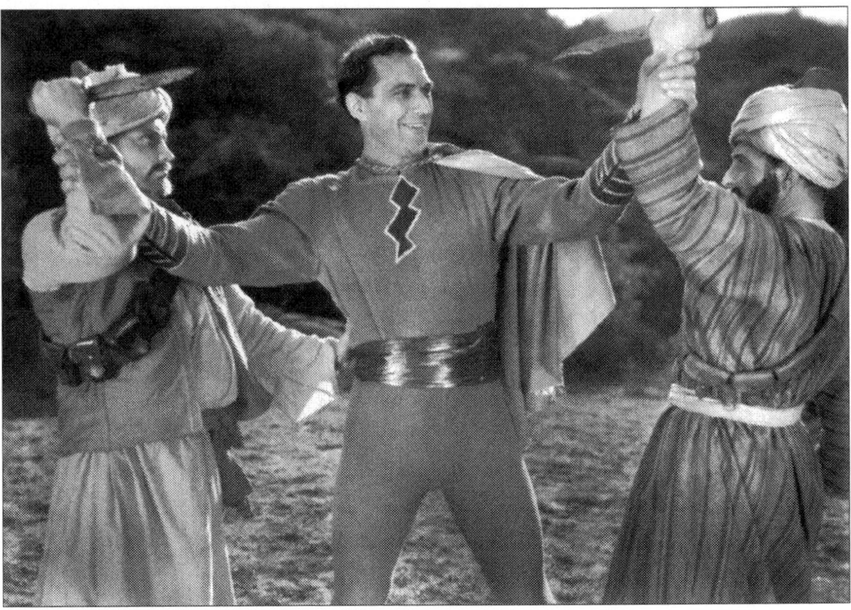

Figure 8.5. Turbaned thugs are no match for Tom Tyler in the Republic serial *The Adventures of Captain Marvel* (1941). Image in the public domain.

Tyler's professionalism was no less evident a few years later in portraying another comic superhero. His character, the Phantom, created by writer/cartoonist Lee Falk, debuted in a King Features Syndicate comic in February 1936 which preceded Superman by two years. It was a composite of tales drawn from literary works and legends such as Johnston McCulley's Zorro; Emma Orczy's *The Scarlett Pimpernel*, and Robin Hood. According to Falk, the Phantom resulted from his "great interest as a kid in hero stories, the great myths and legends—Greek, Roman, Scandinavian, the Songs of Roland, El Cid in Spain, King Arthur and others. There's a heroic thing about him, he's sort of a legendary character. He started out fairly simple and gradually I've added more and more legendary things about him till he has a whole folklore around him."[59] The Phantom became the first superhero to appear in a skin-tight bodysuit. It was usually purple with a cowl, accented by blue trunks with diagonal black stripes, a black belt with a skull design, a black mask, and riding boots. His tools and weapons consisted of two revolvers, homing pigeons to communicate with his Jungle Patrol, a death's head ring on his right hand, and a ring marked "P" on his left hand to leave an imprint on anyone under the Phantom's protection.[60]

His legend can be traced to the sixteenth century, when his alter ego Kit Walker, after surviving a pirate attack and rescued by pygmies to the mythical land of Bangalla, swore to avenge his father's death by devoting his life to fighting evildoers. The skull he found of the pirate who stabbed his father became his inspiration, according to Rovin. "Hiking to a remote section of the Deep Woods, he sets up housekeeping in Skull Cave," the mouth of which had been carved by "eons of wind and rain (and serendipity) into the likeness of a skull." Encapsulating the Phantom's mission was the Oath of the Skull: "I swear to devote my life to the destruction of piracy, greed, cruelty, and injustice, and my sons and their sons shall follow me." What made the Phantom unique was his survival through each generation of his family. "Upon the death of each Phantom," Rovin explains, "his son carries him to a family vault in the cave; while the natives chant, 'The Phantom is dead, long live the Phantom,' he takes the 'Oath of the Skull,' dons the rings and costume, and becomes the new Phantom. However, the rest of the world believes him to be immortal, hence the cognomen 'the Ghost Who Walks.'"[61] While the Phantom may have lacked the strength, speed, and ability to fly of other superheroes, none could match his ancestral endowments of reincarnation.

Tom Tyler, of course, was incapable of portraying a multigenerational character in his fifteen-part serial for Columbia in 1943. Otherwise the

Phantom seemed a perfect fit for the studio's desire to produce exhilarating cliffhangers that could be quickly and inexpensively filmed. The understated costume adapted well to the screen, notes Misiroglu, and Tyler commanded "a believable presence in the garb."[62] In his 1966 *Big Reel* essay, William Cline estimated that "no other character could have resembled the main character more than Tom Tyler. . . . Dressed up in the form-fitting outfit topped by the cowl and mask of Falk's mystery hero, he was the Phantom. In that regard, he even surpassed his portrayal of Captain Marvel. . . . The Phantom stands in the company of the best serials Columbia Pictures made."[63] Six decades later, Tyler's performance as the Phantom continues to impress as movie buffs leave their praise in film forums; as one viewer notes,

> He projected a strong and quietly heroic screen presence, and was athletic enough to look good in the Phantom suit. He is believable in the fight scenes. Superhero suits look good in comic strips, but usually on the screen they look completely stupid. Tom Tyler, a former champion weight lifter, could pull it off. He was also a decent actor. Totally serious, but never camp or inadvertently goofy. I rate him as being almost as good as Buster Crabbe, as far as serial heroes go. Definitely head and shoulders above Kirk Alyn or either of the poor guys that played Batman in the serials.[64]

Despite lead roles in several superhero epics, all of which were box office hits, Tyler remained outside the purview of stardom.

Part of this neglect may be attributed to his being relegated to B movies with weak scripts and poor production standards. Yet he was able to overcome these liabilities through a strong work ethic and an even stronger physical screen presence. "He was imposing in appearance. His acting was restrained, and more than satisfactory," observes Don Miller in *Hollywood Corral*. "The intriguing thing about Tyler was his somewhat sinister attitude, underlined by piercing eyes and deep but repressed speaking voice, as if the sounds were coming from the shadows. More than any other range hero, Tyler gave the impression of tensile, quiet menace—that if he were on the prowl for an adversary."[65] Tyler's screen persona, more than any superhero of his era, projected the strongman he was in real life. However much his menacing, bold, and manly demeanor led to leading roles requiring action or the appearance of action, Tyler's acting was one-dimensional and lacked the sort of nuance that propelled less physically endowed men to stardom.

One also suspects, from responses by Tyler's supporting actors in *Adventures of Captain Marvel*, that his inability to project an engaging personality also plagued his off-screen relationships. Louise Currie, who played Bettie Wallace in the serial, regarded Tyler as "a wonderful, but quiet man. . . . A nice fellow, attractive, a good person, but was he shy! Frank Coghlan, Jr., Billy Benedict and I had lots of fun together, but Tom never seemed to join us in our good times."[66] Shyness was hardly acceptable for a star, much less for an actor with the best muscles in Hollywood.

Notes

1. Eugen Weber, *Movements, Currents, Trends: Aspects of European Thought in the Nineteenth and Twentieth Centuries* (Lexington, MA: D. C. Heath, 1992), 264–67.

2. Oldfield's films include *Barney Oldfield's Race for a Life* (1913) and *The First Auto* (1927).

3. Elzie C. Segar, *Thimble Theatre, Introducing Popeye: A Complete Compilation of the First Adventures of Popeye, 1928–1930* (Westport, CT: Hyperion, 1977).

4. Frank Fiegel, obituary, *Chester (IL) Herald Tribune*, March 28, 1947, quoted in Fred M. Grandinetti, *Popeye: An Illustrated Cultural History*, 5; Constantine Nasr and Mark Nassief, dirs., *I Yam What I Yam: The Story of Popeye the Sailor* (New York: Fleischer Studios, 2007), Daily Motion, http://www.dailymotion.com/video/xjj86l.

5. Dave Fleischer, dir., *Popeye the Sailor* (Los Angeles: Paramount, 1933), clip, YouTube, http://www.youtube.com/watch?v=L7XwesDbZzk; Dave Fleischer, quoted in Leonard Maltin, *Of Mice and Magic: A History of American Animated Cartoons*, 103. "Where does his strength come from?" queried Richard Fleischer, Dave's son. "Interestingly enough, in the comic strip, Popeye's strength came from rubbing the head of a magic whiffle hen, not from eating spinach." Richard Fleischer, *Out of the Inkwell: Max Fleischer and the Animation Revolution* (Lexington: University Press of Kentucky, 2005), 54–55.

6. Grandinetti, *Popeye*, 30.

7. Dave Fleischer, dir., *Popeye in I Yam What I Yam* (Los Angeles: Paramount, 1933), YouTube, http://www.youtube.com/watch?v=8kWIYfMeuZM; Maltin, *Of Mice and Magic*, 101–2. No sanitized version of Popeye appeared until 1989, when he became the official mascot of the Boy Scouts of America; he was then presented in a peaceful setting, without his pipe and with his forearms reversed to hide the anchor tattoos. Grandinetti, *Popeye*, 114.

8. Nasr and Nassief, "I Yam What I Yam."

9. Grandinetti, *Popeye*, 183; Izzy Sparber, dir., *Friend or Phony* (Los Angeles: Paramount, 1952), Daily Motion, http://www.dailymotion.com/video/x5uttvj.

10. Maltin, *Of Mice and Magic*, 66; Grandinetti, *Popeye*, 30, 116–25, 140–47.

11. Nasr and Nassief, "I Yam What I Yam."

12. Brad Ricca, *Super Boys: The Amazing Adventures of Jerry Siegel and Joe Shuster, The Creators of Superman* (New York: St. Martin's, 2013), 92–93, 96, 119–35; Larry Tye,

Superman: The High-Flying History of America's Most Enduring Hero, 10. Dennis Dooley, quoting a *Saturday Evening Post* reporter, reveals that on a warm summer night the story of Superman came to Siegel "in a blinding flash as he lay unable to sleep. . . . 'all of a sudden it hits me. I conceive a character like Samson, Hercules and all the strong men I ever heard tell of rolled into one.'" Dennis Dooley, "The Man of Tomorrow and the Boys of Yesterday," in Dennis Dooley and Gary Engle, *Superman at Fifty: The Persistence of a Legend*, 25–26.

13. Tye, *Superman*, 10–11. Wylie's "superhuman" was likely a derivation of *Ubermensch*, coined by Friedrich Nietzsche in *Thus Spoke Zarathustra* (1883) to refer to a human whose creative powers transcended normal human limitations. For a Krypton genealogy of Clark Kent, see Jeff Rovin, *The Encyclopedia of Superheroes*, s.v. "Superman."

14. Dooley, "The Man of Tomorrow," 30.

15. Les Daniels, *Superman: The Complete History, The Life and Times of the Man of Steel*, 18.

16. Tye, *Superman*, 11.

17. Tye, *Superman*, 14; Gina Misiroglu, *The Superhero Book: The Ultimate Encyclopedia of Comic-Book Icons and Hollywood Heroes*, 539.

18. Jerry Siegel, "Superman Joins the Circus," *Action Comics* 7, quoted in Tye, *Superman*, 315; Misiroglu, *The Superhero Book*, xi; Tye, *Superman*, 38, 47, 52.

19. Daniels, *Superman*, 37, 41.

20. Maltin, *Of Mice and Magic*, 117–18.

21. "The New Pictures," *Time*, July 20, 1942, 81.

22. Tye, *Superman*, 98. Alyn's early film idol was the muscular hero Eddie Polo, "who came out of every fight scene in a blaze of glory and rode off on a white horse over hills and gullies, diving off of cliffs into a lake which looked as though it was a mile straight down." Kirk Alyn, *A Job for Superman*, 3.

23. Kirk Alyn, "Superman Remembers," Superman through the Ages, http://www.superman.nu/theages/kirk/interview.php. "Kirk looked like Clark Kent. That's what impressed me," noted producer Spencer Bennet. Gary Grossman adds that unlike his more celebrated successor, George Reeves, "Alyn didn't use padding. He simply wore a cutaway sweat shirt beneath his costume to keep the perspiration from showing." But Alyn "sat out the earliest tumbles and falls in favor of a double named Paul Stader." Gary Grossman, *Superman: From Serial to Cereal*, 23.

24. Alyn, *A Job for Superman*, 10–12; Daniels, *Superman*, 74.

25. Mannie Pineta, a Pasadena sportswriter who once sparred with Reeves, described him as "the greatest ring prospect of 1932." Grossman, *Superman*, 40, 45.

26. Daniels, *Superman*, 92.

27. Tye, *Superman*, 137. Also, after three years, Reeves's waistline had "thickened to the point where he first had to put on a corset underneath the rubber muscles." Sam Kashner and Nancy Schoenberger, *Hollywood Kryptonite: The Bulldog, the Lady, and the Death of Superman*, 43.

28. Grossman, *Superman*, 52, 160.

29. Super Museum, "Talk of the Town: George Reeves Special, Superman Museum Owner Jim Hambrick," panel discussion, 1992, YouTube, http://www.youtube.com /watch?v=9F2JmAfAkQM.

30. Kashner and Schoenberger, *Hollywood Kryptonite*, 38, 102–3, 140–41.

31. Tye, *Superman*, 157; Kashner and Schoenberger, *Hollywood Kryptonite*, 71.

32. Maltin, *Of Mice and Magic*, 137.

33. Rovin, *Encyclopedia*, s.v. "Mighty Mouse."

34. Paul Terry, quoted in Maltin, *Of Mice and Magic*, 138–39.

35. Stephen Holden, "Marshall Barer, 75, Lyricist For 'Mattress' and Mighty Mouse" (obituary), *New York Times*, August 28, 1998.

36. James Kakalios, "Preface," in E. Paul Zehr, *Becoming Batman: The Possibility of a Superhero*, x; Zehr, *Becoming Batman*, 10.

37. Rovin, *Encyclopedia*, s.v. "Batman"; James Kakalios, *The Physics of Superheroes* (New York: Gotham Books, 2005), 15.

38. Les Daniels, *Batman: The Complete History*, 17–21.

39. Jim Steranko, *The Steranko History of Comics*, vol. 1 (Reading, PA: Supergraphics, 1970), 44. See also Mark S. Reinhart, *The Batman Filmography: Live-Action Features, 1943–1997*, 5–9.

40. Misiroglu, *The Superhero Book*, 62; Daniels, *Batman*, 59.

41. Daniels, *Batman*, 113, 137; Reinhart, *The Batman Filmography*, 86.

42. Daniels, *Batman*, 164.

43. "A Tim Burton Classic!" viewer review of *Batman* (1989), September 19, 2002, Internet Movie Database, http://www.imdb.com/title/tt0096895/reviews?ref_=tt_urv.

44. Zehr, *Becoming Batman*, 261.

45. Jill Lepore, *The Secret History of Wonder Woman*, xi.

46. Rovin, *Encyclopedia*, s.v. "Wonder Woman"; William Moulton Marston, "Why 100,000,000 Americans Read Comics," *American Scholar* 13, no. 1 (Winter 1943–44): 42–43; William Moulton Marston, "Noted Psychologist Revealed as Author of Best-Selling 'Wonder Woman,'" press release, 1942, quoted in Lepore, *Secret History*, 220, 373; Trina Robbins and Catherine Yronwode, *Women and the Comics* (Rolla, MO: Eclipse Books, 1985), 60.

47. The Teen Titans Filmation series was part of *The Superman/Aquaman Hour of Adventure*, which included Aqualad, Kid Flash, and Speedy as complementary superheroes. See "Teen Titans—1967 Filmation #1" (Los Angeles: Filmation Associates, 1967), YouTube, http://www.youtube.com/watch?v=19uz74OcGUM.

48. "It's All Greek to Me," episode of *The Brady Kids* (Los Angeles: Filmation Associates / Redwood Productions, 1972), Big Cartoon Database, http://www.bcdb.com/cartoons /Filmation_Associates/A-G/The_Brady_Kids/.

49. Misiroglu, *The Superhero Book*, 634.

50. Misiroglu, *The Superhero Book*, 634; Jeannie Epper, "Interview with Jeannie Epper Stuntwoman, Part 2," Wonderland, http://www.wonderland-site.com/html/interviews7 .htm; "Jeannie Epper: Biography," Internet Movie Database, http://www.imdb.com/name

/nm0258346/bio?ref_=nm_dyk_trv_sm#trivia. See also Behind the Stunts, "Jeannie Epper–Hollywood Stunt Double," YouTube, http://www.youtube.com/watch?v=m8Hr8E x5QFI; and Chris Nashawaty, "Danger Is Their Middle Name," *Entertainment Weekly*, October 19, 2007, 94.

51. Misiroglu, *The Superhero Book*, 125–26.

52. Misiroglu, *The Superhero Book*, 127.

53. William Witney, *In a Door, into a Fight, out a Door, into a Chase: Moviemaking Remembered by the Guy at the Door*, 182.

54. *Famous Monsters of Filmland*, September 1973, 21, quoted in Mike Chapman, *The Tom Tyler Story: From Cowboy Star to Super Hero*, 78; Witney, *In a Door*, 185.

55. John G. Hagner, *Falling for Stars*, 49–50; John Baxter, *Stunt: The Story of the Great Movie Stunt Men*, 235–36.

56. Frankie Coghlan Jr., interview with Gregory Jackson Jr., *Serial World*, 1974, quoted in Chapman, *The Tom Tyler Story*, 77.

57. Witney, *In a Door*, 183; John G. Hagner, interview with John D. Fair, Moab, Utah, September 3, 2015; Hagner, *Falling for Stars*, 46.

58. William C. Cline, "Tom Tyler, Super Hero," *Big Reel*, March 1966, 108, quoted in Chapman, *The Tom Tyler Story*, 78. According to Alan Barbour, *The Adventures of Captain Marvel* became "Republic's favorite and most respected serial." Alan Barbour, *Cliffhanger: A Pictorial History of the Motion Picture Serial*, 64.

59. Anthony Tollin, "A Visit with Lee Falk," *Comics Revue* 1, no. 27 (1988), quoted in Chapman, *The Tom Tyler Story*, 83.

60. Misiroglu, *The Superhero Book*, 377.

61. Rovin, *Encyclopedia*, s.v. "The Phantom."

62. Misiroglu, *The Superhero Book*, 379.

63. Cline, "Tom Tyler," quoted in Chapman, *The Tom Tyler Story*, 84.

64. "The Phantom's Zone," viewer review of *The Phantom* (1943), February 7, 2008, Internet Movie Database, http://www.imdb.com/title/tt0036262/reviews?ref_=tt_urv.

65. Don Miller, *Hollywood Corral*, 48.

66. Louise Currie, interview, in Michael G. Fitzgerald and Boyd Magers, *Ladies of the Western: Interviews with Fifty-One More Actresses from the Silent Era to the Television Westerns of the 1950s*, 2002, quoted in Chapman, *The Tom Tyler Story*, 79.

IX. DAYS OF GREEK GODS

These Hollywood men of muscle don't have to say a word—their figures speak for themselves!

—Hildegarde Johnson, "Meet the Champs"

The Physique Genre

STARTING WITH THOMAS Edison's primitive, flickery film of Eugen Sandow in 1894, it was clear that moviemakers had long been adept at exploiting the well-built body for entertainment, spectacle and profit. Films had affixed various meanings to muscular male bodies—sometimes representing courage, power, and strength—in both brutish and noble forms. At other times men on the screen were physical ideals that most moviegoers could only aspire to. These, however, were not the only messages embedded in films featuring good-looking, muscular men; there was also often an erotic element. It consequently took gay men little time to demonstrate that there was a market for films catering to this component. Thus, after World War II a new genre became prominent: the physique film. The history of gay-oriented photography has been well documented. Likewise, the presence of gay themes in mainstream cinema has been told, but few have examined physique films as a distinct phenomenon.[1]

It could not have been a secret that many still photographs of muscular, scantily clad men produced since the invention of the camera ended up with gay men, but in the days before home theaters, inexpensive projectors, or venues where films of a questionable nature could be shown, moving pictures were not an option. It was not until the late 1940s that postwar prosperity made production, distribution, and consumption of physique films possible. Still, there were plenty of predecessors, including muscle control and posing films taken at early bodybuilding competitions. It is unclear who watched these poorly made amateur productions, but they were sufficiently well known to be passed around and preserved among cognoscenti. Sandow and other bodybuilders had been filmed since the 1890s, but they were not well known because access was limited. A few films might have made it to movie screens in newsreels and short features, but the still physique photograph reigned supreme until the late 1940s, when the inception of viewing devices made moving pictures relatively inexpensive to enjoy at home.

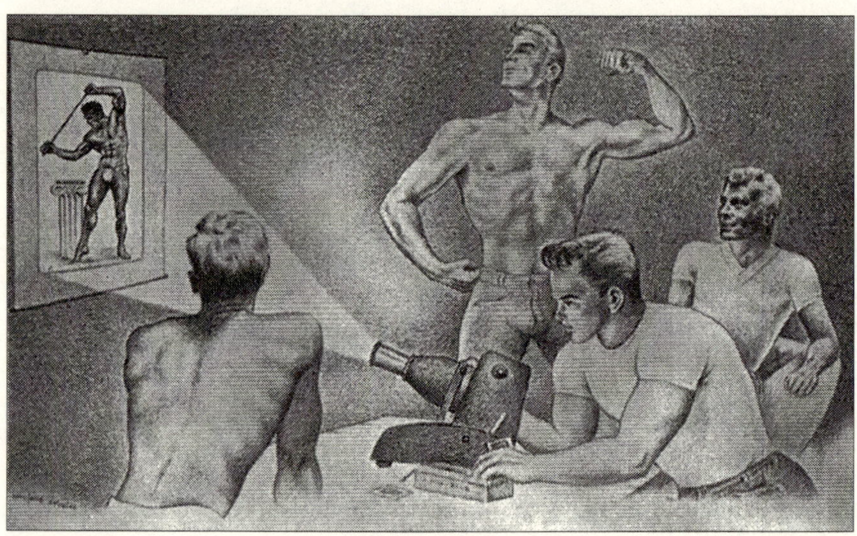

Figure 9.1. *Home Show* (ca. 1955), by artist William MacLane, which depicts men who are inspired by projected images of physique athletes. Collection of David L. Chapman.

There was always a certain mystique about a moving image, and this was especially true for physique films. A major difference between bodybuilding and physique films is that there is frequently a story (however simplistic) which makes watching the latter more immersive. As Thomas Waugh observes, "In comparison to that frozen portrait of corporal perfection that was the still physique photo, physique films proved dreamlike structures of narrative momentum and fulfillment, and thus an even richer document of our sexual imagery of the period."[2] In addition to having story lines, physique films usually featured subjects who were muscular but not massive. The men in physique films were fit and healthy, but hardly overly built. Unlike bodybuilders who merely wanted to display as much musculature as possible, physique performers generally wore loin coverings that clearly outlined their genitals, and since they were unrestrained by any need to pose formally, they could move around and create a more erotic effect as they jiggled and swung their bodies. Their goal was to showcase their sculpted bodies to rev up viewers' libidos. One of the downsides to being the object of audience gaze is that, ironically, it made muscular men often seem less manly.[3] When a man becomes a potential object of beauty to be observed, appreciated, and perhaps lusted after, he unwittingly assumes a traditionally feminine role. To divert this threat to virility, a man must behave in aggressively masculine ways (fighting, boasting, motorcycling, flexing, etc.). This excessively virile behavior seemed not to bother either the performers or consumers of physique films. The audience, the models, and the economy were thus set; all that was needed was someone to make them.[4]

Richard Fontaine

The earliest physique film (featuring muscular men on display for a gay audience) was made in 1949 by would-be actor, director, and go-getter Richard Fontaine. He was born in February 1923 in Minnesota, but his family moved to California when he was seven. Like many showmen, Fontaine was attracted to the theater, where he acted and worked backstage. In the 1940s he went to New York, hoping to become a stage actor while also dabbling in photography and film. On the East Coast Fontaine got a few theater gigs, but mainly he had to scramble for work in radio, on the stage, and in films, eking out a living with his meager talents and undoubted chutzpah. Eventually he found a niche by filming screen tests for other would-be actors. One of these hopefuls was Guy Mayor, a handsome, muscular dancer and actor who had lots of ambition but little money. He suggested a deal: if Fontaine would make the screen test for nothing, he would pose in a physique film the moviemaker could market.[5] The resulting film, shot on sixteen-millimeter stock, and with high-quality sound, was a revelation. Fontaine would often title his films provocatively to telegraph their erotic subtext. Thus, *Always Obtainable* (1949) was revolutionary as well as incendiary. Whether Mayor ever got another screen role is unknown, but his fame spread to articles and covers of at least two magazines in the mid-1950s.

Always Obtainable lasts less than three minutes, but it presents some leitmotifs that later appear in other films of the genre. A handsome model receives a telephone call early in the morning, and he answers it while sprawled nearly naked on a messy bed; the rumpled sheets are a result of "what happened last night." We hear the voice of an artist who calls the young man and requests that his friend come over because he "wants to finish what we started." Guy gets up and the camera follows him to the shower, where he removes his tighty-whities and performs his ablutions with his naked backside to the camera. The scene then dissolves to the artist's atelier, where the young man speaks directly to the camera (and viewers). "It only took me twenty minutes," Guy announces as he bursts through the door. "Just call me speedy." The unseen artist asks the model to "get ready," meaning to remove his street clothes in front of a large mirror, which reveals his entire body. The camera modestly turns aside as Guy removes his trousers, and when it returns he is wearing a posing strap.[6] The artist's hand then emerges from the frame and begins to oil his subject. Guy next assumes a series of poses in front of the mirror, and the camera (with the viewer) is treated to various movements that show the model's musculature and grace. The film ends as the unseen "artist" suggests they go to the sun deck and enjoy the rest of the afternoon.

At least two things are clear from this early physique film. First, the suggestive dialogue is filled with double entendres and sly jokes that likely reflect a previous physical relationship between Guy and the artist/viewer. Second, the film uses the visual vocabulary of older bodybuilding films, with numerous posing set pieces that allow the model to display his muscular physique and move around in an imagined setting. We are far from the bodybuilding dais, however, and spectators can make judgments based on criteria far from muscularity alone. There is nothing feminine about the model's actions. Although the situation drips with homoeroticism, Guy is not a sissy; he is manly in appearance and actions. His muscularity and beauty are designed to awaken the viewer's libido. As Fontaine later confirmed, the film was made "with a tongue-in-cheek idea sort of teasing the audience that there was something going on."[7]

Always Obtainable established a principal trope of the physique film: the artist who asks a muscular, nude model to pose for him (and us). In his next film Fontaine tried another ploy to stir viewers—comparing living bodies with ancient statuary. *Days of Greek Gods* (1954) starred three well-known New York bodybuilders: Jimmy Apollo, Bob Delmonteque, and Artie Zeller. They get together and start talking about three mythological Greek characters. The film alternates images of statuary of the gods with the three men who reinterpret them by displaying their bodies in tiny posing pouches with silvery fig leaf pasties. The "star" is Delmonteque (né Mike Diaks) who talks about the ancient characters, and then has Artie Zeller pose as Hercules, Jimmy Apollo as Narcissus, and himself as Apollo Belvedere. The bodybuilders look convincing as modern versions of ancient icons, but the dialogue is so poorly delivered and corny that it makes concentrating on the artistic, the educational, or even the erotic content challenging. Despite its drawbacks there is an Ed Woodish sincerity and naive tone-deafness to the film that conveys a pathetic charm.

These and other early physique films featured young, virile, and handsome athletes who displayed posing routines that could have been taken directly from a competition. They flex their muscles in a prescribed way—one that would have been familiar to any bodybuilder. These motions and poses are put in a narrative context, but their inspiration came from the sports world, not the homosexual milieu or the realm of fine art. Later Fontaine agreed that his first two physique films could not be specifically called gay, since there was no overt expression of manly affection or same-sex desire, but they were intended for male enjoyment. Even the most unobservant viewer could have seen obvious homoerotic intent. As Fontaine explained, "We were using the body in erotic ways and suggesting the enjoyment of the human form."[8] He may also have intrigued two of the film's performers with their own ideas about recording muscular bodies since both Delmonteque and Zeller later became skilled physique photographers.

In 1950 Fontaine made a film, *Daydreams*, that involves a young man (Art Ullrich) at the beach who is sighing because he wants to meet a model (Tom DeCarlo) whose physique photos he arrays on a blanket. His dream comes true when Tom appears magically, and the two men strip to posing pouches and pose for each other. Then Tom disappears. Alas, it was an illusion, but in the second half of the film Tom reappears in another point-of-view episode. He poses repeatedly wearing his skimpy pouch, and after we have surfeited ourselves on his muscular body, the unseen cameraman invites the bodybuilder to his beach house for cocktails. Tom agrees to this "swell idea," but first he turns over on his blanket and presents his well-formed derriere to viewers—as, perhaps, a preview of coming attractions.

These three films were made at roughly the same time, but Fontaine was at a loss about marketing. Few consumers in 1949 had sixteen-millimeter sound projectors, which made it difficult to find an audience. It was not until 1954 that ads began to appear in gay physique magazines. The first of them appeared unobtrusively in the back of *Tomorrow's Man*. Fontaine managed to sell a few copies of the talkie version of his films, but he soon learned that most people preferred eight-millimeter silent films, which could be shown privately.[9] Coinciding with Fontaine's popular shorts, other producers began to suss out possibilities of cashing in on physique films. One of the first was based in Cincinnati.

Spectrum Films

In 1951 Spectrum Films became the second motion picture company to court a gay audience when it produced *Body Builders*. Perhaps reflecting its stolid Midwestern roots, there was no camp humor or suggestive dialogue, just handsome athletes earnestly posing. Another difference was the modeling attire. "All wear swim trunks," announced an early ad in bold type; customers hoping to see men in posing straps would be disappointed. Models included some minor stars of the bodybuilding world, including Paul Ashley, the ubiquitous Delmonteque, Arman Ozon, and hand balancers Renald and Rudy. Unlike Fontaine's films, the producer seems to have given its potential market more thought. One brochure explains that spectators will be encouraged to work out after they see this film because "the athletes in the film are built like they would like to be themselves." It "makes excellent advertising for gymnasiums who show it to groups of men and boys in their town to interest them in joining their gym for a bodybuilding course." The athletes are not "Mr. Americas, but rather young men whose build would appeal more to the average non-bodybuilder."[10]

If the advertising flier sounds evangelical, it might be due to the distributor's other clients. The same person who marketed this and other cinematic works also produced religious films, and his greatest previous hit was *The Ninety and Nine* (1950), a dramatization of the biblical parable of the shepherd who left ninety-nine of his sheep to search for the one that was lost. The proprietor of Spectrum Films was Edwin T. Schnatz, an elusive and retiring entrepreneur who founded Cathedral Films in Cincinnati after World War II. A *Film World* ad identifies him as a producer and purveyor of religious movies.[11] While he was spreading the Good News, the distributor was also promoting the physiques of healthy young men. There would be no pagan Greek gods in the world of Edwin Schnatz. A year after *Body Builders*, Spectrum Films released a sequence of films titled the Masculine Physique Series. Eventually, various short films were added, and Spectrum models wore less and less until they ended up with the same posing straps that other physique studios used. The films also got increasingly seductive in intent until it was virtually impossible to distinguish Spectrum films from others. They were soon being advertised in gay and cryptogay publications like *Adonis, Body Beautiful,* and *Tomorrow's Man*; thus, the target audience shifted from those encouraging physical culture in the gym and at the YMCA to those with more prurient interests. Despite this, Schnatz seemed perfectly happy to descend to the Cities of the Plain to make a few shekels.

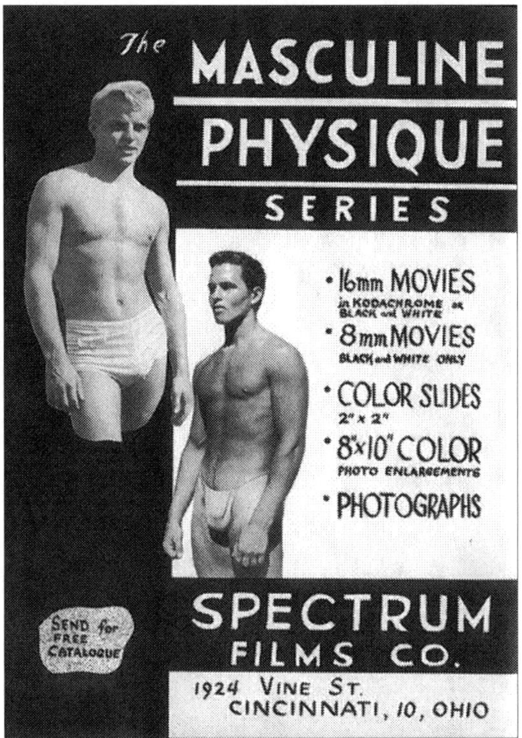

Figure 9.2. An advertisement for Spectrum physique films, from *Physique Pictorial*, December 1953. Collection of David L. Chapman.

In addition to producing posing films, Spectrum began a popular wrestling series. Wrestling was a common activity in physique movies, since it provided a lot of man-on-man contact within the context of masculine sport. One could throttle a partner but never embrace him with affection. Spectrum films were remarkable because the grappling in them was real. Participants in physique films had no murderous intent, with wrestlers mostly playacting and rarely acquiring more than bruises and scratches. Despite its realism, the transitory and slightly salacious nature of Spectrum's films (and indeed the genre) meant that most films were never copyrighted; the only references to them come from advertisements or brochures. Hence, information about them is often as skimpy as the costumes worn by the young models. The subjects in Spectrum films were handsome, athletic young men who were seriously (though not excessively) muscled. Nearly all were healthy-looking, corn-fed Midwestern white men; there were no African Americans, Latinos, or other minorities. Spectrum also insisted on keeping its models well covered; there were never any frontal nudes, even after that became permissible.

Bob Mizer

It was not until about 1958 that a critical mass of physique films featuring muscular men aimed at a gay audience was achieved and exploded with force. Moviemakers determined that eight-millimeter film was optimal for projection, the audience was identified, disposable incomes were rising, advertising media were in place, and gay men were eager consumers. With Fontaine assuming a lower profile, Bob Mizer, head of the Athletic Model Guild, the renowned Los Angeles "physique factory" that produced thousands of still photographs of seminude men, stepped forward. In an issue of Mizer's magazine *Physique Pictorial* from the mid-1950s, he explained that "several years ago" he had attempted to film some of his models. It was "so much random footage with no special plot," but it featured Richard DuBois, winner of the 1954 Mr. America title. The film was "just so much posing and horseplay" produced "when we first got a movie camera, and we beg you not to judge us too harshly."[12] Fans were prepared to give him the benefit of the doubt so long as plenty of scantily clad muscles were displayed.

Coincidentally, Fontaine and Mizer had known one another for years because Fontaine had been a schoolmate of Mizer's nephew, who got Mizer's permission to make movies in his photography studio. The results were promising enough to set both men on the road to becoming physique movie moguls. Since the field was virtually wide open, they decided to market the films under several names; "I had to start my own competitors," Fontaine explained. He released films under the names Apollo, Midwest, RA Enterprises, and Zenith, in addition to AMG (Athletic Model Guild), Mizer's company. It is easy to see Fontaine's hand in films turned out later by AMG. Mizer would become the most prolific producer of films highlighting muscular physiques. In a 1957 issue of *Physique Pictorial* Mizer announced, "AMG is going into the movie business!" He told eager fans that he was going to film "simple little stories which will give the models an opportunity to display their bodies in natural activities, rather than in strictly stilted posing."[13] That unpretentious formula served Mizer well for three decades.

According to Thomas Waugh, all physique films can be categorized as posing, wrestling, or narrative.[14] In the first group the subject moves from one attitude to another, pausing briefly so the viewer can absorb the combination of muscularity, grace, and beauty. It is rooted in both the artist's atelier and the posing dais of a bodybuilding competition. The wrestling film offers an opportunity for two or more models to engage in physical combat and semi-legitimate bodily contact. The narrative film, however, was by far the most popular, and an enterprising director could combine all three categories into one extravagant display. When Fontaine began turning out films at AMG, he showed Mizer how the movies were made and marketed and in the process put a lasting mark on the genre. Fontaine's films were conspicuous by their sly, humorous, wink-wink quality. The vast majority have the feel of saucy seaside postcards or off-color jokes. They are not obscene or indecent, but by using innuendo, suggestion, and in-jokes they pushed the boundaries of acceptability and conveyed a message of male affection in obvious but subtle ways. Mizer adopted this tongue-in-cheek style and stuck with it for the rest of his life.

Many of the plots and themes were undoubtedly joint efforts. Fontaine would make the films, and Mizer would supply performers, take still photos, and market them in his magazine. At the height of its popularity in the late 1950s and early 1960s *Physique Pictorial* allegedly sold over forty thousand copies per month, which aided greatly in spreading the word.[15] It required much effort to keep both the cinematic and publishing enterprises going, thus accounting for the often sloppy production values and absurd plots. The work was made quickly, with little regard for quality. Fontaine and Mizer liked to infuse their films with humor and timely references. Since the epic *Ben-Hur* was released in 1959 and peplum films starring Steve Reeves and other muscular stars had become popular, it is not surprising that many physique productions featured scenarios set in ancient times. A typical result of this passion for all things Greco-Roman is Fontaine's *Ben-Hurry* (1960). It takes place supposedly on the backlot of a studio where a Roman epic is being shot, but is obviously filmed around AMG's backyard pool. As historian Richard Lindsay remarks, the film "takes the homoerotic suggestiveness of the Greco-Roman aesthetic and combines it with the cultural juggernaut of the grandest biblical film of that year."[16] It might not have been as epic as Fontaine hoped, but the film made its mark in the gay universe.

Like most physique films, the plot is simple and silly. Two muscular actors enter carrying spears and wearing peplums. They are extras, and they approach another similarly accoutred associate who is seated and in a glum mood. "What's buggin' you, Ben?" inquires one of the newly arrived "Romans," initiating a dialogue. "My wife's in the hospital having a baby, and I have to sit here dressed in a skirt!" "Gee, Ben," the other man replies, "if that's all that's bothering you . . ." and as he says so, he casually tears off the man's peplum, revealing Ben in nothing more than a posing strap. "Feel better now?"[17] It is not long before all three young men drop their skirts and start tussling with one another; eventually two of them are pushed into the nearby swimming pool. And then they reattach their peplums and return to spear carrying. While the plot is inane and derivative, the film succeeds in displaying the men's physiques in suggestive ways. Amid all the horseplay, the men's erotically charged muscles, clenched buttocks, and jiggling genitals are evident. Though hardly a Hollywood epic, *Ben-Hurry* is a classic of soft-core physique cinema. The acting and script are execrable, but AMG customers clamored for more. The filmmakers responded by making many films that exploited the ancient world, cowboys, juvenile delinquents, monsters, and even satirized the melodrama *Advise and Consent* (1962) with *Advice without Consent* (1962). In this version, the action takes place as one shirtless tough gives another advice on how to repair his motorcycle.[18]

With space alien movies the rage in the early 1960s, AMG had to tap this market. Mizer made several such movies, but his most whimsical is *Muscles from Outer Space* (1961), which features a young (and unaccountably seminude) scientist sitting in front of some ersatz electronics when he "apparently manages to tune in the right frequency" and beams down "a dashing, handsome spaceman" wearing a hubcap-like object over his genitals and a tinfoil helmet. Initially the spaceman is unhappy about being materialized, and the two men struggle, but viewers are told in the synopsis that the characters do little fighting because "Dick Fontaine, the production manager, abhors violence and feels wrestling sequences should be kept to an absolute minimum." After a quick reconciliation, the spaceman whisks the young scientist off to outer space.[19]

Eventually Fontaine parted ways with Mizer and began his own productions. These were redolent of his first films featuring Delmonteque and Zeller, and he continued using "celebrities." One of them, *The Master*, starring Richard DuBois, shows him going through poses in the open air, but then the film switches to the wooded hills around Los Angeles, where another bodybuilder pops out of nowhere and attempts to duplicate "the Master's" poses. The intruder upsets DuBois, who forces the other bodybuilder to pull him around in a little two-wheeled cart. *Day of Fury* (ca. 1957), starring bodybuilder Ed Fury, is only slightly less artless. Wearing a brief costume, Fury bounds up the steps of an elegant Mediterranean mansion and strikes some poses. He stops abruptly and goes down to the swimming pool to answer a telephone. There is a cut to a woman talking on the other end. A title card carries the caption: "I saw you posing on your veranda. I'm sorry you stopped. Please do some more."[20] Ed then fulfills the lady's—and presumably the viewer's—request for more flexing. Fury would star in two other physique films. In one he romps at the beach, and in another he is a cowboy who rescues a young man from an angry Indian who has stripped his victim of his clothing and staked him out spread-eagle on the ground.[21]

Although an occasional star appears in the thousands of physique films produced in the 1950s and 1960s, the great majority feature anonymous young men wanting to display their bodies and/or needing extra dollars. As the genre developed, the actors became less muscular, less healthy looking, and more sensual in intent. The films also lose their heterosexual alibis of referencing models' wives or girlfriends. With the sheer number of films produced, it is no surprise that almost every permutation of the original triad of posing, wrestling, and story line was tried. Most consumers were not interested in compelling stories, expensive sets, or high-quality production. So long as the actors showed off their bodies, wiggled their naughty bits, and had some fun, that was all anyone wanted. In retrospect, they seem silly and innocent. But it is easy for contemporary audiences to miss the subversive nature of these short flicks; for better or worse, they were chipping away at heteronormative hegemony. The success of physique films encouraged an increased number of producers to join in the fray.

One of them was Bruce Bellas, who sold thousands of still physique photos during his career as Bruce of Los Angeles. Bellas began to market physique movies in 1961, and according to the *Encyclopedia of Gay History*, his films "offered even more erotic playfulness" than his photography.[22] He was not nearly as prolific as Mizer, making only twenty-six physique films. Often Bellas would film one version in posing straps and make another version where the model was nude, naturally adding not only an extra frisson to the films but also making them illegal. Bruce often took nude photos, and to circumvent legal authorities would travel around the country and sell them out of a suitcase in hotel rooms. His movies were similar to others', consisting of exercise, posing, and wrestling, but with less narrative. Bruce also had a cowboy fetish, and many of his movies depicted models in western hats, boots, and little else. He would have a few young men put on war paint and feathers, pretending to be Native Americans. After censorship of nude photography loosened in the mid-1960s, Bruce had a ready inventory of films to satisfy the nude model market. The alibi of physique display was soon jettisoned in favor of more sensual phallic displays. These "danglies" (featuring models with exposed genitals) spelled the end for physique films. Now that customers could see what had been concealed, musculature became secondary to erotic content—even with sex, simulated or real.

In the 1960s several other physique photographers made movies. One Chicago studio, Kris, was headed by Domingo Orejudos and Charles Renslow, who operated magazines, ran bars, and eventually produced twenty physique films. In 1955 Renslow and a group of models came to Hollywood, where they met Fontaine and made *A Date with the Boys*. It purports to show two young men who go out to Vasquez Rocks for a film shoot accompanied by "The Kris Studio staff photographers." It features a glamorized version of what goes on when this sort of film is made, including scouting locations, stripping down to posing straps, oiling up, and posing for cameras. The most extraordinary sequence in this five-minute film shows Orejudos removing a few wisps of pubic hair poking out of the posing pouches with a pair of clippers, thereby eroticizing the action and making a mockery of the rule that no extraneous groin hair could be shown.

Eventually Kris moviemakers began regular production. Renslow built the sets and ran the camera, while Orejudos directed and wrote the screenplays. They had few illusions about the quality of their work. "Sure, [they're] corny and whatnot," Renslow later admitted, "but at the time people wanted them."[23] Like those of other producers, the films relied on innuendo, suggestion, and the viewer's dirty imagination to create desirable effects. It was important to show actors with musculatures impressive enough to make them believable as physique-centric works and with enough humor to make them palatable to audiences. Kris films sometimes contained a dash of mysticism and sadomasochism, as in their first independent film *Black Magic* (1963), in which a muscular young man conjures up a devil. First, he must remove all his clothing (except for a posing pouch) and perform a ritual. After a blinding flash, the devil and his well-built assistant chain and pretend to whip him. Eventually, the bodybuilder discovers how to send the devils back to hell and free himself of their torments.[24] Thus, Kris's physique films often involved a bit of kink. AMG preferred humor, Spectrum liked wrestling, and all of them featured models reflecting American stereotypes and values, but the vocabulary of physique mythology also acquired a foreign flavor.

Until the mid-1960s, Americans more or less monopolized physique films, but eventually outsiders found ways to cash in. In the early 1960s the Frontier Athletic Club, based in Tijuana, made a film with Mizer's assistance, but it was one of the few physique films ever shot south of the border.[25] Much more was going on north of the forty-ninth parallel, largely due to Alan Stone, a genial Montreal photographer whose studio, Mark One, specialized in cityscapes as well as French Canadian athletes. Stone began his career in physique photography by taking pictures of local bodybuilders wanting to sell their images at competitions. This entrée encouraged Stone to sell photos through physique magazine ads during the 1960s. Around 1962 he began selling eight-millimeter films of his most popular models. The films were repetitive, with handsome, muscular lads romping around in posing straps and brief bathing suits exposing their bodies to the camera. Despite visual vocabulary similarities, the settings varied. They were often shot deep in the woods of rural Quebec, along the St. Lawrence River near the Lachine Rapids, or in various industrial settings.

Unlike North Americans, overseas producers were not as fast or eager to make physique films. Problems of production, shipping, and overzealous customs agents tended to keep many of them out of the lucrative US market. The talented Niçois photographer Jean Ferrero made a few films of his models, but his principal source of income was nude photos of muscular men in the French Riviera's hills and beaches. In 1957 John Graham's Knightsbridge studio in London announced that he was offering "Britain's first muscle movie in Glorious Colour." Titled *Physique Studio*, it featured Canadian wrestling champ Gordon Nelson, "star model" Bob Sneddon, and "a cast of youthful bodybuilders."[26] Apparently this was Graham's only muscle movie. In Munich, the minor bodybuilding star and physique photographer Frank Hollfelder produced a five-minute epic around 1966 titled *Gone with the River*. A young man named Hansi is sunbathing nude on a secluded Bavarian river bank, and his clothing accidentally falls into the torrent. Clad only in a tiny towel, the muscular lad goes off searching for clothing. He steals a car and ends up at the ornate palace Schloß Linderhof, where instead of finding attire, he lounges on an outdoor staircase until a guard shoos him away. When Hansi returns to his stolen car, he sees a handsome policeman writing out a parking ticket, and he runs back into the woods, losing his towel along the way. The policeman picks it up and smiles knowingly at the camera. *Gone with the River* is an extraordinary combination of physique film and travelogue, miles ahead of most films produced elsewhere. Blond-haired Hansi is not heavily muscled, but he displays much of his gymnast's body. This drama could not have been made by an amateur, suggesting Hollfelder had help from Munich photographer-filmmaker Jan Eyck. Both men were active in the mid-1960s and advertised films, among other products. Eyck's contribution to the genre was titled *Oktoberfest in Munich* (ca. 1965), with "Axel and Alex."[27]

Whether produced at home or abroad, physique films shared similar characteristics: muscular men posing; doing manly, athletic things; or simply horsing around. The ostensible goal was to display men's muscles in a pleasing way, but the true (and not deeply hidden) raison d'être was to provide a male burlesque show for gay men. Instead of feather fans, mesh stockings, or sequined G-strings, men in these films had only muscles and a posing pouch; yet the teasing, vamping, and humor would have been at home at Minsky's. It is difficult to get a definitive count, but it seems that Fontaine made around seventy films (both nude and featuring posing straps), Spectrum Films sixty, Bruce of Los Angeles forty-one (both nude and in posing straps), Alan Stone forty, and Kris nineteen, but the most prolific was Bob Mizer, who made an estimated three thousand reels.[28] On average, Mizer was turning out two or three films weekly. It also means his customers showed an insatiable demand for these briefly made and often artless films.

When strict antipornography laws began to dissipate in the mid- to late 1960s, the reason for physique films vanished. Spectators no longer wanted to see men in posing straps when they could see what they concealed. With the totally nude "danglies" of the 1970s, there was more to see, but it was usually shown with much less style and humor. One of the few directors to buck this trend was Richard Fontaine, who tried making what amounted to the old physique films, but with nude actors. He often filmed his amusing little photoplays with the help of an outrageous drag queen named Glory Holden—a sort of foul-mouthed Divine with a Texas drawl—who starred in the films and then gave sarcastic, suggestive voice-over commentary.[29] Unfortunately, this was not enough to save the genre, and pornography soon ended the brief "dangly" era. After the demise of nude films, there was a short period of simulated sex where men could be filmed kissing and having physical contact but nothing more (except in viewers' perfervid imaginations). By 1980 all restrictions were gone, and anything went. What remained of physique films was a sense of nostalgia for innocence and romantic charm. They demonstrated what a gay man could look and act like, but they no longer reflected the wider spectrum of queer sensibilities.

Issues of masculinity and gender identification are problematic with a gay audience. How can one be a real man if he is not attracted to women? A solution to this conundrum is that many gay men measure masculinity by how closely they ape the behavior and appearance of straight men. In the golden age of physique films it would have been unthinkable for anyone to come across as fey, feminine, or swishy when they appeared in the movies. It would have cast doubts on the rationale for the films—that they were designed to inspire young men to build their muscles in order to be healthy, strong and "manly." Few were taken in by this ruse, but the facade had to be maintained.

It is no accident that Mizer and other physique photographers began to flourish by the 1940s. There was a growing awareness that not all gay men were effeminate—that there was a wide divergence between mincing pansies and leather-clad cyclists. Charles Kaiser in *The Gay Metropolis* posits that this change was stimulated by the huge number of gay soldiers who flooded American cities after World War II and caused a realization that one could be both homosexual and traditionally masculine.[30] Physique films celebrated this shift from one paradigm of gayness to another. Additionally, anecdotal and statistical data show that many gay men tried to improve their musculature after the war. Researcher Erick Alvarez has noted that for many gay men today "masculinity is, for the most part a nonnegotiable demand whether from potential partners or from ourselves."[31] Naturally, physique films were not the only forces that made gay men see that they could be both gay and masculine, but they were early paradigms for an emerging gay culture. Eventually, other forms of gay manhood began to appear in physique films. As soon as the bonds of censorship had relaxed, Glory Holden could join in and camp it up with the muscle boys.

One critic remarked of the 1960 film *Ben-Hurry* that despite all the drawbacks, the physique film was still entertaining and "enjoyable to watch today because of its playful eroticism—the lack of production values or actual sex between the models only adds to its charm."[32] Unfortunately, these charms hardly made much difference for later audiences. The days of the gay Greek gods would never return, and while mainstream cinema trended toward perfecting illusions on screen, the subgenre of physique films represented a novel and more explicit form of realism to moviemaking.

Notes

1. The best works of this genre are Thomas Waugh, *Hard to Imagine: Gay Male Eroticism in Photography and Film from Their Beginnings to Stonewall*; Kenneth Krauss, *Male Beauty: Postwar Masculinity in Theater, Film, and Physique Magazines* (Albany: State University of New York Press, 2014); Vito Russo, *The Celluloid Closet: Homosexuality in the Movies* (New York: Harper and Row, 1981); and Richard Barrios, *Screened Out: Playing*

Gay in Hollywood from Edison to Stonewall (New York: Routledge, 2003). The showing of Kenneth Anger's 1947 experimental gay film *Fireworks* at the Coronet Theater in Los Angeles led to the arrest of distributor Raymond Rohauer on obscenity charges. See Whitney Strub, "Vice's Devices: The Sexual Politics of Obscenity in Postwar Los Angeles," in *Film and Sexual Politics*, ed. Kylo-Patrick R. Hart (Newcastle, UK: Cambridge Scholars Press, 2006), 90.

2. Waugh, *Hard to Imagine*, 255.

3. *Laura Mulvey explores this concept in "Visual Pleasure and Narrative Cinema," in Visual and Other Pleasures, 14–30.*

4. David K. Johnson, *Buying Gay: How Physique Entrepreneurs Sparked a Movement* (New York: Columbia University Press, 2019). Johnson traces the importance of the genre and how it united gay men into a more cohesive group as both consumers and victims of discrimination.

5. Gerald Strickland, "Applause for Dick Fontaine," *Spree News Pictorial* 4, no. 3 (March 1972), n.p.

6. Photos of models wearing posing straps (or even nude, shown from the rear or with genitals inked out) were common in "legitimate" bodybuilding magazines in the 1930s through 1950s.

7. Richard Fontaine, "Cover Story: Richard Fontaine, Pioneer of Gay Films since 1949," interview with Michael Goetsch, *Victory News*, n.d., collection of David L. Chapman.

8. Fontaine, "Cover Story."

9. Fontaine, "Cover Story."

10. Spectrum Films advertising brochure, collection of David L. Chapman.

11. Advertisement in *Film World and A-V World*, August 1946, 372.

12. Bob Mizer, caption to a photo of Richard Du Bois, *Physique Pictorial* 7, no. 4 (Winter 1957): 10.

13. Fontaine, "Cover Story"; Bob Mizer, "AMG Is Going into the Movie Business," *Physique Pictorial* 7, no. 4 (Winter 1957): 2.

14. Waugh, *Hard to Imagine*, 258.

15. F. Valentine Hooven III, *Beefcake: The Muscle Magazines of America 1950–1970* (Cologne: Taschen, 1995), 74.

16. Richard Lindsay, *Hollywood Biblical Epics: Camp Spectacle and Queer Style from the Silent Era to the Modern Day*, 135.

17. Richard Fontaine, dir., *Ben-Hurry* (Los Angeles: AMG, 1960), on the DVD *Richard Fontaine's Days of Greek Gods*, released (El Cerrito, CA: Athletic Model Guild, 2009).

18. *Physique Pictorial* 12, no. 2 (November 1962): 10.

19. Bob Mizer, descriptive caption for "Muscles from Outer Space," *Physique Pictorial* 10, no. 3 (January 1961): 6–7.

20. Richard Fontaine, dir., *Day of Fury* (Los Angeles: AMG, ca. 1957), on the DVD *Richard Fontaine's Days of Greek Gods*. The film's title is a pun on the star's name and a comic reference to the Universal Studios' Western, *A Day of Fury*, which had appeared the previous year.

21. The latter film is Richard Fontaine, dir., *Because of Him* (Los Angeles: AMG, ca. 1957), on the DVD *Days of Greek Gods*.

22. Thomas Waugh, "Bruce of Los Angeles," in *Encyclopedia of Gay Histories and Cultures*, vol. 1, ed. George Haggerty (New York: Routledge, 2012), 146.

23. Tracy Baim and Owen Keehnen, *Leatherman: The Legend of Chuck Renslow*, 59. In an interview in 1991, Renslow explained that he made films because "there was a demand for it, supply and demand. Customers wanted movies of our models." Chuck Renslow, interview with an unnamed correspondent, *Outcome*, 1991, Tim in Vermont, http://www.timinvermont.com/vintage2/krinterview2.html (which requires membership). There is no publication information given, and Kenneth Krauss, in *Male Beauty: Postwar Masculinity in Theater, Film and Physique Magazines* (Albany: State University of New York Press, 2014), 277, claims that the interview was never actually published.

24. Renslow was interested in unconventional religions and magic. Allegedly he had in his home a special room for magic where he read tarot cards and "performed a variety of rituals and took on students." Baim and Keehnen, *Leatherman*, 184–85.

25. See Bob Mizer's caption to a lineup of cast members, *Physique Pictorial* 14, no. 4 (June 1965): 29. The AMG movie *Frontier Fun* was shot by Bob Mizer with ten models in posing straps on the beach in Ensenada, Mexico. Five models were supplied by AMG; the others were from the Frontier Athletic Club in San Diego and Tijuana.

26. Advertisement in *Man's World*, September 1957, 12. Graham had a basement studio near Buckingham Palace; bodybuilder Vic Burdett claims that Graham persuaded many guardsmen from the nearby barracks to pose for him. Vic Burdett to Tim Wilbur, email communication, ca. 2000, at Tim in Vermont, http://www.timinvermont.com/vintage2/jgindex.html (which requires membership).

27. Advertisements for Jan Eyck and Frank Hollfelder, *Young Physique* 6, no. 5 (July–August 1965): 81, 87. Apparently Eyck was the earlier photographer, since he advertises photos of Hollfelder.

28. Bob Mizer Foundation, "Film & Video Collection," http://bobmizer.org/film-video-collection.

29. Her name was likely based on B-movie actress Gloria Holden, and "glory hole" is gay slang for a hole in a public lavatory stall wall through which a man can be fellated.

30. Charles Kaiser, *The Gay Metropolis: The Landmark History of Gay Life in America* (New York: Grove, 1997), 28–30.

31. Erick Alvarez, *Muscle Boys: Gay Gym Culture* (New York: Routledge, 2008), 124–25. Alvarez surveyed gay men and discovered that in answer to the question "How important is it for you to (behave and appear) masculine?" the vast majority replied that it is important to extremely important, and that "behavior" is the principal marker of what makes a man masculine.

32. Lindsay, *Hollywood Biblical Epics*, 137.

X. FEMALE MUSCLES IN ACTION

Action is eloquence

—William Shakespeare, *Coriolanus*

WHILE FEMALE FILM stars have typically achieved ample recognition from the movie media and an adoring public for their acting talent, they are often relegated to glamorous, romantic, or sexy scenarios. So as not to risk sacrificing financially lucrative identities, physical dexterity and athletic prowess are usually reserved for male action heroes and producers are apt to assign the "weaker sex" to softer roles where they can be cuddled, coaxed, and rescued. But in the act of rescuing the ubiquitous "her" from danger, an element of physicality was necessary. Indeed, if seemingly helpless women could exercise strength while maintaining femininity, it would enhance the kind of thrills audiences craved. Such roles demanded a high degree of fitness and a screen persona often contradictory to reality and expectations of the male-dominated world. While the female actor could dispel her sisterhood's appearance of weakness by displaying what she could do with her muscles, it was often not possible to exercise the same degree of control in private life. This illusion of feminine strength was evident in the back stories of such major Hollywood stars as Pearl White (in acrobatics), Sonja Henie (in ice skating), and Esther Williams (in swimming), where beauty and athleticism led to tragic outcomes.

Perilous Pearl

We have seen in chapter 3 how in the early years of moviemaking Pearl White became perhaps the most visible embodiment of the "new woman," but she also served as a model of female physical empowerment. White created her own image as a daredevil star who rivaled the athletic feats of her male counterparts. In a 2001 essay Eve Golden expresses pity for potential biographers of Pearl White: "When it comes to throwing smoke screens and oil slicks behind her to put pursuers off the trail, James Bond had nothing on Pearl." That she "gleefully lied her head off to interviewers" and published an autobiography of dubious credibility, *Just Me*, helps explain why the only extant life story, *The Peerless Fearless Girl*, is "not so much a biography as a collection of musings and questionable dialogues."[1] While much of the drama and romantic allure relating to White's life and screen performances is undoubtedly movie hype, fabrications by the actress herself, and vivid imaginations of pundits, there had to be a high degree of authenticity; a rationale behind her physically challenging feats that cannot so easily be dismissed. As *Photoplay* columnist John Ten Eyck observed at her career height, " 'The Perils of Pauline,' the 'Elaine' serials, 'The Iron Claw' and 'Pearl of the Army' are her heroic enterprises, but around these exalted monuments are glittering fields of comedies, two-reelers, five-reelers, and new stunts of inconceivable physical daring." Even Golden admits that White, not unlike Douglas Fairbanks and Harold Lloyd, used doubles, but she did "more stunts than many actresses: She gamely leaped, swam, and fought her way through many a scene."[2] Notwithstanding the stunts, it was a "strenuous" life when for two and a half years she did only serials, which White described as "very hard work." While satisfying public desire for "thrilling pictures" with "hairbreadth escapes," she suppressed an inner desire to be a "real" actress: "The only joy you derive from appearing in them is when it is all over and you find yourself still alive." In a film career lasting from 1910 to 1924, White garnered 228 screen credits, including two hundred shorts and eleven multireleased serials. And in 1920 *Who's Who on the Screen* pronounced her "an expert at almost every branch of athletics."[3]

Only White's autobiography and interviews, though deemed unreliable, provide an inkling of how she got that way. From an early age she had "a positive fondness for doing reckless things," she recalled in 1917, "and the more danger that is connected with them, the more pleasure I have taken in them."[4] She had a very physical upbringing. White describes her younger self with such unendearing terms as "brat," "roughneck," "outlaw," "juvenile delinquent," "and tomboy," and claims she was "as ugly as a child ever was." At twelve, she writes, "I could lick any kid my size and I would even defy my father." Her craving for stunts she attributes to early exposure to the circus and the stern influence of her father, who, after damping her desire for ballooning, allowed her to hang trapezes from the rafters of an old evaporator shed. "Thus, all the kids in the village, under my leadership, became acrobats. This was one thing my father didn't object to my brother and myself doing. Perhaps he thought it would develop our muscles, and the one thing he always adored was strength." It was the strength and skill she developed on that apparatus, according to White, that "made my venture into the circus business possible." Her circus career was "not long-lived, but oh how happy I was working with that act on traps, and the same time learning to be a bareback rider, which . . . is about the greatest ambition I ever had." It was also where she became enamored of the entertainment industry and "got the nerve and some of the training for the adventurous deeds people think are so wonderful. But it is born in every Western girl to like outdoor life and to do all kinds of wild, daring things."[5]

These early athletic experiences led to stage productions on the road and eventually to New York in search of stardom. But it was her voice more than her body that was utilized. That she gravitated to motion pictures resulted from straining her vocal chords in ceaseless melodramas. Acting on a tip from a fellow actress, White decided to "get a little work in some of the studios until my voice got better."[6] She soon developed a liking for the new medium. For her role as Mercy Merrick in *The New Magdalen* for Powers Picture Plays in 1910 White was favorably received as "an emotional actress of great intensity" with "a great future before her." What's more, she was more adept at conveying this intensity in the silence of film through her background in physical training. "My motion picture experiences have been valuable to me in developing my capacity for expressing emotion independent of the spoken word. I now realize how the actors in the theater are, except in the great plays, handicapped by the dialogue, the artificial scenery and other limitations."[7] Little did she realize the risks entailed until she read the contract for her first serial, *The Perils of Pauline* (1914):

In the first three episodes I had to play tennis, which I could not. I had to take a flight in an aeroplane, which I didn't like much, because it was supposed to crash to the ground in a wreck; then I had to drive a motor car through water fire and sand. This also didn't sound reasonable. Then I had to go out to sea in a yacht, which was all right, only that I was to jump overboard just as the boat was blown up by the villain, and I couldn't swim. Then I was to be in a captive balloon—but ah! The villain was to cut the rope and I was to go sailing about for a while, then drop an anchor, which was to catch in a tree, and I was to descend some two hundred and fifty feet on this, reaching a cliff on the side of a mountain, then I was to be showered with rocks.

Protesting to the director that she was "too clumsy" and had "too much respect for my life," White believed he wanted an acrobat rather than an actress; nonetheless, she signed.[8]

Although she never learned to swim, play tennis, or golf, and never considered herself an all-round athlete, White believed "all sports depend more or less on the schooling of one's muscles, and in the old trapeze days I had developed and trained mine until I could control my entire body fairly easy." For *Perils of Pauline*, White had to expand her skill set. Cuts, bruises, and sprains were inevitable consequences of the roles she performed, but a far more serious injury occurred during the filming of *Pauline* when she fell backward on her head from a flight of stairs and displaced several vertebrae. "The pain was terrible," she recalled in 1920. "For two years I simply lived with osteopaths, and to this day I have some pretty bad times with my back."[9] With her film career declining in the early 1920s, and after two unsuccessful marriages, she retired to become a successful businesswoman in France. But she was no longer athletic. She became overweight, and to cope with enduring back pain she turned to alcohol and drugs, which led to her death at age forty-nine of liver disease.

Yet she remained, as their early "queen," a symbol of physical feats of high intensity and an inspiration to young women who aspired to a movie career. In one sense White and others of her ilk symbolized female empowerment, but their proclivity for violent action and stunt roles also embodied an obverse message of victimization. "The serials put on display a new mobility of woman within public space," argues Marina Dahlquist, "but the heroines' abilities are at times on the verge of being eclipsed as the freedom this new mobility supposedly gave them simultaneously put them in life-threatening situations." These dangers did not deter White, who took a liking to taking chances. "I am an athlete," she admitted, "so it seems like I'm in the right place after all." Pearl White, concludes film biographer Shelley Stamp, "urged young women interested in the film business to be strong, to learn hobbies, to be fearless, and to keep physically fit. Traits such as these," White insisted, "would boost a young woman's chances in the motion picture industry much more readily than painstaking beauty treatments or fancy skin creams."[10] She proved that there was beauty in peril, though of a different kind.

Pavlova of the Ice

While the athleticism of Pearl White is often overshadowed on the screen by her daring feats, the athletic attributes of Sonja Henie defined her public image. Even the beauty and grace of her performances could not diminish the collective memory of her three Olympic gold medals (1928, 1932, and 1936) and ten world championship titles (1927–36) in figure skating.

On her "brilliant path to glory," notes a 1937 *Photoplay* article, she won "more medals, cups, titles and honors than any other human being, man or woman, in the world today."[11] More than any other athlete, Henie put the newly established (1924) Olympic Winter Games on firm footing. By the time she retired in 1936, she was able to enter Hollywood a ready-made star. She wanted to "do with skates what Fred Astaire [was] doing with dancing," Henie told the *New York Times* in March 1936, soon after the Olympics; "no one has ever done it in the movies and I want to." But she also aspired to be known as an actress and filmed in color. What she demanded from Twentieth Century Fox producer Darryl Zanuck was straight dramatic roles. "I don't mind one skating scene," she reasoned, "but I don't want to make pictures forever showing a tiny, dumpy Sonja flying around on ice. I want to act and prove that I can be a great actress like [Greta] Garbo."[12] Henie aspired to combine her early ballet training with ice skating and use these athletic skills as a basis for a career in movies. But much would depend on her ability to convert audience appeal from an activity relying chiefly on her muscles to roles calling for an expression of her personality.

Henie's athleticism was both inherited and acquired during her Norwegian childhood. Her father, Wilhelm, was a wealthy furrier and a versatile sportsman who, according to her brother Leif's account, twice won the world bicycling championship. "He also excelled in speed skating, ski jumping, and cross-country racing, winning medals in these events and setting records that were not bettered for years."[13] Henie's early passion was dancing, so her mother, Selma, engaged an Oslo ballet master, Love Krohn, who once trained the world famous Russian ballerina Anna Pavlova. "I decided it would be nice to be the best dancer in the world," Henie recalled. "Mother remarked that there was a ballerina named Pavlowa [*sic*] whom the world considered incomparable, and that she might give me some competition. . . . Later I wanted to bring dancing into skating, transport the ballet onto ice."[14] Eventually Henie turned from dancing to ice skating, craving the exhilaration of the winter sports she learned at the family's mountain hunting lodge in Geilo, Norway. With expert tutelage, she passionately pursued the sport. She worked so hard that her parents, fearing exhaustion, curtailed her skating hours. "Sometimes she felt as though her muscles were bundles of live wires that would electrocute her if she made the wrong move," observed her brother. By the time she went to bed, her body was an immovable lead mass.[15]

Not surprisingly, with such a rigorous training regimen, Henie won her first world championship in 1927 at age fifteen in Oslo. The following summer, with her focus on the upcoming Winter Olympics in St. Moritz, she saw Pavlova perform in London. She later wrote in her autobiography,

> She was a dancer whose performance went beyond dancing, transcending technique to such an extent that the onlooker was unaware of technique. So she became my idol more than ever. The influence she had on me was twice as great now that she had become a reality. My old and constant passion for dancing burst into new flame. Coming back to the ice in the autumn, I wanted more than anything else to make my free skating program a blend of dancing and figure skating. I wanted it to have the choreographic form of ballet solo and the technique of the ice.

Henie's virtuoso performance at the 1928 Olympics took figure skating to a new level. Before then it had been "rather stiff and pedantic in its competitive form," she explained. "The free skating programs, the half of each contestant's performance that is left to his invention and taste, had been little more than series of school figures and minor stunt figures strung together." Her coach, Martin Stixrud, suggested "the jumps and spins I should incorporate into the number to show the judges my skill, while I arranged them in a sequence that would have something of the patterned continuity and mood of dancing."[16] So accomplished was her blend of artistry with athleticism that audiences were unaware of the muscular effort required to perform her spins and leaps or the grueling hours of training required to master them. At this climactic point in her skating career, Henie confided to her parents that she aspired to a grander place in the entertainment realm: "I have decided to become a movie star."[17]

With each world championship and Olympic victory, as well as other performances, Henie's popularity grew on both sides of the Atlantic. She soon realized the difficulty of satisfying her growing number of fans while staying healthy and fit and maintaining the hectic life of a champion skater. "Everywhere I went, parties were arranged for me, all with such kind intent and flattering purpose that I could hardly refuse to attend," she recalled. Although often deprived of sleep because of her busy schedule, Henie abstained from alcohol and smoking and avoided rich and indigestible foods, noting, "Nothing is so senseless as to risk ruining the condition you've built up with long care." She applied the conditioning and dexterity gained from skating to other sports. In 1931 the Norwegian government awarded her a medal for athletic "versatility and achievement," a first for a woman. In addition to her championship figure skating, Henie was runner-up in the national tennis tournament and displayed proficiency in skiing, swimming, ballet, and horsemanship.[18]

Hollywood, to which she migrated in 1936, would require a new set of skills to further test her versatility. The setting for her film debut, however, was New York City's Madison Square Garden, the world's largest entertainment venue turned into a giant ice rink. Featuring dashing costar Don Ameche, comedy relief by the Ritz Brothers, and Henie's celebrity status, *One in a Million* (1936) seemed a surefire box office hit. *Photoplay* predicted she would "steal her own picture. Nothing can compete with her effortless skating and dancing. And if she can act half as well as she skates—well 20th Century Fox has another new feminine star to find roles for."[19] Not surprisingly, the narrative of the film mimics Henie's brilliant skating career. She stars as Greta, an amateur Swiss skater discovered by the leader of an American theatrical troupe, played by Adolphe Menjou, who almost spoils her by putting her in a professional show. Ameche, as charismatic reporter Bob Harris, rescues Greta from the same fate that had taken Jim Thorpe's greatest accolade from him a generation earlier; Bob's advice to remain an amateur enables Greta to compete in the 1936 Olympics and thereby achieve greater stardom with a climactic performance at the Garden. *Variety*'s assessment was that "a sweet demeanor, engaging personality, an intriguing Scandinavian accent and an abundance of poise" were among Henie's assets. Her skating scenes were "Pavlovaesque on frozen water." *Photoplay* reported that the diminutive Norwegian (at five foot two and 110 pounds) was "knocking them dead all over the country" and that her finale exhibition, "an interpretation of Pavlova's 'Swan Dance' shook the rafters of Madison Square Garden. . . . Sonja loves acting, thinks Hollywood is 'terrific.' Hollywood thinks Sonja is likewise."[20] This film and her next, *Thin Ice* (1937), together grossed $2.6 million and enabled Henie to earn $260,000 for 1937—making her, according to Leif Henie, "the highest salaried woman in show business and probably the world. . . . Never in the history of films had anyone risen to such heights so quickly." But owing to the wizardry of her financial broker, Arthur Wirtz, Henie's movie income was "peanuts compared to the net profits from her ice tours," which he negotiated for $2 million in 1938.[21]

To continuously perform feats befitting a world class athlete and meet the expectations of audiences in two entertainment genres required that

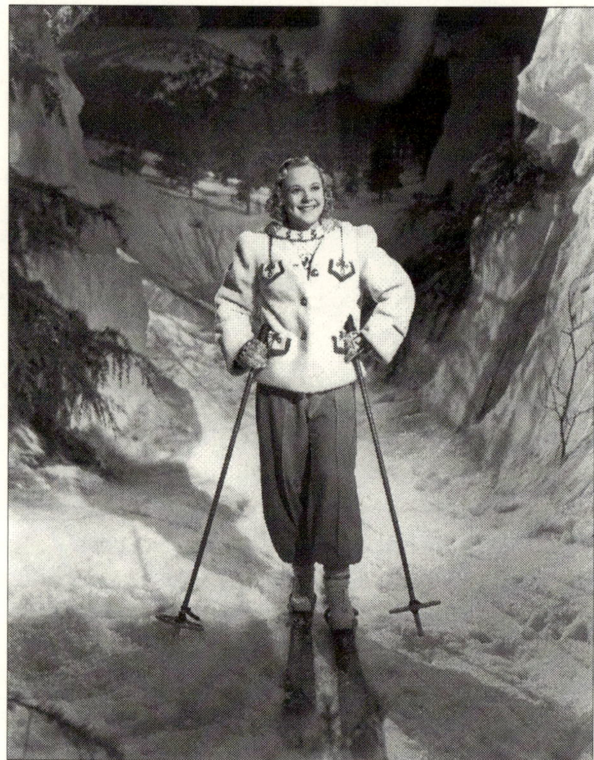

Figure 10.1. Sonja Henie poses on skis in this publicity still from the 1939 feature *Everything Happens at Night*. Collection of David L. Chapman.

Henie remain in top physical condition. Since childhood she had been known for her self-discipline. Most evident in an interview with Madame Sylvia of Hollywood, the women's fitness guru, was that Henie's fitness and figure stemmed from endless hours of practice and performance. Henie told her that her exercise came mostly from working out and practicing new stunts and fancy tricks for her exhibitions. "After you see her, you'll agree that's plenty," noted Sylvia. "These stunts are not easy to master but she floats through the air like a feather. Her figure is healthy, firm and nicely proportioned and when you consider that she has spent half her life on skates, it's all the more outstanding for its lack of knotty muscles."[22] From a broader perspective, fitness guru and *Photoplay* publisher Bernarr Macfadden argued that movie stars, as role models, could have a positive influence on the well-being of Americans. He cited Popeye, who inspired children to eat spinach, and Marlene Dietrich for popularizing straight lines and knobby bones. To Macfadden, Henie was a perfect example of how open-air exercise could vitalize women: "Here we have a heroine whose overflowing vitality is the source of joyous delight. She is a poem on skates, an inspiring song from iceland [*sic*]. She outdoes the panther in grace and suppleness. There, indeed, is femininity at its best—life, animation, beauty and gorgeous force that moves with such ease, and uncanny skill that no musical accompaniment is needed.[23] To maintain her health, despite a grueling schedule of training and performances, Henie exercised ruthless self-discipline and followed a strict diet. While working on a picture in Hollywood, she would rise at five in the morning, work twelve hours, and retire early. On the road she would stay up all night and sleep half the day. Her dietary staple was steak tartare with raw eggs; she consumed few fruits and vegetables. Much to others' dismay, she would regurgitate her food to control her weight. She also took daily vitamin shots in her arms and legs and received massages twice a day, aware as she entered middle age that an athlete's body could be used up. But Henie also indulged in another form of physicality. Although she conveyed an image of wholesomeness on-screen, she pursued lustful relationships with men vulnerable to her star power. As her brother attests, "this guileless, simple girl was one of the most voracious sexy broads in town. She really loved to fuck."[24]

The stamina acquired from her athletic performances and lifestyle enabled Henie to star in nine more feature films from 1938 to 1948, but they always took place in cold weather settings, highlighted by skating scenes.[25] Producer Milton Sperling, reflecting on her most famous film, *Sun Valley Serenade* (1941), confirms that Henie, "always hungry for sex," was especially intimate with good-looking ski instructors. "I think she ran through the whole bunch of them, one at a time," he recalled. "Sonja got away with a lot simply because she was a star and making money. Even her worst films made money." Her ambition to become a great actress, however, was never fulfilled, largely because public demand for her skating overshadowed her noteworthy acting talent. "If she could not be the first lady of the screen, then she would be the first lady of finances," notes her brother.[26] What enabled Henie to become one of the world's wealthiest women was the creation of her *Hollywood Ice Revue* with Arthur Wirtz to tour major cities during winter months, as well as the sale of Henie-related bric-a-brac.

With the accumulation of her fortune, however, people seemed to matter less than personal goals and material well-being. It was a Napoleonic complex attributable to her spoiled upbringing. "Sonja loved money more than anything," recalled her personal assistant, Dorothy Stevens. "People didn't count as much as objectives," according to her brother. Skating partner Michael Mikeler resented her "penchant for tossing people aside or putting them on standby until she needed them again." By the mid-1950s, having endured two failed marriages and a relentless routine for decades, her personality and skating showed signs of deterioration. Henie sought relief in alcohol, remembers skating partner Marshall Beard. "She had an interest in Black and White Scotch and would fill 7-Up bottles with Scotch so nobody would know what she was drinking. She took that 7-Up bottle into restaurants with her. She was never without it." Beard also recalls that Henie talked like a stevedore: "'Mother fucker' was her favorite expression, and she knew how to talk to the union people. She could get down and dirty better than any woman I ever met in my life. She was a hard-nosed bitch." Henie was paranoid about other skaters, insisting on her own private rehearsal time, once even forcing them to stand outside in the cold while she rehearsed. Leif remembers that Henie was "no longer merely drinking all night after the show. She now was belting scotch by the glassful before the show," neither skating well nor following the music. Worst of all, "chorus skaters were skating better and getting better hands. She was merely wobbling around on the ice." Still, she retained her muscular might. "Sonja was as strong as an ox," recalls Stevens. "You'd never know it to look at her, but all those years of athletics gave her tremendous strength" and "when she was drunk and angry she was almost superhuman."[27] Her idyllic life had turned into a nightmare, and she became suicidal. Her death, though premature, was natural. She succumbed to leukemia at age fifty-seven in 1969.

Henie's tragic outcome, not unlike that of Pearl White, was how to descend from the heights of stardom. "The hardest thing is to quit at the top," argues former champion skater Aja Zanova Steindler. "You want to stay—this is your life. A marvelous life. How do you leave? It's a terrible thing. And Sonja was going through that." Aside from brightening the lives of countless thousands of movie and sports fans, Henie was probably most successful in creating an illusion of perfection. Her brother concludes that she was "one of the magicians who convinced the world that Hollywood was truly a magic factory."[28]

The Million Dollar Mermaid

If Sonja Henie could lay claim to the nickname Pavlova of the Ice, Esther Williams could be called Pavlova of the Water. Both shared not only an unrivaled mastery of their respective sports but a desire to combine it with traditional ballet and the ability to make their way to stardom in a man's world. Unlike Henie, however, Williams was never an Olympic champion. Although she was Pacific Coast Champion twice and won several national American Athletic Union swimming titles in the freestyle and breaststroke in the late 1930s, no Olympic games were held until 1948 because of World War II.[29] After serving an entertainment apprenticeship at Billy Rose's San Francisco Aquacade, starring opposite Johnny Weissmuller, Williams attracted the attention of Metro-Goldwyn-Mayer (MGM) head Louis B. Mayer who, as she explained in her autobiography, was "determined to find a female athlete and turn her into big box office, much as 20th Century-Fox had done with Sonja Henie. . . . 'Melt the ice, get a swimmer, make it pretty!' " cried Mayer. Upon signing her MGM contract, Williams recalled "never-ending photo sessions and interviews with fan magazines. These were the MGM stepping stones to 'stardom.' " One summer she appeared on twenty-seven fan magazine covers. As *Screenland* predicted, "Esther Williams will get along swimmingly in her new career."[30]

With Henie as her role model, Williams starred in *Bathing Beauty* (1944), Hollywood's first swimming movie, alongside Red Skelton and Basil Rathbone. It necessitated construction of a deep pool on the MGM lot with camera cranes for overhead shots.[31] Williams soon acquired the nickname Mermaid after a memorable kiss in a screen test with Clark Gable. Although she established her acting credentials in subsequent films, she found it impossible to "break out of the 'swimming star' straitjacket." Likewise, she felt confined by the "pretty pink bubble the studio had constructed around you and your outwardly perfect personal life. The public desperately wanted to believe that you lived a fairy tale existence." There was also predictability in Williams's films: "Audiences had come to expect a certain kind of film from me, and these movies were immensely popular."[32] In five of the postwar productions in which Williams starred—*Thrill of a Romance* (1945), *Easy to Wed* (1946), *On an Island with You* (1948), *Neptune's Daughter* (1949), and *Duchess of Idaho* (1950)—box office receipts ($28,054,000) nearly tripled the original budgets ($9,546,000).[33]

A beautiful face and figure were critical to Williams's appeal, but her most popular screen roles, unlike those of other female stars, usually required minimal makeup and clothes. Such relentless scrutiny of her unadorned body required rigorous conditioning to sustain perfection of form and function.[34] Fortunately, skin was in, but for Williams it was devoid of prurient intent. She exuded a healthy image from swimming and pursuit of the Greek

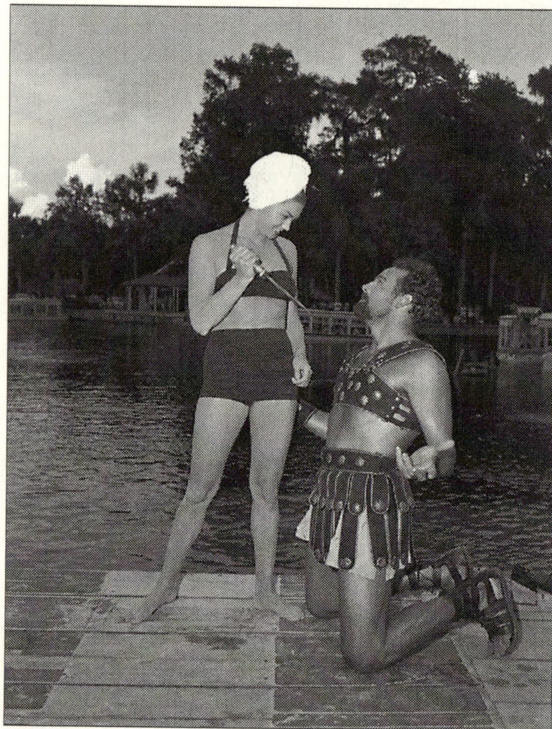

Figure 10.2. Esther Williams and Howard Keel horse around on the set of *Jupiter's Darling* in Silver Springs, Florida. Image in the public domain.

ideal of *mens sana in corpore sano* (a sound mind in a sound body). Even at age fifteen, she recalls, "the years of hard swimming had packed muscle on my frame and made me very strong."[35] Williams believed that mental and physical health went hand-in-hand and caring of the body enabled one to "get the most out of life." Diet and exercise were keys to vitality: "I get most of my exercise through swimming . . . and I find it tunes up not only my body, but my state of mind, too. When I get out of the pool after a swim, there's an absolute 'zing' to the way I feel." What seems remarkable is that Williams could stay in excellent condition despite a hectic life outside the studio. In 1951, at the height of her career, she signed a ten-year contract with MGM that would pay her $2,500 a week, with three months' annual vacation and radio and television performance rights. Williams also owned some profitable enterprises, including a restaurant, a construction company, a factory, and sizable interest in a swimsuit company, as well as property in Mexico. With little help from her alcoholic and spendthrift husband, she was a caring mother for three small children and provided swimming lessons for blind and disabled youth.[36] Despite this intense but highly glamorous life, Williams embarked on what was likely the most ambitious film of her career.

MGM executives, Williams recalled, "thought they were giving me the *crème de la crème* when they cast me in *Million Dollar Mermaid* [1952]." Indeed, producer Arthur Hornblow Jr. and director Mervyn LeRoy were among Hollywood's most respected executives, and her male costars, Walter Pidgeon and Victor Mature, were veteran actors of substance. She also liked the biographical nature of the script, which featured a world-renown female swimmer: "For once, swimming was really part of the story and didn't have to be shoehorned into the rest of the plot. I loved the idea of playing Annette Kellerman, a real person, rather than a superficial character created to give me an excuse to swim." Kellerman was "a woman whose career foreshadowed my own, who started out as a champion swimmer but ended up in the movies on the high wire."[37] It seemed like an opportunity to be her alter ego. Kellerman, however, was ambivalent. When she learned from Hollywood agent Abe Lastfogel that Williams was going to play her in an MGM extravaganza, she burst into tears. "She'd seen the younger star's remake of *Neptune's Daughter* [1949], which bore no resemblance at all to her [1914] film of the same title," notes Emily Gibson. "There were no fabulous fairy grottos or beautiful mermaids; instead, Esther played a swimsuit manufacturer, and Keenan Wynn was her wisecracking manager." At first Kellerman rejected the idea but then met Williams and "realized she really wanted to do my life story." Subsequently MGM bought the rights to *My Story*, Kellerman's autobiography, and enlisted her as technical adviser.[38] Neither of these potential assets, however, was tapped to lend authenticity to the film. Only once did Kellerman appear on the set. Although she gazed approvingly at a replica of the New York Hippodrome where she once performed, she responded disapprovingly to the American casting of her, to which Williams responded, "I'm the only swimmer in the movies, Miss Kellerman. I'm all you've got." After watching some of the shooting, Kellerman left, never to return—not even for the premier.[39]

"It's the most dazzling of all musical spectacles," exclaimed a 1952 publicity blurb for *Million Dollar Mermaid*, "inspired by the true story of the queen of bathing beauties!"[40] Although both women broke new ground for their gender by integrating athleticism and screen acting with water ballet, Williams's portrayal hardly resembles a true story. It romanticizes Kellerman's lifelong progression from polio victim to movie queen, and much is made of Kellerman's Australian origins, including an ersatz boxing kangaroo. But the centerpiece of the film is the made-up love triangle between Kellerman, her promoter Jimmy Sullivan (who in real life was her husband), and Hippodrome manager Alfred Harper. Enough of Kellerman's swimming background is included to make the story plausible, but the drama surrounding her professional development hinges on her love life, not her swimming or acting attributes. Nor is there mention of her ideal feminine form as an alleged "perfect woman," or that she was the first major Hollywood actress to appear nude. Kellerman once confided to an interviewer that although she liked Williams, "she couldn't dive higher than that bed." She claimed to know an Olympic diver "who had been Esther's double for ten years" and got $1,000 per picture. Kellerman, on the other hand, was famous for her daring dives, including the first-ever leap from an airplane without a parachute. Even riskier was her tightrope walking across a waterfall at Yosemite National Park.[41] She was also a proficient fencer, golfer, and ballet dancer. These were athletic feats Williams could never duplicate.

Most unrealistic was the film's characterization of Jimmy Sullivan as a carnival huckster. Kellerman's "quiet unassuming husband" was in real life quite unlike that "hunk of a man," Victor Mature, who plays Sullivan in *Million Dollar Mermaid*. The on-screen romance between Mature and Williams was complemented by their torrid sexual affair off-screen. "Vic was a strong and fulfilling lover. Even better than I had fantasized," Williams recalled. "Fictional desire and real desire blended during the making of *Million Dollar Mermaid*, and it's obvious, to me at least, in every scene." Kellerman couldn't stand Mature, according to biographer Emily Gibson, "and when the film came out poor Jimmie [*sic*] was taunted relentlessly by friends who greeted him with: 'Here comes Samson,'" a reference to Mature's famous screen role. No less overblown is the climactic scene at the reconstructed Hippodrome, with dazzling costumes, lights, special effects and an elaborate synchronized swimming routine that hardly existed in Kellerman's day. Gibson notes that choreographer Busby Berkeley "used more than 100 swimmers, 55-foot high streams of yellow and red smoke, and ramps upon which the swimmers slid into the water while carrying lit torches. Then Williams (or her double) dived from a 50-foot high swing into the mass of swimmers, who immediately went into one of Berkeley's Ferris wheel effects (shot from an overhead camera). In the finale, several hundred lit sparklers emerged from the water and formed a backdrop to the ensemble." Kellerman called the film a "silly little yarn," a "namby pamby attempt" to tell her life story. A *New York Times* review called it a "Technicolored shindig which laughingly pretends to be a biography"; lacking was "a reasonably fascinating script." Indeed, the scriptwriter and director "and occasionally even the actors seem to have strolled out for a smoke. It is in these yawning stretches that *Million Dollar Mermaid* tries to weave the stilted romance that is presented as Miss Kellerman's biography."[42] It bore little resemblance to her actual life.

Admittedly, romantic sensitivities—far more than realistic depictions—permeated the film, yet there existed an eerie semblance in the real lives of these athletic screen heroines. Both came close to death while filming her most famous motion picture. In 1913 Kellerman was performing an underwater scene in Bermuda for *Neptune's Daughter* in a five-thousand-gallon tank with director Herbert Brenon. Suddenly the three-quarter-inch glass broke and they were sucked through a hole in the aquarium wall. "Their bodies lay motionless among the wreckage," observed a reporter, "and we thought them surely dead." Kellerman was badly cut on the foot and required hospitalization for six weeks. When *Neptune's Daughter* premiered in April 1914 at New York's Globe Theater, however, she became an overnight star. It played for nineteen weeks to packed houses, eventually earning over $1 million while eliciting enthusiastic responses nationwide. "Never before in the annals of picturedom has a film created such a furore," proclaimed the *Pittsburgh Leader*.[43]

Kellerman's accident was dramatically staged as a nearly fatal spinal injury in the climax to *Million Dollar Mermaid* and used to provide a romantic angle in which Kellerman, recovering in her hospital bed, reconciles with erstwhile boyfriend Sullivan. Not only was the scene out of sync chronologically, but in real life no breakup or reconciliation ever occurred between the two. Completely uncontrived, however, was Williams's own nearly fatal accident while filming the spectacular water show. Perched on a tiny platform fifty feet above the pool to perform a swan dive, Williams was afflicted with acrophobia and loss of equilibrium because of rupturing her eardrums on seven different occasions as a result of years of underwater swimming. As she later recalled,

> Hurtling down, I muttered a silent, "Oh, shit." I suddenly realized what was going to happen next. *The gold crown on my head.* Instead of being made with something pliable like cardboard, it was lightweight aluminum, a lot stronger and less flexible than my neck.
>
> I hit the water with tremendous force. The impact snapped my head back. I heard something pop in my neck. I knew instantly that I was in

big trouble. . . . I could kick my legs, so I desperately treaded water, but my arms and shoulders were virtually paralyzed. The back of my neck was in screaming pain. In my mind's eye I saw the headlines. "Esther Williams Drowns in MGM Studio Pool."

At the hospital Williams blacked out from pain, and X-rays showed three broken vertebrae in her neck. "I'd come as close to snapping my spinal cord and becoming a paraplegic as you could without actually succeeding." For six months Williams was relegated to a full body cast while the rest of the filming took place around her.[44] Yet *Million Dollar Mermaid* became a major holiday attraction at New York's Radio City Music Hall, where it played for eight weeks and grossed nearly $5 million nationwide.[45] While it was Kellerman who swam underwater in a fishtail costume and introduced underwater choreography, it was Esther Williams who would forever be remembered as the Million Dollar Mermaid.

It appeared that Williams, much in the manner of Sonja Henie, would capitalize on this image for additional fame. While she made several more aquatic-themed films, and her face, figure, and stories still appeared in fan magazines, her fortunes declined following severance of her contract with MGM in 1956. For refusing to accept the lead role in *The Opposite Sex*, Williams lost nearly $3 million in deferred payments set aside for retirement. Most distressing, however, was the disintegration of her marriage to Ben Gage, who had squandered the rest of his wife's fortune. When confronted by her attorney, Paul Ziffrin, he confessed to having lost $250,000 on the restaurant she had bought for him to manage. He had also made some disastrous investments, made loans to personal friends, lost money at the racetrack, and even used the star's money to send his bookkeepers on a luxury vacation. In the end Williams discovered that she was broke: "Everything was gone. All the saving and investing and frugal living I'd done, choosing to give up the jewelry and fancy cars to live like a normal person instead of like a movie star, had all been for nothing."[46]

With the loss of her fortune, divorce from her husband, a declining film career, $750,000 in unpaid taxes, and the responsibility of raising three children, Williams realized her life in the fairy-tale bubble of Hollywood had fallen apart: "Never was I more 'unraveled' than in 1959, when being Esther Williams became an exercise in schizophrenia." In desperation, after learning how it had lifted fellow actor Cary Grant from similar depths of despair, she resorted to the novelty drug LSD at the Psychiatric Institute of

Beverly Hills. It seemed like "instant psychoanalysis." It enabled her to trace the roots of her distress to unreal expectations during her childhood—that she would fulfill, as a female in a man's world, the early promise of her older brother, cut short by his untimely death. This stress was exacerbated by her extraordinary athletic ability and subsequent movie career.[47]

Contrary to the impression that her glamorous movies and fan magazines had created over previous decades, Williams was living a troubled existence. Her idyllic screen image was merely an illusion: "The public desperately wanted to believe that you lived a fairy tale existence, a projection of all their romantic fantasies, so much so that despite everything, you tried to believe it yourself." The stark reality of her personal life had at last intruded on the fantasy world generated by her spectacular aquatic displays on-screen. Her LSD trip had brought a modicum of escape, but Williams was also consoled that she was not alone. She could reflect on how other female stars such as Bette Davis "who rose to the top of our professions and were so successful in our public lives, could have such disastrous private lives." Although she did not die broken and penniless at age ninety-one, Williams realized that her "personal life had become as different as it could be from my All-American screen image."[48]

Williams's suffering was not unlike that of other women, such as Pearl White and Sonja Henie, who sought empowerment outside their traditional sphere of social identity. As Sabine Hake observes, reflecting on views of female images by German journalist Kurt Tucholsky, "Female beauty and eroticism are equated with the ephemeral, whereas female suffering and sacrifice come to symbolize the eternal values of life."[49] But to go against the grain of normal expectations could be dangerous. For Williams, Pearl White was "a true heroine—she wasn't dependent on men to rescue her from danger."[50] Once, in a rescue scene for *The Fatal Ring* (1917), White nearly paid the ultimate price for stepping out of her assigned feminine role. To dodge a monstrous ferryboat, the script called for her partner to grab a rope flung by longshoremen, and

the hero was the only one supposed to grab for the rope thrown us, but, believe me, I forgot for the time being that I was the heroine and was expected to be real ladylike and allow the hero to save me in the proper fashion, and I grabbed for that rope too. . . . I was supposed to let him do all the rescue stunt, but when I grabbed the rope it threw him out of his plan. The only thing I know was that I was thankful that the longshoremen were two husky ones and were used to handling the ferryboat. They yanked us out of the water in rapid fashion.[51]

What Williams admired most about White was that she "performed her own stunts. As we finished *Pagan Love Song* [1950], I felt as though I'd inherited Pearl White's mantle. Part actress, part stuntwoman, I knew I was doing all this on my own, and that's how it was always going to be. No guys were going to save me."[52] Yet she was unable to save herself.

Even more appealing and more successful as a role model was Annette Kellerman, whom Williams viewed as "Shades of Pearl White (The Perils of Pauline)!" While Williams's own life story was corrupted by the financial concerns of Hollywood executives, scriptwriters, and filmdom's fickle fan base, Kellerman appeared to be a "real person" who had sidestepped the gender trap.[53] Though describing herself as an individualist rather than a feminist, Kellerman encapsulated the feminine ideal. According to her biographer, "Annette could see that men, not women, were enjoying life most. She liked to do the things that men did—drive, swim, fence and ride. Often she was as good, if not better, than them. She wanted other women to share her enjoyment and made it her life's work to convert her sisters to the joys of physical exercise. There was a kind of religiosity in her zeal, but there was also a genuine wish for everyone to feel as good as she did."[54] Part of the secret to Kellerman's success as a woman in a man's world was that she retired after her last film in 1924 and never looked back on the contrived culture of movieland. She then pursued more meaningful endeavors, spreading the gospel of proper diet and exercise and creating a contented home life. Unlike Pearl White, Sonja Henie, and Esther Williams, who employed their athletic skills to soar to the heights of popularity but ultimately failed at the more serious business of life, Kellerman shunned public acclaim, pursuing athletic feats more for their own sake and personal fulfillment. She found happiness throughout her entertainment career, and beyond, just by being herself.

Notes

1. Eve Golden, *Golden Images: 41 Essays on Silent Film Stars*, 198. See also Pearl White, *Just Me*; and Manuel Weltman and Raymond Lee, *Pearl White: The Peerless Fearless Girl* (New York: A. S. Barnes, 1969).

2. John Ten Eyck, "Speaking of Pearls," *Photoplay*, September 1917, 26; Golden, *Golden Images*, 201.

3. Pearl White, quoted in Hector Ames, "The Champion Heroine of Movie Perils, Exploits, Plots, and Conspiracies," 50, 52; "Pearl White (1889–1938)," Golden Silents, http://goldensilents.com/stars/pearlwhite.html. Marina Dahlquist notes, however, that many other female stars of this era, including Grace Cunard, Helen Holmes, Ruth Roland, Marie Walcamp, and Kathlyn Williams, were known for their athleticism in thrilling films. What made White unique was that Pathé films "perpetuated a set of myths mixing her private self with the film character Pauline that added to White's action persona." Marina Dahlquist, "Introduction: Why Pearl?, in *Exporting Perilous Pauline: Pearl White and the Serial Film Craze*, ed. Marina Dahlquist, 10–11.

4. Pearl White, "Thrills in Serial Making," 423.

5. White, *Just Me*, 18–19, 49, 52; Ames, "The Champion Heroine," 50.

6. White, *Just Me*, 99.

7. "Picture Personalities," *Moving Picture World* 7, no. 23 (December 3, 1910): 1281.

8. White, *Just Me*, 158–59.

9. Golden, *Golden Images*, 201.

10. Dahlquist, "Introduction," 12. Ben Singer elaborates on this theme in *Melodrama and Modernity: Early Sensational Cinema and Its Contexts*, 254–60; White, *Just Me*, 161; Mabel Condon, "Sans Grease Paint and Wig," *Motography* 12, no. 8 (August 22, 1914): 279; Shelley Stamp, *Movie-Struck Girls: Women and Motion Picture Culture after the Nickelodeon* (Princeton, NJ: Princeton University Press, 2000), 144.

11. Howard Sharpe, "Skating through Life," *Photoplay*, November 1937, 15.

12. Pear White, quoted in Lincoln A. Werden, "Miss Henie Turns Pro; Tour May Net $150,000," *New York Times*, March 18, 1936; Raymond Strait and Leif Henie, *Queen of Ice, Queen of Shadows: The Unsuspected Life of Sonja Henie*, 125.

13. Strait and Henie, *Queen of Ice*, 16.

14. Sonja Henie, *Wings on My Feet*, 3, 7–8.

15. Strait and Henie, *Queen of Ice*, 28.

16. Henie, *Wings on My Feet*, 25–26, 8.

17. Strait and Henie, *Queen of Ice*, 31.

18. Henie, *Wings on My Feet*, 32–33, 44.

19. James Reid, "We Cover the Studios," *Photoplay*, January 1937, 36.

20. "One in a Million," *Variety*, December 31, 1935, http://variety.com/1935/film/reviews/one-in-a-million-1200411200/; "Ask the Answer Man," *Photoplay*, May 1937, 80.

21. Strait and Henie, *Queen of Ice*, 130, 138–39.

22. Madame Sylvia, "Cutting a Figure for Yourself," *Photoplay*, March 1937, 73.

23. Bernarr Macfadden, "The Movies Can Break Us," *Photoplay*, April 1937, 4.

24. Strait and Henie, *Queen of Ice*, 199–200, 207, 116.

25. Henie's filmography includes *Happy Landing* (1938), *My Lucky Star* (1938), *Second Fiddle* (1939), *Everything Happens at Night* (1939), *Sun Valley Serenade* (1941), *Iceland* (1941), *Wintertime* (1943), *It's a Pleasure* (1945), and *The Count of Monte Cristo* (1948).

26. Strait and Henie, *Queen of Ice*, 170, 172.

27. Strait and Henie, *Queen of Ice*, 291, 161, 245, 278–79, 294.

28. Aja Zanova Steindler, quoted in Laura Jacobs, "Sonja Henie's Ice Age," *Vanity Fair*, February 11, 2014, http://www.vanityfair.com/hollywood/2014/02/sonja-henie-ice-skating-queen; Strait and Henie, *Queen of Ice*, 197.

29. Penelope Smith, "Hollywood's Water Baby," *Picturegoer* (September 28, 1948), Scrapbook No. 8, Esther Williams Collection, Margaret Herrick Library.

30. Esther Williams, *The Million Dollar Mermaid*, 57, 74; "Mickey's Back in Circulation!" *Screenland*, December 1942, 41.

31. "Gold Medallion, 2007: Esther Williams, Swimmer," International Swimming Hall of Fame, http://ishof.org/esther-williams.html.

32. Williams, *The Million Dollar Mermaid*, 87, 161, 163, 182.

33. Eddie Mannix Ledger, Margaret Herrick Library.

34. Penelope Smith, however, commenting on Williams's film *This Time for Keeps*, observed that she "certainly does plenty of swimming . . . but some of her best scenes are those which simply give you Miss Williams fully clothed, acting." Smith, "Hollywood's Water Baby."

35. Williams, *The Million Dollar Mermaid*, 29.

36. Lloyd Shearer, "Wet She's a Star, Dry She Ain't," Scrapbook No. 6, Esther Williams Collection, Margaret Herrick Library.

37. Williams, *The Million Dollar Mermaid*, 209, 211, 213.

38. Emily Gibson, *The Original Million Dollar Mermaid: The Annette Kellerman Story*, 206.

39. Williams, *The Million Dollar Mermaid*, 214.

40. Advertisement for *Million Dollar Mermaid*, *Modern Screen*, December 1952, 3.

41. Gibson, *The Original Million Dollar Mermaid*, 208, 175, 177. For an interview with one of Williams's doubles, see Regina Ford, "Stand-In for a Star: Esther Williams' Double Still a Water Babe," *Green Valley (AZ) News*, June 8, 2013, http://www.gvnews.com/news/local/stand-in-for-a-star-esther-williams-double-still-a/article_1a1626aa-d081-11e2-a80c-0019bb2963f4.html.

42. Williams, *The Million Dollar Mermaid*, 213; Gibson, *The Original Million Dollar Mermaid*, 209.

43. Gibson, *The Original Million Dollar Mermaid*, 121–23.

44. Williams, *The Million Dollar Mermaid*, 219–21. That Williams attempted a high dive seems at odds with Gibson's observation that she was inept at diving. It also explains why Williams appears in so many previews and promotions wearing a gold crown and gold fishnet bodysuit but appears in the actual movie wearing a malleable scarlet headdress and bodysuit, hoisted with a hand-held ring, and plunging feet first into the water.

45. Williams, *The Million Dollar Mermaid*, 222; Mannix Ledger.

46. Williams, *The Million Dollar Mermaid*, 297.

47. Williams adds, "With my eyes closed, I felt my tension and resistance ease away as the hallucinogen swept through me. Then, without warning, I went right to the place where the pain lay in my psyche." Williams, *The Million Dollar Mermaid*, 10, 14.

48. Williams, *The Million Dollar Mermaid*, 161, 275, 299.

49. Sabine Hake, "Faces of Weimar Germany," in *The Image in Dispute: Art and Cinema in the Age of Photography*, ed. Dudley Andrew, 141. Ben Singer notes that what he calls "lurid victimization" is prevalent in three Pearl White films—*The Perils of Pauline* (1914), *The Exploits of Elaine* (1914), and *The Fatal Ring* (1917)—where the notion of female agency is coupled with "an equally vivid exposition of female defenselessness and weakness." Ben Singer, "Machine-Made Melodrama: Social Contexts of Popular Sensationalism and American Cinema before 1920" (PhD diss., New York University, 1996), 184, quoted in Jennifer M. Bean, "Technologies of Early Stardom and the Extraordinary Body," *Camera Obscura* 48, no. 16 (2001): 20.

50. Williams, *The Million Dollar Mermaid*, 193.

51. White, "Thrills in Serial Making," 423.

52. Williams, *The Million Dollar Mermaid*, 193.

53. Williams, *The Million Dollar Mermaid*, 211, 213.

54. Gibson, *The Original Million Dollar Mermaid*, 76.

XI. MANLY MEN OF MUSCLE

In dance, because of its enormous physical expenditure, which is a springboard to true psychological release, the human personality is revealed in all its nakedness.

—Burt Lancaster, "The Dance: What It Means to Me"

BURT LANCASTER WAS not a dancer, but he was a versatile athlete who used his exceptional physical skills to enhance the impact of his acting on-screen. Although he and other male stars of the 1950s were known chiefly for their rugged good looks and manly demeanor, audiences were also drawn to the appearance of their bodies. It was a slow process befitting the conservative culture of a nation recovering from the twin throes of economic depression and war. Hollywood, following the demise of silent movies in the late 1920s, had shunned male nudity. Then, perhaps in affirmation of a new sense of masculinity associated with America's superpower status, male film stars began appearing without shirts in scenes. The first such film was the 1949 biblical epic *Samson and Delilah*, starring Hedy Lamarr and Victor Mature. While Mature amply displays his manliness by performing heroic deeds, his body hardly seems Samson-like or consistent with expectations of unbridled strength. But change was on the horizon, facilitated by developments in physical culture. For many decades competitive bodybuilding did not exist and was regarded as a by-product of Olympic weightlifting. Then in 1939 there were six physique contests, including two titled Mr. America.[1] As bodybuilding emerged as a sport fostered by rival organizations in the 1950s, greater attention was paid by moviemakers to the musculature of actors, but their foremost attribute remained an ability to mesmerize viewers with their dialogue and athletic skills.

Mr. Muscles and Teeth

No other leading man of this era personifies this formula of success more than Burt Lancaster. His foremost role model was Douglas Fairbanks, whose athletic acting he witnessed in *The Mark of Zorro* (1920) at a local theater at age seven. He returned daily and stayed through every show, skipping lunch and dinner, until it closed. Lancaster memorized every move and "absorbed the image of a graceful hero doing battle against the bad guys, armed with little besides a big toothy grin and an agile body." The seductive element, notes his biographer Kate Buford, "was what the Russian filmmaker Lev Kuleshov most admired in Fairbanks, a physical expressiveness that emphasized the rhetoric of movement over feeling, a kind of updated [François] Delsarte. The watching eye in the audience followed the body on the screen because the way it moved told a story. When the short, pudgy Burton got home and began imitating his new idol, jumping off, on, and over every piece of furniture in the apartment, he was only practicing to be a movie star, to tell stories with his body." It was not until age thirteen, with a growth spurt and realizing his physical potential, that this Manhattan-born descendant of Irish immigrants could emulate Fairbanks. "His body was coordinated and muscular," notes Buford. It "moved well" and responded to training, enabling him, like his brother, to excel in basketball. Lancaster "discovered he was an athlete." That he was attracted to the entertainment medium owes much to his interest in gymnastics and acquaintance with Nick Cravat, a young Italian American with whom he shared a fascination with circus acrobats. They formulated a routine as "Lang & Cravat" and in 1932 joined a circus for several years on the road. Then with the Depression-born Federal Theater Project they perfected their act. Buford describes it as "a syncopated routine in which each would work from the opposite end of the bars executing full twisters and giant swing finish with in-air somersaults back to the ground." Lancaster perfected his acting and acrobatic skills by entertaining troops overseas as a member of the Army Service Forces from 1942 to 1945. He also acquired the manly look of a soldier, with a forty-one-inch chest.[2]

His rugged physique and natural good looks soon led to a Hollywood, where he starred as an ex-boxer alongside Ava Gardner in the 1946 Universal Studios production of *The Killers*. In 1948 was Lancaster able to utilize his athletic prowess to enhance the plot of *Kiss the Blood Off My Hands*. In the thrilling chase described by cinema historian David Fury, he "runs, jumps slides and climbs fences in a successful attempt to elude the police." In *Rope of Sand* (1949) his athleticism was equally evident in a spectacular fistfight staged (without a double) while tumbling down a sand dune in Arizona. Most personally fulfilling, however, was *The Flame and the Arrow* (1950), in which Lancaster played a Robin Hood–like hero who, with Cravat, rescues the people of Lombardy from the tyranny of Count Ulrich and his Hessian soldiers during the time of Frederick Barbarossa. His rollicking and frolicking execution of acrobatic stunts seemed a flashback to his childhood. "Falling backwards out of a tree, carrying two men stacked on his shoulders, tightroping on a pole across a courtyard. And swinging like Tarzan from pole to pole were just a few of the stunts performed by Lancaster and Cravat," notes Fury.[3] And a *New York Times* reviewer exclaimed,

> Not since Mr. Fairbanks was leaping from castle walls and vaulting over the rooftops of ancient story-book towns has the screen had such a reckless and acrobatic young man to display these same inclinations as it has in Mr. L. Not even Mr. [Errol] Flynn, the dauntless, in the happy days of his youth, when he (or his energetic double) was swinging elastically from ropes or the trees of Sherwood Forest, could match gymnastics with him. . . . With a brilliance matched only by the dazzle of his gleaming white teeth when he smiles, he hoists himself up to the tops of houses, leaps onto castle balconies, glides down the folds of great cloth hangings and swings from chandeliers. He rides like the wind on horses, shoots like a fool with bow and arrow and battles hordes of spearmen with blazing torches in his hands. Who says that derring-do is dead?[4]

On completion of the film, Lancaster embarked on a promotional tour during which he performed the same stunts. Further to lend authenticity, Warner Brothers offered $1 million to anyone who could prove that the Lancaster and Cravat stunts were not done by "strength alone." With a budget of $1.5 million, *The Flame and the Arrow* was a box office success, earning $2.9 million.[5]

It also firmly fixed Lancaster's star status and reputation as Hollywood's most athletic actor. What appeared easy and fun on the screen, however, required lots of training. Lancaster described how he and Cravat started working out three months prior to shooting to avoid using doubles: "We'd never done any fencing or archery worth mentioning, so we had to study it together. We put up our high bar and rope swings in my garden so we could work out there every day. Then we got in a lot of hand balancing, tumbling, handball and swimming."[6] Buford explains that the duo also trained under noted vaudeville acrobat Shotsy O'Brien: "He brushed up their perch pole routine (with a 225-foot climb at the top of which Lancaster could still hold

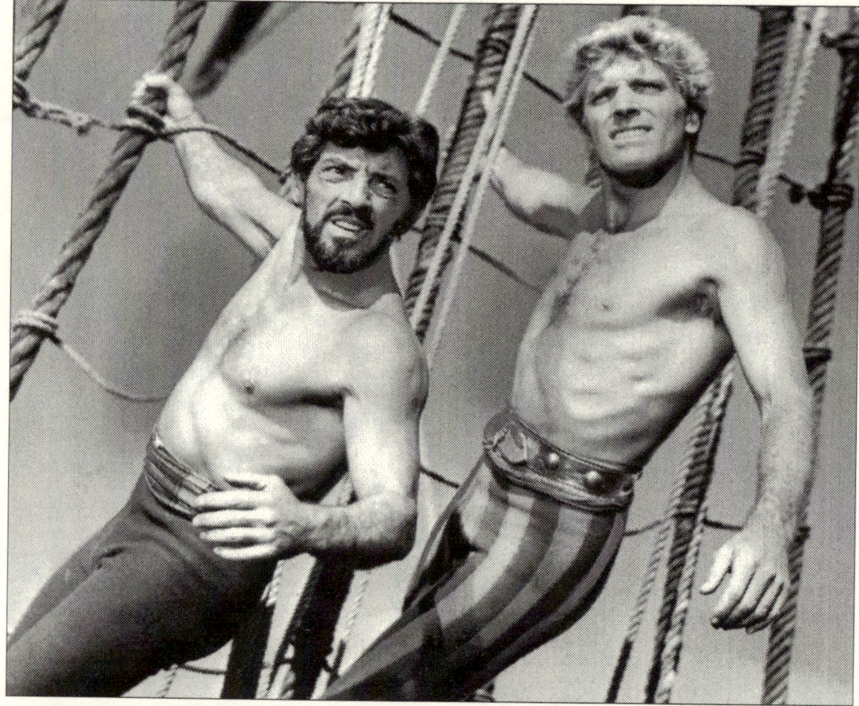

Figure 11.1. Nick Cravat and Burt Lancaster display their physiques and acrobatic skills in the 1952 swashbuckler *The Crimson Pirate*. Collection of David L. Chapman.

himself out like a flag), parallel bar flips, hand-over-hand rope climbs up a thirty-foot rope done with no camera cuts, somersaults and pirouettes from horizontal bars twenty feet above the ground, and so on. Up at 5 a.m. they ran three miles, did tumbling workouts, archery, sword and dagger practice, memorized lines, and—significant for the star's future work—lots of horseback riding lessons." The payoff for such exertions was perfect acrobatic performances on-screen. What Buford discerns in *The Flame and the Arrow* is a "kind of trust and admiration of the risk taken" between performer and viewer. "So instinctive that nobody thought much about it, in the truthful grace of Lancaster's movements there was something god-like, an ancient presumption of the good." It projected in viewers an illusion that authenticity on-screen persisted off-screen as well: "If he could move through space with joy and beauty he was what the earth-bound people sitting in the dark watching him wished they could be."[7] Absorption of Lancaster's physical artistry intruded on the stark reality of viewers' mundane existence.

Typecast as an athlete, Lancaster seemed ideal to depict Jim Thorpe, the sports hero who was not only an Olympic gold medalist but recognized by four hundred sports writers in 1950 as the greatest football player of the early twentieth century.[8] To project the illusion that Lancaster could sprint a hundred yards in ten seconds as well as kick, block, pole-vault, throw the javelin and high-jump, Warner Brothers enlisted the University of California–Los Angeles (UCLA) football coach, the University of Southern California (USC) track coach, a welterweight boxing champion, and Thorpe himself as consultants. Although Lancaster had to learn to play football, he was roughly the same size as his subject and seemed to rival the somewhat bigger UCLA and USC players drafted for gridiron scenes. "With the exception of a couple pole-vault and long-jump shots," notes Buford, "the star did his own jock work. All he had to do, he said, was 'look pretty good doing it'—the distances could be manipulated—as if that were simple." Thorpe's reaction to "watching Burt doing the things I did" was "I don't think I was ever that handsome." Other incongruities show up more in the script than in Lancaster's athletic mimesis. In what Fury dubs a somewhat "romanticized and capsulized version" of Thorpe's life, only the first of his three marriages and first of multiple children are featured. He was allegedly "a natural at virtually every sport he tried, including boxing, wrestling, swimming, golf, bowling, and marksmanship." A 2008 reviewer deems much of Thorpe's real life was distorted by the movie: "Burt Lancaster is OK in the role, physically he seems perfect for the part, but the script doesn't help him understand this man by making up most of his personal life." Despite the phony story, Buford finds merit in the athletic aspects of *Jim Thorpe—All American* (1951): "The athlete in Lancaster and the audience watching him saw the story as their own, the metaphor of striving to the perfect action that hooks fans to sports and movies alike."[9] Lancaster's portrayal enabled audiences to become absorbed in the heroism and pathos of Thorpe's life.

After solidifying his reputation as the screen's most athletic swashbuckler in several more adventure films, Lancaster reached a performance peak that again played out youthful aspirations. "I may do the circus picture I'm evolving from my own memories," he revealed as early as 1950. "I want to do for the circus what 'Red Shoes' did for the ballet."[10] *Trapeze* (1956) was loosely based on Max Catto's 1950 novel *The Killing Frost*, though it replaced the homosexual undercurrent (unacceptable in the mid-1950s) with a love triangle between Lancaster, Tony Curtis, and Gina Lollobrigida in a thrilling aerial act hinged on completing the elusive triple somersault. Although a

Ringling Brothers Circus artist had to be hired for the most difficult feats, Lancaster did most of his stunts. The stars spent many hours training in the gym and practicing on the trapeze, often at forty-five feet above ground, with no safety net. "Lancaster was still at the pinnacle of his superior athletic prowess," Fury notes, "and his physique, at age 43, was as near perfect as ever." In his autobiography, Tony Curtis recalls that "some of the aerial stunts were so dangerous, even the *doubles* had doubles. . . . I did a good chunk of the early bar work in the film, and that was really Burt and me walking on our hands." Although the film was panned by the *New York Times*, it performed well at the box office, earning $3.5 million and rewarding United Artists with its largest gross ever.[11]

Although Lancaster rarely displayed the same energy and athleticism in subsequent films, he followed a rigorous health regimen into his fifties that included morning jogs on the UCLA track or along the Pacific Coast Highway, breakfasts of skim milk, juice, coffee, and soft-boiled eggs, and protein milkshakes later in the day. He was still doing giant swings on the bar into his sixties. But he was also a heavy smoker of unfiltered Camels and had martinis every night.[12]

That he retained his usual vigor was evident in *The Train* (1965), in which he performed without any doubles "the most physically dynamic portrayal of his career," observes Fury. Disregarding personal safety, he slid down the rails of a twenty-foot ladder, jumped onto a moving train, got kicked off the train, scaled a brick wall, jumped off another fast train, ran full-speed across a wooden railroad bridge, stumbled when shot, slid a dozen feet, got up and limped off, and, finally, "when coming to the far side of a large grassy hill, Burt rolled, slid and tumbled as he descended the giant mound." For added realism, he learned to drive his train without an engineer's assistance.[13] Director John Frankenheimer called Lancaster "the strongest man physically I've ever known. He was one of the best stuntmen who ever lived. I don't think anybody's ever moved as well on the screen." But Lancaster's perfect physique and adaptability, as revealed in *The Swimmer* (1968), were waning. Although his performance was sufficient, he had no experience or aptitude for swimming according to his tutor, UCLA swim coach Bob Horne. "He was a strong enough swimmer, but terribly uncomfortable in the water. He didn't put his head in, or breathe properly, and the first time he flutter-kicked he went backwards. But he's very disciplined and he made good progress." Nor did Lancaster display an appetite for daring feats in the sky. Although he could prepare and pack a parachute for his role in *The Gypsy Moths* (1969), he did no skydiving. Still, he lived a charmed existence throughout his long career. "I had the luck," he reflected, "to have an obedient body. I told it to 'March like a prince' and it marched like a prince."[14]

The Ragman's Son

Not unlike Lancaster, the rise of Kirk Douglas to superstardom was a rags-to-riches story. Born Issur Danielovitch on December 9, 1916, in Amsterdam, New York, he was the son of Russian immigrant parents who were poor, Jewish, and social outsiders. His father was a purveyor of junk, and young Kirk struggled to attain respectability. One form of escaping reality was the theater, which first captured his imagination while playing charades with classmates in first grade. The fascination continued into high school, fostering dreams of becoming an actor.[15] But it was not until he entered St. Lawrence University in 1934 and joined the wrestling team that he was awakened to the realities of manhood. "I felt a desperate need to express myself physically. In Amsterdam, I had never had a chance to go out for sports, because I was always working." He craved adventure. "I wanted to risk danger. I needed to *do* something." He soon encountered danger when he was lured into an impromptu wrestling match with a six-foot-three football player. At only five foot nine, and weighing 145 pounds, Douglas had to rely on dexterity alone. As the giant lumbered toward him

> I made a feint to his head, dropped to my knees, and spun around, grabbing his leg and pulling him up, knocking him to the mat. I quickly put a scissors around his body and rode him, on his back. He was very powerful, but when he bucked, I hung on to him, my legs wrapped around him. When he rolled, I rolled with him, squeezing his stomach with my legs. Then he was lying flat out. He started to get up with me clinging to his back. I waited until he was on his knees with both arms straight. With all my strength, I thrust my palms against his elbows. He collapsed. His face smashed into the mat, his nose ran blood. He became furious, howling and trying to shake me off. I wouldn't let go. He bucked and flailed; I squeezed and squeezed. Finally the pressure on his stomach made him throw up. That ended the match.

Douglas won the match but also won "respect." He went on to defeat other formidable opponents and win recognition as a leader in other areas during his collegiate years, including as student body president. His earliest dramatic training occurred in the summers, when he wrestled at carnivals with a "huge and intimidating" teammate dubbed the Masked Marvel, and at the Tamarack Playhouse in the Adirondacks, where he mingled with professional actors. Although his college wrestling coach hoped he would try out for the 1936 Olympic team, Douglas set his sights elsewhere. "Wrestling was just something that I needed emotionally, and a way to get that sparkling white sweater with the crimson 'L.' I wanted to be an actor."[16]

Although he attended the American Academy of Dramatic Arts in New York, Douglas confined his initial acting to radio soap operas and stage plays, never thinking he fit the image of the tall and handsome movie actor. But classmate Lauren Bacall recommended him to producer Hal Wallis for a leading role in *The Strange Love of Martha Ivers* (1946), with Barbara Stanwyck and Van Heflin, and this paved his way to Hollywood. Initially he played weak characters. It was not until his fourth film, *I Walk Alone* (1947), in which he costarred with Burt Lancaster, that his role as a tough guy emerged. Although these hypermasculine personalities frequently clashed, Douglas credits Lancaster as an impresario of filmmaking. By 1955 "Burt was no longer just a movie star—he was making *other* people into stars." In film and popular image, the two manly men would be paired together. As Lancaster biographer Kate Buford recognizes, Douglas was "shorter than Lancaster by several inches and without the physical mass or grace of the athletic, slightly older star." But Douglas compensated for any shortcoming in size or athletic ability by cultivating a fiercely physical screen presence. Both men had thereby "sunk their teeth" into the industry, with Douglas as "the feisty terrier" and Lancaster as "the great big lion," images that would have immense box office appeal.[17]

Douglas's opportunity to reveal his physicality emerged in 1949 with a boxer's role in *Champion*, based on a 1916 novel by sportswriter Ring Lardner. Douglas regarded the character Midge Kelly as "one of the first antiheroes" and "here was a chance to play a really physical role." He first had to overcome the reservations of producer Stanley Kramer and screenwriter Carl Foreman about whether he could play a boxer. "I finally realized what they wanted," he reckoned. "I took off my jacket and shirt, bared my chest and flexed my muscles. They nodded approvingly, satisfied that I could play a boxer. I was probably the only *man* in Hollywood who's had to strip to get a part." Conditioning, however, was critical to playing it, an experience Douglas already gained during his college wrestling days, and he chose not to use a double. To learn how to punch and develop a style, he hired former welterweight champion Mushy Callahan. Most of his ring opponents were also ex-pugs, not actors. But to make movie punching look real required two people—"one to miss the punch when it's thrown, the other to react as if he's been hit. It's very difficult for a real boxer to pretend he's hitting someone; he's trained to hit, not to miss." Once, however, he was knocked out by an opponent who miscalculated. Although it looked great in the movie, Douglas advised against getting "knocked out to make a scene look realistic."[18]

Response to his performance in *Champion* was almost uniformly glowing. "Dynamite with Dimples!" was the heading for a *Screenland* article on Douglas's film personality. Another review called him the "Meanest Mug in the Movies" for his realistic portrayal of a ruthless and amoral fighter, noting, "It's Kirk's most difficult role to date, with rugged workouts in the gym and bruising fight scenes as part of his daily routine. Playing the role of a heel who pulls every dirty trick in the book may be artistically satisfying, but physically it's a little like being trapped inside an active cement mixer."[19] For Bosley Crowther of the *New York Times* the movie's scenes in training gyms, managers' offices, and boxing rings were "strongly atmospheric and physically intense." As the hero, Douglas, though occasionally overeager, "does a good, aggressive job." *Variety* concurred that the fight scenes "match for realism and impact any seen recently" and Douglas's depiction of a boxer "makes the character live." *Champion* won the Academy Award for Film Editing, and Douglas was nominated for the Best Actor award. On a $595,000 investment, box office returns were $2.1 million. That one role, observes biographer John Parker, enabled Douglas's ascent from "journeyman stardom into the superleague."[20]

A different kind of physical challenge confronted Douglas in 1953 when he took on the role of a trapeze artist in "Equilibrium," starring with Italian actress Pier Angeli in the third part of the romantic trilogy *The Story of Three Loves*. Unlike Lancaster, Douglas had no circus or trapeze experience, just raw physical courage and desire. He later admitted it was frightening at first, even with a net:

The real danger was how you fell into the net. It would save you, but if you fell wrong, you could easily break a leg or an arm or your neck. When I missed and was able to adjust to falling flat into the net, I lost all fear of falling. From then on, I enjoyed it very much. And I was good at it. Within a month I was swinging on a trapeze, making a crossover to the catcher, being swung back, turning around in the midair, catching the bar that was hurled to me by one of the girls, and then swinging back up to the platform. I could do a bird's nest—swing by my calves, body arched up—and cross to the catcher.[21]

Over a half century later, one perceptive viewer thought Douglas was in peak physical form. He looked "Hollywood hunky and totally like a leading man, one who was almost too handsome for his own good." The trapeze sequences looked "realistic," and the viewer suspected that "Douglas did most of his stunts himself. He was quite the athlete, and he looked convincing in the part."[22] Indeed, the image of Douglas standing on the platform before a takeoff is as convincing a depiction of an athletic physique as one could expect in Hollywood.

In *The Vikings* (1958), the physical prowess of Douglas is again evident in a complicated plot where he plays a Norwegian prince who struggles with an English king and a slave for the love of a captive princess. Shot mostly in Norway by his own production company, Bryna, it enabled Douglas to display his masculine persona, which is evident in the action scenes with lots of drinking, carousing, and violence. But two scenes require unusual strength and dexterity. The first occurs when Douglas's character performs a traditional Viking feat known as running the oars, for which director Richard Fleischer was going to hire a double. In the scene the sailors get drunk, lock the oars, climb off the boat, and run from oar to oar. "They all told me I couldn't do it," Douglas recounted. "That was all I needed to hear. 'I'm going to do it.'" What he needed to do was "get a rhythm going, keep the momentum from oar to oar. If you slowed down, you had time to lose your balance—and fall into the freezing waters of the fjord. I did the stunt myself, and only slipped once—deliberately. After all, my character was supposed to be drunk."[23] Less convincing is the scene where Douglas climbs to the entrance of the king's castle on hatchets tossed by his Viking hoard into the drawbridge. Tellingly, it is shot from a distance. Crowther called it a "gaudy action film" in which there was "scarcely a minute in its almost two hours that something muscular isn't happening on the screen." *The Vikings* was a box office success, earning an estimated $7.6 million. But it had a greater impact by spawning a half dozen derivative Viking sagas in the early 1960s and serving as a Scandinavian accompaniment to the popular Italian peplum films of that era.[24] American bodybuilder Gordon Mitchell (Charles Pendleton) provided muscular performances in both genres.

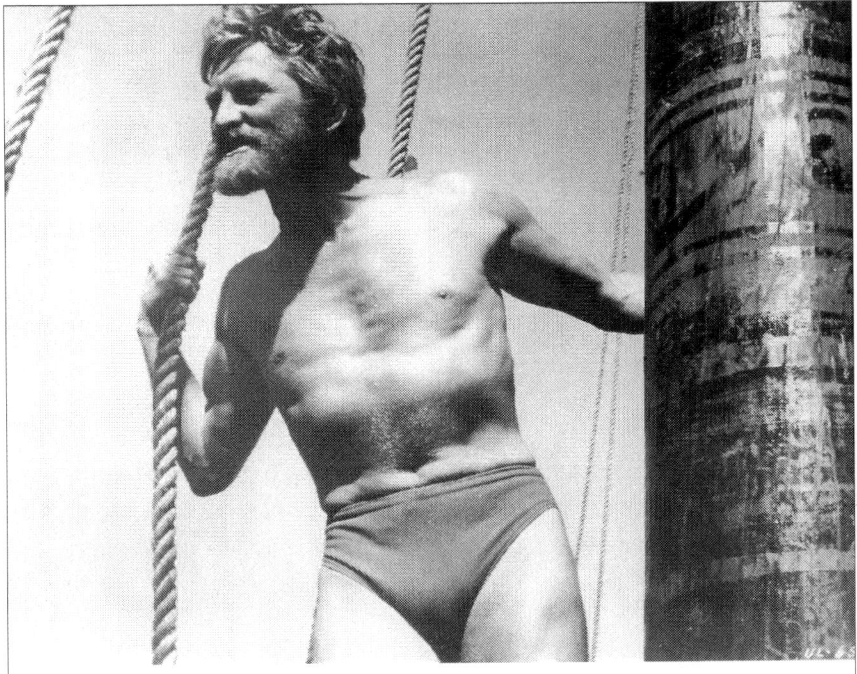

Figure 11.2. Kirk Douglas covers up his dimpled chin with a beard (although he leaves almost everything else exposed) in the 1954 production of *Ulysses*. Collection of David L. Chapman.

Mitchell also performed as a gladiator (as did bodybuilders Joe Gold and Zabo Koszewski) in Douglas's most celebrated film, *Spartacus* (1960), based on a Howard Fast novel, the story of a Thracian slave who led a revolt against the Romans in the first century BCE. Douglas headed a star-studded cast, including Tony Curtis, Charles Laughton, Laurence Olivier, Jean Simmons, and Peter Ustinov. As Spartacus, Douglas encountered many risks that tested his mettle, but "whenever possible, I did my own stunts." One of them required climbing and leaping off a high fence, hand-to-hand fighting, and realistic swordplay. At one point Lancaster accidentally broke an actor's jaw when he was supposed to drown the man by holding his head under liquid in a cauldron of soup. Ironically, the shot was not used in the final cut. So great were the physical demands during the *Spartacus* filming that it was "amazing" to Douglas that no one died.[25] Though not known for his muscularity, Tony Curtis encountered the same challenges, and he trained accordingly to stay fit and convey the appearance of a slave warrior. Once Olivier asked Curtis, "Where do you get arms like that?" Curtis escorted him behind the dressing rooms and said, " 'Let's do push-ups.' So we did push-ups, and from then on we did them every day before we went to work. . . . He got into it, and one day he said, 'I owe you one.' " Crowther panned *Spartacus* in the *New York Times* as "heroic humbug" that was "full of historical inaccuracies" and "pitched about to the level of a lusty schoolboy's taste." But it enjoyed spectacular success, earning a lifetime gross of $60 million, exceeding its budget fivefold.[26]

Reflecting on his long film career, Douglas realized the illusory nature of the business, much in keeping with Ben Singer's concept of absorptive realism. "When you become a movie star, you create an image for the public," Douglas explained. "They begin to believe it, and you start buying into that fiction yourself. In some ways, I had come to believe that I was one of the tough guys I played."[27] Biographer Michael Munn describes how Douglas encountered that reality late one night when he entered a Los Angeles bar after the release of *Champion*:

From a group of drinkers stepped a rather large and very drunk man who eyed Douglas, recognizing the actor who'd been so tough as a boxer on the screen. He ambled over to Kirk and without a word drove his fist into that famous dimpled chin. The whole place suddenly fell silent.

All eyes were on Kirk, the Champ, waiting for him to retaliate. It promised to be a fight greater than any featured in *Champion*. But Kirk was to disappoint the eager crowd. He stood against the bar and shouted, "Anyone in this bar can lick me." The drunk staggered back with a puzzled look on his face. He seemed to be trying to figure this one out. This movie star who was so tough on the screen just had no inclination to prove himself and even admitted that he wasn't up to a fight.[28]

Moviemaking, Douglas came to realize, was "an unnatural life, just being wrapped up in make-believe characters." Indeed, absorption by movie stars in the fiction of their screen images could have more serious consequences than the few hours of fantasy enjoyed by moviegoers. A key factor to his survival in this fragile environment, Douglas believed, was "to learn how to cope with my success and not let it destroy me, as it has destroyed so many people." Indeed, he survived to the age of 103, despite smoking two packs of cigarettes daily for forty years.[29]

Muscles That Dance

It would be easy to dismiss Gene Kelly as a fitting subject for a study of muscles in film. Admittedly, he rarely displayed his unclothed body, but he exemplifies, perhaps more than any actor, the essence of Lancaster's observation about the enormous physical expenditure of dance. Kelly's life was all about movement, a trait he inherited during his Pittsburgh childhood from his father James, who, according to biographer Clive Hirschhorn, was "a fine athlete who worked out with dumb-bells and Indian clubs" and was "a first-rate ice-skater and hockey player." By the time he was six, Kelly recalled, he could "skate like a wizard," and by age eight "there wasn't a kid in the neighbourhood who could outskate me."[30] At fifteen he was working out with the semiprofessional Pittsburgh Yellow Jackets ice hockey team. Although he was not interested in going professional, Kelly believed "much of my style as a dancer springs from that early training in ice hockey." Meanwhile, his mother subjected him to dancing lessons, an activity he initially disliked because it was considered unmanly by his peers. As a "sports nut," Kelly was more interested in hockey, as well as football, baseball, and gymnastics, and in all he displayed exceptional ability.[31] Like Burt Lancaster, his source of inspiration to become an athletic actor came from viewing Douglas Fairbanks in *The Mark of Zorro*: "I don't think it's exaggerating to say that had the movie I saw that day been a gangster picture or, let's say anything other than a Doug Fairbanks picture, my life might have taken a different course. For Doug Fairbanks was my ideal from that day on and his dashing athletic prowess was what really inspired me to become a dancer."[32] That experience enabled Kelly to overcome any inhibitions about dancing being unmasculine. It became his "lifelong belief," according to Hirschhorn, "that dancing and athletics are inextricably linked, and that muscular contractions for, say, a dance movement in the second position have their athletic equivalent on the gym floor or in other areas of sport."[33] These sentiments were later echoed in a 1958 NBC *Omnibus* documentary episode, "Dancing: A Man's Game," in which he choreographed the moves of a group of star athletes, including Bob Cousy, Mickey Mantle, and Sugar Ray Robinson, to dispel the effeminate stereotype of dance. "What drives a man to take up dancing?" Kelly reflected in that program. "The same things that drive painters, sculptors—he wants to express himself and he has a basic love of movement."[34]

Although Kelly earned a degree in economics from Pennsylvania State University, managed two Pittsburgh dance schools, and even attended law school during the 1930s, it was the summer offerings by the Chicago

Association of Dance Masters of ballet in the Russian mode that had the greatest impact on his film career. Much in the manner of Sonja Henie, who blended ballet with figure skating, Kelly would combine it with his style of dance. According to biographers Cynthia and Sara Brideson, he had already "integrated elements of modern dance into tap" in which he incorporated his "masculine strength and jazz-inspired movement." Now he sought to blend ballet with tap. After searching for opportunities in New York to showcase his distinctive style for several years, Kelly was propelled into stardom in the Broadway production of the Richard Rodgers and Lorenz Hart musical *Pal Joey*. "The importance of *Pal Joey* in Gene's career cannot be overstated," the Bridesons observe. "In this production, he created a blueprint for all of his succeeding works. . . . Gene strove to give his dances meaning and allow them to communicate more than dialogue."[35]

Kelly encountered a new challenge, however, when migrating to Hollywood in 1941. Film was an unfamiliar medium, and there had been only one song and dance man since George M. Cohan a generation earlier. Often partnered in musicals with Ginger Rogers, Fred Astaire became renowned in the 1930s for his sense of rhythm, perfectionism, and elegance, but his public appeal was different from Kelly's. "Fred represents the aristocracy when he dances," remarked Kelly. "I represent the proletariat."[36] Yet mutual admiration, not hostility or rivalry, governed their lifelong friendship. The Bridesons recognize that the two dancers had similarities, "but Astaire lacked the athletic prowess Gene saw as vital to American expression." Kelly regarded himself as too big physically for Astaire's kind of dancing. His own style "wasn't elegant, but it was me."[37] That Kelly's eye-popping brand of dance had a future in film became evident in several performances during World War II with Judy Garland and other leading ladies. His style coincided with the mood of the country. "It was a different world," explains actress Nina Foch. "We were macho, this country. Along comes this muscular young man who takes dance and puts it somewhere that all Americans could appreciate it."[38] Culminating this wartime sentiment was the 1945 musical *Anchors Aweigh*, in which Kelly, costarring with Kathryn Grayson and Frank Sinatra, fully exposes his extraordinary athleticism. Hirschhorn describes a fantasy wooing scene with Grayson in a romantic Spanish courtyard where Kelly, "dressed in a dazzling gold shirt, red and black cape and black trousers, gives full expression to his athletic prowess in a fandango-style routine that has him scaling battlements, leaping over parapets and making a forty-five foot vine-swinging jump from a rooftop to the balcony of his señorita in the noblest

Fairbanks tradition."[39] Bosley Crowther called it a "humdinger of a musical" and Kelly an "Apollonian marvel." Box office receipts exceeded expenditures by $4,895,000, and Kelly was nominated for an Academy Award as Best Actor.[40]

Anchors Aweigh provided a template for Kelly's two more athletic films, both in the Fairbanks tradition. *The Pirate* (1948), based on a Broadway play by S. N. Behrman, was a romantic musical costarring Garland as Manuela, a Spanish señorita engaged to the local mayor, who dreams of escaping with the legendary pirate Mack the Black. Kelly, playing the troubadour Serafin, seeks to win her heart by impersonating the pirate. In the process, note the Bridesons, he would "take on the persona of his boyhood hero, Douglas Fairbanks with all his swashbuckling bravado."[41] To facilitate Kelly's capacity for athletic dancing, according to film biographers Earl Hess and Pratibha Dabholkar, art director Jack Martin Smith designed a set in the plaza of the port of San Sebastián, Spain, "studded with props, hand holds, and foot holds, many of them inconspicuously placed so as to blend in with the everyday life of the town." Smith marveled at how Kelly could run up and down the set "like a cat."[42] In a piece Kelly wrote for journalist Dorothy Kilgallen, he described how, on the fifty-yard set, "I do a number in which I dance (and sing) down one side of the street, climb a couple of balconies en route, then up to the top of a building, a leap to another building, then down a water spout and a dance down the other side of the street."[43] Kelly's most daring feat was a tightrope walk to Manuela's room. Safety precautions, including wires on his back, a mattress below, and a backup double (Muscle Beach acrobat Russ Saunders), were unnecessary, but director Vincent Minnelli devised a camera trick to make Kelly appear unsteady to induce greater suspense. The most strenuous scene, "Be a Clown," featured a hit song by Cole Porter and an acrobatic sequence of Kelly with two talented black dancers, a Hollywood first. The Bridesons note that, with a hangman's noose awaiting Serafin at the center of the dance floor, "The three dancers pirouette about it with carefree steps as if the prospect of death is something comedic. 'No noose is good noose!' Serafin quips only moments before launching into his performance. The number employed more athleticism and gymnastics than any Gene had yet achieved, utilizing 'splits, handsprings, and turnovers' and Gene's trademark move in which he 'bounces sideways on his hand and toes—body extended in push up position.'"[44] The "Pirate Ballet," the most elaborate scene in the film, was demanding and daring, replete with explosives, swordplay, and swinging ropes. Kelly's slide down a rope, note Hess and Dobholkar, epitomized his "bravura moviemaking" style, "reminiscent of Fairbanks sliding down the sails of a ship by slicing them with a knife in *The Black Pirate*" (1926). No less striking was the costume Minnelli designed for Kelly, modeled after Fairbanks, that consisted of a pair of short trousers: "To show off Kelly's extremely muscular legs, he made them much shorter and tighter than the ones Fairbanks had worn. It was the only time in Kelly's film career that he wore short trousers."[45] Although he never exposed his torso, it was obvious to viewers of *The Pirate* how Kelly could release so much kinetic energy.

Critical reviews were uniformly favorable. "Gene Kelly is doing some of the fanciest gymnastic dancing of his career," concluded the *New York Herald Tribune*, "and he's good, very good, indeed." Overall public appeal, however, fell far short of expectations, with production costs of $3,768,496 exceeding the film's revenue of $2,956,000.[46] The film did evoke a special interest among gay male viewers who, according to Richard Dyer, sensed a strong element of camp that focused on "a play of sex roles and spectacular illusion." Film theorist David Gerstner was captivated by Kelly's revealing costume and the low-angle camera shots that enhanced his body image. Together they "emphasized Kelly's well-defined thighs, pumped biceps, and well-announced manly bulge." For Dyer, *The Pirate* "fully allows Kelly as a sex object, to a more sustained degree than any male star between Rudolph Valentino and John Travolta; and at the same time plays around with him as spectacle, so that he is both turn-on and send-up." Providing insight into why *The Pirate* did not play as well among general audiences, legendary producer Arthur Freed believed it was "twenty years ahead of its time."[47]

As a sort of sequel to his muscle mimicry of Fairbanks in *The Pirate*, Kelly took on the leading role of D'Artagnan in another film adaptation of Alexandre Dumas's 1844 novel *The Three Musketeers* (1948). The plot features the romantic, swashbuckling adventures of a young provincial nobleman who comes to Paris to become a musketeer. He joins three comrades to thwart the plans of the chief minister, Cardinal Richelieu, to usurp the king's power. Kelly was already at the peak of fitness but had to learn the art of fencing. To this end, Metro-Goldwyn-Mayer hired Jean Heremans, a Belgian champion and instructor at the Los Angeles Athletic Club, to practice fencing routines with Kelly. "The resulting action scenes were strikingly set up and executed, and are among the best of their kind," observes film historian Rudy Behlmer. "The early encounter of D'Artagnan, Athos, Porthos and Aramis with the Cardinal's Guards—filmed at (the old)

Busch Gardens in Pasadena—was particularly effective. As this sequence progresses and the Cardinal's Guards are being disposed of, D'Artagnan singles out Jussac, Captain of the Guard (Saul Gorss), and the two engage in an acrobatic—and comedic—choreographed routine, accompanied by burlesqued Tchaikowsky. It runs five minutes, and was, up to that time, the longest duel on record. It's a delight."[48] Some critics found Kelly's "bouncing, tumbling, vaulting, flipping and leaping performance tending toward burlesque," notes film historian Tony Thomas, "but it is entirely conceivable that the man Dumas described as the finest swordsman in France would be this kind of zesty athlete." Indeed, "no other actor had ever come this close to matching the performances of Fairbanks, Sr. at his swashbuckling best."[49] Kelly was so overzealous and strong that he inadvertently injured Lana Turner, his leading lady, by throwing her down in a staged quarrel. This incident caused a kink in the shooting, but *The Three Musketeers* earned $4,507,000, for a profit of $1,828,000.[50]

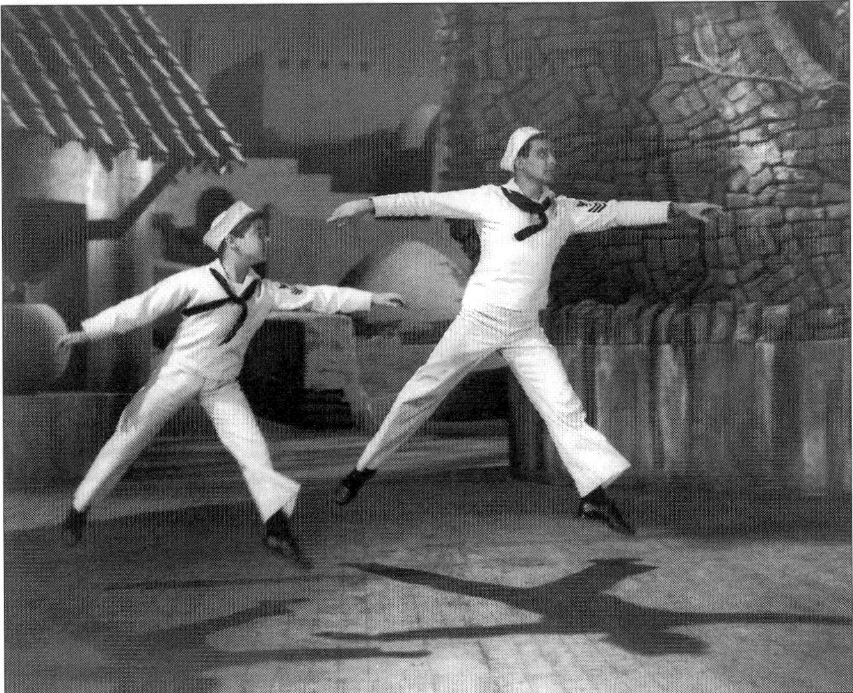

Figure 11.3. Gene Kelly with child actor-dancer David Kasday in a scene from *Invitation to the* Dance (1956). Collection of David L. Chapman.

Although none of his subsequent films could match the manly exuberance of *The Pirate* and *The Three Musketeers*, Kelly entered the climactic phase of his storied career with such blockbuster hits as *On the Town* (1949), *An American in Paris* (1951), and *Singin' in the Rain* (1952), in which he continued to wow audiences with his athletic dancing. André Previn deemed *Singin' in the Rain* to be "the best musical ever made. Full stop." Leonard Bernstein called it "a reaffirmation of life."[51] But Kelly's iconic stature diminished somewhat in successive lackluster pictures until a skiing accident in Switzerland in 1958, at age forty-six, ended his serious dancing. "The older you get as a dancer the harder it is to grind up your physical forces," he admitted. "The dancer's life is probably the shortest artistic life in the world and you have to face that fact when you get into it."[52] In fact, he had been coping with reality ever since arriving in Hollywood. Not unlike Kirk Douglas, he refused to buy into the illusion of stardom. Hollywood was merely "a state of mind," his first wife Betsy Blair explained. The studio system was designed to keep stars "childish. If an actor wasn't as tough and intelligent as Kelly, he was likely to believe his own publicity and lose track of himself."[53] His daughter, Kerry Kelly Novick, remembers that when she was growing up, "every adult I knew was in analysis except my father." Unlike many major stars, Kelly was free of self-delusion, but misapprehension persisted for moviegoers who immortalized this fit and vibrant personality in their memories as he was during his glory days. "His last years were sad," recalls Novick. "For someone whose physical prowess had been so central to his identity to be old and ill . . . was very hard."[54] He was the superman of dance.

The Strongman

Anthony Quinn, best known for his starring role in *Zorba the Greek* (1964), shared the masculine image of Lancaster, Douglas, and (less overtly) Kelly during the 1950s. Quinn's breakthrough, after seventy-two screen appearances dating back to 1936, came from playing Zampanò the strongman in *La strada* (The street, 1954), which won an Academy Award for Best Foreign Language Film. It also marked a climactic episode in cinematic history for its innovative director Federico Fellini and a phase of Italian filmmaking dubbed neorealism. Arising after World War II from the ashes of a damaged and beleaguered nation, neorealism traces its origins to the genius of Roberto Rossellini and his depiction of the shattered lives and edifices of Rome under Nazi occupation in *Open City* (1945). What Fellini learned from Rossellini was a "lesson of humility," conveying reality of situations and characters in "an extremely simple way," and trying "to relate what had been actually seen." According to film historians Peter Bondanella and Manuela Gieri, neorealism was "primarily a way of seeing the world and its problems honestly" and "remaining open to the poetic potential of even the most banal daily events." But Fellini's brand of neorealism differed from Fascist- and Marxist-driven approaches. He departed from characterizations reflecting social and economic conditions "to a more fanciful world" of a character's "emotions, dreams and psychology." How a character presented an "authentic 'face'—by his subconscious aspirations, ideals, and instincts" was most clearly presented in *La strada*.[55]

At first glance, Anthony Quinn's role as a strongman might appear to be a reformulation of the classic configuration Bartolomeo Pagano's Maciste. Quinn, however, was a Mexican American with limited strength and athletic background. Living as an unemployed factory worker as a youth in Los Angeles, he became a welterweight boxer, earning twenty to fifty dollars per fight. He once even sparred with world champion Primo Carnera, but lacked the competitive instinct: "Although I liked the glamorous part of boxing, the performance part of it, I didn't like the competitiveness. I liked the drama, those bright lights, the kind of strangely festive atmosphere in the audience, and the comradeship with the guys. I hated the dressing room with its odors of rubbing alcohol, iodine, wet leather, cheap soap and dirty, stained towels. I hated the tawdriness behind the scenes, all those sweating bodies, the frantic efforts to achieve something with your fists." Quinn also tried dancing, but winning first prize in the tango on Santa Monica Pier was less memorable than his initial sexual experience afterward. His transition into acting resulted from fortuitous circumstances. It was inspired partly by his appreciation of the philosophy of Arthur Schopenhauer, which imparted to Quinn the notion that "life was precious; you shouldn't waste time; you should spend every minute of your waking day advancing yourself." At one time he had envisioned himself a future Jack Dempsey or Gene Tunney, but now, at age twenty-one, he gravitated from athletics to acting in little theater groups.[56] His first professional exposure came as an aging alcoholic thespian resembling John Barrymore in *Clean Beds* (1936), staged at the Hollytown Theatre by Mae West, one of the most "amazing women" Quinn had ever met. In addition to Quinn's "physique, voice, animal magnetism and instinctual comprehension of human motivation," journalist Alvin Marill attributes his rise to a natural ability to "guide an audience's thinking along the lines a play requires."[57] This kind of investment in a stage character enabled Quinn to provide viewers with experiences in absorptive realism on-screen.

In one of his earliest films Quinn met and soon married Katherine DeMille, daughter of famed filmmaker Cecil B. DeMille, which securely invested him in the Hollywood scene for two decades. But his star did not truly rise until he exported his talents to five Italian productions in the early 1950s. In *Ulysses* (1954), starring Kirk Douglas, Quinn played an antihero in what was widely deemed an impressive failure. "Kirk Douglas plays the Greek superhero with brawn and vitality," notes Tony Thomas, "but he all too obviously looks like an American actor cast in an Italian picture. Anthony Quinn also appears but it is a small and unimportant part and he is completely wasted."[58] While performing in *Donne proibite* (Forbidden women, 1954, but known in the United States under the title *Angels of Darkness*), however, he met Giulietta Masina, the wife of Federico Fellini, with whom he would play the starring role of Zampanò in *La strada*.[59]

In retrospect, Fellini's choice of Quinn had less to do with any preconceived notions of the appearance or abilities of a strongman than his wife's recommendation of Quinn as someone who could convey the sense of exploitation and despair inherent in the script. It features Zampanò, a brutish and violent itinerant, purchasing Gelsomina (Masina), a simple-minded peasant girl, from her mother to assist his strongman stunts in local piazzas and country fairs. He mistreats her, emotionally and physically, as he also does the tightrope walker known as the Fool (played by Richard Basehart), who empathizes with her. Zampanò's insensitivity leads to the death of both traveling companions and leaves him in isolation and despair. Unlike other men in muscle depictions of this period, there are no daring feats or overt displays of physicality, only a few faux fight sequences. In all three scenes in which Quinn alleges to display "superhuman strength" the audience is merely given the same stunt and description: "Ladies and gentlemen, here is a chain and a hook a half-centimeter thick made of pig iron, stronger than steel. With the simple expansion of my pectoral muscles—that is to say, my chest—I shall shatter this hook. This piece of cloth is not meant to protect me but to spare the public the sight of blood if the hook tears my flesh. If anybody in the audience is squeamish, it's better not to watch."[60] Anyone familiar with these kinds of carnival acts knows they are usually improvised with chains easily broken by a previously chiseled weak link. Indeed, Zampanò hardly seems to be trying. In the final scene, some sword-swallowing and fire-eating apparatus is lying on the ground, if only to give the impression that he intended to use it.

The tightrope walking scene between two high buildings by the Fool is real, but as film critic Luigi Giacosi points out, it was an uncredited stuntman, not Richard Basehart, on the high wire.[61] No less misleading are movie posters showing Zampanò with flexed muscles breaking chains when in fact Quinn's musculature as depicted in the film resembles that of a brawny stevedore or amateur boxer at best and not even that of an average bodybuilder, not to mention strongman, of the 1950s. Ironically, for a film that exemplifies the neorealism genre of the era, so much of it is unreal.

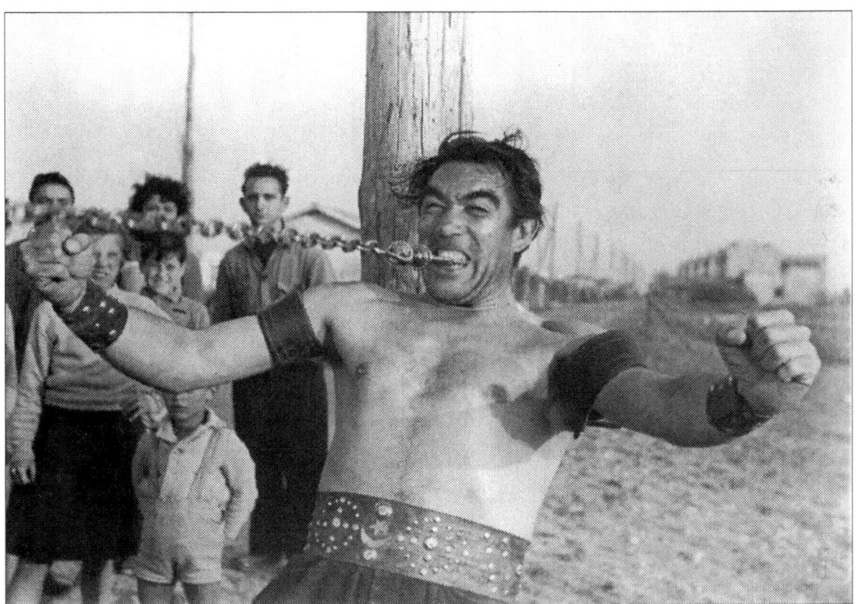

Figure 11.4. Anthony Quinn as the evil strongman Zampanò performing his chain-breaking stunt in *La strada*. Collection of David L. Chapman.

It is a cruel irony that *La strada* reflects the *giganti buoni* (good giant) movies of the early twentieth century when characters like Maciste protected the weak and punished the guilty. Contrary to the heroic depictions of earlier *forzuti* (strongmen), it depicts the depressed reality of postwar Italy: Zampanò is portrayed as evil and conniving, where Maciste was good. Fellini turns his strongman into a masochistic tyrant who preys on those who are too kind-hearted and stupid to recognize the phony strongman's duplicity. The film combines the fantasy of the good giant with the harsh realities of Italy's grim recent history using the metaphor of the itinerant strongman. What makes it relevant to this study of muscles in the movies is that *La strada* tapped into and bolstered a vibrant resurgence of Italian filmmaking after World War II. This so-called Italian film renaissance, according to Robert Kass, was aided by fiscal policies of the government, forcing foreign filmmakers to make more pictures in Italy, and US tax laws exempting actors and directors living abroad for seventeen months or longer from income tax on their earnings. Equally critical to this revival were two relics of Benito Mussolini's Fascist regime—the state-sponsored Centro sperimentale di cinematografia, which trained actors, directors, writers, and technicians, and the Cinecittà complex of fourteen full-size stages, larger than any European studio and comparable to any in Hollywood. "Moreover," Kass notes, "production costs in America had risen so high that American producers could take few chances on new film ideas. But in Italy, by shooting in the streets, with a minimum of costume and set changes, a producer could easily take a chance on an off-beat story which *might* catch on. And so, in a world market weary of the repetitiously commercial, the Italians made a considerable impression, gained an elan, and began to develop box office personalities with an international appeal." That the Italians were mounting a challenge to Hollywood was obvious at the 1955 Italian Film Festival in London, attended by Queen Elizabeth and the Duke of Edinburgh, where an outlay of £20,000 earned an estimated £1 million worth of publicity. By 1961 fears by journalists that producers were deserting America for greener pastures overseas became frequent; Christopher North commented at the time that "US companies now produce so many films abroad that employment in the movie industry in Hollywood is reduced and there is danger that Hollywood may ultimately cease to be the locus of the best trained, and most-talented, practitioners of the motion picture arts and technics."[62] Admittedly, Anthony Quinn at best was only a manly illusion of a strongman, but *La strada* proved to be a centerpiece of the Italian film renaissance in the 1950s and, not unlike *The Vikings*, helped lay the foundation for the explosion of peplum films in the 1960s.

Notes

1. See John D. Fair, *Mr. America: The Tragic History of a Bodybuilding Icon.*
2. Kate Buford, *Burt Lancaster: An American Life*, 24, 34, 49.
3. David Fury, *The Cinema History of Burt Lancaster*, 33, 40, 45.
4. Bosley Crowther, "The Screen: Adventure Theme in New Films," *New York Times*, July 8, 1950.
5. Fury, *The Cinema History*, 45; Buford, *Burt Lancaster*, 104.

6. Burt Lancaster, quoted in Ben Maddox, "Burt's Private Life," 60.

7. Buford, *Burt Lancaster*, 105.

8. After his decathlon and pentathlon victories at the 1912 Olympics, Thorpe was recognized by King Gustav V of Sweden as "the greatest athlete in the world," but his medals were taken from him because he had violated amateur rules by playing semiprofessional baseball the previous summer. John Durant and Otto Bettmann, *Pictorial History of American Sports: From Colonial Times to the Present* (New York: A. S. Barnes, 1952), 143, 150.

9. Buford, *Burt Lancaster*, 110, 111; Fury, *The Cinema History*, 56; "Not Really Jim Thorpe's Life," viewer review of *Jim Thorpe—All American*, July 29, 2008, Internet Movie Database, http://www.imdb.com/title/tt0043687/reviews?ref_=tt_ov_rt.

10. Maddox, "Burt's Private Life," 61.

11. Fury, *The Cinema History*, 101–2; Tony Curtis, *Tony Curtis: The Autobiography*, 128; Bosley Crowther, "Greatest of Ease: Monotonous 'Trapeze' Swings into Capitol," *New York Times*, June 5, 1956; "Top Film Grossers of 1956," *Variety Weekly*, January 2, 1957; Buford, *Burt Lancaster*, 151.

12. Buford, *Burt Lancaster*, 217, 264.

13. Fury, *The Cinema History*, 173.

14. John Frankenheimer, quoted in Buford, *Burt Lancaster*, 239; Fury, *The Cinema History*, 190; Buford, *Burt Lancaster*, 226.

15. Fredda Dudley, "Dynamite with Dimples!," 37.

16. Kirk Douglas, *The Ragman's Son: An Autobiography*, 45–46, 57–59.

17. Kirk Douglas, *I Am Spartacus! Making a Film, Breaking the Blacklist*, 31; Buford, *Burt Lancaster*, 165.

18. Douglas, *The Ragman's Son*, 128–29.

19. Dudley, "Dynamite," 37; "Meanest Mug in Movies," *Screenland*, May 1949, 38.

20. "Champion," *Variety*, March 16, 1949; John Parker, *Michael Douglas: Acting on Instinct* (London: Headline, 1994), 23. Douglas confirms that "*Champion* made me a star and earned me my first Academy Award nomination." Kirk Douglas, *Climbing the Mountain: My Search for Meaning*, 103.

21. Douglas, *The Ragman's Son*, 174.

22. Viewer review of *The Story of Three Loves* (1953), Internet Movie Database, http://www.imdb.com/title/tt0046374/reviews?start=20.

23. Douglas, *The Ragman's Son*, 259.

24. Bosley Crowther, "Norse Opera," *New York Times*, June 12, 1958; "Some of the Top UA Grossers," *Variety*, January 6, 1960. See also Howard Hughes, *Cinema Italiano: The Complete Guide from Classics to Cult* (London: I. B. Tauris, 2011), 29–32.

25. Douglas, *I Am Spartacus!*, 112.

26. Curtis, *Tony Curtis*, 186; *New York Times*, October 7, 1960; "Box Office/Business for *Spartacus*," *Spartacus* (1960), Internet Movie Database, http://www.imdb.com/title/tt0054331/.

27. Douglas, *Climbing the Mountain*, 27–28.

28. Michael Munn, *Kirk Douglas*, 33–34.

29. Douglas, *The Ragman's Son*, 306; Douglas, *I Am Spartacus!*, 12.

30. Gene Kelly, quoted in Clive Hirschhorn, *Gene Kelly: A Biography*, 10–11.

31. Tony Thomas, *The Films of Gene Kelly: Song and Dance Man*, 10–11.

32. Kelly, quoted in "Gene Kelly," *Parade*, August 3, 1957, quoted in Cynthia Brideson and Sara Brideson, *He's Got Rhythm: The Life and Career of Gene Kelly*, 21. It is likely, however, that Kelly saw Fairbanks's sequel, *Don Q, Son of Zorro* (1925), not *The Mark of Zorro*. Earl J. Hess and Pratibha A. Dabholkar, *The Cinematic Voyage of* The Pirate: *Kelly, Garland, and Minnelli at Work*, 59.

33. Hirschhorn, *Gene Kelly*, 27. Professor Patricia Vertinsky contends that a precedent was set for male dancing by Springfield College physical educator Ted Shawn in the 1930s. Although Shawn was "determined to overturn the popular notion that men who danced were 'sissies,'" it was "not men, but women who drove the dance culture he built upon in the leap from the nineteenth and into the twentieth century." Patricia Vertinsky, "'This Dancing Business Is More Hazardous Than Any "He-Man" Sport': Ted Shawn and His Men Dancers," *Sociology of Sport Journal* 35, no. 2 (2018): 168, 174. "Virile *and* sexy, his dancing has an erotic potential that disturbs the manly/effeminate antithesis imposed upon it" is the view in Steven Cohan, "Dancing with Balls in the 1940s: Sissies, Sailors and the Camp Masculinity of Gene Kelly," in *The Trouble with Men: Masculinities in European and Hollywood Cinema*, ed. Phil Powrie, Ann Davies, and Bruce Babington, 20.

34. Gene Kelly, quoted in "Dancing: A Man's Game," episode of *Omnibus*, December 21, 1958, NBC, quoted in Brideson and Brideson, *He's Got Rhythm*, 47.

35. Brideson and Brideson, *He's Got Rhythm*, 48, 89.

36. Gene Kelly, in Robert Trachtenberg, dir., *Gene Kelly: Anatomy of a Dancer* (New York: Warner Brothers, 2002), DVD.

37. Brideson and Brideson, *He's Got Rhythm*, 49; Gene Kelly, quoted in Albin Krebs, "Gene Kelly, Dancer of Vigor and Grace, Dies," *New York Times*, February 3, 1996.

38. Nina Foch, in Trachtenberg, *Gene Kelly*.

39. Hirschhorn, *Gene Kelly*, 119. Enhancing Kelly's physicality in the role was his technical ingenuity: he blended live action with animation in a dance routine with Jerry the Mouse and, in an alter ego scene, cinematic double exposure enabled him to dance with himself.

40. Bosley Crowther, "'Anchors Aweigh,' Gay Musical Film, with Gene Kelly, Frank Sinatra and Miss Grayson, Opens at the Capitol Theatre," *New York Times*, July 20, 1945; Eddie Mannix Ledger, Margaret Herrick Library.

41. Brideson and Brideson, *He's Got Rhythm*, 184.

42. Hess and Dabholkar, *Cinematic Voyage*, 98.

43. Gene Kelly, in Dorothy Kilgallen, "Voice of Broadway," undated clipping, in Scrapbook 4, Box 7, Gene Kelly Collection, Howard Gotlieb Archival Research Center, Boston University, quoted in Hess and Dabholkar, *Cinematic Voyage*, 98.

44. Brideson and Brideson, *He's Got Rhythm*, 190.

45. Hess and Dabholkar, *Cinematic Voyage*, 121–22. As Fairbanks's biographer notes, "he shows off his legs by wearing nothing but a doublet and ragged, thigh-length trousers

for most of the film." Gary Carey, *Doug & Mary: A Biography of Douglas Fairbanks and Mary Pickford* (New York: E. P. Dutton, 1977), 167.

46. "'The Pirate,' with Gene Kelly, Judy Garland and Walter Slezak at Music Hall," *New York Herald Tribune*, May 21, 1948, quoted in Hess and Dabholkar, *Cinematic Voyage*, 139, 141.

47. Richard Dyer, *Heavenly Bodies: Film Stars and Society* (Basingstoke, UK: St. Martin's, 1986), 182–85; David A. Gerstner, "Dancer from the Dance: Gene Kelly, Television, and the Beauty of Movement," *The Velvet Light Trap* 49 (Spring 2002): 55–59; Arthur Freed, quoted in Hess and Dabholkar, *Cinematic Voyage*, 150.

48. Rudy Behlmer, "Swordplay on the Screen," *Films in Review* 16, no. 6 (June–July 1965): n.p.

49. Thomas, *The Films of Gene Kelly*, 86.

50. Brideson and Brideson, *He's Got Rhythm*, 203–4. The authors note that Cyd Charisse, who performed with Kelly in *Singin' in the Rain*, "once claimed that her husband always knew she had been dancing with Gene Kelly if she came home with bruises and with Fred Astaire if she came home unmarked."

51. André Previn, and Leonard Bernstein, in Trachtenberg, *Gene Kelly*. Perhaps the most remarkable feature of Kelly's performance is that, at the time, he had a temperature of 103.

52. Gene Kelly, quoted in Thomas, *The Films of Gene Kelly*, 10.

53. Betsy Blair, *In Memory of All That: Love and Politics in New York, Hollywood, and Paris* (New York: Alfred A. Knopf, 2003), 143.

54. Kerry Kelly Novick, in Trachtenberg, *Gene Kelly*.

55. Federico Fellini, "My Experiences as a Director," in *Federico Fellini: Essays in Criticism*, ed. Peter Bondanella (Oxford: Oxford University Press, 1978), 3; Peter Bondanella and Manuela Gieri, "Fellini's *La Strada* and the Cinema of Poetry," in *La Strada: Federico Fellini, Director*, ed. Peter Bondanella and Manuela Gieri, 7, 9.

56. Anthony Quinn, *The Original Sin: A Self-Portrait* (Boston: Little, Brown, 1972), 151, 159, 164, 186.

57. Anthony Quinn, quoted in "Mae West: Quinn in Clean Beds," January 9, 2014, *Mae West* (blog), http://maewest.blogspot.com/2014/01/mae-west-quinn-in-clean-beds.html; Alvin H. Marill, "Anthony Quinn," *Films in Review* 19, no. 8 (October 1968): 465.

58. Tony Thomas, *The Films of Kirk Douglas* (Secaucus, NJ: Citadel, 1972), 111.

59. Marill, "Anthony Quinn," 471.

60. Federico Fellini, dir., *La strada* (Rome: Ponti–De Laurentiis Cinematografica), script, in Bondanella and Gieri, eds., *La Strada*, 42.

61. Luigi Giacosi, "The Most Strenuous Film in a Career of Forty-Three Years," in Bondanella and Gieri, eds., *La Strada*, 190.

62. Robert Kass, "The Italian Film Renaissance," *Films in Review* 4, no. 7 (August–September 1953): 338–39, 346–47; Christopher Brunel, "London's Italian Festival," *Films in Review* 6, no. 3 (March 1955): 180; Christopher North, "The Abandonment of Hollywood," *Films in Review* 12, no. 1 (January 1961): 14.

PART III.

MUSCLES FOR SHOW

XII. ATHENA

When two hearts are entwined
Venus waltzes with Mars
hand in hand we will find
love can change the stars.

> —Ralph Blane and Hugh Martin, "Love Can Change the Stars"

As Jackie Robinson broke the color barrier in baseball, I broke the physique barrier in show business.

> —Steve Reeves, quoted in Dave Dowling and George Helmer,
> *Steve Reeves: His Legacy in Films*

THE METRO-GOLDWYN-MAYER (MGM) 1954 production of *Athena*, dubbed "the musical with young ideas," appeared at a propitious time in film history.[1] With an abundance of talented singers and dancers and increased application of Technicolor and CinemaScope, the musical reached its zenith as a popular genre.[2] This postwar pathway to cinematic success featured the 1951 remake of *Showboat*, which, with many hit songs, proved to be the most financially successful and memorable of film and stage versions since 1927. It was followed in 1952 by *Singin' in the Rain*, starring Donald O'Connor (who won a Golden Globe for best actor), Gene Kelly, and Debbie Reynolds. In 1953 *Gentlemen Prefer Blonds* featured two of the most potent sex symbols of the decade, Marilyn Monroe and Jane Russell, with the former singing "Diamonds Are a Girl's Best Friend." By the time *Athena* was released in November, the year 1954 had already spawned four blockbuster musicals, including *A Star Is Born*, with Judy Garland and James Mason; *Brigadoon*, with Gene Kelly singing "Almost Like Being in Love"; the award-winning *Seven Brides for Seven Brothers*; and *White Christmas*, a romantic comedy that demonstrated how financially rewarding musicals could be. It was a banner year for musicals, and *Athena* was expected to be part of this seemingly endless flow of box office triumphs.

The credentials of *Athena's* cast provided ample reason for optimism. Starring roles were filled by Jane Powell, whose fame was established as the leading bride in *Seven Brides for Seven Brothers*, and Edmund Purdom, a British actor who starred in the 1954 production of *The Student Prince*, in which he lip-synched the voice of famed tenor Mario Lanza. Other leading roles were filled by Debbie Reynolds, whose career was taking off after sharing the limelight with Kelly, and Vic Damone, a classic crooner best known for his renditions of "You're Breaking My Heart" (1949), "My Heart Cries for You" (1950), and "My Truly Truly Fair" (1951). Second billing was reserved for veteran Louis Calhern, whose career as a contract player peaked in the 1950s for many films, including *The Student Prince*, and Linda Christian, a Mexican actress dubbed by MGM as "the anatomic bomb."[3] Neither, however, could sing or dance.

It was not the string of romantic musicals that inspired *Athena's* creation, however, but a series of upbeat aquatic productions starring Esther Williams. It was during lunch breaks while shooting *Easy to Love* (1953) that Williams, director Charles Walters, and writer Leo Pogostin conceived *Athena* along the same lines. Their idea, explains Turner Classic Movies writer Frank Miller, "was to cast Williams as a reincarnated Greek goddess swimming her way to happiness."[4] As Williams observes in her 1999 autobiography, "the fifties and into the sixties was the Age of Antiquity for the Hollywood studios. Any story that had its foot in Athens, Rome, or Jerusalem was part of the Hollywood mindset," and her script was "right on the money." While Williams was on maternity leave, however, studio head Dore Schary put the film into production without her and turned all of her swimming sequences into singing scenes for Powell, who was no swimmer. "Schary's actions were absolutely indefensible," fumes Williams. "What he'd done was 'legal' since we were all under contract, and everything we did on company time belonged to the studio; but it went to the heart of my sense of values about fair play. . . . The gossip wags wrote: 'The Mermaid on the Lot has been beached.'" Williams insists that Schary, unlike Louis B. Mayer, "didn't like movie stars." She "loathed" Schary, whom she describes as smooth, snide, and condescending. It seemed fitting that this "turkey" was fired on Thanksgiving Day 1956.[5]

Although Williams eventually received recognition as cowriter of *Athena*, the musical was launched on a sour note. Originally titled *Adam and Athena*, the plot centers on a handsome but unfit young lawyer, Adam Shaw (Purdom), who becomes romantically entangled with Athena Mulvain

(Powell) and her fitness-crazed family of grandparents and six sisters (oddly, no parents or brothers are present) who operate a health food store and live in a hilltop compound where everyone follows a strict diet and exercises regularly. This new age family's beliefs include numerology, spiritualism, astrology, vegetarianism, abstinence from nicotine and alcohol, weight training, and group singing. The singing, featuring Damone, Powell, and Reynolds, accompanies the cheerful but often conflicting love matches that instill some intrigue to this fitness paradise. They are joined by a troupe of bodybuilders, including such leading lights as Malcolm Brenner; Richard DuBois (Mr. America 1954), billed in the film as Richard Sabre; Joe Gold, the founder of Gold's Gym; Ed Holovchik, billed in the film as Ed Fury; Irvin "Zabo" Koszewski; Steve Reeves (Mr. Universe 1950), and Jerry Ross, whose physiques, it is implied, are produced by the barbells strewn about the grounds.[6] Despite the efforts of this cult-like aggregation to achieve nirvana through a holistic lifestyle, much is made of the role of fate. A climax is provided by a televised Mr. Universe contest in which Ed Perkins (Reeves) displays his classic physique and wins a weightlifting challenge. When Adam (Purdom), after an altercation, devalues Ed's fit body by tossing him over his shoulders, it appears that Athena, embarrassed by this affront to her family's ideals, seems fated to marry Ed. But she chooses love (Adam) over muscles. "People are better than vegetables" thus becomes the movie's signature line.[7]

Much fault can be found in the film. The script seems wacky and simplistic, the acting is often wooden, and the songs are unmemorable. Furthermore, *Athena* does nothing to remove existing stereotypes at a time when bodybuilders were often stigmatized as muscle-bound, narcissistic, and homosexual and health food aficionados viewed as kooks. Jane Powell recalled that after each scene, director Richard Thorpe usually would "toss the pages of the script over his shoulder and walk away." For Reynolds, who "hated the script," it was a picture she "didn't want to do." Critics have treated it harshly. The *New York Times* reviewer called it "energetic, sincere and strangely unimaginative. Despite its cheerful approach, 'Athena' appears to be an augury of a cold, hard winter" for films.[8] It is hardly surprising that *Athena* was a flop and that MGM endured a $511,000 loss. Nor would it fare better in posterity; it is conspicuous by omission from most compilations of memorable musicals in the ensuing six decades.[9]

Yet much can be discerned about how physical culture was perceived in the 1950s by examining the way it was portrayed in *Athena* and permeated its actors. Health and fitness loom large, but the leading men show no indication of being healthy or fit. Hedda Hopper describes Purdom as "handsome in the romantic tradition—wavy black hair, dark eyes, and classic features."[10] Behind the character Adam's appearance as a reluctant convert to physical culture on-screen, however, movie wags were more intrigued by Purdom's physical prowess off-screen—ironically, with the woman his character had spurned for Athena. As Reynolds explains in her autobiography, "the only relief on the set was the action going on off camera" between Purdom and Linda Christian, either in dressing trailers or the studio gardens.[11] On-screen, however, a faux physicality is projected with the harebrained notion that the judo that Adam Shaw learned in the navy enables him to overpower the superior strength and athleticism of Ed Perkins. The effect is enhanced by a reporter asking Adam afterward if he had "ever fought professionally" and a phone call enquiring if he intended to "make a personal appearance at the stadium." It is believable that Reeves, who did most of his own stunt work, took the fall on his back, but a sudden scene shift enabled the swapping of a double for Purdom. That Johnny Nile (Vic Damone), who is exhibited as a weakling in an early scene, is able to flatten Bill Nichols (Richard DuBois) with one arm near the end of the film is likely a result of the latter simply performing a somersault. "The bigger they are, the harder they fall," boasts Johnny, but it has a hollow ring.

The lifestyle and demeanor of the leading women, on the other hand, was more authentic and in sync with the film's theme. Unlike Damone, Powell was a talented dancer and singer. She recalled taking "every kind of dancing lesson" as a child at the Peters Dancing School in Portland, Oregon—"acrobatic, tap, ballet." She was also health conscious: "I counted calories even before I was a teenager, following in Mama's footsteps. . . . I exercise almost every day and I try not to waste calories; there's nothing worse to me than wasting calories eating food that doesn't taste good. If it isn't delicious, I don't bother." Befitting her film role, Powell described herself as "wholesome, not sexy," and what attracted her to her first husband, Geary Steffen, was his athletic background as a skater, skier, and water-skier. "He introduced me to that outdoor world I'd always yearned for," she explained.[12]

Likewise, the exercise credentials of Debbie Reynolds, who projected a clean-living image, were impeccable. A Texas transplant, she had played sports with the guys as a kid and aspired, even as a contract player at Warner Brothers, to become a gym teacher. Between her studio school classes, she developed an admiration for physical culture by sneaking into the adjacent gym where Kirk Douglas was receiving boxing training for *The Champion*. "It was very exciting," she recalled. "Boy, did they have great bodies. Mae West would have loved their pecs."[13] Films requiring physical exertion presented no obstacle, but working with accomplished dancers Kelly and O'Connor in *Singin' in the Rain* proved to be trial by fire: "Gene was in great condition. His legs were like pistons; he had the strongest thighs of any man alive. Donald was slim and not nearly as muscular but very strong. My body was strong from sports and barre work. Fortunately I didn't have to build the body, but I was still worn out."[14] Kelly concurred that Reynolds, though lacking singing and dancing experience, "proved able to master the basics of dancing" through "long hours of demanding physical effort" (and later in life Reynolds would produce an exercise video, *Do It Debbie's Way*).[15] Her dancing and singing duet with Powell, "I Never Felt Better," proved to be a musical highlight of *Athena*. Yet she was also involved in a behind-the-scenes love affair. Reynolds recalled that "the most memorable thing about making this movie was meeting Eddie Fisher . . . then a famous singer with his own TV show."[16] They met on the set of *Athena* in response to a request from Fisher, and their budding romance aroused far more attention and acclaim than her film role and provided an emotional substitute for her contrived and unconvincing screen romance with Damone.

In striking contrast to the perky athleticism of Reynolds was the phony fitness of Louis Calhern as Grandpa Ulysses Mulvain, the patriarch and chief trainer of this physical culture paradise. Portraying a seventy-eight-year-old superman who could perform giant swings on the high bar and do back flips, Calhern was only fifty-nine at the time of filming and benefited from a stuntman, again with scene changes, when demonstrating his swinging ability. Although he was on a special diet after suffering a heart attack, Calhern seemed unconcerned about his health. Reynolds recalls having lunches with him where she exchanged the bologna sandwiches with pickle and potato chips prepared by her mother for Spartan concoctions of egg whites and the white chicken meat Calhern's wife had prepared.[17] He died of a heart attack less than two years after *Athena*'s release.

The most obvious quality of Athena's sisters is their athletic demeanor (their Isadora Duncan–inspired dance movements reveal professional training) and healthy appearance. All have names of ancient derivation; in addition to Minerva (Reynolds), the family includes Aphrodite, Calliope, Ceres, Medea, and Niobe. While the film attempts to exemplify the Greek maxim of a sound mind in a sound body, two of the sisters are named after Roman goddesses. Grandpa Ulysses Mulvain's name is not just Greek but Homeric, though Grandma Mulvain (Evelyn Varden) is clearly out of sync.

Her name, Salome, is of Hebrew derivation, and she regularly communes with the Indian deity Narada.

What compensates for the weak and wimpy male leads is the beefy cast of bodybuilders under the tutelage of Grandpa Ulysses. Despite their physical culture symbolism and importance to the flow and climax of the story (the Mr. Universe contest) they are given short shrift by the producers. Mostly extras recruited from nearby gyms, they are displayed as a motley lot, zombie-like nonentities who appear collectively in four short scenes. First, after parading past the puzzled Adam Shaw (Purdom), nine of them engage in light exercise on the patio while Bill (DuBois) and Ed (Reeves) receive special treatment inside the compound. Eight of the extras show up for the two community meal scenes, while a full fourteen, including the anonymous character played by Joe Gold, compete for the Mr. Universe title. Aside from the principals—DuBois, Fury, Gold, Goodrich (who never appears on camera), Koszewski, and Reeves—their names are ignored in the credits and thus lost to obscurity. Even Reeves receives no more than secondary billing. The producers seem almost embarrassed by their presence, and as actors they appear unable to act.

Yet their presence does not go unnoticed in the dialogue, where their bodies and culture are treated with the same disdain as their personalities. Such treatment occurs in a scene at the health food store when Minerva (Reynolds) asks Bill Nichols (DuBois) to carry a bulky sack of walnuts to the storeroom. The ease with which he completes the task leads Johnny Nyle (Damone) to ask, "Who was that?," and the following exchange takes place:

Minerva: Bill Nichols, a special friend of mine.
Johnny: Were those his own muscles?
Minerva: Oh, anybody can do what he did.
Johnny: Don't bet on it.
Minerva: Thanks, Bill.
Bill: Oh, it's all right. I'll see you up on the hill after supper.
Johnny: I guess between a guy like that and a guy like me, anybody would rather have a guy like that.
Minerva: Muscles aren't everything. Sometimes it's personality and the way a fella smiles.

Minerva confirms her disregard for brawn after watching Adam and Athena kiss on the patio. When Johnny asks "What are you looking so pleased about?" she responds, "Nothing. It's just that it's amazing what you can do without muscles." Later Minerva scolds Ed Perkins (Reeves) for eating the orchids Johnny brought her, saying, "Wish you'd go on a diet." Then Athena reinforces a commonplace stereotype of bodybuilders when Ed complains, "I just can't keep my mind on my workouts" because of her obsession with Adam. "Well, you just tell Grandpa to give you a steam bath," she replies. "And stop thinking. It always upsets you." And when Adam and Johnny encounter Bill Nichols, who is barring their way to the hilltop compound in the final scene, Johnny orders him, "Stop thinking. You'll strain a muscle." Stereotyping bodybuilders as all brawn and no brains was hardly new. In a *Life* magazine interview shortly after he won the Mr. America contest, Reeves's statement that he next planned to attend college was twisted to read, "When my muscles stop expanding in a couple of years, I will start expanding my brain." Reeves and gym owners resented this misquotation, which made bodybuilders sound like nothing but muscleheads.[18]

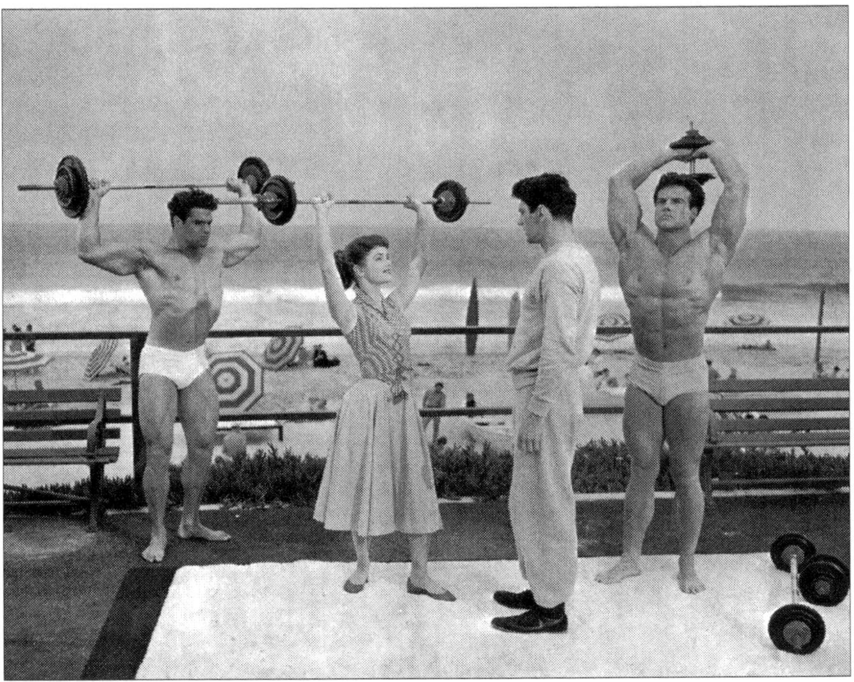

Figure 12.1. An off-the-set publicity photo of bodybuilders Richard DuBois and Steve Reeves with Debbie Reynolds and Ed Purdom, who starred in the 1954 film *Athena*. Collection of David L. Chapman.

A later scene in Grandpa's gym reveals a profound ignorance of the body when Grandpa Ulysses (Calhern) tells Adam (Purdom), "The minute you walked in here I liked the look of your Sartorius muscle, boy. It's a man's pinnings that count." While Adam retorts sharply, "Your opinion of my pinnings is of no importance," the dialogue seems pointless inasmuch as his leg muscles are undetectable under the loose-fitting trousers he is wearing. One wonders also why Grandpa's finest physical specimens (Ed Perkins and Bill Nichols) are made to lie motionless under sheets on massage tables. Repeatedly Ulysses utters, "No excitement. Take it easy. Take it easy, boy. Ed, keep your mind a blank. . . . That's the boy, dead dog." He then introduces Adam to the hapless Johnny, saying, "You've seen pictures of the before and after, haven't you? Well, this is before." On arising, there is a disparaging reaction from Ed and Bill to Adam:

> Bill: Hey Ed, what's the dude?
> Ulysses: A friend of Athena's.
> Ed: No muscle tone.
> Bill: No muscle, period. Ha Ha.
> Ed: They seem to be getting a new class of people around here.

No less a mockery of muscle is the way in which weightlifting props are displayed. It is evident in a scene when the nonathletic Adam enters his home after midnight wearing a three-piece suit and carrying what appears to be a one-hundred-pound barbell in one hand, and then effortlessly places it on the floor while holding a large batch of vegetables and flowers in the other arm. Equally absurd is the phony efforts by the two Mr. Universe finalists (played by Fury and Reeves) to break a tie by negotiating a continental clean and press, made to look and sound like three hundred pounds. A photo appearing in the December 1954 issue of *Muscle Builder* gives lie to this strength feat by showing Bert Goodrich in suit and tie grinning while holding the gigantic ersatz stage barbell off camera to the amusement of onlooking bodybuilders.[19]

Nevertheless, expectations were high in the bodybuilding community that the appearance in *Athena* of two of its greatest champions, DuBois and Reeves, would open doors for others to become stars. Citing Marlon Brando, Kirk Douglas, Burt Lancaster, and Victor Mature as stars who trained with weights for leading roles, an article titled "How Would You Like to Be a Movie Star?" argued,

There are new and great opportunities open for the man of muscle as a professional actor. TV, the stage, night clubs and Hollywood have all suddenly taken a new interest in the male physique. Hollywood, it seems, leads the field and in its search for new talent has shown a decided preference for muscular males. . . . Under certain favorable conditions, the physique may be just as important, or even more so than acting ability. . . . The sky is the limit when you are strong and healthy.[20]

Iron game sage Earle Liederman predicted that *Athena* would "do more for the bodybuilding game than anything that has happened during the past few years." Bert Goodrich was even more sanguine, estimating that with over five million barbell users in America, the film would "do more for weight training than anything ever before attempted."[21]

The highest hopes were invested in DuBois, who as the 1954 Mr. America won paeans of praise as an ideal symbol of the nation's manhood. York Barbell Company president Bob Hoffman described him as "superbly developed, handsome, smiling, likeable, popular." Despite being only twenty, and the youngest Mr. America yet, DuBois looked and acted the part. "He was all that a person would visualize a Mr. America to be," remarked California gym owner George Bruce. "If only more young Americans would follow his example, we could wipe out sickness, ill health and lack of bodily vigor."[22] Especially appealing was the rags-to-riches story of how DuBois had risen from poverty in the South Bronx. When his father died he was sent to a Catholic orphanage, where he excelled in swimming, diving, and boxing. But DuBois also displayed an artistic bent. While shining shoes and selling newspapers in Manhattan's Theater District, he was befriended by actors who secured minor stage roles for him. After starting serious bodybuilding, he was drawn to Los Angeles, where he could maximize his dual talents in Hollywood and at Muscle Beach. "A typical American Horatio Alger story" is how a publicity release described DuBois, "a 21 year old, athletically-built, clean-cut young man, with natural acting ability and a willingness to work hard for a career." He combined "the romantic aspects of Mature with the masculinity of [Clark] Gable's virility, blended with the dash of [Douglas] Fairbanks and the woman appeal of [Charles] Boyer." With a long-term contract at Universal Studios in the offing, Liederman predicted DuBois's cinema career would "rise with meteoric speed and he will become the most commercial Mr. America of them all."[23]

With stars in his eyes, DuBois adopted the name Richard Sabre, assuming it would help propel him to fame and fortune. Liederman, however, expressed concern that he was giving up the name recognition he had already earned, albeit in the limited sphere of bodybuilding, for a name no one would recognize. DuBois's experience began as one of the three magi in his orphanage Christmas play and extended to Los Angeles little theater productions. Nevertheless, he fancied himself "a Shakespearean actor," predicting that "within five years I will be the greatest actor that Hollywood has ever known!"[24] By happenstance, Liederman observed DuBois just after he had worked out, showered, and dressed at George Eiferman's gym, "And the first thing that happened was Dick dramatically and loudly rehearsing lengthy lines from Shakespeare—Hamlet and Caesar. Man! He must have felt himself right on stage for he gave it all he had—gestures and acting. As you know by now, Dick has been studying dramatics for a long time and has aspirations for a full theatrical career, rather than a muscular prize winning future." By virtue of his New York theater connections and Mr. America title, DuBois secured his role in *Athena* and was told he might get a follow-up slot in Esther Williams's forthcoming film *Jupiter's Darling* (1955); as Charles Smith confidently predicted in *Muscle Builder*, "His future is assured."[25] DuBois's promise was never fulfilled in *Athena*, however; he appears stiff and overacts his brief lines—likely a result of trying too hard to become a star on his first outing. And his affected tough-guy, big-city accent hardly endeared him to moviegoers in the hinterlands. With few further opportunities to exploit, he turned his muscles into quick cash by joining Eiferman, Gold, Koszewski, Armand Tanny, and others in Mae West's road show and was soon playing in Las Vegas for $1,000 a week.[26] Eventually DuBois became a born-again Christian, and disappeared from both the muscle and movie scenes; he died in 2007 at age seventy-four.

Steve Reeves's on-set demeanor and speech was little better than DuBois's. According to one reviewer, Reeves, like the film's dancing sisters, received no close-ups and "doesn't show any great skill at delivering a dialogue line."[27] But he was better known than DuBois, more mature, and could draw on more acting experience. He also had the most proportional physique and handsome face in bodybuilding. These qualities provided him with his first movie opportunity, years before *Athena*. Just prior to the Mr. America contest at the Lane Tech Auditorium in Chicago, promoter Dick Trusdale arranged for Montreal photographer Tony Lanza to take some photos of Reeves along the city's lakeshore for mail-order marketing. As they searched for an appropriate place and pose, "Lanza had an inspiration. He asked Steve to stand erect and while flexing his biceps to raise his arms in roughly a 'U' shape over his head. It was the perfect pose to accentuate the athlete's ample chest, thick arms, and narrow waist. The sheen of perspiration caused by the hot Midwestern sun, the earnest expression on the bodybuilder's face, and the beautifully sculpted muscles, all combined to create one of the most sublime moments in the history of the human body. The resulting picture was destined to be an unqualified masterpiece of physique art." Superimposed on a mountain of clouds, the photographer titled it "Perfection in the Skies."[28]

Its impact, Reeves later explained, resulted after one of Cecil B. DeMille's talent scouts spotted Reeves when he was taking acting lessons in New York and doing a vaudeville act on weekends. After passing a screen test for *Samson and Delilah*, Reeves was offered a seven-year contract and was flown to Hollywood, where he relocated near Paramount Studios. As he would later recall,

> I arrived at Paramount and walked into Mr. DeMille's office. He had five two-foot blow-ups of pictures on his wall. The pictures were of Bob Hope, Bing Crosby, Dorothy Lamour, Alan Ladd, and me, in a pose called "Perfection in the Clouds," where I'm standing with my hands over my head stretching toward the sky. And he said, "This is my Samson." Then he added, "But you must realize that the motion picture camera puts on 15 pounds, so you're going to have to lose 15 pounds." . . . So I'd lose five pounds, then I'd go out to the beach on Sunday and all my friends would say, "Steve, you're looking terrible. You're ruining yourself. . . . Once a week I would have to do a skit for him. . . . I did this on and off . . . for about three months. Then he called me into his office and said, "You've lost seven pounds in three months. Some days your skits are really good; and some days they're terrible. It looks like you're preoccupied with something."

Needing to start filming in just a month, DeMille told Reeves that he was going to use Victor Mature, who was not ideal but experienced and dependable.[29]

It is easy to trivialize the physique of Mature and his physical culture credentials, especially in comparison to Reeves and succeeding generations of superbuff bodybuilders, but even as a worker in an aircraft plant in 1942 he was lifting York barbells, avidly reading *Strength and Health*, and corresponding with York president Bob Hoffman. Mature sensibly capitalized on his physique and sex appeal. As he told *Life* magazine in 1941, "I can act, but what I've got that the others don't have is this," pointing to his body. *Life* described him as "proportioned like a frappe glass" with a "33-inch waist, 25-inch [*sic*] biceps, a

45-inch chest and standing 6 feet 2½ inches tall" and noted that "300 New York models had chosen him as the man they would most like to be marooned with on a desert island."[30] By the end of the 1940s Mature was helping to introduce male muscle and flesh to film audiences. Esther Williams remembers him as a "big man" with a "great swagger" and "well-developed pectorals. . . . How he maintained his muscular physique, given his peculiar diet, I'll never know. Vic was the only person I ever knew who could—and would—eat anything at all." Mature eventually played a major role in the success of *Samson and Delilah*, which received two Academy Awards and took in $25.6 million, making it the highest-grossing film for 1950. According to *Variety*, it was a "lusty action story with a heavy coating of torrid-zone romance," and Mature "fits neatly into the role of the handsome but dumb hulk of muscle."[31] Whether Reeves could have filled the bill for a "dumb hulk of muscle" and engaged in "torrid-zone romance" seems doubtful. But Mature, with broad manly shoulders and husky physique, proved ideal and able to display the strength and passion needed for the part.

For Reeves, the years after his release were full of frustrations. Although he continued winning physique contests, including the title Mr. Universe 1950, Reeves yearned to act: "I was still trying very hard every month to convince certain Hollywood companies, like MGM, Universal, and others, that I was perfect for movies, and that if they could just see around the fact that bodybuilders didn't belong in the movies, I could prove them wrong. But I was turned away constantly, so it was tough trying to persuade them to give me a shot. It was a never ending battle."[32] Meanwhile, he was gaining valuable stage experience, and television exposure through minor appearances in the pilot for the proposed *Kimbar of the Jungle* series and on *The Dinah Shore Show*, *The Ralph Edwards Show*, *The Red Skelton Show*, and *Topper*. More serious commitments included his role as a cop in *Jail Bait* (1954), which enabled him to earn his Screen Actors Guild card, and a spot in the Broadway musical *Kismet*, in which he played a Wazir guard. Thus by the time Reeves, in his late twenties, was offered the role of Ed Perkins in *Athena*, he had gained lots of experience.

It seemed appropriate that his long apprenticeship should end with a character befitting his background. Of all the cast members, Reeves was probably the most health conscious. When asked on a visit to Canada what he cherished most in life, he replied, "Health is the thing. I expect to live to the ripe old age of 100 years, no problem!"[33] To ensure longevity, he developed a set of fourteen "rules to live by" that he later revealed in his memoir *Building the Classic Physique the Natural Way*. Few physical culturists have come so close to realizing the Greek ideal of *mens sana in corpore sano* as Reeves.[34] He should have suspected, however, that even in a film on physical culture, his body-builder role would be marginalized and not in sync with the lifestyle of others in the cast or even the theme of the film. Reeves discovered that "while my muscles were an asset in winning physique contests, they proved an absolute liability in obtaining roles in Hollywood. As most of the actors in Hollywood were not physical culturists, very few of them had well-developed physiques, which made most of them insecure with my appearing alongside them. It's ironic that I would eventually be able to make my own mark in Hollywood solely because I refused to play the emaciated leading man, preferring to show audiences the beauty and value of a fully developed male physique."[35] Reeves and his comrades were not only shunned on the set; their characters were also denied any heroic role in the outcome of the story. Although Adam Shaw's display of physical superiority over Mr. Universe in the penultimate scene seemed to evoke sympathy for Ed Perkins and virtually assured his marriage to Athena, Adam then displayed his moral courage by challenging Grandpa's notion that fate is determined by numbers and the stars:

Adam: I'm tired of your theories. Maybe the berries and the nuts and
the sunshine saved your lives. Maybe they didn't. Maybe you and
Grandma were just too much in love to give up. Maybe what kept
you going was that you were both fighting to have a life together.
Isn't Athena entitled to that much too?
Ulysses: Until you came along we were very happy. All we want is to
live our lives in our own way.
Adam: Oh, no. You want everyone else to live in your way too. You
talk big—live and let live. I love you, let us be friends. It's just talk.
You're a fraud, Mr. Mulvain. You're narrow-minded, pigheaded, and
obstinate. I don't know what the stars say or what the numbers add
up to, but in my book love is better than lettuce, and people are more
important than vegetables.

The impact of this reproach is obvious when Athena pays Adam a surprise visit the next morning for a ham-and-eggs breakfast, signifying a break with her family's fitness cult and submission to the ways of the world: "I just had a long talk with Grandma and Grandpa, and we agreed that if two people loved each other enough, they could solve everything. And they think people are much more important than vegetables." Athena then ends the musical by singing "Life is fun if you harmonize" followed by a chorus of "Love will change the stars if it's strong enough." She thus reinforces existing cultural norms by rejecting alternative lifestyles in the staid and homogeneous 1950s.[36]

The film's legacy, however, was quite different. Reeves recalls that on completing *Athena* he took up employment with American Health Studios and virtually abandoned his search for a show business career. But famed Italian filmmaker Pietro Francisci had written a script for a movie titled *Hercules* and spent five years looking for an actor to play the title role. "One day his daughter, who was 13, went to the theater and saw *Athena*," according to Reeves, "which had gotten to Italy by then. And she ran home and said, 'Daddy, I think I have your Hercules.'" The director went to the theater the next day and decided on his star. Reeves was paid $10,000 for his role as Hercules. The movie cost $500,000 to make and became the biggest box office draw of 1958. In the United States, where it was purchased by Joseph E. Levine, *Hercules* grossed $40 million.[37] Reeves biographer Milton Moore estimates that millions of young men were inspired by it to take up bodybuilding; within months of Reeves's appearance in *Hercules*, "the spa movement proliferated in America and spread throughout the world. Sparked by the sight of Reeves on film, millions of men enrolled in the nearest gymnasium or reducing salon."[38] *Hercules* enabled Reeves to display his body in a way that was denied in *Athena*—and with worldwide consequences.

It also inspired many other peplum films of the 1960s, including numerous *Hercules* copycats. As bodybuilding mogul Joe Weider recognized in a 1965 issue of *Muscle Builder*,

> Many others have played Hercules or herculean roles, yet none has symbolized the great Hercules as has Steve. Steve seems to be eternally innocent . . . the clean-cut, handsome boy whom we all love and can hardly wait for another of his exploits. Other herculean stars might be more muscular, more massive, and stronger, but they represent . . . the type of man the public doesn't especially care for. When other Hercules appear on the screen, we can hardly wait for them to be destroyed . . . eaten by the lions . . . so we can get the heck out of the theater.[39]

Weider was saying that Reeves made bodybuilding more palatable to the mainstream moviegoer. This popularity not only inspired countless young men to take up bodybuilding but more broadly laid the groundwork for

Arnold Schwarzenegger, the 1977 film *Pumping Iron*, and the fitness craze that swept America and the world in the 1970s. In a 1978 *Playboy* interview, Sylvester Stallone admitted that Reeves's portrayal of Hercules stirred his interest: "I remember seeing things like *On the Waterfront*, and I'd always end up in a deep snore. But one day I saw Steve Reeves in *Hercules Unchained*, and I thought, Hey, it's one thing for Brando to stand up to the union, but this weird guy with the beard and big calves can pull down a temple all by himself." A decade later Stallone elaborated: "The day I saw Steve Reeves was the day my life changed. It was like seeing the Messiah. I said, 'This is what I want to be.'"[40] Schwarzenegger, who also starred in a Hercules movie, realized Reeves's impact: "As far as the general public was concerned, in the 1950s—except for the perennial Charles Atlas—there was only one famous bodybuilder: Steve Reeves." Even decades later *Iron Man* author David Prokop viewed the Reeves physique as immortal: "If the definition of ultimate bodybuilding greatness is to look better—from head to toe—than any man who ever lived, Steve Reeves has to rank as the greatest bodybuilder of all time." And though he sported an antithetical look, modern champion Sergio Oliva agreed that "Steve Reeves' physique is perfect."[41] Chris LeClaire concludes that "it is almost impossible to imagine a time when Hollywood didn't want leading men with muscular builds. Today casting directors can't get enough of muscle and brawn. Actors are encouraged to lift weights, hire trainers and build muscle so that they can take on the look of a Jean-Claude Van Damme, Sylvester Stallone and of course Arnold Schwarzenegger."[42]

However much *Athena*'s depiction of physical culture and bodybuilding was dismissed as irrelevant within the context of its time, it foreshadowed major societal changes. Representing the views of an average film aficionado in 2011, Todd Mason argues that "looking backwards, from a great and wise old age, I see the movie's obvious faults and yet I can't help but think that all the *nonsense* the Mulvains spouted has come home to roost. What seemed arcane and weird then—the vegetarianism, the devotion to exercise, the star gazing, is all main stream [*sic*] now."[43] In her 1988 autobiography Jane Powell recognized that *Athena* was "not brilliant social commentary, but I thought it really deserved a better reception than it got." She believed the movie was "way ahead of its time" and "would have done better twenty years later!"[44] But *Athena* can be appreciated as a barometer of the times in which it appeared. Not unlike the film itself, which never lived up to its billing at the box office or in critical acclaim, those who pursued physical culture and bodybuilding as a healthy and fulfilling lifestyle were regarded as odd or, to use relevant lines from the movie, "off the beam" and failing to "fit in with the rest of the rest of the world." At best, *Athena* represents a parody of the Mulvains, cult-like idealists who refuse to conform to society's expectations. Yet it is their nonconformity, however awkwardly conveyed, that presages the cultural revolution that would sweep America a decade later. Though the Mulvains were misfits in the 1950s, their favorite salutation, "I love you. Let us be friends," became a familiar mantra for the flower children of the 1960s.[45]

Notes

1. According to Wayne Schmidt's Box Office Data Page, the average number of new releases per year from 1945 to 1959 were 451.8 (1945–49), 560 (1950–1954), and 470 (1955–59). "Wayne Schmidt's Box Office Data Page," Wayne's This and That, http://www. waynesthisandthat.com/moviedata.html.

2. Twentieth Century Fox producer and executive Darryl Zanuck observed that in the early 1950s, an era notable for Senator Joseph McCarthy's communist witch hunt and the Korean War, "audiences seem to be shopping for anything that sounds like adventure or escape." Producer and screenwriter Aubrey Solomon adds that this refocusing at Fox "resulted in a disproportionate number of musicals, light comedies, and action films." Darryl Zanuck to Philip Dunne, May 7, 1953, Philip Dunne Collection, Cinema-Television Library, University of Southern California, quoted in Aubrey Solomon, *Twentieth Century-Fox: A Corporate and Financial History* (Metuchen, NJ: Scarecrow, 1988), 71–72.

3. "Atomic Bomb," *Life*, September 3, 1945, 53.

4. Frank Miller, "Athena," Turner Classic Movies, http://www.tcm.com/this-month/article/135978%7C0/Athena.html.

5. Esther Williams, *The Million Dollar Mermaid*, 259, 185, 292, 210, 266.

6. As technical director, Hollywood gym owner and 1939 Mr. America Bert Goodrich did not appear on-screen but was in charge of recruiting bodybuilders, mostly from nearby Muscle Beach, and for the film's staging of the Mr. Universe contest. Earle Liederman, "Let's Gossip," *Muscle Power*, November 1954, 63.

7. Richard Thorpe, dir., *Athena* (Los Angeles: Metro-Goldwyn-Mayer, 1954); all dialogue quoted herein is transcribed from the DVD (Burbank, CA: Turner Entertainment / Warner Brothers, 2011). Reeves later noted that in the scene with Purdom tossing him over his shoulder, it was "definitely me landing on the canvas not a stunt double. To do that scene and get the right effect, I basically threw myself over Edmund's shoulder. We had to rehearse the scene several times before the director Dick Thorpe and the two of us felt it looked real. If you watch closely, there's a quick cut and you never actually see Edmund totally throw me over his shoulder." Steve Reeves, quoted in Dave Dowling and George Helmer, *Steve Reeves: His Legacy in Films*, 2–9.

8. Jane Powell, *The Girl Next Door . . . And How She Grew*, 160; Debbie Reynolds, *Debbie: My Life* (New York: William Morrow, 1988), 102; "At the Globe," *New York Times*, December 22, 1954.

9. See, for example, Stanley Green, *Encyclopedia of the Musical Film* (New York: Oxford University Press, 1981), s.v. "Athena." Rare exceptions include Clive Hirschhorn, *The Hollywood Musical* (New York: Octopus Books, 1981) and John Howard Reid, *Hollywood Movie Musicals: Great, Good and Glamorous* (Raleigh, NC: Lulu Press, 2006), but the former calls *Athena* a "slightly off-beat story in a routine screenplay . . . and an equally routine set of songs" (343), and the latter rates *Athena* "routine at best, glaringly incompetent at worst" (8).

10. Hedda Hopper, "Edmund Purdom: From Pauper to Prince," *Modern Screen*, October 1954, 72.

11. Reynolds, *My Life*, 102–4.

12. Powell, *The Girl Next Door*, 19, 32, 104, 118.

13. Debbie Reynolds, *Unsinkable: A Memoir*, 189, 184.

14. Reynolds, *My Life*, 90, 92.

15. Peter Wollen, *Singin' in the Rain* (London: British Film Institute, 1992), 32; Reynolds, *My Life*, 427.

16. Reynolds, *Unsinkable*, 222.

17. Reynolds, *My Life*, 68.

18. Chris LeClaire, *Worlds to Conquer: Steve Reeves, An Authorized Biography*, 83.

19. "How Would You Like to Be a Movie Star?" *Muscle Builder*, December 1954, 16.

20. "How Would You Like to Be a Movie Star?," 52–53.

21. Liederman, "Let's Gossip"; Bert Goodrich, quoted in "What the Champs Are Saying," *Muscle Power*, September 1954, 54.

22. Bob Hoffman, "1954 Mr. America Contest," *Strength and Health*, October 1954, 46; George R. Bruce, "Richard DuBois, Mr. America, 1954," *Strength and Health*, November 1954, 49.

23. Earle Liederman, "From Poverty and Weakness to Muscles and the Movies," *Muscle Power*, September 1954, 46, 48, 62.

24. Liederman, "From Poverty and Weakness," 46–47; "What the Champs Are Saying," *Muscle Power*, January 1955, 65. As it happened, DuBois never appeared in *Jupiter's Darling*.

25. Charles A. Smith, "Richard DuBois, Newly Crowned King of Bodybuilding," *Muscle Builder*, October 1954, 48.

26. Earle Liederman, "Richard DuBois Crowned 'Mr. America 1954,'" *Muscle Power*, September 1954, 62. DuBois also posed frequently for physique photos (principally those of gay publisher Bob Mizer) and sold autographed seminude photos of himself to fans. See, for example, "Richard DuBois at 21," *Physique Pictorial* 6, no. 2 (Summer 1956): 4.

27. Glenn Erickson, Review of *Athena*, 2011, DVD Talk, http://www.dvdtalk.com/dvdsavant/s3606athe.html.

28. David Chapman, "Perfection in Chicago: Lanza Photographs Steve Reeves," *Iron Game History: The Journal of Physical Culture* 6, no. 4 (December 2000): 16–19.

29. Steve Reeves, interview, *Perfect Vision* 6, no. 22 (July 1994), Drkrm, http://www.drkrm.com/reeves.html.

30. Victor Mature to Bob Hoffman, March 26, 1942, Bob Hoffman Papers, in the possession of John D. Fair; Aljean Harmetz, "Victor Mature, Movie Idol Noted for His Physique in Loincloths and Togas, Is Dead," *New York Times*, August 10, 1999, http://www.nytimes.com/1999/08/10/movies/victor-mature-movie-idol-noted-for-his-physique-in-loincloths-and-togas-is-dead.html.

31. Williams, *Million Dollar Mermaid*, 211–13; "Top Grosser in 1950: 'Samson and Delilah,'" *Box Office*, December 30, 1950, 16; "Samson and Delilah," *Variety*, December 31, 1949.

32. Steve Reeves, quoted in LeClaire, *Worlds to Conquer*, 122.

33. Steve Reeves, quoted in LeClaire, *Worlds to Conquer*, 125.

34. Steve Reeves, *Building the Classic Physique the Natural Way*, 129. Following his Mr. America victory in 1947, physique photographer Lon Hanagan drew exactly this comparison. He was "sure if one of these Ancient Greeks came to life today and saw our new MR. AMERICA, Steve Reeves—he would find it hard to believe that Steve was not a re-incarnation of the body of one of those superior beings from Mount Olympus." Lon Hanagan, quoted in Arthur F. Gay, "Results of the Mr. America Contest," *Your Physique*, September 1947, 11.

35. Reeves, *Building the Classic Physique*, 41. Reeves later concluded that "too many muscles can get in your way. You've got to have enough to get people interested, but not so much that you scare them off." "Matter Over Mind," *Newsweek*, August 29, 1960, 86.

36. A sign of the times was a 1957 article about Muscle Beach in the *Saturday Evening Post*: "Mention Muscle Beach to Southern California regional cynics, its wise guys, its soft in the body, and you are liable to draw only sniggers or snorts." Joel Sayre, "The Body Worshipers of Muscle Beach," 35.

37. Reeves interview.

38. Milton T. Moore Jr., *Steve Reeves: A Tribute* (Dallas: self-published, 1982).

39. Joe Weider, "The Training Wisdom of Joe Weider," *Muscle Builder*, January 1965, 29.

40. Sylvester Stallone, quoted in LeClaire, *Worlds to Conquer*, 184.

41. Arnold Schwarzenegger, *Encyclopedia of Modern Bodybuilding*, with Bill Dobbins (New York: Simon and Schuster, 1985), 44; David Prokop, "Grimek, Reeves, Oliva, Immortals of Muscle," *Iron Man*, May 1995, 99; Sergio Oliva, quoted in Prokop, "Grimek, Reeves, Oliva," 113.

42. LeClaire, *Worlds to Conquer*, 122.

43. Todd Mason, "Tuesday Overlooked Films: ATHENA (1954)," October 4, 2011, *In So Many Words* (blog), http://yvettecandraw.blogspot.com/2011/10/tuesday-overlooked-films-athena-1954.html.

44. Powell, *The Girl Next Door*, 159–60. That this change was starting to occur by 1966 was evident to cardiologist Carleton Chapman, who observed that for decades "the

tradition was that physical vigor was not a concern of the American adult, the topic was more or less suspect; the compulsive focus of health faddists rather than the legitimate interest of the rank and file." Carleton B. Chapman, "Introduction," in *Prescription for Life*, ed. M. F. Graham (New York: D. McKay, 1966), xvii.

45. For an account of this cultural transition, see Todd Gitlin, *The Sixties: Years of Hope, Days of Rage* (New York: Bantam Books, 1987).

XIII. MIGHTY SONS OF HERCULES

Every era has the revival of antiquity that it deserves.

—Abraham Moritz Warburg,
"L'antichità italiana nell'epoca di Rembrandt"

THE SWORD-AND-SANDAL FILMS of the 1960s were full of contradictions. They starred massively built bodybuilders whose acting abilities were rarely as enormous as their biceps, they were cheaply made in Italy and poorly dubbed elsewhere, and they recycled the same plot. Despite their low production values and the opprobrium heaped on them, the films often enjoyed spectacular worldwide success. Why, then, did moviegoers love them? By what alchemy did these lowbrow "cheap, trash films" turn simplistic plots set in ancient times into box office gold?[1] The answer to this riddle reveals much about the times and audiences of these popular movies. They featured ancient mythological heroes who performed incredible feats of strength while the camera lovingly focused on—almost caressed—their bulging muscles. It hardly mattered that many of these men of muscle could barely budge the heavy objects or perform the miraculous feats depicted on-screen, but it was important that they look like they could to enable viewers to suspend disbelief. Special effects were critical to perfecting this illusion. Between 1958 and 1968, around two hundred of these Italian costume dramas were produced. While important precedents were set with such works as the *Maciste* films of the 1920s, the *Last Days of Pompeii* (1938), and *Julius Caesar* (1953), the genre began with Steve Reeves's *Hercules* (1958) and had a meteoric impact on moviegoers, who could not get enough of these stories of ancient empires and mighty men.

Most cinema scholars have settled on the term *peplum films* for these vivid representations of the distant or imaginary past. It was first used by French critics in 1962 and refers to the pleated skirts many of the heroes wear while performing feats of strength and daring.[2] As the genre developed, the shirtless heroes often left their habitat in ancient Greece and began appearing in unusual and incongruous places: Incan Peru, Calvinist Scotland, seventeenth-century Spain, and even nineteenth-century Russia. The inconsistencies and inaccuracies in peplum films are often as glaring and monumental as the cardboard sets: Egyptian pharaohs are played by Caucasians, Sappho has a boyfriend, Salome dances to *save* John the Baptist, and the actors in *Spartacus* wear wristwatches.[3] But there is also majesty and drama that is easily overlooked. These are stories of powerful, muscular men who solve problems with little mental action. They delight in crashing down marble temples, gilded palaces, and institutions that oppress helpless people.

These "sons of Hercules" had long been destroying buildings and knocking petty tyrants down a peg or two. The heyday of peplum films was the 1960s, but they are derived from a film genre that began in Italy before the Great War and extended through to the *giganti buoni* (good giants) of the interwar period to the post–World War II bodybuilding world. The actors had wide shoulders, tiny waists, and bulging, clearly defined muscles, and these bare-chested demigods saved innocent and powerless peasants from depredations of various tyrants—often a Mephistophelian monarch or malevolent queen with too much makeup and big hair. But almost always it is the man's body that is at the center of attention, not the woman's. These Herculean performers proved to be immensely popular worldwide, and they brought muscular athletes to the screen in unprecedented numbers, largely because the protagonists were invariably American bodybuilders. Unlike in other genres, the hero's massive body rather than his inner conflicts or philosophical struggles are emphasized. The star's muscularity is central to the action in these films; it is the only thing standing between justice and injustice, freedom and servitude, life and death.

The postwar years were awful for most Italians; it was a misery reflected in such dark and gritty neorealist films as *Roma città aperta* (Rome open city, 1945), *Ladri di biciclette* (Bicycle thieves, 1948) and *La strada* (The street, 1954). Conditions improved slowly, but there were few entertainment resources. As late as 1951, over 70 percent of family expenditures were on food, housing, and clothes, leaving little for movie tickets.[4] During the next decade, however, rapid economic development transformed the country from a largely rural to a major industrial power. Italians called it *il miracolo economico*. As a result of the Marshall Plan and the determination of Italians, businesses reopened, employment increased, and salaries improved. For many citizens, *la vita* was starting to be *dolce*.[5] Some perceptive moviemakers saw an opportunity for another type of film. "Italy was sick of neorealism," screenwriter Ennio de Concini explained. It was "a country in transformation that wanted to identify with a wholesome and colossal strongman who solved everything with a punch and a kick in the butt and with almost no weapons."[6] Austerity and a grim black-and-white world was fading, to be replaced by a new Technicolor fantasy universe—but where good and evil were just as discernable as in older films.

As the economy revved up in 1957 and Italians were generally feeling better about themselves, Lionello Santi, president of Galatea Film, decided to make a picture that would revive one of Italy's favorite characters: the good giant Hercules. He would have many traits of the earlier hero: a champion who was free and unattached, strong and good with neither master nor mistress. The movie would reflect the optimism of the revitalized Italy, but the main character would fight against tyrants, greedy landlords, and oppressive invaders—all of whom were fresh in postwar minds. The principal audience would be Italians in the countryside or those living in the soulless apartments that were built on the outskirts of cities and rapidly filling up with those escaping rural poverty and seeking work in newly opened northern factories.[7]

To direct this film the producers chose Pietro Francisi, a successful moviemaker from Rome who had directed several historical films, most recently *Attila* (1953). "The epic attracted Francisi irresistibly," explains film historian Michele Giordano; "so much so that he embarked on research trips to Segesta, Agrigento and Pompeii."[8] Inspired by these classical sites, he set to work in 1957 on *Le fatiche di Ercole* (The labors of Hercules), the movie that would launch a thousand imitations and variations. The film is comprised of a jumble of mythical stories, but its principal plot line concerns the mighty hero and his quest to restore order to the kingdom of Iolcus. Along the way he encounters Pelias, the usurper king, and his beautiful daughter, Iole. Hercules and a group of adventurers (including Jason, the rightful king of Iolcus) are sent in quest of the Golden Fleece. After a brief detour among a group of lovely Amazons, the troupe arrives at Chalcis, where Hercules and the crew fight a band of ape-men while Jason finds the Golden Fleece and slays the dragon protecting it. Upon their return to Iolcus, Pelias steals the Golden Fleece and imprisons Hercules. A battle follows, but Hercules breaks free and scatters the enemy troops by toppling the royal palace portico onto the attackers. Pelias swallows poison, Jason ascends the throne, Iole admits her love for Hercules, and the two lovers sail into the sunset.

The story was set, but Francisi had to find someone to play the main part. There are differing versions of how he settled on Steve Reeves. The most commonly accepted one says that the director's thirteen-year-old daughter saw Reeves in the movie *Athena* (1954), and told her father, "I think I've found your Hercules." Supposedly, Francisi checked out the movie and agreed, but there are other versions of the discovery of Reeves. The tall, husky actor Mimmo Palmara says that Francisi came to him and said, "You're the only Italian actor who can play the role of Hercules because you have the strongest, most muscular body." Even so, the director admitted that he would like to find someone who was even bigger and more muscular, but he was unsure if such a person existed. Palmara told him that he needed to find an American bodybuilder. Francisi was reportedly amazed. "Who are these bodybuilders?" he asked. Palmara responded, "They are semiathletes who lift weights all day long, so their muscles swell and become enormous." He warned Francisi that these men were huge and strong, though "they all had ugly faces." But one of them, Steve Reeves, possessed "the face of an angel." Another version of how Reeves got the role, told by film historian Steve Della Casa, is that director of photography Mario Bava saw Reeves's photo in an American bodybuilding magazine and told Francisi that he had found the perfect Hercules. The director hired Reeves, but required one change. "Grow a beard," was his laconic advice.[9]

This was likely the only instruction the thirty-two-year-old Reeves, whose early career was fraught with economic and artistic problems, needed.[10] That changed after the actor received a round-trip ticket to Rome along with half his promised salary of $10,000. Filming took three months; interiors were shot at the Lux-Titanus studios in Rome, and exteriors were filmed near Anzio. The most dramatic sequence was the destruction of the tyrant's palace, when Hercules wrapped chains around the pillars and, like Samson, knocked down the oppressor's haven. By the end of shooting, Reeves was exhausted and suffering from several injuries as a result of doing his own stunts. Not enthusiastic about the film's chances, he returned to California.[11] Indeed, Reeves never felt secure as an actor, and he became increasingly disillusioned with moviemaking. French actress Mylène Demongeot, who costarred with him in a later peplum film, described him as "a very sweet guy who told me that he didn't have the slightest interest in making movies. The only thing that interested him was the money that they paid him. . . . His goal was very simple: he wanted to go back to America. He said that he had no acting talent. He hoped to make several more films. 'Maybe two or three more if I'm lucky. And with the money that I earn I'll buy me a ranch.' He was completely serious about what he said." Meanwhile, *Le fatiche di Ercole* was becoming popular in Europe, easily outgrossing blockbusters like *Giant* (1956) and *Bridge on the River Kwai* (1957). A week after its release in Italy and France, it recovered its production costs and eventually took in $7 million in Europe.[12]

With the success Francisi's film was receiving, it is hardly surprising that it attracted the attention of a cinematic entrepreneur with the expertise and chutzpah to market the film beyond the means of the original producers. Joseph E. Levine saw its potential appeal to a wider audience. Short, chubby, foul-mouthed, and the son of Russian Jewish immigrants, Levine was an unlikely champion of muscular heroes, but he had an instinctive sense of what postwar middle-class Americans would want to see at the local bijou. "A streetwise hustler, hawker and flim-flam man," he reportedly "could sell a sack of shit to a ladies' group."[13] His first success came in 1956, when he headed a group of investors who discovered a cheap and cheesy Japanese monster movie called *Gojira* which he dubbed into English and retitled *Godzilla, King of the Monsters.* Levine was supposedly not impressed by Francisi's mythological epic when he viewed it two years later. He thought it had bad color and a botched soundtrack, but he could see beyond its drawbacks. The film also had "musclemen, broads and a shipwreck and a dragon for the kids."[14] It was also cheap. Levine consequently bought the American rights for a paltry $120,000 and retitled it *Hercules.* He then spent another $120,000 on dubbing and reediting to make the film palatable to Americans. These expenses pale by comparison to the $1.2 million the mogul spent on promotions. He began to court exhibitors months before its release by hosting a gigantic "Explodation" luncheon for twelve hundred theater owners and guests. Next came a lavish press book, a three-story cardboard cutout of Steve Reeves, and a recorded version of the *Hercules* theme song by honey-toned crooner Vaughn Monroe. The luncheon cost $15,000, but that was chicken feed when balanced against potential profits. The crafty promoter knew that if he could convince US audiences to identify with Reeves the American athlete rather than some ancient demigod, then the potential for even greater profits would increase, so the star's physique was emphasized in many ads and merchandising materials that were distributed to the public.[15] But Levine did not stop there; he was perfectly willing to crawl into bed with the enemy if it meant larger audiences and greater profits. Hence he decided to make use of the flickering black-and-white screens that had invaded almost every American home. Television was the great bugbear of the movie industry at this time, but Levine knew he could use the "idiot box" to spread the word about his movie. The wily publicist used every trick, gimmick, and stunt he could think of to make potential audiences think it was essential to see this spectacle.

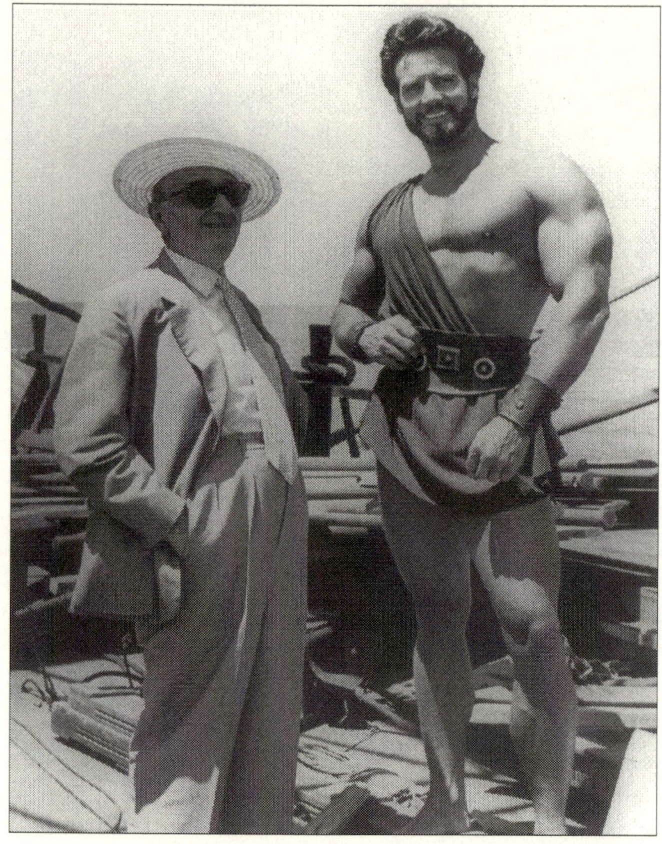

Figure 13.1. Producer Joseph E. Levine visits Steve Reeves on the set of *Hercules Unchained* (1960). Collection of David L. Chapman.

Levine's scheme for selling a movie was "saturation booking." Rather than opening in a few theaters and gradually trickling down to second- and third-tier cinemas, *Hercules* would open everywhere at once. Thus, Levine invested $360,000 to produce 635 prints for same-day showing. Saturation booking was "designed for a quick kill," explained one historian. This stratagem "could be used for a picture of poor quality to skim off the curious before bad reviews or negative word-of-mouth took effect." Or, as Levine famously said, "You can fool all of the people all of the time if the advertising is right and budget is big enough."[16] Fortunately, there was little fooling that had to be done after audiences viewed *Hercules*; the trick was getting them into the theaters initially. No matter how fabulous the publicity, if a film does not deliver what audiences expect, it is doomed. *Hercules*, however, was seen by some twenty-four million people in over eleven thousand theaters. Its North American profits were an estimated $18 million.[17]

A major reason for the film's massive success was its charismatic star. As film scholar Robert Rushing notes, "The camera loved Steve Reeves— like [Bartolomeo] Pagano, Reeves had a natural and dominating physical presence. He was not a gifted actor and rarely conveyed an emotion with any success, but his body convinced where his voice and face did not."[18] Largely because of his physique, Reeves became the highest-paid film star in Europe by the early 1960s, and peplum films experienced a sudden surge in popularity in Italy and abroad. Aside from simply stumbling on a winning formula, other forces were at work in Italy to make the public receptive to films set in ancient times. Most important was the Seventeenth Olympiad, held in Rome in 1960. There was a new emphasis on strong bodies set amid ancient reminders of the past. Another motivation for pride was the "miraculous" prosperity that returned in the late 1950s. Along with new consumer gadgets came entertainment opportunities. It was time to shake off the recent past and create a new and glamorous ancient past. Peplum films were made to order. Finally, there were the American mega-epics like *Ben-Hur* (1959) and *Spartacus* (1960) that strode onto screens like colossi. These were American Italian coproductions made in Hollywood sul Tevere (Hollywood on the Tiber). When US moviemakers went home, they often left behind sets and costumes, as well as technicians who knew how to make movies— usually less expensively.[19] It was too good an opportunity for savvy Italian producers to miss out on; they sensed that peplum films would be profitable for a long time.

When Italians discovered a vein of cinematic gold, they tended to mine it until it ran out; this led to the *filone*, or series film.[20] Thus, if Hercules was successful, why not come up with similar productions? After peplum *filone* petered out in the mid-1960s, Italians turned to spaghetti Westerns and then to James Bond knockoffs. The proof that the *filone* was on course came in 1960 when a new star, Mark Forest, seized the franchise with *La vendetta di Ercole* (The revenge of Hercules). Audiences eagerly accepted him, and peplum films were off and running. Steve Reeves had been an

American bodybuilder, so the obvious course was to comb American gyms for new stars. Forest was a prominent Italian American bodybuilder who began life as Lou Degni. Ed Holovchik was another minor physique star of the 1950s and 1960s tapped to play in peplum films. But he changed his name to the more euphonious and aggressively masculine Ed Fury when his acting career escalated. By the early 1960s the race was on to locate any American bodybuilder who could appear halfway presentable on screen. The cast, crew, and producers were European, but with dubbing and action-heavy scripts, linguistic ineptitude and acting deficits could be concealed. When there were not enough Americans to satisfy the insatiable demand of the peplum machine, a few Italians filled the gap, but they had to assume Anglo-sounding names. One of the most popular rechristened hunks was Alan Steel, born in Rome as Sergio Ciani. According to *Newsweek*, he had organized "the Society to Protect Italian Musclemen," which encouraged native strongmen to appear in peplum films.[21] If Ciani's group ever actually existed, it was unnecessary, because at the height of the genre, there was plenty of work for all.

With hundreds of peplum films produced in the 1960s, it is easy to track their themes: they are usually celebrations of manly, muscular power over the machinations of cruel, conniving women or pitiless, effeminate men who seek to destroy or humiliate the hero. Hercules (or a proxy) is a manifestation of individualism; even if he places his muscles in the service of every widow and waif inhabiting the surrounding countryside, he extricates himself from any situation by his strength and fighting skill, not his intellect. Nature and a bit of boulder lifting or tree uprooting have bestowed on him perfect musculature, and he is transformed into a virile fantasy. As Steve Della Casa and Marco Giusti note, after Reeves invented the genre's modern form, the peplum hero was born; it was now "not enough to be a fit and good-looking young man or even someone with an athletic background; the protagonist must display that exponential harmony that only the discipline of bodybuilding is able to forge."[22] In addition to being superbly muscular, the peplum hero never worries about the righteousness of his cause, and his audience is never in doubt. As Spanish cinema historian Oscar Lapeña Marchena notes, "There are no gradations of color in peplum films; there are only two categories of characters: good and evil. Almost every film relates the confrontation between two entities that aspire to command the tribe, city, kingdom or empire—the legitimate and the illegitimate."[23] These films always feature a Manichean struggle between evil pagan Romans and

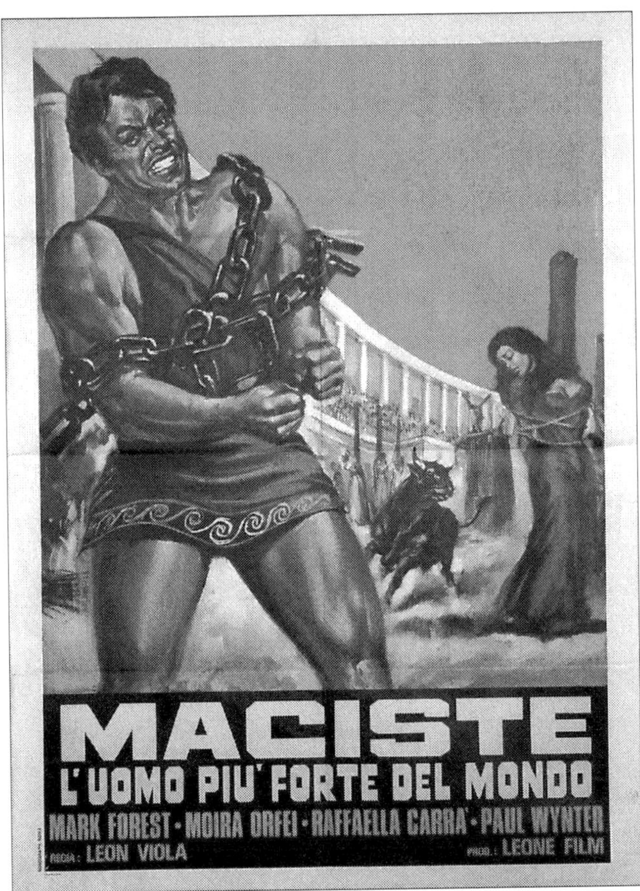

Figure 13.2. Mark Forest on an Italian poster for the 1961 peplum film *Maciste: L'uomo più forte del mondo* (Maciste: The strongest man in the world). In the United States it carried the less grandiose title *Mole Men against the Son of Hercules*. Collection of David L. Chapman.

virtuous Christians, Egyptians and Jews, decadent Romans and savage barbarians, and solar and lunar forces. To underscore this trope, the crowned heads and villainous usurpers in peplum films are always devious, ruthless, cruel, and mired in malice. "Happy feelings have always disgusted me," admits one tyrant. Another says of his helpless prisoners, "If they are hungry, feed them the whip. If they are thirsty, let them drink blood—their own, of course." No one could doubt the depravity of a man who declares, "Have all the suspects tortured. Start with the women and children."[24]

Sword-and-sandal evils are always easily determined. The films may have been shot in gorgeous Technicolor, but the moral issues are always black and white. The hero might never be bothered by spiritual doubts, but he occasionally gets injured. The strongman's wounds, however, are always superficial—scratches that draw attention to the beautiful curvature of his biceps or pectorals. Besides, there is usually a pretty maiden around to serve his medical needs.

The injured body she sympathetically tends to is at the heart of the genre and differentiates it from other films. The peplum strongman inhabits the kingdom of the body, and it is a realm that sets the hero apart from others. It is never clear where the protagonist's strength and beauty originate— perhaps a gift of the gods or a product of hard work and clean living. Or maybe the Hercules of the moment is a sport of nature. Usually he arrives on the scene from nowhere, restores justice (or establishes the just and rightful ruler), and then returns to nature, where he remains until the next film. The genre fixes a steely and admiring gaze on physiques; it emphasizes athletic and exaggerated bodies for men and shapely, magnificent, and sensual forms for women. The bodies sometimes resemble those of Renaissance frescoes or Greek statuary, but the peplum hero sports a form that exceeds the historic bounds of muscularity because it is mainly molded in a modern gym. The robust bodies of these men were often revelations to audiences with little knowledge of physical culture. Nowhere was this new vision of masculinity more apparent than in midcentury Italy. The *Hercules* and *Maciste* films presented a new vista to viewers who remembered the deprivations of both postwar eras. To film critic Giacomo Manzoli they represented "a world where malnutrition and poverty are no longer constant companions and where it is no longer possible to imagine the male body covered in twitchy and undernourished muscles, with unkempt hair—a body encased in a rumpled, baggy undershirt like Massimo Girotti in *Ossessione*." The ideal man was inspired by ancient artworks and trained to create a futuristic body to inspire men of the present. In fact, the films ignited a desire to emulate the bodies on the screen in real life, and Italy consequently experienced an upsurge of interest in bodybuilding, thanks partly to the success of peplum films. Steve Reeves was a major inspiration for this renaissance. The first modern Italian book on bodybuilding was John Vigna's *Muscoli e bellezza* (Muscles and beauty), which came out the same year *Athena* was released (1954), and Reeves was featured on the cover of the 1957 edition after *Hercules* became a hit.[25] In fact, according to a journalist in *Newsweek* magazine, Reeves was responsible for inspiring a resurgence of interest in bodybuilding and a permanent fascination with peplum films in the United States too. The article claims that the muscular actor was the unwitting catalyst for a new "muscle boom" that was sweeping America: "For the past fifteen years there has been a growing physical-culture drive in the U.S. It's coming to a head now. What they call the muscle picture is here to stay, like Westerns."[26]

While more men were pumping iron in the gyms, their heroes in the cinemas were continuing the fight against monstrous oppressors and their infernal devices. In many peplum films the hero is quite literally forced to pit himself against diabolical machines. The evil rulers always make the same mistake, often uttering things like "Your death is not enough; you must *suffer!*" This invariably sets up a situation where Hercules can destroy the torture device and bring about the villain's downfall. It also allows the protagonist to show his superiority to technology and give audiences an opportunity to view his muscles close up as the camera lovingly pans across his straining biceps, knotted deltoids, and swelling pectorals. Sometimes the hero's antitechnological bent reflects the real world of the 1960s. Critics have detected a similarity between peplum films and Cold War events. In both, a strong and healthy American bursts onto the scene of European carnage and desperation; he sets the situation right with his powerful body, then leaves to fight other battles. Some Italian directors reworked their films to comment on political situations and present-day perils. In *Ercole alla conquista di Atlantide* (Hercules conquers Atlantis, 1961), one of the most prescient of peplum film directors, Vittorio Cottafavi, presents a bleak picture of the modern world by way of the ancient. From prophesy, Androcles, the king of Thebes, fears the evil island kingdom of Atlantis will eventually conquer the world. To prevent it, he organizes an expedition to the island where he and Hercules find a civilization that oppresses and brainwashes its people. It is ruled by the beautiful but wicked Queen Antinea, who dreams of world conquest. She has an army of supersoldiers who follow orders blindly and an atomic bomb–like destructive power that threatens to destroy any opposition. According to Cottafavi, he wanted to show the dangers of a Hitlerian demagogue, but he was careful to bury his movie's allegorical elements in a rich humus of mythology and special effects: "There are many symbols that are easily understood in this film, like the new race that needs to be created in order to conquer the rest of the earth. Those are Nazis with real concentration camps, men whose only goal is to kill. Naturally, all this is suggested—hinted at between a catastrophe and a battle—both indispensable elements of the genre. But naturally, the producers cannot put a moral or social concept in the middle of a battle."[27] As the astute director realized, this is precisely where moviemakers attempt to make their pitch—where it is seldom expected. Cottafavi knew that his message had to be subtle. The audience that moviemakers targeted was not the intellectual elite, and any intrinsic theme had to be carefully packaged.

That same proletarian, anti-intellectual audience still enjoys peplum films. Although the heyday of the sword-and-sandal movie was more than sixty years ago, the genre shows little sign of fading. Modern films like *Conan the Barbarian* (1982), *Gladiator* (2000), and *300* (2006) demonstrate that the genre is a perennial favorite with moviegoers. Its popularity can be attributed to its celebration of the body—especially the hypermuscular male body—and its ability to deflect many of the slings and arrows of modern society. The muscular hero is a protector of the people, a righter of wrongs who puts his strength, courage, and life on the line to subvert fearsome monsters or monstrous tyrants. As Robert Rushing notes, the peplum film has served as a cinematic intervention "that offers the spectator an imagined form of the ideal male body, overflowing with health, muscular energy, and natural vitality, one that appears as a defense against menacing forms of alterity on the outside."[28] That intervention might be illusory and temporary, but for as long as the images flicker on the screen, audiences can feel assured that all will be well.

Peplum films also changed the parameters of masculinity. They introduced bona fide bodybuilders to an international audience, and the male body became the center of attention in a unique way. It was a developed, muscular body that accustomed moviegoers to a more aesthetically pleasing physique. Muscular heroes were no longer thought of as big lummoxes; now they were the stuff of heroism. A man might go to the cinema to see men who were better built than he or anyone else, but owing to the manly events happening on the screen, he could watch it with society's "permission." Marcus van Ackerman and Rowena Chapman described this shift: " 'Younger men aren't afraid to look at themselves anymore.' Nor, it seemed, were they afraid of looking openly at the newly-proliferating images of other men, whose 'aquiline features' and 'well-rounded musculature' were . . . 'a common denominator.' " They were discussing the films of the Ronald Reagan–era 1980s, but their words are also surprisingly apt for the early 1960s.[29]

Notes

1. Gerald Mast, *A Short History of the Movies*, 364.

2. According to French historian Claude Aziza, scholars used the term *peplum* as early as August 1961, but in 1962 an article in *Les cahiers du cinéma* titled "L'âge du péplum" virtually cemented it into film criticism. Claude Aziza, "Le mot et la chose," in *Le Péplum: L'antiquité au cinéma*, ed. Charles Corlet (Paris: Corlet-Télérama, 1998), 10.

3. This is true of almost any film set in ancient Egypt; see, for example, *Sappho, Venus of Lesbos* (1960), *Salome* (1953), and *Spartacus* (1960). See also Bill Givens, *Roman Soldiers Don't Wear Watches: 333 Film Flubs—Memorable Movie Mistakes* (Secaucus, NJ: Carol, 1996).

4. Luca Gorgolini, *L'Italia in movimento: Storia sociale degli anni Cinquanta* (Milan: Mondadori, 2013), 53.

5. For Italy's economic miracle, see Guido Crainz, *Storia del miracolo italiano: Cultura, identità, trasformazioni fra anni Cinquanta e Sessanta* (Rome: Donzelli, 2005) and, for the change from neorealism to less socially engaged films, especially 154–62.

6. Ennio de Concini, quoted in Michele Giordano, *Giganti buoni: Da Ercole a Piedone (e oltre) il mito dell'uomo forte nel cinema italiano*, 38. Some might argue that Italy had just removed a ruler who solved problems with violence and hypermasculinity, but Benito Mussolini was constrained by reality; Hercules was not.

7. Giordano, *Giganti buoni*, 33. Some ideological directors like Giuseppe de Santis hoped films would cause a "proletarianization of the middle classes," but according to Ennio de Concini, what happened was a "middle-classicization of the proletariat." Peter Bondanella, *A History of Italian Cinema*, 170.

8. Giordano, *Giganti buoni*, 35.

9. Mimmo Palmara, in Steve Della Casa, dir., *Uomini Forti: Iron Men* (Rome: Terminal Video Italia SRL, 2006), DVD; Steve Della Casa, *Splendor: Storia (inconsueta) del cinema italiano* (Bari, Italy: Laterza, 2013), 50; Chris LeClaire, *Worlds to Conquer: Steve Reeves, An Authorized Biography*, 170.

10. Reeves occasionally resorted to prostitution, according to Scotty Bowers. "I once sent Steve Reeves over to [director] George Cukor as a trick [paid assignation]. Steve was a little hard up at the time and did it purely for the cash." Scotty Bowers, *Full Service: My Adventures in Hollywood and the Secret Sex Lives of the Stars* (New York: Grove, 2012), 189.

11. LeClaire, *Worlds to Conquer*, 170–74.

12. Mylène Demongeot, quoted in Christophe Champclaux and Linda Tahir Meriau, *Le Péplum* (Paris: Le Courriere du livre, 2016), 103, 177.

13. A. T. McKenna, *Showman of the Screen: Joseph E. Levine and His Revolutions in Film Promotion*, 1.

14. Nan Robertson, "Joseph E. Levine, a Towering Figure in Movie Making, Is Dead," *New York Times*, August 1, 1987, http://www.nytimes.com/1987/08/01/obituaries/joseph -elevine-a-towering-figure-in-movie-makingis-dead.html?pagewanted=all&mcubz=0.

15. McKenna, *Showman*, 45; Maria Wyke, "Herculean Muscle! The Classicizing Rhetoric of Bodybuilding," *Arion: A Journal of Humanities and the Classics*, third ser., 4, no. 3 (Winter 1997): 51–79.

16. Brian Hannan, *The Making of* The Magnificent Seven: *Behind the Scenes of the Pivotal Western* (Jefferson, NC: McFarland, 2015), 255; Tino Balio, *United Artists: The Company That Changed the Film Industry* (Madison: University of Wisconsin Press, 1987), 211; McKenna, *Showman*, 14.

17. Bondanella, *A History of Italian Cinema*, 167.

18. Robert A. Rushing, *Descended from Hercules: Biopolitics and the Muscled Male Body on Screen*, 46.

19. Not every American production left sets behind. After the filming of *Ben-Hur* (1959), many lavish sets were destroyed to prevent Italian directors from reusing the massive stadiums and palaces in cheaper productions. Abby McGanney Nolan, "Lights, Camera, Destruction! The 10 Most Ecologically-Unfriendly Films," *Guardian*, November 21, 2007, http://www.theguardian.com/film/filmblog/2007/nov/21/lightscameradestruction.

20. For a fuller discussion of *filone*, see Austin Fisher, "Italian Popular Film Genres," in *A Companion to Italian Cinema*, ed. Frank Burke (Chichester, UK: John Wiley and Sons, 2017), 250–66.

21. "Matter over Mind," *Newsweek*, August 29, 1960, 86.

22. Steve Della Casa and Marco Giusti, *Il grande libro di Ercole: Il cinema mitologico in Italia*, 13.

23. Oscar Lapeña Marchena, *Guida al cinema peplum: Ercole, Ursus, Sansone e Maciste alla conquista di Atlantide* (Rome: Profondo Rosso, 2009), 15.

24. Della Casa and Giusti, *Il grande libro di Ercole*, 17.

25. Giacomo Manzoli, *Da Ercole a Fantozzi: Cinema popolare e società italiana dal boom economico alla neotelevisione (1958–1976)* (Rome: Carocci, 2012), 11. See also John Vigna, *Muscoli e bellezza: Trattato italo-americano di alto culturismo fisica* (Turin: Editrice Esclusiva M.E.B., 1954). For a history of Italian bodybuilding, see Umberto Devetak and Giuseppe Corbetta, "La cultura fisica in Italia," in *Enciclopedia universale della cultura fisica* (Milan: Casa Editrice Madison, 2009), 434–81.

26. "Matter over Mind," *Newsweek*, August 29, 1960, 86.

27. Vittorio Cottafavi, quoted in Bernard Tavernier, "Je n'aime pas les films historiques," in *Ai poeti non si spara: Vittorio Cottafavi tra cinema e televisione*, ed. Adriano Aprà, Giulio Bursi, and Simone Starace (Bologna: Edizioni Cineteca Bologna, 2010), 225.

28. Rushing, *Descended from Hercules*, 3.

29. Marcus van Ackerman, interviewed in Jonathan Rutherford, "Who's That Man?" (1996) and Rowena Chapman, "The Great Pretender: Variations on the New Man" (1996), quoted in Pamela Church Gibson, "Queer Looks, Male Gazes, Taut Torsos and Designer Labels: Contemporary Cinema, Consumption and Masculinity," in *The Trouble with Men: Masculinities in European and Hollywood Cinema*, ed. Phil Powrie, Ann Davies, and Bruce Babington, 179.

XIV. BEACH MUSCLE BODIES

When 5,000 Pairs of Biceps meet 5,000 Bare Bikinis . . . You KNOW what's gonna happen!

—*Muscle Beach Party* advertising concept, 1964

Uneasily situated between counterculture images projected by James Dean in *Rebel without a Cause* (1955) and the dawning of the so-called Age of Aquarius a decade later, there emerged a motion picture interlude of innocence on the beaches of Southern California.[1] It was first fostered by *Gidget* (1959) and then by thirty "surf and sex" movies that focused on young attractive bodies and beach escapades rather than serious social causes.[2] The films, argues Kirse Granat May, "created an ideal teenage existence, marked by consumption, leisure, and little else." In *History of the Hollywood Teen Movie*, Stephen Tropiano explains how fan magazines helped create "the first true teenagers of the American cinema," thereby "shaping the archetypal image of the American teenager." It was reinforced by the surfing sounds of the Beach Boys, Jan and Dean, and other recording groups that "turned America's attention to the Southern California coastline, and those who never set foot on its sandy shores were led to believe that life on the West Coast was a twenty-four-hour beach party."[3] *Muscle Beach Party* (1964) was a notable film of this genre that deployed two nascent forms of physical culture, building muscles and using muscles, to exhibit this playful spirit. Its depictions reveal much about American attitudes about fitness in the 1960s.

While the Cold War and fears of a nuclear holocaust were paramount for most Americans of this era, a nagging concern emerged in the early 1950s that the nation's domestic tranquility was endangered by disenchanted and alienated youth.[4] Postwar teens, according to psychologists and educators, were spoiled, irresponsible, disrespectful of authority, and increasingly violent. This obsession with wayward youth stemmed partly from US Senate investigations into organized crime spearheaded by Estes Kefauver of Tennessee. So successful was his probe, according to biographer Joseph Gorman, that 866 cases were referred to the US Department of Justice for indictment, resulting in 593 convictions. It also spawned a CBS television series, *Crime Syndicated* (1951–53); a Hollywood film, *The Enforcer* (1951), starring Humphrey Bogart; and Kefauver's book *Crime in America* (1951), which became a *New York Times* best seller. The senator emerged "as an important national hero" and a leading presidential candidate in 1952.[5]

Much the same scenario transpired in a lead-up to the 1956 election when Kefauver headed a the US Senate Subcommittee on Juvenile Delinquency, which investigated depictions of violence and sex in film, television, and comic books.[6] "America had overnight discovered juvenile delinquency," explains Gorman, "and studies, analyses, and recommendations became favorite pastimes of all those groups that focus on what seems to be the major problem of the season."[7] Although Kefauver gained much favorable publicity, he never made it to the White House, and his subcommittee was unable to establish a clear link between the media and teen delinquents. An unexpected opportunity emerged in its wake, however, for a new kind of film that would exploit a different type of teen. Ironically, it was brought to life by the producer of such parent-stressing titles as *The Beast with a Million Eyes* (1955), *I Was a Teenage Werewolf* (1957), *Reform School Girl* (1957), and *Hot Rod Gang* (1958). What Sam Arkoff of American International Pictures (AIP) understood was the impact of television, by the mid-1950s, on the movie industry. He observed that "AIP and Disney were the only film companies . . . that consistently made a profit, year after year. While the major companies struggled to stay in the black, we never had a money-losing year. We weren't doing things big, but we were doing them right."[8] Arkoff also found a niche market ignored by what he called "arty-farty" major studios. While downtown movie palaces were shrinking, teenagers were flocking to suburban drive-ins to watch AIP's exploitative films through steamed-up windshields, listening on tinny speakers and crunching on buttered popcorn. *Teenage Werewolf* was shot in six days for $100,000 and earned $2 million its first year.[9]

Arkoff's successful product, however, flew in the face of middle-class America's need for wholesome entertainment to protect its potentially delinquent juveniles. Soon after *Teenage Werewolf*'s release in 1957, Illinois senator Paul Douglas, a Kefauver ally, urged Arkoff to "take a responsible stand in the movies it makes for young audiences, rather than making movies that are scandalous and immoral." AIP soon changed its fare, but not from pressure by do-gooders. By 1959 the market was inundated with copy-cat films. With profits down, Arkoff turned to Italy, where he purchased the US rights to some of the newly popular sword-and-sandal movies starring American bodybuilders. While filming a modern setting of an adult beach party in the summer of 1962, he imagined it would be a perfect scenario for an American teenage movie, especially with cute girls in skimpy bathing suits. Soon Arkoff's writer, Lou Rusoff, was probing West Coast beaches for ideas for a *Beach Party* script.[10]

Southern California provided an ideal setting for some serious cinematic mythmaking. There, as a 1959 issue of *Cosmopolitan* observed, "the boys and girls grow bigger and more beautiful. They are longer of leg, deeper of chest, better muscled than other American youngsters." And the young women, *Life* rhapsodized in 1962, were "the prettiest, biggest, lithest, tannest, most luscious girls this side of the international date line." Kirse Granat May attributes the emergence of these super suburban kids to a relaxed, anxiety-free lifestyle, "typified by healthy eating, year-round swimming, skiing, surfing, sailing, and sports."[11] California imagery of the good life where teens need not worry about the future provided the leitmotif for Arkoff's newest venture. In the wake of Disney's successful theme park and television ventures (Disneyland and *The Mickey Mouse Club*), wholesomeness, not delinquency, seemed the most marketable commodity. That Hollywood had exhausted its genre of teenage crime and was ready to capitalize on patron tastes for nicer teens was evident in *Gidget*, starring Sandra Dee. Released by Columbia in 1959, it fostered a clean teen movement personified by Dick Clark on *American Bandstand* and provided a template for Arkoff's "sex and surf" films in the early 1960s.[12]

Utilizing the abundant sun, sand, and surf of Malibu, *Beach Party* (1963), starring Frankie Avalon as Frankie and Annette Funicello as Dee Dee, was a huge hit. Its sequel, *Muscle Beach Party* (1964), drew on many of the same sites, sounds, scenarios, and stars, but bodybuilders replaced the rowdy motorcycle gang of *Beach Party* to disrupt the surfers' paradise. In *Muscle Beach Party* the rivalry between these groups for control of the beach is complicated by a romantic triangle between Dee Dee, Frankie, and an Italian contessa, Julie (Luciana Paluzzi). The zany plot is enlivened by comedians Morey Amsterdam, Buddy Hackett, and Don Rickles; the rocking rhythms of Dick Dale and His Del-Tones and Little Stevie Wonder; and the twisting frenzy of dancer Candy Johnson. Notable bodybuilders include Peter Lupus (Mr. Indiana 1960), strongman Steve Merjanian, Larry Scott (Mr. America

1962), Gene Shuey (Mr. America 1960), and Chester Yorton (who would go on to become Mr. Universe 1966).

An AIP promotional circular calls the eight musclemen "perfect representatives of the muscle cult kidded [about] in the film" and makes much of their dietary habits, which include an avoidance of starches and a preference for beef:

> Former "Mr. America" Larry Scott exists mainly on steak, cottage cheese, milk, butter and cashew nuts, while "Mr. America" Gene Shuey concentrates strictly on steak and cottage cheese. Rock Stevens, the former "Mr. Hercules" and "Mr. International Health" who portrays "Mr. Galaxy" in the musical comedy, eats only steak and cottage cheese twice daily plus 200 food supplement vitamin pills daily and a high protein special drink. The same pattern is followed by Bob Seven, Steve Merjanian, Chester Yorton, Gordon Cohn and Dan Haggerty—all of whom also have great big muscles too.

While the surfers, led by Frankie, are depicted as clean-cut all-American kids bent on having fun in the sun, the bodybuilders serve as a foil, fitting the stereotype of self-possessed muscleheads who care for little else but the size and shape of their bodies. Surfers aside, the bodybuilders provide a parody of physical culture.[13]

They are introduced as "muscles anonymous," strutting out in pink cloaks, like horses on the track. "Well if it isn't Seabiscuit," taunts Frankie. "Isn't this ridiculous?" Their coach, Don Rickles, with the unappealing cognomen of Jack Fanny (a conflation of Jack LaLanne and Vic Tanny), orders them to stand tall and look smart. "Today is the day of the latissimus dorsi!" he shouts, after which he lapses into double-talk, saying that "all muscles are beautiful. The latissimus is beautiful too because it's a muscle. . . . To make the muscles beautiful, you must always have beautiful muscles." Surfer Johnny (John Ashley) then shouts, "That creep's on my blanket! . . . I'm not afraid of those muscle-bound jerks." "Yeah, they're not for real anyway," adds Deadhead (Jody McCrea). To prove they are real, the musclemen drag Johnny away on the blanket.[14] The irony underlying this encounter is that it's the surfers who are unreal. Most of their scenes in the film either employed stock footage or stuntmen to make the stars appear athletic. "Real surfers were not overjoyed," notes beach historian Tom Lisanti, "and cringed whenever the pretty boy actors got in front of the waves with the romantic subplots."[15] Only

McCrea had surfing experience, while the diminutive Avalon, a land-lubber from inner-city Philadelphia, had difficulty lifting a nine-foot surfboard. Funicello, whose only claim to credibility was getting her hair wet in a mock surfing scene, disliked swimming and surfing and hated the beach.

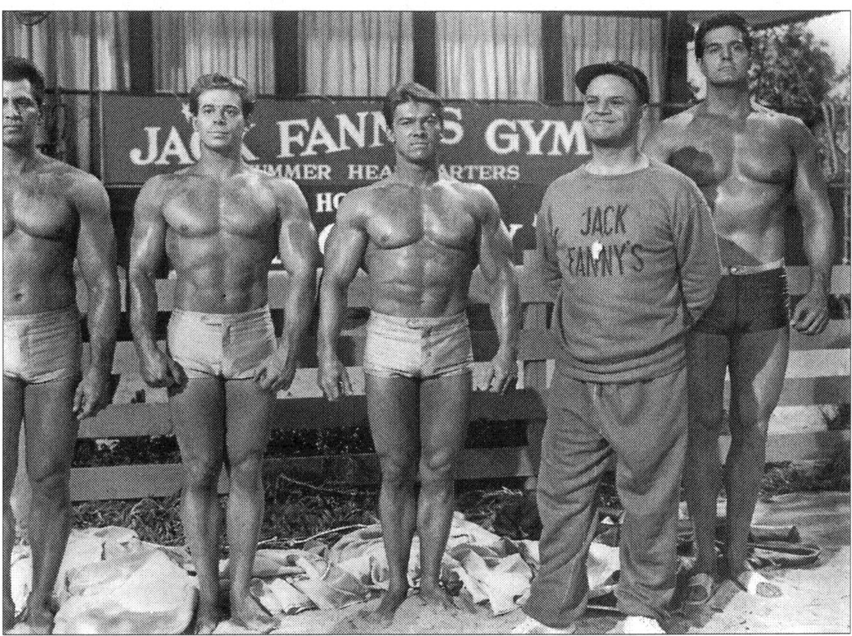

Figure 14.1. Don Rickles as trainer Jack Fanny invades the surfers' beach with his dumb but superbuff "pupils" in the 1964 film *Muscle Beach Party.* Collection of David L. Chapman.

In the next scene, on the contessa Julie's yacht, her attorney Theodore sneers, then frowns, as he watches the bodybuilders flexing on the beach. But the superrich Julie, smitten by musclemen she has seen in *Muscle Magazine,* sailed five thousand miles to meet Fanny's leading protégé, Flex Martian, aka Mr. Galaxy (Peter Lupus). "I think it's ridiculous falling in love with a picture," retorts her business manager S. Z. Matts (Buddy Hackett), who refers to Flex unflatteringly as "that beast in the flesh." Further commodification ensues when he tries to satisfy the contessa's bizarre tastes by asking Fanny whether "this magnificently shaped, perfectly carved piece of human real estate" would belong to her, then asking, "Can I buy just him, or do I have to take the whole set?"—which includes Biff, Clod, Mash, Riff, Rock, Sulk, and Tug. Julie finally meets Flex, but he seems totally obsessed with his own size, strength, and good looks. When she declares "I want to be alone with you," he responds, "Did you see this tricep—the way I can make it ripple?" Sex, or even relating to another person outside his clique, seems impossible. Although they spend most of the day together, it is obvious that sparks never fly. Flex is then escorted to his muscle compound by Fanny for a bowl of mush—and then to bed.

Julie, unfulfilled, retires to the beach, where she falls in love with a lonely Frankie, who is crooning "A Boy Needs a Girl." But their romantic rendezvous is disturbed when a sarcastic Dee Dee shows up and confronts her rival with one of the film's signature lines: "Did you run out of musclemen?" Julie's fickle taste in love interests soon becomes obvious when S. Z. gleefully announces that he had purchased "seventeen Kongs" for her. "I don't want them now," she responds. "I found someone to love." No less confounded than her aides to this reneging of a signed contract are the musclemen, who resent this insult to their lifestyle, and this sets the stage for a showdown with the pygmy surfers. Most indignant is Flex Martian. Though uninterested in a sexual encounter, he is riled over the rejection of his most coveted asset—his muscles.

Jack Fanny: She's hurt Flex's feelings.
Julie: It's not that I don't like muscles anymore, but I found something even more exciting. *Him.* (She gestures toward Frankie.)
Flex: You mean that little thing?"
Frankie: "You heard her, Gargantuan."
Jack Fanny: "You mean you would trade Gargantuan—Mr. Galaxy—for that undernourished mouse?"
Julie: "I sure would."
Jack Fanny: "You think we ain't got dignity, ain't got honor? Flex for that mouse? Well we ain't standing for it, and that can only mean one thing. War!

The scene for war shifts to Cappy's Café, where the surfers are rudely mimicking the muscle movements and poses of bodybuilders to the tunes of Dick Dale and His Del-Tones: "It's the latest dance that is going round. Flex your biceps, turn your head and you strike up a pose. Do the mashed potato and stick out your chest. Movin' in the muscle bound. And if you can't go muscle bound, do the muscle shuffle." Observing from a distance, a bodybuilder shouts, "They're doing exercises!" "Exercises my trapezius," Fanny retorts. "They're making fun of us. That's it, that's the last straw." To prepare a final assault to crush the puny upstarts with their size and strength, Fanny orders his troops back to their compound to "lift something heavy."

In the ensuing calm before the coming storm, Frankie escapes the clutches of the contessa, but no sooner does he make amends with Dee Dee than Fanny and his behemoths appear. "Onward men!" Fanny shouts. "The war has begun!" He orders his men to "break their bones, stamp on their eyes, snap their necks, twist them like a wet bathing suit—but don't hurt your muscles." Not only are their big muscles ineffective against the wily surfers, but the surfers' female allies prove surprisingly adept at manhandling. The frenzied twisting of dancer Candy Johnson is so powerful, in fact, that it sweeps the biggest muscleman, Tug (Steve Merjanian), across the room. In a final humiliation, Fanny's benefactor, the weird Mr. Strangdour (Peter Lorre), enters and introduces himself as "the strongest man in the world." He ends the melee by leading a whining Flex Martian away by the ear, calling him a "young creep" and saying he's "much too young to look at girls." Flex's unmanly response is "Don't spank me, Papa. Please don't spank me, Papa." It's a counterintuitive outcome, where physical culture becomes a travesty and muscularity is trivialized.

Critical reviews found little value in the film. The *New York Times* described it as "a tangle of vigorous young people with beautiful bodies and empty heads." The *New York Post* called its IQ level "abysmal"—with surfing, new dances, and displays of musculature "so vulgarized in this picture that it can't miss with millions of morons." *Variety* regarded *Muscle Beach Party* as "very mechanical," the only novelty being "the gallery of extraordinary musclemen—as spectacularly repulsive an array of beefcake as probably has ever crossed the screen."[16] Yet the film was a hit with young teens fantasizing about an idyllic life in the sun and sand of the Golden State. It was also a box office success, owing to producer Arkoff, who had already exploited the economic power of youthful moviegoers. Heavily promoted, it was already outdrawing *Beach Party* by 31 percent in its opening weeks.[17] Arkoff was oblivious to art and reputation, and his model was to make entertaining films that earn "enough money to finance the next movie."[18] Perhaps the biggest payoff of *Muscle Beach Party* was its social message. With no overt sex, violence, or alcoholism, it placated white, middle-class, suburban parents who feared the specter of juvenile delinquency and were as yet unaware of the drug culture looming on the horizon.[19] "In spite of Walt Disney's anxiety," insists Arkoff, "there wasn't anything more wholesome on the screen than our beach movies."[20] But the surf and sex genre soon lost its appeal and profitability as the innocence of the early 1960s gave way to the cynicism of the latter part of the decade. "Before anyone had heard of Vietnam or LSD or Lee Harvey Oswald," observe Jane and Michael Stern, "the surfers' dream of life as an endless summer really did appear to be a possibility. For a few years on the cusp of the age of Aquarius, it was a seductive ideal."[21]

However much *Muscle Beach Party* romanticized the lifestyle of surfers and the California ideal, its depiction of bodybuilding was different. But what was the movie's message? Simply that bodybuilding was a frivolous culture and bodybuilders deserved little more respect than animals or children. "Couldn't you send them to a zoo?" queries Julie in one of the more telling lines of the film.[22] Repeatedly, Jack Fanny and the men of his "muscle farm" are humiliated verbally and even physically. The film perpetuates existing stereotypes that serious weight training makes one muscle-bound, narcissistic, and witless.[23] In retrospect, special effects played an important role in sustaining these well-ingrained illusions, but for all the wrong reasons. Bodybuilders and even surfers are treated as nonentities and regarded more as props than as stars. *Muscle Beach Party* illustrates how physical culture served other agendas and was of little concern for mainstream Americans.[24]

Notes

1. Jane and Michael Stern contend that "like many other inhabitants of their decade, surfers, twisters, and party animals yearned to escape the status quo. But they had a quicker and cleaner way to reach bliss than either psychedelic drugs (too confusing) or political struggle (too hard)." Jane Stern and Michael Stern, *Sixties People*, 79.

2. See Frederick Kohner, *Gidget: The Little Girl with Big Ideas*; and Paul Wendkos, dir., *Gidget* (Los Angeles: Columbia Pictures, 1959). According to Thomas Lisanti, the combined impact of the novel and the film was huge on the development of surfing: "The novel had brought so much attention to the sport that its popularity skyrocketed. . . . It is estimated that the number of surfers in the U.S. went from approximately 2,000 to hundreds of thousands due to the success of *Gidget*." Thomas Lisanti, *Hollywood Surf and Beach Movies: The First Wave, 1959–1969*, 10.

3. Kirse Granat May, *Golden State, Golden Youth: The California Image in Popular Culture, 1955–1966*, 123; Stephen Tropiano, *Rebels & Chicks: A History of the Hollywood Teen Movie* (Washington, DC: Back Stage, 2005), 10, 79.

4. Juvenile delinquency emerged as an important public issue during the early war years from social strains on the family caused by a lack of parental supervision. James Gilbert, *A Cycle of Outrage: America's Reaction to the Juvenile Delinquent in the 1950s*, 26.

5. Joseph Bruce Gorman, *Kefauver: A Political Biography*, 98–99.

6. Data indicate that 1954–56 were the peak years for public concern. In 1955, according to cultural historian James Gilbert, about two hundred bills were pending in the US Congress relating to juvenile delinquency, largely in response to local outrage. But he concludes that observers exaggerated and misinterpreted the problem. Gilbert, *A Cycle of Outrage*, 66.

7. Gorman, *Kefauver*, 197–98. Bill Mauldin called postwar teens the "most publicized, analyzed, speculated-upon, worried-about, frowned-upon generation of teen-agers in modern times." Bill Mauldin, "Today's Teen-Agers—'What Gives?,'" *Collier's* 135, no. 2 (January 21, 1955): 46.

8. Sam Arkoff, *Flying through Hollywood by the Seat of My Pants: From the Man Who Brought You* I Was a Teenage Werewolf *and* Muscle Beach Party, 1, 4, 7. AIP president Jim Nicholson concurs, admitting that their films subscribed to the Peter Pan Syndrome and targeted men and boys, ages nineteen and younger. "These are busy pictures," he asserted. "They don't even have to make sense if they move fast enough—so long as nobody stops to analyze until he's on his way home. . . . We're out to make *moving* pictures. That's the name of the game." Alan Levy, "Peekaboo Sex, or How to Fill a Drive-in," 82, 84.

9. Arkoff notes that by 1958, with car registrations booming, there were 4,063 drive-ins, compared to only 820 in 1948, and his company tapped nearly all of them. Arkoff, *Flying through Hollywood*, 58–59.

10. Arkoff, *Flying through Hollywood*, 65, 95–96, 128–29.

11. Stanley Gordon, "California Co-eds: Beauties from Two Top Campuses," *Look* 23, no. 21 (September 29, 1959): 28; "California Lassie, Universally Classy," *Life* 53, no. 16 (October 19, 1962): 119; May, *Golden State*, 24. For classic portrayals of Southern California beach culture, see Joel Sayre, "The Body Worshipers of Muscle Beach," 34–35, 136–40; "Muscle Queen, Miss Muscle Beach, July 1954," UCLA Film and Television Archive, Los Angeles.

12. According to Annette Funicello, Clark "played a huge role" in making rock 'n' roll a strong cultural force. "Without intending to do so, he proved to parents and doubters everywhere that good, clean-cut kids could enjoy rock 'n' roll and still be good kids." She also argues that *The Mickey Mouse Club* was not merely an idealization but "an honest if exaggerated reflection of an America that, sadly, has faded into history." Annette Funicello, *A Dream Is a Wish Your Heart Makes: My Story* (New York: Hyperion, 1994), 40, 89.

13. *Muscle Beach Party*, promotional circular, MPAA/AIP 1963, Margaret Herrick Library.

14. William Asher, dir., *Muscle Beach Party* (Los Angeles: American International Pictures, 1964); all dialogue quoted herein is transcribed from the DVD (Chicago: Olive Films, under license from Twentieth Century Fox Home Entertainment / Metro Goldwyn Mayer Studios, 2015).

15. Lisanti, *Hollywood Surf and Beach Movies*, 17.

16. Bosley Crowther, "Donahue and Suzanne Pleshette in Western," *New York Times*, May 28, 1964; *New York Post*, May 28, 1964, quoted in "Muscle Beach Party," Turner

Classic Movies, June 25, 2020, http://www.tcm.com/this-month/article/202640%7C0 Muscle-Beach-Party.html; "Film Reviews: Muscle Beach Party," *Variety*, March 25, 1964.

17. The film was launched at a gala premier in San Francisco attended by Amsterdam, Avalon, Funicello, and McCrea. According to a report of the events, "Among the highlights of the three day series was a gigantic autograph party given by the stars at the world's largest shopping center, Hillsdale Center in San Mateo. More than 20,000 teenagers home on Easter vacation attended that session, with thousands more present at the afternoon teen-age 'blue-jeans' premieres of 'Muscle Beach Party' in San Francisco and Oakland. Jet flown from Hollywood into more than 40 cites, nine stars and five company officials chalked up a record 286 radio interviews, 215 TV appearances and 197 newspaper interviews to launch 'Muscle Beach Party' as another box office blockbuster." "Muscle Beach Party," *Greater Amusements*, April 24, 1964, 8.

18. Arkoff, *Flying through Hollywood*, 4. Much of a film's success, argues Jim Nicholson, depends on title choice. AIP's simple formula was that "70% of a picture's appeal to an audience is in the title," and the corollary was that "one good title deserves another." Jim Nicholson, quoted in Levy, "Peekaboo Sex," 81.

19. Though the supposed juvenile delinquency crisis in the 1950s was largely chimeric, James Gilbert attaches its significance to AIP's *Bikini Beach* series as the "most benign spin-off of the delinquency genre." Gilbert, *A Cycle of Outrage*, 193.

20. Arkoff, *Flying through Hollywood*, 131. Despite the popularity of its beach offerings, the filmography of AIP reveals that it continued producing low-budget exploitation movies throughout the 1960s and into later decades. "American International Pictures," filmography, Internet Movie Database, http://www.imdb.com/company/co0022781/.

21. Lisanti, *Hollywood Surf and Beach Movies*, 26; Stern and Stern, *Sixties People*, 80–81. The sleazy side of bodybuilding was quickly mined in other less prestigious works like the sexploitation movie *Beauty and the Body* (1963), starring second-string bodybuilder Kip Behar and a bevy of giggling, jiggling women. The film, which is supposed to be an anthropological depiction of weird things one could find in Los Angeles, was a sad knock-off of the Italian *Mondo Cane* series.

22. Not atypical of this era was the attitude expressed by the business manager of fitness guru Jack LaLanne, that "people tend to associate a muscular body with a muscle-bound mind." Huston Horn, "LaLanne: A Treat and a Treatment," *Sports Illustrated* 13, no. 25 (December 19, 1960): 31.

23. Tolga Ozyurtcu argues that beach party movies, however superficial, helped create and sustain the myth upon which the bodybuilding empire of Joe Weider was constructed and sustained in Southern California in subsequent decades. Tolga Ozyurtcu, "Flex Marks the Spot: Histories of Muscle Beach" (PhD diss., University of Texas at Austin, 2014), 96–97.

24. *Muscle Beach Party* was not the first film to make fun of big muscular lugs. In the 1951 opus *Mister Universe*, Vince Edwards plays a good-looking, naive, and muscular young man who wins an elaborately staged physique contest. Edwards, along with veteran actors Jack Carson and Bert Lahr (and a phalanx of colorful pro wrestlers like

Delightful Dave, Gorilla Hogan, and Newton the Teuton) join to mock bodybuilders, phony wrestling matches, and the people who encourage them. The film shows that the distance between true strength and muscularity and its various simulacra was broad and (in this case) laughable.

XV. PURSUING THE AMERICAN DREAM

The American dream is real. I know because it happened to me.

—Arnold Schwarzenegger, "Living the American Dream"

I want to be remembered as a man of raging optimism, who believes in the American dream.

—Sylvester Stallone, quoted in Marsha Daly,
Sylvester Stallone: An Illustrated Life

THE LIVES AND film careers of Arnold Schwarzenegger and Sylvester Stallone are often equated with the fulfillment of the American dream. "Arnold" is easily recognized by his first name alone, "Sly" by his nickname, and Schwarzenegger is one of few foreign surnames not questioned by a computer spell-check. The two men are synonymous with muscles in the movies.

Muscles That Dazzle

A self-made man who migrated to the United States as a bodybuilding sensation, Schwarzenegger won fourteen world physique titles, married into the family of President John F. Kennedy, and skyrocketed to film fame in blockbuster hits like *Conan the Barbarian* (1982) and *The Terminator* (1984) in which he displayed his muscularity. From Hollywood he muscled his way into politics, gaining election twice as governor of California.

Born Arnold Alois Schwarzenegger in 1947 in Thal bei Graz, Austria, he had a disciplined upbringing; was proficient in skiing, ice skating, and soccer; and at age thirteen started lifting weights. He rapidly rose to the top of European bodybuilding during the 1960s, winning multiple Mr. Universe titles with his fifty-seven-inch chest and twenty-two-inch arms. In 1968 bodybuilding mogul Joe Weider brought Schwarzenegger to the United States, where, within a decade, he became the greatest physique champion of his era. It was his first step in pursuing the American dream, which stemmed from reading muscle magazines about men with well-developed bodies who achieved success in the movies. Most impressive was the "rough, massive look" of British champion Reg Park:

> The man was an animal. That's the way I wanted to be—ultimately: big. . . . I dreamed of big deltoids, big pecs, big thighs, big calves; I wanted every muscle to explode and be huge. I dreamed about being gigantic. Reg Park was the epitome of that dream, the biggest, most powerful person in bodybuilding.
>
> From then on in my mid-teens, I kept my batteries charged with the adventure movies of Steve Reeves, Mark Forrest, Brad Harris, Gordon Mitchell, and Reg Park. I admired Reg Park more than the others. He was rugged, everything I thought a man should be. I recall seeing him for the first time on the screen. The film was *Hercules and the Vampires*, a picture in which the hero had to rid the earth of an invasion of thousands of bloodthirsty vampires. Reg Park looked so magnificent in the role of Hercules I was transfixed. And, sitting there in the theater, I knew that was going to be me.[1]

For Schwarzenegger it was an intense experience of absorptive realism that awakened a lifelong passion for achievement. His California girlfriend, Barbara Outland Baker, confirms that Reg Park "captured his visceral imagination." That he could earn a lucrative income through his physique inspired him to see all seven of Park's *Hercules* films, and "his ambition seemed encoded into his DNA." A defining moment occurred when he was "watching himself win the Mr. Olympia title on the popular *Wide World of Sports* television program. . . . The idea of Big Screen success grew much deeper roots that Saturday afternoon."[2]

Schwarzenegger's first serious venture into filmdom occurred by happenstance when Weider touted his acting ability to New York producers looking for a muscular lead in an adventure movie, *Hercules in New York*, assuring them that Schwarzenegger had been a Shakespearean actor in Vienna and had outstanding stage presence. Schwarzenegger eagerly seized the opportunity, and as Hercules played opposite veteran Arnold Stang, who portrayed a street vendor named Pretzie. Schwarzenegger recalls it as "a low-budget spoof on the big sword-and-sandal epics," in which his character is accidently sent by his father Zeus on a lightning bolt to earth, where he enters bodybuilding and encounters the challenges of an immortal demigod plopped into a world of mortals.[3] Biographer Larry Leamer calls the film a "campy romp," with Hercules attired in what appears to be giant Pampers and a sheet and speaking pidgin English. "Arnold had none of the magical aura of a great undiscovered star shining through this most dismal of projects," Leamer notes. What he projected was "an immense likeability, a gentle giant driving his chariot through Times Square, and a subtle, ironic distance—both crucial aspects of his eventual screen persona."[4] Critics panned the film. Even Weider's in-house editor, Rick Wayne, though wowed by the star's "all-action" scenes and dazzling muscle displays, was restrained: "It's as though the young Austrian phenomenon has been set a series of Herculean tasks with very little time in which to perform them." Yet Schwarzenegger claims he learned "what acting is all about" when shooting a farewell scene between Hercules and Pretzie. "I really got into it, just like they always talk about in acting. The director came over afterward and said, 'I got goose bumps when you did that.'" He predicted a promising career for Schwarzenegger. In a 2012 interview, however, Schwarzenegger observed "this political battle over (torture technique) water-boarding at places like Guantanamo Bay. I think they (interrogators) should just say, 'Hey, if you guys don't talk, you'll have to see Hercules in New York.' I guarantee those guys would talk much faster with that treatment."[5]

To Schwarzenegger's credit, he started to take acting as seriously as his bodybuilding. He not only took lessons but also accepted a more serious role in a movie based on a novel by Charles Gaines that explored the bodybuilding subculture. When informed he had to lose thirty pounds to be less intimidating to audiences and other actors, he decided he had to "let go of my vision of myself as the world's most muscular guy." Unable to "have it both ways," he retired from competition.[6] In *Stay Hungry* (1976), set in Birmingham, Alabama, Schwarzenegger plays Joe Santo, a Mr. Austria training to be Mr. Universe. The story involves an attempt by a young Southerner (Jeff Bridges) to take over the gym where Schwarzenegger is training on behalf of a shady real estate syndicate, but he falls in love with the receptionist (Sally Field), foils the plot of his bosses, and becomes a fitness convert. Struggling to understand the point of the film, Vincent Canby reported that it "isn't all bad." In fact, he noted there were "some awfully good things in it," including performances by Bridges and Field and less assuredly Schwarzenegger who appears as "a nice, honorable young man who appears to be trapped inside a huge, grotesquely muscled body that has no relation to the conventional head on top of it." Disconcerting to Canby was how, unlike other films, *Stay Hungry* intended to respect bodybuilding, "and as long as Mr. Schwarzenegger keeps his clothes on, it does. However, when the camera, at the end of the film, roams over physiques so carefully and lovingly exaggerated they seem about to burst, you suspect the movie of being a freak show that couldn't care less about its freaks." No less jolting was a chase scene of elite bodybuilders pouring into downtown Birmingham. The would-be actors take advantage of this attention to stage impromptu posing displays, which are imitated by the crowd. Bodybuilder Roger Callard recalls the director "screaming over his megaphone, 'Please do not touch the bodybuilders!' People were rushing us, even scratching us!"[7] But *Stay Hungry* was a box office hit, signifying a defining moment in the fitness revolution emerging in the 1970s and the film career of Schwarzenegger, who received a Golden Globe Award for Best Acting Debut.

Stay Hungry also served as segue for an even greater muscle movie with Schwarzenegger as star. Inspired by the creative niche he found in the subculture of bodybuilding, Gaines collaborated with photographer George Butler to produce a nonfiction book titled *Pumping Iron: The Art and Sport of Bodybuilding* (1974). They likened their experience to nineteenth-century explorers "because we found bodybuilding to be as primeval and unmapped as parts of Labrador." It was an activity that advertised itself with "consummate tackiness" and "occupied the same shadowy corners in national consciousness as dildos and raincoat exhibitionists."[8] The book, Leamer notes, was an unlikely best seller and the first exposure for many readers to bodybuilding: "There is no stench of sweat, no foul epithets, no gay hustlers, no steroid dealers, no diuretics, and no sore losers. The book is a classic of sports journalism, but as much as it purports to be the truth about bodybuilding, the words and photos are an ideal that the sport has rarely achieved. And above it all stands Arnold. . . . Nobody posed better. No bodybuilder was better at creating the illusion of physical perfection."[9]

The movie version of *Pumping Iron* that followed in 1977 reveals Schwarzenegger preparing and ultimately winning his sixth consecutive Mr. Olympia title against rival Lou Ferrigno and other champions. Playing himself came naturally to Schwarzenegger, but he chose to avoid any one-dimensional approach to bodybuilding by focusing on his personality. "My model was Muhammad Ali," he recalls. "What separated him from other heavyweights wasn't only his boxing genius. . . . Ali was always willing to say and do memorable and outrageous things. But outrageousness means nothing unless you have the substance to back it up—you can't get away with

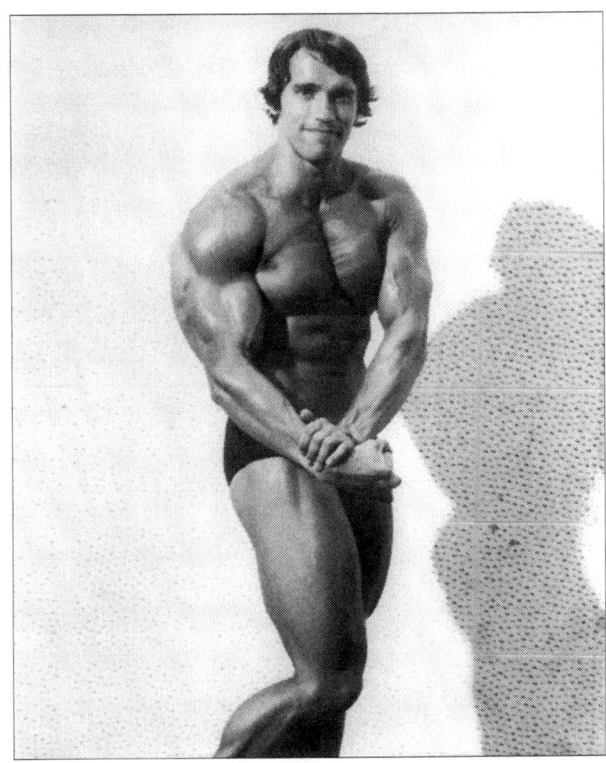

Figure 15.1. Arnold Schwarzenegger in *Stay Hungry* (1976). Courtesy of Mark Joules and David New.

it if you're a loser."[10] The 1975 Mr. Olympia Contest in South Africa provided the setting for the film, but during the editing process the production ran out of money. So Butler staged a fundraising event at the Whitney Museum of American Art in February 1976 that featured a photo exhibit, a panel discussion by local art, literature and medical professors, and a living sculpture display by Schwarzenegger and two other bodybuilders on rotating platforms. The overflow audience, largely of physique aficionados, greeted Schwarzenegger's appearance with "deafening" applause and "loud shouts for Arnold! Arnold! Arnold!" reported Al Antuck. The ensuing discussion centered mostly on the ancient Greek ideal of beauty. But the academics were dismissive of its modern variant, and one of them likened the bodybuilders' poses to "personification of 19th century camp. I do not find it beautiful."[11] The event proved far more successful in fundraising than anticipated, but was considered questionable with regard to taste and acceptance by the non-bodybuilding public trying to understand how this flagrant display of muscle fit into American culture.

This reaction was reflected somewhat in the film reviews. In the *New York Times* Richard Eder seemed underwhelmed and skeptical about the muscle spectacle, calling it "an interesting, rather slick and excessively long documentary" and Schwarzenegger "a handsome man with a body as knotted as an especially lumpy vegetable soup." As an outsider, Eder's realization from the film was that "the object of all that weight-lifting is neither strength nor prowess, but appearance." Gary Arnold provided a more insightful assessment in the *Washington Post*, writing, "Schwarzenegger is the first personality since Bruce Lee who might become a unique and credible physical star, idolized in particular by kids but enjoyed and admired by a vast cross section of the public. In his own way his physical self-possession seems as remarkable as Lee's, or Fred Astaire's. Like them, Schwarzenegger can make unusual physical attributes appear to be the most natural thing in the world." Most effusive in praising the film was Richard Schickel in *Time*: "It is a very good film, beautifully shot and edited, intelligently structured and—to risk what will surely seem at first a highly inappropriate term—charming."[12] In retrospect, Butler considers their film as successful not so much for artistic or entertainment merit as its groundbreaking impact. What was "fun and interesting" was that "we went for an audience outside of the sport and we defined bodybuilding to a world who knew nothing about bodybuilding." Likewise, Leamer views it more as a crucial step in constructing a Schwarzenegger iconography: "Gaines and Butler helped elevate Arnold to a unique place, not only in bodybuilding but in American popular culture."[13]

Indeed, *Pumping Iron* provided a jumping-off point for Schwarzenegger's movie career by helping to legitimize bodybuilding. Showy muscles, once anathema to moviegoers, soon became a desirable staple. As Schwarzenegger explains, producer Ed Pressman and partner Terrence Malick were looking for an actor to play the 1930s pulp fiction warrior Conan "when they saw a rough cut of *Pumping Iron*. Right away they decided I would be perfect for Conan." Upon signing the contract for *Conan the Barbarian* in 1978, Schwarzenegger was "confident that I would be among the million dollar players in the movie business." To prepare for his role, Schwarzenegger undertook a training routine formulated by director John Milius that was unlike anything in bodybuilding. He was subjected to "masters in martial arts, armorers, stunt people who were horse-riding specialists. For three months I was tutored in broadsword combat two hours a day. Unlike the samurai sword, which is very light and very sharp—designed for lopping off heads and limbs and slicing bodies in half—the broadsword is massive and double edged. . . . I had to learn which parts of the body are vulnerable to attack and how to swing the sword, not to mention what happens if you miss." Schwarzenegger also had trainers in Japanese *kenjutsu* (swordsmanship) and the Brazilian martial arts form capoeira. Additionally, "A stuntman taught me climbing techniques, how to fall and roll, and how to jump fifteen feet onto a mat. . . . The training was as intense and time consuming as getting ready for a bodybuilding competition and I took to it completely." Now it was time for his big break. He likened his selection as Conan to winning his first major physique title.[14]

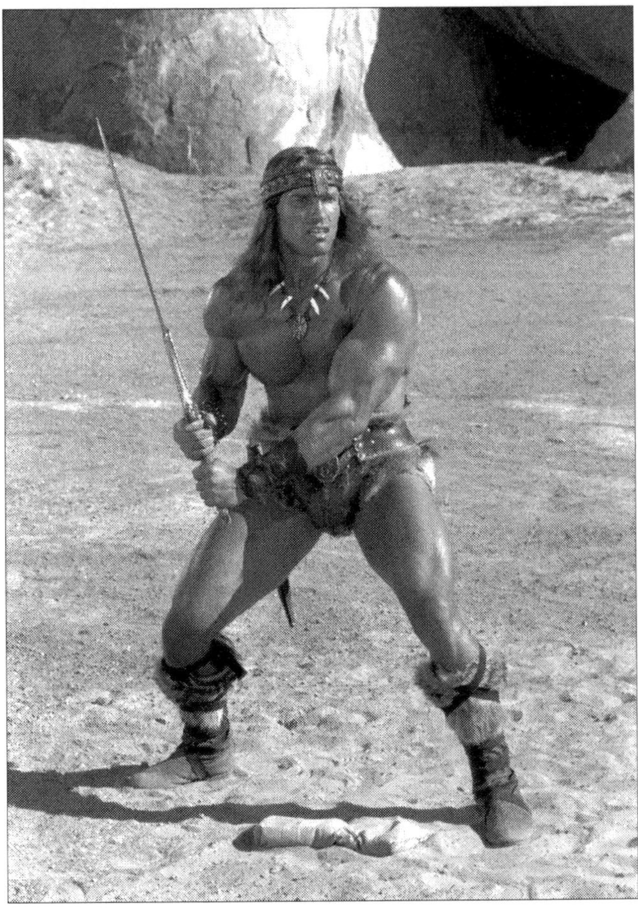

Figure 15.2. Wielding the Sword of Crom, Arnold Schwarzenegger looks appropriately fearsome in the 1982 feature *Conan the Barbarian*. Collection of David L. Chapman.

What Schwarzenegger did not anticipate was that his training would lead him back temporarily to bodybuilding competition. Although recruited by CBS to provide color commentary for the 1980 Mr. Olympia Contest in Sydney, he repeatedly assured friends that he had no intention of coming out of retirement. Yet during the summer, to build a body reflecting the muscular image of Conan, thoughts of reentering competition emerged. As Schwarzenegger recalls, his role required transformation from "a lean young warrior of about 215 pounds to a full-bodied, robust king" of about 230. He started training in August, but when the production schedule was moved up to October from the following January, he had to "get big, and fast." He adopted a rigorous "double-split, six-days-a-week" program, and friends started saying that he was within 80 to 90 percent of contest shape and should consider competing in Sydney. Joe Weider concurred, reminding him, "You're a champion. If you can get in shape and want to enter the contest, go ahead." Schwarzenegger's decision came as a Zen moment:

> One day, just a few weeks before the contest, I woke up and the idea of competing was fixed firmly in my mind, "Yes," my mind seemed to be saying to me, almost beyond my control, "you must compete." . . . The same thing happened one day when I suddenly realized I should become an actor. There's an inevitability about such a feeling that you can't analyze or you'll destroy it. It's just a gut instinct.[15]

In the ensuing contest, Schwarzenegger's hastily prepared physique did not compare favorably with others, whose bodies had advanced during his five-year absence, yet he eked out a victory with the help of a rigged judging panel. "For the first time in his heralded career," reported Jack Neary, "Arnold was booed—by approximately 40% of the more than 2000 fans who filled the posh seats of the opera house." Schwarzenegger, however, seemed oblivious to the swirl of controversy. "You know the applause was very clearly overwhelming for me," he recollected decades later.[16] Yet the experience convinced him that his future stardom was no longer in bodybuilding but acting.

These inclinations were reinforced by Schwarzenegger's off-the-set interactions with veteran actor James Earl Jones, who played Conan's foe, the villainous Thulsa Doom. Jones was a Shakespearean actor with a powerful voice who had won an Academy Award nomination as boxer Jack Johnson in *The Great White Hope* (1970). "I spent days hanging out in his trailer,"

Schwarzenegger recalls. "He wanted to keep in shape, so I helped him with his training, and in return, he coached me on my acting." Schwarzenegger's swordsmanship became useful in a scene in which he encountered a thirty-six-foot remote-controlled boa constrictor. In one swift motion he had to grab a heavy broadsword and "strike a precise point behind the snake's head to trigger the exploding blood pack. . . . I'm proud to say that two and a half years of training paid off, and I nailed it in the first take."[17] Part of Schwarzenegger's secret of success, claims director Milius, was that he wanted his fledgling star to not only *act* Conan but *be* Conan: "I wanted him to think as a Zen warrior. When he was Conan, he owned Conan, it was part of him." Much like Kirk Douglas and Gene Kelly before him, Schwarzenegger never lost his sense of self. "He never lost his self-esteem or his ego," observed Milius. "He was always completely Arnold. . . . I just made suggestions and he *knew* what to do."[18] Unlike many movie and bodybuilding buffs who were incapable of separating fantasy from reality, Schwarzenegger was able temporarily to absorb the reality of his character. And unlike peplum film stars, Schwarzenegger always spoke with his own voice.

Producer Dino De Laurentiis was no less complimentary about Schwarzenegger's promotional skills, which owed to his bodybuilding background and international appeal; he "knew how to sell the movie so people would really want to go out and see it." This appeal was reflected at the Houston and Las Vegas test screenings. "The studio had been banking on die-hard fans of *Conan* in the comics and fantasy novels to make the movie a success," Schwarzenegger explains. "What Universal didn't count on was my guys: the bodybuilders. They made up probably a third of the audience" in Las Vegas. "Without them, the film might have gotten maybe an 88, but with them it was again 93, just like Houston. . . . After that night, *Conan* was unstoppable."[19] Critics, however, were not so enamored of Schwarzenegger or this nontraditional film genre. Putting the best face on what he regarded as "a perfect fantasy for the alienated preadolescent," Roger Ebert called the movie "a triumph of production design, set decoration, special effects and makeup. At a time when most of the big box-office winners display state-of-the-art technology, 'Conan' ranks right up there with the best." *TV Guide* called it a "sweaty, musclebound ode to mythic masculinity." Vincent Canby, notable for his condescending remarks about Schwarzenegger in *Stay Hungry*, was scathing in his *Conan* review: "Though the landscapes are sometimes pretty, the images are as empty as the narrative, which, among other wrong things, begins on a fairly exciting note and then becomes progressively less suspenseful until it just sort of stops. This could be a film to be run backward." As for the character Conan, "Mr. Schwarzenegger looks overdressed even when he is undressed, but then there is no way he can unzip that overdeveloped physique and slip into something more comfortable."[20] Yet success for *Conan the Barbarian* was determined ultimately at the box office, which registered $79.1 million in receipts, a nearly fourfold increase over its $20 million budget.[21]

Its toned-down sequel, *Conan the Destroyer* (1984), elicited slightly less unfriendly receptions. *Variety* called it "the ideal sword and sorcery picture," while *Time Out* welcomed the lack of intellectual pretensions and gratuitous sex of its predecessor, fulfilling "creator Robert E. Howard's preference for small minds in big bodies—a requirement Schwarzenegger fills wonderfully." Ebert, too, welcomed this less gloomy version of the heroic saga, noting that Conan "doesn't take himself as seriously. He's not just a muscle-bound superman, but a superstitious half-savage who gets very nervous in the presence of magic." Canby, though unrepentant of earlier anti-Schwarzenegger sentiments, called this Conan "a sort of cut-rate Hercules" and seemed pleased with the special effects and fewer decapitations.[22] Again Schwarzenegger's movie muscle was demonstrated at the box office, yielding an estimated $100 million from an $18 million budget.[23] Ebert and Canby concurred that this film could lead to an indefinite series of Conan adventures, possibly rivaling Tarzan in fulfilling moviegoers' ongoing need for a noble savage.

That no further sequels transpired owes to Schwarzenegger getting sidetracked to star in *The Terminator*, a science-fiction action film in which showy or functional muscles were expendable. For Schwarzenegger, now nearing the age of forty and feeling the effects from decades of intense training, "the idea of going from muscles to mainstream action movies gained stronger and stronger appeal." In this instance, his performance as a machine would be computer programmed: "When he kills, there will be absolutely no expression on the face, not joy, not victory, not anything." It would require just action, with fewer lines spoken than in the Conan films—just eighteen, Schwarzenegger noted. "Here was a project that would get me out of a loincloth and into real clothes! The selling point would be the acting and the action, not just me ripping off my shirt. The Terminator was the ultimate tough character, with cool outfits and cool shades. I knew it would make me shine." Training for Schwarzenegger's new role consisted of perfecting his technical skills; he repeatedly stripped and reassembled guns until his actions were automatic. He spent "endless hours at the shooting range, learning techniques for a whole arsenal of different weapons. . . . You have to practice each move thirty, forty, fifty times until you get it. From the bodybuilding days on, I learned that everything is reps and mileage." Beyond technology, awe-inspiring action was supplied not by Schwarzenegger's muscles but by "stunt guys" whom director James Cameron found nearly indispensable.[24] Yet this film firmly established Schwarzenegger's acting identity and generated the iconic line, "I'll be back."

The Terminator attracted critical acclaim and topped the box office for two weeks. Significantly, over half the total gross of $78.4 million came from the foreign market, a notable feature of *Conan the Barbarian* and *Conan the Destroyer.*[25] It coincided with the trajectory of his film career and image he would project off-screen. Critical to developing his public persona was Charlotte Parker, of the public relations firm of Rogers and Kallin, who started working with Schwarzenegger after his first Conan film. "He was masterful," she recalls, adding,

> Initially there were a lot of people who thought of him as a sort of dumb joke, a big dumb bodybuilder. But as I got to know him I saw what a superbly intelligent interesting dynamic person he was, and I began to understand his business acumen. Then I began to put together that whole campaign of him being a businessman and I had him dress in suits. That whole thing was under my purview, and I moved into it and created that image. I think that helped a lot in terms of people understanding who he really was and how smart he was. . . . Together we were an incredible team. He had a tremendous self-understanding of where he wanted to go, and I was able to execute those things, and have visions of my own.[26]

Laurence Leamer concurs that Parker had an immense influence on Schwarzenegger and Hollywood executives' acceptance of *The Terminator* as greater than its commercial value: "This was Parker's contribution to the *perception* of the film in the City of Dreams." For Leamer, "not the reality but the public perception of reality had become the higher truth. Hollywood is not only a creator of myth but a consumer of it."[27]

Commando (1985) and *The Predator* (1987) were Schwarzenegger's final two muscle movies, yet he never lost his bodybuilder image. He admits that his continued attraction as a muscular action star was reinforced by an increasingly buff Sylvester Stallone, whose *Rambo: First Blood Part II* and *Rocky*

IV appeared the same year as *Commando*. Both of their films were box office blockbusters and received critical acclaim. In *Commando*, Schwarzenegger plays a retired special agent who takes on a band of South American mercenaries who are holding his daughter hostage until he can carry out a political assassination to restore the dictator he was instrumental in overthrowing. It is a violent film, where Schwarzenegger single-handedly kills scores of well-armed bad guys and displays superhuman strength, breaking chains, lifting a telephone booth, and holding a fully grown man over the edge of a cliff with one arm. Glimpses of his physique, aside from a brief early scene, are masked by a tight green shirt and ammo vest. In the climactic final fight, the illusion of action is facilitated by a blend of special effects, stuntmen, and lots of facial rather than full body shots. Virtually no direct muscular action can be attributed to Schwarzenegger alone. Most distinctive is his employment of dialogue; enhanced by bits of dark humor, close-up expressions, and the memorable "I'll be back" line from *Terminator*, words were replacing body movements as the defining aspect of Schwarzenegger's screen persona.

Likewise, in *The Predator*, Schwarzenegger employs his body to complement his burgeoning acting skills. In the film his character, Alan "Dutch" Schaeffer, leads a team of commandos on a rescue mission for possible survivors of a helicopter crash in a South American jungle and find themselves hunted down by an extraterrestrial predator. Again, special effects and stunt performers loom large in lieu of any spectacular muscular action from Schwarzenegger. His physique is still striking, but views of it are limited to repeated exposure of his arms, often toting a weapon, with his torso partially hidden behind an ammo vest. This fixation with Schwarzenegger's arms is notable in an arm-wrestling match in an opening scene with Carl Weathers (best known for his role as Apollo Creed in four *Rocky* films), yet neither actor shows any of the strain normally exhibited in any real such contest. Schwarzenegger's comfort level is further sustained by humorous quips and cigar smoking, traits that carry over to the actor's real life. And the Hollywood debut of professional wrestler Jesse Ventura to play his comrade-in-arms reinforces his tough-guy image. Although Schwarzenegger would retain his reputation as a bodybuilder, these films were more about manliness than muscle.

Perhaps even more important to his cinematic impact is the legacy left by Schwarzenegger. Other stars—notably, Chuck Norris, Claude Van Damme, and Bruce Willis—were being lured into the muscle action mode. "Even guys like Clint Eastwood, who were doing action movies all along, started bulking up and ripping off their shirts and showing off muscles," notes Schwarzenegger. "In all this, the body was key. The era had arrived where muscular men were viewed as attractive. Looking physically heroic became the aesthetic." Just the appearance of powerful muscles conveyed the impression of superhuman capabilities: "No matter how outlandish the stunt, you would think, 'Yeah, he could do that.'"[28] In a 2016 overview of his career from *Hercules in New York* to *Predator*, English pundit Jake Wilson suggests that as his career developed, Schwarzenegger

> proved he was much more than just unisex eye-candy, developing his aesthetic allure into real Hollywood charisma. Arnold would come to blossom in attracting a younger market, mixing action roles in *Terminator 2* and *Total Recall* with *Kindergarten Cop* and *Junior*. Not only did *Kindergarten Cop* have no right to be as good as it is, but Arnold had no right to be so enjoyable to watch. His size became a point of contrast rather than one of awe, towering over others without menace but humour. He became his own character, a phenomenon for a reason beyond his look. He became the epitome of the American Dream, persevering and succeeding more than anyone thought he could.[29]

Yet Schwarzenegger's appeal owed much to the success of the action genre popularized by Sylvester Stallone in the early 1980s. Though he vehemently denied it, "much of his publicity and positioning campaign had linked him with Stallone," concludes Leamer. "The reality was that Parker's plan had worked brilliantly."[30] Schwarzenegger framed his muscular persona to become a permanent fixture in the Hollywood firmament.

Muscles That Do

Sylvester Stallone found a different muscular route to the American dream. As a youth growing up in Maryland, he struggled to overcome a speech defect and personality disorders. "I was not an attractive child," he recalls, "I was sickly and I even had rickets. My personality was abhorrent to the other children. So I enjoyed my own company and did a lot of fantasizing." His vivid imagination hampered him from distinguishing fantasy from reality. The popular comic-book hero Superboy became Stallone's idol, leading him to devise his own costume at age eight and to jump off the roof of the family home at eleven. His rebellious temperament led a therapist to diagnose him incorrigible and destined for a reformatory or jail. Biographer Marsha Daly recognizes the movies as a childhood escape for Stallone, writing, "Lost in the illusions of the silver screen, he could be anybody or anything from a hero to the handsome leading man finding sexy and beautiful women. The one movie that left the greatest impression on him was *Hercules*, starring Steve Reeves as the strongest man in the universe. Like a lot of thirteen-year-old boys, Sly wanted to rescue pretty maidens and do good deeds that would be appreciated by weaker mortals." Delusions of emulating Hercules led to an interest in training at a Philadelphia gym operated by his divorced mother Jacqueline. His father Frank provided negative reinforcement, saying, "You weren't born with much of a brain, so you'd better develop your body." Stallone went on to complete his education at a Pennsylvania high school for troubled youth, where he played football and excelled in boxing.[31]

To avoid homelessness, he accepted a leading role in *The Party at Kitty and Stud's* (1970), a soft-core porn film in which he first displayed his body on-screen. In succeeding years he played in numerous theater and cinema productions, the most significant being a starring role in *The Lords of Flatbush* (1974), with Henry Winkler, who would go on to fame as Fonzie in the TV series *Happy Days*. Stallone's role as a motorcycle gang member did not require lots of muscle so much as looking bigger and tougher than his five-foot-ten frame suggested. Toward this end, he started training at the local Jack LaLanne Health Spa. Although his "pumping up" proved adequate, it was insufficient for the muscleman role producers envisioned for *Stay Hungry*, which set the stage for Schwarzenegger's cinematic career and longtime rivalry with Stallone.[32] Prior to moving to the West Coast in 1974, and with his career going nowhere, Stallone turned to writing. But his scripts were "entrenched in pessimism"—to fit America's mood as the Vietnam War was ending—and dictated that "all the heroes must die in the end and go down in the one big blaze of glory." After realizing that his writing was "trite" and "simply yielding to a vogue," Stallone rediscovered himself: "What did I really enjoy seeing up on the screen? I enjoyed heroism. I enjoyed great love. I enjoyed stories of dignity, of courage, of man's ability to rise above his station and take life by the throat and not let go until he succeeded." This self-realization culminated on March 15, 1975, when Stallone attended the Muhammad Ali / Chuck Wepner fight in Richfield, Ohio. As Stallone writes, "Wepner, a battling bruising type of club fighter who had never really made the big, big time, was now having his shot. But the fight was not regarded as a serious battle. It was called a public joke. He would barely go three rounds, most of the predictions said. Well, the history books will read that he went fifteen rounds and he established himself as one of the few men who had ever gone the distance with Muhammad Ali and he can hold his head up high forever no matter what happens." Wepner would provide the inspiration for Stallone's story of Rocky Balboa, soon to become one of the greatest screen characterizations of muscle. "He was America's child," Stallone explains. "He was to the seventies what Chaplin's Little Tramp was to the twenties."[33] For Marsha Daly, the fight was a Cinderella story that transformed Stallone's career: "Sly saw a lot of himself in Chuck Wepner. Somewhere in the deepest regions of his subconscious, Rocky was born that night."[34] And if Rocky was born, Stallone was reborn as an actor destined for stardom.

After much haggling with United Artists over sale of the script and Stallone's demand to play the lead, he delved into boxing culture. He hired a trainer who whipped him into shape, putting him on a rigorous schedule from 4:00 a.m. to 6:00 p.m. lifting weights, running, jumping rope, calisthenics, and sparring. "I didn't know how I was going to fool the public into thinking that I was a professional fighter with twelve to fifteen years' experience," Stallone admits. "It wasn't going to be easy because I couldn't even fool myself. I was clumsy. I couldn't hit the speed bag. My timing on the heavy bag was ridiculous; I continually sprained my wrist and bent my thumbs back and brought smiles to the faces of observing fighters." He also studied thousands of feet of fight footage, concluding that "boxing is a muscular dance of sorts." The secret was to go with the flow. To play his partner, Apollo Creed, Stallone chose former professional football player Carl Weathers, whom he judged to have "one of the finer bodies in the world; it's perfectly sculptured—a natural body that was perfect for the champion." He worked with Weathers daily to perfect his fighting skills and was induced by the director to utilize a stunt coordinator to further fool the public. But to impart emotion into each scene, Stallone became his own choreographer. His concern was to "submerge myself far enough into this fantasy, into this character, to make the audience, and me, believe."[35] However contrived, it had to look real.

To this end, a training montage was included, showing Stallone running past familiar Philadelphia landmarks and getting smashed in the gut by a medicine ball so hard that his pain would "register as real." Likewise, he was scripted to perform two-hand push-ups in the ring. "But something crazy happens every time that camera rolls and before I knew it, I was flying from one hand to another doing an exercise that no boxer in his right mind would ever do," Stallone recalled. "I think I inflamed every joint in my body." For the memorable scene of him punching slabs of beef in a meat locker, Stallone had his hands taped to prevent broken bones. "But after eight hours, the cold penetrated the bandages and hitting the meat finally caused me to crack a knuckle and drive it back into the middle of my hand." The film's most dramatic moments feature Stallone sprinting along the pier and ascending the steps of the Philadelphia Museum of Art. He was concerned about having enough speed to convey dynamism, but when the camera started to roll, "I felt my feet moving so fast that I thought I was going to topple forward and scrape my teeth along the asphalt until they were nothing but stumps." That Stallone had trained his body so well that he could lose himself in his character enhanced the film's impact. That it could also have the same effect on those observing the action was evident in a serious incident after filming the final round. The script called for each fighter to be carried from the ring by respective fans:

> We had hired stunt men to play the individuals who would hoist us up and carry us out of the arena while we were surrounded by the extras but the scene did not go according to plan. As Carl was picked up and carried out of the ring, I saw several hundred people converge on him and I could see hands groping up toward him and fists lashing out and the man that played his trainer, Tony Burton, and his corner men were also being punched and jabbed. And then it was my turn to go into these . . . over-zealous fans. . . . In those few minutes, the crowd had inflicted more pain on Carl and myself than all the training and the four days of fighting combined.[36]

For self-preservation's sake, the end of the fight was reshot in the ring. "America did fall in love with Stallone," notes Daly; the public was "won over because they mistakenly believed he really was Rocky." And Roger Ebert, in his review of the film, wrote, "It involves us emotionally, it makes us commit ourselves: We find, maybe to our surprise after remaining detached during so many movies, that this time we care."[37] With an estimated budget of only $1 million, *Rocky* earned $225 million, becoming the highest-grossing picture for 1976; it also garnered seven Academy Award nominations and three wins, including Best Picture.[38]

This widespread adulation enabled moviegoers to vicariously live the American dream. It also had the effect of nurturing the once fragile ego of Stallone, who became too famous too fast. According to Daly, his "halo began to slip . . . Hollywood could not help noticing the subtle change in Sly—from a modest, appreciative, level-headed young writer/actor to a high-handed, arrogant egomaniac."[39] The most unnerving aspect of this newly created persona was its emotional toll, leading to the breakup of his marriage and the need to satisfy unrealistic public expectations for more cinematic miracles. Sylvester, whose name became synonymous with Rocky, precipitously seized on a script about the entanglements of a Hoffa-like Cleveland Teamster with organized crime and the government. When *F.I.S.T.* (which stood for Federation of Inter-State Truckers) was released in 1978, it was greeted with Andrew Sarris's *Village Voice* review, "Waking Up from the Dream," which castigated Stallone as "miscast as Hoffa" and unable to get inside the firebrand labor leader. "Whereas *Rocky* celebrated the American Dream, *F.I.S.T.* memorializes the American Nightmare," Sarris concluded. "After *Rocky*, the drift to damnation of Johnny Kovac [Stallone] may strike audiences as a downer, and downers seldom pay off at the bottom line."[40] *F.I.S.T.* was successful enough at the box office, perhaps because it was Stallone's post-Rocky debut.[41] What it lacked was the heroic appeal of an overt display of muscles in action.

Even less well received was *Paradise Alley* (1978), in which three Italian American brothers struggle to get out of New York City's Hell's Kitchen neighborhood through the rough-and-tumble world of professional wrestling. The plot was ill conceived, and devoid of the raw muscularity one might expect from the nature of the sport. David Denby of *New York* magazine thought it dim-witted, "so synthetic you don't believe a word of it." The opinion of Vincent Canby was that Stallone needed help. "If he continues to write, direct and star in movies like 'Paradise Alley,' the career that only really began with 'Rocky' may turn out to have been an extremely brief dream."[42] By this time, *Rocky II* was in the works, and Stallone was seeking to recapture his earlier formula of success. "It would be his make-or-break movie," notes Daly.[43]

In his reprise of *Rocky*, Stallone sought to reinstill the kind of realism lacking in his two previous productions by replaying some of the more popular scenes from the first *Rocky* film, such as his harsh training regimen, his dramatic run up the stairs of the art museum, and his devotion to his girlfriend Adrian, whom he marries in *Rocky II*. The principals in the cast also remain the same, but one significant change is in the plot: this time Rocky wins. While rehearsing their boxing scenes, Stallone and Weathers pulled no punches, and Stallone tore his chest and abdomen muscles, leaving him with pain and no lateral movement. "There must be something buried inside Sylvester Stallone that makes him want to prove himself not only as a movie star but as a man," observed Roger Ebert in 1980, adding,

> He needs to take the risks himself, and in the four years since "Rocky" he has deliberately put himself into dangerous situations that were not necessarily required by his scripts. During the filming of last summer's "Rocky II," he insisted on doing all the fight scenes himself and doing them for real, even though doubles could have been used and punches could have been pulled. He suffered internal injuries, and now, on location in Hungary, he pulls up his shirt to show the scar left by an operation to mend his torn pectoral muscle: "The operation lasted four hours and took 120 stitches," he explains.[44]

Box office figures of over $200 million from an estimated $7 million budget justified his commitment.[45]

Victory (1981) provided another opportunity for Stallone to star in a physical culture flick. The plot features the escape of Allied prisoners of war during a soccer match with an all-star Nazi team in Paris during World War II. To play goalkeeper, Stallone again underwent serious physical conditioning. "It was his most rigorous program to date," notes Daly; "not only did he trim down to 159 pounds, but he hired a trainer who literally reshaped his body into a lean lithe machine, the same kind real soccer stars display on the field." His diet consisted of egg whites and cheese every morning for weeks.[46] Even with veteran actor Michael Caine playing coach and soccer superstar Pelé to complement the action scenes, the film was only a moderate commercial success. It was followed by *Nighthawks* (1981), a police drama somewhat less infused with muscle appeal. The challenge for Stallone, however, came with stunts he insisted on doing himself. "Running through the tunnels of an un-built subway station was very dangerous, but exciting and we were only given one hour to do it," he stated in a 2006 question-and-answer session. "Hanging from the cable car was probably one of the more dangerous stunts I was asked to perform because it was untested and I was asked to hold a folding Gerber knife in my left hand so if the cable were to snap, and I survived the 230 foot fall into the East River with its ice cold 8 mile an hour current, I could cut myself free from the harness."[47] In *Victory*, explains film scholar Mark Gallagher,

Stallone's body matters less to the film's narrative and thematics than does his ability to be European. . . . He appears in a tank top in one scene and shirtless for the brief scene of his night-time escape from the camp, for which he climbs into the roofing of a shower area. For the rest of the film he is fully clothed—even the football-training sequences keep him in a shirt and trousers, with the team members wearing shorts only in the third-act match against the Germans. *Nighthawks* also withholds displays of Stallone's muscled body, perhaps in so doing limiting its commercial appeal.

Nighthawks, Gallagher concludes, "tests the professionalism of Stallone's character more than his purely physical attributes," likely in an effort to broaden his star persona.[48]

To resurrect his sagging stardom, Stallone called on *Rocky* a third time. He later admitted his training for *Rocky III* was "a bit of an overkill." He would run three miles in the morning, spar fifteen rounds, lift weights for two hours, perform five hundred sit-ups, and jump rope for thirty minutes; then after lunch go through a similar routine, ending with a long swim. "It was difficult to turn off the desire to train," he confessed. "I'd think about it obsessively. Sometimes, I would even leave a movie or dinner party at night and drive home to work out no matter what the time—one or two in the morning." Subsisting on tuna, burnt toast, water, and espresso for six months enabled Stallone to develop a chiseled physique at 2.8 percent body fat.[49]

Much originality is evident in the script, and the film is highlighted by wrestling sensations Hulk Hogan and Mr. T, but it was Stallone's directing and acting that made it a hit. *Rocky III* incorporates the main character's former adversary Apollo Creed as his trainer when his erstwhile trainer, played by Burgess Meredith, dies, causing loss of the championship. Creed convinces him he could regain the title by believing in himself again. "You lost that fight, Rock, for all the wrong reasons. You lost your edge," advises Creed, and it is a statement that could just as easily be applicable to Stallone's career at that point. "You had that eye of the tiger, man, the edge. And now you've gotta get it back—the eye of the tiger."[50] This ingredient for Rocky's success applied also to audiences who absorbed his dramatic comeback into their own lives. Stallone's movies were successful, he told Ebert, because of their simplicity: "Most successful art reflects the exact ideas of the viewer— whether or not the viewer knows it. . . . Paintings that endure are paintings that inspire people to say, hey, that's the way I feel; those are the colors I see in my dreams."[51] Box office payoff was immense, at $270 million worldwide against a budget of $17 million. "*Rocky III* became the first 'triquel' in history to outgross its predecessors," notes Daly.[52]

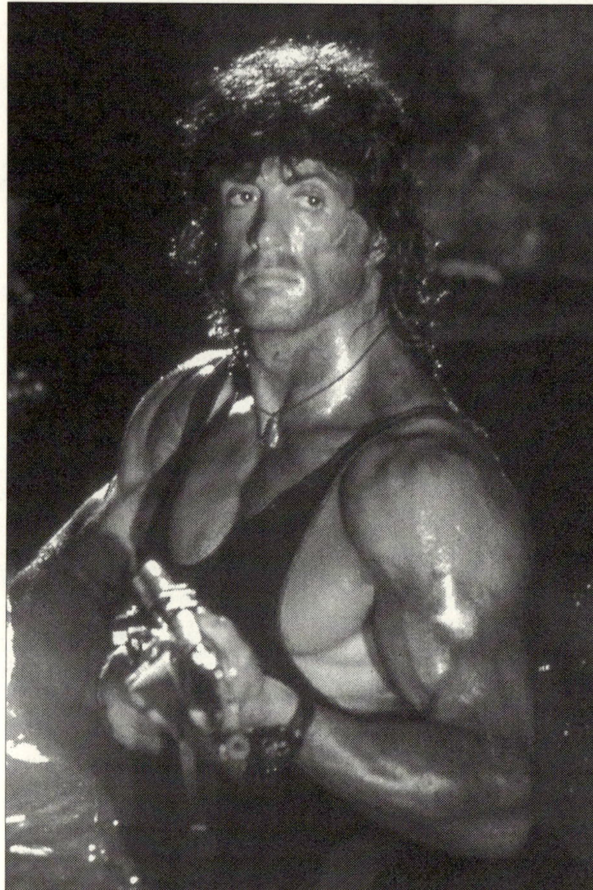

Figure 15.3. Reeking of sweat, anger, and testosterone, Sylvester Stallone takes on his enemies as John Rambo in *Rambo III* (1988). Image in the public domain.

This spectacular success can be attributed largely to Stallone getting back in the groove of using his muscles to highlight his action scenes. This effect was enhanced by creative camera alterations between accelerated motion during Rocky's river run in training and slow motion in ring bouts with Hulk Hogan and Mr. T, including several minutes of repetitious knock-out blows with the latter in the film's finale. What is distinctive about *Rocky III* is that Stallone's muscles appear larger and shapelier than in earlier episodes, which likely explains why Stallone repeatedly stressed his extreme, almost superhuman, workouts, danger-ridden stunts, and dietary restrictions. Later, in an ad for his dietary supplement company, he even claimed that he was able to reduce from 18 percent to 2.8 percent body fat by "downing nothing but tuna fish and water for six months."[53] It strains credulity, however, to imagine how any of these extreme measures could be deemed authentic or that he constructed such a body by natural means at age thirty-six. Even so, Yvonne Tasker seems dismissive about his use of performance-enhancing drugs. Although the actor was busted in 2007 by Australian customs officials for trying to import forty-eight vials of human growth hormone (HGH), Tasker rationalizes it as a lone incident that got little media attention, far less significant than the high-profile doping scandals in baseball and cycling, and excusable on the grounds that "the fake sport of the movie world stands for inauthentic achievements" and should be judged by a different standard from real sports. She adds, "While Hollywood and sports media equally revel in Cinderella stories of talent and ambition realized, cheating in movies is not really an issue in the same way as is cheating in sports. Indeed, both movie stars themselves and the cinema as a medium are self-conscious constructions; . . . desired to produce pleasure through illusion, movies deal in fantasy and spectacle. Thus, within Stallone's films, despite both scandals over HGH and the physical impact of aging, the credibility of the star's body as a sign of authentic struggle remains undiminished." Still, with all due allowance for artistic license, Tasker must admit that the stakes for cheating in movie sports are no less high than in real sports: "Stallone's built body was—and remains—crucial to his film roles and his star persona."[54] That no other chapter besides Tasker's grapples with such a "crucial" issue in *The Ultimate Stallone Reader* seems remarkable.

In the absence of bona fide research by academic authors, perhaps owing to libel concerns, one must rely on plausible extrapolations from existing evidence. Most of these accounts cite Stallone's 2007 drug conviction, his two candid admissions, and his obvious increase in muscularity in subsequent *Rocky* films and others.[55] "Hollywood is fertile ground for people seeking a fountain of youth at any price," notes Ned Zeman in a 2012 article in *Vanity Fair*. "These days, though, nothing is hotter than Hollywood's latest health and fitness craze: H.G.H. therapy." The hormone is used by many Hollywood actors, and it is said to be particularly popular with older stars. Zeman explains that its effects are pretty easy to spot, and quotes the talent manager of a still-muscular celebrity who is well into middle age: "Any actor over 50 you're still seeing with a ripped stomach and veins in his forearms is probably taking H.G.H." As Zeman notes, "The trend arrived in Hollywood by way of the city's flourishing community of bodybuilders, who passed it on to their confederates in show business. Hollywood's early adopters were action stars."[56]

Most allegations of Stallone's drug use, however, are based on prima facie evidence—largely, pictorial and video representations of his screen appearances over succeeding decades. Isaac Haynes speculates that Stallone has taken clenbuterol, a supplement that "acts as a thermogenic that elevates one's metabolic rate while burning excessive fats and calories. It explains Sly's development of red skin, reduced body fat, increased muscle mass, and a well-toned physique. Clenbuterol also improves cardiovascular endurance and *one's general health*, leading to a more intense workout session."[57] Ernst Peibst concurs about Stallone's use of clenbuterol, noting,

> Sly hired 2 time Mr Olympia champion Franco Colombu when prepping for Rocky IV. Franco was in the same era as Arnold Schwarzenegger and Lou Ferrigno in the 70's, a cluster of bodybuilders who were known to be taking steroids.
>
> So, if Sylvester told Franco that he wanted to get as shredded as possible for Rocky IV, it'd make sense for Franco to tell him about the best fat-burning steroids (that he may have used in the past)—such as clenbuterol.

Stallone's muscularity culminated in 1993 with *Demolition Man*, the first film in which, notes Peibst,

> Sly really looks "BIG." Usually he looks pretty muscular with his top off, but in this film he even looks like a beast with his t-shirt on. . . .
>
> However, he doesn't look like he's put on enough mass to warrant taking bulking steroids, so my guess is that Stallone's taken **some form of HGH**; which could be the reason why he's gained a decent amount of lean muscle tissue. Bulking steroids on the other-hand like dianabol or anadrol would've got Sly huge. . . .
>
> The structure of Stallone's face has also changed over the years. . . . HGH not only causes your internal organs to grow, but also your skull and nose. . . . Sly's head has got considerably bigger over the years and now has a more square appearance, including a wider jaw. These are all common signs of HGH-use. . . .

So, technically Sly may not have taken "*steroids*," as clenbuterol and HGH aren't officially classed as anabolic steroids. However, it's almost certain he's used illegal substances like these to help him burn fat and build muscle, as he was busted for smuggling HGH in 2007.[58]

The assertion of Reda Almardi is that Stallone "steered clear of strong anabolic steroids such as Trenbolone, Turinabol or Dbol." But given that he used HGH and perhaps a strong fat burner, "he may not be 100% natural." Almardi adds, "At the same time we wouldn't be shocked if he was using nothing but HGH as his work rate is second to none."[59]

Whether or not these opinions have any basis in fact, the larger issue is not so much that Stallone might have been using drugs to enhance his screen appeal as the potential hypocrisy of his actions. How many thousands of young bodybuilders were led to believe they could develop Stallone-like muscles by following his tortuous workouts and restrictive diets cannot be determined. Many, no doubt, were deluded into thinking the on-screen illusion could become a reality.

Flagrant depictions of Stallone's built body, however, are infrequent in *Rambo, First Blood* (1982). Aside from an early shower scene, he is at least partially clothed, befitting the chilly temperatures during the British Columbia filming. Emphasis is on the dramatic action of Stallone's muscles, despite six stuntmen and lots of special effects. John Rambo, a returned Green Beret from the Vietnam War, uses his skills in wilderness survival and combat to avenge gross mistreatment by a small-town sheriff and deputies, providing a vivid reminder of the public disregard for the sacrifices of veterans at home and abroad. As Roger Ebert noted in his review of the film, "Sylvester Stallone is one of the great physical actors in the movies, with a gift for throwing himself so fearlessly into an action scene that we can't understand why somebody doesn't really get hurt. When he explodes near the beginning of 'First Blood,' hurling cops aside and breaking out of a jail with his fists and speed, it's such a convincing demonstration of physical strength and agility that we never question the scene's implausibility. In fact, although almost all of 'First Blood' is implausible, because it's Stallone on the screen, we'll buy it." And buy it the movie-watching public did: against a budget of $14 million, *First Blood* earned over $125 million worldwide.[60] What made Rambo successful, Stallone believed, "was that the character spoke with his body." In the absence of dialogue, Rambo "was completely emotional and physical. It turned out that words were pointless with Rambo." Not unlike the stars of silent era films, "he expressed himself clearly with sinewy catlike moves and haunted eyes."[61] Stallone mastered an ability to unleash his physique in emotion-driven action scenes, even clothed.

In *Rambo: First Blood Part II* (1985), Stallone's muscular torso is flamboyantly revealed in many scenes from all angles and is well-oiled for maximum effect as he takes on the Vietnamese and Russian armies to rescue American prisoners of war imprisoned in the jungle. In preparation for the film, his workouts were pushed "to new limits" to create a "ferocious look to match a plot that was equally pumped up." Stallone sought to turn Rambo "into a physical specimen even bodybuilders would appreciate." He indulged in "an extremely intense training regimen" and "a repetitive high-protein diet." It was hard-core training, during which Stallone "lived in the gym. Then I would come home at night and before bed I'd do 200 sit-ups, 250 push-ups, 100 chin-ups."[62] In *Action Movie Freak*, Katrina Hill celebrates the serious "ass kicking" he inflicts on hundreds of bad guys with spectacular weapons, including a bow that shoots arrows with exploding heads. A *Los Angeles Times* reviewer, however, was unimpressed with Stallone's "muscle-flexing optimism," noting, "If a character can seemingly do anything, it's hard to feel tension or concern about his fate. (At least, Superman had kryptonite.) We are left with nothing but detached aesthetic appreciation: watching Rambo race through several million dollars worth of explosions and aerial attacks, coruscant fireballs billowing everywhere and bodies flying hither and yon. Except for anyone irretrievably into violent power fantasies, this will probably soon pall." *Newsweek* was impressed that Stallone could portray superheroes simultaneously in two blockbuster films, *Rocky IV* and *Rambo: First Blood Part II* in 1985. His success "with two series at once, and with two grunt heroes, is unprecedented in the industry."[63] Notwithstanding the use of twenty stuntmen and spectacular special effects to complement Stallone's strapping body, both muscle movies achieved stunning profits, together earning about $547 million over budget.[64]

By 1988, at age forty-two, Stallone felt compelled to sustain the physical image he had created in successive renditions of *Rocky* and *Rambo*. He needed a physique that would convince fans he was still a killer machine capable of taking on the Russian invaders of Afghanistan. The challenge was not "just about getting into great shape" but "*maintaining* the look." Shooting the film in the Dead Sea environs, one of earth's hottest places, presented an additional challenge. Stallone also reminds us that *Rambo III* "was made before the days of computer-generated effects, so we had to do everything for real—rappelling out of helicopters, lying under a moving tank running through explosions. The closest call came when a French Puma helicopter banked the wrong way during the shooting of a fight and nearly decapitated me and one of the stuntmen. I have such admiration for the men and women who do this type of stunt work for a living, and I owe them a great deal."[65] *Washington Post* reviewer Hal Hinson called the movie "lamebrained," asserting that it was "full of empty action, minimalistic dialogue and more explosive material than the mind can fathom." Stallone, he observed, "has developed his musculature to the point that he hardly seems human. . . . All of Stallone's preparation for the role seems to have been done in the weight room; he's become the chief exponent of the Mr. Universe school of acting."[66] That *Rambo III* was not as popular or profitable as expected may be attributed in part to the moral of its story. Unlike its predecessors, whose story lines portrayed retribution from a guilt-ridden public for ill treatment of Vietnam War veterans, the release of *Rambo III*, which sought justification for American foreign policy, coincided with the withdrawal of Soviet troops from Afghanistan.

In succeeding decades Stallone continued to cash in with several dozen action movies, including two in the *Rambo* franchise and four more *Rocky* spin-offs, and Schwarzenegger has capitalized from the genre with four more *Terminator* installments. While both superstars reinforced each other by utilizing their bodies in fantasy action films, their personal relations, until Schwarzenegger's entry into politics, endured serious clashes off-screen. Laurence Leamer concludes that they were "such different types that they would not have gotten along no matter where they encountered each other—on the school playground, the athletic field, the corporate world, or Hollywood." Resentful that Stallone starred in two action films at once, Schwarzenegger "had a proprietor's sense of his own turf, and Stallone was stepping into what Arnold considered his territory" after his *Conan* breakthroughs. In a 1985 interview for *News of the World*, Schwarzenegger denigrated his rival, saying, "Stallone uses body doubles for some of the close-ups in his movies. I don't. . . . We probably kill more people in *Commando* than Stallone did in *Rambo*, but the difference is that we don't pretend the violence is justified by patriotic pride. All that flag waving is a lot of bull." And in a 1986 *GQ* interview, Schwarzenegger berated Stallone for his acting persona: "There's no love there. And people see that. You can fake your way through for a year, but for ten years, that's hard. Eventually, it catches up with you."[67]

More fundamental to understanding their conflict is how they responded to the evolution of public perceptions of muscle. Although Schwarzenegger helped inspire the so-called fitness revolution of the late 1970s, few physical culturists or moviegoers could relate to the steroid-induced freaks who succeeded him in the 1980s and beyond. As Robert Rushing notes, "Schwarzenegger shed thirty pounds for *Conan the Barbarian,* and the bodybuilders in other 1980s peplums are conspicuously less massive than their 1950s and 1960s counterparts." For Rushing, the oversize muscles of competitive bodybuilders are irrelevant to cinema; he asserts that "the central terms of value in bodybuilding—mass, volume, definition—all seem to be opposed to cinematic body, which is in its very name a body in movement."[68] Schwarzenegger simply followed this trend toward movement rather than mass, relying on his still robust frame and reputation to achieve the desired heroic illusion. Not unlike Schwarzenegger, Stallone achieved the same effect by constructing an iconic muscular image to complement his actions. Both superstars achieved their widespread appeal by perfecting the art of illusion through copious use of stuntmen, special effects, shifting camera speeds and angles, and, it is alleged, performance-enhancing drugs. Overwhelmingly viewers, though able to distinguish fantasy from reality, found their films compelling. Rushing, citing André Bazin and Plato, attributes this tendency to a "perennial desire that cinema, an art form based on a host of optical illusions, could be somehow honest and direct with us, rather than illusory and deceptive. But this desire is strangely self-deceptive, since it is the illusion itself that we enjoy." Both Schwarzenegger and Stallone exploited this desire by creating unreal but inspiring action scenarios. Katrina Hill designates Stallone as "the most influential actor in the genre . . . while Schwarzenegger moved on to politics and let his physique go soft."[69] But attaining superhero status in the 1980s by no means ended their pursuit of the American dream.

Notes

1. Arnold Schwarzenegger, *Arnold: The Education of a Bodybuilder* (New York: Simon and Schuster, 1977), 17–18.

2. Barbara Outland Baker, *Arnold and Me: In the Shadow of the Austrian Oak* (Bloomington, IN: AuthorHouse, 2006), 22–23, 94.

3. Arnold Schwarzenegger, *Total Recall: My Unbelievably True Life Story,* 113.

4. Laurence Leamer, *Fantastic: The Life of Arnold Schwarzenegger*, 89.

5. Rick Wayne, "Hercules Visits New York and How!!" *Muscle Builder / Power*, October 1970, 39; Schwarzenegger, *Total Recall*, 114–15; "Arnold Schwarzenegger Recommends Film Flop for Terrorist Interrogators," *Express*, August 5, 2012.

6. Schwarzenegger, *Total Recall*, 176.

7. Vincent Canby, "'Stay Hungry': Rafelson Film Is about 'New' South," *New York Times*, April 26, 1976; Irene Hause, "Mike Mentzer's Venture," *MuscleMag International* no. 33 (January 1983): 25.

8. Charles Gaines and George Butler, *Pumping Iron: The Art and Sport of Bodybuilding* (London: Sphere, 1974), 7–8.

9. Leamer, *Fantastic*, 107.

10. Schwarzenegger, *Total Recall*, 194–95.

11. Al Antuck, "Bodybuilding in the Whitney Museum," *MuscleMag International* 2 (Summer 1976): 69–70.

12. Richard Eder, "Muscles Galore: Bulging Physique," *New York Times*, January 19, 1977; Gary Arnold, "A Whitty Psych-Out," *Washington Post*, February 19, 1977; Richard Schickel, "A Delicate Beefcake Ballet," *Time*, January 24, 1977, 79.

13. George Butler, "Pumping Iron at 25: The Film That Almost Wasn't," *Iron Age*, April 28, 2009, https://web.archive.org/web/20090428110042/http://www.ironage.us/articles/butler.html; Leamer, *Fantastic*, 106.

14. Schwarzenegger, *Total Recall*, 229, 235–36.

15. Arnold Schwarzenegger, "My Olympia Comeback," *Muscle and Fitness* 42, no. 2 (February 1981): 6, 148. See also John D. Fair, "The Intangible Arnold: The Controversial Mr. Olympia Contest of 1980," *Iron Game History* 11, no. 1 (September 2009): 4–22.

16. Jack Neary, "Olympia Report, Arnold's Victory Creates Controversy & Bitterness," *Muscle and Fitness* 42, no. 2 (February 1981): 161, 164; Arnold Schwarzenegger, quoted in Leamer, *Fantastic*, 147.

17. Schwarzenegger, *Total Recall*, 210–71.

18. Jim Steranko, "John Milius: Behind-the-Scenes Interview with the Writer/Director of Conan," *Prevue* 48 (1982), https://web.archive.org/web/20020805203203/http://www.prevuemagazine.com/Articles/Thevault/240.

19. Dino De Laurentiis, quoted in Leamer, *Fantastic*, 158; Schwarzenegger, *Total Recall*, 279–80.

20. Roger Ebert, "Conan the Barbarian," January 1, 1982, http://www.rogerebert.com/reviews/conan-the-barbarian-1982; "Conan the Barbarian," *TV Guide*, http://www.tvguide.com/movies/conan-the-barbarian/review/111376/; Vincent Canby, "Fighting, Fantasy in 'Conan the Barbarian,'" *New York Times*, May 15, 1982.

21. "Conan the Barbarian (1982)," The Numbers, https://www.the-numbers.com/movie/Conan-the-Barbarian#more.

22. "Conan the Destroyer," *Variety*, December 31, 1983; "Conan the Destroyer," *Time Out*, https://www.timeout.com/london/film/conan-the-destroyer; Roger Ebert, "Conan the Destroyer," January 1, 1984, http://www.rogerebert.com/reviews

/conan-the-destroyer-1984; Vincent Canby, "Schwarzenegger in New 'Conan,'" *New York Times*, June 29, 1984.

23. "Conan the Destroyer (1984)," The Numbers, http://www.the-numbers.com /movie/Conan-the-Destroyer#tab=summary; "Conan the Destroyer," Box Office Mojo, https://www.boxofficemojo.com/release/rl4182410753/weekend/.

24. Schwarzenegger, *Total Recall*, 299–302, 308–10.

25. *The Terminator* was budgeted at $6.4 million. Box Office Mojo, https://www.box officemojo.com/release/rl3480585729/weekend/.

26. Charlotte Parker, interview with John D. Fair, Los Angeles, June 7, 2011.

27. Leamer, *Fantastic*, 172.

28. Schwarzenegger, *Total Recall*, 337.

29. Jake Wilson, "Arnold Schwarzenegger's Greatest Muscle Flexes," *Den of Geek!*, June 16, 2016, http://www.denofgeek.com/uk/movies/arnold-schwarzenegger/41486 /arnold-schwarzeneggers-greatest-muscle-flexes.

30. Leamer, *Fantastic*, 182.

31. Marsha Daly, *Sylvester Stallone: An Illustrated Life*, 12–17.

32. Daly, *Sylvester Stallone*, 35, 39–40.

33. Sylvester Stallone, *The Official Rocky Scrapbook*, 18–19.

34. Daly, *Sylvester Stallone*, 44.

35. Stallone, *The Official Rocky Scrapbook*, 24–25, 30–32, 38.

36. Stallone, *The Official Rocky Scrapbook*, 47–48, 58.

37. Daly, *Sylvester Stallone*, 60; Roger Ebert, "Rocky," January 1, 1976, https://www. rogerebert.com/reviews/rocky-1976.

38. Sheldon Hall and Stephen Neale, *Epics, Spectacles, and Blockbusters: A Hollywood History* (Detroit: Wayne State University Press, 2010), 214.

39. Daly, *Sylvester Stallone*, 63.

40. Andrew Sarris, "Waking Up from the American Dream," *Village Voice*, May 1, 1978.

41. With a budget of $8 million, *F.I.S.T.* took in $20,388,920. "*F.I.S.T.*," Wikipedia, https://en.wikipedia.org/wiki/F.I.S.T.

42. David Denby, "Movies," *New York*, November 20, 1978, quoted in Daly, *Sylvester Stallone*, 88; Vincent Canby, "Rocky Goes to Limbo in 'Paradise Alley': Rocky as Wrestler," *New York Times*, November 10, 1978.

43. Daly, *Sylvester Stallone*, 88.

44. Roger Ebert, "Interview with Sylvester Stallone," Budapest, Hungary, July 13, 1980, https://www.rogerebert.com/interviews/interview-with-sylvester-stallone-1980.

45. "*Rocky II*," Wikipedia, https://en.wikipedia.org/wiki/Rocky_II.

46. Daly, *Sylvester Stallone*, 103.

47. Moriarty, "Round One with Sylvester Stallone Q&A!!," December 3, 2006, Ain't It Cool News, http://www.aintitcool.com/node/30861. The problem with Stallone's stunt performance in *Nighthawks* is that it does not seem death-defying, and there is nothing to convince viewers from long-shots and close-ups that it is not a stuntman.

48. Mark Gallagher, "Stallone and Hollywood in Transition," in *The Ultimate Stallone Reader: Sylvester Stallone as Star, Icon, Auteur*, ed. Chris Holmlund, 114.

49. Sylvester Stallone, *Sly Moves: My Proven Program to Lose Weight, Build Strength, Gain Will Power, and Live Your Dream*, 30; Michael Berg, "Sylvester Stallone, Fitness' Renaissance Man," *Muscle & Fitness* 65, no. 9 (September 2004): 115.

50. Sylvester Stallone, dir. *Rocky III* (Los Angeles: Metro-Goldwyn-Mayer, 1982); YouTube, https://www.youtube.com/watch?v=OhEHV2JGpM8.

51. Roger Ebert, "Interview with Sylvester Stallone," Budapest, Hungary, July 21, 1980, https://www.rogerebert.com/interviews/interview-with-slyvester-stallone.

52. Daly, *Sylvester Stallone*, 116.

53. Sylvester Stallone, "Feel What All the Buzz Is About," *Muscle and Fitness* 65, no. 9 (September 2004): 25.

54. Yvonne Tasker, "Stallone, Ageing and Action Authenticity," in *The Ultimate Stallone Reader: Sylvester Stallone as Star, Icon, Auteur*, ed. Chris Holmlund, 245, 247–48.

55. "As you get older, the pituitary gland slows and you feel older, your bones narrow. This stuff gives your body a boost and you feel and look good," he stated in 2007. "Doing Rambo is hard work." Sylvester Stallone, quoted in "Was Sylvester Stallone on Steroids in Rocky IV?" Quora, https://www.quora.com/Was-Sylvester-stallone-on-steroids-in-Rocky-IV. "HGH (human growth hormone) is nothing," Stallone told a *Time* interviewer in 2008. "Anyone who calls it a steroid is grossly misinformed—testosterone to me is so important for a sense of well-being when you get older. Everyone over 40 years old would be wise to investigate it because it increases the quality of your life. Mark my words. In 10 years it will be over the counter." Sylvester Stallone, quoted in Joel Stein, "On a Mission," *Time*, February 4, 2008, 59.

56. Ned Zeman, "Hollywood's Vial Bodies," *Vanity Fair*, March 2012, https://archive.vanityfair.com/article/2012/3/hollywoods-vial-bodies.

57. Isaac Haynes, "Is Sylvester Stallone on Steroids, or Is He Natural?," Fitness Donkey, May 20, 2020, https://www.fitnessdonkey.com/blog/sylvester-stallone-steroids-natural.

58. "Ernst Peibst, "Sylvester Stallone: Steroids or Natural?" Muscle + Brawn, last updated June 11, 2020, https://muscleandbrawn.com/sylvester-stallone-steroids/.

59. Reda Almardi, "Did Sylvester Stallone Take Steroids?" Strong Chap, April 1, 2020, https://strongchap.com/sylvester-stallone/.

60. Roger Ebert, "First Blood," January 1, 1982, https://www.rogerebert.com/reviews/first-blood-1982; "First Blood (1982)," *The Numbers*, http://www.the-numbers.com/movie/First-Blood#tab=summary.

61. Stallone, *Sly Moves*, 32.

62. Stallone, *Sly Moves*, 33–34.

63. Katrina Hill, *Action Movie Freak*, 81–82; Michael Wilmington, "Why a 'Rambo II'? For Muddiest of Reasons," *Los Angeles Times*, May 22, 1985, http://articles.latimes.com/1985-05-22/entertainment/ca-16965_1_john-rambo; "Showing the Flag: Rocky, Rambo, and the Return of the American Hero," *Newsweek*, December 23, 1985, 58.

64. "*Rocky IV*," Wikipedia, https://en.wikipedia.org/wiki/Rocky_IV; "*Rambo: First Blood Part II*," Wikipedia, https://en.wikipedia.org/wiki/Rambo:_First_Blood_Part_II.

65. Stallone, *Sly Moves*, 37, 40.

66. Hal Hinson, "Rambo III," *Washington Post*, May 25, 1988, http://www.washington post.com/wp-srv/style/longterm/movies/videos/ramboiiirhinson_a0c8ef.htm.

67. Leamer, *Fantastic*, 176–77; Ian Harmer, "Stallone Slugs It Out for Real with Arnold," *News of the World*, October 20, 1985; Arnold Schwarzenegger, quoted in Jean Vallely, "The Promoter," *GQ*, July 1986, quoted in Wendy Leigh, *Arnold: An Unauthorized Biography* (Chicago: Congdon and Weed, 1990), 222.

68. Robert A. Rushing, *Descended from Hercules: Biopolitics and the Muscled Male Body on Screen*, 121–23. See also Jennifer Barker, *The Tactile Eye: Touch and the Cinematic Experience* (Berkeley: University of California Press, 2009).

69. Rushing, *Descended from Hercules*, 135; Hill, *Action Movie Freak*, 249.

XVI. A HEROIC TRADITION?

The greatest satisfaction to me is to hear another unbiased human being whose heart has been touched and honestly says, "Hey, here is someone real!"

—Bruce Lee, quoted in Linda Lee, *The Bruce Lee Story*

Enter the Dragon

IN A SPECIAL June 1999 issue, *Time* magazine recognized Chinese martial artist Bruce Lee as one of the one hundred most influential "Heroes and Icons of the Twentieth Century," along with such notables as Muhammad Ali, Albert Einstein, and Franklin Delano Roosevelt. "With nothing but his hands, feet and a lot of attitude," noted Joel Stein, "he turned the little guy into a tough guy." In 1959 Lee Jun-fan, "a short, skinny, bespectacled 18-year-old kid from Hong Kong traveled to America and declared himself to be John Wayne, James Dean, Charles Atlas and the guy who kicked your butt in junior high."[1] But he wasn't just any small-statured, muscular guy; he was a tough and well-built *Asian* man, universally admired for his ripped physique, his fighting ability, and his intense focus on winning. He was virtually alone as a heroic role model for Asian audiences. Before Lee's films, there were plenty of evil exemplars of the so-called Yellow Peril: perfidious "Chinamen," "Japs," or Vietcong who represented violence, sorrow, and opium use in Western lore. Bruce Lee's energetic fighting prowess, benevolent screen persona, and aesthetic musculature changed all that. His physique never bulged with Schwarzeneggian muscles, but he became a star with his own unique look and with lethal fighting moves that Arnold Schwarzenegger could never have mastered.

Remarkably, Lee did all of this in a tragically brief career, as he died in 1973 at the young age of thirty-two. "His short, yet illuminating life, on this earth has left an indelible impression," write Sid Campbell and Greglon Yimm Lee in *Remembering the Master*. "He was a man of undaunted vision, driven by perfection and striving to reach incredible plateaus." Reminiscences by Lee's friends and colleagues on his life and legacy reveals similar sentiments. "There was no one like him and nobody ever since" asserts Paul Heller, co-producer of Lee's landmark film *Enter the Dragon* (1973). "I think anybody who has worked in the action genre recognizes the brilliance he brought to it, he was truly, truly brilliant." Protégé Richard Bustillo recalls that he thought he had "seen it all" until he witnessed Lee's speed and power. In reconstructing Lee's legacy, Paul Bowman concludes that "the impact of Lee's films on the global awareness of East Asia martial arts cannot be overstated."[2] Critical to this formulation of heroic historiography are the reminiscences of Linda Lee, his grieving widow, in *Bruce Lee: The Man Only I Knew* (1975) and *The Bruce Lee Story* (1989), on which the 1993 film *Dragon: The Bruce Lee Story*, was based.

Lee's introduction to motion pictures stemmed from the influence of his father, Lee Hoi-chuen, a Cantonese opera star who featured three-month-old Bruce as a "prop baby" in *Golden Gate Girl*, set in San Francisco, where Bruce Lee was born. It was followed by many more roles as a child actor in Hong Kong, the city of his youth, where audiences nicknamed him Little Dragon. A rebellious child, Lee joined a street-fighting gang, then took up wing chun–style martial arts under grandmaster Ip Man. At age seventeen his extraordinary physical talents gained public notice when he employed his straight-line wing chun punching to win an intracity boxing match and a cha-cha contest for which he improvised dozens of dance steps. Upon returning to the United States, Bruce enrolled at the University of Washington to study philosophy and collaborated with jun fan gung fu practitioner James Yimm Lee in Oakland. As a California weightlifting champion and gym operator, James Yimm Lee's fitness world included the likes of Jack Delinger (Mr. America 1949), the legendary Jack LaLanne, and numerous boxing notables. George Lee, an early protégé who made equipment for their gym, remembers Bruce for his "vigorous and very serious workouts." Bruce not only developed the many facets of jeet kune do during his Oakland years in the early 1960s but would also "spend the better portion of each day working out and bettering his physical ability." Soon he was becoming "extremely muscular and taking on a well-conditioned physique. He used to show us at the beginning of each session how much he was developing." Ironically, Lee was classified 4-F when drafted by the US Army for poor eyesight, an undescended testicle, and a sinus disorder—no doubt the fittest recruit it ever rejected.[3]

Lee's multifaceted principles of *jeet* (parry) *kune* (fist) and *do* (way) transcended all previous fighting styles. The emphasis, as Charles Russo explains, was on "streamlining everything to a tangible effectiveness: economy of movement and direct attacks. The focus was on speed and power." It was "fighting without fighting." Utilizing the traditional Chinese concepts of yin and yang, wu wei (Taoism), and Zen Buddhism, Lee believed the more that muscles relaxed, the more power they could generate—softness yielded hardness. To illustrate the hand's importance, he performed two-finger push-ups on each hand to perfect his famous one-inch punch. Lee's kicking power was no less lethal, observed student Jesse Glover. A would-be karate-trained challenger was once subjected to a "furious barrage of straight punches to his face" and then a kick to the head. "The man took a long time to regain consciousness. I thought he was dead." Subsequently Lee displayed his authenticity less violently. As Glover recalled, "Paradoxically, Bruce was pushing for realism even as he was also constantly stoking the imaginations of observers toward the unrealistic. In this sense—of kicking the eyeglasses cleanly off someone's face—his feats of speed and agility were not only drawing students to his business but were also weaving their own mythology in the process. Bruce's students would increasingly attest to how he had become virtually 'untouchable' in sparring sessions. George Lee remembers how Bruce could snatch a quarter out of someone's palm and leave a dime in exchange before the person could even close his hand." Another precept of jeet kune do was converting an opponent's energy to one's advantage by combining defense with attack. To Paul Bowman, Lee's nonclassical approach coincided with such countercultural motifs as cultural hybridity, postcolonialism, interdisciplinarity, globality, multiculturalism, and post-modernism in the Vietnam era.[4]

Bruce Lee's film career began unobtrusively, however, on the small screen. In 1966 he was offered a role in *The Green Hornet* as Kato, the Japanese chauffeur for a millionaire publisher who by night became a crime-fighting vigilante in a Lone Ranger style mask. Originally a 1930s radio series, *The Green Hornet* reemerged as a spin-off of ABC's *Batman* series in the 1960s. It only ran for six months in twenty-six half-hour episodes, but critics and the public were impressed by Lee's athleticism. "Those who watched him," wrote one critic, "would bet on Lee to render Cassius Clay [Muhammad Ali] senseless if they were put in a room and told that anything goes." Another reviewer noted that Lee struck with "such speed that he makes a rattler look like a study in slow motion."[5] Lee's Hong Kong popularity was so great that

Green Hornet episodes were marketed as *The Kato Show*. He also appeared as Kato in two *Batman* episodes. Eventually *The Green Hornet* became a cult classic, observed a 2001 reviewer, but Lee "was limited by the Hollywood system," which could not decide how to use him. "Bruce Lee was ahead of his time because he did action moves that were considered too fast for television."[6]

Yet Lee aspired to make a name for himself in Hollywood and display the worth of Chinese culture to the world. His "ultimate goal," observed fellow martial artist Leo Fong, was "to show his stuff on the movie screen."[7] Lee's striking *Green Hornet* presence earned him various minor roles as actor and choreographer of action scenes. Most important, he gained the respect of numerous celebrities, including James Coburn, James Garner, Lee Marvin, and Steve McQueen, as well as Kareem Abdul-Jabbar, who hired him as personal trainer for $250 an hour. Tired of being relegated to supporting roles, Lee consulted with his friends about making films in foreign countries. "TV wastes genius," advised Coburn; "follow [Clint] Eastwood and [Charles] Bronson; make a movie abroad."[8] In 1971 Lee signed a contract with Hong Kong–based Golden Harvest Pictures to star in *Big Boss*, playing the role of Cheng Chao-an, a young man who ventures to Bangkok to live and work with relatives in an ice plant. When two of his cousins mysteriously disappear after discovering a cache of drugs embedded in ice, Cheng exacts retribution by using his ferocious fighting skills to wreak destruction on the gangsters operating the drug smuggling ring. "Lee's physical gifts are undeniable," observed film critic Jeremy Beday in retrospect, "the blinding speed of his fists and feet must be seen to be believed." To screenwriter Donald Guarisco, *Big Boss* "has a predictable plot line, cartoonish acting, and awful dubbing," but it benefits from "solid direction" by filmmaker Lo Wei and the presence of Lee, who "carries himself with charisma of a star and brings a singular blend of gracefulness and macho swagger to the fight scenes." The finale features him "taking on a gang of hired killers and their vicious boss without ever showing a second of fear or doubt."[9] *Big Boss* was a low-budget film at a cost of $100,000, but it earned nearly $6 million. It was the highest-grossing film in Hong Kong history, and Lee became famous throughout East Asia and a rising star in the American market.

Fist of Fury (1972), again directed by Lo Wei, grossed even more, at over $7.8 million. It features Lee as Chen Zhen, who, upon returning to Shanghai, learns that his martial arts sifu (master), Huo Yuanjia, has died. At the funeral, where members of a local Japanese dojo insult Chinese students, Cheng learns that Huo was poisoned on orders of the dojo's master. Lee, described by *New York Times* reviewer A. H. Weiler as a hero with "a low boiling point, avenges the murder of his revered teacher with an éclat that would charm Superman." It was, Weiler estimates, Lee's "personal dish of tea." The handsome actor, "with the muscular build of a welterweight champ, doesn't let the Kung-Fu lovers down. He is decidedly an eye-catching figure as he takes on all comers, singly or in whimpering groups, in stylized, Karate-like bouts with swift, balletic moves, baleful stares, deadly flying fists and legs and, of course, all the necessary eerie shouts."[10] *The Way of the Dragon* (1972), written and directed by Lee, outdistanced his earlier films, with $10.5 million in receipts. As Tang Lung, he arrives in Rome to assist his cousins who are being pressured to relinquish their restaurant to a criminal syndicate. Tang defends the family's rights by handily defeating the European and Japanese martial artists hired to destroy him. "A lot of the action is for laughs," remarks Roger Ebert, "as when goons attempt to copy Lee and succeed only in knocking themselves out, or when Lee himself, momentarily stunned by an opponent, goes into the Muhammad Ali shuffle to confuse him. It goes without saying that Lee is invincible—although only if they play by his rules. Sixteen goons come at him one at a time, allowing him to methodically stack them up in unconscious heaps while the reserves stand around waiting their turn."[11] The movie's climax takes place in the historic Roman Colosseum, where Tang squares off with American hireling Colt, played by Chuck Norris; the role was critical in launching Norris to stardom. This scenario sets a precedent in cinematic norms: no longer are Asians portrayed as treacherous, violent, yellow-skinned, evildoers; rather, they can assume a protagonist role while the Westerner becomes a villainous heavy.

Bruce Lee's stardom is based largely on his performance in *Enter the Dragon*, in which his character Lee is recruited by British intelligence to infiltrate an island owned by a one-handed criminal named Han to take part in an invitational martial arts competition. Upon learning that Han is dealing in drugs and prostitution and responsible for his sister's death, Lee exacts revenge by decimating the compound. The many amazing fight scenes, notes Katrina Hill, include "a young extra named Jackie Chan, but the finale is what really breaks into crazy awesome territory—an all-out brawl between, literally, four hundred billion martial artists."[12] An iconic moment in the film is when Lee uses trickery to illustrate the "art of fighting without fighting." Challenged by a bully while journeying to Han's island, Lee lures him to a dinghy set adrift in the open sea. Not only do martial arts displays achieve a new level of intensity, but the casting, cinematography, directing, and acting of *Enter the Dragon* far surpass Lee's previous films. *New York Times* reviewer Howard Thompson found it "downright fascinating" how Lee's portrayal of a "supermaster killer" created the impression of a "fine actor." Thompson noted that "Lee, who also staged the combats, died very recently. Here he could not be more alive."[13]

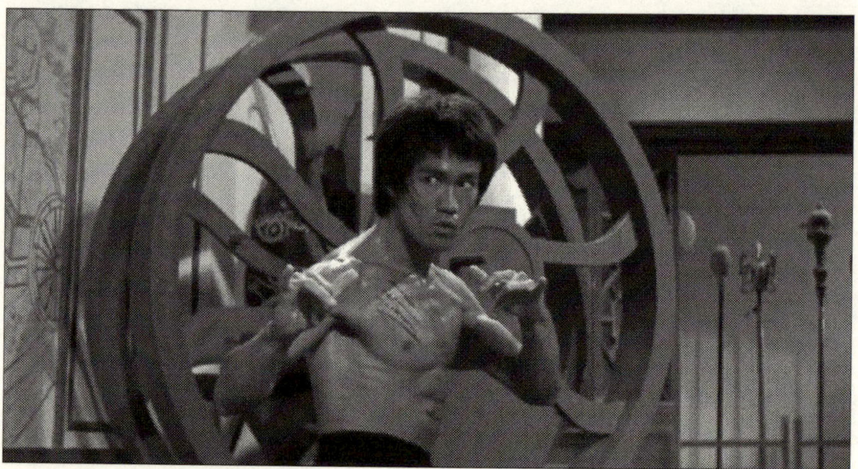

Figure 16.1. Bruce Lee prepares to unleash a whirlwind of righteous fury in the film *Enter the Dragon* (1973). Image in the public domain.

Unsettled Matters

The unexpected death of Lee in 1973 at age thirty-two, and at the height of his physical prowess and cinematic fame, shocked Hollywood and the martial arts community. A coroner's inquest confirmed the physician's opinion at Hong Kong's Queen Elizabeth Hospital that Lee died from hypersensitivity to Equagesic, a pain medication he had been taking since injuring his back in a training accident with weights in 1970. As Linda Lee explains, the doctor told him that he would "never do his kung fu kick again" and recovery would require prolonged rest. "Normally telling Bruce even to take it easy was like trying to tell a grasshopper not to jump but when he set his mind to it, he could do anything. He stayed in bed for three months—enduring a period of great mental and physical pain, stress and financial problems. Altogether it was more than six months before he could resume even light training." Bruce continued to exhibit his "usual life and energy," but Linda sensed during the making of *Enter the Dragon* that "tensions and pressures were reaching their peak." He seemed preoccupied with death and even suggested that it was imminent and not an unwelcome option to his stressed existence: "Maybe that's the only place where I'll find peace." A premonition occurred in May 1973 when he collapsed at the Golden Harvest studios. Although traces of cannabis were discovered in his system when he died two months later of cerebral edema, there was no evidence of foul play, and Linda concluded that his death was "a natural one."[14]

Still, much uncertainty prevailed about how it could have happened to such a fit and healthy action star, in the prime of life and with a successful career and loving family. These doubts motivated screenwriter Tom Bleecker to reveal an alternative explanation of Lee's tragic outcome. Bleecker was a black belt martial artist who had met Lee in 1963 and became a good friend. In 1988 he met Linda Lee at a tribute to a Bruce Lee protégé at the Bonaventure Hotel in Los Angeles. Afterward they had dinner, and she asked Bleecker to assist with the book she was writing, *The Bruce Lee Story*.

In *Unsettled Matters*, based on first- and secondhand sources, Bleecker unveils a scenario of Lee's troubled life leading up to his death, including his weight loss, near fatal collapse in May 1973, violent mood swings, depression and paranoia, alcohol and drug dependence, womanizing, and "his ongoing battle with the press and seemingly endless list of enemies."[15] While the veracity of some of these assertions might be questioned, undoubtedly the personal impressions Bleecker derived from his friendship with Lee were enhanced by two years of marriage to his widow.

Bleecker, however, ventures farther afield. The testimony of physicians who treated Lee confirm that he did have a back ailment, but Dr. Lionel Walpin calls it a "back spasm . . . triggered during an episode of sexual intercourse in June 1970." After a complete physical examination, including X-rays, Walpin "concluded there was little wrong with him . . . and with the help of a Jacuzzi, Bruce straightened out and returned to his usual workouts and running." Dr. Herbert Tanney, after administering lab tests and X-rays, could find "nothing seriously the matter with Bruce" but he "began injecting cortisone into his spine." Likewise, Dr. Ellis Silberman, following more X-rays in December 1970, concluded that the lumbosacral region of Lee's spine, and his pelvis, were "within normal limits." Then in November 1972 Dr. Otto Y. T. Au treated Lee for some other ailments—sunken cheeks, profuse sweating, severe acne, and weight loss. Bleecker believes Lee had become "obsessed with his on-screen body image" and desired a "highly defined musculature" like that of "ripped" bodybuilders. To achieve it "he began taking anabolic steroids" and became "a frequent user of diuretics." Along with well-defined muscle mass, Lee also allegedly displayed "roid rage" that threatened the lives of others. "In an effort to quell his episodes of rage, besides his use of marijuana," argues Bleecker, "Bruce began drinking heavily." An *Enter the Dragon* cameraman testifies that he often dined at a local restaurant with Lee, who would drink ten to twenty ceramic bottles of sake in an evening, then proceed in the predawn hours to the apartment of his girlfriend Betty Ting Pei. "His runaway drug use had finally turned his world into a nightmare of spinning plates."[16] Bleecker calls the inquest into Lee's death a "sham," believing that "he was either poisoned or died of adrenal failure."[17]

A 2012 scientific investigation by a registered nurse, Duncan Alexander McKenzie, concurs with much of Bleecker's explanation but finds no evidence of anabolic steroid or diuretic use. After meticulously analyzing numerous theories and false leads, McKenzie concludes that the official verdict that Lee died from an adverse reaction to Equagesic was correct.[18] In by far the most thorough biography of Lee, however, Matthew Polly argues that heat stroke "is the most plausible scientific theory for his death." On May 10, 1973, "Lee collapsed after working in a boiling hot room. He displayed multiple symptoms of central nervous system dysfunction (nausea, vomiting, staggering, collapse), and his temperature was dangerously elevated—the two diagnostic criteria for hyperthermia. Bruce had a long history of being vulnerable to heat. His risk factor was increased by sleep deprivation, extreme weight loss, and the recent surgical removal of his armpit sweat glands." July 20 was "the hottest day of the month in tropical Hong Kong," explains Polly. "In Betty Ting Pei's small apartment, Bruce demonstrated scene after kung fu scene from *Game of Death*," leaving him tired and thirsty. "Just like on May 10, Bruce exerted himself in a hot enclosed space and ended up feeling faint and suffering from a headache—two early signs of heat stroke. He wandered into Betty's bedroom, fell onto her bed, and never got up again."[19] Though it is admittedly circumstantial, Polly's evidence offers a convincing scenario for Lee's untimely demise.

None of these dysfunctional behaviors fit public portrayals of Lee as a flawless on-screen idol. Nor were they obvious to his martial arts confreres. Yet it was obvious that he could not continue his highly stressed lifestyle and remain in top physical condition to satisfy the demands of adoring fans. That Lee "pushed himself to the limit" is how martial artist George Dillman explains his death: "The human body can only take so much. He had a drive.

And maybe he knew he was going to die, but he would constantly do pushups, sit ups, practice with a piece of wood. And on the movie set when they would take a break, and everybody would sit down, people tell me Bruce went over and would do pushups, pumping up for the next scene so he looked strong." Fellow actor Jon T. Benn concurs that "one of the reasons he passed away was he was non-stop." Lee would train on the set throughout an eight-hour shooting, then go home and train another eight hours in his basement gym. "He was active 16 hours a day. And that's what killed him, he was right on the edge all the time."[20] Even Linda Lee, while publicly accepting the verdict of his death, admits that her husband was "always a very emotionally involved person" and at that time was "suffering many emotional ups and downs." His legacy would be not unlike that of "earlier great screen figures such as Rudolph Valentino and James Dean who had died before their time." He would become "the nexus of a world cult."[21] However real Bruce Lee's abbreviated screen life may have been, it assumed mythic proportions after his death. As historian Richard Ian Kimball explains, "an early death protects an athlete from the inevitable loss of skill, fame, and youth." Immortality occurs when "athletes escape the inevitability of aging and decline of skill, with only the prime of their youth to be remembered."[22]

Darth Vader

One of the most striking images of cinematic villainy emerged from the imagination of filmmaker George Lucas with his trilogy *Star Wars* (1977), *The Empire Strikes Back* (1980), and *The Return of the Jedi* (1983), all of which quickly came to be considered classics. Few realize, however, that the man behind the dark mask and cloak who played a primal force of evil was David Prowse, a champion weightlifter and bodybuilder whose main claim to fame came from portraying a force for good. His role as the Green Cross Code Man, a superhero who for two decades promoted a road safety campaign for British children, earned him a knighthood as a Member of the Most Excellent Order of the British Empire in 2000. Prowse's athletic prowess dates back to his childhood, when he outperformed his peers in sprinting, jumping, and throwing events at his grammar school after World War II. His conversion to physical culture occurred on a cold January day in 1951 when he bought an issue of *Health and Strength* that featured French bodybuilder Robert Duranton, whose physique he likened to "a Greek god," on the cover. "From that momentous day onwards, I became hooked on the concept of the 'body beautiful.' My whole life became dedicated to health, fitness strength and physique and my body eventually became my passport to fame and a wonderful career."[23] While working as an accountant, Prowse started exercising with a Charles Atlas course, then gravitated to free weights, where he could only press seventy pounds and bench press eighty pounds. After a decade of training he could press 330, bench press 500, and deadlift 660 pounds. In 1962 he became British Heavyweight Weightlifting Champion and competed in the world championships in Budapest and the British Empire and Commonwealth Games in Perth, Australia. He also entered the 1960 Mr. Universe contest in London. Although Prowse never ascended to the peak of either sport, he parlayed his impressive strength and size into numerous profitable ventures.

As physical fitness became increasingly popular, he promoted merchandise in Britain for the American-based Weider organization and took advantage of the isometric craze of the 1960s by marketing a German home fitness device called the Bullworker, which attracted over thirty thousand buyers its first year. He also started a mail order business, and with profits from these enterprises launched a short-lived physical culture magazine called *Power* in 1967 and a long-lasting gym in South East London in 1969. His acting career began by happenstance when he played the character Death in a black comedy titled *Don't Let Summer Come* at the Mermaid Theatre; this was followed by other minor roles. His film career started with television commercials when he played a huge Viking warrior for Kit-Kat chocolate bars. "I never considered myself to be an actor," he recalled. "I hadn't attended drama school or received any dramatic training and I didn't have a resume that listed any stage work. I was a 6ft 7in bodybuilder who didn't look like a boxer or all-in wrestler and I seemed to fill a niche in the acting world."[24] That his muscles, not his acting ability, could arouse the interest of filmgoers hardly occurred to Prowse.

What enabled him to capitalize on his muscles was not so much their strength or appearance but how they complemented his size. It became apparent in his first cinematic breakthrough in 1971 when he played Julian, a manservant in Stanley Kubrick's dystopian crime film *A Clockwork Orange*. Prowse never plays a violent role but appears somewhat menacingly on the side while others engage in dialogue. Despite protestations that he was so "exhausted" from holding and carrying wheelchair-bound Frank Alexander down several flights of stairs that it took "a couple of days off to recover," Prowse appears on camera barely ten minutes, speaking only twenty words, and never shirtless. He was listed so far down the credits that he merited virtually no attention from movie critics. Nevertheless, he was striking in his horn-rimmed glasses and with his muscly appearance. The image Prowse conveyed was not unlike that of Olympic weightlifter Harold Sakata, who, as one reviewer noted, "will forever be remembered as the villainous 'Odd Job' in the ultimate [James] Bond film, *Goldfinger* (1964), with his lethal martial arts and steel-brimmed bowler hat."[25] Indeed, Prowse was soon chosen by filmmaker Russ Meyer for a minor role in *Black Snake* (1973), where he was again typecast as a monstrous, uncouth, muscleman. More consequentially, it paved the way for a major/minor role in George Lucas's *Star Wars*.

By the time he was tapped to play Darth Vader in that epic production, Prowse was one of the most experienced actors on the set, having appeared in a dozen films and countless television shows, none of which were major or sustaining. Yet his body would be hidden under a cumbrous costume of quilted leather and fiberglass and his West Country English accent replaced by the deep and resonant voice of American actor James Earl Jones: "So there I was, supposedly the most awe-inspiring villain in the universe, sweating like a pig and as blind as a bat!" For as many as six continuous hours, Prowse suffered the indignity of sweltering studio lights with nobody able to recognize what he looked like or how he sounded. He consoled himself by imagining that he spoke through his lumbering gait:

> Body acting and bodybuilding are more closely related than most people would imagine, and all that posing I'd done to impress the judges in my early years now began to pay dividends. From within the black leather suit, I treated Vader's every gesture as a bodybuilding pose, refining here and exaggerating there, until my character "spoke" with every tilt of his head or movement of his arms. When I watch those *Star Wars* movies . . . I'm quietly pleased at the amount of expression that Vader manages to convey without a facial expression to his name, save for the fixed menace of that mask.

Prowse's character appeared only infrequently in the *Star Wars* trilogy, and it was the suit, not the actor, that received acclaim. It became most apparent to Prowse at personal appearances where he was denied the right to do Darth Vader. For the studio it was far cheaper and convenient to put any large guy in the suit, hoping fans would not know the difference. Nor was he allowed to speak or write his name as Vader. To complete the unreality of his film portrayal, stuntmen were substituted for Prowse in all three *Star*

Wars renditions, not only for the light saber exchanges but in other scenes necessitating neither skill nor risks.[26] Unprecedented use of special effects further detracted from his presence.

The 1977 version, which cost about $11 million to produce, grossed $775,398,007 by 2011, the second highest gross of all time for a film.[27] It also won six Academy Awards, including Best Costume Design and Best Visual Effects. Resentment boiled over for Prowse when he was not allowed to wear his suit when it appeared onstage with designer John Mollo, who collected the Oscar. *The Empire Strikes Back* and *Return of the Jedi* were also highly successful box office attractions and again won awards for special effects. Prowse went unmentioned in any of the reviews despite his costume's featured role. By 1983 it was obvious to John Simon, drama critic for *New York* magazine, that movies of this ilk, which he called "malodorous offal," were "dehumanizing." They're for children or childish adults," Simon noted. "They're not for adult mentalities. . . . They're making children dumber than they need to be. . . . Special effects are like the tail of the dog which should not wag the whole animal. When you have a film that's 90% special effects (and that's a kindly estimate) you might just as well be watching an animated cartoon." Fellow critic Roger Ebert struck back: "I think all movies are special effects. Movies are not real. They're two dimensional. The film goes through the camera, the projector throws the light on the screen, and that makes the special effect. It's a dream. It's an imagination. As to whether this film is good enough, it made me laugh, it made me thrilled." Ebert claimed that he had been "thoroughly entertained."[28] Although Prowse received a modicum of personal recognition and financial compensation, and his character achieved cult status, the mysterious "force" behind all the action benefited little from his muscles, which were never seen and rarely used.

Further disillusionment stemmed from Prowse being rejected for the role of the superhero in the 1978 remake of *Superman*, which would have allowed the viewing public to appreciate his muscular might and acting attributes. "Of all the films I've been involved in, I've never tried so hard to get a part as I did for the role of Superman." The selection was made more bitter not only by the choice of a "skinny" American actor named Christopher Reeve, who was six foot four and 175 pounds, but the request that Prowse be the one to put some muscles on Reeve's frame so that he would look the part. Although Reeve improved steadily under his tutelage, gaining five or six pounds of "healthy muscle" a week, "developing a fine taper from chest to waist," and improved "fitness and physical presence,"

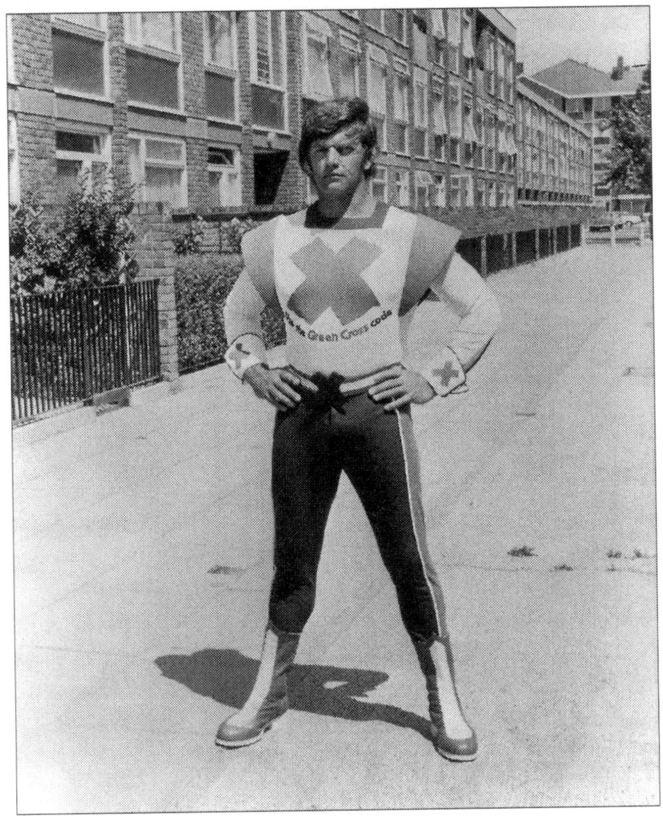

Figure 16.2. Before he became the body of Darth Vader, Dave Prowse was the Green Cross Code Man, a superhero who promoted road safety. Collection of David L. Chapman.

an altercation on the set over his appearance resulted in a parting of ways. Prowse attributed it to the American's developing a "big star" attitude to complement his superhero role.[29]

Far more satisfying to Prowse's own aspirations to stardom was his selection in 1976 to portray the Green Cross Code Man, an attempt by the British Department for Transport to reduce the road accident figures involving children, estimated annually at forty thousand. Catering to kids' tastes by mimicking Superman helped compensate for earlier shortcomings. "My tasteful green costume was pure superhero," he recalled, "with a fetching pair of green tights below my body-hugging, long-sleeved tunic. Accessories included a fine pair of shoulder extensions, green and white gauntlets and compulsory superhero knee boots. My chest was emblazoned with a huge green cross, and various smaller green crosses re-emphasised the theme throughout the ensemble." Prowse's message of "stop, look, listen, and think" was broadcast to children and adults through public information films, television ads, and visits to schools in seven hundred cities throughout the United Kingdom and the world over two decades. Whether his message saved as many as 250,000 children from being killed and injured on the roads, as he claimed, seems doubtful, but being the Green Code Man was "the best gig I ever had."[30] Prowse never showed or used his muscles, but the sight of his imposing size and striking attire had a far greater impact.

The Karate Kid

Much in the manner of Sylvester Stallone's *Rocky* (1976), *Karate Kid* (1984) and its sequels *Karate Kid Part II* (1986) and *Karate Kid Part III* (1989), relate the oft-told heroic tale of how an underdog defies overwhelming odds to defeat superior opponents. Greater strength and size of muscles in this instance is superseded by martial arts skills imparted to a young protégé named Daniel (Ralph Macchio) by Mr. Miyagi (Pat Morita), a Japanese handyman. There is no evidence that *either* Macchio or Morita had extensive athletic or martial arts backgrounds. The former was a singer and dancer, while the latter was known chiefly as a stand-up comedian who played in minor television and movie roles. What qualifies *Karate Kid* as a muscles movie, aside from its impressive contrived action sequences, is its conception by producer Jerry Weintraub, who was inspired by a tele-vised story he watched on five-o'clock news at his Los Angeles home: "It was about a kid in the [San Fernando] Valley who had been getting beat up every day on his way home from school. He took it and took it, until, tired of taking it, he found a teacher and learned karate. The next time the bullies came, it was lights out for the bad guys. I loved the story. It remind-ed me of the ninety-pound weakling ads they used to have for Charles Atlas." It was a captivating story that Weintraub immediately associated with the immensely successful *Rocky* series, which was by now in its third installment. He envisioned *The Karate Kid* as "just Rocky another way—it was an underdog story, a Cinderella story and a fantasy, the world as you wish it would be."[31] For the teenage kid, the scrawny, innocent, fatherless image conveyed by Macchio (who was actually twenty-two) seemed per-fect, while the choice of Morita to breathe life into an otherwise hopeless character depended as much on his fatherly manner as any physical pedagogy. And Morita's Japanese cultural background provided a vital link to the martial arts.

Further to reinforce the film's theme, Weintraub hired *Rocky* Academy Award winner John Avildsen as director. The plot for *Karate Kid*, as biographers Larry Powell and Tom Garrett note, was "essentially a combination of *Rocky* and teenage alienation." Weintraub also enlisted black belt karate expert Robert Kamen as screenwriter. By contributing to the perception of realism in the film, Avildsen believed Kamen deserved much of the credit for its success. To ensure at least some familiarity with the script, Macchio took a six-week crash course in karate, and Pat Johnson, a protégé of martial artist and actor Chuck Norris "provided karate instruction to the actors during the filming and appears as the referee in the final match." Still, it was necessary to hire fifteen stuntmen, a stunt coordinator, a special effects director, two sound effects editors, and a martial arts choreographer to achieve the desired degree of realism.[32] Lest viewers misconstrue muscles for might, however, the filmmakers infused Miyagi (Morita) with a mysterious superpower reviewer Roger Ebert identifies as "applied serenity. In a couple of scenes where he has to face down a hostile karate coach, Miyagi's words are so carefully chosen they don't give the other guy any excuse to get violent. Miyagi uses the language as carefully as his hands or arms to ward off blows and gain an advantage."[33] Belying the impressive shape, size, and strength of muscular bodies in action was the inner strength of the old man's wisdom to reinforce the illusion that he and his weak protégé could transform the impossible (à la Charles Atlas) into the miraculous. Weintraub succeeds in creating the ultimate fantasy of a world most viewers wish it would be. Building on the emotional bond between the kid and his mentor, Weintraub employs an extra layer of credibility to make fantastic physical feats seem real.

Audiences agreed. Made with a budget estimated at $8 million, the movie was regarded as a "sleeper," earning only $5,031,753 during its first week in June 1984. But it caught on quickly, and by the end of its run in 1985 earned $90,815,558. Popular acceptance of the underdog story generated a momentum that led to *Karate Kid II* in 1986, which earned $115,103,979.[34] Totally disregarding its phony depictions of athleticism, audiences, journalists, and Academy of Motion Picture Arts and Sciences members, consumed by Miyagi's applied serenity, rewarded *The Karate Kid* handsomely. Pat Morita received Academy Award and Golden Globe nominations for

Best Actor in a Supporting Role, and the film was named Best Family Motion Picture at the Young Artist Awards. "The movie really belongs to Pat Morita," concludes Ebert.[35]

The Raging Bull

Unlike Kirk Douglas, Burt Lancaster, or Steve Reeves, Robert De Niro was an actor with no athletic credentials, but he was adept at infusing reality into any role. As he conveyed to the *New York Times* in 1973, "You try to get as close as possible to the reality of a character. You learn his lifestyle, how he holds his fork, how he carries himself, how he talks, how he relates to other people." He believed that "you've got to physically and mentally become that person you are portraying." Furthermore, observes biographer Andy Dougan, De Niro had a "third eye" that enabled him to gauge his performances from an audience point of view, "And it is only through the audience that an actor can tell whether or not the performance is real. If the audience accepts it, then it is real. In the theater 'fake acting' cannot be hidden from the audience. The cinema, however, survives on the suspension of disbelief. Film acting has to be fake." Otherwise, "it would take days to get a single take in the can" and "stuntmen and special effects teams would be redundant. . . . Movie acting is an elaborate optical illusion which the audience unconsciously indulges."[36] For De Niro to convey realism in action scenes requiring a display and use of muscles would not be impossible by this rationale.

Yet only two movies required him to portray an athlete. *Bang the Drum Slowly* (1973) is based on Mark Harris's 1956 novel about the friendship between star pitcher Henry Wiggen (Michael Moriarty) and a half-witted catcher, Bruce Pearson (De Niro) on a fictitious major league baseball team and how they cope with the latter's terminal illness. De Niro first had to master the Southern culture of his character, "So I went to Georgia and stayed in a small town. I found an old-fashioned country store and I bought the kind of clothes Bruce would buy. I wore them all around. Then I started with the way that Bruce would talk. The people in the town were really nice and they didn't mind me copying the way they talked. . . . After a while I began to move like Bruce and I began to feel like him."[37] Mastering the sport of baseball was another matter, however. Having never played the game, it was imperative that De Niro read as many books, watch as many players, and study as many films as possible. He and other members of the crew also spent two hours daily playing baseball before the shooting commenced in and around New York.[38] To learn how to swing a bat, De Niro practiced with a pitching machine. Then, after shooting the film all day, he would do more batting practice and run several miles. On days off, he watched baseball on television: "I saw in every baseball game how relaxed the players were. . . . I could practice in my room watching them do nothing." Mastering the art of tobacco chewing was another challenge. Despite the appearance of a plug in his cheek in many scenes, there was virtually no spitting.[39] Much of the actual baseball sequences consisted of clips from stock footage provided by major league teams. Little more dedication to the reality of the sport was required for De Niro, since most of the action consisted of dramatic scenes off the field. Although Ebert calls *Bang the Drum Slowly* "the ultimate baseball movie," he notes that "there isn't a lot of play-by-play action, only enough to establish the games and make the character points."[40]

Raging Bull (1980) required a different skill set. The film relates the turbulent life of boxer Jake La Motta (De Niro), whose raging temperament led to winning the World Middleweight Championship and eventually wrecking his personal life. Although director Martin Scorsese was not a boxing fan and was disinclined to make the film, De Niro became absorbed in the character after reading La Motta's autobiography, discerning "a few good scenes around which to build the plot." Perhaps the most telling feature of their collaboration was their aversion to sports. "The one sure thing was that it wouldn't be a film about boxing!" Scorsese had proclaimed at the outset. "We didn't know a thing about it and it didn't interest us at all."[41] For two years De Niro became preoccupied with the project, originally dubbed *Prizefighter*, and had a major influence in developing the script with screenwriters Mardik Martin and Paul Schrader and enlisting La Motta's assistance with the boxing scenes. He had also been training to get in shape and frequently engaged in prolonged shadow boxing sessions. As shooting approached, De Niro started taking boxing lessons from La Motta, sparring with him and trying to perfect his Bronx accent, all under the supervision of Al Silvani, Sylvester Stallone's trainer for his *Rocky* films. Although both boxers wore headgear and mouthpieces, the bouts were intense enough that both got black eyes and La Motta required minor dental work. Baxter observes that "De Niro's body was thickening with all the exercise, helped by a high protein diet. Make-up built up his nose, and his hair was darkened and curled. Once he was proficient in the ring, De Niro, whom La Motta, with typical hyperbole, said he'd rate among the twenty top middleweights in the world, sparred through three fights in a Brooklyn boxing ring. Spieled by the ring announcer as 'a young La Motta,' he outpointed opponents in two of the three." Notwithstanding these realistic efforts, virtually all acting scenes were carefully contrived for dramatic effect. According to Baxter, the production team "plotted the movements like dance routines, with diagrams of feet, and arrows showing the direction of movement."[42] Little was left for the spontaneity one expects to see in an actual boxing match.

Arguably the greatest physical exertion required for *Raging Bull* stemmed not from the boxing but its filming. "The fight scenes would take some really critical physical stamina on the part of Bob and everyone else," Scorsese recalls. "They had to be shot over and over again."[43] Actors were also coached precisely on when they were going to get hit and how to avoid injury. "In the fight scenes the punches are all choreographed," De Niro explains. "Your opponent has to move his head in a certain direction when you hit him and the camera has to be at a certain angle so that it looks like he's been hit. Then you lay in the sound later." Defensive moves required additional stamina one could not replicate in shadow boxing: "When there's another person there you have to rehearse so that nobody gets hurt accidently."[44] These protective measures, seemingly at odds with the avowed purpose of boxing to inflict bodily harm, were reinforced by the manner of filming, where, Andy Dougan notes, the fight scenes

> had to be shot in slow motion so that they would have as much impact as possible in the film. That required an additional discipline from De Niro. . . . To shoot the fight scenes properly Scorsese had quartered the ring and would work in one section at a time. De Niro had a punch-bag put in one of the other corners of the ring. While Scorsese was setting up, De Niro would be working up a sweat. When the time came to roll the cameras he would simply move to the spot where they were shooting, already looking as if he was in the middle of a title fight. For De Niro the scenes in the ring were rather like being at the Arthur Murray School of Dancing.[45]

Furthermore, De Niro had no interest in fighting for its own sake. He admits he did not intend to "make a meal of it. . . . What Jake taught me was how to take punishment, but I'm not anxious to prove a point. I know I'm supposed to be the actor who carries his role over into private life. There is a small spillage, but I don't flip out. I'm not eating glass for breakfast or beating up the wife as a result of getting inside Jake La Motta's skin."[46] Although De Niro tried to get inside his character's head, he failed to get inside his skin. When the actor was in the ring, his only costume was his nearly naked body. He had to bare his body and soul for the camera, and there was nowhere to hide.

Ultimately De Niro's lack of realism carries into actual movie fight scenes. Unlike real matches, there is no footage devoted to fighters bobbing and weaving or dancing around the ring to detect an opponent's vulnerabilities or the right moment to strike. Every scene consists of nonstop slugging, and no real boxer has that much stamina or capacity for punishment. Nor would La Motta's major rival for the crown, Sugar Ray Robinson, have been a part of a slugfest. While the Bronx Bull describes his own style as "punch, punch, punch," Robinson was "a real cutie when it came to boxing."[47] It should be obvious to any serious observer of the manly art that virtually every fight scene in this film has been subjected to varying camera speeds, typically slow to fast motion to depict savage power and violence, and close-up camera angles to display the pain and agony from faux blows, all of which reverberate with the same studio sound effect. In *The Making of Raging Bull*, Mike Evans describes how

> Scorsese would even change the size and shape of the ring to enhance what he wanted to convey about Jake's emotional state. The first time we see him knock down Sugar Ray in the ring is large and sweeping, the lighting is bright, reflecting the elation of the moment. But later, when Sugar Ray defeats him, the ring—as well as being dark and smoky—is smaller, enveloping its occupants almost like a prison cell. . . . Other sequences use devices such as stop-frames, extreme close-ups, and jump-cut editing to convey the dynamic of the combat in an impressionistic, sometimes almost surreal way. But all the time, Scorsese retains a sense of "realism" in his portrayal of the action, despite the images themselves being highly contrived.

Much of the film's fabrications may be credited to cinematographer Michael Chapman and to Thelma Schoonmaker, whose film editing earned an Oscar. Not only did the fight scenes, lasting less than twenty minutes of a two-hour-plus movie, require 50 percent of the filming time, but the postproduction process, "scheduled to take seven weeks, ended up taking six months," according to Evans.[48] To avoid further delays, Scorsese resorted to cinematic shortcuts to mask the film's phony physicality. Many of La Motta's lesser matches are depicted in stills or at a distance from stock footage where De Niro's face and body cannot be discerned. One can only imagine how much more the credited stunt and special effects coordinators added to the films' "realism." Indeed, the brawl scenes outside the ring in *Raging Bull* are more convincing than the fights.

More realistic is the portrayal of the aftermath of La Motta's fight career, for which De Niro gained sixty pounds, going from 165 to 215, to fit into his character's dissipated existence at his Florida nightclub. Scorsese was alarmed by his star's condition after a two-month break in shooting. "Bobby's weight was so extreme that his breathing was like mine when I have an asthma attack," he observed. "With the bulk he put on there was no more doing forty takes. There were three or four takes. The body dictated things. He just became that person."[49] Contrary to his remarks about how he improvised his athleticism, De Niro justified his later life characterization of La Motta: "I just can't fake acting," he said. "I know movies are an illusion and the first rule is to fake it, but not for me. . . . I want to deal with all the facts of the character, thin or fat." For the sake of realism, De Niro was willing to sacrifice his body. "I reached the point where I couldn't tie my shoes and I was huffing and puffing and my breath started to sound strange. . . . I looked like an animal."[50] But it was precisely the look Scorsese wanted for the climactic scenes. Much has been made of De Niro's dramatic weight gain and how it contributed to the portrayal of La Motta. It underscores the fact that the realistic portions of *Raging Bull* are not so much the scenes about boxing and brawn but the dramatic scenes where muscle becomes fat.

Although box office receipts exceeded the film budget by only about $5 million, *Raging Bull* garnered eight Academy Award nominations and took two of the awards: De Niro won for Best Actor and the film also took the Best Film Editing prize.[51] Critical reviews in the *Monthly Film Journal*, the *New York Times*, *Newsweek*, and *Time* lent credence to these accolades. Decades later *Raging Bull* was deemed a modern classic. Roger Ebert called it the best film of the 1980s and one of the ten best films of all time. Likewise, Leonard Maltin included it in his 100 Must-See Films of the Twentieth Century, most notably for its dramatic content and for De Niro's physical transformation. For general audiences as well as critics, the action scenes in *Raging Bull* seemed real, Dougan explains, through "the third eye" where images projected on the human retina twenty-four times per second elicits the principle of persistence of vision, enabling the eye to "retain the image and trick the brain into thinking that it is moving. Cinema survives on the suspension of disbelief." Indeed, biographer Shawn Levy's 2014 conclusion that "in *Raging Bull*, he is one of the most plausible movie-screen boxers ever filmed" underscores how effectively De Niro used his unathletic body to perfect an illusion. "To call it a boxing picture is ridiculous," Scorsese admitted. "It's sports but it's something to do with living." The irony was evident also to La Motta, who concurs that although "they took a lot of footage of fighting," the story is "*really* about three people—a man, his wife, and his brother."[52] Notwithstanding its boxing tableau and De Niro's reputation for realism, *Raging Bull* is not a muscle movie.

G. I. Jane

During the mid-1990s, as the women's empowerment movement was gaining strength, there appeared an action movie that seemingly symbolized many of the goals women were fighting for, including respect, intelligence, and the opportunity to show that they could perform many of the same physical feats as men. *G. I. Jane* (1997) was never a smash hit, but it made a powerful cinematic statement on behalf of many women who had only heretofore been passive participants in the cause. In the film, Demi Moore portrays the fictional Lieutenant Jordan O'Neil, the first woman to undergo training in the US Navy Special Warfare Group, Moore had formerly been recognized in Hollywood as a model, songwriter, and actor in low-budget film and television productions; starting in 1984 she enjoyed a long string of successes, culminating in *Ghost* (1990), which became the highest-grossing film of the year and earned Moore a Golden Globe nomination.[53] By 1995 she was Hollywood's highest-paid actress. By no means the least important asset for Moore was her photogenic face and her curvaceous figure, which she frequently bared, most significantly in *Striptease* (1996), for which she received a record-breaking salary of $12.5 million.

Aside from its gender-charged message, *G. I. Jane* was significant as the first instance in which Moore, despite her lack of athletic experience or inclination, displayed her physical talents as part of a movie's central theme. What made it possible was the predisposition of its potential director, Ridley Scott, with whom she had developed a congenial relationship over the years. Scott, as his biographer Vincent LoBrutto points out, was "fascinated by war." After graduating from West Hartlepool College in England, he entered national service in the Royal Marines. "Art was in his blood but so was the military," LoBrutto notes, owing to Scott's father's service and his brother's career in the Merchant Navy: "Below the surface the young Ridley Scott was attracted to self discipline and organization. The inner workings of war fascinated and obsessed him."[54] But it was Moore, not Scott, who brought *G. I. Jane* to the fore. "What's interesting is that *Jane* wasn't the first project she'd brought to my attention," Scott recalls. "I'd met Demi on a couple of prior occasions, where we'd swapped ideas; in fact, she'd tried to offer me one film I didn't go for. And with Demi it's always better to be frank. So I'd said 'no.' This is why, I think, she came back later with something that was more appropriate for her and me—*G.I. Jane*."[55]

According to Paul Sammon's 1998 account, *G. I. Jane* fit perfectly into Scott's filmmaking trademark, featuring "mature nuances resting comfortably alongside big budgets, big stars, state-of-the-art visuals, and multiplex-friendly plots." Sammon assures readers that there "often *is* more to the cinema of Ridley Scott than what meets the eye."[56] Indeed, one suspects the viewer's eye is missing an important aspect of reality. What never becomes convincing to educated physical culturists is how Moore could condition her body so quickly from that of a shapely film star with minimal workout experience into a physical specimen comparable to the men in America's most elite and fit commando unit. *G. I. Jane*, after all, is all about conditioning the female body for the most rigorous combat experience any male soldier might encounter in the field. We are told from multiple sources that Moore would start her daily workout routine at 4:00 a.m. by running around Manhattan's Central Park with multiple security guards, but with no indication of how far, how fast, how long it lasted, or its impact on her filming for the day. For more comprehensive training she tapped the expertise of two personal trainers, noted celebrity guru Gregory Joujon-Roche for physical conditioning, and Navy Seal, Air, and Land Forces (SEALs) instructor Stephen Helvenston to "gain that visceral, Navy SEAL mindset" to assure suspicious viewers that her actions are real. For two weeks prior to filming on location, her daily workout routine allegedly consisted of a combination of ninety minutes on a 2 percent incline treadmill at varying speeds (with frequent abdominal intervals) for cardio fitness. The abdominal exercises included accordion crunches, side bridges, and "Supermans." Chest and shoulder routines consisted of one to two hours of weightlifting, stressing one-arm pushups, "dive bombers," dumbbell bench presses, overhead presses, front raises, and a combination of chest, cable, lateral, and barrel flys. Instead of specifying a certain number of repetitions, Moore's trainers recommended she "do sets of each circuit until you feel 'you've killed it.'"[57] Rest assured, any experienced college or professional strength and conditioning coach will dismiss any notion that such a routine can transform an average healthy and fit man or woman into a highly trained and perfectly conditioned Navy

SEAL in two weeks as pure fantasy. The normal training period for SEALs is seventeen weeks, and only then after careful screening. Even after a day or two of intense physical exertion, Moore's sore and stiff muscles would have seriously impaired her acting and ability to continue training.[58]

What, then, can account for Moore's amazing ability to convince viewers that the transformation of her body and ability to turn gender assumptions upside down is real? It is chiefly attributable to the cinematic artistry of director Scott, whose 1998 interviews with Paul Sammon form the basis for all subsequent assessments of *G. I. Jane*.[59] Much of his background, Scott reveals, comes from working with material in commercials and rock videos featuring "style over content. But style is, in turn, shaped by a piece's visual effects which directly connects to the cameraman." Scott admits that "the Seal training you see in the film is a bit of the real and the fanciful mixed together." Having observed Seal trainees perform basic exercises at bases at Parris Island, South Carolina, and in Pensacola, Florida, he concluded that "those weren't very photogenic—they were more repetitious than anything else" and would not transmit well to film. Knowing the importance of spectacle to the success of any film, Scott "decided to mix fact with invention." It took the form of many of the same artifices Scorsese and De Niro employed in *Raging Bull*, including the distant filming of action scenes where Moore cannot be distinguished from anyone else in the unit, along with unending sequences of her face only, usually in response to action occurring elsewhere. The only display of strenuous physical exertion occurs in the much heralded one-arm push-up scene, leading Scott to insist that "Demi did almost all of what you see in the movie. She was rarely doubled. In fact, Demi put on about twenty pounds of muscle for the part, much to her horror. She kept insisting she looked like Atlas from the back. I thought she looked fantastic. That's how she was able to do those one-handed push-ups in the film. That really is Demi. She's really doing those. Remarkable."[60] Yet the film shows her doing only seven such push-ups, lasting barely nineteen seconds, and her body descends just halfway to the floor; it is a pretty simple exercise that any moderately fit athlete could execute. Even more unimpressive, reminiscent of the sudden scene shift that enabled muscular Steve Reeves to be overpowered in *Athena* (1954), Moore is shown doing a chin-up, displaying first her lower body, then her face and arms, and then her shoulders finishing the hoist. Her only complete body exposure occurs in a (nonsexual) nude shower scene in which she converses with Commander Master Chief John James Urgayle (Viggo Mortensen). What completed the unrealistic scenario of the movie was that Scott was prohibited from using any real SEALs or government operational facilities and that the US Department of Defense, though initially cooperative, opposed virtually all of the filmmakers' requests. "It later became clear that the Navy and DOD didn't want this film to happen," recalls Scott.[61]

That it did happen owes much to Scott's commitment to an ideal of female empowerment being acted out in the real world by courageous women who were asserting their rights in the wake of the Navy's 1991 Tailhook scandal and Shannon Faulkner's bid to enter the Citadel military college in 1994. "I thought *G. I. Jane* just reflected the way the world is really working," Scott asserts. "It was basically a parable of a woman trying to make it in the most manly of male worlds . . . a woman fighting back and refusing to be beaten down. . . . I was trying to show what a woman has to do just to have the same chances as a man."[62] The film was a moderate hit, earning "two thumbs up" from Gene Siskel and Roger Ebert and praise from the latter for Demi Moore as "one of the most venturesome of current stars." He found it "intriguing to watch her work with the image of her body" and admired her ability to "test the tension between a woman's body and a woman's ambition and will. 'G.I. Jane' does it most obviously, and effectively." At the box office, however, it earned only about $80 million worldwide. "Not great," Scott lamented. "I thought we'd do better."[63] This outcome could hardly be attributed to lack of talent. Demi Moore, already one of the brightest starts in Hollywood, put in a first-class performance as Lieutenant O'Neil. Likewise, Viggo Mortensen and Anne Bancroft were outstanding in respective supporting roles as Commander Master Chief John James Urgayle and Senator Lillian DeHaven. What's more, Scott's ability to make a hard-hitting statement on a hot-button issue was amply demonstrated. It reaches an apogee in the torture scene when Master Chief Urgayle, thinking he has beaten down his beleaguered female trainee, tells her to "seek life elsewhere." O'Neil sharply retorts, "Suck my dick," which is echoed repeatedly by "suck my dick" chants from the male prisoners in the chamber, and again later at a fraternizing bar scene, where one of her comrades readily accepts her equal status saying, "Hey O'Neil, I'd go to war with you any day."

As a muscle movie, however, *G. I. Jane* fails on multiple counts. What detracts most from the film's credibility is its heavy reliance on dramatic dialogue, a cinematic tradition since talkies replaced the physical histrionics that had been so characteristic of silent films until the late 1920s. Yet the film's feminist plot is contingent on physical performance, not verbal manipulations. This adverse effect is further compromised by the gloomy aspect of black-and-white images, with splashes of color here and there that pervade the film. Even the action scenes appear murky, thereby inducing ennui rather than interest or excitement. Finally, the director, despite existing trends in moviemaking trends by the 1990s, makes only minimal use of the most obvious techniques for creating spectacles that have been around since the days of Georges Méliès. His bag of tricks included only eight special effects experts, two stunt coordinators, five utility stuntmen, and one double for Demi Moore. *G. I. Jane* fails to achieve the desired level of illusion of a woman displaying parity with men in the most intense arena of masculine hegemony. Far from fulfilling his vision of conveying a sense of reality, Ridley Scott proves only to be the master of make believe.

The Rock

The athletic credentials of Dwayne "the Rock" Johnson are unquestionable. They are apparent in each of his films as heroic feats of action accompanied by overt displays of muscle. Scion of two generations of professional wrestlers on both sides of his family and physically gifted in size and strength, it is hardly surprising that he would showcase his body publicly. His father, the late Rocky Johnson (Wayde Douglas Bowles) was a champion wrestler, an accomplished boxer who sparred with George Foreman, and a proficient swimmer and gymnast. The Rock remembers him as "one of the first guys in our business to have a complete package: a great, muscular body, tremendous athleticism, real wrestling talent, and a strong personality."[64] With his father as a role model, the Rock was introduced to mat life at age five when "I was with my dad down in the wrestling ring and in the weight room, watching all these guys wrestle, jack iron all day. It was a different world. Everything was dirty: dirty gym, dirty mats. My dad said, 'I'm getting up at six; you're gonna get up at six, too. I'm having my coffee; you have your orange juice. I'm going to the gym; you come to the gym with me.' And then on the mats, I would roll around and these guys would throw me around and wrestle around with me."[65] By age thirteen Johnson was lifting weights seriously and was already over six feet tall and weighing 170 pounds. At Freedom High School in Bethlehem, Pennsylvania, he decided that amateur wrestling was not his style, concluding that he was more an entertainer than a wrestler. But he excelled in football, making fourteen sacks and over a hundred tackles his senior year.[66] Named a high school All-American, Johnson accepted a scholarship to the University of Miami, where he played defensive tackle on the Hurricanes' 1991 national championship team. After briefly playing linebacker for the Calgary Stampeders, he returned to his family in Miami to become a wrestler under the guidance of his father, who "grinded me out every day for months."[67]

The professional wrestling world Johnson stepped into has long been surrounded by controversy over whether it is sport or entertainment, real or fake. Broderick Chow, Eero Laine, and Claire Warden argue that it is "a live performance" that is "intensely physical and relies heavily on various aspects of spectacle . . . overlaid with an over-the-top theatricality that animates and drives the narrative forward." Perhaps the most realistic aspect of this artistry is the practice of "blading," where a wrestler simulates serious injury by extracting blood from his forehead with a concealed razor blade. Unlike movie and stage depictions of pugilism, it is the sight of real blood spurting on the athletic body. The competition "is at once scripted, theatrical, and fake, and improvised, and real" with wrestlers "actually doing the things we see them do, but their motivations for doing them are highly theatrical. . . . Professional wrestling does what theatre cannot do or can only do by means of illusion: enact violence in a live performance."[68] World Wresting Entertainment (WWE) star Mark Henry explains that professional wrestling is not fake but predetermined:

> It's scripted. But there's a lot to it. It's a special business. There's nothing else on earth like professional wrestling. You have to be an actor. You have to be an athlete, and you have to be smart enough to understand psychology and what works and doesn't work, and it's regional. Wherever you go is different. So you have to be able to have a multiplicity in your skill set and psychology base. It's simple sometimes. You're the big guy. He's the small guy. He's the good guy, you're the bad guy. But after that, you have to be able to make people respect you for your abilities but emotionally get invested in you as an individual. That's when you're really hitting your audience. In pro wrestling we call it suspended disbelief. They have to be able to feel your pain.[69]

The power of this staged event to electrify audiences, explains Stephen Di Benedetto, stems "not from its veracity as athletic competition, but rather from the crowd's propensity to become enthralled and unable to determine when a [scripted] 'work' becomes a [spontaneous] 'shoot.'" Philosopher Roland Barthes contends more generally that "the public is completely uninterested in knowing whether the contest is rigged or not, and rightly so; it abandons itself to the primary virtue of the spectacle, which is to abolish all motives and all consequences: what matters is not what it thinks but what it sees."[70]

What the public sees in Dwayne Johnson is an accomplished athlete with impressive size and strength and a charismatic personality whose punishments of and by opponents seem real. For Johnson, wrestling also fit his family's chosen lifestyle, comparable to that of Mickey Rourke's real-life character in *The Wrestler* (2008). "That was my dad, that was my uncles, that was so many members of my family, explains Johnson. "It was the only thing they knew." When asked about the accuracy of *The Wrestler*, Johnson answers, "It's very accurate. I would do blade jobs. I get a call once from the WWE, saying, 'Vince [McMahon] would like to see you in Stamford.' I went to his office and he says, 'I really think you have a lot of potential, but you're not ready for the WWE. You should go to Memphis, Tennessee. That's where I want you to learn the business.' And as I was leaving, he said, 'You keep working hard, but don't go down there and cut your fucking forehead with razor blades, you understand me?' "[71]

From 1998 to 2001 Johnson gained fame as one of the circuit's most talented and popular wrestlers, winning and reclaiming the World Wrestling Federation (WWF) championship belt six times. Meanwhile, he decided to showcase his talents beyond television gigs to the big screen. The earliest evidence of his physicality appears in a low-budget documentary titled *Beyond the Mat*, written, produced, directed, and narrated by Barry Blaustein (cowriter of *The Nutty Professor*, 1996), which focuses on the lives of three prominent wrestlers: Mick Foley, Terry Funk, and Jake Roberts. While the Rock is included only in a portion of the final segment on Foley, who was WWF world champion, the film displays one of the most violent scenes ever witnessed in this brutal sport. It records the January 24, 1999, Royal Rumble, and an "I quit" match in which the Rock first boasts that he is "the most electrifying man in sport entertainment today," then demonstrates his physicality by doing serious damage to his opponent's face and skull.[72] As pundit Nathan Birch observes, Johnson mercilessly "pummels Foley with 11 vicious unprotected chair shots to the head (he was only supposed to hit five, but got carried away), leaving the hardcore legend with a deep gash in his scalp and a dislocated jaw. To add family trauma to injury, Foley's wife and kids were at ringside to witness the whole thing." "It is a show, yes," writes Roger Ebert. "'Beyond the Mat' makes no secret of the fact that every match is scripted and that the outcomes are not in doubt. But we knew that. What I didn't fully realize, until I saw this film, is how real the show is."[73] Indeed, the sight of the Rock manhandling the six-foot-two, 287-pound Foley in and out of the ring on live footage left no doubt about his athleticism. Readers of *Pro Wrestling Illustrated* voted the Royal Rumble 1999 Match of the Year. The production also proved riveting to wrestling and movie fans: with an estimated budget of only $500,000, it grossed $2,053,648. *Beyond the Mat* was also named Best Documentary at the Cinequest Film Festival in San Jose, California, and nominated by the Directors Guild of America for Best Documentary and Best Director.[74]

It also provided a rationale for the Rock to test the waters in a bona fide Hollywood production. As he explained in an interview, "I never quite understood why if you're successful in something, and then you want to make the transition to Hollywood, why wouldn't you apply the same discipline and processes that you did with wrestling and football?"[75] Whereas his wrestling career had revealed his real-life strength, agility, and entertainment ability, the movie camera demanded little more than the appearance of his muscular body. In *The Mummy Returns*, a 2001 sequel to *The Mummy* (1999), Johnson plays the villainous Scorpion King, whose designs for world conquest are thwarted, but his soul emerges from a mummified body shipped to the British Museum, where it resurfaces as an evil incarnation to wreak havoc and destruction. Ebert found it curious that too much movie action could be boring. "Imagine yourself on a roller coaster for two hours. After the first 10 minutes, the thrills subside. The mistake of 'The Mummy Returns' is to abandon the characters, and to use the plot only as a clothesline for special effects and action sequences." Most disappointing to Ebert were misleading billings for the Rock as a star: "To call his appearance a 'cameo' would be stretching it. He appears briefly at the beginning of the movie, is transmuted into a kind of transparent skeletal wraith and disappears until the end of the film, when he comes back as the dreaded Scorpion King. I am not sure, at the end, if we see the real Rock or merely his face, connected to computer-generated effects."[76] Critical consensus for reviewers in *Rotten Tomatoes* was that "the special effects are impressive, but the characters seem secondary to the computer-generated imagery." Still, this flawed spectacle, thanks in part to Johnson's muscular cameo, earned over $433 million against a budget of just $98 million. Johnson won the 2001 Teen Choice Award for Choice Sleazebag.[77]

The Rock's appearance, however, led to a starring role in a prequel titled *The Scorpion King* (2002), which garnered even more scathing reviews.

"Another grandiose, hyperactive crock, full of lame jokes and gorgeous, stupefying images" was Michael Wilmington's view in the *Chicago Tribune*. In the *New York Times*, Stephen Holden attributed the violent mayhem to fakery from special effects:

The Rock may be the first movie action hero made of flesh and blood who appears more digital than human. With his bulging eyes, skinny plucked-looking eyebrows, heavy-metal mane and monotone voice, he suggests a lobotomized Billy Crystal on stilts and steroids. But it's his body language more than his physiognomy that makes the Rock resemble something cooked up in a digital laboratory. The muscle-bound star moves laboriously, as if beneath all that bulk an ordinary human were straining to maneuver an extra hundred pounds of grafted-on muscle and tissue. . . . In "The Scorpion King," the balance between digital fakery and live action tips so decisively toward the artificial that the entire movie looks like an overblown cartoon.

At the website Reelviews, James Berardinelli likened the Rock to a young Schwarzenegger: "He has the same kind of physique, the same complete lack of acting ability, the same screen presence, and the same general appeal. Only the accent is missing." Critics on *Rotten Tomatoes* estimated that "action adventure doesn't get much cheesier than The Scorpion King," and Nick Rogers listed it in "Movies You Aught Not Watch" at The Film Yelp: "Boasting sword-and-sandal action more sluggish than a Ye Olde Renaissance Faire, The Rock putting someone through a table would be a welcome anachronism."[78]

Indeed, the film relies almost totally on stunt performers and special effects to reconstruct reality. To complement the acting component, the production company enlisted an army of moving picture technical experts to augment the action: 108 in visual effects (including twenty-four animators and eighteen compositors), 106 in stunt work (including eight coordinators), twenty-six in special effects, four in sound effects, and three choreographers, for a total of 247. Ironically, little real use was made of the Rock's muscles. It sufficed for most viewers who remembered his athleticism in the ring and could see his impressive physique to suspend any disbelief in the miraculous feats he appeared to be performing. Hence, *The Scorpion King* earned $165,333,180 against a $90 million budget.[79]

It was much the same stunt/special effects scenario that was used in such subsequent films starring Johnson: *Walking Tall* (2004, with seventy-seven hired experts), *Get Smart* (2008, with 344), *G.I. Joe: Retaliation* (2013, with 1,068), and *Baywatch* (2017, with 144). In *Hercules* (2014), his first classical role since *The Scorpion King*, there were 1,074 individuals recruited to enhance viewer appeal. What Johnson hoped to achieve was "a look that had never been seen before on-screen by any actor." He realized that Arnold Schwarzenegger had "set the bar very high" in *Conan*. Now forty years old, Johnson felt "the role of Hercules came around for me at a great time where everything kind of came together," enabling him to acquire "that experienced, aged muscle . . . that can only come with time." In contrast to his look at age twenty-nine, when he made *The Scorpion King*, it would feature a mature body type: "It required a lot of prep—a longer prep than I'm typically used to. We started the prep about 6–8 months out." Meanwhile, Johnson, who had retired from wrestling to devote more time to moviemaking after *Scorpion King*, continued serious weight training, reentered the "squared ring" full-time in 2011, and regained his championship belt. On April 3, 2013, he sustained serious injury in a WrestleMania 29 match with John Cena in which he tore the rectus tendon and adductor muscle from his pelvis and sustained a triple hernia, just as filming was about to start on *Hercules* in Budapest: "There was four weeks that I couldn't do anything, there was no cardio there was no anything—that helped me tremendously. . . . I actually came into *Hercules* a bit bigger, fuller, and more vascular." Indeed, his powerful-looking physique gives credence to the mythical Greek hero as conveyed in the comic book *Hercules: The Thracian Wars* on which the movie is based.[80]

Having witnessed Johnson appear on-screen nearly two dozen times since *Scorpion King*, it is not surprising that critics had become more attuned to his acting persona and inured to over-the-top special effects, especially for a fantasy film about a mythical story. "Hercules is tongue-in-cheek revisionist mythology, pitched at classics students who prefer to attend their lectures stoned," noted Ben Kenigsberg in the *New York Times*. "Hercules' gang of merry mercenaries roves Greece, killing pirates and other fourth-century B.C. riffraff. . . . Emphasizing tribalism and family treachery, 'Hercules' clearly aims to tap into the 'Game of Thrones' craze," Kenigsberg concluded. For Sherilyn Connelly in the *Village Voice*, the movie displayed both brawn and brains. Johnson was "not just physically strong, but with all apologies to Steve Reeves, Lou Ferrigno, and Ryan Gosling, he's by far the best actor to ever play this role. That's not damning with faint praise, either. Johnson is genuinely talented." In *Variety*, Scott Foundas concurred that "Hercules'

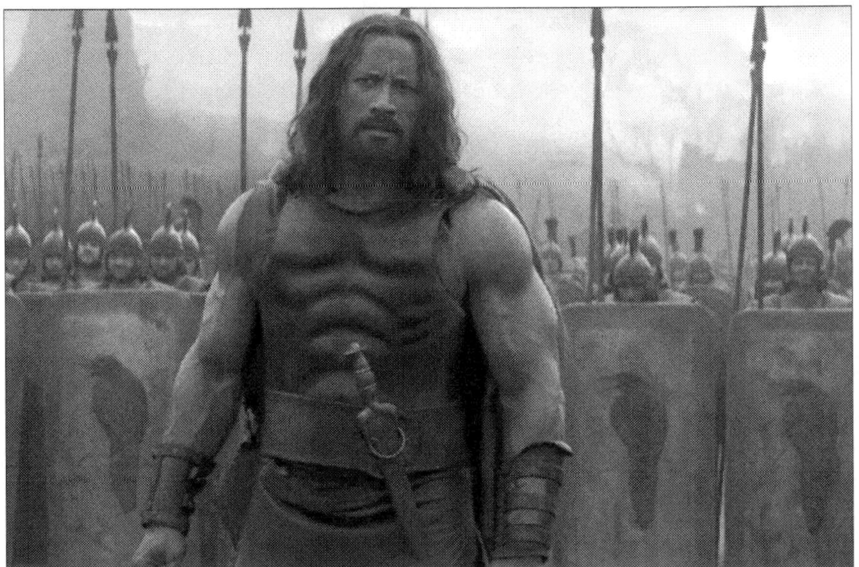

Figure 16.3. Dwayne Johnson brings the mythical hero down to earth as a dark, brooding protagonist in the 2014 film *Hercules*. Image in the public domain.

strongest asset is surely Johnson, who continues to foster one of the most affable, guileless screen personas in movies today. Johnson may have been born with screen presence wired into his DNA, but he's gradually cultivated the skills of a canny actor who knows just how to play to the camera and whose brute physical prowess is cut with a sly self-awareness." "The effects are impressive," wrote Elizabeth Weitzman in the *New York Daily News*, "but there are none bigger than the star's biceps. As [director Brett] Ratner cheerfully acknowledges, The Rock's preposterously oversized bulk is perfectly suited to a preposterously oversized movie." She identifies the Rock as "one of those actors who's always fully committed to his audience" and "never, ever forgets that we've paid good money to be entertained." This sensitivity to audience approval no doubt stems from the nature of his professional wrestling audience, prompting James Berardinelli's observation that *Hercules*, with its "endless computer generated special effects . . . seems geared toward boys in the age 10–14 range who have nothing better to do than watch a big-screen version of stuff they're used to seeing in video games."[81]

While the artificial means used to display Johnson's athleticism and appearance is not unlike that employed for other twenty-first-century stars, he seemingly stands apart in not having to resort to performance enhancing drugs to achieve an edge. Johnson admits he started popping an oral steroid just after high school graduation, but after seeing no results, he stopped taking it:

> I remember expressing complete and utter dissatisfaction to one of my football buddies, the only guy who knew what I was doing: "This is bullshit, man. It's not working." And that was it. That was my run-in with steroids. My size, unfortunately, led other people to suspect that I was on something. . . . And it simply wasn't true! At the same time, I wouldn't have known how or where to obtain steroids. I was genetically predisposed to being big and strong. And I worked out—a lot! That's it. There was no magic formula, no special drug.[82]

Although no subsequent hard evidence has appeared, bloggers seized upon his admitting once again to teenage steroid use in the October 2014 issue of *Fortune* to speculate. For Erny Peibst, "it seems he's lying when he stated he hasn't touched them since, because he's blown up and has several steroid side-effects." Most respondents on the Generation Iron Fitness Network suspect the Rock was on steroids, but writer Jonathan Salmon asserts that "it isn't fair to label him a 'roidhead' because of the hard work Johnson puts in the gym. Even if Johnson currently used steroids, which we doubt he does, it shouldn't take away from the fact that he's a great actor, role model, and human being."[83] That the Rock's story has remained consistent through repeated interviews attests to his insistence that he just wanted to "build my body, because the men who were successful that I know of—Stallone, Arnold, Bruce Willis— were men of action." Ironically, his actions on the screen, primarily executed through the employment of special effects and stunt performers, allowed fewer opportunities to use his body than professional wrestling. Hence his return to the squared ring and subsequent injury before filming *Hercules*; It resulted in an ongoing two-year feud with John Cena that Johnson insists was "very real. When I came back, I needed something real to sink my teeth into, as a performer."[84] While Hollywood enabled audiences to suspend their disbelief by its display of a muscular body that seemed capable of executing heroic feats, it was professional wrestling, often regarded as fake, that con-vinced those same audiences that the Rock was really strong, athletic, and talented. By blending appearance with reality, Johnson, more than any other performer of his generation, perfected the art of illusion.

Notes

1. Joel Stein, "Heroes and Icons of the Twentieth Century," *Time*, June 14, 1999, 118.

2. Sid Campbell and Greglon Yimm Lee, *Remembering the Master: Bruce Lee, James Yimm Lee, and the Creation of Jeet Kune Do*, xvii; Paul Heller, quoted in Fiaz Rafiq, *Bruce Lee: Conversations: The Life and Legacy of a Legend*, 25; Charles Russo, *Striking Distance: Bruce Lee and the Dawn of Martial Arts in America*, 118; Paul Bowman, *Beyond Bruce Lee: Chasing the Dragon through Film, Philosophy, and Popular Culture*, 20.

3. Campbell and Lee, *Remembering the Master*, 34, 176. Rafiq describes Lee's physique as "covered with rippling muscles. With his lean, muscular and striated physique, he was an envy of even the bodybuilders." Rafiq, *Bruce Lee*, 289.

4. Russo, *Striking Distance*, 8, 114, 70, 124; Bowman, *Beyond Bruce Lee*, 36, 23.

5. Linda Lee, *The Bruce Lee Story*, 74.

6. "Introduces the Entertainment World to Martial Arts Genius Bruce Lee," viewer review of *The Green Hornet* (1966–67), Internet Movie Database, http://www.imdb.com /title/tt0059991/reviews?ref_=tt_ov_rt.

7. Leo Fong, quoted in Rafiq, *Bruce Lee*, 62.

8. James Coburn, quoted in Campbell and Lee, *Remembering the Master*, 194.

9. Jeremy Beday, "Synopsis: Fists of Fury," AllMovie, http://www.allmovie.com/movie /fists-of-fury-v17615; Donald Guarisco, "Review: Fists of Fury," AllMovie, http://www. allmovie.com/movie/fists-of-fury-v17615/review#sseMlsxlYOeMfqL6.99.

10. A. H. Weiler, "A Chinese 'Fist of Fury': Stark Tale of Revenge Opens at Pagoda Shanghai," *New York Times*, November 8, 1972.

11. Roger Ebert, "Return of the Dragon," August 8, 1974, http://www.rogerebert.com /reviews/return-of-the-dragon-1974.

12. Katrina Hill, *Action Movie Freak*, 131.

13. Howard Thompson, "'Enter Dragon,' Hollywood Style," *New York Times*, August 18, 1973, http://www.nytimes.com/1973/08/18/archives/enter-dragon-hollywood-style. html.

14. Linda Lee, *Bruce Lee: The Man Only I Knew* (New York: Warner Books, 1975), 15, 17, 205.

15. Tom Bleecker, *Unsettled Matters: The Life and Death of Bruce Lee*, 5.

16. Bleecker, *Unsettled Matters*, 59, 84–86, 110, 197.

17. Question and Answer Session with Tom Bleecker, Temple of the Unknown website, March 7, 2001, http://www.cityonfire.com/unknown/interviews/tombleecker/index.htm. Bleecker alleges that Linda Lee told him "she never believed the autopsy or the inquest but saw no point in raising the issue."

18. Duncan Alexander McKenzie, *The Death of Bruce Lee: A Clinical Investigation* (Morrisville, NC: LuLu, 2012), 106–10.

19. Matthew Polly, *Bruce Lee: A Life* (New York: Simon and Schuster, 2018), 473–74.

20. Rafiq, *Bruce Lee*, 119, 215.

21. Lee, *Bruce Lee*, 14, 18.

22. Richard Ian Kimball, *Legends Never Die: Athletes and Their Afterlives in Modern America* (Syracuse, NY: Syracuse University Press, 2017), 3.

23. Dave Prowse, *Straight from the Force's Mouth: The Autobiography of Dave Prowse, MBE*, 94.

24. Prowse, *Straight from the Force's Mouth*, 183.

25. "Harold Sakata: Biography," Internet Movie Database, http://www.imdb.com /name/nm0757138/bio?ref_=nm_ov_bio_sm.

26. Prowse, *Straight from the Force's Mouth*, 4, 10, 48–49, 64–65.

27. "Star Wars: Episode IV—A New Hope," Box Office Mojo, http://www.boxofficemo jo.com/movies/?id=starwars4.htm.

28. "Star Wars Nightline Discussion—Summer of 1983," ABC News *Nightline*, You-Tube, http://www.youtube.com/watch?v=rB3V3qyZiFM.

29. Prowse, *Straight from the Force's Mouth*, 228–30.

30. Prowse, *Straight from the Force's Mouth*, 286, 293–94; David Prowse, "Being the Green Cross Man Beats Being Darth Vader Any Day," *Guardian*, November 25, 2014, http://www.theguardian.com/commentisfree/2014/nov/25/david-prowse-green-cross -man-darth-vader-children-road-safety.

31. Jerry Weintraub, *When I Stop Talking, You'll Know I'm Dead: Useful Stories from a Persuasive Man* (New York: Grand Central, 2010), 207–8.

32. Larry Powell and Tom Garrett, *The Films of John G. Avildsen: Rocky, The Karate Kid and Other Underdogs* (Jefferson, NC: McFarland, 2014), 132, 137–38, 141.

33. Roger Ebert, "The Karate Kid," January 1, 1984, http://www.rogerebert.com /reviews/the-karate-kid-1984.

34. "The Karate Kid (1984)," Internet Movie Database, http://www.imdb.com/title /tt0087538/; "Franchise: The Karate Kid," Box Office Mojo, http://www.boxofficemojo. com/franchise/fr2521272069/?ref_=bo_frs_table_83.

35. Ebert, "The Karate Kid."

36. Robert De Niro, quoted in Andy Dougan, *Untouchable: A Biography of Robert De Niro*, 61, 106, 246–47.

37. Robert De Niro, quoted in Dougan, *Untouchable*, 50.

38. Dougan, *Untouchable*, 51.

39. Robert De Niro, quoted in John Baxter, *De Niro: A Biography*, 98–99.

40. Roger Ebert, "Bang the Drum Slowly," August 26, 1973, http://www.rogerebert. com/reviews/bang-the-drum-slowly-1973.

41. Martin Scorsese, quoted in Michael Henry, "Raging Bull," in *Martin Scorsese Inter-views*, ed. Peter Brunette (Jackson: University Press of Mississippi, 1999), 85.

42. Baxter, *De Niro*, 117, 164, 198, 200.

43. Martin Scorsese, quoted in Dougan, *Untouchable*, 128.

44. Robert De Niro, quoted in Dougan, *Untouchable*, 128.

45. Dougan, *Untouchable*, 128.

46. Robert De Niro, quoted in Dougan, *Untouchable*, 129.

47. Jake La Motta, *Raging Bull: My Story*, 76, 92.

48. Mike Evans, *The Making of Raging Bull* (London: Unanimous, 2006), 72–73, 76, 90.

49. Robert De Niro, quoted in Dougan, *Untouchable*, 133.

50. Robert De Niro, quoted in " 'I Just Can't Fake': De Niro's Method of Getting a Fat Part," *New York Daily News*, October 28, 1980, quoted in Shawn Levy, *De Niro: A Life*, 335.

51. "Raging Bull," Box Office Mojo, http://www.boxofficemojo.com/movies/?id=rag ingbull.htm.

52. Dougan, *Untouchable*, 246–47; Levy, *De Niro*, 341–42; Martin Scorsese, quoted in Fred Ferretti, "The Delicate Art of Creating a Brutal Film Hero," *New York Times*, November 23, 1980.

53. "Domestic Box Office for 1990," Box Office Mojo, http://www.boxofficemojo.com /yearly/chart/?view2=worldwide&yr=1990&p=.htm.

54. Vincent LoBrutto, *Ridley Scott: A Biography*, 11, 21.

55. Ridley Scott, quoted in Paul M. Sammon, "Joining the Club: Ridley Scott on *G.I. Jane*," in *Ridley Scott: Interviews*, ed. Laurence F. Knapp and Andrea F. Kulas, 135.

56. Sammon, "Joining the Club," 133.

57. Chris Davis, "Demi Moore Workout & Diet: Transforming Into G.I. Jane," March 15, 2013, Pop Workouts, http://www.popworkouts.com/demi-moore-workout-gi-jane/.

58. Two-time Olympian Bruce Wilhelm contends that "it's hard to have a guy come in and coach you. If he's coaching me and doesn't really know you, he can't spend quality time with you. So it's sort of a superficial deal." Bruce Wilhelm, interview with John D. Fair, San Carlos, California, June 17, 2019.

59. See Paul M. Sammon, *Ridley Scott: Close Up: The Making of His Movies* (London: Orion, 1999); Richard A. Schwartz, *The Films of Ridley Scott* (Westport, CT: Praeger, 2001); and LoBrutto, *Ridley Scott*.

60. Ridley Scott, quoted in Sammon, "Joining the Club," 139, 148–49, 153. Moore's personal trainer, Gregory Joujon-Roche, explains that the single-arm push-up is not so much about strength and will power but technique and flexibility: "A one-armed push-up doesn't come from your shoulder. I tell (Demi Moore). It comes from your butt. From your stomach. Most especially, it comes from the big toe on the opposite side of your supporting arm. It's all about distributing your power. It's a support-system move, more than a power move. Gregory Joujon-Roche, quoted in Davis, "Demi Moore Workout."

61. Ridley Scott, quoted in Sammon, "Joining the Club," 143–45.

62. Ridley Scott, quoted in Sammon, "Joining the Club," 167.

63. Roger Ebert, "G.I. Jane," August 22, 1997, http://www.rogerebert.com/reviews/gi-jane-1997; Ridley Scott, quoted in Sammon, "Joining the Club," 166.

64. The Rock [Dwayne Johnson], *The Rock Says . . . : The Most Electrifying Man in Sports Entertainment*, 25.

65. Dwayne Johnson, quoted in Scott Raab, "The Rock Is Dead. Long Live Dwayne Johnson, American Treasure," *Esquire*, June 29, 2015, http://www.esquire.com/entertainment /interviews/a36037/dwayne-johnson-the-rock-0815/.

66. The Rock, *The Rock Says*, 39, 52.

67. Dwayne Johnson, quoted in Raab, "The Rock Is Dead."

68. Broderick Chow, Eero Laine, and Claire Warden, "Introduction: Hamlet Doesn't Blade: Professional Wrestling, Theatre, and Performance," in *Performance and Professional Wrestling*, ed. Broderick Chow, Eero Laine, and Claire Warden, 2–4.

69. Mark Henry, interview with John D. Fair, March 21, 2019.

70. Stephen Di Benedetto, "Playful Engagements," in Chow, Laine, and Warden, eds., *Performance and Professional Wrestling*, 27; Roland Barthes, *Mythologies*, trans. Annette Lavers (New York: Hill and Wang, 1972), 15.

71. Dwayne Johnson, quoted in Scott Raab, "Dwayne Johnson," 17.

72. Barry Blaustein, dir., *Beyond the Mat* (Los Angeles: Imagine Entertainment, 1999).

73. Nathan Birch, "Cooking Up Beefs: The Raucous Real-Life Feuds of Dwayne 'The Rock' Johnson," Uproxx, August 11, 2016, http://uproxx.com/prowrestling/the-rock-real-life-feuds/; Roger Ebert, "Beyond the Mat," March 17, 2000, http://www.rogerebert.com/reviews/beyond-the-mat-2000.

74. "Beyond the Mat," Box Office Mojo, http://www.boxofficemojo.com/movies/?id=beyondthemat.htm.

75. Dwayne Johnson, quoted in Raab, "The Rock Is Dead." Mark Henry, however, traces Johnson's maturity as an actor to *The Grid Iron Gang* (2006) because "you could see him coming out of being The Rock and being Dwayne Johnson. The Grid Iron Gang was about kids that were in a reform school, and he let them know that he was one of them. And if he could get out of that situation, they could get out of that situation. And they went through their toils and strifes as any movie would, but the emotional value in that film paid dividends because he was able to work a muscle that he hadn't worked before." Henry interview.

76. Roger Ebert, "The Mummy Returns," May 4, 2001, http://www.rogerebert.com/reviews/the-mummy-returns-2001.

77. "The Mummy Returns," Rotten Tomatoes, http://www.rottentomatoes.com/m/mummy_returns; "The Mummy Returns," Box Office Mojo, http://www.boxofficemojo.com/movies/?id=mummyreturns.htm; "Dwayne Johnson," Awards and Winners, awardsandwinners.com/winner/?name=dwayne-johnson&mid=/m/014g_s.

78. Michael Wilmington, "Rock Schlock," *Chicago Tribune*, July 20, 2002; Stephen Holden, "In a Prequel to the 'Mummy' Series, a Mountain of Muscle Makes a Parody," *New York Times*, April 19, 2002; James Berardinelli, "The Scorpion King," Reelviews, http://preview.reelviews.net/movies/s/scorpion_king.html; "The Scorpion King," Rotten Tomatoes, http://www.rottentomatoes.com/m/scorpion_king/; Nick Rogers, "Movies You Aught Not Watch: The Scorpion King," The Film Yap, http://www.thefilmyap.com/2010/10/13/the-scorpion-king/.

79. "The Scorpion King," Box Office Mojo, http://www.boxofficemojo.com/movies/?id=scorpionking.htm.

80. Dwayne Johnson, quoted in Matt Tuthill, "Mythical Proportions: An Exclusive Interview with Dwayne 'the Rock' Johnson, *Muscle and Fitness*, n.d., http://www.muscleandfitness.com/athletes-celebrities/interviews/mythical-proportions

-exclusive-interview-dwayne-rock-johnson; Steve Moore and Admira Wijaya, *Hercules: The Thracian Wars* (Carpinteria, CA: Radical Books, 2008).

81. Ben Kenigsberg, "All Tribalism and Treachery, Dude," *New York Times*, July 25, 2014; Sherilyn Connelly, "Hercules Surprisingly Has Both Brains and Brawn," *Village Voice*, July 23, 2014; Scott Foundas, "Film Review: 'Hercules,'" *Variety*, July 23, 2014; Elizabeth Weitzman, "'Hercules': Movie Review," *New York Daily News*, July 25, 2014; James Berardinelli, "Hercules," Reelviews, July 25, 2014, http://www.reelviews.net/reelviews /hercules_2783.

82. The Rock, *The Rock Says*, 44.

83. Daniel Roberts, "How Dwayne Johnson Rocked the Film Industry," *Fortune*, October 30, 2014, http://fortune.com/2014/10/30/dwayne-johnson-best-advice-entertainment -star/; Erny Peibst, "Is Dwayne Johnson (The Rock) On Steroids?" Muscle and Brawn, September 20, 2016, updated June 11, 2020, http://muscleandbrawn.com/dwayne -johnson-the-rock-steroids/; Jonathan Salmon, "Dwayne 'the Rock' Johnson Comes Clean on Steroid Use," Generation Iron Fitness Network, November 6, 2014, http://gen erationiron.com/dwayne-rock-johnsons-steroid-use/.

84. Dwayne Johnson, quoted in Tuthill, "Mythical Proportions."

XVII. PERFECTING THE ILLUSION

A true hero isn't measured by the size of his strength but by the
strength of his heart.

—*Hercules*, 1997

DWAYNE "THE ROCK" Johnson's racial heritage includes African American
and Polynesian ancestors, and thus his cinematic career exemplifies how the
function and display of multiracial muscles has enriched the lives of countless millions of moviegoers in America and the world. What is not so obvious
is the technological and psychological basis for its impact on the subgenre
of melodrama. From the late nineteenth century to the early twenty-first
century, the depiction of muscles in the movies has served to satisfy two
contradictory tendencies common to moviemakers and moviegoers: the
desire for realism and the need for illusion to sustain it. The potential for this
anomaly, as identified by Plato and other philosophers, is rooted in human
nature, and later the media that emerged to represent it. "In cinema man's
innate drive to self-assertion finds one of its fullest and most direct means
of realization," declared Henri Bergson, the first philosopher of film. "A film
is an emotional reality, and that is how the audience receives it—as a second
reality."[1] For the first two decades after Eugen Sandow's debut, motion pictures were little more than curiosities that provided limited entertainment
or cultural enrichment for a public eager for realistic depictions of worldly
wonders. In addition to juggling realism and illusion, movies with muscular
heroes showed audiences what action and strength looked like—both in real
and fantastic varieties. Vaudeville and circus audiences had long watched
professional strongmen lift huge weights and perform astounding stunts
(some real), but moviemakers quickly learned to put actors into situations
they could never accomplish on a stage set.

It was French illusionist and film director Georges Méliès who transformed filmmaking into an art form by creating such camera techniques as
the double exposure, stop action, reverse action, fast and slow motion, the

dissolve, and animation. These innovations dramatically stimulated viewer interest and enthusiasm by generating yet more ambiguity between the real and unreal and by enhancing elements of action and spectacle. Through imaginative editing, observes Nicholas Vardac, the projection of fantasies "became a personal, subjective experience of the audience," thereby ensuring widespread reception and robust box office receipts. "If the essence of the drama of [Henrik] Ibsen and his colleagues was dialogue, theme, and character, that of the photoplay was action and spectacle," argues Vardac. "Spectacle was, from the start, and by definition, one of the basic elements of the film. Yet it was not exploited as such in any great way until such productions as *Quo Vadis?*, *Cabiria*, *Judith of Bethulia*, *The Birth of a Nation* . . . about 1912–1915."[2] Indeed, Bartolomeo Pagano's appearance in *Cabiria* (1914) was a defining moment in the history of filmmaking and movie muscles. For the first time, a cinematic hero had sufficient muscularity to make audiences believe he might actually be able to perform the fantastic feats shown on the screen. Audiences were conditioned to see handsome, muscular men as selfless protagonists rather than dim-witted freaks or monstrous villains. It is no accident that muscular bad guys in movies are much rarer than their more virtuous counterparts.

Cabiria also fulfilled the two most critical of the five elements Ben Singer defines for modern photo melodrama: "moral polarization and sensational action and spectacle." Pagano as Maciste, no less than other silent media stars such as Francis X. Bushman, Douglas Fairbanks and Tom Mix, capitalized on this formula for success. As technology advanced quickly in the early twentieth century, the crowds that filled the cinemas adjusted to the new gizmos and the faster pace of life with amazing ease. A key point in Singer's modernization model is that "the modern individual somehow internalized the tempos, shocks, and upheavals of the outside environment, and this generated a taste for hyperkinetic amusements."[3] This view not only cites the intensification of sensations of urban life as a precondition for film but also the observations of philosopher Walter Benjamin, the so-called Patron Saint of Visual Studies, that film emerged to meet "a new and urgent need for stimuli." Benjamin conceived of the world through "an optical media device" that he described as "phantasmagoria" or illusions. "People respond popularly not to cinema per se," asserts Lauren Rabinovitz, "but to cinema only when it is in the service of a spectacle." Such was Méliès's impact for ten years as "the most popular film maker in the world" that Richard Rickitt argues he "could justifiably lay claim to being the cinema's first star."[4] Unfortunately, the innovative Frenchman's reign was brief, and his stagy, artificial fantasies were overtaken by the vast scale and greater realism of early Italian super-productions. Bartolomeo Pagano as Maciste, and Bruto Castellani as Ursus, soon rose to the top of the cinematic heap through their creative display of prodigious muscularity. It was something audiences could understand better than the gossamer fantasies spun by Méliès, but greater transformations were on the way.

The impact of action and spectacle was complemented by the emergence of a celebrity culture. It was hardly coincidental that five of the earliest cinema stars—Francis X. Bushman, Douglas Fairbanks, Bartolomeo Pagano, Rudolph Valentino, and Pearl White—were acclaimed for their muscles in motion. Celebrity culture is a nebulous concept, Kevin Brownlow admits, that is the creation of moviegoers as much as moviemakers: "The star system was based on myth and imagination, and through ingenious fabrication it would flourish."[5] In *Intimate Strangers*, Richard Schickel identifies the illusion of intimacy as an internal motivation that links movie audiences with stars: "Not only do we think we know them, we think we know what makes them tick, which makes us want to tick as they do."[6] For Richard Allen it is projective illusion that provides a Kantian allusion that compromises a viewer's grip on reality:

> The star persona blurs the boundary between character role and the real-life body of the actor, conflating the distinction between "nominal" and "physical" portrayal. Our identification with, say, the star persona of Robert de Niro, encourages us to fuse the particular role of Jake La Motta in *Raging Bull* (1980) with the range of intertextual associations that accrete around the body of de Niro, the actor, to form de Niro, the star. We are encouraged to switch from the realistic perception of de Niro the actor, playing La Motta, to the projective illusion of de Niro as "Jake La Motta."[7]

Although today bodybuilders are often considered the ne plus ultra of masculinity, it was not always so. Prior to films like *Pumping Iron* (1977) and *Conan the Barbarian* (1982), bodybuilders were often outlandish and repellant to moviegoers and ordinary citizens. There was a suspicion that oversize musclemen were freaks, narcissists, gay, or an unsavory combination of the three. According to bodybuilder Eddie Giuliani, "Nobody liked guys with the lumps back then. They thought we are all morons and fairies."[8] After

Arnold Schwarzenegger became a superstar, all of that changed, coinciding with a rebirth of traditional masculinity in American cinema that transformed the freaks into heroes. It resulted in a reevaluation of masculinity during the administration of President Ronald Reagan. Many moviemakers veered away from the disaster films, gritty urban dramas, and space operas popular in the 1970s and began to speculate on what a real man looked and acted like. He was, in their estimation, big, violent, and usually ticked off.

Moviemakers sensed that the public was tired of sensitivity and acceptance of malaise. Viewers wanted tough guys with big bodies and low boiling points. They wanted heroes, men whom no one was going to push around anymore—especially not red-blooded American men. When Sylvester Stallone as Rambo trots around the forest carrying a rocket launcher blasting his enemies to smithereens and Arnold Schwarzenegger uses his muscles to outfight and outsmart a hideously ugly alien in *Predator* (1987), they are not only redefining and reinforcing traditional masculinity but are also repudiating the failures of the Vietnam War, discarding the inroads of feminism, and showing why capitalism triumphed over communism. When American working-class men have felt themselves under attack from women, dark-skinned immigrants, liberals, or those whose gender identification is uncomfortably fluid, they have struck out most visibly in film. The current popularity of morally unambiguous comic book heroes in film, fantasy films, and violent adventure movies can probably be traced to the perceived malaise of men who feel their privileges being expropriated by those whom they consider less than manly. Gender wars never go away; they merely assume new forms as they fight the same adversaries.

More than any other factor, it was movie fans and fan magazines that encouraged viewer enthusiasm for stars. As film analyst Anthony Slide attests, it was the writers and publishers of those magazines that "embraced what the studios chose to reveal about their stars because that was also what the public wanted to read about those stars. 'Fan book readers don't want to hear anything derogatory about the star. They want the myth,' explained one fan magazine editor in 1948. . . . 'We paint beautiful pictures of love, excitement, wealth, prestige, security and glamour.' "[9] At least that was the design until 1950s, when scandal magazines like *Confidential* started spilling unsavory secrets, and then continuing into the late 1960s, when such equally sleazy tabloids as *National Enquirer* (coinciding not incidentally with the counterculture revolution of that era) began more realistically focusing on flawed celebrity lifestyles, thus further enhancing their public profile. Only then did the public learn of the private peccadillos and shenanigans that the stars got up to when the cameras were turned off. Was Douglas Fairbanks a philanderer? Was Rock Hudson gay? Did Arnold Schwarzenegger father a love child? As it turned out, moviegoers with inquiring minds were interested not just in the studio-censored details of a star's life but also—and even more—in the less savory details that showed that beautiful people had the same weaknesses, moral blemishes, and feet of clay as the rest of us.

Meanwhile, muscles remained a focus of fan enthusiasm with such animated representations as Mighty Mouse, Popeye, and Superman, along with the dramatic roles played by Kirk Douglas, Sonja Henie, and Burt Lancaster. Likewise, the stupid, clumsy, but superbly muscular bodies featured prominently in *Athena* (1954) and *Muscle Beach Party* (1964) allowed movie audiences to simultaneously laugh at and admire the physiques on the screen. For Yvonne Tasker, the concept of star as hero was the "key aspect" of the visual excess that Hollywood offered its audiences amid a montage of pyrotechnics, military hardware, archvillains, overwhelming obstacles, overblown budgets, and expansive landscapes and soundtracks. Still, the essential ingredient remained "the body of the star as hero, characteristically functioning as spectacle."[10] Nowhere was it more obvious than in the sword-and-sandal genre of the 1960s, and especially its biggest star, Steve Reeves. As Robert Rushing observes, moviemaking had reached a stage where muscles were no longer as important to depicting movement. Although the peplum film

> privileges musculature perhaps more than any other film genre, its muscles appear to have little to do with movement. Indeed, they seem decidedly opposed to it. It was almost impossible for viewers or critics to miss the midcentury bodybuilder's stiff and awkward walking and often comically poor choreography in sword-fighting sequences; at times, even for the bodybuilder to turn his head seemed to require a massive effort, as if the dense and inflated musculature was there to hinder the body's movements. Even in the silent period, Maciste was often paired with another character who could provide movements that were acrobatic to give a sense of brio and sprezzatura to the filmic body. Maciste, by contrast was heavy, at his best, he was an immovable obstacle, a piece of machinery. The central terms of value to bodybuilding— mass, volume, definition—all seem to be opposed to cinematic body, which is in its very name a body in movement.[11]

No less aware of this anomaly is Richard Dyer, who recognizes that body-builders "are not necessarily agile or acrobatic; the point is their size and shape, frozen in moments of maximum tension. Holding a boulder aloft in a clinch with a lion, these and many other set-ups incorporate not only the posing vocabulary of bodybuilding competitions but also the *mise-en-scènes* of such non-narrative forms as physique photography and strongman acts."[12] It was not that bodybuilders were muscle-bound—though that myth persisted—but that their craft and casting required set pieces of posing rather than dexterity. Furthermore, the same impact could be achieved through special effects, abdominals enhanced through computer-generated imagery, and stuntmen without endangering the actors' health or waste of production time and money.

Notwithstanding their continued reliance on such acting aids, Arnold Schwarzenegger and Sylvester Stallone were able to combine muscularity with motion. Their impact was aided also by an illusion of familiarity with the context of their bodies, owing mainly to the increased popularity of weight training, health clubs, fitness diets, and steroids. In striking contrast to the functional and muscular physiques that were parodied in *Athena* and *Muscle Beach Party* in the 1950s and 1960s, they became a familiar and spectacular visage, thanks in part to Schwarzenegger's popularity and the fitness revolution that swept the world in the 1970s. E. H. Gombrich captures the essence of that new outlook in his book *Art and Illusion*, where he argues that environmental expectations create illusions: "One must have experienced these effects to realize how elusive they make the idea of 'appearance' as distinct from the object itself. . . . The illusions of art presuppose recognition; to repeat the phrase from Philostratus, 'no one can understand the painted horse or bull unless he knows what such creatures are like.' . . . That perspective creates its most compelling illusion where it can rely on certain ingrained expectations and assumptions on the part of the beholder."[13] Somewhat more abstruse but apropos is the explanation of novelist Walker Percy for how audiences "certify" illusions they see on the screen: "Nowadays when a person lives somewhere, in a neighborhood, the place is not certified for him. More than likely he will live there sadly and the emptiness which is inside him will expand until it evacuates the entire neighborhood. But he sees a movie which shows his very neighborhood, it becomes possible for him to live, for a time at least, as a person who is Somewhere and not Anywhere."[14] It was this kind of familiarity that enabled audiences to envisage Robert De Niro, celebrated for his authenticity in previous roles, exhibiting the muscularity and moves of professional boxer Jake La Motta. For Dwayne Johnson, however, moviegoer recognition has taken a more realistic turn. What viewers see in his movies is a transmogrification of his famous role as a professional wrestler, made more believable by his reentry to the ring in 2011 at age thirty-nine.

It is important to remember that special effects and stuntmen are hardly new. They have been a critical aspect in creating the illusions that have made movies entertaining since the early days of filmmaking. The display of functional and fit physiques has added an important inspirational and aspirational element ready for absorption by average viewers. Since the era of Douglas Fairbanks and Maciste, however, special effects have bolstered the movie industry through the vehicle of celebrities and spectacles. As John Hagner, founder of the Hollywood Stuntmen's Hall of Fame, explains, "In almost every film there's that one moment of extraordinary action which is the focal point of the entire movie, a moment seldom forgotten by the public."[15] Dwayne Johnson echoed this sentiment with his heroic leap from a crane to the open window of a towering inferno in *Skyscraper* (2018). "Every film has a moment designed to take your breath away when you see the final moment on screen," he mused. "This is one of those moments." For Johnson, such over-the-top scenes incorporated a work ethic that combined movies and wrestling. "People work very hard for their money," he rationalized, "and I want to give them a great show. That's it. Bottom line."[16] When sheer muscle was not enough to thrill viewers, producers and actors always relied on stunts, creative makeup, massive sets, and special effects.

That special effects and stuntmen allowed actors to exhibit less real strength and agility did not seem to matter, as long as the stars looked like they could perform the miraculous feats that dazzled audiences, and as long as it created celebrities with whom audiences could identify. "The beauty of movies is that they don't have to be logical," concludes *Terminator* director James Cameron. "They just have to have plausibility. If there's a visceral, cinematic thing happening that the audience likes, they don't care if it goes against what's likely."[17] While Gene Kelly and Bruce Lee had to justify their celebrity status through active use of muscles, it mattered little whether Arnold Schwarzenegger or Steve Reeves were really strong. Today, in the time of Dwayne Johnson, who has sometimes been dubbed the Arnold of the new century, the medium of muscle, utterly adulterated by artificial means, is an inherent part of action movies. Kung fu fighters fly through the air, Maciste hefts an automobile overhead, Hercules knocks down a huge temple single-handedly, and all is well so long as audiences can think to themselves, "It could happen." In the imagination of viewers, performance remains an inherent part of the genre, no matter how many special effects are tapped to mimic reality. It is a marriage of bodily function and form, and the psychic tension it creates, that perfects the art of illusion.

Notes

1. Henri Bergson, *Time and Free Will: An Essay on the Immediate Data of Consciousness*, trans. F. L. Pogson (New York: Harper, 1960), 177.

2. Nicholas Vardac, *Stage to Screen: Theatrical Method from Garrick to Griffith*, 192, 219, 239.

3. Ben Singer, *Melodrama and Modernity: Early Sensational Cinema and Its Contexts*, 58, 119.

4. James Elkins, *Visual Studies: A Skeptical Introduction* (New York: Routledge, 2003), 94; Walter Benjamin, *The Writer of Modern Life: Essays on Charles Baudelaire*, ed. Michael W. Jennings and trans. Howard Eiland (Cambridge, MA: Harvard University Press, 2006), 191; Walter Benjamin, "The Production, Reproduction, and Reception of the Work of Art," trans. Edmund Jephcott, in Benjamin, *The Work of Art in the Age of Its Technological Reproducibility, and Other Writings on Media*, ed. Michael W. Jennings, Brigid Doherty, and Thomas Y. Levin (Cambridge, MA: Harvard University Press, 2008), 11; Lauren Rabinovitz, "The Fair View: Female Spectators and the 1893 Chicago World's Columbian Exposition," in *The Image in Dispute: Art and Cinema in the Age of Photography*, ed. Dudley Andrew, 111; Richard Rickitt, *Special Effects: The History and Technique*, 13.

5. Kevin Brownlow, *Hollywood: The Pioneers*, 156.

6. Richard Schickel, *Intimate Strangers: The Culture of Celebrity*, 29.

7. Richard Allen, "Representation, Illusion, and the Cinema," 44.

8. Eddie Giuliani, quoted in Paul Solotaroff, "Venice Beach, Gold's Gym, and the Dawn of Bodybuilding," *Men's Journal*, November 18, 2012, http://www.mensjournal.com /features/the-dawn-of-bodybuilding-20121118/.

9. Anthony Slide, *Inside the Hollywood Fan Magazine: A History of Star Makers, Fabricators, and Gossip Mongers* (Jackson: University Press of Mississippi, 2010), 80.

10. Yvonne Tasker, "Dumb Movies for Dumb People," in *Screening the Male: Exploring Masculinities in Hollywood Cinema*, ed. Steven Cohan and Ina Rae Hark, 233.

11. Robert A. Rushing, *Descended from Hercules: Biopolitics and the Muscled Male Body on Screen*, 46, 120–21.

12. Richard Dyer, *White: Essays on Race and Culture*, 167.

13. E. H. Gombrich, *Art and Illusion: A Study in the Psychology of Pictorial Representation* (Princeton, NJ: Princeton University Press, 1960), 260.

14. Walker Percy, *The Moviegoer* (New York: Alfred A. Knopf, 1961), 63.

15. John Hagner, in "The Hollywood Stuntmen's Hall of Fame," *Starr Talk with Sonny Starr* (Springfield, OR: Northwest Productions), DVD in possession of John D. Fair.

16. Dwayne Johnson, quoted in "Dwayne 'The Rock' Johnson Is The Hero We All Need," and Dwayne Johnson, quoted in "Behind the Scenes of *Skyscraper*," *Hollywood Story: Dwayne "The Rock" Johnson* (New York: Centennial Media, 2018), 6, 8.

17. James Cameron, "Creator James Cameron on Terminator's Origins, Arnold as Robot, Machine Wars," *Wired*, March 23, 2009, http://www.wired.com/2009/03/ff-cameron/.

SELECTED BIBLIOGRAPHY

ARCHIVES

Bob Hoffman Papers, in the Possession of John D. Fair

Margaret Herrick Library, Academy of Motion Picture Arts and Sciences, Beverly Hills

Audrey Chamberlin Scrapbooks

Douglas Fairbanks Collection

Eddie Mannix Ledger

Esther Williams Collection

James Raker Papers

Paramount Pictures Collection, 1959

Rudy Behlmer Papers

Maurice Zolotow Papers, University of Texas at Austin

Museo Nazionale del Cinema, Turin, Italy

Robert De Niro Papers, University of Texas at Austin

UCLA Film and Television Archive, University of California–Los Angeles

INTERVIEWS

Dyer, Richard. London, September 11, 2012. Interview by John D. Fair.

Hagner, John. Moab, Utah, September 3, 2015. Interview by John D. Fair.

Henry, Mark. Austin, Texas, March 21, 2019. Interview by John D. Fair.

Parker, Charlotte. Los Angeles, June 7, 2011. Interview by John D. Fair.

Slide, Anthony. Los Angeles, May 24, 2017. Interview by David L. Chapman

Wilhelm, Bruce. San Carlos, California, June 17, 2019. Interview by John D. Fair.

Wyke, Maria. London, September 17, 2015. Interview by John D. Fair.

BOOKS AND ARTICLES

Abel, Richard, ed. *Encyclopedia of Early Cinema*. New York: Routledge, 2005.

Allen, Richard. "Representation, Illusion, and the Cinema." *Cinema Journal* 32, no. 2 (February 1993): 21–48.

Allister, Ray. *Friese-Greene: Close-up of an Inventor*. New York: Arno, 1972.

Alyn, Kirk. *A Job for Superman*. Los Angeles: K. Alyn, 1971.

Ames, Hector. "The Champion Heroine of Movie Perils, Exploits, Plots, and Conspiracies." *Motion Picture Classic*, June 1916, 50–52.

Andrew, Dudley, ed. *The Image in Dispute: Art and Cinema in the Age of Photography*. Austin: University of Texas Press, 1997.

Arkoff, Sam. *Flying through Hollywood By the Seat of My Pants: From the Man Who Brought You* I Was a Teenage Werewolf *and* Muscle Beach Party. With Richard Trubo. Secaucus, NJ: Birch Lane, 1992.

Ashe, Arthur R., Jr. *A Hard Road to Glory: A History of the African-American Athlete, 1619—1918*. New York: Warner Books, 1988.

Baim, Tracy, and Owen Keehnen. *Leatherman: The Legend of Chuck Renslow*. Chicago: Prairie Avenue, 2011.

Barbera, Alberto, and Gian Luca Farinelli. *Maciste: L'uomo forte*. Bologna: Cineteca di Bologna, 2009.

Barbour, Alan G. *Cliffhanger: A Pictorial History of the Motion Picture Serial*. New York: A and W, 1977.

Baxter, John. *De Niro: A Biography*. New York: HarperCollins, 2002.

———. *Stunt: The Story of the Great Movie Stunt Men*. Garden City, NY: Doubleday, 1974.

Bean, Jennifer M. "Technologies of Early Stardom and the Extraordinary Body." *Camera Obscura* 16, no. 3 (2001): 8–57.

Bertetto, Paolo, and Gianni Rondolino, eds. *Cabiria e il suo tempo*. Turin, Italy: Museo Nazionale del Cinema, 1997.

Birchard, Robert S. *King Cowboy: Tom Mix and the Movies*. Burbank, CA: Riverwood, 1993.

Bleckman, Matias. *Harry Piel: Ein Kino-Mythos und seine Zeit*. Düsseldorf: Filminstitut der Landeshauptstad Düsseldorf, 1992.

Bleecker, Tom. *Unsettled Matters: The Life and Death of Bruce Lee*. Lompoc, CA: Gilderoy, 1996.

Blom, Ivo. "The Beauty of the Forzuti: Irresistible Male Bodies on and Offscreen." In *Corporeality in Early Cinema: Viscera, Skin, and Physical Form*, edited by Marina Dahlquist, Doron Galili, Jan Olsson, and Valentine Robert, 146–55. Bloomington: Indiana University Press, 2018.

Bondanella, Peter. *A History of Italian Cinema*. New York: Continuum, 2009.

Bondanella, Peter, and Manuela Gieri, eds. *La Strada: Federico Fellini, Director*. New Brunswick, NJ: Rutgers University Press, 1987.

Bonomo, Joe. *The Strongman: A True Life Pictorial Autobiography of the Hercules of the Screen Joe Bonomo*. New York: Bonomo Studios, 1968.

Bowman, Paul. *Beyond Bruce Lee: Chasing the Dragon through Film, Philosophy, and Popular Culture*. London: Wallflower, 2013.

Brady, William A. *Showman: My Life Story*. New York: E. P. Dutton, 1937.

Braun, Marta. "The Expanded Present: Photographing Movement." In *Beauty of Another Order: Photography in Science*, edited by Ann Thomas, 150–85. New Haven, CT: Yale University Press / National Gallery of Canada, 1997.

———. *Picturing Time: The Work of Etienne-Jules Marey (1830–1904)*. Chicago: University of Chicago Press, 1992.

Brideson, Cynthia, and Sara Brideson. *He's Got Rhythm: The Life and Career of Gene Kelly*. Lexington: University Press of Kentucky, 2017.

Brownlow, Kevin. *Hollywood: The Pioneers*. New York: Alfred A. Knopf, 1979.

Brunetta, Gian Piero. *Cent'anni di cinema italiano: Dalle origini alla seconda guerra mondiale*. Bari, Italy: Laterza, 1995.

———. *Il cinema muto italiano*. Rome: Laterza, 2008.

Buford, Kate. *Burt Lancaster: An American Life*. New York: Alfred A. Knopf, 2000.

Burke, Frank, ed. *A Companion to Italian Cinema*. Chichester, UK: John Wiley, 2017.

Bushman, Francis X. "How I Keep My Strength." *Photoplay*, June 1915, 59–62.

Cafagna, Dino. *L'uomo più forte del mondo: La leggenda di Giovanni Raicevich da Trieste*. Trieste, Italy: Luglio, 2015.

Campbell, Sid, and Greglon Yimm Lee. *Remembering the Master: Bruce Lee, James Yimm Lee, and the Creation of Jeet Kune Do*. Berkeley, CA: Blue Snake Books, 2006.

Chandler, Charlotte. *Nobody's Perfect: Billy Wilder, a Personal Biography*. New York: Applause, 2002.

Chapman, David L. *Sandow the Magnificent: Eugen Sandow and the Beginnings of Bodybuilding*. Urbana: University of Illinois Press, 1994.

Chapman, Mike. "Gallery of Tarzans." *Strength and Health*, January 1982, 38–41.

———. *The Tom Tyler Story: From Cowboy Star to Super Hero*. Newton, IA: Culture House Books, 2005.

Chow, Broderick, Eero Laine, and Claire Warden, eds. *Performance and Professional Wrestling*. London: Routledge, 2017.

Cohan, Steven, and Ina Rae Hark, eds. *Screening the Male: Exploring Masculinities in Hollywood Cinema*. London: Routledge, 1993.

Connor, Edward. "The Twelve Tarzans." *Films in Review* 11, no. 8 (October 1960): 452–63.

Cooke, Alistair. *Douglas Fairbanks: The Making of a Screen Character*. New York: Museum of Modern Art, 1940.

Copeland, Bobby J. *Trail Talk*. Madison, NC: Empire, 1996.

Curtis, Tony. *Tony Curtis: The Autobiography*. With Barry Paris. New York: William Morrow, 1993.

Dahlquist, Marina, ed. *Exporting Perilous Pauline: Pearl White and the Serial Film Craze*. Urbana: University of Illinois Press, 2013.

Dall'Asta, Monica, ed. *Non solo dive: Pioniere del cinema italiano.* Bologna: Cineteca di Bologna, 2008.

———. *Trame spezzate: Archeologia del film seriale.* Recco, Italy: Le Mani, 2009.

———. *Un cinéma musclé: Le surhomme dans le cinéma muet italien (1913–1926).* Crisnée, Belgium: Editions Yellow Now, 1992.

Daly, Marsha. *Sylvester Stallone: An Illustrated Life.* New York: St. Martin's, 1984.

Daniels, Les. *Batman: The Complete History.* San Francisco: Chronicle Books, 1999.

———. *Superman: The Complete History, The Life and Times of the Man of Steel.* San Francisco: Chronicle Books, 1998.

Davis, Lon, and Debra Davis. *King of the Movies: Francis X. Bushman.* Albany, GA: BearManor Media, 2016.

Della Casa, Steve, and Marco Giusti. *Il grande libro di Ercole: Il cinema mitologico in Italia.* Rome: Edizioni Sabinae, 2013.

DeMarco, Mario. *Tom Tyler and George O'Brien: "The Herculeses of the Cinema Range."* N.p.: self-published, 1987.

Donev, Stef. *The Fun of Living Dangerously: The Life of Yakima Canutt.* New York: McGraw-Hill, 1997.

Dooley, Dennis, and Gary Engle. *Superman at Fifty: The Persistence of a Legend.* New York: Collier, 1987.

Dougan, Andy. *Untouchable: A Biography of Robert De Niro.* New York: Hachette, 1996.

Douglas, Kirk. *Climbing the Mountain: My Search for Meaning.* New York: Simon and Schuster, 1997.

———. *I Am Spartacus! Making a Film, Breaking the Blacklist.* New York: Open Road, 2002.

———. *The Ragman's Son: An Autobiography.* New York: Simon and Schuster, 1988.

Dowling, Dave, and George Helmer. *Steve Reeves: His Legacy in Films.* Malibu, CA: Classic Image, 2003.

Dudley, Fredda. "Dynamite with Dimples!" *Screenland,* March 1949, 37, 61–63.

Dyer, Richard. *White: Essays on Race and Culture.* London: Routledge, 1997.

Egan, J. C. "A Coterie of the Strongest Men in the United States: Athletics of the Los Angeles Athletic Club." *Strength,* July 1920, 18–19, 32.

Essoe, Gabe. *Tarzan of the Movies: A Pictorial History of More Than Fifty Years of Edgar Rice Burroughs' Legendary Hero.* Secaucus, NJ: Citadel, 1972.

Eubanks, L. E. "Strong Men of the Movies." *Strength,* July 1922, 28–32.

Fair, John D. *Mr. America: The Tragic History of a Bodybuilding Icon.* Austin: University of Texas Press, 2015.

———. *Muscletown USA: Bob Hoffman and the Manly Culture of York Barbell.* University Park: Pennsylvania State University Press, 1999.

Fairbanks, Douglas. *Douglas Fairbanks: In His Own Words.* New York: iUniverse, 2006.

Fairbanks, Douglas, Jr. *The Salad Days.* New York: Doubleday, 1988.

Faludi, Susan. *Stiffed: The Betrayal of the American Man.* New York: HarperCollins, 1999.

Farassino, Alberto, and Tatti Sanguineti, eds. *Gli uomini forti*. Milan: Mazzotta, 1983.

Fields, Armond. *James J. Corbett: A Biography of the Heavyweight Boxing Champion and Popular Theater Headliner*. Jefferson, NC: McFarland, 2001.

Fontaine, Richard. "Cover Story: Richard Fontaine, Pioneer of Gay Films since 1949." Interview with Michael Goetsch. *Victory News*, n.d. Collection of David L. Chapman.

Fury, David. *The Cinema History of Burt Lancaster*. Minneapolis: Artist's Press, 1989.

Gammel, Irene. "Lacing Up the Gloves: Women, Boxing, and Modernity." *Cultural and Social History* 9, no. 3 (September 2012): 369–90.

Gandert, Gero, ed. *Der Film der Weimarer Republik 1929: Ein Handbuch der zeitgenössischen Kritik*. Berlin: Walter de Gruyter, 1993.

Gibson, Emily. *The Original Million Dollar Mermaid: The Annette Kellerman Story*. With Barbara Firth. Crows Nest, New South Wales, Australia: Allen and Unwin, 2005.

Gilbert, James. *A Cycle of Outrage: America's Reaction to the Juvenile Delinquent in the 1950s*. New York: Oxford University Press, 1988.

Gils, Bieke. "Flying, Flirting, and Flexing: Charmion's Trapeze Act, Sexuality and Physical Culture at the Turn of the Twentieth Century." *Journal of Sport History* 41, no. 2 (Summer 2014): 251–68.

Giordano, Michele. *Giganti buoni: Da Ercole a Piedone (e oltre) il mito dell'uomo forte nel cinema italiano*. Rome: Gremese, 1998.

Golden, Eve. *Golden Images: 41 Essays on Silent Film Stars*. Jefferson, NC: McFarland, 2001.

Gorman, Joseph Bruce. *Kefauver: A Political Biography*. New York: Oxford University Press, 1971.

Grace, Dick. "'Stunt Men,' the Boys Who Risk Their Lives to Thrill." *Photoplay*, August 1925, 32–35, 129–30.

Grandinetti, Fred M. *Popeye: An Illustrated Cultural History*. 2nd ed. Jefferson, NC: McFarland, 2004.

Grieveson, Lee, and Peter Krämer, eds. *The Silent Cinema Reader*. London: Routledge, 2004.

Griffin, Scott Tracy. *Tarzan: The Centennial Celebration*. London: Titan Books, 2012.

Grossman, Gary. *Superman: From Serial to Cereal*. New York: Popular Library, 1977.

Gunning, Tom. "'Now You See It, Now You Don't': The Temporality of the Cinema of Attractions." In *The Silent Cinema Reader*, edited by Lee Grieveson and Peter Krämer, 41–50. London: Routledge, 2004.

Hagner, John G. *Falling for Stars*. Reseda, CA: self-published, 1973.

Henie, Sonja. *Wings on My Feet*. New York: Prentice-Hall, 1940.

Hess, Earl J., and Pratibha A. Dabholkar. *The Cinematic Voyage of* The Pirate: *Kelly, Garland, and Minnelli at Work*. Columbia: University of Missouri Press, 2014.

Hill, Katrina. *Action Movie Freak.* Iola, WI: Krause, 2012.

Hirschhorn, Clive. *Gene Kelly: A Biography.* New York: St. Martin's, 1984.

Holmlund, Chris, ed. *The Ultimate Stallone Reader: Sylvester Stallone as Star, Icon, Auteur.* New York: Wallflower, 2014.

Hornblow, Arthur, Jr. "Douglas Fairbanks, Dramatic Dynamo." *Motion Picture Classic,* March 1917, 48–50.

Hughes, Laurence A., ed. *The Truth about the Movies by the Stars.* Los Angeles: Hollywood Publishers, 1924.

Hylan[d], Dick. "Risking Life and Limb for $25." *Photoplay,* November 1927, 30–33, 122–23.

Jensen, Erik N. *Body by Weimar: Athletes, Gender, and German Modernity.* New York: Oxford University Press, 2010.

Kaes, Anton, Martin Jay, and Edward Dimendberg, eds. *The Weimar Republic Sourcebook.* Berkeley: University of California Press, 1994.

Kashner, Sam, and Nancy Schoenberger. *Hollywood Kryptonite: The Bulldog, the Lady, and the Death of Superman.* New York: St. Martin's, 1996.

Kasson, John F. *Houdini, Tarzan, and the Perfect Man: The White Male Body and the Challenge of Modernity in America.* New York: Hill and Wang, 2001.

Kibler, M. Alison. *Rank Ladies: Gender and Cultural Hierarchy in American Vaudeville.* Chapel Hill: University of North Carolina Press, 1999.

Knapp, Laurence F., and Andrea F. Kulas, eds. *Ridley Scott: Interviews.* Jackson: University Press of Mississippi, 2005.

Kohner, Frederick. *Gidget: The Little Girl with Big Ideas.* New York: G. P. Putnam's, 1957.

La Motta, Jake. *Raging Bull: My Story.* With Joseph Carter and Peter Savage. Englewood Cliffs, NJ: Prentice-Hall, 1970.

Lahue, Kalton C. *Bound and Gagged: The Story of the Silent Serials.* New York: Oak Tree, 1968.

Lant, Antonia. "Spazio per la razza in Cabiria." In *Cabiria e il suo tempo,* edited by Paolo Bertetto and Gianni Rondolino, 212–22. Turin, Italy: Museo Nazionale del Cinema, 1998.

Leamer, Laurence. *Fantastic: The Life of Arnold Schwarzenegger.* New York: St. Martin's, 2005.

LeClaire, Chris. *Worlds to Conquer: Steve Reeves, An Authorized Biography.* South Chatham, MA: USN Dive Locker Press, 1999.

Lee, Linda. *The Bruce Lee Story.* Santa Clarita, CA: Black Belt, 1989.

Lepore, Jill. *The Secret History of Wonder Woman.* New York: Alfred A. Knopf, 2014.

Levy, Alan. "Peekaboo Sex, or How to Fill a Drive-in." *Life,* July 16, 1965, 81–88.

Levy, Shawn. *De Niro: A Life.* Farmington Hills, MI: Crown/Archetype, 2014.

Lindsay, Richard. *Hollywood Biblical Epics: Camp Spectacle and Queer Style from the Silent Era to the Modern Day.* Santa Barbara, CA: Praeger, 2015.

Lisanti, Thomas. *Hollywood Surf and Beach Movies: The First Wave, 1959–1969.* Jefferson, NC: McFarland, 2005.

LoBrutto, Vincent. *Ridley Scott: A Biography*. Lexington: University Press of Kentucky, 2019.

Maddox, Ben. "Burt's Private Life." *Screenland*, March 1950, 26–27, 58–61.

Magers, Boyd, and Michael G. Fitzgerald. *Westerns Women: Interviews with 50 Leading Ladies of Movie and Television Westerns from the 1930s to the 1960s*. Jefferson, NC: McFarland, 1999.

Maltin, Leonard. *Of Mice and Magic: A History of American Animated Cartoons*. New York: McGraw-Hill, 1980.

Marill, Alvin H. "Anthony Quinn." *Films in Review* 19, no. 8 (October 1968): 461–81.

Martinelli, Vittorio, and Mario Quargnolo. *Maciste & Co.: I giganti buoni del muto italiano*. Gemona del Friuli, Italy: Cinepopolare Edizioni, 1981.

Mast, Gerald. *A Short History of the Movies*. Indianapolis: Bobbs-Merrill, 1976.

Mathews, Nancy Mowll. *Moving Pictures: American Art and Early Film, 1880–1910*. Manchester, VT: Hudson Hills, 2005.

Maturi, Richard J., and Mary Buckingham Maturi. *Francis X. Bushman: A Biography and Filmography*. Jefferson, NC: McFarland, 1998.

May, Kirse Granat. *Golden State, Golden Youth: The California Image in Popular Culture, 1955–1966*. Chapel Hill: University of North Carolina Press, 2002.

McKenna, A. T. *Showman of the Screen: Joseph E. Levine and His Revolutions in Film Promotion*. Lexington: University Press of Kentucky, 2016.

Menefee, David W. *George O'Brien: A Man's Man in Hollywood*. Albany, GA: BearManor, 2009.

Miller, Don. *Hollywood Corral*. Edited by Leonard Maltin. New York: Popular Library, 1976.

Mintz, Steven, and Randy Roberts, eds. *Hollywood's America: United States History through Its Films*. 3rd ed. St. James, NY: Brandywine, 2001.

Misiroglu, Gina. *The Superhero Book: The Ultimate Encyclopedia of Comic-Book Icons and Hollywood Heroes*. Detroit: Visible Ink, 2004.

Mitchell, George, and William K. Everson. "Tom Mix, of His Many Contributions to the Western, the Greatest Was Showmanship." *Films in Review* 8, no. 8 (October 1957): 387–97.

Mulvey, Laura. "Visual Pleasure and Narrative Cinema." In *Visual and Other Pleasures*, 14–30. New York: Palgrave Macmillan, 2009.

Munn, Michael. *Kirk Douglas*. New York: St. Martin's, 1985.

Musser, Charles. *The Emergence of Cinema: The American Screen to 1907*. New York: Scribner, 1990.

———. "'A Personality So Marked': Eugen Sandow and Visual Culture." In *Moving Pictures: American Art and Early Film, 1880–1910*, ed. Nancy Mowll Mathews, 104–10. Manchester, VT: Hudson Hills, 2005.

Myler, Patrick. *Gentleman Jim Corbett: The Truth behind a Boxing Legend*. London: Robson Books, 1998.

Paddock, Charley. "Why Athletes Fail in Pictures." Photoplay, September 1928, 52–53, 124.

Plato. *The Republic.* New York: Oxford University Press, 1941.

Powell, Jane. *The Girl Next Door . . . And How She Grew.* New York: William Morrow, 1988.

Powrie, Phil, Ann Davies, and Bruce Babington, eds. *The Trouble with Men: Masculinities in European and Hollywood Cinema.* London: Wallflower, 2004.

Prolo, Maria Adriana. "Introduzione." In *Cabiria: Visione storica del III secolo A.C.,* edited by Roberto Radicati and Ruggero Rossi, 5–16. Turin, Italy: Museo Nazionale del Cinema, 1977.

Prowse, Dave. *Straight from the Force's Mouth: The Autobiography of Dave Prowse, MBE.* Clacton on Sea, UK: Apex, 2011.

Quargnolo, Mario. *Luciano Albertini: un divo degli anni "venti."* Udine, Italy: CSU, 1977.

Rafiq, Fiaz. *Bruce Lee: Conversations: The Life and Legacy of a Legend.* New York: HNL, 2009.

Reeves, Steve. *Building the Classic Physique the Natural Way.* Calabasas, CA: Little Wolf, 1995.

Reich, Jacqueline. *The Maciste Films of Italian Silent Cinema.* Bloomington: Indiana University Press, 2015.

Reinhart, Mark S. *The Batman Filmography: Live-Action Features, 1943–1997.* Jefferson, NC: McFarland, 2004.

Reynolds, Debbie. *Unsinkable: A Memoir.* With Dorian Hannaway. New York: William Morrow, 2013.

Rickitt, Richard. *Special Effects: The History and Technique.* New York: Billboard Books, 2000.

Roberts, Randy. *Papa Jack: Jack Johnson and the Era of White Hopes.* New York: Free Press, 1985.

Rock, the [Dwayne Johnson]. *The Rock Says . . . : The Most Electrifying Man in Sports Entertainment.* With Joe Layden. New York: Regan Books, 2000.

Rogowski, Christian, ed. *The Many Faces of Weimar Cinema: Rediscovering Germany's Filmic Legacy.* Rochester, NY: Camden House, 2010.

Rose, Bob. "Cheating Death for a Living." *Popular Mechanics,* February 1935, 226–29, 128A.

Rovin, Jeff. *The Encyclopedia of Superheroes.* New York: Facts on File, 1985.

Rushing, Robert A. *Descended from Hercules: Biopolitics and the Muscled Male Body on Screen.* Bloomington: Indiana University Press, 2016.

Russo, Charles. *Striking Distance: Bruce Lee and the Dawn of Martial Arts in America.* Lincoln: University of Nebraska Press, 2016.

Sadoul, Georges. *Histoire générale du cinéma.* Vol. 3, *Le cinéma devient un art.* Paris: Denoel, 1951.

Sandow, Eugen. *Sandow on Physical Training.* Edited by G. Mercer Adam. New York: Selwin Tait and Sons, 1894.

———. *Strength and How to Obtain It.* London: Gale and Polden, 1897.

Sayre, Joel. "The Body Worshipers of Muscle Beach." *Saturday Evening Post,* May 25, 1957, 34–35, 136–40.

Schickel, Richard. *His Picture in the Papers*. New York: Charterhouse, 1973.

———. *Intimate Strangers: The Culture of Celebrity*. Garden City, NY: Doubleday, 1985.

Schwarzenegger, Arnold. *Encyclopedia of Modern Bodybuilding*. New York, Simon and Schuster, 1985.

———. *Total Recall: My Unbelievably True Life Story*. With Peter Petre. New York: Simon and Schuster, 2012.

Shirley, Lois. "The Enemy of Beauty—Over-Exercise." *Photoplay*, August 1931, 30–31, 112.

Singer, Ben. *Melodrama and Modernity: Early Sensational Cinema and Its Contexts*. New York: Columbia University Press, 2001.

Slide, Anthony. *Early American Cinema*. New York: A. S. Barnes, 1970.

Spehr, Paul C. *The Man Who Made Movies: W. K. L. Dickson*. New Barnet, UK: John Libbey, 2008.

Stallone, Sylvester. *The Official Rocky Scrapbook*. New York: Grosset and Dunlap, 1977.

———. *Sly Moves: My Proven Program to Lose Weight, Build Strength, Gain Will Power, and Live Your Dream*. New York: HarperCollins, 2005.

Stern, Jane, and Michael Stern. *Sixties People*. New York: Alfred A. Knopf, 1990.

Strait, Raymond, and Leif Henie. *Queen of Ice, Queen of Shadows: The Unsuspected Life of Sonja Henie*. New York: Stein and Day, 1985.

Streible, Dan. *Fight Pictures: A History of Boxing and Early Cinema*. Berkeley: University of California Press, 2008.

———. "On the Canvas: Boxing, Art, and Cinema." In *Moving Pictures: American Art and Early Film, 1880–1910*, ed. Nancy Mowll Mathews, 111–16. Manchester, VT: Hudson Hills, 2005.

Studlar, Gaylyn. *This Mad Masquerade: Stardom and Masculinity in the Jazz Age*. New York: Columbia University Press, 1996.

Thomas, Tony. *The Films of Gene Kelly: Song and Dance Man*. Secaucus, NJ: Citadel, 1974.

Tye, Larry. *Superman: The High-Flying History of America's Most Enduring Hero*. New York: Random House, 2012.

Usai, Paolo Cherchi. *Giovanni Pastrone: Gli anni d'oro del cinema a Torino*. Turin, Italy: Unione Tipografico-Editrice Torinese, 1986.

Vance, Jeffrey. *Douglas Fairbanks*. Berkeley: University of California Press, 2008.

Vardac, A. Nicholas. *Stage to Screen: Theatrical Method from Garrick to Griffith*. Cambridge, MA: Harvard University Press, 1949.

Walter, Denie. "The Tarzan Blueprints." *MuscleMag International*, August 1976, 40–45.

Waugh, Thomas. *Hard to Imagine: Gay Male Eroticism in Photography and Film from Their Beginnings to Stonewall*. New York: Columbia University Press, 1996.

White, Pearl. *Just Me*. New York: George H. Doran, 1919.

———. "Thrills in Serial Making." *Moving Picture World* 33, no. 3 (July 21, 1917): 423–24.

Williams, Carl Easton. "Analyzing Douglas Fairbanks." *Physical Culture* 46, no. 5 (November 1921): 21–24, 80, 82, 84.

Williams, Esther. *The Million Dollar Mermaid.* New York: Simon and Schuster, 1992.

Williams, John Alexander, ed. *Weimar Culture Revisited.* New York: Palgrave Macmillan, 2011.

Willoughby, David P. *The Super-Athletes.* New York: A. S. Barnes, 1970.

Witney, William. *In a Door, into a Fight, out a Door, into a Chase: Moviemaking Remembered by the Guy at the Door.* Jefferson, NC: McFarland, 1996.

Zehr, E. Paul. *Becoming Batman: The Possibility of a Superhero.* Baltimore: Johns Hopkins University Press, 2008.

Zhen, Zhang. *An Amorous History of the Silver Screen: Shanghai Cinema, 1896–1937.* Chicago: University of Chicago Press, 2005.

INDEX